Signed in at Barnes & Noble, Fresno, with Eddie, Jr. on knee — 8½ most

Executive Editor: Deborah Hoffman Emry
Executive Editor: Annie Todd
Development Editor: David Cohen
Editorial Assistant: Jane Avery
Editor-in-Chief: PJ Boardman
Executive Marketing Manager: Beth Toland
Production Editor: Lynda Paolucci
Project Manager: Susan Rifkin
Managing Editor: Bruce Kaplan
Senior Manufacturing Supervisor: Paul Smolenski
Manufacturing Manager: Vincent Scelta
Designer: Jill Little
Design Manager: Patricia Smythe
Photo Research Supervisor: Melinda Lee Reo
Image Permission Supervisor: Kay Dellosa
Photo Researcher: Teri Stratford
Cover Design: Lorraine Castellano
Cover Photo: UNIPHOTO Stock Photography, Washington, D.C.
Composition: Carlisle Communications, Ltd.

Library of Congress Cataloging-in-Publication Data

Horngren, Charles T., 1926–
    Introduction to financial accounting / Charles T. Horngren, Gary
L. Sundem, John A. Elliott. — 7th ed.
      p. cm.
    Includes bibliographical references and index.
    ISBN 0-13-905993-8
    1. Accounting.   I. Sundem, Gary L.   II. Elliott, John A.
III. Title.
HF5635.H813   1999
657—dc21

98-24280
CIP

Photo credits for this textbook appear on page I12.

Prentice-Hall International (UK) Limited, *London*
Prentice-Hall of Australia Pty. Limited, *Sydney*
Prentice-Hall Canada, Inc., *Toronto*
Prentice-Hall Hispanoamericana, S.A., *Mexico*
Prentice-Hall of India Private Limited, *New Delhi*
Prentice-Hall of Japan, Inc., *Tokyo*
Pearson Education, Asia Pte. Ltd., *Singapore*
Editora Prentice-Hall do Brasil, Ltda., *Rio de Janeiro*

Printed in the United States of America
Printed with corrections, July, 1999
10 9 8 7 6 5 4 3

INTRODUCTION TO FINANCIAL ACCOUNTING

Seventh Edition

CHARLES T. HORNGREN
Stanford University

GARY L. SUNDEM
University of Washington—Seattle

JOHN A. ELLIOTT
Cornell University

PRENTICE HALL, *Upper Saddle River, NJ 07458*

Charles T. Horngren Series in Accounting
Charles T. Horngren, Consulting Editor

Auditing: An Integrated Approach, 7/E
Arens/Loebbecke

Financial Statement Analysis, 2/E
Foster

Government and Nonprofit Accounting: Theory & Practice, 6/E
Freeman/Shoulders

Financial Accounting, 3/E
Harrison/Horngren

Cases in Financial Reporting, 2/E
Hirst/McAnally

Cost Accounting: A Managerial Emphasis, 9/E
Horngren/Foster/Datar

Accounting, 4/E
Horngren/Harrison/Bamber

Introduction to Financial Accounting, 7/E
Horngren/Sundem/Elliott

Introduction to Management Accounting, 11/E
Horngren/Sundem/Stratton

To Joan, Scott, Mary, Susie,
Cathy, Liz, Garth, Jens,
Laura, Dawn, and little guy

Charles T. Horngren is the Edmund W. Littlefield Professor of Accounting, Emeritus, at Stanford University. A graduate of Marquette University, he received his MBA from Harvard University and his Ph.D. from the University of Chicago. He is also the recipient of honorary doctorates from Marquette University and DePaul University.

A Certified Public Accountant, Horngren served on the Accounting Principles Board for six years, the Financial Accounting Standards Board Advisory Council for five years, and the Council of the American Institute of Certified Public Accountants for three years. For six years, he served as a trustee of the Financial Accounting Foundation, which oversees the Financial Accounting Standards Board and the Government Accounting Standards Board.

Horngren is a member of the Accounting Hall of Fame.

A member of the American Accounting Association, Horngren has been its President and its Director of Research. He received its first annual Outstanding Accounting Educator Award.

The California Certified Public Accountants Foundation gave Horngren its Faculty Excellence Award and its Distinguished Professor Award. He is the first person to have received both awards.

The American Institute of Certified Public Accountants presented its first Outstanding Educator Award to Horngren.

Horngren was named Accountant of the Year, Education, by the national professional accounting fraternity, Beta Alpha Psi.

Professor Horngren is also a member of the Institute of Management Accountants, where he received its Distinguished Service Award. He was a member of the Institute's Board of Regents, which administers the Certified Management Accountant examinations.

Horngren is the author of these books published by Prentice-Hall: *Cost Accounting: A Managerial Emphasis,* Ninth Edition, 1997 (with George Foster and Srikant Datar); *Introduction to Management Accounting,* Eleventh Edition, 1999 (with Gary L. Sundem and William O. Stratton); *Accounting,* Fourth Edition, 1999 (with Walter T. Harrison, Jr. and Linda Bamber); and *Financial Accounting,* Third Edition, 1999 (with Walter J. Harrison, Jr.).

Horngren is the Consulting Editor for the Charles T. Horngren Series in Accounting.

Gary L. Sundem is the Julius A. Roller Professor of Accounting and Co-Chair of the Department of Accounting at the University of Washington, Seattle. He received his B.A. degree from Carleton College and his MBA and Ph.D. degrees from Stanford University.

Professor Sundem was the 1992–93 President of the American Accounting Association. He was Executive Director of the Accounting Education Change Commission, 1989–91, and served as Editor of *The Accounting Review,* 1982–86.

A member of the National Association of Accountants, Sundem is past president of the Seattle chapter. He has served on NAA's national Board of Directors, the Committee on Academic Relations, and the Research Committee.

Professor Sundem has numerous publications in accounting and finance journals including *Issues in Accounting Education, The Accounting Review, Journal of Accounting Research,* and *The Journal of Finance.* He was selected as the Outstanding Accounting Educator by the American Accounting Association in 1998 and by the Washington Society of CPAs in 1987. He has made more than 150 presentations at universities in the United States and abroad.

John A. Elliott is Associate Dean and Professor of Accounting at the Johnson Graduate School of Management at Cornell University. He received his B.S. and MBA degrees from the University of Maryland and his Ph.D. degree from Cornell University.

A certified public accountant, Elliott worked for Arthur Andersen & Co. and for Westinghouse before returning for his advanced degrees. He currently teaches financial accounting and international accounting at the Johnson School. Prior teaching experience has included auditing and taxation as well as intermediate accounting and financial statement analysis. With over 25 years as an educator, Professor Elliott has taught at the University of Maryland, St. Lawrence University, Central Washington State College, and the University of Chicago. In addition to executive teaching for Cornell, he has conducted various corporate training programs in the United States and internationally.

As a member of the American Accounting Association, he was the founding president of the Financial Accounting and Reporting Section. As a member of the Financial Accounting Standards Committee he frequently responded to FASB exposure drafts and worked to integrate academic study with practice. His research has been published in accounting and economics journals and deals primarily with the use of accounting information to assess the financial condition of an enterprise.

Professor Elliott served on the Hangar Theatre Board of Trustees for nine years, and was president for four of those years. He currently serves as Chairman of the Board of the Cayuga Medical Center at Ithaca.

Brief Contents

CONTENTS

PREFACE

"You have to know what something is before you know what it is used for."

Introduction to Financial Accounting, 7/E describes the most widely used accounting theory and practice with an emphasis on what accounting is rather than on what it should be.

IFA, 7/E takes the view that business is an exciting process and that accounting is the perfect window through which to see how economic events affect businesses. Because we believe that accounting aids the understanding of economic events and that accounting builds on simple principles, this book introduces a number of concepts earlier than other textbooks. These early introductions are at the simplest level and are illustrated with carefully chosen examples from real companies.

OUR PHILOSOPHY

Introduce the simple concepts early, revisit concepts at more complex levels as students gain understanding, and provide appropriate real-company examples at every stage— that's our philosophy.

We want students to view accounting as a tool that enhances our understanding of economic events. Students should be asking, "After this transaction, are we better or worse off?"

One of our colleagues, Hal Bierman, often focuses on an economic event by asking, "Are you happy or are you sad?" We believe that accounting provides a way to understand what is happening and to answer that question. You might think of the basic financial statements as scorecards in the most fundamental economic contests. Each year the financial statements help you answer the most important questions: Are you happy or sad? Did you make or lose money? Are you prospering or just surviving? Will you have the cash you need for the next big step?

WHO SHOULD USE THIS BOOK?

IFA, 7/E presupposes no prior knowledge of accounting and is suitable for any undergraduate or MBA student enrolled in a financial accounting course. It deals with important topics that all business students should study. Our goals have been to choose relevant subject matter, and to present it clearly and accessibly.

This text is oriented to the user of financial statements but gives ample attention to the needs of potential accounting practitioners. *IFA,* 7/E stresses underlying concepts yet makes them concrete with profuse illustrations, many taken from recent corporate annual reports. Moreover, accounting procedures such as transaction analysis, journalizing, and posting are given due consideration where appropriate.

IMPORTANT CHANGES TO THIS EDITION

LEANER ORGANIZATION. Time is of the essence! Because we are aware of the time constraints on both instructors and students, we have reduced this text from 16 to 14 chapters, cutting more than 100 pages. However, we refused to sacrifice content for length. Instead, we chose to integrate topics and tighten our discussions. Specific changes from the sixth edition include:

- Our discussion of the accounting cycle has been tightened and condensed from five chapters to four.
- Ch. 8, "Internal Control and Ethics" from the sixth edition has been eliminated. Coverage of ethics and internal control has been strengthened by integrating these topics into the text where appropriate.
- Chapter 8, "Liabilities and Interest," and Chapter 9, "Valuing and Accounting for Bonds and Leases," replace Chapter 10 from the sixth edition. This material was divided into two chapters based on reviewer feedback.
- Ch. 14, "Income Taxes," has been eliminated in response to reviewer input.

NEW CHAPTER-OPENING VIGNETTES WITH "ON LOCATION!" VIDEOS. To give students a better idea of accounting's role in today's business world, each chapter begins with a look at how the chapter's topic affects a familiar, real-world company. "On Location!" video segments, specially produced for this text, reinforce and expand upon these vignettes.

NEW GAP ANNUAL REPORT. Students often have trouble seeing how the accounting concepts they learn fit together in actual business practice. To help students "put it all together," we have included the complete annual report of GAP, Inc., both in its original form (shrink-wrapped to the text) and reproduced in Appendix A of the text. Many chapters refer to the information in this report and all chapters include a homework problem designed specifically to test students on their abilities both to integrate concepts and to apply those concepts to a real company.

TAKE IT TO THE WEB! A huge assortment of financial information is available on the Web—a resource *IFA, 7/E* utilizes. Each chapter features an Internet Exercise tied to the chapter's opening vignette and video. In addition, the PHLIP (Prentice Hall Learning on the Internet Partnership) Web site guides students through many sites and links that make accounting realistic and accessible. The PHLIP Web site also contains links to many of the companies featured as text examples, as well as on-line tutoring, and much more. For instructors, we provide a passcode protected resource area where instructors can download key supplements. Check out our Web site at www.prenhall.com/.

COLLABORATIVE LEARNING EXERCISES. For those instructors trying to facilitate group learning, each chapter now includes a Collaborative Learning Exercise. Each of these exercises has been specifically designed to promote classroom and student interaction through research, role playing, and other popular learning techniques.

ENHANCED ACCESSIBILITY.   Students learn best if a text appeals to them. Accordingly, *IFA,* 7/E has adopted a more open, attractive four-color design. Also, the text's art and photo programs have been improved and expanded, and, perhaps most importantly, the writing style of the text has been simplified and tightened to provide a more student-friendly topical presentation.

RETAINED FEATURES

- *Introduction to Financial Accounting,* 7/E is part of a matched set of texts that enable any instructor to teach a full year of financial and management accounting. This text can be followed with *Introduction to Management Accounting,* 11/E, also available in a new edition by Horngren, Sundem, and Stratton. Both texts share authors, chapter organization, pedagogy, commitment to emphasizing accounting's importance in business decisions, and depth and breadth of available problem material. The new editions of each text have been designed to work together as seamlessly as possible.
- Boxed material, highlighting real-world issues, has been streamlined and revised.
- As in every edition, *Introduction to Financial Accounting,* 7/E continues to offer the best problem sets available in both quality and quantity. Problem material has been updated and expanded.

SUPPLEMENTS FOR INSTRUCTORS

INSTRUCTOR'S RESOURCE MANUAL BY JOHN MARTS, UNIVERSITY OF NORTH CAROLINA, WILMINGTON.   The *Resource Manual* includes: chapter overviews, chapter outlines organized by objectives, teaching tips, chapter quizzes, transparency masters, student notes derived from textbook exhibits, and suggested readings. This edition also includes Financial Statement Problems based on The Gap, Inc. Annual Report and Collaborative Learning Techniques based on selected end-of-chapter assignments. Included is a Video Guide that carefully integrates the videos into your classroom lectures.

SOLUTIONS MANUAL AND TRANSPARENCIES BY TEXT AUTHORS.   Solutions are provided for all of the end-of-chapter assignments. The Solutions Manual is also available in acetate form and on disk to adopters.

TEST ITEM FILE BY THOMAS CARMENT, NORTHEASTERN STATE UNIVERSITY. Completely new for this edition, the Test Item File contains over 1700 test items. Each chapter includes multiple choice, true/false, exercises, comprehensive problems, short answer problems, critical thinking essay questions, and questions based on The Gap, Inc. Annual Report, which is packaged with each student version of the text. Each test item is tied to the corresponding learning objective, has an assigned difficulty level, provides a page reference, and identifies what skill (i.e., comprehension, recall, analysis, application, etc.) is tested.

PRENTICE HALL CUSTOM TEST, BY ENGINEERING SOFTWARE ASSOCIATES (ESA), INC. This easy-to-use computerized testing program is available on 3.5″ diskettes. Instructors can create an exam and track student results. The PH Custom Test also provides on-line testing capabilities.

ON LOCATION! VIDEO LIBRARY BY BEVERLY AMER, NORTHERN ARIZONA UNIVERSITY. Video segments, created for this book, contain all the fast-paced and engaging qualities of TV while focusing on the successful accounting activities of the real-world companies highlighted in each chapter's opening vignettes. A Video Guide in the Instructor's Resource Manual carefully integrates the videos into your classroom lectures.

PH PROFESSOR: A CLASSROOM PRESENTATION ON POWERPOINT. This computerized supplement provides the instructor with an interactive presentation for each chapter of the text. It is not necessary to have PowerPoint in order to run the presentation. However, having PowerPoint will provide instructors with the flexibility to add slides or modify the existing ones to meet the course's needs.

SUPPLEMENTS FOR STUDENTS

WORKING PAPERS BY LYNN MAZZOLA, NASSAU COMMUNITY COLLEGE. This supplement includes tear-out forms to solve all the end-of-chapter assignments in the text. Forms are numbered and arranged in the same order as the textbook.

STUDY GUIDE BY LYNN MAZZOLA, NASSAU COMMUNITY COLLEGE. Contains a pretest, a chapter overview, a detailed chapter review including study tips, practice test questions, and demonstration problems with worked-out solutions.

ACTIVITIES IN FINANCIAL ACCOUNTING BY MARTHA DORAN, SAN DIEGO STATE UNIVERSITY. This workbook contains interactive learning assignments designed to help students see beyond the technical aspects of accounting through active learning. In addition, these group activities fulfill the AECC recommendations by providing students with the chance to practice and improve their writing, speaking, and reasoning skills. An Instructor's Guide provides an overview of each activity, highlights important content and process objectives, and provides step-by-step instructions for running each activity.

NEW IMPROVED SPREADSHEET TEMPLATES BY ALBERT FISHER, COMMUNITY COLLEGE OF SOUTHERN NEVADA. Selected exercises and problems are identified in the text by a spreadsheet icon. The documentation includes short tutorials on how to use Excel and Lotus 1–2–3 as well as step-by-step instructions for completing each template. We've enhanced our spreadsheet templates by adding more problems and increasing the difficulty level. Students are now provided with the opportunity to enter more formulas to solve problems. Solutions are available on disk to the instructor upon adoption of the text.

CAREER PATHS IN ACCOUNTING-CD-ROM (WINNER OF THE NEW MEDIA INVISION GOLD AWARD IN EDUCATION!) Alone or with the text, this CD-ROM provides students with a dynamic, interactive job-searching tool. Included are workshops in career planning, resume writing, and interviewing skills. Students can learn the latest market trends and facts as well as the skills required to get the right job. In addition, the CD-ROM provides the student with salary information, video clips describing specific jobs, and profiles of practitioners in the field.

ACCOUNTING MADE EASY-CD-ROM. This user-friendly program reviews the accounting cycle and procedures. Students take a pretest to see where they need the most help and then work through new material presented in short learning segments. Performance feedback is provided after each session. Accounting Made Easy is available blister-packed to the textbook or as a stand-alone package. This tutorial comes in two levels:

- Level 1—covers accounting basics such as business organization, accounting information financial statements, the accounting equation, general ledger, and account transactions.
- Level 2—focuses on accounting procedures and covers the following areas: recording transactions, posting transactions, adjustments, and completing the accounting cycle.

PRENTICE HALL ACCOUNTING SOFTWARE-PHAS: A GENERAL LEDGER PACKAGE BY JEAN INSINGA, MIDDLESEX COMMUNITY COLLEGE. This windows-based program covers the accounting cycle and is user-friendly. The program computerizes selected end-of-chapter assignments which are identified in the text with a disk icon. PHAS allows students to enter journal entries, change or delete entries, print journals and other reports, post journal entries, and close the period. This program also provides helpful tips, on-line help, individual problem help, the ability to create new problems and save to a disk, edit journal entries, and establish subsidiary accounts. Quick Tours provide students with quick and easy practice drills that demonstrate how to use the program.

NEW!! MEDIA SUPPORT FOR BOTH INSTRUCTORS AND STUDENTS

PHLIP (PRENTICE HALL LEARNING ON THE INTERNET PARTNERSHIP). Offers a content rich Web site to support both professors and students. **Visit the site at www. prenhall.com/phlip.**

- New bi-monthly updates are integrated into specific chapters of the text.
- Internet resources are linked to a wide variety of sites to enhance and expand the text's coverage of select topics.
- Internet exercises developed specifically for *IFA,* 7/E help students learn how to use the Web as a management resource.
- Companion Web site (On-line Study Guide) capabilities allow students to test their knowledge of chapter learning objectives.

ACKNOWLEDGMENTS

Our appreciation extends to our present and former mentors, colleagues, and students. This book and our enthusiasm for accounting grew out of their collective contributions to our knowledge and experience. We particularly appreciate the following individuals who supplied helpful comments and reviews of the previous edition or of drafts of this edition:

Roderick S. Barclay, University of Texas at Dallas; Mary Barth, Stanford University; Marianne Bradford, The University of Tennesse; David T. Collins, Bellarmine College; Ray D. Dillon, Georgia State University; Patricia A. Doherty, Boston University; Alan H. Falcon, Loyola Marymount University; Anita Feller, University of Illinois; Richard Frankel, University of Michigan; John D. Gould, Western Carolina University; Leon J. Hanouille, Syracuse University; Al Hartgraves, Emory University; Suzanne Hartley, Franklin University; Peter Huey, Collin County Community College; Yuji Ijiri, Carnegie Mellon University; Joan Luft, Michigan State University; Maureen McNichols, Stanford University; Mohamed Onsi, Syracuse University; Patrick M. Premo, St. Bonaventure University; Leo A. Ruggle, Mankato State University; James A. Schweikart, University of Richmond; Robert Swieringa, Cornell University; Katherene P. Terrell, University of Central Oklahoma; Michael G. Vasilou, DeVry Institute of Technology, Chicago; Deborah Welch, Tyler Junior College; Christine Wiedman, College of William and Mary; and Peter D. Woodlock, Youngstown State University.

Finally, our thanks to the following people at Prentice Hall: Annie Todd, Deborah Hoffman Emry, PJ Boardman, Natacha St. Hill, Elaine Oyzon-Mast, Jane Avery, Beth Toland, Bob Prokop, Christopher Smerillo, Lynda Paolucci, Paul Smolenski, Vincent Scelta, Bruce Kaplan, Susan Rifkin, Richard Bretan, Pat Smythe, and Jill Little.

The solutions manual was skillfully produced by Donna Phoenix. Proofing help was provided by Anya Chaliotis, Karren Hills, and Dmitri Semenov.

Comments from users are welcome.

Charles T. Horngren
Gary L. Sundem
John A. Elliott

INTRODUCTION
TO FINANCIAL ACCOUNTING

ACCOUNTING: THE LANGUAGE OF BUSINESS

The World's most recognized arches are associated with more than 21,000 locations in more than 100 countries.

Learning Objectives

After studying this chapter, you should be able to

1 Explain how accounting information assists in making decisions.

2 Describe the components of the balance sheet.

3 Analyze business transactions and relate them to changes in the balance sheet.

4 Compare the features of proprietorships, partnerships, and corporations.

5 Describe auditing and how it enhances the value of financial information.

6 Distinguish between public and private accounting.

7 Evaluate the role of ethics in the accounting process.

D id you ever wonder how McDonald's, which started as a small Pasadena, California, hamburger stand, became a 21,000-location restaurant chain with stores in 101 countries? The first McDonald's employed three carhops to serve hot dogs and shakes to drive-in customers in Pasadena in 1937. In 1940 the two McDonald brothers, Dick and Mac, added a larger drive-in in San Bernardino where 20 carhops served a 25-item menu of sandwiches and ribs. Business was good, and the brothers shared $50,000 per year in profits (and in 1940 $50,000 would buy as much as $500,000 today).

How did accounting affect these entrepreneurs? When they analyzed their sales and costs, they found that 80% of their business came from hamburgers. Other sandwiches and ribs might taste good, but they generated little business. So the McDonald brothers streamlined their product line and focused on low prices, high volume, and a small standardized menu. Twenty-five items were cut to nine, and the price of a burger was slashed from $.30 to $.15. Sales and profits soared. This simple menu and value pricing served McDonald's well for years.

A few people noticed this money machine besides the nightly customers. Carnation Corporation noticed it was selling the McDonald brothers frozen milk shake mix in enormous quantities. The company figured that anyone selling that many shakes was on to something, so Carnation tried to buy the right to open additional McDonald's stores. Dick and Mac declined. Then, in 1954, Ray Kroc entered the picture.

Ray Kroc sold five-spindle "Multi-mixers," machines that made five milk shakes simultaneously. You guessed it: He sold so many such machines to the McDonald brothers that he eventually decided to visit the burger stand that made so many shakes. Kroc spent a day watching the McDonald's operation. He saw an opportunity to sell more shake machines as the company opened more stores. But within days he decided the real golden opportunity was in selling the McDonald's formula to entrepreneurs who wanted to open similar burger stands around the country. A persistent man, Kroc convinced the McDonald brothers to allow him to sell franchises. Kroc's golden opportunity became the golden arches, and a small California burger stand became one of the world's strongest marketing engines. Today McDonald's has become one of the most recognized brand names in the world, mostly by sticking to the strategy worked out years ago using accounting information.

accounting The process of identifying, recording, summarizing, and reporting economic information to decision makers.

financial accounting The field of accounting that serves external decision makers, such as stockholders, suppliers, banks, and government agencies.

Objective 1
Explain how accounting information assists in making decisions.

This book is an introduction to financial accounting. **Accounting** is a process of identifying, recording, summarizing and reporting economic information to decision makers. **Financial accounting** focuses on the specific needs of decision makers external to the organization such as stockholders, suppliers, banks, and government agencies. So you probably expect to see a bunch of rules and procedures about how to record financial information and how to report it to investors. Well, you are correct. You will see all of those. But our philosophy about financial accounting goes beyond rules and procedures. To use your financial accounting training effectively you must also understand the underlying business transactions that give rise to the economic information and why the information is helpful in making the financial decisions.

We hope it is true that you want to know about how businesses work. When you understand that McDonald's sales information by product helped its management make reporting decisions about what products to sell, you will see why we track sales and profitability by product line. Outside investors and internal marketing experts all need this information.

Our goal is to help you understand business transactions. We also want you to know how business transactions create accounting information and how decision makers both inside the company (managers) and outside the company (investors) use this information in deciding how, when, and what to buy or sell. By the end of this course you will understand business transactions, how to record those transactions, and how accountants combine those transactions to create financial reports that decision makers can use. In the process you will get to know some of the world's premier companies. You may wonder about what it costs to develop a theme park such as Disney World. Are these parks worth that kind of huge investment? How many people visit these Disney destinations each year? Can Disney keep track of them all, and are there enough visitors to make the parks profitable? If an investor considers purchasing Disney stock, what does she need to know to decide that the current price is a good one? We cannot answer *every* such question you might ask, but we will explore some exiting aspects of business and use business examples to illustrate the uses of accounting information.

In pursuing actual business examples, we will consider details about many of the 30 companies in the Dow Jones Industrial Average (the DOW), the most commonly reported stock market index in the world. Disney and McDonald's are both among these 30 companies along with many other large, familiar companies listed in Exhibit 1-1. We will also consider some smaller, younger, and faster growing companies such as Timberland, Boston Market, and The Gap. For now, we will start with the basics.

THE NATURE OF ACCOUNTING

Accounting organizes and summarizes economic information so that decision makers can use it. The information is presented in reports called *financial statements*. To prepare these statements, accountants analyze, record, quantify, accumulate, summarize, classify, report, and interpret economic events and their financial effects on the organization.

Exhibit 1-1

Dow Industrials

Assets and Owners' Equity, Fall 1997 ($ in millions)

Company Name	Total Assets	Total Owners' Equity
Allied Signal, Inc.	12,829.000	4,180.000
Aluminum Co. of America	13,449.898	4,462.394
American Express	108,512.000	8,528.000
AT&T Corp.	55,552.000	20,295.000
Boeing Co.	27,254.000	10,941.000
Caterpillar, Inc.	18,728.000	4,115.996
Chevron Corp.	34,854.000	15,623.000
Coca-Cola Co.	16,161.000	6,156.000
Disney	37,306.000	16,086.000
Du Pont (E I) De Nemours	37,987.000	10,709.000
Eastman Kodak Co.	14,438.000	4,734.000
Exxon Corp.	95,527.000	43,542.000
General Electric Co.	272,402.000	31,125.000
General Motors Corp.	222,142.000	23,418.000
Goodyear Tire & Rubber Co.	9,671.796	3,279.100
Hewlett-Packard Co.	27,699.000	13,438.000
Int'l Business Machines Corp.	81,132.000	21,628.000
Int'l Paper Co.	28,252.000	9,344.000
Johnson & Johnson	20,010.000	10,836.000
McDonald's Corp.	17,386.000	8,718.191
Merck & Co.	24,293.098	11,970.500
Minnesota Mining & Mfg. Co.	13,364.000	6,284.000
Morgan (J P) & Co.	222,026.000	11,432.000
Philip Morris Cos. Inc.	54,871.000	14,218.000
Procter & Gamble Co.	27,544.000	12,046.000
Sears Roebuck & Co.	36,167.000	4,945.000
Travelers Group, Inc.	151,067.000	13,214.000
Union Carbide Corp.	6,546.000	2,167.000
United Technologies Corp.	16,745.000	4,740.000
Wal-Mart Stores	39,604.000	17,143.000

The series of steps involved in initially recording information and converting it into financial statements is called the *accounting system.* The exact form of the statements produced by the accounting system can be adjusted to meet the needs of the decision makers who use the information. The accounting systems themselves are actually designed based on the types of information desired by managers and other decision makers. Accountants analyze the needs of these decision makers and create the accounting system that best meets those needs. Bookkeepers and computers then perform the routine tasks of collecting and compiling economic information. Although some accounting systems may be highly complex and require the skills and talents of many people, the real value of any accounting system lies in the information it provides.

Consider the accounting system at your school. It collects information about tuition charges and payments and tracks the status of each student. Your school must be able to bill individuals whose balances are unpaid. It must be able to schedule courses and hire faculty to meet the course demands of students. It must ensure that tuition and other cash inflows are sufficient to pay the faculty and keep the buildings warm (or cool) and well lit. If your experience is like most students, you can find some flaws with your school's accounting system. Perhaps there are too many waiting lines at registration or too many complicated procedures in filing for financial aid that appear to have no purpose. If you are lucky, you have experienced electronic registration for courses and made all of your tuition payments in response to bills received in the mail. The right information system can make the difference.

Note that the various information systems used by your school for registration and billing may be separate or integrated. We have referred to an accounting system, and certainly the billing and collections portion constitute accounting information. The course registration system may be separate from the accounting system at some schools. At these schools you might have to show a paid tuition bill in order to be permitted to register. At other schools the course registration system might create billings for courses on a credit hour basis and students who do not pay will be dropped during the semester. Increasingly, the lines between various information systems are blurring.

Every business maintains an accounting system, from the store where you bought this book to the company that issued the credit card you used to pay. Mastercard and Visa maintain very fast, very complicated accounting systems. At any moment, thousands of credit card transactions are occurring around the globe, and accounting systems are keeping track of them all. When you use your charge card, it is read electronically and linked to the cash register, which transmits the transaction amount over phone lines to the card company's central computer. The computer checks to make sure that your charges are within acceptable limits and approves or denies the transaction. At the same time the computer also conducts some fairly careful security checks. For example, if your credit card were being used simultaneously to buy groceries in Ithaca and to make long distance phone calls in Korea, the credit card computer might sense that something is wrong and require you to call a customer service representative before the charges were approved. Without reliable accounting systems, credit cards simply could not exist.

ACCOUNTING AS AN AID TO DECISION MAKING

Accounting information is useful to anyone who must make decisions that have economic consequences. Such decision makers include managers, owners, investors, and politicians. For example,

- When the engineering department of Apple Computer develops a new personal computer, an accountant develops a report on the potential profitability of the product, including estimated sales and estimated production and selling costs. Managers use the report to help decide whether to produce and market the product.
- Jill runs a small consulting firm and has five employees who service clients. In deciding who to promote (and who to fire), Jill produces reports each month of the productivity of each employee and compares productivity to the salary and other costs associated with the employees' work for the month.
- An investor considering buying stock in either General Motors or Volvo would consult published accounting reports to compare the most recent financial results of the companies. The information in the reports helps her decide which company would be the better investment choice.
- A senator debating a new low-income housing plan needs to know how the proposed plan will affect the country's budget. Accounting information shows how much the plan will cost and where the money will come from.
- A lender considering a loan to a company that wants to expand would examine the historical performance of the company and projections the company provided about how the borrowed funds will be used to produce new business.

Accounting helps decision making by showing where and when money has been spent and commitments have been made, by evaluating performance, and by indicating the financial implications of choosing one plan rather than another. Accounting also helps predict the future effects of decisions, and it helps direct attention to current problems, imperfections, and inefficiencies, as well as opportunities.

Consider some basic relationships in the decision-making process:

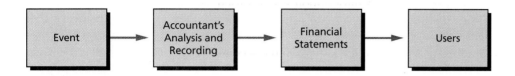

Our focus includes all four boxes. All financial accounting courses cover analysis and recording and preparing financial statements. We will pay more attention to the underlying business process and to the way in which the financial reports help decision makers to take action.

FINANCIAL AND MANAGEMENT ACCOUNTING

The financial statements discussed in this book are common to all areas of accounting. "Financial accounting" is often distinguished from "management accounting." The major distinction between them is their use by two different classes of decision makers. The field of financial accounting serves external decision makers, such as stockholders, suppliers, banks, and government agencies. **Management accounting** serves internal decision makers, such as top executives, department heads, college deans, hospital administrators, and people at other management levels within an organization.[1] The two fields of accounting share many of the same procedures for analyzing and recording the effect of individual transactions.

The primary questions regarding a firm's financial success that decision makers want answered are:

What is the financial picture of the organization on a given day?

How well did it do during a given period?

The accountant answers these questions with three major financial statements: balance sheet, income statement, and statement of cash flows. The balance sheet focuses on the financial picture as of a given day. The other financial statements focus on the performance over time.

The most common source of financial information used by investors and managers is the annual report. The **annual report** is a document prepared by management and distributed to current and potential investors to inform them about the company's past performance and future prospects. Firms distribute their annual report to stockholders automatically. Interested investors may request the report by calling the investor relations department of the company.

You may want to skim over The Gap's annual report in Appendix A to see how firms use photographs and charts extensively to communicate their message. Also, in addition to the financial statements, annual reports include:

1. A letter from corporate management
2. A discussion and analysis of recent economic events by management

management accounting The field of accounting that serves internal decision makers, such as top executives, department heads, college deans, hospital administrators, and people at other management levels within an organization.

3 financial statements answer these questions

annual report A combination of financial statements, management discussion and analysis, and graphs and charts that is provided annually to investors.

---

[1]*For a book-length presentation of the field, see Charles T. Horngren, Gary L. Sundem, and William O. Stratton,* Introduction to Management Accounting, *11th ed. (Upper Saddle River, NJ: Prentice Hall, 1999), the companion volume to this textbook.*

3. Footnotes that explain many elements of the financial statements in more detail
4. The report of the independent auditors
5. A statement of management's responsibility for preparation of the financial statements
6. Other corporate information

Although all of the annual report is important, we will concentrate on the principal financial statements and how accountants collect and report this information.

THE BALANCE SHEET

balance sheet (statement of financial position, statement of financial condition) A financial statement that shows the financial status of a business entity at a particular instant in time.

One of the major financial statements prepared by the accounting system is the **balance sheet,** which shows the financial status of a company at a particular instant in time. The balance sheet has two counterbalancing sections. The left side lists assets, which represent the resources of the firm (everything the firm owns and controls—from cash to buildings, and so on). The right side lists liabilities and owners' equity, which represent the sources of resources used to acquire the assets. Liabilities and owners' equity might be thought of as claims against the resources.

Although *balance sheet* is a widely used term, it is not as descriptive as its newer substitute terms: **statement of financial position** or **statement of financial condition.** But old terms die hard, so balance sheet will be used in this book.

balance sheet = statement of financial position = statement of financial condition.

To illustrate the balance sheet, suppose George Smith, a salaried employee of a local bicycle company, quits his job and opens his own bicycle shop. Smith has heard about the troubles of new businesses that lack money, so he invests plenty: $400,000. Then Smith, acting for the business (which he names Biwheels Company), borrows $100,000 from a local bank for business purposes. That gives Biwheels $500,000 in assets, all currently in the form of cash. The opening balance sheet of this new business enterprise follows:

Biwheels Company
Balance Sheet December 31, 19X1

Assets		Liabilities and Owners' Equity	
Cash	$500,000	Liabilities	
		(note payable)	$100,000
		Smith, capital	400,000
		Total liabilities	
Total assets	$500,000	and owners' equity	$500,000

A = L + OE

The elements in this balance sheet show the financial status of the Biwheels Company as of December 31, 19X1. The company's assets at this point in time ($500,000) are listed on the left. They are balanced on the right by an equal amount of liability and owners' equity ($100,000 liability owed to the bank plus $400,000 paid in by Smith).

Because the balance sheet shows the financial status at a particular point in time, it is always dated. Also, the left and right sides are always kept in balance (thus the name balance sheet). The elements in the balance sheet form the **balance sheet equation:**

$$\text{Assets} = \text{Liabilities} + \text{Owners' equity}$$

The terms in this equation are specifically defined as follows:

Assets are economic resources that are expected to increase or cause future cash inflows or reduce or prevent future cash outflows. Examples are cash, inventories, and equipment.

Liabilities are economic obligations of the organization to outsiders, or claims against its assets by outsiders. An example is a debt to a bank. When a company takes out a loan or other type of liability, a promissory note that states the terms of repayment is usually exchanged. Accountants use the term **notes payable** to describe the existence of promissory notes.

Owners' equity is the residual interest in, or remaining claims against, the organization's assets after deducting liabilities. When the business is first started, the owners' equity is measured by the total amount invested by the owners. As illustrated by "Smith, capital" in the Biwheels Company example, the accountant often uses the term capital instead of owners' equity to designate an owner's investment in the business. The residual, or "leftover," nature of owners' equity is often emphasized by reexpressing the balance sheet equation as follows:

$$\text{Owners' equity} = \text{Assets} - \text{Liabilities}$$ *OE = A − L*

balance sheet equation
Assets = Liabilities + Owners' equity

assets Economic resources that are expected to benefit future cash inflows or help reduce future cash outflows.

liabilities Economic obligations of the organization to outsiders, or claims against its assets by outsiders.

notes payable Promissory notes that are evidence of a debt and state the terms of payment.

owners' equity *(capital)* The residual interest in the organization's assets after deducting liabilities.

BALANCE SHEET TRANSACTIONS

Balance sheets are affected by every transaction that a company, or an entity, has. An **entity** is an organization or a section of an organization that stands apart from other organizations and individuals as a separate economic unit. A **transaction** is any event that both affects the financial position of an entity and can be reliably recorded in money terms. Each transaction has counterbalancing entries on the balance sheet so that the total assets always equal the total liabilities and owners' equity. That is, the equality of the balance sheet equation is maintained for every transaction. An accountant who prepares a balance sheet that does not balance has made a mistake somewhere because the balance sheet must balance.

entity An organization or a section of an organization that stands apart from other organizations and individuals as a separate economic unit.

transaction Any event that both affects the financial position of an entity and can be reliably recorded in money terms.

Let's take a look at some transactions of Biwheels Company to see how typical transactions affect the balance sheet.

TRANSACTION 1, INITIAL INVESTMENT. The first Biwheels transaction was the investment by the owner on December 31, 19X1. Smith deposited $400,000 in a business bank account entitled Biwheels Company. The accounting equation is affected as follows:

Objective 3
Analyze business transactions and relate them to changes in the balance sheet.

	Assets	= Liabilities	+	Owners' Equity
	Cash			Smith, Capital
(1)	+ 400,000 =			+ 400,000
				(owner investment)

This transaction increases both the assets, specifically Cash, and the owners' equity of the business, specifically Smith, Capital. Liabilities are unaffected. Why? Because Smith's business has no obligation to an outside party because of this transaction. A parenthetical note, "owner investment," is used to identify the reason for the transaction's effect on owners' equity. The total amounts on the left side of the equation are equal to the total amounts on the right side, as they should be.

TRANSACTION 2, LOAN FROM BANK. On January 2, 19X2, Biwheels Company borrows from a bank, signing a promissory note for $100,000. The $100,000 is added to the business's cash. The effect of this loan transaction on the accounting equation is:

	Assets	=	Liabilities	+	Owners' Equity
			Note		
	Cash		Payable		Smith, Capital
(1)	+ 400,000	=			+ 400,000
(2)	+ 100,000	=	+100,000		
Bal.	500,000	=	100,000		400,000
	500,000			500,000	

The loan increases the asset, Cash, and increases the liability, Note Payable, by the same amount, $100,000. After the transaction is completed, Biwheels has assets of $500,000, liabilities of $100,000, and owners' equity of $400,000. As always, the sums of the individual account balances (abbreviated Bal.) on each side of the equation are equal.

TRANSACTION 3, ACQUIRE INVENTORY FOR CASH. On January 2, 19X2, Biwheels acquires bicycles from a manufacturer for $150,000 cash.

	Assets		=	Liabilities	+	Owners' Equity
		Merchandise		Note		Smith,
	Cash	Inventory		Payable		Capital
Bal.	500,000		=	100,000		400,000
(3)	−150,000	+150,000	=			
Bal.	350,000	150,000	=	100,000		400,000
	500,000			500,000		

inventory Goods held by a company for the purpose of sale to customers.

This transaction, the cash purchase of inventory, increases one asset, Merchandise Inventory, and decreases another asset, Cash, by the same amount. **Inventory** refers to goods held by the company for the purpose of sale to customers. The form of the assets changed, but the total amount of assets is unchanged. Moreover, the right-side items are completely unchanged.

Biwheels can prepare a balance sheet at any point in time, even after every transaction. The balance sheet for January 2, after the first three transactions, would look like this:

Biwheels Company
Balance Sheet January 2, 19X2

Assets		Liabilities and Owners' Equity	
Cash	$350,000	Liabilities (note payable)	$100,000
Merchandise inventory	150,000	Smith, capital	400,000
Total assets	$500,000	Total liabilities and owners' equity	$500,000

TRANSACTION ANALYSIS

Accountants record transactions in an organization's accounts. An **account** is a summary record of the changes in a particular asset, liability, or owners' equity, and the *account balance* is the total of all entries to the account to date. The analysis of transactions is the heart of accounting. For each transaction, the accountant determines (1) which specific accounts are affected, (2) whether the account balances are increased or decreased, and (3) the amount of the change in each account balance.

Exhibit 1-2 shows how a series of transactions may be analyzed using the balance sheet equation. The transactions are numbered for easy reference. Please examine how the first three transactions that were discussed earlier are analyzed in Exhibit 1-2.

Consider how each of the following additional transactions is analyzed:

4. Jan. 3. Biwheels buys bicycles for $10,000 from a manufacturer. The manufacturer requires $4,000 by January 10 and the balance in 30 days.

5. Jan. 4. Biwheels acquires assorted store equipment for a total of $15,000. A cash down payment of $4,000 is made. The remaining balance must be paid in 60 days.

6. Jan. 5. Biwheels sells a store showcase to a business neighbor after Smith decides he dislikes it. Its selling price, $1,000, happens to be exactly equal to its cost. The neighbor agrees to pay within 30 days.

7. Jan. 6. Biwheels returns some inventory (which had been acquired on January 3 for $800) to the manufacturer for full credit (an $800 reduction of the amount that Biwheels owes the manufacturer).

8. Jan. 10. Biwheels pays $4,000 to the manufacturer described in transaction 4.

9. Jan. 12. Biwheels collects $700 of the $1,000 owed by the business neighbor for transaction 6.

— Jan. 12. Smith remodels his home for $35,000, paying by check from his personal bank account.

Use the format in Exhibit 1-2 to analyze each transaction. Try to do your own analysis of each transaction before looking at the entries shown for it in the exhibit. For example, you could cover the numerical entries with a sheet of paper or a ruler and then proceed through each transaction, one by one.

TRANSACTION 4, PURCHASE ON CREDIT. Most purchases by various types of companies throughout the world are made on a credit basis rather than on a cash basis. An authorized signature of the buyer is usually good enough to assure payment. No formal promissory note is necessary. This practice is known as buying on **open account.** The money owed is shown on the buyer's balance sheet as an *account payable.* Thus an **account payable** is a liability that results from a purchase of goods or services on open account. As Exhibit 1-2 shows for this merchandise purchase on account, the merchandise inventory (an asset account) of Biwheels is increased and an account payable

account A summary record of the changes in a particular asset, liability, or owners' equity.

open account Buying or selling on credit, usually by just an "authorized signature" of the buyer.

account payable A liability that results from a purchase of goods or services on open account.

Exhibit 1-2

Biwheels Company

Analysis of Transactions for December 31, 19X1–January 12, 19X2

Description of Transactions	Cash	+ Accounts Receivable +	Merchandise Inventory +	Store Equipment =	Note Payable +	Accounts Payable +	Smith, Capital
			Assets		**=**	**Liabilities + Owners' Equity**	
(1) Initial investment	+400,000			=			+400,000
(2) Loan from bank	+100,000			=	+100,000		
(3) Acquire inventory for cash	−150,000		+ 150,000	=			
(4) Acquire inventory on credit			+ 10,000	=		+10,000	
(5) Acquire store equipment for cash plus credit	− 4,000			+15,000 =		+11,000	
(6) Sale of equipment		+1,000		− 1,000 =			
(7) Return of inventory acquired on January 3			− 800	=		− 800	
(8) Payments to creditors	− 4,000			=		− 4,000	
(9) Collections from debtors	+ 700	− 700					
Balance, January 12, 19X2	342,700	+ 300 +	159,200 +	14,000 =	100,000 +	16,200 +	400,000
			516,200			516,200	

(a liability account) is also increased in the amount of $10,000 to keep the equation in balance.

	Cash	Merchandise Inventory	Note Payable	Accounts Payable	Smith, Capital
		Assets	**=** **Liabilities**	**+**	**Owners' Equity**
Bal.	350,000	150,000	= 100,000		400,000
(4)		+10,000	=	+10,000	
Bal.	350,000	160,000	= 100,000	10,000	400,000
		510,000		510,000	

TRANSACTION 5, PURCHASE FOR CASH PLUS CREDIT. This transaction illustrates a **compound entry** because it affects more than two balance sheet accounts (two asset accounts and one liability account in this case). Store equipment is increased by the full amount of its cost regardless of whether payment is made in full now, in full later, or partially now and partially later. Therefore Biwheels' Store Equipment (an asset account) is increased by $15,000, Cash (an asset account) is decreased by $4,000, and Accounts Payable (a liability account) is increased by the difference, $11,000.

compound entry A transaction that affects more than two accounts.

	Cash	Merchandise Inventory	Store Equipment	Note Payable	Accounts Payable	Smith, Capital
		Assets		**=** **Liabilities**	**+**	**Owners' Equity**
Bal.	350,000	160,000		= 100,000	10,000	400,000
(5)	− 4,000		+15,000	=	+11,000	
Bal.	346,000	160,000	15,000	= 100,000	21,000	400,000
		521,000			521,000	

TRANSACTION 6, SALE ON CREDIT. This transaction is similar to a purchase on credit except that Biwheels is now the seller. Thus Biwheels is owed money. The cash payment that has been promised counts as an asset. Accounts Receivable (an asset account) of $1,000 is thus created, and Store Equipment (an asset account) is decreased by $1,000. In this case, the transaction affects assets only. Liabilities and owners' equity are unchanged.

| | | | Assets | | = | Liabilities | | Owners' Equity |
	Cash	Accounts Receivable	Merchandise Inventory	Store Equipment		Note Payable	Accounts Payable	Smith, Capital
Bal.	346,000		160,000	15,000	=	100,000	21,000	400,000
(6)		+1,000		−1,000	=			
Bal.	346,000	1,000	160,000	14,000	=	100,000	21,000	400,000
		521,000					521,000	

TRANSACTION 7, RETURN OF INVENTORY TO SUPPLIER. When a company returns merchandise to its suppliers for credit, its merchandise inventory account is reduced and its liabilities are reduced. In this instance, the amount of the decrease on each side of the equation is $800.

| | | | Assets | | = | Liabilities | | Owners' Equity |
	Cash	Accounts Receivable	Merchandise Inventory	Store Equipment		Note Payable	Accounts Payable	Smith, Capital
Bal.	346,000	1,000	160,000	14,000	=	100,000	21,000	400,000
(7)			− 800		=		− 800	
Bal.	346,000	1,000	159,200	14,000	=	100,000	20,200	400,000
		520,200					520,200	

TRANSACTION 8, PAYMENTS TO CREDITORS. A **creditor** is one to whom money is owed. For Biwheels, the manufacturer who supplied the bikes on credit is an example of a creditor. Payments to the manufacturer decrease both assets (Cash) and liabilities (Accounts Payable) by $4,000.

creditor A person or entity to whom money is owed.

| | | | Assets | | = | Liabilities | | Owners' Equity |
	Cash	Accounts Receivable	Merchandise Inventory	Store Equipment		Note Payable	Accounts Payable	Smith, Capital
Bal.	346,000	1,000	159,200	14,000	=	100,000	20,200	400,000
(8)	− 4,000				=		− 4,000	
Bal.	342,000	1,000	159,200	14,000	=	100,000	16,200	400,000
		516,200					516,200	

TRANSACTION 9, COLLECTIONS FROM DEBTORS. A **debtor** is one who owes money. Biwheels' business neighbor is a debtor, and Biwheels is the creditor. Collections from the neighbor increase one of Biwheels' assets (Cash) and decrease another asset (Accounts Receivable) by $700.

debtor A person or entity that owes money to another.

	Assets			=	Liabilities		Owners' Equity
	Cash	Accounts Receivable	Merchandise Inventory	Store Equipment	Note Payable	Accounts Payable	Smith, Capital
Bal.	342,000	1,000	159,200	14,000	= 100,000	16,200	400,000
(9)	+ 700	− 700			=		
Bal.	342,700	300	159,200	14,000	= 100,000	16,200	400,000
		516,200				516,200	

PREPARING THE BALANCE SHEET

A cumulative total may be drawn at any date for each account in Exhibit 1-2. The following balance sheet uses the totals at the bottom of Exhibit 1-2. Observe once again that a balance sheet represents the financial impact of all transactions up to a specific point in time, here January 12, 19X2.

Biwheels Company
Balance Sheet January 12, 19X2

Assets		Liabilities and Owners' Equity	
Cash	$342,700	Note payable	$100,000
Accounts receivable	300	Accounts payable	16,200
Merchandise		Total liabilities	$116,200
inventory	159,200		
Store equipment	14,000	Smith, capital	400,000
Total	$516,200	Total	$516,200

As noted earlier, Biwheels could prepare a new balance sheet after each transaction. Obviously, such a practice would be awkward and unnecessary. Therefore balance sheets are usually produced once a month.

EXAMPLES OF ACTUAL CORPORATE BALANCE SHEETS

To become more familiar with the balance sheet and its equation, consider the following condensed excerpts from one actual recent financial report. Some terms vary among organizations, but the essential balance sheet equation does not.

The DuPont 1996 balance sheet shows that property, plant and equipment is a major asset for the chemical industry, accounting for more than half of total assets. Moreover, the total liabilities is greater than the amount of owners' equity. Other liabilities consist primarily of obligations to employees for future life insurance and medical benefits during retirement.

Appendix A at the end of this book contains a complete set of the actual 1996 financial statements of The Gap, Inc. As you proceed from chapter to chapter, you should examine the pertinent parts of The Gap's financial statements. In this way, you will become increasingly comfortable with actual financial reports. For example, the general format and major items in The Gap's balance sheet (Appendix A) should be familiar by now. Details will gradually become more understandable as each chapter explains the nature of the various major financial statements.

DuPont
Consolidated Balance Sheet
(Dollars in millions, except per share)

December 31	1996
Assets	
Current Assets	
Cash and Cash Equivalents	$ 1,066
Marketable Securities	253
Accounts and Notes Receivable	5,193
Other Current Assets	4,591
Total Current Assets	11,103
Property, Plant and Equipment	50,549
Less: Accumulated Depreciation, Depletion and Amortization	29,336
	21,213
Investment in Affiliates	2,278
Other Assets	3,393
Total	**$ 37,987**
Liabilities and Stockholders' Equity	
Current Liabilities	
Accounts Payable	$ 2,757
Other Liabilities	8,230
Total Current Liabilities	10,987
Long-Term Borrowings and Capital Lease Obligations	5,087
Other Liabilities	10,584
Total Liabilities	26,658
Total Stockholders' Equity	11,329
Total	**$37,987**

TYPES OF OWNERSHIP

Although there are countless different types of companies, there are only three basic forms of ownership structures for business entities: sole proprietorships, partnerships, and corporations.

Objective 4
Compare the features of proprietorships, partnerships, and corporations.

SOLE PROPRIETORSHIPS

A **sole proprietorship** is a separate organization with a single owner. Most often the owner is also the manager. Therefore sole proprietorships tend to be small retail establishments and individual professional businesses such as those of dentists, physicians, and attorneys. From an accounting viewpoint, each sole proprietorship is a separate entity that is distinct from the proprietor. Thus the cash in the dentist's business account is an asset of the dental practice, while the cash in her personal account is not.

sole proprietorship A separate organization with a single owner.

PARTNERSHIPS

A **partnership** is an organization that joins two or more individuals who act as co-owners. Many retail establishments are partnerships, and dentists, physicians, attorneys, and accountants often conduct their activities as partnerships. Partnerships can be gigantic. The largest international accounting firms have thousands of partners. Again, from an accounting viewpoint, each partnership is an individual entity that is separate from the personal activities of each partner.

partnership A form of organization that joins two or more individuals together as co-owners.

CORPORATIONS

corporation A business organization that is created by individual state laws.

limited liability A feature of the corporate form of organization whereby corporate creditors ordinarily have claims against the corporate assets only. The owners' personal assets are not subject to the creditors' grasp.

publicly owned A corporation in which shares in the ownership are sold to the public.

privately owned A corporation owned by a family, a small group of shareholders, or a single individual, in which shares of ownership are not publicly sold.

Corporations are business organizations created under state law in the United States. The most notable characteristic of a corporation is **limited liability** of the owners, which means that corporate creditors (such as banks or suppliers) ordinarily have claims against the corporate assets only. Individuals form a corporation by applying to the state for approval of the company's articles of incorporation, which include information on shares of ownership. Most large corporations are **publicly owned** in that shares in the ownership are sold to the public. The owners of the corporation are then identified as *shareholders* (or *stockholders*). Large publicly owned corporations can have thousands of shareholders. Some corporations are **privately owned** by families, small groups of shareholders, or a single individual, and shares of ownership are not publicly sold. Many states allow having only one shareholder.

In the United States, the laws governing the creation of a corporation vary from state to state. In spite of its small size, Delaware is the state in which many corporations are legally created because its rules are less restrictive than are those of most other states. In addition, its legal and incorporating fees are low and its legal system and the judges who hear business cases are experienced and efficient at resolving disputes and lawsuits. The exact rights and privileges of a corporation vary from state to state and from country to country.

Internationally, organizational forms similar to corporations are common. In the United Kingdom they are frequently indicated by the word limited (Ltd.) in the name. In many countries whose laws trace back to Spain, the initials S.A. refer to a "society anonymous" meaning that multiple unidentified owners stand behind the company. Not surprisingly, countries in the former Soviet Union are formulating legal systems that permit corporate-style companies. They are also creating markets where the owners of these companies can buy and sell their ownership interests.

Whereas the owners of proprietorships and partnerships are typically active managers of the business as well, corporate managers often own only a small part of the public corporation. Because the corporate form is the form in which the majority of U.S. business is conducted, we will use corporate accounting practice exclusively henceforth.

A NOTE ON NONPROFIT ORGANIZATIONS

The major focus of this book is on profit-seeking organizations, such as business firms. However, the fundamental accounting principles also apply to nonprofit (that is, not-for-profit) organizations. Managers and accountants in hospitals, universities, government agencies, and other nonprofit organizations use financial statements. Money must be raised and spent, budgets must be prepared, and financial performance must be judged. Nonprofit organizations need to use their limited resources wisely, and financial statements are essential for judging their use of resources.

ADVANTAGES AND DISADVANTAGES OF THE CORPORATE FORM

The corporate form of organization has many advantages. Limited liability is foremost. If a corporation drifts into financial trouble, its creditors cannot look for repayment beyond the corporation itself. In other words, the owners' personal assets are not subject to the creditors' grasp. In contrast, the owners of proprietorships and partnerships typically have *unlimited liability,* which means that business creditors can look to the owners' personal assets for repayment. For example, if Biwheels were a partnership, each partner would bear a personal liability for full payment of the $100,000 bank loan.

Another advantage of the corporation is easy transfer of ownership. In selling shares in its ownership, the corporation usually issues **capital stock certificates** (often called simply **stock certificates**) as formal evidence of ownership. These shares may be sold and resold among present and potential owners. Numerous stock exchanges exist in the United States and worldwide where long established rules for trading facilitate daily buying and selling of shares. More than 600 million shares are bought and sold on an average day on the New York Stock Exchange (NYSE) alone. Further, trading is not limited to U.S. markets. Shares of many large U.S. firms are also traded on international exchanges such as those in Tokyo and London. And many Japanese and British firms have shares traded on the NYSE. Examples include Nissan, Toyota, and Honda from Japan, British Petroleum, and Glaxo Wellcome from the United Kingdom. The total market value of shares traded in U.S. markets is approximately $7 trillion, compared with some $1 trillion in Japan and $1.5 trillion in London.

In contrast to proprietorships and partnerships, corporations have the advantage of ease in raising ownership capital from hundreds or thousands of potential stockholders. Indeed, AT&T has over 2 million stockholders, owning a total of over 1.6 billion shares of stock as of December 31, 1996.

The corporation also has the advantage of continuity of existence. The life of a corporation is indefinite in the sense that it continues even if its ownership changes. In contrast, proprietorships and partnerships officially terminate upon the death or complete withdrawal of an owner.

The effects of the form of ownership on income taxes may vary significantly. For example, a corporation is taxed as a separate entity (as a corporation). But no income taxes are levied on a proprietorship (as a proprietorship) or on a partnership (as a partnership). Instead the income earned by proprietorships and partnerships is attributed to the owners as personal taxpayers. In short, the income tax laws regard corporations as being taxable entities, but proprietorships or partnerships as not being taxable entities. Whether the corporate form provides tax advantages or disadvantages depends heavily on the personal tax situations of the owners.

Regardless of the economic and legal advantages or disadvantages of each type of organization, some small-business owners incorporate simply for prestige. That is, they feel more important if they can refer to "my corporation" and if they can refer to themselves as "chairman of the board" or "president" instead of "business owner" or "partner."

In terms of numbers of businesses, there are fewer corporations in the United States than there are proprietorships or partnerships. However, the corporation has far more economic significance. Corporations conduct a sheer money volume of business that dwarfs the volume of other forms of organization. Moreover, almost every reader of this book interacts with, owes money to, or invests in corporations. For these reasons, this book emphasizes the corporate form of ownership.

ACCOUNTING FOR OWNERS' EQUITY

The basic accounting concepts that underlie the owners' equity section of the balance sheet are the same for all three forms of ownership. However, owners' equities for proprietorships and partnerships are often identified by the word **capital.** In contrast, owners' equity for a corporation is usually called **stockholders' equity** or **shareholders' equity.** Examine the possibilities for the Biwheels Company that are shown in the accompanying table.

The accounts for the proprietorship and the partnership show owners' equity as straightforward records of the capital invested by the owners. For a corporation, though, the total capital investment by its owners, both at the start of the company and thereafter, is called **paid-in capital.** It is recorded in two parts: capital stock at par value and paid-in capital in excess of par value.

capital stock certificate (stock certificate) Formal evidence of ownership shares in a corporation.

note difference

capital A term used to identify owners' equities for proprietorships and partnerships.

stockholders' equity (shareholders' equity) Owners' equity of a corporation. The excess of assets over liabilities of a corporation.

paid-in capital The total capital investment in a corporation by its owners at the inception of business and subsequently.

Owners' Equity for Different Organizations

Owners' Equity for a Proprietorship **(Assume George Smith is the sole owner)**	
George Smith, capital	$400,000

Owners' Equity for a Partnership *(Assume Smith has two partners)*	
George Smith, capital	$320,000
Alex Handl, capital	40,000
Susan Eastman, capital	40,000
Total partners' capital	$400,000

Owners' Equity for a Corporation	
Stockholders' equity:	
Paid-in capital:	
Capital stock, 10,000 shares issued at par value of $10 per share	$100,000
Paid-in capital in excess of par value of capital stock	300,000
Total paid-in capital	$400,000

THE MEANING OF PAR VALUE

par value (stated value) The nominal dollar amount printed on stock certificates.

Most states require stock certificates to have some dollar amount printed on them. This amount is determined by the board of directors and is usually called **par value** or **stated value.** Typically, the stock is sold at a price that is higher than its par value. The difference between the total amount received for the stock and the par value is called **paid-in capital in excess of par value.** This distinction is of little economic importance and we introduce it here only because you will frequently encounter it in actual financial statements.

paid-in capital in excess of par value When issuing stock, the difference between the total amount received and the par value.

Let's take a closer look at par value by altering our Biwheels example. We will now assume that Biwheels is a corporation and that 10,000 shares of its stock have been sold for $40 per share. The par value is $10 per share, and therefore the paid-in capital in excess of par value is $30 per share. Thus, the total ownership claim of $400,000 arising from the investment is split between two equity claims, one for $100,000 "capital stock, at par" and one for $300,000 "paid-in capital in excess of par" or "additional paid-in capital."

The following formulas show these components of the total paid-in capital account:

$$\text{Total paid-in capital} = \text{Capital stock at par} + \text{Paid-in capital in excess of par}$$
$$\$400,000 = \$100,000 + \$300,000$$

$$\text{Capital stock at par} = \text{Number of shares issued} \times \text{Par value per share}$$
$$\$100,000 = 10,000 \times \$10$$

$$\text{Paid-in capital in excess of par} = \text{Total paid-in capital} - \text{Capital stock at par}$$
$$\$300,000 = \$400,000 - \$100,000$$

$$\text{Total paid-in capital} = \text{Number of shares issued} \times \text{Average issue price per share}$$
$$\$400,000 = 10,000 \times \$40$$

The following financial statement excerpts show par value and paid-in capital at work in real companies:

The Gap, Inc.
Consolidated Balance Sheets

($000)	February 1, 1997	February 3, 1996
Stockholders' Equity		
Common stock $.05 par value		
Authorized 500,000,000 shares; issued 317,864,090		
and 315,971,306 shares	$ 15,895	$ 15,799
Additional paid-in capital	442,049	335,193
Retained earnings	1,938,352	1,569,347
Other	(741,826)	(279,866)
Total Stockholders' Equity	$1,654,470	$1,640,473

AT&T Corp. and Subsidiaries
Consolidated Balance Sheets

Dollars in Millions		
At December 31	1996	1995
Shareowners' Equity		
Common shares, par value $1 per share	$ 1,623	$ 1,596
Authorized shares: 2,000,000,000		
Outstanding shares: 1,623,487,646 at December 31, 1996;		
1,596,005,351 at December 31, 1995		
Additional paid-in capital	15,643	16,614
Other	(49)	(249)
Retained earnings (deficit)	3,078	(687)
Total shareowners' equity	$20,295	$17,274

Note that AT&T has $1 par value common shares, while The Gap has $.05 par value common stock. Whether called common shares or **common stock,** the meaning is the same as that of "capital stock" in the discussion above. Although it would be nice to stick to one phrase at every point in this textbook, the reality is that the world is full of different words for some accounting items. One of our goals is to help you to prepare yourself for reading and understanding actual financial statements and reports. Therefore, we will use many of the various synonyms you are likely to come across when reading financial statements. Another of our goals is to identify distinctions that are important and those that are not. For example there are different par values for these companies, but these values bear no relation to the companies' market prices, as illustrated below:

common stock Stock representing the class of owners having a "residual" ownership of a corporation.

Same as Capital stock.

	AT&T	The Gap
Par Value	$ 1.00	$ .05
Market Value	$44.00	$52.00

The extremely small amount of par value as compared to the additional paid-in capital is common in practice and illustrates the insignificance of "par value" in today's business world. The Gap uses the frequently encountered term, "additional paid-in capital," as a short synonym for "paid-in capital in excess of par value of common stock." Finally, note that the number of "shares authorized" is the maximum number of shares that the company can issue as designated by the company's articles of incorporation.

Both AT&T and The Gap show *retained earnings* and *other* as part of their owners' equity. These values arise from various sources with the passage of time. Our current focus is on the first two lines-common stock and additional paid-in capital. These amounts can be described accurately with a simple term, total paid-in capital. An important point about "paid-in" capital is that it shows amounts that owners actively contributed to the firm.

Individuals buy shares of stock as investments. Sometimes they purchase the stock from the company and the previous discussion describes what happens. The company records cash received and records the par value of shares issued with the excess shown as an increase in paid-in capital. But the majority of stock transactions involving purchase and sale of stock occur between individuals. When Mary sells 100 shares of DuPont to Carlos, the transaction has no effect on DuPont. Mary may have a gain if the shares are sold for more than she paid for them. She will have a loss on the sale otherwise. But this affects DuPont only in terms of keeping track of its owners. When the shares change hands, Mary will be replaced by Carlos on the corporate records as an owner, and Carlos will begin to receive the dividends on the shares and will be allowed to vote on corporate issues.

STOCKHOLDERS AND THE BOARD OF DIRECTORS

In partnerships, top management may be shared by the owners. In corporations, the ultimate responsibility for management is delegated by stockholders to the *board of directors,* as indicated in the following diagram:

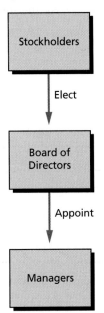

An advantage of the corporate form of organization is that it separates ownership and management. Stockholders invest resources but do not need to devote time to managing, and managers can be selected for their managerial skills, not their ability to invest large sums in the firm. The board of directors is the link between stockholders and the actual managers. It is the board's duty to ensure that managers act in the interests of shareholders.

The board of directors is elected by the shareholders, but the slate of candidates is often selected by management. Sometimes, the chairman of the board is also the top manager and the major shareholder. For example, for over 30 years Henry Ford II was the major stockholder, the chairman of the board, and the chief executive officer (CEO) of the Ford Motor Company. Other top company managers, such as the president, financial vice president, and marketing vice president, are routinely elected to the board of directors of the company they manage. Therefore, the interests of both stockholders and managers are usually represented on the board of directors.

Membership on a board of directors is often extended to CEOs and presidents of other corporations, to university presidents and professors, and to attorneys. For example, the 16-member board of General Mills recently included five General Mills managers, eight present or former CEOs of other companies, two professors, and one attorney. In many cases, these members of the board are also stockholders of the corporation. Many companies are moving toward having smaller boards of directors that include fewer members of the company's management team. For example, in 1996, IBM had an 11-member board, which included only one member of IBM's management. That member was Louis Gerstner, who took over as chief executive officer several years earlier and currently serves as chairman of the board.

CREDIBILITY AND THE ROLE OF AUDITING

If someone told you that smoking cigarettes was not related to the risk of lung cancer, your reaction would be based on when the conversation occurred, on who the speaker was, and on your own knowledge at the time. For instance, when Europeans arrived in North America and first witnessed the act of smoking tobacco, no one knew what lung cancer was, and no one linked disease to behavior. By the middle of the twentieth century, people understood that what you did to your body could easily make you sick, but there wasn't enough evidence about the health risks of smoking. Were people who smoked more likely to have lung cancer? By the mid-1990s, evidence showed that the answer to this question was most certainly yes, although it was not until 1997 that executives of tobacco companies acknowledged a link. Some people continue to consider the additional risk of cancer small and continue to smoke.

This little history lesson shows that when people make statements, those statements will often be affected by the position of the speaker. Tobacco executives cannot say that tobacco causes cancer for to do so would be to acknowledge prior lies and to invite lawsuits. Smokers cannot say that tobacco is really dangerous because to do so would call into question their own behavior. As listeners we discount certain claims because we know the motives of the person or organization making the claim.

Corporate managers are the ones who provide financial statements to both internal and external decision makers, and they may have incentives to make the company's performance look better than it really is. Perhaps doing so will make it easier to raise money to open new stores, or increase the managers' compensation. Managers often believe that company conditions are better than they really are because managers are optimistic about the good decisions they have made and the plans they are implementing. Investors are naturally a little suspicious of what managers tell them. The problem we face as investors is that we need to be able to rely on managers to tell the truth, but we cannot see personally what is really going on in the firm.

One way to solve this credibility problem is to introduce an honorable, expert third party. In the area of financial statements this third party is called the auditor. The **auditor** examines the information that managers use to prepare the financial statements and provides assurances about the credibility of those statements. Upon seeing the auditor's assurance that the financial statements provide a fair and accurate picture of a company's economic circumstances, investors can feel more comfortable about using the information to guide their investing activity. Another way to ensure truthful reporting by managers is by handing out stiff legal penalties for lying. A manager who knowingly misstates performance is subject to both fines and jail sentences under U.S. law.

auditor A person that examines the information used by managers to prepare the financial statements and attests to the credibility of those statements.

THE CERTIFIED PUBLIC ACCOUNTANT

The desire for stockholders and external parties such as banks who lend money to the firm to have third-party assurance about the credibility of financial statements gave rise naturally to a profession dedicated to that purpose. Providing credibility requires individuals who must have both the technical knowledge to assess financial statements and determine their quality as well as the reputation for integrity and honestly telling investors and other interested parties if management has not produced fair financial statements. Enter the certified public accountant.

certified public accountant (CPA) In the United States, a person earns this designation by a combination of education, qualifying experience, and the passing of a two-day written national examination.

A **certified public accountant (CPA)** in the United States earns his or her certification by a combination of education, qualifying experience, and passing a two-day written national examination. The examination is administered and graded by a national organization, the American Institute of Certified Public Accountants (AICPA). The institute is the principal professional association in the private sector that regulates the quality of the public accounting profession. Other English-speaking nations have similar arrangements but use the term chartered accountant (CA) instead of certified public accountant.

The CPA examination covers four major topical areas: auditing, accounting theory, business law, and accounting practice. The last is a series of accounting problems covering a wide variety of topics, including income taxes, cost accounting, and accounting for non-profit institutions.

Although the AICPA prepares and grades the CPA examination on a national basis, the individual states have their own regulations concerning the qualifications for taking and passing the examination and for earning the right to practice as a CPA. These regulations are determined and enforced by state boards of accountancy.

THE AUDITOR'S OPINION

audit An examination of transactions and financial statements made in accordance with generally accepted auditing standards.

To assess management's financial disclosure, public accountants conduct an **audit,** which is an examination of transactions and financial statements made in accordance with generally accepted auditing standards developed primarily by the AICPA. This audit includes miscellaneous tests of the accounting records, internal control systems, and other auditing procedures as deemed necessary. The examination is described in the **auditor's opinion** (also called an **independent opinion**) that is included with the financial statements in a corporation's annual report. Standard phrasing is used for auditors' opinions, as illustrated by the following opinion rendered by a large CPA firm, Ernst & Young, for McDonald's Corporation.

auditor's opinion (independent opinion) A report describing the auditor's examination of transactions and financial statements. It is included with the financial statements in an annual report issued by the corporation.

To the Board of Directors and Shareholders of McDonald's Corporation:

We have audited the accompanying consolidated balance sheet of McDonald's Corporation as of December 31, 1996 and 1995, and the related statements of income, shareholders' equity, and cash flows for each of the three years in the period ended December 31, 1996. These financial statements are the responsibility of the McDonald's Corporation management. Our responsibility is to express an opinion on these financial statements based on our audits.

We conducted our audits in accordance with generally accepted auditing standards. Those standards require that we plan and perform the audit to obtain reasonable assurance about whether the financial statements are free of material misstatement. An audit includes examining, on a test basis, evidence supporting the amounts and disclosures in the financial statements. An audit also includes assessing the accounting principles used and significant estimates made by management, as well as evaluating the overall financial statement presentation. We believe that our audits provide a reasonable basis for our opinion.

In our opinion, the financial statements referred to above present fairly, in all material respects, the financial position of McDonald's Corporation at December 31, 1996 and 1995, and the consolidated results of

its operations and its cash flows for each of the three years in the period
ended December 31, 1996 in conformity with generally accepted account-
ing principles.

ERNST & YOUNG LLP

This book will explore the meaning of such phrases as "present fairly" and "generally accepted accounting principles." For now, reflect on the fact that auditors do not prepare a company's financial statements. Rather, the auditor's opinion is the public accountant's stamp of approval on management's financial statements.

THE ACCOUNTING PROFESSION

There are many ways to classify accountants, but the easiest and most common way is to divide them into public and private accountants. **Public accountants** are those whose services are offered to the general public on a fee basis. Such services include auditing, preparing income taxes, and management consulting. All other accountants would be **private accountants.** This category consists not only of those individuals who work for businesses but also those who work for government agencies, including the Internal Revenue Service, and other nonprofit organizations.

PUBLIC ACCOUNTING FIRMS

Public accounting firms vary in their size and in the type of accounting services they perform. There are small proprietorships, where auditing may represent as little as 10% or less of annual billings. Billings are the total amounts charged to clients for services rendered to them. The bulk of the work of these small proprietorships is usually income taxes and "write-up" work (the actual bookkeeping services for clients who are not equipped to do their own accounting).

There are also a handful of gigantic firms that have more than two thousand partners with offices located throughout the world. Such enormous firms are necessary because their clients also tend to be enormous. For instance, a large CPA firm has reported that its annual audit of one client takes the equivalent of 72 accountants working a full year. Another client has 300 separate corporate entities in 40 countries that must ultimately be consolidated into one set of overall financial statements.

The six largest public international accounting firms are known collectively as the "Big-Six":

- Arthur Andersen & Co.
- Coopers & Lybrand
- Deloitte & Touche
- Ernst & Young
- KPMG Peat Marwick
- Price Waterhouse

Many of these firms trace their origins to England and Scotland during the colonial period when audit firms came to the United States to oversee investments in the colonies. As this text is being written the combination of the largest international accounting firms is continuing. This process began decades ago when the "Big-Eight" experienced two mergers. Ernst & Young was created by joining predecessor firms Ernst & Ernst with Arthur Young while Deloitte & Touche grew out of Touche Ross combining with Deloitte, Haskin & Sells. In early 1998, a merger is pending between Coopers & Lybrand and Price Waterhouse. Thus the "Big-Six" may soon be the "Big-Five."

Objective 6
Distinguish between public and private accounting.

public accountants
Accountants who offer services to the general public on a fee basis including auditing, tax work, and management consulting.

private accountants
Accountants who work for businesses, as well as government agencies, and other nonprofit organizations.

public accounting The field of accounting where services are offered to the general public on a fee basis.

Of the companies listed on the New York Stock Exchange, 97% are clients of the "Big-Six." These accounting firms have annual billings in excess of a billion dollars each. A large part of the billings is attributable to auditing services. The top partners in big accounting firms are compensated on about the same scale as their corporate counterparts. Huge accounting firms tend to receive more publicity than other firms. However, please remember that there are thousands of other able accounting firms, varying in size from sole practitioners to giant international partnerships.

OTHER OPPORTUNITIES FOR ACCOUNTANTS

In the accompanying diagram, the long arrows indicate how accountants often move from public accounting firms to positions in business or government. Obviously, these movements can occur at any level or in any direction.

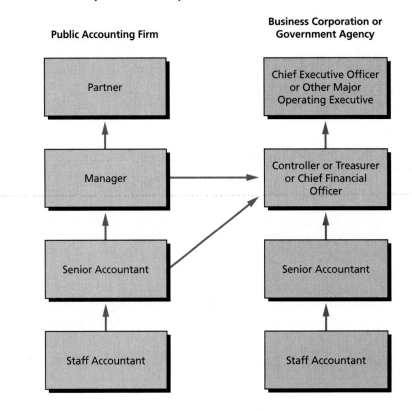

Accounting cuts across all management functions, including purchasing, manufacturing, wholesaling, retailing, and a variety of marketing and transportation activities. It provides an excellent opportunity for gaining broad knowledge. The people responsible for collecting and interpreting financial information about the company develop detailed knowledge about what is occurring and close relationships with key decision makers. Senior accountants or controllers in a corporation are often picked as production or marketing executives. Why? Because they may have impressed other executives as having acquired general management skills.

Accounting is ranked as the most important business school course for future managers. *Business Week* recently reported that "more CEOs [chief executive officers] started out in finance or accounting than in any other area." It is easy to see why accounting is called the language of business.

Objective 7
Evaluate the role of ethics in the accounting process.

PROFESSIONAL ETHICS

Members of the American Institute of Certified Public Accountants must abide by a code of professional conduct. Surveys of public attitudes toward CPAs have consistently ranked the accounting profession as having high ethical standards. The code of professional conduct is especially concerned with integrity and independence. For example, independent auditors are forbidden to own shares of their client corporations. Moreover, the auditors must satisfy themselves that their clients' financial statements are properly prepared.

The emphasis on ethics extends beyond public accounting. For example, members of the Institute of Management Accountants are expected to abide by that organization's code of ethics for management accountants. Auditors and management accountants have professional responsibilities regarding competence, confidentiality, integrity, and objectivity. Professional accounting organizations and state regulatory bodies have procedures for reviewing behavior alleged to violate codes of professional conduct.

SUMMARY PROBLEMS FOR YOUR REVIEW

PROBLEM ONE

Analyze the following additional transactions of Biwheels Company. Begin with the balances shown for January 12, 19X2, in Exhibit 1-2 on page 12. Prepare an ending balance sheet for Biwheels Company (say, on January 16 after these additional transactions).

  i. Biwheels pays $10,000 on the bank loan (ignore interest).
  ii. Smith buys furniture for his home for $5,000, using his family charge account at Macy's.
  iii. Biwheels buys merchandise inventory for $50,000. Half the amount is paid in cash, and half is owed on open account.
  iv. Biwheels collects $200 more from its business debtor.

SOLUTION TO PROBLEM ONE

See Exhibits 1-3 and 1-4. Note that transaction ii is ignored because it is wholly personal. However, visualize how Smith's personal balance sheet would be affected. His assets, Home Furniture, would rise by $5,000 and his liabilities, Accounts Payable, would also rise by $5,000.

Exhibit 1-3

Biwheels Company

Analysis of Additional January Transactions

Description of Transaction	Cash	+	Accounts Receivable	+	Merchandise Inventory	+	Store Equipment	=	Note Payable	+	Accounts Payable	+	Smith, Capital
					Assets			=			**Liabilities + Owners' Equity**		
Balance, January 12, 19X2	342,700 +		300	+	159,200	+	14,000	=	100,000 +		16,200	+	400,000
(i) Payment on bank loan	– 10,000							=	–10,000				
(ii) Personal; no effect													
(iii) Acquire inventory, half for cash	–25,000			+	50,000			=			+ 25,000		
(iv) Collection of receivable	+ 200		–200										
Balance, January 16	307,900 +		100	+	209,200	+	14,000	=	90,000 +		41,200	+	400,000
					531,200			=			531,200		

Exhibit 1-4

Biwheels Company

Balance Sheet January 16, 19X2

Assets		Liabilities and Owners' Equity	
		Liabilities:	
Cash	$307,900	Note payable	$ 90,000
Accounts receivable	100	Accounts payable	41,200
Merchandise inventory	209,200	Total liabilities	$131,200
Store equipment	14,000	Smith, capital	400,000
Total	$531,200	Total	$531,200

PROBLEM TWO

"If I purchase 100 shares of the outstanding stock of General Motors Corporation (or Biwheels Company), I invest my money directly in that corporation. General Motors must record that event." Do you agree? Explain.

SOLUTION TO PROBLEM TWO

Money is invested directly in a corporation when the corporation originally issues the stock. For example, 100,000 shares of stock may be issued at $80 per share, bringing in $8 million to the corporation. This is a transaction between the corporation and the stockholders. It affects the corporate financial position:

Cash $8,000,000   Stockholders' equity $8,000,000

Subsequently, 100 shares of that stock may be sold by an original stockholder (Michael Jordan) to another individual (Meg Ryan) for $130 per share. This is a private transaction; no cash is received by the corporation. Of course, the corporation records the fact that 100 shares originally owned by Jordan are now owned by Ryan, but the corporate financial position is unchanged. Accounting focuses on the business entity; subsequently, private dealings of the owners have no effect on the financial position of the entity, although the corporation records the owners' identities.

PROBLEM THREE

"One individual can be an owner, an employee, and a creditor of a corporation." Do you agree? Explain.

SOLUTION TO PROBLEM THREE

The corporation enters contracts, hires employees, buys buildings, and conducts other business. The chairman of the board, the president, the other officers, and all the workers are employees of the corporation. Thus Katharine Graham could own some of the capital stock of the *Washington Post* and also be an employee (CEO). Because money owed to employees for salaries is a liability, she could be an owner, an employee, and a creditor. Similarly, an employee of a telephone company who is a stockholder of the company could also be receiving telephone services from the same company. She is an owner, employee, customer, and debtor of the company.

PROBLEM FOUR

Refer to the financial statements for The Gap Inc. reproduced in Appendix A in order to respond to the following questions.

1. As of what date is the consolidated balance sheet prepared?
2. What are total assets for The Gap for the two years shown in the consolidated balance sheets? What elements explain the difference in the asset levels for the two years?
3. What is the par value of the common stock?
4. How many share of common stock are authorized and how many shares are outstanding at the latest year-end?

SOLUTION TO PROBLEM FOUR

1. Two balance sheets are presented. One is dated as of February 1, 1997 and the other as of February 3, 1996. The more recent one is in the left column of the page. When the company uses a fiscal year that does not end on December 31 it is sometimes confusing to label the year. In this instance The Gap refers to the year ended February 1, 1997 as fiscal year 1996. We will follow that pattern.
2. Total assets were $2,343,000,000 in fiscal 1995 and $2,626,000,000 in fiscal 1996. The total change of $283 million was primarily due to additional property, equipment, and merchandise inventory. Note that the numbers in the balance sheet omit three zeros. This is indicated by the ($000) in the upper left-hand corner of the statement. Thus the total asset number of $2,626,927 refers to $2.6 billion, $2,626,927,000.
3. The par value is $.05.
4. The Gap has 500,000,000 shares authorized. This is the number of shares The Gap is legally able to issue. As of February 1, 1997, 274,517,331 shares are outstanding. In the caption describing the number of shares, when two numbers appear, as they do for "outstanding," the first number refers to the left-hand column and the second number refers to the right-hand column. Thus, 287,747,984 shares were outstanding on February 3, 1996.

Highlights to Remember

Financial statements provide information for decision making to managers, creditors, and owners of all types of organizations. The balance sheet (or statement of financial position) provides a "snapshot" of the financial position of an organization at any instant. That is, it answers the basic question, Where are we?

The balance sheet equation is Assets = Liabilities + Owners' Equity. This equation must always be in balance.

Transaction analysis is the heart of accounting. A transaction is any event that both affects the financial position of an entity and can be reliably recorded in money terms. For each transaction, an accountant must determine what accounts are affected and by how much.

Corporations are the most important form of business ownership because so much business is conducted by corporations. The ownership equity of a corporation is usually called stockholders' equity. It initially takes the form of common stock at par, or stated, value plus additional paid-in capital.

Separation of ownership from management in corporations creates a demand for auditing, a third-party examination of financial statements. The public accounting profession gives credibility to audits by specifying qualifications for certified public accountants, including ethical standards, and by developing generally accepted auditing standards to ensure thoroughness of audits. Because accountants work with managers in all management functions, accounting positions are fertile training grounds for future top managers.

Accounting Vocabulary

account, p. 11
accounting, p. 4
account payable, p. 11
annual report, p. 7
assets, p. 9
audit, p. 22
auditor, p. 20
auditor's opinion, p. 22
balance sheet, p. 8
balance sheet equation, p. 9
capital, p. 17
capital stock certificate, p. 17
certified public accountant (CPA), p. 22
common stock, p. 19
compound entry, p. 12
corporation, p. 16

creditor, p. 13
debtor, p. 13
entity, p. 10
financial accounting, p. 4
independent opinion, p. 22
inventory, p. 10
liabilities, p. 9
limited liability, p. 16
management accounting, p. 7
notes payable, p. 9
open account, p. 11
owners' equity, p. 9
paid-in capital, p. 17
paid-in capital in excess of par value, p. 18
partnership, p. 15

par value, p. 18
private accountants, p. 23
privately owned, p. 16
public accountants, p. 23
public accounting, p. 23
publicly owned, p. 16
shareholders' equity, p. 17
sole proprietorship, p. 15
stated value, p. 18
statement of financial condition, p. 8
statement of financial position, p. 8
stock certificate, p. 17
stockholders' equity, p. 17
transaction, p. 10

Assignment Material

The assignment material for each chapter is divided into Questions, Exercises, and Problems. The assignment material contains problems based on fictitious companies and problems based on real-life situations. We hope our use of actual companies and news events enhances your interest in accounting.

We identify problems based on real companies by highlighting the name in blue. These problems underscore a major objective of this book: to increase your ability to read, understand, and use published financial reports and news articles. In later chapters, these problems provide the principal means of reviewing not only the immediate chapter but also the previous chapters. Note that the last four problems in each chapter are (1) a problem based on The Gap, whose financial statements are in Appendix A, (2) a financial statement research problem, (3) a Collaborative Learning Exercise, and (4) an Internet-based problem.

QUESTIONS

1-1. Describe *accounting*.

1-2. "It's easier to learn accounting if you avoid real-world examples." Do you agree? Explain.

1-3. Give three examples of decisions that are likely to be influenced by financial statements.

1-4. Give three examples of users of financial statements.

1-5. Briefly distinguish between *financial accounting* and *management accounting*.

1-6. Give two synonyms for *balance sheet*.

1-7. "The balance sheet may be out of balance after some transactions, but it is never out of balance at the end of an accounting period." Do you agree? Explain.

1-8. "When a company buys inventory for cash, total assets do not change. But when it buys inventory on open account, total assets increases." Explain.

1-9. Explain the difference between a *note payable* and an *account payable*.

1-10. Give two synonyms for *owners' equity*.

1-11. Explain the meaning of *limited liability*.

1-12. Why does this book emphasize the corporation rather than the proprietorship or the partnership?

1-13. "International companies with Ltd. or S.A. after their name are essentially the same in organizational form as U.S. companies with Corp. after their name." Do you agree? Explain.

1-14. "The accounting systems described in this book apply to corporations and are not appropriate for nonprofit organizations." Do you agree? Explain.

1-15. "The idea of par value is insignificant." Explain.

1-16. Explain the relationship between the board of directors and top management of a company.

1-17. What is a CPA and how does someone become one?

EXERCISES

1-18 Describing Underlying Transactions

LaTech Company, which was recently formed, is engaging in some preliminary transactions before beginning full-scale operations for retailing laptop computers. The balances of each item in the company's accounting equation are given below for May 10 and for each of the next nine business days.

	Cash	Accounts Receivable	Computer Inventory	Store Fixtures	Accounts Payable	Owners' Equity
May 10	$ 6,000	$ 4,000	$18,000	$ 3,000	$ 4,000	$27,000
11	12,000	4,000	18,000	3,000	4,000	33,000
12	12,000	4,000	18,000	6,000	4,000	36,000
15	9,000	4,000	21,000	6,000	4,000	36,000
16	9,000	4,000	26,000	6,000	9,000	36,000
17	12,000	1,000	26,000	6,000	9,000	36,000
18	7,000	1,000	26,000	13,000	11,000	36,000
19	4,000	1,000	26,000	13,000	8,000	36,000
22	4,000	1,000	25,600	13,000	7,600	36,000
23	2,000	1,000	25,600	13,000	7,600	34,000

Required

State briefly what you think took place on each of these nine days, assuming that only one transaction occurred each day.

1-19 Describing Underlying Transactions

The balances of each item in Monterrey Company's accounting equation are given below for August 31 and for each of the next nine business days.

Required

State briefly what you think took place on each of these nine days, assuming that only one transaction occurred each day.

	Cash	Accounts Receivable	Computer Inventory	Store Fixtures	Accounts Payable	Owners' Equity
Aug. 31	$2,000	$8,000	$ 9,000	$ 7,500	$ 5,500	$21,000
Sept. 1	4,000	6,000	9,000	7,500	5,500	21,000
2	4,000	6,000	9,000	10,000	8,000	21,000
3	1,000	6,000	9,000	10,000	8,000	18,000
4	2,000	9,000	5,000	10,000	8,000	18,000
5	2,000	9,000	11,000	10,000	8,000	24,000
8	1,500	9,000	11,000	10,000	7,500	24,000
9	1,000	9,000	11,000	13,000	10,000	24,000
10	1,000	9,000	11,000	12,700	9,700	24,000
11	4,000	6,000	11,000	12,700	9,700	24,000

1-20 Prepare Balance Sheet

Albany Corporation's balance sheet at March 30, 19X1, contained only the following items (arranged here in random order):

Cash	$11,000	Accounts payable	$ 8,000
Notes payable	10,000	Furniture and fixtures	3,000
Merchandise inventory	40,000	Long-term debt payable	12,000
Paid-in capital	81,000	Building	20,000
Land	6,000	Notes receivable	2,000
Accounts receivable	14,000	Machinery and equipment	15,000

On March 31, 19X1, these transactions and events took place:

1. Purchased merchandise on account, $3,000.
2. Sold at cost for $1,000 cash some furniture that was not needed.
3. Issued additional capital stock for machinery and equipment valued at $12,000.
4. Purchased land for $25,000, of which $5,000 was paid in cash, the remaining being represented by a five-year note (long-term debt).
5. The building was valued by professional appraisers at $45,000.

Required Prepare in good form a balance sheet for March 31, 19X1, showing supporting computations for all new amounts.

1-21 Prepare Balance Sheet

Broadway Corporation's balance sheet at November 29, 19X1 contained only the following items (arranged here in random order):

Paid-in capital	$195,000	Machinery and equipment	$ 20,000
Notes payable	20,000	Furniture and fixtures	8,000
Cash	22,000	Notes receivable	8,000
Accounts receivable	10,000	Accounts payable	16,000
Merchandise inventory	29,000	Building	230,000
Land	46,000	Long-term debt payable	142,000

On the following day, November 30, these transactions and events occurred:

1. Purchased machinery and equipment for $14,000, paying $3,000 in cash and signing a 90-day note for the balance.
2. Paid $6,000 on accounts payable.
3. Sold on account some land that was not needed for $6,000, which was the Broadway Corporation's acquisition cost of the land.

4. The remaining land was valued at $240,000 by professional appraisers. *nothing*

5. Issued capital stock as payment for $23,000 of the long-term debt, that is, debt due beyond one year.

Prepare in good form a balance sheet for November 30, 19X1, showing supporting computations for all new amounts.

1-22 Balance Sheet

General Electric is one of the largest companies in the world with sales of nearly $80 billion. The company's balance sheet on January 1, 1997, had total assets of $272 billion and stockholders' equity (called shareowners' equity by GE) of $31 billion.

1. Compute General Electric's total liabilities on January 1, 1997.

2. As of January 1, 1997, General Electric had issued 1,857,013,000 shares of common stock. The par value was $.32 per share. Compute the balance in the account, "Common stock, par value" on GE's balance sheet.

PROBLEMS

1-23 Prepare Balance Sheet

Sophia Brentano is a realtor. She buys and sells properties on her own account, and she also earns commissions as a real estate agent for buyers and sellers. Her business was organized on November 24, 19X1, as a sole proprietorship. Brentano also owns her own personal residence. Consider the following on November 30, 19X1:

1. Brentano owes $95,000 on a mortgage on some undeveloped land, which was acquired by her business for a total price of $180,000.

2. Brentano had spent $15,000 cash for a Century 21 real estate franchise. Century 21 is a national affiliation of independent real estate brokers. This franchise is an asset.

3. Brentano owes $100,000 on a personal mortgage on her residence, which was acquired on November 20, 19X1, for a total price of $180,000.

4. Brentano owes $3,800 on a personal charge account with Nordstrom's Department Store.

5. On November 28, Brentano hired Benjamin Goldstein as her first employee. He was to begin work on December 1. Brentano was pleased because Goldstein was one of the best real estate salesmen in the area. On November 29, Goldstein was killed in an automobile accident.

6. Business furniture was acquired for $17,000 on November 25, for $6,000 on open account plus $11,000 of business cash. On November 26, Brentano sold a $1,000 business chair for $1,000 to her next-door business neighbor on open account.

7. Brentano's balance at November 30 in her business checking account after all transactions was $9,500.

Prepare a balance sheet as of November 30, 19X1, for Sophia Brentano, realtor.

1-24 Analysis of Transactions

Use the format of Exhibit 1-2 to analyze the following transactions for April of Crystal Cleaners. Then prepare a balance sheet as of April 30, 19X1. Crystal was founded on April 1.

1. Issued 1,000 shares of $1 par common stock for cash, $60,000.

2. Issued 1,000 shares of $1 par common stock for equipment, $60,000.

3. Borrowed cash, signing a note payable for $35,000.

4. Purchased equipment for cash, $20,000.
5. Purchased office furniture on account, $10,000.
6. Disbursed cash on account (to reduce the account payable), $4,000.
7. Sold equipment on account at cost, $8,000.
8. Discovered that the most prominent competitor in the area was bankrupt and was closing its doors on April 30.
9. Collected cash on account, $3,000. See transaction 7.

1-25 Analysis of Transactions

Walgreen Company is a well-known drugstore chain. A condensed balance sheet for August 31, 1996 follows (in thousands):

Assets		Liabilities and Stockholders' Equity	
Cash	$ 8,819		
Accounts receivable	288,538	Accounts payable	691,836
Inventories	1,631,974	Other liabilities	898,705
Property and other assets	1,704,315	Stockholders' equity	2,043,105
Total	$3,633,646	Total	$3,633,646

Required Use a format similar to Exhibit 1-2 to analyze the following transactions for the first two days of September. (Dollar amounts are in thousands.) Then prepare a balance sheet as of September 2.

1. Issued 1,000 shares of common stock to employees for cash, $20.
2. Issued 1,500 shares of common stock for the acquisition of special equipment from a supplier, $30.
3. Borrowed cash, signing a note payable for $120.
4. Purchased equipment for cash, $125.
5. Purchased inventories on account, $90.
6. Disbursed cash on account (to reduce the accounts payable), $354.
7. Sold display equipment to retailer on account at cost, $14.
8. Collected cash on account, $84.

1-26 Analysis of Transactions

Nike, Inc. had the following condensed balance sheet on May 31, 1997 (in thousands):

Assets		Liabilities and Owners' Equity	
Cash	$ 445,421	Notes payable	$ 553,153
Accounts receivable	1,754,137	Accounts payable	687,121
Inventories	1,338,640	Other liabilities	965,095
Equipment and		Total liabilities	$2,205,369
other assets	1,823,009	Owners' equity	3,155,838
		Total liabilities and	
Total assets	$5,361,207	owners' equity	$5,361,207

Consider the following transactions that occurred during the first three days of June (in thousands of dollars):

1. Inventories were acquired for cash, $160.
2. Inventories were acquired on open account, $190.
3. Unsatisfactory shoes acquired on open account in March were returned for full credit, $40.

4. Equipment of $120 was acquired for a cash down payment of $30 plus a six-month promissory note of $90.

5. To encourage wider displays, special store equipment was sold on account to New York area stores for $400. The equipment had cost $400 in the preceding month.

6. Jodie Foster produced, directed, and starred in a movie. As a favor to a Nike executive, she agreed to display Nike shoes in a basketball scene. No fee was paid by Nike.

7. Cash was disbursed on account (to reduce accounts payable), $170.

8. Collected cash on account, $180.

9. Borrowed cash from a bank, $500.

10. Sold additional common stock for cash to new investors, $900.

11. The president of the company sold 5,000 shares of his personal holdings of Nike stock through his stockbroker.

Required

1. Using a format similar to Exhibit 1-2 (p. 12), prepare an analysis showing the effects of the June transactions on the financial position of Nike.

2. Prepare a balance sheet as of June 3.

1-27 Analysis of Transactions

Consider the following January transactions:

1. XYZ Corporation is formed on January 1, 19X1, by three persons, Xiao, Yergen, and Zimbel. XYZ will be a wholesale distributor of PC software. Each of the three investors is issued 20,000 shares of common stock ($1 par value) for $10 cash per share. Use two stockholders' equity accounts: Capital Stock (at par) and Additional Paid-in Capital.

2. Merchandise inventory of $200,000 is acquired for cash.

3. Merchandise inventory of $85,000 is acquired on open account.

4. Unsatisfactory merchandise that cost $11,000 in transaction 3 is returned for full credit.

5. Equipment of $40,000 is acquired for a cash down payment of $10,000 plus a three-month promissory note of $30,000.

6. As a favor, XYZ sells equipment of $4,000 to a business neighbor on open account. The equipment had cost $4,000.

7. XYZ pays $20,000 on the account described in transaction 3.

8. XYZ collects $2,000 from the business neighbor. See transaction 6.

9. XYZ buys merchandise inventory of $100,000. One-half of the amount is paid in cash, and one-half is owed on open account.

10. Zimbel sells half of his common stock to Quigley for $12 per share.

Required

1. Using a format similar to Exhibit 1-2, prepare an analysis showing the effects of January transactions on the financial position of XYZ Corporation.

2. Prepare a balance sheet as of January 31, 19X1.

1-28 Analysis of Transactions

You began a business as a wholesaler of woolen goods. The following events have occurred:

1. On March 1, 19X1, you invested $160,000 cash in your new sole proprietorship, which you call Yukon Products.

2. Acquired $20,000 inventory for cash.

3. Acquired $8,000 inventory on open account.

4. Acquired equipment for $15,000 in exchange for a $5,000 cash down payment and a $10,000 promissory note.

5. A large retail store, which you had hoped would be a big customer, discontinued operations.

6. You take gloves home for your family. The gloves were carried in Yukon's inventory at $600. (Regard this as a borrowing by you from Yukon Products.)

7. Gloves that cost $300 in transaction 2 were of the wrong style. You returned them and obtained a full cash refund.

8. Gloves that cost $800 in transaction 3 were of the wrong color. You returned them and obtained gloves of the correct color in exchange.

9. Caps that cost $500 in transaction 3 had an unacceptable quality. You returned them and obtained full credit on your account.

10. Paid $5,000 on promissory note.

11. You use your personal cash savings of $5,000 to acquire some equipment for Yukon. You consider this as an additional investment in your business.

12. Paid $3,000 on open account.

13. Two scarf manufacturers who are suppliers for Yukon announced a 7% rise in prices, effective in 60 days.

14. You use your personal cash savings of $1,000 to acquire a new TV set for your family.

15. You exchange equipment that cost $4,000 in transaction 4 with another wholesaler. However, the equipment received, which is almost new, is smaller and is worth only $1,500. Therefore the other wholesaler also agrees to pay you $500 in cash now and an additional $2,000 in cash in 60 days. (No gain or loss is recognized on this transaction.)

Required

1. Using Exhibit 1-2 (p. 12) as a guide, prepare an analysis of Yukon's transactions for March. Confine your analysis to the effects on the financial position of Yukon Products.

2. Prepare a balance sheet for Yukon Products as of March 31, 19X1.

1-29 Personal and Professional Entities

Jose Gomez, a recent graduate of a law school, was penniless on December 25, 19X1.

1. On December 26, Gomez inherited an enormous sum of money.

2. On December 27, he placed $80,000 in a business checking account for his unincorporated law practice.

3. On December 28, he purchased a home for a down payment of $100,000 plus a home mortgage payable of $250,000.

4. On December 28, Gomez agreed to rent a law office. He provided a $1,000 cash damage deposit (from his business cash), which will be fully refundable when he vacates the premises. This deposit is a business asset. Rental payments are to be made in advance on the first business day of each month. (The first payment of $700 is not to be made until January 2, 19X2.)

5. On December 28, Gomez purchased a computer for his law practice for $5,000 cash plus a $5,000 promissory note due in 90 days.

6. On December 28, he also purchased legal supplies for $1,000 on open account.

7. On December 28, Gomez purchased office furniture for his practice for $4,000 cash.

8. On December 29, Gomez hired a legal assistant receptionist for $380 per week. She was to report to work on January 2.

9. On December 30, Gomez's law practice lent $2,000 of cash in return for a one-year note from Genie Kulp, a local candy store owner. Kulp had indicated that she would spread the news about the new lawyer.

1. Use the format demonstrated in Exhibit 1-2 (p. 12) to analyze the transactions of Jose Gomez, lawyer. To avoid crowding, put your numbers in thousands of dollars. Do not restrict yourself to the account titles in Exhibit 1-2.

2. Prepare a balance sheet as of December 31, 19X1.

1-30 Bank Balance Sheet
Consider the following balance sheet accounts of Wells Fargo and Co. (in millions):

Assets		Liabilities and Stockholders' Equity	
Cash	$ 11,736	Deposits	$ 81,821
Investment securities	13,505	Other liabilities	12,955
Loans receivable	65,371	Total liabilities	$ 94,776
Premises and equipment	2,038	Stockholders' equity	14,112
Other assets	16,238	Total liabilities and	
Total assets	$108,888	stockholders' equity	$108,888

This balance sheet illustrates how banks gather and use money. More than 60% of the total assets are in the form of investments in loans, and more than 70% of the total liabilities and stockholders' equity are in the form of deposits, the major liability. That is, these financial institutions are in the business of raising funds from depositors and, in turn, lending those funds to businesses, homeowners, and others. The stockholders' equity is usually tiny in comparison with the deposits (only about 13% in this case).

1. What Wells Fargo and Co. accounts would be affected if you deposited $1,000?

2. Why are deposits listed as liabilities?

3. What accounts would be affected if the bank loaned John Solvang $50,000 for home renovations?

4. What accounts would be affected if Isabel Ramos withdrew $4,000 from her savings account?

1-31 Balance Sheet
KLM Royal Dutch Airlines is an international airline with a home base at Schiphol Airport in Amsterdam. It has more than 26,000 employees, 80% of them located in the Netherlands. On March 31, 1997, KLM's non-cash assets were NLG 14,013 million. (NLG stands for the Netherlands' monetary unit, the guilder.) Total assets were NLG 16,083, and total liabilities were NLG 11,346.

1. Compute the following:
   a. KLM's cash on March 31, 1997.
   b. KLM's stockholders' equity on March 31, 1997.

2. Explain the easiest way to determine KLM's total liabilities and stockholders' equity from the information given in this problem.

1-32 Presenting Paid-in Capital
Consider excerpts from two balance sheets (amounts in thousands):

Occidental Petroleum Corporation

Common stock, $0.20 par value; authorized 500 million shares; shares outstanding 329,227,688	$66,000
Additional paid-in capital	4,463

IBM

Common stock, par value $1.25 per share—shares authorized: 750,000,000; shares issued: 509,070,542 shares (includes capital in excess of par value) *Same*	$7,752,000

1. How would the presentation of Occidental's stockholders' equity accounts be affected if one million more shares were issued for $50 cash per share?

2. How would the presentation of IBM's stockholders' equity accounts be affected if one million more shares were issued for $50 cash per share? Be specific.

1-33 Presenting Paid-in Capital

Honeywell, Inc., maker of thermostats and a variety of complex control systems, presented the following in its balance sheet of January 1, 1997:

Common stock—$1.50 par value, 187,809,512 shares issued	?
Additional paid-in capital	3,074,700,000

What amount should be shown on the common stock line? What was the average price per share paid by the original investors for the Honeywell common stock? How do your answers compare with the $70 market price of the stock? Comment briefly.

1-34 Presenting Paid-in Capital

Honda Motor Company is the largest producer of motorcycles in the world, as well as a major auto manufacturer. The following items were presented in its balance sheet of March 31, 1997:

Common stock—¥50 par value, 974 million shares issued and outstanding	?
Additional paid-in capital (in millions of yen)	¥171,910

Note: ¥ is the symbol for Japanese yen.

1. What amount should be shown on the common stock line?

2. What was the average price per share paid by the original investors for the Honda common stock?

3. How do your answers compare with the ¥580 market price of the stock? Comment briefly.

1-35 Prepare Balance Sheet

Microsoft is the world's leading software company. Microsoft's March 31, 1997 balance sheet included the following items (in millions of dollars):

Property, plant, and equipment	1,371
Accounts payable	864
Capital stock	5,016
Cash	?
Total stockholders' equity	?
Long-term debt	0
Total assets	12,613
Accounts receivable	866
Other assets	1,188
Additional stockholders' equity	?
Other liabilities	2,615

Prepare a condensed balance sheet, including amounts for

Required

1. Cash.
2. Additional and total stockholders' equity.
3. Total liabilities.

1-36 Prepare Balance Sheet

May Department Stores, headquartered in St. Louis, operates Lord & Taylor, Filene's, and six other department store chains. It's balance sheet of February 1, 1997 contained the following items (in millions):

Long-term debt payable	$ 3,849
Cash	(1)
Total shareholders' equity	(2)
Total liabilities	(3)
Accounts receivable	2,425
Common stock	118
Inventories	2,380
Accounts payable	872
Property, plant, and equipment	4,159
Additional shareholders' equity	3,532
Other assets	1,083
Other liabilities	1,688
Total assets	10,059

Prepare a condensed balance sheet, including amounts for

Required

1. Cash. What do you think of its relative size?
2. Total shareholders' equity.
3. Total liabilities.

1-37 Accounting and Ethics

A survey of high school seniors and college freshmen by the American Institute of Certified Public Accountants showed that accountants are given high marks for their ethics. Professional associations for both internal accountants and external auditors place much emphasis on their standards of ethical conduct. Discuss why maintaining a reputation for ethical conduct is important for (1) accountants within an organization, and (2) external auditors. What can accountants do to foster a reputation for high ethical standards and conduct.

1-38 The Gap Annual Report

This and similar problems in succeeding chapters focus on the financial statements of an actual company. The Gap, Inc., operates nearly 2,000 retail stores in the United States and abroad.

As each homework problem is solved, readers gradually strengthen their understanding of actual financial statements in their entirety.

Refer to The Gap's balance sheet in Appendix A at the end of the book and answer the following questions:

1. How much cash did The Gap have on February 1, 1997? (Include cash equivalent as part of cash.)   485,644 (p. 29)   2,626,927   2,343,068
2. What were the total assets on February 1, 1997? February 3, 1996?
3. Write the company's accounting equation as of February 1, 1997, by filling in the dollar amounts: 2,626 927

$$\text{Assets} = \text{Liabilities} + \text{Stockholders' equity.}$$ 654,420

Consider long-term obligations under capital leases and deferred income taxes to be liabilities.

1-39 Financial Statement Research

Select the financial statements of any company, and focus on the balance sheet.

Required

1. Identify the amount of cash (including cash equivalents, if any) shown on the most recent balance sheet.

2. What were the total assets shown on the most recent balance sheet? The total liabilities plus stockholders' equity? How do these two amounts compare?

3. Compute total liabilities and total stockholders' equity. (Assume that all items on the right side of the balance sheet that are not explicitly listed as stockholders' equity are liabilities.) Compare the size of the liabilities to stockholders' equity, and comment on the comparison. Write the company's accounting equation as of the most recent balance sheet date, by filling in the dollar amounts.

COLLABORATIVE LEARNING EXERCISE

1-40 Understanding Transactions

Form groups of three to five students each. Each group should choose one of the companies included in the Dow Jones Industrial Average (see Exhibit 1-1), and find its most recent balance sheet. (You might try the company's home page on the Internet; the majority of DOW companies include their financial statements on their web site.) Ignore much of the detail on the balance sheet, focusing on the following accounts: cash, inventory, notes payable, accounts payable, and total stockholders' equity.

Divide the following six assumed transactions among the members of the group:

1. Sold 1 million shares of common stock for a total of $10 million (ignore par value).

2. Bought inventory for cash of $3 million.

3. Borrowed $5 million from the bank, receiving the $5 million in cash.

4. Bought inventory for $6 on open account.

5. Paid $4 million to suppliers for inventory bought on open account.

6. Bought equipment for $8 million cash.

Required

1. The student responsible for each transaction should explain to the group how the transaction would affect the company's balance sheet, using the accounts listed above.

2. Using the most recent published balance sheet as a starting point, prepare a balance sheet for the company assuming that the six transactions above are the only transactions since the date of the latest balance sheet.

1-41 Internet Case

Go to **http://www.mcdonalds.com/a_system/investinfo** to find the McDonald's *Investor Information* menu. Select the most recent annual report from this menu. If your browser allows you to see graphics, select the *Complete Version*. Otherwise, select the *Text Only Version*.

Answer the following questions concerning the McDonald's Annual Report:

1. Select *Letter to Shareholders* from the menu. Does McDonald's intend to grow during the coming year? Does management believe the company's performance was favorable during the year?

2. Select *Performance at a Glance* from the menu. In how many countries does McDonald's operate? In which year did McDonald's earn the most profits (net income)?

3. Select *Investor Perspective—Part I* to read the information. Then read *Part 2*. What type of information is provided in these sections?

4. Select *Financial Statement and Comments,* and examine the *Consolidated Balance Sheet.* What is McDonald's largest asset? Does the amount of McDonald's debt appear to be increasing or decreasing?

5. Select *Financial Statement and Comments,* and examine *Management's Report.* Who is responsible for the preparation, integrity and fair presentation of the consolidated financial statements? Examine the *Report of Independent Auditors.* What is the auditors' responsibility?

MEASURING INCOME TO ASSESS PERFORMANCE

IT'S *just* LUNCH!, a young, fast-growing company, helped these two professionals meet for lunch.

Learning Objectives

After studying this chapter, you should be able to

1 Explain how accountants measure income.

2 Use the concepts of recognition, matching, and cost recovery to record revenues and expenses.

3 Prepare an income statement and show how it is related to a balance sheet.

4 Prepare a statement of cash flows and show how it differs from an income statement.

5 Account for cash dividends and prepare a statement of retained income.

6 Compute and explain earnings per share, price-earnings ratio, dividend-yield ratio, and dividend-payout ratio.

When Andrea McGinty's fiancé walked out on her just weeks before their wedding, the 29-year-old jewelry marketing representative was faced with the prospect of reentering the dating scene. She didn't like what she found: singles bars, video dating services, personal ads. None of the available choices appealed to her instincts as a sophisticated, professional person, and none of them really fit into her lifestyle. Then she hit on an idea. What if there were a service that fit the lifestyle of today's busy professionals, one that let people date over the lunch hour instead of during an entire evening? Ready to take on the challenge, McGinty formed "It's Just Lunch!" in downtown Chicago.

Using her accounting education as a foundation, McGinty knew that she'd need some capital to start the business and generate income. So she used $6,000 from her personal savings to print flyers and lease office space. She also knew that the sales revenue she hoped to generate would be reduced by the expenses of running the business, so she priced her services to be sure she made an acceptable return on her investment. She charged $400 for arranging six dates.

What started as a simple idea for helping single professionals find matches has grown into a multimillion-dollar-a-year business. Sales last year exceeded $2.1 million, and net income totaled $400,000. McGinty relies on her accrual-based income statement and balance sheet reports each month to assess how well the company is doing. Because "It's Just Lunch!" now has many locations across the country, she gets reports for each location. These reports allow her to quickly identify a location that is not performing up to expectations and focus her energy on correcting any problems.

And what about McGinty's own dating life? A Chicago lawyer came in for help and decided he wanted to date the owner. After thinking about it, McGinty refunded his fees and accepted the date. They are now married.

The measurement of income is one of the most important and controversial topics in accounting. Income is calculated as the difference between revenue and expense. The resulting income number is a measure of accomplishment—a means of evaluating an organization's performance over a period of time.

Investors eagerly await reports about a company's annual income. Stock prices generally reflect investors' expectations about income. However, actual reported income often differs from what was expected, which tends to result in large swings in stock prices. For example, Nautica Enterprises, a hot name in the apparel industry, announced its earnings for the first quarter of 1997 during the week of June 30, 1997. The earnings were 13% higher than expected and the share price of Nautica Enterprises rose by $3.38 or 16% during the week. Investors concluded that the company's new designs were even more popular than they had realized and the prospects for future sales and profits were very good.

The Nautica example was the reaction to an actual announcement, but even rumors can have a major effect on stock prices. The September 10, 1997 *Wall Street Journal* attributed the previous day's 2.8% decline in IBM to "rumors about profit problems at IBM, stemming from adverse markets in Southeast Asia." Consider investors in IBM stock during recent years. They saw profits fall from $5.8 billion in 1988 to a loss of $2.8 billion in 1991 before reaching profits of $3.0 billion in 1994 and $5.4 billion in 1996. Share prices followed profits. One IBM share was $120 in 1988, fell to about $45 during 1993 before recovering to $166 at the end of 1996. Meanwhile, investors in McDonald's Corporation saw a steady increase in profits from $0.6 billion in 1988 to $0.9 billion in 1991, $1.2 billion in 1994 and $1.6 billion in 1996. And these investors experienced a fairly steady increase in share values as well. One McDonald's share sold for $12 in 1988, $16 in 1991, and reached $48 by the end of 1996. For comparison sake, $100 invested in a bank account in 1988 would be worth about $148 in 1996. In IBM, a $100 investment would have grown to only $138. But a $100 investment in McDonald's in 1988 would be worth $400 by 1996. These profitability numbers and various other pieces of information in financial statements allow investors to make intelligent decisions about whether to invest more or less in a particular firm.

So profits are a key measure of performance and value. This chapter presents the basics of measuring income, with a special focus on revenues and expenses. It also defines three basic financial statements prepared by accountants: the income statement, statement of cash flows, and statement of retained income.

INTRODUCTION TO INCOME MEASUREMENT

Objective 1
Explain how accountants measure income.

Measuring income is important to everyone, from individuals to businesses, because we all need to know how well we are doing economically. Income is a tool for keeping score. But measuring income is not straightforward. Income is generally regarded as a measure of the increase in the "wealth" of an entity over a period of time. But what is wealth and how do you measure it over a period of time? Accountants have agreed on a common set of rules for measuring income that should be applied by all companies. Decision makers such as investors can more easily compare the performance of one company with that of another when the 'measuring stick', net income, is fairly standard. Let us now take a look at the foundations of these rules.

OPERATING CYCLE

Most companies follow a similar operating cycle (also called a *cash cycle* or *earnings cycle*). During the **operating cycle,** the company uses cash to acquire goods and services, which in turn are sold to customers. The customers in turn pay for their purchases with cash, which brings us back to the beginning of the cycle. A retail business usually engages in some version of the operating cycle in order to earn profits. Consider the following example:

operating cycle The time span during which cash is used to acquire goods and services, which in turn are sold to customers, who in turn pay for their purchases with cash.

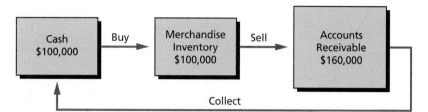

The box for Accounts Receivable (amounts owed to the entity by customers) is larger than the other two boxes because the company's objective is to sell its goods at a price higher than it paid for them. The amount that the selling price rises over costs/expenses is, of course, known as profit. The total amount of profit earned during a particular period depends on the difference between selling price and costs and on the speed of the operating cycle.

THE ACCOUNTING TIME PERIOD

Because it is hard to measure accurately the success of an ongoing operation, the only way to be certain of how successfully a business has performed is to close its doors, sell all its assets, pay all liabilities, and return any leftover cash to the owner. Actually, in the 1400s, Venetian merchant traders did exactly that for each and every voyage. Successful investors might combine their cash to initiate another voyage while investors in failed voyages might have to sell other assets to cover unpaid liabilities. Of course, that system would not be feasible for companies today (imagine a company that needed to close down and restart after every business deal!). Instead, companies need to be able to measure their performances over discrete time periods.

note 1

Revenues = sales

The calendar year is the most popular time period for measuring income or profits. However, about 40% of large companies use a **fiscal year.** Established purely for accounting purposes, the fiscal year does not end on December 31. Instead, the fiscal year-end date is often the low point in annual business activity. For example, Kmart and JC Penney use a fiscal year ending on January 31. Why? Because Christmas sales and post-Christmas sales are over, and inventories, which are at their lowest point of the year, can be counted more easily and valued with greater accuracy.

fiscal year The year established for accounting purposes.

Of course, users of financial statements cannot wait an entire year for financial information. They want to know how well the business is doing each month, each quarter, and each half-year. Therefore, companies prepare financial statements for these **interim periods.**

interim periods The time span established for accounting purposes that are less than a year.

REVENUES AND EXPENSES

Now that we know the "when" and "why" of measuring income, we need to examine the "how." Revenues and expenses are the key components in measuring income. These terms apply to the inflows and outflows of assets that occur during a business's operating cycle. The **revenues (inflows)** also called **sales,** increase the owner's interest (equity) in the

revenues (sales) Increases in owners' equity arising from increases in assets received in exchange for the delivery of goods or services to customers.

Exhibit 2–1

Biwheels Company
Analysis of Transactions for December 31, 19X1–January 12, 19X2 (in dollars)

Description of Transactions	Cash	+	Accounts Receivable	+	Merchandise Inventory	+	Store Equipment	=	Note Payable	+	Accounts Payable	+	Stockholders' Equity
(1) Initial investment	+400,000							=					+ 400,000
(2) Loan from bank	+100,000							=	+100,000				
(3) Acquire inventory for cash	−150,000				+150,000			=					
(4) Acquire inventory on credit					+ 10,000			=			+10,000		
(5) Acquire store equipment for cash plus credit	− 4,000						+ 15,000	=			+11,000		
(6) Sales of equipment			+1,000				− 1,000	=					
(7) Return of inventory acquired on January 3					− 800			=			− 800		
(8) Payments to creditors	− 4,000							=			− 4,000		
(9) Collections from debtors	+ 700		− 700										
Balance, January 12, 19X2	+342,700	+	300	+	159,200	+	14,000	=	100,000	+	16,200	+	400,000
					516,200						516,200		

expenses Decreases in owners' equity that arise because goods or services are delivered to customers.

income (profit, earnings) The excess of revenues over expenses.

retained income (retained earnings, reinvested earnings) Additional owners' equity generated by income or profits.

business while **expenses (outflows) decrease the** owner's interest. Together these items define the fundamental meaning of **income** (or **profit** or **earnings**), which can be defined simply as the excess of revenues over expenses. Revenues arise when McDonald's collects cash in exchange for a "happy meal." Expenses arise when McDonald's uses hamburger, buns and other materials and pays the workers to deliver a completed meal to the customers. The McDonald's store owner is happy when the cash received exceeds the cost to produce and deliver the meal. The additional owners' equity generated by income or profits is called **retained income** (or **retained earnings or reinvested earnings**).

Consider again the Biwheels Company we examined in Chapter 1. Exhibit 2-1 is almost a direct reproduction of Exhibit 1-2, which summarized the nine transactions of George Smith's business. However, the company has now been incorporated, and the owners' equity account is no longer George Smith, Capital. In Exhibit 2-1, it is stockholders' equity.

Now consider some additional transactions. Suppose Biwheels' sales for the entire month of January amount to $160,000 on open account. The cost to Biwheels of the inventory sold is $100,000. Note that the January sales and other transactions illustrated here are recorded as summarized transactions. The company's sales do not all take place at once, nor do purchases of inventory, collections from customers, or disbursements to suppliers.

The accounting for the summarized sales transaction has two phases, a revenue phase (10a) and an expense phase (10b):

	Assets		=	Liabilities	+	Stockholders' Equity
	Accounts Receivable	Merchandise Inventory				Retained Income
(10a) Sales on open account	+160,000		=			+160,000 (sales revenues)
(10b) Cost of merchandise inventory sold		−100,000	=			−100,000 (cost of goods sold expenses)

This transaction is somewhat complex and can be best understood as two things happening simultaneously in the balance sheet equation: an inflow of assets in the form of accounts receivable (10a) in exchange for an outflow of assets in the form of merchandise inventory (10b). This exchange of assets does not affect liabilities, so to keep the equation equal, stockholders' equity must rise by $60,000 ($160,000 (sales revenues) − $100,000 (cost of goods sold expense)).

As entries 10a and 10b show, revenue from sales is recorded as an increase in the asset Accounts Receivable and an increase in Retained Income. In contrast, the expense of the goods sold is recorded as a decrease in the asset Merchandise Inventory and a decrease in Retained Income. You can thus see that revenues are positive entries to stockholders' equity accounts, and expenses are negative entries to stockholders' equity accounts. These relationships can be illustrated as follows:

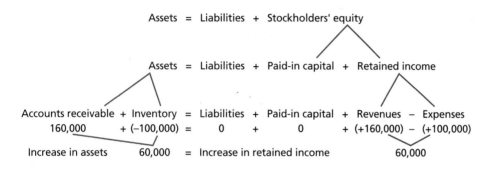

MEASURING INCOME

ACCRUAL BASIS AND CASH BASIS

There are multiple ways to measure income, the most compelling of which are the cash basis and the accrual basis. The **accrual basis** recognizes the impact of transactions in the financial statements for the time periods when revenues and expenses occur. That is, revenue is recorded as it is earned, and expenses are recorded as they are incurred—not necessarily when cash changes hands. In contrast, the **cash basis** recognizes the impact of transactions in the financial statements only when cash is received or disbursed.

For many years accountants debated the merits of accrual-basis versus cash-basis accounting. Supporters of the accrual basis maintained that the cash basis ignores activities that increase or decrease assets other than cash. Supporters of the cash basis pointed out that a company, no matter how well it seems to be doing, can go bankrupt if it does not manage its cash properly. In the end, the debate has been declared a draw. One of the basic financial statements presents the results for the year in terms of cash flows. But in the calculation of income, the accrual basis won out. It is the current standard for income measurement. Although both bases have their merits, the accrual basis has the advantage of presenting a more complete summary of the entity's value-producing activities. The accrual basis recognizes revenues as they are earned and matches costs to revenues. This accrual process was illustrated in our analysis of the sale on open account in transaction 10. Revenue was recognized although no cash was received and an expense was recorded although no cash was paid. Let us now take a look at some of the specifics of the accrual basis.

RECOGNITION OF REVENUES

A major convention accountants use to measure income on an accrual basis is **recognition** of revenues, which is a test for determining whether revenues should be recorded in

accrual basis Accounting method that recognizes the impact of transactions on the financial statements in the time periods when revenues and expenses occur.

cash basis Accounting method that recognizes the impact of transactions on the financial statements only when cash is received or disbursed.

recognition A test for determining whether revenues should be recorded in the financial statements of a given period. To be recognized, revenues must be earned and realized.

the financial statements of a given period. To be recognized, revenues must ordinarily meet two criteria:

Delivery

1. They must be *earned.* Revenues are considered earned when a company delivers goods or services to a customer.

cash

2. They must be *realized.* Revenues are realized when cash or claims to cash are received in exchange for goods or services. "Claims to cash" usually mean credit or some other promise to pay. For a promise to pay to justify revenue recognition, the company must make relatively certain that it will receive the cash it has been promised.

note

Revenue recognition for most retail companies, such as Wal-Mart, Safeway, and McDonald's, is straightforward. Revenue is both earned and realized at the point of sale—when a customer makes payment and takes possession of the goods. For other companies, revenue may be earned and realized at different times. When revenues are earned and realized at different times, the revenue is not recognized until the second event. Consider the following examples:

- *Newsweek* receives prepaid subscriptions. The revenue is realized when the subscription is received, but it is not earned until delivery of each issue.
- A dealer in oriental rugs lets a potential customer take a rug home on a trial basis. The customer has possession of the goods, but no revenue is recorded until the customer formally promises to accept the rug and pay for it.

MATCHING AND COST RECOVERY

product costs Costs that are linked with revenues and are charged as expenses when the related revenue is recognized.

Now that we have seen how revenues are recognized, we should turn our attention to expenses. There are two types of expenses in every accounting period: (1) those linked with the revenues earned that period, and (2) those linked with the time period itself. Some expenses, called **product costs,** are naturally linked with revenues. **Cost of goods sold** (that is, the acquisition cost of the inventory that was sold, also called **cost of sales**) and sales commissions are good examples. If there are no revenues, there is no cost of goods sold or sales commissions. When are product costs recognized? Accountants match such expenses to the revenues they help produce. Expenses are best recognized and recorded in the same period as their related revenues are recognized. This process is known as **matching.**

cost of goods sold (cost of sales) The original acquisition cost of the inventory that was sold to customers during the reporting period.

matching The recording of expenses in the same time period as the related revenues are recognized.

Other expenses, such as rent and many administrative expenses, cannot be linked directly to specific revenues. These expenses go toward supporting a company's operations for a given period and are thus called **period costs.** Period costs are recognized as expense in the period in which they are incurred. Rent expense arises because of the passage of time regardless of the sales level and therefore rent is a good example of a period cost. Consider a McDonald's store. The rent expense for May gives the store operator the right to do business for the month and is best matched to May sales, regardless of whether the sales are high or low.

period costs Items identified directly as expenses of the time period in which they are incurred.

Some expenses can be tricky in that a transaction occurs well before the revenues or benefits they will ultimately help produce. To record the expense in the proper period accountants use the **cost recovery** concept. Under cost recovery, some purchases of goods or services are recorded as assets because the costs are expected to be recovered in the form of cash inflows (or reduced cash outflows) in future periods. For example, the purchase price of goods or services that are acquired in the current period but will be sold or used in a future period should be initially recorded as an asset. When the good or service is sold or used, the accountant reduces the asset account and records an expense.

cost recovery The concept by which some purchases of goods or services are recorded as assets because their costs are expected to be recovered in the form of cash inflows (or reduced cash outflows) in future periods.

Rent paid in advance is such an asset. Suppose a firm pays an annual rental of $12,000 on January 1. An asset account, prepaid rent, is increased by $12,000 because the rental services have not yet been used. Each month the prepaid rent account is reduced by $1,000, and rent expense is increased by $1,000, recognizing the using up of the prepaid rent asset.

APPLYING MATCHING AND COST RECOVERY

To focus on the matching and cost recovery concepts, assume that the Biwheels Company has only two expenses other than the cost of goods sold: rent expense and depreciation expense. Rent is $2,000 per month, payable quarterly in advance. Transaction 11 (see Exhibit 2-2, which merely continues Exhibit 2-1) is the payment of $6,000 worth of store rent, covering January, February, and March of 19X2. (Assume that this initial payment was made on January 16, although rent is commonly paid at the start of the rental period.)

The rent payment gives the company the right to use store facilities for the next three months. The use of the facilities constitutes a future benefit, so the $6,000 is recorded in an asset account, Prepaid Rent. } *recorded initially as an asset*

Transaction 11, the rent payment, shows no effect on stockholders' equity in the balance sheet equation. One asset, cash, is simply exchanged for another, prepaid rent.

Transaction 12 is recorded at the end of January. It recognizes that one-third of the rental services has been used up, so that asset is reduced, and stockholders' equity is also reduced by $2,000 as rent expense for January. This recognition of rent expense means that $2,000 of the asset, Prepaid Rent, has been "used up" in the conduct of operations during January. That $2,000 worth of rent was a period cost for January and is recognized at the end of that period.

Prepaid rent of $4,000 remains an asset as of January 31. Why? Because without the prepayment, Biwheels would have to pay $2,000 in both February and March for rent. So the cost of the prepayment will be recovered in the sense that future cash outflows will be reduced by $4,000.

The same matching and cost recovery concepts that underlie the accounting for prepaid rent apply to **depreciation,** which is the systematic allocation of the acquisition cost of long-lived or fixed assets to the expense accounts of particular periods that benefit from the use of the assets. These assets are tangible physical assets such as buildings, equipment, furniture, and fixtures owned by the entity. Land is not subject to depreciation because it does not deteriorate over time.

In both prepaid rent and depreciation, the business purchases an asset that gradually wears out or is used up. As the asset is being used, more and more of its original cost is transferred from an asset account to an expense account. The sole difference between depreciation and prepaid rent is the length of time taken before the asset loses its usefulness. Buildings, equipment, and furniture remain useful for many years; prepaid rent and other prepaid expenses usually expire within a year.

Transaction 13 in Exhibit 2-2 records the depreciation expense for the Biwheels equipment. A portion of the original cost of $14,000 becomes depreciation expense in each month of the equipment's useful life, say, 140 months. Under the matching concept, the depreciation expense for January is $14,000/140 months, or $100 per month:

depreciation The systematic allocation of the acquisition cost of long-lived or fixed assets to the expense accounts of particular periods that benefit from the use of the assets.

	Assets	=	Liabilities	+	Stockholders' Equity
	Store Equipment				Retained Income
(13) Recognize depreciation expense	−100	=			−100 (increase depreciation expense)

In this transaction, the asset account, Store Equipment, is decreased as is the stockholders' equity account, Retained Income. The general concept of expense under the accrual basis should be clear by now. The purchases and uses of goods and services (for

Exhibit 2-2
Biwheels Company
Analysis of Transactions for January 19X2 (in dollars)

Description of Transactions		Assets				=	Liabilities		+	Stockholders' Equity	
	Cash +	Accounts Receivable +	Merchandise Inventory +	Prepaid Rent +	Store Equipment	=	Note Payable +	Accounts Payable	+	Paid-in Capital +	Retained Income
(1)–(9) See Exhibit 2-1 Balance, January 12, 19X2	342,700 +	300 +	159,200	+	14,000	=	100,000 +	16,200	+	400,000	
(10a) Sales on open account (inflow of assets)		+160,000				=					+ 160,000 (sales revenue)
(10b) Cost of merchandise inventory sold (outflow of assets)			−100,000			=					−100,000 (increase cost of goods sold expense)
(11) Pay rent in advance	− 6,000			+ 6,000		=					
(12) Recognize expiration of rental services				− 2,000		=					−2,000 (increase rent expense)
(13) Recognized expiration of equipment services (depreciation)					− 100	=					− 100 (increase depreciation expense)
Balance, January 31, 19X2	336,700 +	160,300 +	59,200 +	4,000 +	13,900	=	100,000 +	16,200	+	400,000 +	57,900
		574,100				=			574,100		

example, inventories, rent, equipment) ordinarily consist of two basic steps: (1) the acquisition of the assets (transactions 3, 4, and 5 in Exhibit 2-1 and transaction 11 in Exhibit 2-2), and (2) the expiration of the assets as expenses (transactions 10b, 12, and 13 in Exhibit 2-2). As these examples show, when prepaid expenses and fixed assets are used up, the total assets and owners' equity are decreased. Expense accounts are basically deductions from stockholders' equity.

RECOGNITION OF EXPIRED ASSETS

Assets such as inventory, prepaid rent, and equipment may be thought of as costs that are stored to be carried forward to future periods and recorded as expenses in the future. For inventory, the future period of expense recognition is identified by the sale of the item and the recognition of revenue at the time of sale. For rent the future period of recognition is the period to which the rent applies. For equipment, the total cost of the long-lived asset is split up into smaller pieces and a part of that total cost is recognized in each of the periods that benefits from the use of the asset. You might say that inventory costs are product costs that are matched to the revenue they produce. Rent is a period cost that is matched to the period it benefits. Equipment benefits many periods, and its cost is spread over those periods as depreciation expense:

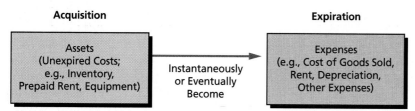

The analysis of the inventory, rent, and depreciation transactions in Exhibit 2-2 distinguishes between acquisition and expiration. Inventory, rent, and equipment are all recorded as assets when they are acquired. The unexpired costs of inventory, prepaid rent, and equipment then remain assets until they are used up and become expenses.

What happens if acquired assets expire, or are used, almost immediately? For example, services such as advertising are often used almost as soon as they are acquired. Conceptually, these costs should, at least momentarily, be viewed as assets upon acquisition before being written off as expenses. For example, suppose a company purchased newspaper advertising for $1,000 cash. To abide by the acquisition-expiration sequence, the transaction could be analyzed in two phases (see alternative 1 below).

		Assets		= Liabilities +	Stockholders' Equity	
Transaction	Cash	+ Other Assets	+ Prepaid Advertising =		Paid-in Capital	+ Retained Income
ALTERNATIVE 1: TWO PHASES						
Phase (a) Prepay for advertising	−1,000		+ 1,000 =			
Phase (b) Use up advertising			−1,000 =			−1,000 (advertising expense)
ALTERNATIVE 2: ONE PHASE						
Phases (a) and (b) together	−1,000		=			−1,000 (advertising expense)

In practice, however, prepaid advertising and many other services are acquired and used up so quickly that accountants do not bother recording them as assets. Instead accountants use the recording shortcut shown in alternative 2. When financial statements are prepared, this alternative presents the correct result, although the two-step alternative 1 more accurately portrays the events. The entity acquires goods and services and these goods and services become expenses as they are used to generate revenue.

Although this chapter is focused on the income statement, it is important to realize that the income statement is really just a way of explaining changes between one balance sheet and another. The balance sheet equation shows revenue and expense items as subparts of owners' equity. The income statement just collects all of these changes in owners' equity for the accounting period and combines them in one place.

(1) Assets (A) = Liabilities (L) + Stockholders' equity (SE)

(2) Assets = Liabilities + Paid-in capital + Retained income

(3) Assets = Liabilities + Paid-in capital + Revenue − Expenses

Revenue and expense accounts are nothing more than subdivisions of stockholders' equity—temporary stockholders' equity accounts, as it were. Their purpose is to summarize the volume of sales and the various expenses so that income can be measured.

The analysis of each transaction in Exhibits 2-1 and 2-2 illustrates the dual nature of the balance sheet equation, which is always kept in balance. If the items affected are confined to one side of the equation, the total amount added is equal to the total amount subtracted on that side. If the items affected are on both sides, then equal amounts are simultaneously added or simultaneously subtracted on each side.

The striking feature of the balance sheet equation is its universal applicability. No transaction has ever been conceived, no matter how simple or complex, that cannot be analyzed via the equation. Business leaders and accountants employ the balance sheet equation constantly to be sure they understand the effects of business transactions they are planning.

THE INCOME STATEMENT

Objective 3
Prepare an income statement and show how it is related to a balance sheet.

income statement (statement of earnings, operating statement) A report of all revenues and expenses pertaining to a specific time period.

net income The remainder after all expenses have been deducted from revenues.

By now you should understand when revenues and expenses are recorded and how they can be used to measure income. The question you should be wondering is: Where are they recorded in the financial statements? Chapter 1 introduced the balance sheet as a snapshot-in-time summary of a company's financial status. However, the balance sheet doesn't show period by period revenue and expense transactions. For that purpose, we need another basic financial statement, the income statement. An **income statement** (also called **statement of earnings** or **operating statement**) is a report of all revenues and expenses pertaining to a specific time period. **Net income** is the famous "bottom line" on an income statement—the remainder after all expenses have been deducted from revenue.

Look back at Exhibit 2-2 and notice that four of the accounting events affect the Biwheels Company's retained income account: sales revenue, cost of goods sold expense, rent expense, and depreciation expense. Exhibit 2-3 shows how an income statement arranges these transactions to arrive at a net income of $57,900.

As we already stated, the income statement measures performance, in terms of revenues and expenses, over a span of time, whether it be a month, a quarter, or longer. Therefore the income statement must always indicate the exact period covered. In Exhibit 2-3, the Biwheels income statement clearly shows it covers the month ended January 31, 19X2.

Public companies in the United States generally publish income statements quarterly. In some other countries, companies publish only semiannual or annual statements. Nevertheless, most companies prepare such statements monthly or weekly for internal management purposes. Some top managers even insist on a daily income statement to keep up-to-date on the performance of their operations.

Exhibit 2-3

Biwheels Company

Income Statement for the Month Ended January 31, 19X2

Sales (revenues)		$ 160,000
Deduct expenses:		
Cost of goods sold	$100,000	
Rent	2,000	
Depreciation	100	
Total expenses		102,100
Net income		$ 57,900

Decision makers both inside and outside the company use the income statement to assess the company's performance or its management over a span of time. The income statement shows how the entity's operations for the period have increased net assets through revenues and decreased net assets through expenses. Net income measures the amount by which the increase in newly acquired assets (revenues) exceeds the expiration of other assets (expenses). (A net loss means that expenses exceeded revenues.) In essence, net income is one measure of the wealth created by an entity during the accounting period. By tracking net income from period to period, and examining changes in the revenue and expense components of net income, investors and other decision makers can evaluate the success of the period's operations.

For example, the management of Sunglass Hut International explained its 15.2% increase in net income in 1996 in its annual report by addressing the revenue and cost elements separately. Revenues rose by 26% due primarily to new stores opened during the year. Comparable store sales rose by only 2.5%. Comparable stores are those that have been open for several years. Note that net income did not increase as much as revenue did. Management explained that during 1996 new stores were often opened in high-priced international locations which resulted in lower profits.

RELATIONSHIP BETWEEN INCOME STATEMENT AND BALANCE SHEET

The income statement is the major link between two balance sheets:

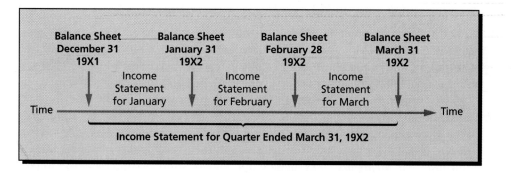

Remember that the balance sheet provides a snapshot of an entity's financial position at an instant of time. In contrast, the income statement provides more of a moving picture of events over a span of time. You can think of income statements as filling in the gaps between balance sheets. The balance sheets show the financial position of the company at discrete points in time, and the income statements explain the changes that have taken place between those points.

For example, the balance sheet for Biwheels Company on December 31, 19X1 showed assets of $500,000 and, to balance the equation, liabilities of $100,000 plus stockholders' equity of $400,000. There was no retained income. The January transactions analyzed in Exhibit 2-2 showed revenues of $160,000 and expenses of $102,100 recorded in the retained income account. The income statement in Exhibit 2-3 displays these revenues and expenses for the time span, the month of January. The next balance sheet, on January 31, 19X2, will include these changes in retained earnings (sales revenue of $160,000 less expenses of $102,100). The stockholders' equity account, Retained Income, will be $160,000 − $102,100 = $57,900 greater on January 31, 19X2 than it was on December 31, 19X1.

STATEMENT OF CASH FLOWS

INCOME VERSUS CASH FLOWS

You can think of income as a measure of the entity's performance in generating net assets (that is, assets less liabilities). Increases in retained income are accompanied by increases in assets or decreases in liabilities. However, income, especially when using accrual basis accounting, does not measure the entity's performance in generating cash. Because a business enterprise is usually formed to return cash to the owners, and because creditors must be paid in cash, many decision makers want a financial statement focused on cash in addition to the income statement that focuses on changes in net assets. The statement of cash flows is prepared to fill this need. Since the 1970's companies have been required to provide this statement in addition to the income statement. This is why we said earlier that the debate over whether to use cash or accrual accounting, was really a draw. Accountants do both.

statement of cash flows (cash flow statement) A required statement that reports the cash receipts and cash payments of an entity during a particular period.

The **statement of cash flows** (or **cash flow statement**) reports the cash receipts and cash payments of an entity during a particular period. Like the income statement, it summarizes activities over a span of time, so it must be labeled with the exact period covered. Furthermore, like the income statement, which shows details about how operating activities produce changes in retained income, the statement of cash flows details the changes in one balance sheet account, the cash account.

INTRODUCTION TO STATEMENT OF CASH FLOWS

The creation of the statement of cash flows is simple. First, list the activities that increased cash (that is, cash inflows) and those that decreased cash (cash outflows). Second, place each cash inflow and outflow into one of three categories according to the type of activity that caused it: operating activities, investing activities, and financing activities.

Operating activities include the sale and the purchase or production of goods and services, including collecting accounts payable from customers, paying suppliers or employees, and paying for items such as rent, taxes, and interest. *Investing activities* include acquiring and selling long-term assets and securities held for long-term investment purposes. *Financing activities* include obtaining resources from owners and creditors and repaying amounts borrowed. When The Gap sells you clothing, it is an operating cash flow. When The Gap buys a new storefront in New York City to open a new store, it is an investing activity. When The Gap issues additional common stock to investors in order to raise money to finance growth and the new store, it is a financing activity.

Consider our Biwheels example from its inception in December 19X1 through the end of January 19X2. Part I of Exhibit 2-4 lists the transactions that affect cash, and Part

Exhibit 2-4

Biwheels Company

Statement of Cash Flows for the Two Months Ended January 31, 19X2

PART I: TRANSACTIONS AFFECTING CASH

Transaction	Amount	Type of Activity
(1) Initial investment	$400,000	Financing
(2) Loan from bank	100,000	Financing
(3) Acquire inventory for cash	(150,000)	Operating
(5) Acquire store equipment for cash	(4,000)	Investing
(8) Payments to trade creditors	(4,000)	Operating
(9) Sale of store equipment	700	Investing
(11) Pay rent in cash	(6,000)	Operating

PART II: STATEMENT OF CASH FLOWS

CASH FLOWS FROM OPERATING ACTIVITIES	
Cash payments to suppliers	$(154,000)
Cash payments for rent	(6,000)
Net cash used for operating activities	$(160,000)
CASH FLOWS FROM INVESTING ACTIVITIES	
Cash payments for purchases of equipment	$ (4,000)
Cash receipts from sales of equipment	700
Net cash used for investing activities	$ (3,300)
CASH FLOWS FROM FINANCING ACTIVITIES	
Proceeds from initial investment	$ 400,000
Proceeds from bank loan	100,000
Net cash provided by financing activities	$ 500,000
Net increase in cash	$ 336,700
Cash balance, December 1, 19X1	0
Cash balance, January 31, 19X2	$ 336,700

II shows the statement of cash flows. Notice that at the bottom of the statement the changes in cash during the month are added to the beginning balance to give the January 31, 19X2, balance in the cash account.

The statement of cash flows gives a direct picture of where cash came from and where it went. The dominant reason that Biwheels' cash increased by $336,700 is that the company obtained $500,000 of new financing. No cash came in from operating activities. In fact, a total of $160,000 was paid to support operating activities. It is not unusual to have large cash outflows for operating activities in the early periods of a business's life or when an entity is growing quickly. Cash payments for inventories and prepayments for operating expenses often exceed receipts. In the Biwheels example, all sales were on open account, and no cash was received before the end of January, so all operating cash flows were outflows. Despite having an income of $57,900 for January, Biwheels has not yet started to generate any cash from operating activities.

SUMMARY PROBLEM FOR YOUR REVIEW

PROBLEM ONE

Biwheels' transactions for January were analyzed in Exhibits 2-1 and 2-2. The balance sheet, January 31, 19X2, is

Biwheels Company
Balance Sheet January 31, 19X2

Assets		Liabilities and Stockholders' Equity		
Cash	$336,700	Liabilities:		
Accounts receivable	160,300	Note payable		$100,000
Merchandise		Accounts payable		16,200
inventory	59,200	Total liabilities		$116,200
Prepaid rent	4,000	Stockholders' equity:		
Store equipment	13,900	Paid-in capital	$400,000	
		Retained income	57,900	
		Total stockholders' equity		457,900
		Total liabilities and		
Total assets	$574,100	stockholders' equity		$574,100

The following series of transactions occurred during February:

(14) Collection of accounts receivable, $130,000.

(15) Payments of accounts payable, $15,000.

(16) Acquisitions of inventory on open account, $80,000, and for cash, $10,000.

(17) Merchandise carried in inventory at a cost of $110,000 was sold for $176,000, of which $125,000 was on open account and $51,000 was for cash.

(18) Recognition of rent expense for February.

(19) Recognition of depreciation expense for February.

(20) Borrowing of $10,000 from the bank was used to buy $10,000 of store equipment on February 28.

Required

1. Prepare an analysis of transactions, employing the equation approach demonstrated in Exhibit 2-2.

2. Prepare a balance sheet as of February 28, 19X2, and an income statement and statement of cash flows for the month of February.

SOLUTION TO PROBLEM ONE

1. *Analysis of transactions.* The answer is in Exhibit 2-5. All transactions are straightforward extensions or repetitions of the January transactions.

2. *Preparation of financial statements.* Exhibit 2-6 contains the balance sheet, income statement, and statement of cash flows, which have been described earlier. Notice that the balance sheet lists the ending balances in all the accounts in Exhibit 2-5. The income statement summarizes the revenue and expense entries in retained income, and the statement of cash flows summarizes the entries to the cash account.

ACCOUNTING FOR DIVIDENDS AND RETAINED INCOME

Objective 5
Account for cash dividends and prepare a statement of retained income.

A corporation's revenues and expenses for a particular time period are recorded in the stockholders' equity account, Retained Income. Because net income is the excess of revenues over expenses, retained income increases by the amount of net income reported during the period. If expenses exceed revenues, retained income decreases by the amount of the period's **net loss.**

Exhibit 2-5
Biwheels Company

Analysis of Transactions for February 19X2 (in dollars)

Description of Transactions	Cash	+	Accounts Receivable	+	Merchandise Inventory	+	Prepaid Rent	+	Store Equipment	=	Notes Payable	+	Accounts Payable	+	Paid-in Capital	+	Retained Income
											Liabilities				Stockholders' Equity		
Balance, January 31, 19X2	336,700	+	160,300	+	59,200	+	4,000	+	13,900	=	100,000	+	16,200	+	400,000	+	57,900
(14) Collection of accounts receivable	+130,000		−130,000														
(15) Payments of accounts payable	− 15,000									=			− 15,000				
(16) Acquisitions of inventory on open account and for cash	− 10,000				+ 90,000					=			+80,000				
(17a) Sales on open account and for cash	+ 51,000		+125,000							=							+176,000 (increase sales revenue)
(17b) Cost of inventory sold					−110,000					=							−110,000 (increase cost of goods sold expense)
(18) Recognize expiration of rental services							−2,000			=							− 2,000 (increase rent expense)
(19) Recognize expiration of equipment services (depreciation)									− 100	=							− 100 (increase depreciation expense)
(20a) Borrow from bank	+ 10,000									=	+10,000						
(20b) Purchase store equipment	− 10,000								+10,000	=							
Balance, February 28, 19X2	492,700	+	155,300	+	39,200	+	2,000	+	23,800	=	110,000	+	81,200	+	400,000	+	121,800

713,000

713,000

Exhibit 2-6

Biwheels Company

Balance Sheet February 28, 19X2

Assets		Liabilities and Stockholders' Equity		
Cash	$492,700	Liabilities:		
Accounts receivable	155,300	Notes payable	$110,000	
Merchandise		Accounts payable	81,200	$191,200
inventory	39,200			
Prepaid rent	2,000	Stockholders' equity:		
Store equipment	23,800	Paid-in capital	$400,000	
		Retained income	121,800	521,800
Total	$713,000	Total		$713,000

Biwheels Company

Income Statement for the Month Ended February 28, 19X2

Sales		$176,000
Deduct expenses:		
Cost of goods sold	$110,000	
Rent	2,000	
Depreciation	100	112,100
Net income		$ 63,900

Biwheels Company

Statement of Cash Flows for the Month Ended February 28, 19X2

CASH FLOWS FROM OPERATING ACTIVITIES	
Cash collections from customers	$ 181,000
Cash payments to suppliers	(25,000)
Net cash provided by operating activities	$ 156,000
CASH FLOWS FROM INVESTING ACTIVITIES	
Purchase of store equipment	$ (10,000)
Net cash used for investing activities	$ (10,000)
CASH FLOWS FROM FINANCING ACTIVITIES	
Loan from bank	$ 10,000
Net cash provided by financing activities	$ 10,000
Net increase in cash	$ 156,000
Cash balance, February 1, 19X2	336,700
Cash balance, February 28, 19X2	$ 492,700

CASH DIVIDENDS

net loss The name given to the difference between revenues and expenses when expenses exceed revenues.

cash dividends Distributions of cash to stockholders that reduce retained income.

In addition to revenues and expenses, **cash dividends,** distributions of cash to stockholders, are recorded in the Retained Income account. These distributions reduce retained income. Corporations pay out cash dividends to stockholders to provide a return on the stockholders' investment in the corporation. The ability to pay dividends is fundamentally a result of profitable operations. Retained income increases as profits accumulate, and it decreases as dividends are paid out. Although cash dividends decrease retained income, they are not expenses like rent and depreciation. They should not be deducted from revenues because dividends are not directly linked to the generation of revenue or the costs of operating activities. For example, assume that on February 28, cash dividends of $50,000 are disbursed to stockholders. This transaction (21) is analyzed as follows:

	Assets	=	Liabilities	+	Stockholders' Equity
	Cash				Retained Income
(21) Declaration and payment of cash dividends	−50,000	=			−50,000 (dividends)

Transaction 21 shows the decrease in Retained Income and the decrease in Cash.

Cash dividends distribute some of the company's assets (cash) to shareholders, thus reducing the economic value of their remaining interest in Biwheels. Of course, companies must have sufficient cash on hand to pay cash dividends. Because dividends require so much cash, many companies try to avoid paying dividends that exceed the amount of cash provided by operating activities.

Not all companies pay dividends. Microsoft retains all of its income to finance future growth. McDonald's also paid no dividends during its early, highest growth years. However, as a successful company grows, the Retained Income account can soar enormously if dividends are not paid. It can easily be the largest stockholders' equity account. Its balance is the cumulative, lifetime earnings of the company less its cumulative, lifetime losses and dividends. For example, Eastman Kodak's retained earnings are $4,469 million, and its paid-in capital is only $1,161 million.

The board of directors of a company decides how much will be paid in dividends. Many factors affect the decision. Firms that are growing rapidly tend not to pay dividends because their growth requires continuous cash investment in plant, property, and equipment, leaving little cash for distribution. Stable, mature companies tend to pay consistent dividends year after year, in part because their investors expect them. For example, retirees might invest in stable companies that historically pay dividends so that the quarterly dividends provide cash for living expenses. Generally we might expect next quarter's dividend payment to be similar to today's, unless something significant happened. Not surprising, investors react significantly to sudden increases, and especially decreases, in dividends. Generally dividend decreases signal difficulty in finding the cash to maintain historical levels of dividend distributions.

DIVIDEND TRANSACTIONS

Transaction 21 presented the payment of a dividend as a single transaction. However, corporations usually approach dividend matters in steps. The board of directors declares— announces its intention to pay—a dividend on one date (declaration date), payable to those stockholders on record as owning the stock on a second date (record date), and actually pays the dividend on a third date (payment date).

Barron's lists dividend announcements as follows:

Company	Period	Amt.	Payable Date	Record Date
Allied Signal	Q*	$.15	3-2-98	2-9-98
Amoco	Q*	.75	3-10-98	2-11-98

*Q indicates that the dividend is typically declared quarterly.

Such dividend actions entail two accounting transactions. First, the declaration affects the corporation's financial position because the shareholders also become creditors for the amount of the legally declared dividend. Second, the resulting liability is reduced only when the cash is disbursed. Consequently, transaction 21 must be divided into two phases:

	Assets	=	Liabilities	+	Stockholders' Equity
	Cash	=	Dividends Payable	+	Retained Income
(21a) Date of declaration		=	+50,000		−50,000 (dividends)
(21b) Date of payment	−50,000	=	−50,000		
The net effect is eventually the same as in 21 above	−50,000	=	0		−50,000

Although the ultimate effect here is the same as that shown originally in transaction 21, a balance sheet prepared between the date of declaration and the date of payment will show dividends payable as a liability. For example, if Amoco issued a balance sheet on February 27, 1998 it would show about $367.5 million of dividends payable because it is paying a $.75 dividend per share on each of its 490 million outstanding shares. Note too that although a corporation may be expected to pay dividends, it is not legally required to do so until its board of directors formally declares a dividend.

RETAINED INCOME AND CASH

The existence of retained income and cash enable a board of directors to declare a dividend. However, Cash and Retained Income are two entirely separate accounts, sharing no necessary relationship. Consider the following illustration:

Step 1. Assume an opening balance sheet of

Cash	$100	Paid-in capital	$100

Step 2. Purchase inventory for $50 cash. The balance sheet now reads

Cash	$ 50	Paid-in capital	$100
Inventory	50		
Total assets	$100		

Step 3. Now sell the inventory for $80 cash, which produces a retained income of $80 − $50 = $30:

Cash	$130	Paid-in capital	$100
		Retained income	30
		Total owners' equity	$130

At this stage, the retained income seems to be directly linked to the cash increase of $30. It is, but do not think that retained income is a claim against the cash specifically. Remember it is a claim against total assets. This relationship can be clarified by the transaction that follows.

Step 4. Purchase inventory and equipment, in the amounts of $60 and $50, respectively. Now,

Cash	$ 20	Paid-in capital	$100
Inventory	60	Retained income	30
Equipment	50		
Total assets	$130	Total owners' equity	$130

Where is the $30 in retained income reflected? Is it reflected in Cash? It cannot be, because there is only $20 in Cash, and Retained Income is $30. Part of the cash from profitable sales has been reinvested in inventory and equipment. This example helps to explain the nature of the Retained Income account. It is a residual claim, not a pot of gold. A residual claim means that if the company went out of business, and all of its assets were sold and converted to cash, the owners would receive the amount left over after all of the liabilities were paid. Retained income (and also paid-in capital) is a general claim against, or undivided interest in, total assets, not a specific claim against cash or against any other particular asset. Do not confuse the assets themselves with the claims against the assets.

STATEMENT OF RETAINED INCOME

Naturally, if owners are interested in tracing the amount of retained income in a company, accountants have created a financial statement to do just that. Exhibit 2-7 shows the **statement of retained income,** which lists the beginning balance (in this case, January 31) in Retained Income, followed by a description of any major changes (in this case, net income and dividends) that occurred during the period, and the ending balance (February 28) for the Biwheels Company.

Frequently, the statement of retained income is added to the bottom of the income statement. In such cases, the combined statements are called a **statement of income and retained income.** For example, the income statement in Exhibit 2-6 combined with the statement of retained income in Exhibit 2-7 appear reformatted, and retitled, in Exhibit 2-8 as a statement of income and retained income.

Note how Exhibit 2-8 is anchored to the balance sheet equation:

Asset = Liabilities + Paid-in capital + Retained income

$$\text{Ending balance} = \left[\text{Beginning balance} + \text{Revenues} - \text{Expenses} - \text{Dividends} \right]$$

$$\text{Bal. Feb. 28 after dividends} = \left[57{,}900 + 176{,}000 - 112{,}100 - \$50{,}000 \right] = 71{,}800$$

statement of retained income A statement that lists the beginning balance in retained income, followed by a description of any changes that occurred during the period, and the ending balance.

statement of income and retained income A statement that includes a statement of retained income at the bottom of an income statement.

CUSTOMS OF PRESENTATION

Exhibits 2-7 and 2-8 illustrate some customs that accountants follow when they prepare financial statements. To save space accountants often place a subtotal on the right side of the final number in a column, as is illustrated by the $112,100 in Exhibit 2-8.

Exhibit 2-7

Biwheels Company
Statement of Retained Income for the Month Ended
February 28, 19X2

Retained income, January 31, 19X2	$ 57,900
Net income for February	63,900
Total	$121,800
Dividends declared	50,000
Retained income, February 28, 19X2	$ 71,800

Exhibit 2-8

Biwheels Company

Statement of Income and Retained Income for the Month Ended
February 28, 19X2

Sales		$176,000
Deduct expenses:		
Cost of goods sold	$110,000	
Rent	2,000	
Depreciation	100	112,100
Net income		$ 63,900*
Retained income, January 31, 19X2		57,900
Total		$121,800
Dividends declared		50,000
Retained income, February 28, 19X2		$ 71,800

* Note how the income statement ends here. The $63,900 simultaneously
becomes the initial item on the statement of retained income portion of this
combined statement.

Dollar signs are customarily used at the beginning of each column of dollar amounts and for net income. Some statements also use dollar signs with the subtotals, for example, the $63,900 and the $121,800 in Exhibit 2-8. Double-underscores (double rulings) are typically used to denote final numbers.

SUMMARY PROBLEM FOR YOUR REVIEW

PROBLEM TWO

The following interpretations and remarks are frequently encountered with regard to financial statements. Do you agree or disagree? Explain fully.

1. "Sales show the cash coming in from customers, and the various expenses show the cash going out for goods and services. The difference is net income."
2. Consider the following December 31, 1996 accounts of Motorola, Inc., a U.S. company that is a leading worldwide provider of wireless communications, semiconductors and advanced electronic systems, and components and services. You may have used one of their cell phones:

Motorola

Consolidated Balance Sheets

(In millions, except per share amounts)   Motorola, Inc. and Consolidated Subsidiaries

December 31	1996	1995
Stockholders' equity		
Common stock, $3 par value		
Authorized shares: 1996 and 1995, 1,400		
Issued and outstanding shares: 1996, 593.4; 1995, 591.4	**1,780**	1,774
Preferred stock, $100 par value issuable in series		
Authorized shares: 0.5 (none issued)	—	—
Additional paid-in capital	**1,672**	1,750
Retained earnings	**8,343**	7,461
Total stockholders' equity	**$11,795**	$10,985

A Motorola employee commented, "Why can't that big company pay higher wages and dividends too? It can use its hundreds of millions of dollars of retained earnings to do so."

3. "The total Motorola stockholders' equity measures the amount that the shareholders would get today if the corporation were liquidated."

SOLUTION TO PROBLEM TWO

1. Cash receipts and disbursements are not the basis for the accrual accounting recognition of revenues and expenses. Sales could easily be credit sales for which no cash has yet been received, and expenses could be those that have been incurred but not yet paid out. Therefore, under accrual accounting sales and expenses are not equivalent to cash inflows and outflows.

   To determine net income under accrual accounting, expenses are subtracted from revenues (expenses are linked to revenues via matching). Cash flow from operations can be larger or smaller than net income.

2. As the chapter indicated, retained earnings is not cash. It is a stockholders' equity account that represents the accumulated increase in ownership claims due to profitable operations. This claim may be lowered by the payment of cash dividends, but a growing company will reinvest cash in receivables, inventories, plant, equipment, and other assets so necessary for expansion. As a result, the ownership claims measured by retained earnings may not be covered by cash. In fact, some companies might not be able to pay out their retained earnings without liquidating many or all of their assets.

3. Stockholders' equity is the excess of assets over liabilities. If the assets were carried in the accounting records at their liquidating value today and the liabilities were represented exactly at their market values, the remark would be true. However, the numbers on the balance sheet are historical numbers, not current numbers. Intervening changes in markets and general price levels in inflationary times may mean that the assets are woefully understated. Investors may make a critical error if they think that balance sheets indicate current values.

FOUR POPULAR FINANCIAL RATIOS

Now that you know quite a bit about financial statements, you are ready to learn how the information in these statements is used. Numbers are hard to understand out of context. Is $10 a lot to pay for a share of stock? Is $1 a good dividend? To show you how investors think about such questions, we will gradually introduce you to various financial ratios.

A financial ratio is computed by dividing one number by another. For a set of complex financial statements, literally hundreds of ratios can be computed if desired. Every analyst has a set of favorite ratios, but one is so popular that it dwarfs all others: **earnings per share of common stock (EPS).** In fact, EPS data must appear on the face of the income statement of publicly held corporations. This is the only instance in which a financial ratio is required as a part of the body of financial statements. Let us now examine some popular ratios based on financial statement information.

Objective 6
Compute and explain earnings per share, price-earnings ratio, dividend-yield ratio, and dividend-payout ratio.

EARNINGS PER SHARE (EPS)

When the owners' equity is relatively simple, the computation of EPS is straightforward. For example, consider Pepsico Corporation, the well-known beverage and food company. It reported EPS of $.68, $.98 and $.72 in 1990, 1993, and 1996, respectively. The 1996 EPS

Earnings per share (EPS)
Net income divided by average number of common shares outstanding.

is calculated by dividing 1996 income of $1,149 million by average shares outstanding during the year of 1,606,000,000.

$$EPS = \frac{\text{Net income}}{\text{Average number of shares outstanding}}$$

$$1993\ EPS = \frac{\$1,587,900,000}{1,620,000,000} = \$.98 \quad 1996\ EPS = \frac{\$1,149,000,000}{1,606,000,000} = \$.72$$

The Pepsico computation is relatively simple because the company has only one type of capital stock, little fluctuation of shares outstanding throughout the year, and no unusual items affecting the computation of net income. EPS calculations can become more difficult when such complications arise. Investors interested in Pepsico might ask whether EPS was growing over time and might ask especially why EPS was lower in 1996.

PRICE-EARNINGS (P-E) RATIO

price-earnings ratio (P-E)
Market price per share of common stock divided by earnings per share of common stock.

Another popular ratio is the **price-earnings (P-E) ratio:**

$$P\text{-E Ratio} = \frac{\text{Market price per share of common stock}}{\text{Earnings per share of common stock}}$$

The numerator is typically today's market price for a share of the company's stock. The denominator is the EPS for the most recent 12 months. Thus the P-E ratio varies throughout a given year, depending on the fluctuations in the company's stock price. For example, Pepsico's P-E ratio would be:

Pepsico

	Using Highest Market Price During Fourth Quarter	Using Lowest Market Price During Fourth Quarter
1996 P-E	$\frac{\$32.88}{\$.72} = 45.7$	$\frac{\$28.13}{\$.72} = 39.1$
1993 P-E	$\frac{\$21}{\$.98} = 21.4$	$\frac{\$18}{\$.98} = 18.4$

The P-E ratio is sometimes called the earnings multiple. It measures how much the investing public is willing to pay for a chance to share the company's potential earnings. Note especially that the P-E ratio is determined by the marketplace. This earnings multiplier may differ considerably for two companies within the same industry. It may also change for the same company through the years. In general, a high P-E ratio indicates that investors predict that the company's net income will grow rapidly. Consider Microsoft's 1996 ratio of 53 compared with the P-E ratio of 8 for Chrysler. These ratios tell us that Microsoft's earnings are expected to grow much more rapidly than Chrysler's. History certainly suggests this is likely. Microsoft earnings per share have grown almost 50% each year during the last decade while Chrysler's EPS grew at about 5% per year over the same period. The *Wall Street Journal* publishes P-E ratios daily on its stock pages.

DIVIDEND-YIELD RATIO

dividend-yield ratio
Common dividends per share divided by market price per share.

Individual investors are usually interested in the profitability of their personal investments in common stock. That profitability takes two forms: cash dividends and market-price appreciation of the stock. The **dividend-yield ratio** (the current dividend per share divided by the current market price of the stock), also simply called dividend yield, gauges dividend payouts. It is computed as follows:

Pepsico

	Using Highest Market Price During Fourth Quarter	Using Lowest Market Price During Fourth Quarter
1996 Dividend yield =	$\dfrac{\$.50}{\$32.88} = 1.5\%$	$\dfrac{\$.50}{\$28.13} = 1.8\%$
1993 Dividend yield =	$\dfrac{\$.30}{\$21} = 1.4\%$	$\dfrac{\$.30}{\$18} = 1.7\%$

Dividend ratios may be of particular importance to those investors in common stock who seek regular cash returns on their investments. For example, an investor who favored high current returns would not buy stock in growth companies. Growth companies have conservative dividend policies because they are using most of their profit-generated resources to help finance expansion of their operations.

Market prices at which stocks are traded in organized marketplaces, such as the New York Stock Exchange, are quoted in the daily newspapers. The dividend yields are also published, as measured by annual disbursements based on the last quarterly dividends.

Consider the following stock quotations for Pepsico regarding trading on September 9, 1997:

52 Weeks										
High	Low	Stock	Div.	Yld. %	P-E Ratio	Sales 100s	High	Low	Close	Net Chg.
39¾	28⅛	Pepsico	.50	1.3	47	33,103	38½	37¹⁵⁄₁₆	38⁷⁄₁₆	⁵⁄₁₆

Reading from left to right, the highest price at which Pepsico common stock was traded in the preceding 52 weeks was $39.75 per share; the lowest price, $28.125. The current dividend rate for 12 months is $.50 per share, producing a yield of 1.3% based on the day's closing price of the stock. The P-E ratio is 47, also based on the closing price. Total sales for the day were 3,310,300 shares. The highest price at which the stock was traded was $38.50 per share; the lowest $37.93. The closing price was that of the last trade for the day, $38.43, which was $.31 lower than the preceding day's last trade.

Keep in mind that transactions in publicly traded shares are between individual investors in the stock, not between the corporation and the individuals. Thus a "typical trade" results in the selling of, say, 100 shares of Pepsico stock held by Ms. Johnson in Minneapolis to Ms. Davis in Atlanta for $3,843 in cash. These parties would ordinarily transact the trade through their respective stockbrokers. Pepsico Corporation would not be directly affected by the trade except that its records of shareholders would be changed to show that 100 shares were now held by Davis, not Johnson.

DIVIDEND-PAYOUT RATIO

Although not routinely published, the **dividend-payout ratio** also receives much attention from analysts. Consider McDonald's, the well-known fast-food chain. The formula for its payout computation is given below, followed by McDonald's ratio, using figures from its 1996 annual report:

dividend-payout ratio Common dividends per share divided by earnings per share.

$$\text{Dividend-payout ratio} = \frac{\text{Common dividends per share}}{\text{Earnings per share}}$$

$$\text{Dividend-payout ratio} = \frac{\$.42}{\$2.91} = 14\%$$

Exhibit 2-9

Some Synonyms in Accounting

Term Initially Used in This Book	Examples of Synonyms	Example of Companies
1. Net income		Anheuser-Busch, H.J. Heinz, Colgate-Palmolive
	Net earnings	General Mills, Chrysler, Johnson & Johnson
	Profit	Caterpillar
2. Retained income		General Motors
	Retained earnings	Anheuser-Busch, H. J. Heinz, Colgate-Palmolive
	Reinvested earnings	Scott Paper, Coca-Cola
	Earnings retained for use in the business	Ford Motor
	Profit employed in the business	Caterpillar

McDonald's fits into the category of a low-payout company. As long as McDonald's continues its worldwide expansion, a minimal payout can be anticipated. Some fast-growing companies such as Microsoft pay no dividends. In contrast, companies without exceptional growth tend to pay a higher percentage of their earnings as dividends. Public utilities will ordinarily have high payout ratios. For instance, recently Pacific Gas and Electric Company paid dividends amounting to 80% of its earnings. Chrysler falls between the extremes, with a 1996 payout ratio of ($1.40 ÷ $5.03) = 28%.

THE LANGUAGE OF ACCOUNTING IN THE REAL WORLD

At this point you have learned a great number of accounting terms. Unfortunately, organizations use different terms to describe the same concept or account. As a result, the terms you see in real financial statements might not correspond to the ones you just learned. To ease your potential terminology worries, a number of synonyms are presented in Exhibit 2-9. These terms are not introduced here to confuse you. Our objective is to acquaint you with the real world of accounting vocabulary so that you will not be surprised when a company's financial statement uses different terms than you learned initially.

SUMMARY PROBLEM FOR YOUR REVIEW

PROBLEM THREE

During 1996 Liz Claiborne stock sold for about $40 per share. The company had net income of $155,665,000, had an average of 72,402,326 shares outstanding during the year and paid dividends of $.45 per share. Calculate the following:

Earnings per share	Dividend-Yield ratio
Price-Earnings ratio	Dividend-Payout ratio

SOLUTION TO PROBLEM THREE

$$\text{Earnings per share} = \$155,665,000/72,402,326 = \$2.15$$

$$\text{Price-Earnings ratio} = \$40/\$2.15 = 18.6$$

$$\text{Dividend-Yield ratio} = \$.45/\$40 = 1.1\%$$

$$\text{Dividend-Payout ratio} = \$.45/\$2.15 = 21\%$$

Highlights to Remember

Accountants can measure income, the excess of revenues over expenses for a particular time period, on an accrual or cash basis. In accrual accounting, revenue is recorded when it is earned, and expenses are recorded when they are incurred. In cash accounting, revenues and expenses are recorded only when cash changes hands. Accrual accounting is the standard basis for accounting today.

The concept of revenue recognition means that revenues are assigned to the period in which they are earned and realized. Under the concepts of matching and cost recovery, expenses are assigned to a period in which the pertinent goods and services are either used or appear to have no future benefit. Revenues and expenses are components of stockholders' equity. Revenues increase stockholders' equity, and expenses decrease stockholders' equity.

An income statement shows an entity's revenues and expenses for a particular span of time. The net income (loss) during the period increases (decreases) the amount of retained income on the balance sheet.

Accrual accounting is an excellent way to follow a company's use of its overall assets, but it does not trace cash flows. To satisfy decision makers' need to follow a company's use of cash, accountants use a statement of cash flows. This statement can easily be linked to both the income statement and the balance sheet.

Cash dividends are not expenses. They are distributions of cash to stockholders that reduce retained income. Corporations are not obligated to pay dividends, but once dividends are declared by the board of directors they become a legal liability until paid in cash.

Accounting Vocabulary

accrual basis, p. 45
cash basis, p. 45
cash dividends, p. 56
cash flow statement, p. 52
cost of goods sold, p. 46
cost of sales, p. 46
cost recovery, p. 46
depreciation, p. 47
dividend payout ratio, p. 63
dividend-yield ratio, p. 62
earnings, p. 44
earnings per share (EPS), p. 61
expenses, p. 44

fiscal year, p. 43
income, p. 44
income statement, p. 50
interim periods, p. 43
matching, p. 46
net income, p. 50
net loss, p. 56
operating cycle, p. 43
operating statement, p. 50
period costs, p. 46
price-earnings ratio, p. 62
product costs, p. 46
profit, p. 44

recognition, p. 45
reinvested earnings, p. 44
retained earnings, p. 44
retained income, p. 44
revenues, p. 44
sales, p. 44
statement of cash flows, p. 52
statement of earnings, p. 50
statement of income and
   retained income, p. 59
statement of retained income,
   p. 59

Assignment Material

QUESTIONS

2-1. How long is a company's operating cycle?

2-2. "Expenses are negative stockholders' equity accounts." Explain.

2-3. What is the major defect of the cash basis of accounting?

2-4. What are the two tests of recognition of revenue?

2-5. Give two examples where revenue is not recognized at the point of sale, one where recognition is delayed because the revenue is not yet earned, and one because it is not yet realized.

2-6. "Expenses are assets that have been used up." Explain.

2-7. "The manager acquires goods and services, not expenses per se." Explain.

2-8. "The income statement is like a moving picture; in contrast, a balance sheet is like a snapshot." Explain.

2-9. "Cash dividends are not expenses." Explain.

2-10. Identify the three categories of cash flows found on the statement of cash flows and list two activities that might appear in each of the categories.

2-11. "Retained income is not a pot of gold." Explain.

2-12. "Financial ratios are important tools for analyzing financial statements, but no ratios are shown on the statements." Do you agree? Explain.

2-13. "Fast growing companies have high P-E ratios." Explain.

2-14. Give two ratios that give information about a company's dividends, and explain what each means.

2-15. "Companies with a high dividend-payout ratio are good investments because stockholders get more of their share of earnings in cash." Do you agree? Explain.

2-16. Give two synonyms for *income statement.*

2-17. Give two synonyms for *income* and for *retained income.*

2-18. Why is it important to learn synonyms that are used for various accounting terms?

EXERCISES

2-19 Synonyms and Antonyms

Consider the following terms: (1) expenses, (2) unexpired costs, (3) reinvested earnings, (4) net earnings, (5) prepaid expenses, (6) undistributed earnings, (7) statement of earnings, (8) used-up costs, (9) net profits, (10) net income, (11) revenues, (12) retained income, (13) sales, (14) statement of financial condition, (15) statement of income, (16) statement of financial position, (17) retained earnings, (18) operating statement and (19) cost of goods sold.

Required   Group the items into two major categories, the income statement and the balance sheet. Answer by indicating the numbered items that belong in each group. Specify items that are assets and items that are expenses.

2-20 Special Meanings of Terms

A news story described the disappointing sales of a new model car, the Nova. An auto dealer said: "Even if the Nova is a little slow to move out of dealerships, it is more of a plus than a minus. . . . We're now selling 14 more cars per month than before. That's revenue. That's the bottom line."

Required   Is the dealer confused about accounting terms? Explain.

2-21 Nature of Retained Income

This is an exercise on the relationships between assets, liabilities, and ownership equities. The numbers are small, but the underlying concepts are large.

1. Assume an opening balance sheet of:

Cash	$1,500	Paid-in capital	$1,500

2. Purchase inventory for $700 cash. Prepare a balance sheet. A heading is unnecessary in this and subsequent requirements.

3. Sell the entire inventory for $950 cash. Prepare a balance sheet. Where is the retained income in terms of relationships within the balance sheet? That is, what is the meaning of the retained income? Explain in your own words.

4. Buy inventory for $400 cash and equipment for $700 cash. Prepare a balance sheet. Where is the retained income in terms of relationships within the balance sheet? That is, what is the meaning of the retained income? Explain in your own words.

5. Buy inventory for $500 on open account. Prepare a balance sheet. Where is the retained income and account payable in terms of the relationships within the balance sheet? That is, what is the meaning of the account payable and the retained income? Explain in your own words.

2-22 Asset Acquisition and Expiration

The Lougee Company had the following transactions:

a. Paid $2,000 for stationery and wrapping supplies.
b. Paid $18,000 cash for rent for the next six months.
c. Paid $4,000 cash for an advertisement in the New York Times.
d. Paid $9,000 cash for a training program for employees.

Show the effects on the balance sheet equation in two phases: at acquisition and upon expiration at the end of the month of acquisition. Show all amounts in thousands.

Required

2-23 Find Unknowns

The following data pertain to the Cruz Corporation. Total assets at January 1, 19X1 were $100,000; at December 31, 19X1, $124,000. During 19X1, sales were $354,000, cash dividends were $4,000, and operating expenses (exclusive of cost of goods sold) were $200,000. Total liabilities at December 31, 19X1, were $55,000; at January 1, 19X1, $40,000. There was no additional capital paid in during 19X1. Compute the following:

1. Stockholders' equity, January 1, 19X1, and December 31, 19X1.
2. Net income for 19X1
3. Cost of goods sold for 19X1

2-24 Income Statement

A statement of an automobile dealer follows:

Warner Toyota, Inc.
Statement of Profit and Loss
December 31, 19X3

Revenues:		
Sales	$1,000,000	
Increase in market value of land		
and building	200,000	$1,200,000
Deduct expenses:		
Advertising	$ 100,000	
Sales commissions	50,000	
Utilities	20,000	
Wages	160,000	
Dividends	100,000	
Cost of cars purchased	700,000	1,130,000
Net profit		$ 70,000

[handwritten: should not be shown at all]

[handwritten: never deducted on an income statement taken out after]

[handwritten: cost of goods]

List and describe any shortcomings of this statement.

2-25 Income Statement and Cash Flow Statement

KLM Royal Dutch Airlines flies to more than 350 cities in 80 countries. In the year ended March 31, 1997, KLM had revenues of NLG 10,550 million (where NLG is Netherlands Guilders). Total expenses were NLG 10,323 million. Cash flows from operating activities were NLG 786 million, cash flows from investing were NLG (108), and cash flows from financing activities were NLG (981) million.

1. Compute KLM's net income for the year ended March 31, 1997.
2. Compute the increase (decrease) in cash for KLM for the year ended March 31, 1997.

2-26 Balance Sheet Equation

(Alternates are 2-27 and 2-42.) For each of the following independent cases, compute the amounts (in thousands) for the items indicated by letters, and show your supporting computations:

	Case 1	Case 2	Case 3
Revenues	$140	$ K	$280
Expenses	120	200	240
Dividends declared	–0–	5	Q
Additional investment by stockholders	–0–	40	35
Net income	E	20	P
Retained income:			
Beginning of year	30	60	100
End of year	D	J	110
Paid-in capital:			
Beginning of year	15	10	N
End of year	C	H	85
Total assets:			
Beginning of year	80	F	L
End of year	95	280	M
Total liabilities:			
Beginning of year	A	90	105
End of year	B	G	95

2-27 Balance Sheet Equation

(Alternates are 2-26 and 2-42.) Eastman Kodak's terminology and actual data (in millions of dollars) follow for a recent fiscal year:

Total cost	$ B
Net earnings	1,288
Dividends	539
Additional investments by stockholders	111
Assets, beginning of period	14,477
Assets, end of period	E
Liabilities, beginning of period	A
Liabilities, end of period	9,704
Additional capital paid-in, beginning of period	1,777
Additional capital paid-in, end of period	D
Retained earnings, beginning of period	2,097
Retained earnings, end of period	C
Total revenues	16,244

Find the unknowns (in millions), showing computations to support your answers.

Required

2-28 Nonprofit Operating Statement

Examine the accompanying statement of the Edinburgh University Faculty Club. Identify the Edinburgh classifications and terms that would not be used by a profit-seeking hotel and restaurant. Suggest terms that the profit-seeking entity would use instead. (£ is the British pound.)

Edinburgh Faculty Club
Statement of Income and Expenses for Fiscal Year 1997–1998

Food Service:		
Sales		£545,130
Expenses:		
Food	£287,088	
Labor	272,849	
Operating costs	30,537	590,474
Deficit		£ (45,344)
Bar:		
Sales		£ 90,549
Expenses:		
Cost of liquor	£ 29,302	
Labor	5,591	
Operating costs	6,125	41,018
Surplus		49,531
Hotel:		
Sales		£ 33,771
Expenses		23,803
Surplus		9,968
Surplus from operations		£ 14,155
General income (members' dues, room fees, etc.)		95,546
General administration and operating expenses		(134,347)
Deficit before university subsidy		£ (24,646)
University subsidy		31,000
Net surplus after university subsidy		£ 6,354

2-29 Earnings and Dividend Ratios

Cadbury Schwepps, the British candy and beverage company, had 1996 earnings of £340 million. Cash dividends per share were £.17. The company had an average of 996 million common shares outstanding. No other type of stock was outstanding. The market price of the stock at the end of the year was £6 per share.

Compute (1) earnings per share, (2) price-earnings ratio, (3) dividend yield, and (4) dividend-payout ratio.

Required

2-30 Earnings and Dividend Ratios

Chevron Corporation is one of the largest oil companies in the world. The company's revenue in 1996 was $42.8 billion. Net income was $2,607,000,000. EPS was $3.99. The company's common stock is the only type of shares outstanding.

Required

1. Compute the average number of common shares outstanding during the year.
2. The dividend-payout ratio was 52%. What was the amount of dividends per share?

ASSIGNMENT MATERIAL 69

3. The average market price of the stock for the year was $58 per share. Compute (a) dividend yield and (b) price-earnings ratio.

PROBLEMS

2-31 Fundamental Revenue and Expense

Bowen Corporation was formed on June 1, 19X2, when some stockholders invested $100,000 in cash in the company. During the first week of June, $80,000 cash was spent for merchandise inventory (sportswear). During the remainder of the month, total sales reached $110,000, of which $70,000 was on open account. The cost of the inventory sold was $60,000. For simplicity, assume that no other transactions occurred except that on June 28, Bowen Corporation acquired $25,000 additional inventory on open account.

Required

1. Using the balance sheet equation approach demonstrated in Exhibit 2-2 (p. 48), analyze all transactions for June. Show all amounts in thousands.
2. Prepare a balance sheet, June 30, 19X2.
3. Prepare two statements for June, side by side. The first should use the accrual basis of accounting to compute net income, and the second the cash basis to compute net cash provided by (or used by) operating activities. Which basis provides a more informative measure of economic performance? Why?

2-32 Accounting for Prepayments

(Alternates are 2-34, 2-36, 2-38, and 2-41.) The Ordonez Company, a wholesale distributor of home appliances, began business on July 1, 19X2. The following summarized transactions occurred during July.

1. Ordonez's stockholders contributed $230,000 in cash in exchange for their common stock.
2. On July 1, Ordonez signed a one-year lease on a warehouse, paying $60,000 cash in advance for occupancy of twelve months.
3. On July 1, Ordonez acquired warehouse equipment for $100,000. A cash down payment of $40,000 was made and a note payable was signed for the balance.
4. On July 1, Ordonez paid $24,000 cash for a two-year insurance policy covering fire, casualty, and related risks.
5. Ordonez acquired assorted merchandise for $35,000 cash.
6. Ordonez acquired assorted merchandise for $190,000 on open account.
7. Total sales were $200,000, of which $30,000 were for cash.
8. Cost of inventory sold was $160,000.
9. Rent expense was recognized for the month of July.
10. Depreciation expense of $2,000 was recognized for the month.
11. Insurance expense was recognized for the month.
12. Collected $35,000 from credit customers.
13. Disbursed $80,000 to trade creditors.

For simplicity, ignore all other possible expenses.

Required

1. Using the balance sheet equation format demonstrated in Exhibit 2-2 (p. 48), prepare an analysis of each transaction. Show all amounts in thousands. What do transactions 8 to 11 illustrate about the theory of assets and expenses? (Use a Prepaid Insurance account, which is not illustrated in Exhibit 2-2.)
2. Prepare an income statement for July on the accrual basis.
3. Prepare a balance sheet, July 31, 19X2.

2-33   Net Income and Cash Flows from Operating Activities
(Alternates are 2-35, 2-37, and 2-39.) Refer to the preceding problem. Suppose Ordonez measured performance on the cash basis instead of the accrual basis. Compute the net cash provided by (or used for) operating activities. Which measure, net income or net cash provided by (or used for) operating activities, provides a better measure of overall performance? Why?

2-34   Analysis of Transactions, Preparation of Statements
(Alternates are 2-32, 2-36, 2-38, and 2-41.) The Guenther Company was incorporated on April 1, 19X2. Guenther had ten holders of common stock. Rita Guenther, who was the president and chief executive officer, held 51% of the shares. The company rented space in chain discount stores and specialized in selling ladies' shoes. Guenther's first location was in a store that was part of The Old Market in Omaha.

The following events occurred during April:

1.   The company was incorporated. Common stockholders invested $140,000 cash.
2.   Purchased merchandise inventory for cash, $45,000.
3.   Purchased merchandise inventory on open account, $35,000.
4.   Merchandise carried in inventory at a cost of $37,000 was sold for cash for $25,000 and on open account for $65,000, a grand total of $90,000. Guenther (not The Old Market) carries and collects these accounts receivable.
5.   Collection of the above accounts receivable, $15,000.
6.   Payments of accounts payable $28,000. See transaction 3.
7.   Special display equipment and fixtures were acquired on April 1 for $36,000. Their expected useful life was thirty-six months. This equipment was removable. Guenther paid $12,000 as a down payment and signed a promissory note for $24,000. Also see transaction 11.
8.   On April 1, Guenther signed a rental agreement with The Old Market. The agreement called for a flat $2,000 per month, payable quarterly in advance. Therefore, Guenther paid $6,000 cash on April 1.
9.   The rental agreement also called for a payment of 10% of all sales. This payment was in addition to the flat $2,000 per month. In this way, The Old Market would share in any success of the venture and be compensated for general services such as cleaning and utilities. This payment was to be made in cash on the last day of each month as soon as the sales for the month had been tabulated. Therefore Guenther made the payment on April 30.
10.   Employee wages and sales commissions were all paid for in cash. The amount was $34,000.
11.   Depreciation expense of $1,000 was recognized ($36,000/36 months). See transaction 7.
12.   The expiration of an appropriate amount of prepaid rental services was recognized. See transaction 8.

Required

1.   Prepare an analysis of Guenther Company's transactions, employing the equation approach demonstrated in Exhibit 2-2 (p. 48). Show all amounts in thousands.
2.   Prepare a balance sheet as of April 30, 19X2, and an income statement for the month of April. Ignore income taxes.
3.   Given these sparse facts, analyze Guenther's performance for April and its financial position as of April 30, 19X2.

2-35   Net Income and Cash Flows from Operating Activities
(Alternates are 2-33, 2-37, and 2-39.) Refer to the preceding problem. Suppose Guenther measured performance on the cash basis instead of the accrual basis. Compute the net

cash provided by (or used for) operating activities. Which measure, net income or net cash provided by (or used for) operating activities, provides a better measure of overall performance? Why?

2-36 Analysis of Transactions, Preparation of Statements

(Alternates are 2-32, 2-34, 2-38, and 2-41.) H. J. Heinz Company's actual condensed balance sheet data for April 30, 1997, follows (in millions):

Cash	$ 157	Accounts payable	$ 865
Accounts receivable	1,119	Other liabilities	5,132
Inventories	1,433	Paid-in capital	284
Other assets	3,250	Retained earnings	2,157
Property, plant, and equipment	2,479		
Total	8,438	Total	8,438

The following summarizes some transactions during May (in millions):

1. Ketchup carried in inventory at a cost of $3 was sold for cash of $2 and on open account of $8, a grand total of $10.
2. Acquired inventory on account, $6.
3. Collected receivables, $4.
4. On May 2, used $12 cash to prepay some rent and insurance for 12 months.
5. Payments on accounts payable (for inventories), $2.
6. Paid selling and administrative expenses in cash, $1.
7. Prepaid expenses of $1 for rent and insurance expired in May.
8. Depreciation expense of $1 was recognized for May.

Required

1. Prepare an analysis of Heinz's transactions, employing the equation approach demonstrated in Exhibit 2-2 (p. 48). Show all amounts in millions. (For simplicity, only a few transactions are illustrated here.)
2. Prepare a statement of earnings for the month ended May 31 and a balance sheet, May 31. Ignore income taxes.

2-37 Net Income and Cash Flows from Operating Activities

(Alternates are 2-33, 2-35, and 2-39.) Refer to the preceding problem. Suppose Heinz measured performance on the cash basis instead of the accrual basis. Compute the net cash provided by (or used for) operating activities. Which measure, net income or net cash provided by (or used for) operating activities, provides a better measure of overall performance? Why?

2-38 Analysis of Transactions, Preparation of Statements

(Alternates are 2-32, 2-34, 2-36, and 2-41.) Wm. Wrigley Jr. Company manufactures and sells chewing gum. The company's actual condensed balance sheet data for a recent December 31 follows (in millions):

Cash	$ 301	Accounts payable	$ 75
Receivables	165	Dividends payable	20
Inventories	233	Other liabilities	241
Other current assets	31	Paid-in capital	16
Property, plant, and equipment	388	Retained earnings	882
Other assets	116		
Total	$1,234	Total	$1,234

The following summarizes some major transactions during January (in millions):

1. Gum carried in inventory at a cost of $40 was sold for cash of $32 and on open account of $40, a grand total of $72.
2. Collection of receivables, $50.
3. Depreciation expense of $3 was recognized.
4. Selling and administrative expenses of $24 were paid in cash.
5. Prepaid expenses of $5 expired in January. These included fire insurance premiums paid in the previous year that applied to future months. The expiration increases selling and administrative expense and reduces other current assets.
6. The December 31 liability for dividends was paid in cash on January 25.
7. On January 30, the company declared a $2 dividend, which will be paid on February 25.

1. Prepare an analysis of Wrigley's transactions, employing the equation approach demonstrated in Exhibit 2-2 (p. 48). Show all amounts in millions. (For simplicity, only a few major transactions are illustrated here.) **Required**
2. Prepare a statement of earnings and also a statement of retained earnings for the month ended January 31. Also prepare a balance sheet, January 31. Ignore income taxes.

2-39 Net Income and Cash Flows from Operating Activities
(Alternates are 2-33, 2-35, and 2-37.) Refer to the preceding problem. Suppose Wrigley measured performance on the cash basis instead of the accrual basis. Compute the net cash provided by (or used for) operating activities. Which measure, net income or net cash provided by (or used for) operating activities, provides a better measure of overall performance? Why?

2-40 Prepare Financial Statements
The Loretti Corporation does not use the services of a professional accountant. At the end of its second year of operations, 19X2, the company's financial statements were prepared by its office manager. Listed below in random order are the items appearing in these statements:

Accounts receivable	$ 27,800	Office supplies inventory	$ 2,000
Paid-in capital	100,000	Notes payable	7,000
Trucks	33,700	Merchandise inventory	61,000
Cost of goods sold	156,000	Accounts payable	14,000
Salary expense	86,000	Notes receivable	2,500
Unexpired insurance	1,800	Utilities expenses	5,000
Rent expense	19,500	Net income	4,200
Sales	280,000	Retained income:	
Advertising expense	9,300	January 1, 19X2	18,000
Cash	14,400	December 31, 19X2	22,200

You are satisfied that the statements in which these items appear are correct except for several matters that the office manager overlooked. The following information should have been entered on the books and reflected in the financial statements:

a. The amount shown for rent expense includes $1,500 that is actually prepaid for the first month in 19X3.
b. Of the amount shown for unexpired insurance, only $800 is prepaid for periods after 19X2.
c. Depreciation of trucks for 19X2 is $5,000.

d. About $1,200 of the office supplies in the inventory shown above was actually issued and used during 19X2 operations.

e. Cash dividends of $3,000 were declared in December 19X2 by the board of directors. These dividends are to be distributed in February 19X3.

Required Prepare in good form the following corrected financial statements, ignoring income taxes:

1. Income statement for 19X2
2. Statement of retained income for 19X2
3. Balance sheet at December 31, 19X2

It is not necessary to prepare a columnar analysis to show the transaction effects on each of the elements of the accounting equation.

2-41 Transaction Analysis and Financial Statements, Including Dividends
(Alternates are 2-32, 2-34, 2-36, and 2-38.) Consider the following balance sheet of a wholesaler of party supplies:

Partco Supplies Company
Balance Sheet December 31, 19X7

Assets		Liabilities and Stockholders' Equity		
		Liabilities:		
Cash	$ 300,000	Accounts payable		$ 800,000
Accounts receivable	400,000	Stockholders' equity:		
Merchandise inventory	860,000	Paid-in capital	$300,000	
Prepaid rent	40,000	Retained income	600,000	
Equipment	100,000	Total stockholders'		
		equity		900,000
Total	$1,700,000	Total		$1,700,000

The following is a summary of transactions that occurred during 19X8:

a. Acquisitions of inventory on open account, $1 million.

b. Sales on open account, $1.4 million; and for cash, $200,000. Therefore, total sales were $1.6 million.

c. Merchandise carried in inventory at a cost of $1.2 million was sold as described in b.

d. The warehouse twelve-month lease expired on September 1, 19X8. However, the lease was immediately renewed at a rate of $84,000 for the next twelve-month period. The entire rent was paid in cash in advance.

e. Depreciation expense for 19X8 for the warehouse equipment was $20,000.

f. Collections on accounts receivable, $1.25 million.

g. Wages for 19X8 were paid in full in cash, $200,000.

h. Miscellaneous expenses for 19X8 were paid in full in cash, $70,000.

i. Payments on accounts payable, $900,000.

j. Cash dividends for 19X8 were paid in full in December, $100,000.

Required

1. Prepare an analysis of transactions, employing the equation approach demonstrated in Exhibit 2-2 (p. 48). Show the amounts in thousands of dollars.
2. Prepare a balance sheet, statement of income, and statement of retained income. Also prepare a combined statement of income and retained income.
3. Reconsider transaction j. Suppose the dividends were declared on December 15, payable on January 31, 19X9, to shareholders of record on January 20. Indicate

which accounts and financial statements in requirement 2 would be changed and by how much. Be complete and specific.

2-42 Balance Sheet Equation
(Alternates are 2-26 and 2-27.) Nordstrom, Inc., the fashion retailer, had the following actual data for its 1997 fiscal year (in millions):

Assets, beginning of period	$2,733
Assets, end of period	2,703
Liabilities, beginning of period	A
Liabilities, end of period	E
Paid-in capital, beginning of period	168
Paid-in capital, end of period	D
Retained earnings, beginning of period	1,255
Retained earnings, end of period	C
Sales and other revenues	4,453
Cost of sales, and all other expenses	4,305
Net earnings	B
Dividends	40
Additional investment by stockholders	15

Find the unknowns (in thousands), showing computations to support your answers. **Required**

2-43 Statement of Cash Flows
D. Ng Company imports Asian goods and sells them in eight import stores on the East Coast. On August 1, 19X4, Ng's cash balance was $166,000. Summarized transactions during August were:

1. Sales on open account, $580,000.
2. Collections of accounts receivable, $450,000.
3. Purchases of inventory on open account, $305,000.
4. Payment of accounts payable, $280,000.
5. Cost of goods sold, $325,000.
6. Salaries and wages expense, $105,000, of which $90,000 was paid in cash and $15,000 remained payable on August 31.
7. Rent expense for August, $35,000, paid in advance in July.
8. Depreciation expense, $46,000.
9. Other operating expenses, $60,000, all paid in cash.
10. Borrowed from bank on August 31, $50,000, with repayment (including interest) due on December 31.
11. Purchased fixtures and equipment for the Baltimore store on August 31, $120,000; half paid in cash and half due in October.

1. Prepare a statement of cash flows, including the cash balance on August 31. **Required**
2. Prepare an income statement.
3. Explain why net income differs from net cash provided by (or used for) operating activities.

2-44 Two Sides of a Transaction
For each of the following transactions, show the effects on the entities involved. As was illustrated in the chapter, use the A = L + OE equation to demonstrate the effects. Also name each amount affected, show the dollar amount, and indicate whether the effects are increases or decreases. The following transaction is completed as an illustration.

ILLUSTRATION

The Seattle General Hospital collects $1,000 from the Blue Cross Health Care Plan.

Entity	Cash	Receivables	Trucks		=	L + OE Payables
		A			=	**L + OE**
Hospital	+1,000	−1,000			=	
Blue Cross	−1,000				=	−1,000

1. Borrowing of $100,000 on a home mortgage from Fidelity Savings by Kenneth Berg.
2. Payment of $10,000 principal on the above mortgage. Ignore interest.
3. Purchase of a two-year subscription to *Time* magazine for $80 cash by Carla Paperman.
4. Purchase of trucks by the U.S. Postal Service for $10 million cash from the U.S. General Services Administration. The trucks were carried in the accounts at $10 million by the General Services Administration.
5. Purchase of U.S. government bonds for $100,000 cash by Lockheed Corporation.
6. Cash deposits of $10 on the returnable bottles sold by Safeway Stores to a retail customer, Philomena Simon.
7. Collections on open account of $100 by Sears store from a retail customer, Kenneth Debreu.
8. Purchase of traveler's checks of $1,000 from American Express Company by Michael Sharpe.
9. Cash deposit of $500 in a checking account in Bank of America by David Kennedy.
10. Purchase of a United Airlines "super-saver" airline ticket for $400 cash by Robert Peecher on June 15. The trip will be taken on September 10.

2-45 Net Income and Retained Income

McDonald's Corporation is a well-known fast-food restaurant company. The following data are from a recent annual report (in millions):

McDonald's Corporation

Retained earnings, beginning of year	$ 9,831.3	Dividends paid	$ 230.9
Revenues	10,686.5	General, administrative, and selling expenses	1,320.6
Interest and other non-operating expenses	381.6	Franchise expenses	570.1
Provisions for income taxes	678.4	Retained earnings, end of year	11,173.0
Food and packaging expense	2,546.6	Occupancy and other operating expenses	1,706.8
Wages and salaries	1,909.8		

Required

1. Prepare the following for the year:
   a. Income statement. The final three lines of the income statement were labeled as income before provision for income taxes, provisions for income taxes, and net income.
   b. Statement of retained earnings.
2. Comment briefly on the relative size of the cash dividend.

2-46 Earnings Statement, Retained Earnings

~~General Electric~~ is usually rated among the best-managed companies in the United States. The following amounts were in the financial statements contained in its 1996 annual report (in millions):

Total revenues	$79,179	Retained earnings at	
Cash	4,191	beginning of year	34,528
Provision for income taxes	3,526	Cost of goods sold	24,578
Accounts payable	10,205	Dividends declared	3,138
Cash provided by operations	17,851	Other expenses	43,795

Required

Choose the relevant data and prepare (1) the income statement for the year and (2) the statement of retained income for the year. The final three lines of the income statement were labeled as earnings before income taxes, provision for income taxes, and net earnings.

2-47 Financial Ratios

Following is a list of several well-known companies and selected financial data included in a letter sent by a stock brokerage firm to some of its clients:

	Per-share Data			Ratios and Percentages		
Company	Price	Earnings	Dividends	Price-Earnings	Dividend Yield	Dividend-Payout
Airborne Freight	$24	$1.28	$ —	$ —	—%	25%
B. F. Goodrich	50	—	1.12	—	—	40
Lockheed Martin	—	6.04	1.60	15.2	—	—
Northern States Power	54	—	2.75	14.2	5.1	—
Texaco	92	7.52	—	—	3.6	—
USX Corp.	24	3.00	1.00	—	—	—
Wells Fargo	—	—	5.20	—	1.4	43

The missing figures for this schedule can be computed from the data given.

1. Compute the missing figures and identify the company with
   a. The highest dividend yield
   b. The highest dividend-payout percentage
   c. The lowest market price relative to earnings

2. Assume that you know nothing about any of these companies other than the data given and the computations you have made from the data. Which company would you choose as
   a. The most attractive investment? Why?
   b. The least attractive investment? Why?

2-48 Revenue Recognition and Ethics

Kendall Square Research Corporation (KSR), located in Waltham, Massachusetts, produced high-speed computers and competed against companies such as Cray Research and Sun Microsystems.

In August 1993 the common stock of KSR reached an all-time high of $25.75 a share; by mid-December it had plummeted to $5.25. Its financial policies were called into question in an article in *Financial Shenanigan Busters,* Winter 1994, p. 3. The main charge was that the company was recording revenues before it was appropriate.

KSR sold expensive computers to universities and other research institutions. Often the customers took delivery before they knew how they might pay for the computers.

Sometimes they anticipated receiving grants that would pay for the computers, but other times they had no prospective funding. KSR also recorded revenue when computers were shipped to distributors who did not yet have customers to buy them and when computers were sold contingent on future upgrades.

Required

Comment on the ethical implications of KSR's revenue recognition practices.

2-49 The Gap Annual Report

Refer to the financial statements of the actual company, The Gap, in Appendix A at the end of the text and answer the following questions:

Required

1. What was the amount of net sales (total revenues) for the year ended February 1, 1997? The net earnings?

2. What was the total amount of cash dividends for the year ended February 1, 1997?

3. Compute the increase in retained earnings for the year ended February 1, 1997.

2-50 Financial Statement Research

Select the financial statements of any company.

Required

1. What was the amount of sales or total revenues for the most recent year? The net income?

2. What was the total amount of cash dividends for the most recent year?

3. What was the amount of cash provided by (or used for) operating activities in the most recent year? Compare the amount to the net income.

4. What was the ending balance in retained income in the most recent year? What were the two most significant items during the year that affected the retained income balance?

COLLABORATIVE LEARNING EXERCISE

2-51 Financial Ratios

Form groups of four to six persons each. Each member of the group should pick a different company and find the most recent annual report for that company. (If you do not have printed annual reports, try searching the Internet for one.)

Required

1. Each member should compute the following ratios for his or her company:
   a. Earnings per share
   b. P-E ratio
   c. Dividend-yield ratio
   d. Dividend-payout ratio

2. As a group, list two possible reasons that each ratio differs across the selected companies. Focus on comparing the companies with the highest and lowest values for each ratio, and explain how the nature of the company might be the reason for the differences in ratios.

2-52 Internet Case

Go to **http://www.disney.com/investors** to find the *Investor Relations* section of The Walt Disney Company's home page. Select *Investor Relations* from the menu, then select *Fact Book* of the most recent year to find financial information.

Answer the following questions about The Walt Disney Company:

1. From the company's *Consolidated Statements of Income,* identify the company's three segments of revenue. Which type is the largest? Go back to the *Fact Book* menu and select this segment of revenue. What revenue producing activities are included in this segment?

2. From the company's *Consolidated Statements of Income,* identify the company's fiscal year. Why do you suppose The Walt Disney Company chose this period?

3. What expenses on Disney's *Consolidated Statements of Income* are considered product costs? What revenues are these product costs linked to?

4. Is Disney's income statement prepared using the cash or accrual basis? What assets on the balance sheet are clues that help you answer this?

5. From the company's *Consolidated Statement of Cash Flow,* identify the largest source of cash inflows, and the largest source of cash outflows? What type of activities are each of these? Did total cash increase or decrease during the year?

6. Do you think that The Walt Disney Company is a nonprofit or a profit-seeking organization? What clues on the financial statements help you answer this?

RECORDING TRANSACTIONS

One Gap Storefront from a firm with over 2,000 casual apparel specialty stores, including Bannana Republic and Old Navy locations.

Learning Objectives

After studying this chapter, you should be able to

1 Use double-entry accounting.

2 Analyze and journalize transactions.

3 Post journal entries to the ledgers.

4 Prepare and use a trial balance.

5 Correct erroneous journal entries and describe how errors affect accounts.

6 Use T-accounts to analyze accounting relationships.

7 Explain how computers have transformed processing of accounting data.

Have you ever bought a shirt, a pair of jeans, or anything else from a Gap Store? If so, your purchase was just one of hundreds of transactions that The Gap had to record that day. With so many transactions happening, you might think that yours would get lost in the shuffle. Yet you can read a report on it in any major newspaper in a press release such as this one:

"**Gap, Inc. Reports Results for Second Quarter; Earnings Per Share Up 13% on Revenue Gain of 20%**—San Francisco, CA, August 14, 1997—Gap, Inc. (NYSE-GPS) today reported record sales and earnings for the fiscal second quarter which ended August 2, 1997. Second Quarter: Net sales grew 20% to $1.345 billion compared to $1.120 billion in 1996. Comparable store sales grew 4% compared with 9% growth last year. Net earnings increased 6% to $69.5 million, compared with $65.8 million last year. The net earnings gain is on top of a 103% increase in last year's second quarter. Earnings per share, reflecting the Company's ongoing share repurchase activities, grew 13% to $.26 from $.23 last year."

Are you not seeing that shirt you bought? Read between the lines. The information contained in this news article comes directly from The Gap's corporate headquarters and is designed to inform investors, stockholders, and other interested parties about the financial performance of the organization. The Gap's corporate headquarters gets this information directly from the company's accounting records. Of course, these records contain every single Gap transaction—including your shirt purchase.

Gap, Inc.'s accounting system records the financial effect of every transaction in the appropriate accounts. Transactions can take many forms—for example, merchandise sales for cash or credit or purchases of inventory to stock in its stores. When summarized at the end of the month, quarter, or year, the totals for each account can be used to prepare the financial reports that tell the financial story for that period. As you can see from The Gap, Inc.'s press release, their net sales totaled $1.345 billion for the quarter. After deducting expenses and other items, net earnings came to $69.5 million, or 5.2% of net sales ($69.5 ÷ $1,345). Now you know that only 5.2% of what you paid for your shirt was actually net earnings for The Gap.

Methods of processing accounting data have changed dramatically in the last decade or two, as computerized systems have replaced manual ones. However, the steps in recording, storing, and processing accounting data have not changed. Switching from pencil-and-paper accounting records to computerized ones is a little like switching from a car with a stick shift to an automatic. You spend less time worrying about routine tasks, but you still need to understand the way the basic system works. Whether the data are entered into the system by pencil, keyboard, or optical scanner, the same basic data are required to produce accounting reports.

To use intelligently the financial statements we learned about in the last two chapters, decision makers must understand the methods used to record and analyze the data in those reports. This chapter focuses on those methods. In particular, this chapter explains the double-entry accounting system that is universally used to record and process information about a company's transactions. As you will find, a working knowledge of this system is essential for anyone engaged in business. Ultimately the accounting practices are a language that managers in all organizations use to understand the economic progress of their organization.

THE DOUBLE-ENTRY ACCOUNTING SYSTEM

Objective 1
Use double-entry accounting.

double-entry system The method usually followed for recording transactions, whereby at least two accounts are always affected by each transaction.

In large businesses such as McDonald's and the Disney Stores, hundreds or thousands of transactions occur hourly. With so much activity, it is easy to lose track of one or two transactions. However, even one lost transaction could wreak havoc on a company's accounting (just think of what happens when you miss one transaction in your checking account record) and lead to some very serious consequences. As a result, accountants must carefully keep track of and record these transactions in a systematic manner. Usually accountants will record all of a business entity's transactions using a **double-entry system,** in which at least two accounts are always affected by each transaction. Each transaction must be analyzed to determine which accounts are involved, whether the accounts are increased or decreased, and how much each account balance will change.

Recall the first three transactions of the Biwheels Company introduced in Chapter 1:

	A		=	L	+	SE
	Cash	Merchandise Inventory		Note Payable		Paid-in Capital
(1) Initial investment by owner	+400,000		=			+400,000
(2) Loan from bank	+100,000		=	+100,000		
(3) Acquire inventory for cash	−150,000	+150,000	=			

This balance sheet equation format illustrates the basic concepts of the double-entry system by showing two entries for each transaction. It also emphasizes that the equation Assets = Liabilities + Stockholders' Equity must always remain in balance. Unfortunately, this format is too unwieldy for recording each and every transaction that occurs. In practice, accountants use ledgers to record the individual transactions in the proper accounts.

LEDGER ACCOUNTS

A **ledger** contains the records for a group of related accounts. The ledger may be in the form of a bound record book, a loose-leaf set of pages, or some kind of electronic storage element such as magnetic tape or disk, but it is always kept current in a systematic manner. For simplicity's sake, you can think of a ledger as a book with one page for each account. When you hear about "keeping the books" or "auditing the books," the word books refers to the ledger. A firm's **general ledger** is the collection of accounts that accumulate the amounts reported in the firm's major financial statements.

The ledger accounts used here are simplified versions of those used in practice. They are called **T-accounts** because they take the form of the capital letter T. They capture the essence of the accounting process we need to understand as accountants and managers without burdening us with too many details that bookkeepers use. The vertical line in the T divides the account into left and right sides for recording increases and decreases in the account. The account title is on the horizontal line. For example, consider the format of the Cash account:

Cash	
Left side	Right side
Increases in cash	Decreases in cash

ledger The records for a group of related accounts kept current in a systematic manner.

general ledger The collection of accounts that accumulates the amounts reported in the major financial statements.

T-account Simplified version of ledger accounts that takes the form of the capital letter T.

The T-accounts for the first three Biwheels Company transactions are as follows:

Assets				=	Liabilities + Stockholders' Equity			
Cash					**Note Payable**			
Increases		Decreases			Decreases		Increases	
(1)	400,000	(3)	150,000				(2)	100,000
(2)	100,000							
Merchandise Inventory					**Paid-in Capital**			
Increases		Decreases			Decreases		Increases	
(3)	150,000						(1)	400,000

Note that two accounts are affected by each numbered transaction, as is the rule under the double-entry system.

In practice, accounts are created as needed. The process of creating a new T-account in preparation for recording a transaction is called *opening the account.* For transaction 1, we opened Cash and Paid-in Capital. For transaction 2, we opened Note Payable, and for transaction 3, we opened Merchandise Inventory.

Each T-account summarizes the changes in a particular asset, liability, or owners' equity. Because T-accounts show only amounts and not transaction descriptions, each transaction is keyed in some way, such as by the numbering used in this illustration or by the date or by both. This keying helps the rechecking (auditing) process by aiding the tracing of entries in the ledger account to the original transactions, which are written down in chronological order as they occur.

A **balance** is the difference between the total left-side and right-side amounts in an account at any particular time. Asset accounts have left-side balances. They are increased by entries on the left side and decreased by entries on the right side. Liabilities and owners' equity accounts have right-side balances. They are increased by entries on the right side and decreased by entries on the left side.

balance The difference between the total left-side and right-side amounts in an account at any particular time.

Take a look at the analysis of the entries for each Biwheels transaction. Notice that each transaction generates a left-side entry in one T-account and a right-side entry of the same amount in another T-account. Helpful hint: When analyzing a transaction, initially pinpoint the effects (if any) on cash. Did cash increase or decrease? Then think of the effects on other accounts. In this way, you get off to the right start. Usually, it is much easier to identify the effects of a transaction on cash than it is to identify the effects on other accounts.

1. Transaction: Initial Investment by owners, $400,000 cash.
     Analysis: The asset **Cash** is increased.
                The stockholders' equity **Paid-in-Capital** is increased.

	Cash			Paid-in Capital	
(1)	(400,000)		(1)		(400,000)

2. Transaction: Loan from bank, $100,000.
     Analysis: The asset **Cash** is increased.
                The liability **Note Payable** is increased.

	Cash			Note Payable	
(1)	400,000		(2)		(100,000)
(2)	(100,000)				

3. Transaction: Acquired inventory for cash, $150,000.
     Analysis: The asset **Cash** is decreased.
                The asset **Merchandise Inventory** is increased.

	Cash		
(1)	400,000	(3)	(150,000)
(2)	100,000		

	Merchandise Inventory	
(3)	(150,000)	

Accounts such as these exist to keep an up-to-date record of the changes in specific assets and equities. Financial statements can be prepared at any instant if the account balances are up to date. The information accumulated in the accounts provides the necessary summary balances for the financial statements. For example, Biwheels' balance sheet after its first three transactions would contain the following account balances:

Assets		**Liabilities + Owners' Equity**	
Cash	$350,000	Liabilities:	
Merchandise		Note payable	$100,000
inventory	150,000	Stockholders' equity:	
		Paid-in capital	400,000
Total	$500,000	Total	$500,000

DEBITS AND CREDITS

debit An entry or balance on the left side of an account.

credit An entry or balance on the right side of an account.

charge A word often used instead of debit.

You have just seen that the double-entry system features entries on left sides and right sides of various accounts. Accountants use the term **debit** (abbreviated dr.) to denote an entry on the left side of any account and the term **credit** (abbreviated cr.) to denote an entry on the right side of any account. Many people make the mistake of thinking that credit means increase and debit means decrease. Trust us—when used in accounting they do not. Left and right would be much easier and more descriptive to use, but debit and credit are the standard terms for the double-entry system. The word **charge** is often used instead of debit, but no single word is used as a synonym for credit. Just remember that debit means left and credit means right and you will be fine.

Debit and credit are used as verbs, adjectives, and nouns. "Debit $1,000 to cash, and credit $1,000 to accounts receivable" are examples of uses as verbs, meaning that $1,000 should be placed on the left side of the Cash account and on the right side of the Accounts Receivable account. Similarly, in phrases such as "a debit is made to cash" or "cash has a debit balance of $12,000," the word debit is a noun or an adjective that describes the status of a particular account. From this point on you will be seeing an awful lot of *debit* and *credit*. Be sure you understand their uses completely before moving on.

THE RECORDING PROCESS

In the earlier section we entered Biwheels' transactions 1, 2, and 3 directly in the ledger. In actual practice the recording process does not start with the ledger. The sequence of steps in recording transactions is as follows:

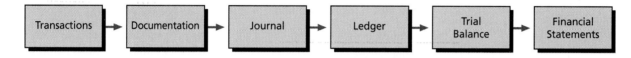

Transactions → Documentation → Journal → Ledger → Trial Balance → Financial Statements

The recording process begins with **source documents.** These are the original records of any transaction. Examples of source documents include sales slips or invoices, check stubs, purchase orders, receiving reports, cash receipt slips, and minutes of the board of directors. As soon as a transaction occurs, it generates a source document. For example, when a company sells a product to a customer, a receipt is made for the sale. Source documents are kept on file so they can be used to verify the details of a transaction and the accuracy of subsequent records if necessary.

In the second step of the recording process, an analysis of the transaction, based on the source documents, is placed in a **book of original entry,** which is a formal chronological listing of each transaction and how it affects the balances in particular accounts. The most common example of a book of original entry is the **general journal.** The general journal is basically a diary of all of the events (transactions) in an entity's life. Each transaction is listed in its entirety in one place in the journal.

When transactions are entered into the ledger, which is the third step of the recording process, they are not entered in a single place. Instead, as we have seen, they are divided up into components that affect the various accounts and entered under the appropriate accounts. Information in the ledger is updated periodically by recording each piece of each transaction from the journal in the ledger account where it belongs. This process might occur weekly, or even less frequently in very small organizations. The timing of the steps will differ. Transactions occur constantly and source documents are prepared continuously. Depending on the size and nature of the organization, the accounting operation may be very large and transaction analysis may also occur continuously or the operation may be small and the analysis of transactions and recording in the journal may be less frequent. Basically, the timing of the steps in the recording process must conform to the needs of the users of the data.

The fourth step of the recording process is the preparation of the **trial balance,** which is a simple listing of the accounts in the general ledger together with their balances. This listing aids in verifying clerical accuracy and in preparing financial statements. Thus it occurs as needed, perhaps each month or each quarter as the firm prepares its financial statements. The final step, the preparation of financial statements, occurs at least once a quarter, every three months, for publicly traded companies in the United States. Although they are required to produce financial statements only once a quarter for external reporting, some companies prepare financial statements more frequently for management's

source documents The supporting original records of any transaction.

receipts are source documents

book of original entry A formal chronological record of how the entity's transactions affect the balances in pertinent accounts.

general journal The most common example of a book of original entry; a complete chronological record of transactions.

trial balance A list of all accounts in the general ledger with their balances.

benefit. For example, Springfield ReManufacturing Corp. in the Ozark Mountains of southern Missouri prepares monthly financial statements. Springfield is a leader in "open-book management," which refers to the open availability of the company's accounting results. Management and all employees meet monthly to examine the results in detail. Extensive training is provided to employees on how the accounting process works and what the numbers mean. This new management process increased efficiency and profitability at Springfield.

JOURNALIZING TRANSACTIONS

journalizing The process of entering transactions into the journal.

journal entry An analysis of the effects of a transaction on the accounts, usually accompanied by an explanation.

Objective 2
Analyze and journalize transactions.

The process of entering transactions into the journal is called **journalizing**. A **journal entry** is an analysis of all the effects of a single transaction on the various accounts, usually accompanied by an explanation. For each transaction, this analysis identifies the accounts to be debited and credited. The top of Exhibit 3-1 shows how the opening three transactions for Biwheels are journalized.

The conventional form for recording in the general journal includes the following:

1. The date and identification number of the entry make up the first two columns.
2. The accounts affected are shown in the next column, Accounts and Explanation. The title of the account or accounts to be debited is placed flush left. The title of the account or accounts to be credited is indented in a consistent way. The journal entry is followed by the narrative explanation of the transaction, which can be brief or extensive. The length of the explanation depends on the complexity of the transaction and whether management wants the journal itself to contain all relevant information. Most often, explanations are brief because details are available in the file of supporting documents.
3. The Post Ref. (posting reference) column contains the number that is assigned to each account and is used for cross-referencing to the ledger accounts.
4. The debit and credit columns are for recording the amounts that are to be debited (left) or credited (right) for each account. No dollar signs are used.

CHART OF ACCOUNTS

chart of accounts A numbered or coded list of all account titles.

To make recording and understanding recordings easier, organizations have a **chart of accounts,** which is normally a numbered or coded list of all account titles. These numbers are used as references in the Post Ref. column of the journal, as Exhibit 3-1 demonstrates. The following is the chart of accounts for Biwheels:

Account Number	Account Title	Account Number	Account Title
100	Cash	202	Note payable
120	Accounts receivable	203	Accounts payable
		300	Paid-in capital
130	Merchandise inventory	400	Retained income
		500	Sales revenues
140	Prepaid rent	600	Cost of goods sold
170	Store equipment	601	Rent expense
170A	Accumulated depreciation, store equipment (explained later)	602	Depreciation expense

Although an outsider will not know what each code means without referring to the chart of accounts, accounting employees become so familiar with the various codes that

General Journal

Date	Entry No.	Accounts and Explanation	Post Ref.	Debit	Credit
19X1					
12/31	1	Cash	100	400,000	
		Paid-in capital	300		400,000
		Capital stock issued to Smith			
12/31	2	Cash	100	100,000	
		Note payable	202		100,000
		Borrowed at 9% interest on a			
		one year note.			
19X2					
1/2	3	Merchandise inventory	130	150,000	
		Cash	100		150,000
		Acquired inventory for cash.			

General Ledger

CASH — Account No. 100

Date	Explanation	Journ. Ref.	Debit	Date	Explanation	Journ. Ref.	Credit
19X1				19X2			
12/31	(often blank because the explanation is already in the journal)	1	400,000	1/2		3	150,000
12/31		2	100,000				

MERCHANDISE INVENTORY — Account No. 130

Date	Explanation	Journ. Ref.	Debit	Date	Explanation	Journ. Ref.	Credit
19X2							
1/2		3	150,000				

NOTE PAYABLE — Account No. 202

Date	Explanation	Journ. Ref.	Debit	Date	Explanation	Journ. Ref.	Credit
				19X1			
				12/31		2	100,000

PAID-IN CAPITAL — Account No. 300

Date	Explanation	Journ. Ref.	Debit	Date	Explanation	Journ. Ref.	Credit
				19X1			
				12/31		1	400,000

Exhibit 3-1

Journal Entries—Recorded in General Journal and Posted to General Ledger Accounts

they think, talk, and write in terms of account numbers instead of account names. Thus an outside auditor may find Biwheels' entry 3, the acquisition of Merchandise Inventory (Account 130) for Cash (Account 100), journalized as follows:

19X2			dr.	cr.
Jan. 2	130	....	150,000	
	100	....		150,000

This journal entry was made using the employee's shorthand, which uses codes and does not bother with account names. Its brevity and lack of explanation would hamper any outsider's understanding of the transaction, but the entry's meaning would be clear to anyone within the organization.

POSTING TRANSACTIONS TO THE LEDGER

posting The transferring of amounts from the journal to the appropriate accounts in the ledger.

Posting is the transferring of amounts from the journal to the appropriate accounts in the ledger. To demonstrate, consider transaction 3 for Biwheels. Exhibit 3-1 shows with bold arrows how the credit to cash is posted using the information and values from the journal entry. Note that the sample of the general ledger in Exhibit 3-1 uses fairly complete structures for the account rather than the simplified T-accounts format. Dates, explanations and journal references are provided in detail on paper formatted with special columns. The structure is repeated for debits on the left side of the page and for credits on the right side.

Objective 3
Post journal entries to the ledgers.

Because posting is strictly a mechanical process of moving numbers from the journal to the ledger, many accountants feel it is most efficiently done by a computer. In such cases, the accountant would journalize a transaction in an electronic general journal, and the computer would automatically transfer the information to an electronic version of the ledger. Note how cross-referencing occurs between the journal and the ledger. The date is recorded in the journal and the ledger, and the journal entry number for each transaction is placed in the reference column of the ledger. The process of using numbering, dating, and/or some other form of identification to relate each posting to the appropriate journal entry is known as the **keying of entries,** or **cross-referencing.** Transactions from the journal are often posted to several different accounts, but keying allows users to find all the components of the transactions in the ledger no matter where they start. It also helps auditors to find and correct errors and reduces the frequency of initial errors.

keying of entries (cross-referencing) The process of numbering or otherwise specifically identifying each journal entry and each posting.

RUNNING BALANCE COLUMN

Ledger entries do not always take the form of a T-account. Exhibit 3-2 shows another popular ledger account format, one that adds an additional column to the presentation to

	CASH				Account No. 100	
Date	Explanation	Journ. Ref.	Debit	Credit	Balance	
19X1						
12/31	(often blank because the explanation is already	1	400,000		400,000	
12/31	in the journal)	2	100,000		500,000	
19X2						
1/2		3		150,000	350,000	

Exhibit 3-2
Ledger Account with Running Balance Column

provide a *running balance* of the account holdings. This format should look familiar to you because it is very similar to the format found in a checkbook. The running balance feature is a nice addition because it provides a status report for an account at a glance. Although it can certainly be tallied manually, the running balance is most easily tracked by computers.

Note that regardless of the account format used—T-account (Exhibit 3-1) or running balance (Exhibit 3-2)—the same journal information is reflected in the posting.

ANALYZING, JOURNALIZING, AND POSTING THE BIWHEELS TRANSACTIONS

We have seen that the accountant reviews source documents about a transaction, mentally analyzes the transaction, records that analysis in a journal entry, and then posts the result to the general ledger where all transactions affecting an account are grouped together. We can now apply this process to additional transactions from the Biwheels company.

4. Transaction: Acquired inventory on credit, $10,000.
    Analysis: The asset **Merchandise Inventory** is increased.
            The liability **Accounts Payable** is increased.
      Entry: In the journal (explanation omitted):

Merchandise inventory	10,000	
Accounts payable		10,000

Post to the ledger (postings are indicated by circled amounts):

Merchandise Inventory*		Accounts Payable	
(3) 150,000		(4) (10,000)	
(4) (10,000)			

*If it is the only type of inventory account, it is often simply called Inventory.

Transaction 4, like transactions 1, 2, and 3, is a **simple entry** in that only the two accounts shown are affected by the transaction. Note that the balance sheet equation always remains in balance.

simple entry An entry for a transaction that affects only two accounts.

5. Transaction: Acquired store equipment for $4,000 cash plus $11,000 trade credit.
    Analysis: The asset **Cash** is decreased.
            The asset **Store Equipment** is increased.
            The liability **Accounts Payable** is increased.
      Entry: In the journal:

Store equipment	15,000	
Cash		4,000
Accounts payable		11,000

Post to the ledger:

Cash			Accounts Payable	
(1) 400,000	(3) 150,000		(4) 10,000	
(2) 100,000	(5) (4,000)		(5) (11,000)	

Store Equipment	
(5) (15,000)	

Transaction 5 is a **compound entry,** which means that more than two accounts are affected by a single transaction. Whether transactions are simple (like transactions 1 through 4) or compound, the total of all left-side entries always equals the totals of all right-side entries. The net effect is always to keep the accounting equation in balance:

compound entry An entry for a transaction that affects more than two accounts.

$$\text{Assets} = \text{Liabilities} + \text{Stockholders' equity}$$
$$15,000 - 4,000 = + 11,000$$

6. Transaction: Sold unneeded showcase to neighbor for $1,000 on open account.

Analysis: The asset **Accounts Receivable** is increased.

The asset **Store Equipment** is decreased.

Entry: In the journal:

Accounts receivable	1,000	
Store equipment		1,000

Post to the ledger:

Accounts Receivable

(6)	1,000	

Store Equipment

(5)	15,000	(6)		1,000

In transaction 6, one asset goes up, and another asset goes down. Only one side of the accounting equation is involved because no liability or owners' equity account is affected.

7. Transaction: Returned inventory to supplier for full credit, $800.

Analysis: The asset **Merchandise Inventory** is decreased.

The liability **Accounts Payable** is decreased.

Entry: In the journal:

Accounts payable	800	
Merchandise inventory		800

Post to the ledger:

Merchandise Inventory					Accounts Payable			
(3)	150,000	(7)	800	(7)	800	(4)	10,000
(4)	10,000					(5)	11,000

8. Transaction: Paid cash to creditors, $4,000.

Analysis: The asset **Cash** is decreased.

The liability **Accounts Payable** is decreased.

Entry: In the journal:

Accounts payable	4,000	
Cash		4,000

Post to the ledger:

Cash					Accounts Payable			
(1)	400,000	(3)	150,000	(7)	800	(4)	10,000
(2)	100,000	(5)	4,000	(8)	4,000	(5)	11,000
		(8)	4,000				

9. Transaction: Collected cash from debtors, $700.

Analysis: The asset **Cash** is increased.

The asset **Accounts Receivable** is decreased.

Entry: In the journal:

Cash	700	
Accounts receivable		700

Post to the ledger:

Cash

(1)	400,000	(3)	150,000
(2)	100,000	(5)	4,000
(9)	700	(8)	4,000

Accounts Receivable

(6)	1,000	(9)	700

Transactions 7, 8, and 9 are all simple entries. In transactions 7 and 8, an asset and a liability both go down. In transaction 9, one asset goes up while another asset goes down.

REVENUE AND EXPENSE TRANSACTIONS

Revenue and expense transactions deserve special attention because their relation to the balance sheet equation is less obvious. To help focus on this relationship, you should review how the owners' equity section of the balance sheet equation can be broken down

$$\text{Assets} = \text{Liabilities} + \text{Stockholders' equity} \tag{1}$$

$$\text{Assets} = \text{Liabilities} + (\text{Paid-in capital} + \text{Retained income}) \tag{2}$$

Recall from Chapter 2 that if we ignore dividends, retained income is merely accumulated revenue less expenses. Therefore the T-accounts can be grouped as follows:

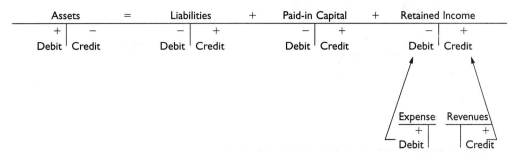

You may wonder why we do not simply increase the Retained Income account directly. To do so would make it harder to prepare an income statement because revenue and expense items would be mixed together in the Retained Income account. By accumulating information separately for categories of revenue and expense, a more meaningful income statement can be easily prepared.

Expense and Revenue accounts are part of Retained Income. You can think of them as separate compartments within the larger Retained Income account. Expense and Revenue accounts are types of accounts, just as an asset account is a type. Cash is a specific asset account and we will discuss a variety of specific revenue and expense accounts. A Revenue account collects items that increase retained income. Thus, any credit to Revenue is essentially a credit to Retained Income (both revenue and retained income are increased by such a credit entry). Sales revenue is an example of a revenue account. The Expense account collects items that decrease retained income. Thus, a debit to Expense is essentially a debit to Retained Income. Although a debit entry increases expenses, it results in a decrease in retained income. Wage expense is an example of an expense account. Revenue and expense accounts are really "little" stockholders' equity accounts. That is, they are fundamentally a part of stockholders' equity.

We can now examine a few transactions involving revenues and expenses. Consider Biwheels' transactions 10a and 10b in detail:

10a. Transaction: Sales on credit, $160,000.
      Analysis: The asset **Accounts Receivable** is increased.
                    The stockholders' equity **Sales Revenues** is increased.
          Entry: In the journal:
                    Accounts receivable   160,000
                        Sales revenues   160,000
                    Post to the ledger:

Accounts Receivable			Sales Revenues	
(6)	1,000	(9)	700	(10a)	160,000
(10a)	160,000				

The Sales Revenues account is increased by a credit, or right-side, entry in this transaction, essentially increasing the stockholders' equity account, Retained Income.

10b. Transaction: Cost of merchandise inventory sold, $100,000.
      Analysis: The asset **Merchandise Inventory** is decreased.
                    The stockholders' equity is decreased by creating an expense account,
                    Cost of Goods Sold, which is essentially a negative stockholders' equity account.
          Entry: In the journal:
                    Cost of goods sold   100,000
                        Merchandise inventory   100,000
                    Post to the ledger:

Merchandise Inventory				Cost of Goods Sold	
(3)	150,000	(7)	800	(10b)	100,000
(4)	10,000	(10b)	100,000		

In this transaction, the expense account, Cost of Goods Sold, is increased by a debit, or left-side, entry. The effect is to decrease the stockholders' equity account, Retained Income.

Before proceeding, reflect on the logic illustrated by transactions 10a and 10b. These transactions illustrate the general relationship of revenue and expense to retained income using actual journal entries and showing the effects on the ledger accounts. Revenues increase stockholders' equity because the revenue accounts and the stockholders' equity accounts are right-side balance accounts. Expenses decrease stockholders' equity because expenses are left-side balance accounts. They are offsets to the normal right-side balances of stockholders' equity. Therefore increases in expenses are decreases in stockholders' equity. The following analysis shows that the $100,000 Cost of Goods Sold expense could be recorded directly in the Stockholders' Equity Account, in the Retained Income account, or in an expense account. This third alternative captures the most information.

If only a lone stockholder's equity account is used:	Stockholders' Equity	
	Decreases (100,000)	Increases

If two stockholders' equity accounts are used without a revenue or expense account:	Paid-in Capital		Retained Income	
	Decreases	Increases	Decreases (100,000)	Increases

If revenue and expense accounts are created that will eventually be summarized into a single net effect on retained income:	Expenses		Revenues	
	Increases (100,000)			Increases

Exhibit 3-3 presents the rules of debit and credit and the normal balances of the accounts discussed in this section. It demonstrates the basic principles of the balance sheet equation and the double-entry accounting system:

$$\text{Left side} = \text{Right side}$$
$$\text{Debit} = \text{Credit}$$

Exhibit 3-3

Rules of Debit and Credit and Normal Balances of Accounts

RULES OF DEBIT AND CREDIT

ASSETS	=	LIABILITIES	+	OWNERS' EQUITY

Assets	=	Liabilities	+	Paid-in Capital	+	Retained Income

+	−	−	+	−	+	−	+
Increase	Decrease	Decrease	Increase	Decrease	Increase	Decrease	Increase
Debit	Credit	Debit	Credit	Debit	Credit	Debit	Credit
Left	Right	Left	Right	Left	Right	Left	Right
Normal Bal.			Normal Bal.		Normal Bal.		Normal Bal.

	Revenues	
	−	+
	Decrease	Increase
	Debit	Credit
	Left	Right
		Normal Bal.

	Expenses	
	+*	−
	Increase	Decrease
	Debit	Credit
	Left	Right
	Normal Bal.	
	*Remember that *increases* in expenses *decrease* retained income.	

Normal Balances

Assets	Debit	
Liabilities		Credit
Owners' Equity (overall)		Credit
Paid-in Capital		Credit
Revenues		Credit
Expenses	Debit	

The exhibit also emphasizes that revenues increase stockholders' equity; hence they are recorded as credits while expenses decrease stockholders' equity and are recorded as debits. Keeping revenues and expenses, which are changes in retained income resulting from operations, in separate accounts makes it easier to prepare an income statement. Revenues and expenses are summarized and used to calculate net income (or net loss) on the income statement providing a detailed explanation of how operations caused the retained income shown on the balance sheet to change during the period.

PREPAID EXPENSES AND DEPRECIATION TRANSACTIONS

Recall from Chapter 2 that prepaid expenses, such as prepaid rent and depreciation expenses, relate to assets having a useful life that will expire some time in the future. Biwheels' transactions 11, 12, and 13 demonstrate the analysis for journalizing and posting of prepaid rent expenses and depreciation of store equipment.

11.	**Transaction:**	Paid rent for three months in advance, $6,000.
	Analysis:	The asset **Cash** is decreased.
		The asset **Prepaid Rent** is increased.
	Entry:	In the journal:

Prepaid rent	6,000	
Cash		6,000
Post to the ledger:		

Cash			
(1)	400,000	(3)	150,000
(2)	100,000	(5)	4,000
(9)	700	(8)	4,000
		(11)	(6,000)

Prepaid Rent	
(11)	(6,000)

Transaction 11 represents the prepayment of rent as the acquisition of an asset. It affects only asset accounts—Cash is decreased (credited) and Prepaid Rent is increased (debited). Transaction 12 represents the subsequent expiration of one-third of the asset as an expense.

12.	**Transaction:**	Recognized expiration of rental services, $2,000.
	Analysis:	The asset **Prepaid Rent** is decreased.
		The negative stockholders' equity **Rent Expense** is increased.
	Entry:	In the journal:

Rent expense	2,000	
Prepaid rent		2,000
Post to the ledger:		

Prepaid Rent				Rent Expense	
(11)	6,000	(12)	(2,000)	(12)	(2,000)

Remember that in this transaction, the effect of the $2,000 increase in Rent Expense is a decrease in stockholders' equity on the balance sheet.

13.	**Transaction:**	Recognized depreciation, $100.
	Analysis:	The asset-reduction account **Accumulated Depreciation, Store Equipment** is increased.
		The negative stockholders' equity **Depreciation Expense** is increased.
	Entry:	In the journal:

Depreciation expense	100	
Accumulated depreciation, store equipment		100
Post to the ledger:		

Accumulated Depreciation, Store Equipment			Depreciation Expense	
	(13)	(100)	(13)	(100)

contra account A separate but related account that offsets or is a deduction from a companion account. An example is accumulated depreciation.

contra asset A contra account that offsets an asset.

book value (net book value, carrying amount, carrying value) The balance of an account shown on the books, net of any contra accounts. For example, the book value of equipment is its acquisition cost minus accumulated depreciation.

accumulated depreciation (allowance for depreciation) The cumulative sum of all depreciation recognized since the date of acquisition of the particular assets described.

In transaction 13, a new account, ~~Accumulated Depreciation~~, is opened. While it is described as an *asset-reduction* account in our analysis and corresponding journal entry, a more popular term is *contra account.* A **contra account** is a separate but related account that offsets or is a deduction from a companion account. A contra account has two distinguishing features: (1) it always has a companion account, and (2) it has a balance on the opposite side than the companion account. In our illustration, accumulated depreciation is a **contra asset** account because it is a contra account offsetting an asset. While the normal balance of the asset account is a debit, the normal balance of accumulated depreciation is a credit. The asset and contra asset accounts on January 31, 19X2, are:

Asset:	Store equipment	$14,000
Contra asset:	Accumulated depreciation, equipment	100
Net asset:	Book value	$13,900

The **book value** or **net book value** or **carrying amount** or **carrying value** is defined as the balance of an account shown on the books, net of any contra accounts. In our example, the book value of Store Equipment is $13,900, the original acquisition cost less the contra account for accumulated depreciation.

A NOTE ON ACCUMULATED DEPRECIATION

The balance sheet distinguishes between the store equipment's original cost and its accumulated depreciation. As the name implies, **accumulated depreciation** (sometimes called **allowance for depreciation**) is the cumulative sum of all depreciation recognized since the date of acquisition of the particular assets described. Published balance sheets routinely report both the original cost and accumulated depreciation.

Why is there an Accumulated Depreciation account? Why not reduce Store Equipment directly by $100? Conceptually, a direct reduction is indeed justified. However, accountants have traditionally preserved the original cost in the original asset account throughout the asset's useful life. Accountants can then readily refer to that account to learn the asset's initial cost. Such information may be sought for reports to management, government regulators, and tax authorities. Moreover the original $14,000 cost is the height of accuracy—it is a reliable, objective number. In contrast, the Accumulated Depreciation is an estimate, the result of a calculation whose accuracy depends heavily on the accountant's less reliable prediction of an asset's useful life. Recall that the $100 of depreciation was calculated by dividing the $14,000 cost by an assumed useful life of 140 months. We have no assurance regarding how long an asset will be useful. Some cars run for several hundred thousand miles over 20 years, while others become impossible to keep running after 10 years of use. In calculating depreciation, we must make estimates that are imperfect, but there is no other way to allocate the cost of the equipment over the periods that it benefits.

In practice investors can estimate the average age of the assets by computing the percentage of the original cost that has been depreciated. For example, Microsoft has accumulated depreciation of $314 million on an original cost of plant and equipment of $1,037 million, making it 30% depreciated. Most of Microsoft's assets must be quite young, which is what would be expected for a fast-growing company. In contrast, the German diversified industrial company VIAG Aktiengesellschaft has accumulated depreciation of DM 17.1 billion on an original cost of DM 24.5 billion (DM stands for the German currency deutsche marks). Therefore, its assets are 17.1 ÷ 24.5 = 70% depreciated.

Exhibit 3-4 shows the formal journal entries for Biwheels' transactions 4 through 13 as analyzed in the previous section. The posting reference (Post Ref.) column uses the account numbers from the Biwheels chart of accounts on page 86. These account numbers also appear on each account in the Biwheels general ledger.

Exhibit 3-5 shows the Biwheels general ledger in T-account form. Pause and trace each of the following journal entries to its posting in the ledger:

1. Initial investment
2. Loan from bank
3. Acquire merchandise inventory for cash
4. Acquire merchandise inventory for credit.

Exhibit 3-4
General Journal of Biwheels Company

Date	Entry No.	Accounts and Explanation	Post Ref.	Debit	Credit
19X2	4	Merchandise inventory	130	10,000	
		Accounts payable	203		10,000
		Acquired inventory on credit.			
	5	Store Equipment	170	15,000	
		Cash	100		4,000
		Accounts payable	203		11,000
		Acquired store equipment for cash plus credit.			
		(This is an example of a *compound journal entry*,			
		whereby more than two accounts are affected by			
		the same transaction.)			
	6	Accounts receivable	120	1,000	
		Store equipment	170		1,000
		Sold store equipment to business neighbor.			
	7	Accounts payable	203	800	
		Merchandise inventory	130		800
		Returned some inventory to supplier.			
	8	Accounts payable	203	4,000	
		Cash	100		4,000
		Payments to creditors.			
	9	Cash	100	700	
		Accounts receivable	120		700
		Collections from debtors.			
	10a	Accounts receivable	120	160,000	
		Sales	500		160,000
		Sales to customers on credit.			
	10b	Cost of goods sold	600	100,000	
		Merchandise inventory	130		100,000
		To record the cost of inventory sold.			
	11	Prepaid rent	140	6,000	
		Cash	100		6,000
		Payment of rent in advance.			
	12	Rent expense	601	2,000	
		Prepaid rent	140		2,000
		Recognize expiration of rental service.			
	13	Depreciation expense	602	100	
		Accumulated depreciation, store equipment	170A		100
		Recognize depreciation for January.			

Exhibit 3-5

General Ledger of Biwheels Company

Assets	Liabilities and Stockholders' Equity
(Increases on left, decreases on right)	*(Decreases on left, increases on right)*

Cash   Account No. 100

(1)	400,000	(3)	150,000
(2)	100,000	(5)	4,000
(9)	700	(8)	4,000
		(11)	6,000
1/31 Bal. 336,700			

Note Payable   202

		(2)	100,000

Paid-in Capital   300

		(1)	400,000

Accounts Receivable   120

(6)	1,000	(9)	700
(10a)	160,000		
1/31 Bal.	160,300		

Accounts Payable   203

(7)	800	(4)	10,000
(8)	4,000	(5)	11,000
		1/31 Bal.	16,200

Retained Income   400

	1/31 Bal. 57,900*

Expense and Revenue Accounts

Merchandise Inventory   130

(3)	150,000	(7)	800
(4)	10,000	(10b)	100,000
1/31 Bal.	59,200		

Cost of Goods Sold   600

(10b)	100,000	

Sales Revenues   500

		(10a)	160,000

*The details of the revenue and expense accounts appear in the income statement. Their net effect is then transferred to a single account, Retained Income, in the balance sheet. In this case, $160,000 − $100,000 − $2,000 − $100 = $57,900.

Prepaid Rent   140

(11)	6,000	(12)	2,000
1/31 Bal.	4,000		

Rent Expense   601

(12)	2,000	

Store Equipment   170

(5)	15,000	(6)	1,000
1/31 Bal.	14,000		

Depreciation Expense   602

(13)	100	

Accumulated Depreciation, Store Equipment   170A

	(13)	100

Note: An ending balance is shown on the side of the account with the larger total.

5. Acquire store equipment for cash plus credit
6. Sale of equipment on credit
7. Return of merchandise inventory for credit
8. Payments to creditors
9. Collections from debtors

10a. Sales on credit
10b. Cost of merchandise inventory sold
11. Pay rent in advance
12. Recognize expiration of rental services
13. Recognize depreciation

It is customary not to use dollar signs in either the journal or the ledger. You should also note that negative numbers are never used in the journal or the ledger to show the effect of a given transaction on an account. Instead the effect on the account is conveyed by the side on which the number appears. Debits and credits tell the whole story in the recording process, so be sure you understand them fully.

In the ledgers that do not keep a running balance column, the account balance may be updated from time to time as desired. There are many acceptable techniques for updating, and accountants' preferences vary. The double horizontal lines in Exhibit 3-5 signify that these accounts have been updated. (Many accountants prefer to use single horizontal lines instead of the double lines used in this book.) All postings above the double lines are summarized as a single balance immediately below the double lines. Accountants would use this single balance as a starting point for computing the next updated balance.

The accounts in Exhibit 3-5 that contain only one lone number do not have a double line. Why? If there is only one number in a given account, this number automatically serves also as the ending balance. For example, the Note Payable entry of $100,000 also serves as the ending balance for the account.

PREPARING THE TRIAL BALANCE

Once journal entries have been posted to the ledger, the next step in the process of recording transactions is the preparation of a trial balance. A trial balance is a list of all of the accounts with their balances. It is prepared as a test or check—a trial as the name says—before proceeding further. Thus the purpose of the trial balance is twofold: (1) to help check on accuracy of posting by proving whether the total debits equal the total credits, and (2) to establish a convenient summary of balances in all accounts for the preparation of formal financial statements. Basically, you can think of the trial balance as a kind of worksheet for checking the figures when preparing financial statements, much like a worksheet you might use when preparing a math exam. Just as your professor gets only your exam and not your worksheet, the public sees only the published financial statements, not the trial balance.

Objective 4
Prepare and use a trial balance.

A trial balance may be taken at any time the accounts are up to date. For example, we might take a trial balance for Biwheels on January 2, 19X2, after the company's first three transactions:

Biwheels Company
Trial Balance January 2, 19X2

Account Number	Account Title	Balance	
		Debit	Credit
100	Cash	$350,000	
130	Merchandise inventory	150,000	
202	Note payable		$100,000
300	Paid-in capital		$400,000
	Total	$500,000	$500,000

Obviously, the more accounts there are, the more detailed (and the more essential for checking multiple figures) the trial balance becomes.

Exhibit 3-6 shows the trial balance of the general ledger in Exhibit 3-5. As shown, the trial balance is normally prepared with the balance sheet accounts listed first, in the order of assets, liabilities, and stockholders' equity. These are followed by the income statement accounts, Revenues and Expenses. Note that the last stockholders' equity account listed, Retained Income, has no balance here because it was zero at the start of the period in our example. The revenues and expenses for the current period that are on the list constitute the change in retained income for the current period. When the accountant prepares a formal balance sheet, the revenue and expense accounts will be deleted and their net effect will be added to the Retained Income account.

DERIVING FINANCIAL STATEMENTS FROM THE TRIAL BALANCE

As you can see, the trial balance assures the accountant that the debits and credits are equal. It is also the springboard for the preparation of the balance sheet and the income statement, as shown in Exhibit 3-7. The income statement accounts are summarized later as a single number, net income, which then becomes part of Retained Income in the formal balance sheet. Note that the retained income in the balance sheet in Exhibit 3-7 is $57,900 although the retained income in the trial balance is $0. This is because the balance sheet shows the ending balance in retained income, the beginning balance of zero plus net

Exhibit 3-6

Biwheels Company

Trial Balance January 31, 19X2

	Debits	Credits
Cash	$336,700	
Accounts receivable	160,300	
Merchandise inventory	59,200	
Prepaid rent	4,000	
Store equipment	14,000	
Accumulated depreciation, store equipment		$ 100
Note payable		100,000
Accounts payable		16,200
Paid-in capital		400,000
Retained income		0*
Sales revenues		160,000
Cost of goods sold	100,000	
Rent expense	2,000	
Depreciation expense	100	
Total	$676,300	$676,300

*If a Retained income balance existed at the start of the accounting period, it would appear here. However, in our example Retained Income was zero at the start of the period.

income during the period. In future periods when the trial balance is prepared, the beginning balance will be the ending balance of the previous period. The beginning balance for next period will be $57,900.

Although the trial balance helps alert the accountant to possible errors, a trial balance may balance even when there are recording errors. For example, an accountant may misread a $10,000 cash receipt on account as a $1,000 receipt and erroneously record that amount in both the Cash and Accounts Receivable accounts. Then both Cash and Accounts Receivable would be in error by offsetting amounts of $9,000. Another example would be the recording of a $10,000 cash receipt on account as a credit to Sales Revenues rather than as a credit reducing Accounts Receivable. Sales Revenues and Accounts Receivable would both be overstated by $10,000. Nevertheless, the trial balance would still show total debits equal to total credits.

EFFECTS OF ERRORS

Objective 5
Correct erroneous journal entries and describe how errors affect accounts.

When a journal entry contains an error, the entry can be erased or crossed out and corrected—if the error is discovered immediately. However, if the error is detected later, typically after posting to ledger accounts, the accountant makes a correcting entry, as distinguished from a correct entry. Basically, the idea behind correcting entries is to counteract the erroneous entries into the incorrect accounts and to make sure that all correct accounts are either credited or debited. The correcting entry is recorded in the general journal and posted to the general ledger exactly as regular entries are. But the end result is that the balances in the accounts are corrected to what they should have been originally. The focus is on the final balances, not on the flow of entries through the accounts. The balances are used in preparing the financial statements and therefore it is the balances that must be correct.

Exhibit 3-7

Trial Balance, Balance Sheet, and Income Statement

Biwheels Company
Trial Balance
January 31, 19X2

	Debits	Credits
Cash	$336,700	
Accounts receivable	160,300	
Merchandise inventory	59,200	
Prepaid rent	4,000	
Store equipment	14,000	
Accumulated depreciation, store equipment		$ 100
Note payable		100,000
Accounts payable		16,200
Paid-in capital		400,000
Retained income		0
Sales revenue		160,000
Cost of goods sold	100,000	
Rent expense	2,000	
Depreciation expense	100	
Total	$676,300	$676,300

Biwheels Company
Balance Sheet
January 31, 19X2

Assets		
Cash		$336,700
Accounts receivable		160,300
Merchandise inventory		59,200
Prepaid rent		4,000
Store equipment	14,000	
Less accumulated depreciation	100	13,900
Total assets		$574,100

Liabilities and Stockholders' Equity		
Liabilities:		
Note payable	$100,000	
Accounts payable	16,200	
Total liabilities		$116,200
Stockholders' equity:		
Paid-in capital	$400,000	
Retained income	57,900	
Total stockholders' equity		457,900
Total liabilities and stockholders' equity		$574,100

Biwheels Company
Income Statement
For the Month Ended January 31, 19X2

Sales revenues		$160,000
Deduct expenses:		
Cost of goods sold	$100,000	
Rent	2,000	
Depreciation	100	
Total expenses		102,100
Net income		$ 57,900

99

Consider the following examples:

1. A repair expense was erroneously debited to Equipment on December 27. The error is discovered on December 31:

CORRECT ENTRY

12/27 Repair Expense	500	
Cash		500

ERRONEOUS ENTRY

12/27 Equipment	500	
Cash		500

CORRECTING ENTRY

12/31 Repair Expense	500	
Equipment		500

The correcting entry shows a credit to Equipment to cancel or offset the erroneous debit to Equipment. Moreover, the entry debits Repair Expense correctly. Notice that the credit to Cash was correct and therefore was not changed.

2. A collection on account was erroneously credited to Sales on November 2. The error is discovered on November 28:

CORRECT ENTRY

11/2 Cash	3,000	
Accounts Receivable		3,000

ERRONEOUS ENTRY

11/2 Cash	3,000	
Sales		3,000

CORRECTING ENTRY

11/28 Sales	3,000	
Accounts Receivable		3,000

The debit to Sales in the correcting entry offsets the incorrect credit to Sales in the erroneous entry. The credit to Accounts Receivable in the correcting entry places the collected amount where it belongs. The correcting entry moves the 3,000 from the Sales account to the Accounts Receivable account where it belongs. The correct debit to Cash in the erroneous entry is unaffected by the correcting entry.

SOME ERRORS ARE COUNTERBALANCED

Accountants' errors that are undetected can affect a variety of items, including revenues and expenses for a given period. Some errors are counterbalanced by offsetting errors in the ordinary bookkeeping process in the next period. Such errors misstate net income in both periods, but by the end of the second period the errors counterbalance or cancel each other out, and they affect the balance sheet of only the first period, not the second.

Consider a payment of $1,000 in December 19X1 for rent. Suppose this was for January 19X2's rent. Instead of recording it as prepaid rent, the payment was listed as Rent Expense:

INCORRECT ENTRY

12/X1 Rent expense	1,000	
Cash		1,000
One month's rent.		

CORRECT ENTRY

12/X1 Prepaid rent	1,000	
Cash		1,000
Payment for January 19X2's rent.		
1/X2 Rent Expense	1,000	
Prepaid rent		1,000
Expiration of January's rent.		

The effects of this recording error would be to (1) overstate rent expense (which understates pretax income) and understate year-end assets by $1,000 (because the prepayment would not be listed as an asset waiting to be expired) for the first year and (2) understate rent expense (which overstates income by $1,000) for the second year. These errors have no effect on the second year's ending assets because the same *total* assets exist whether the rent is recorded as paid in January of that year or recorded as paid in full the previous year. The total of the incorrect pretax incomes for the two years would be identical with the total of the correct pretax incomes for the two years because the first year's understatement of $1,000 would counterbalance the second year's overstatement of $1,000. The retained income balance at the end of the second year would thus be correct on a pretax basis.

SOME ERRORS ARE NOT COUNTERBALANCED

Errors that are not counterbalanced in the ordinary bookkeeping process will keep subsequent balance sheets in error until specific correcting entries are made. For example, overlooking a depreciation expense of $2,000 in only one year would (1) overstate pretax income, assets, and retained income by $2,000 in that year, and (2) continue to overstate assets and retained income on successive balance sheets for the life of the fixed asset. But observe that pretax income for each subsequent year would not be affected unless the same error is committed again.

INCOMPLETE RECORDS

Objective 6
Use T-accounts to analyze accounting relationships.

A company's accounting records are not always perfect. Records may be stolen, destroyed, or lost, and accountants are left to make journal and ledger entries and create financial statements with incomplete records. Luckily, T-accounts can help accountants to discover unknown amounts. For example, suppose the proprietor of a local sports shop asks you for help in calculating her sales for 19X5. She provides the following accurate but incomplete information:

List of customers who owe money:	
December 31, 19X4	$ 4,000
December 31, 19X5	6,000
Cash receipts from customers during 19X5	
appropriately credited to customer's accounts	280,000

She further tells you that all sales were on credit, not cash. How can you use T-accounts to solve for the missing credit sales figure? There are two basic steps to follow:

Step 1: Enter all known items into the key T-account. Of course, you need to understand this account and all of its components to properly work the problem. In this case, we are looking for credit sales, which are debited to Accounts Receivable. Substituting S for the unknown credit sales, we get the following T-account values:

Accounts Receivable			
Bal. 12/31/X4	4,000	Collections	280,000
Sales	S		
Total debits	(4,000+S)	Total credits	280,000
Bal. 12/31/X5	6,000		

INCOMPLETE RECORDS **101**

Step 2: Solve for the unknown. Finding this solution is usually just a simple arithmetic exercise. However, we can also use the debit and credit relationships we have just learned to solve our problem:

$$\text{Total debits} - \text{Total credits} = \text{Balance}$$
$$(4,000 + S) - \quad 280,000 = 6,000$$
$$S = 6,000 + 280,000 - 4,000$$
$$S = 282,000$$

Obviously, the analyses of missing data become more complicated if there are more entries in a particular account and if there is more than one unknown value. Nevertheless, the key idea is to fill in the account with all known debits, credits, and balances, and then solve for the unknown.

DATA PROCESSING AND COMPUTERS

data processing The totality of the procedures used to record, analyze, store, and report on chosen activities.

Objective 7
Explain how computers have transformed processing of accounting data.

Data processing is a general term referring to the procedures used to record, analyze, store, and report on chosen activities. An accounting system is a data-processing system. Computers have been refining data-processing systems for the last decade, and the accounting system is no exception. (Although for simplicity's sake we focus on manual methods for record keeping.) Today almost all organizations use advanced technology, ranging from a simple cash register to bar-code scanners at grocery store checkouts to massive computer systems that automatically record and bill billions of telephone transactions per month.

Today journals and ledgers are more likely to be computerized than they are to be in the traditional paper book format. Regardless of their *format,* journals and ledgers still maintain the same *form* and still require the same inputs. So, whether you enter them into a book or into a computer, the transaction data in ledgers and journals remains the same. Of course, if you enter journal amounts into a computerized accounting program, the computer can automatically generate the subsequent ledger postings.

The personal computer has enabled small organizations to process data more efficiently than ever. In fact, managers can get computers to produce daily financial statements. However, the benefits of computers affect not only the outputs of a recording system, but the inputs as well. When you check out at a CVS drug store or The Limited clothing store, the cash register often does more than just record a sale. It may be linked to a computer that also records a decrease in inventory. It may activate an order to a supplier if the inventory level is low. If a sale is on credit, the computer may check a customer's credit limit, update the accounts receivable, and eventually prepare monthly statements for mailing to the customer. Most importantly, the computer can automatically enter each and every transaction into the journal as each transaction occurs, thereby reducing the amount of source document paperwork and moving from step 2 of the recording process to step 3 in the blink of an eye.

Because computers reduce the need for paperwork and for accountants to analyze every transaction, data processing costs have plummeted recently. Consider the oil companies. Amoco Oil Company once received 650,000 separate sales slips daily. But today most credit sales are recorded by computers reading the magnetic strips on credit cards. Many gas stations have the card-reading equipment built into the gasoline pumps, eliminating the need for sales clerks. Information about each credit sale is electronically submitted to a central computer, which prepares all billing documents and financial statements. Millions of transactions are recorded automatically into the general journal without any paperwork or keyboard entry, producing huge savings in time and money while increasing accuracy.

SUMMARY PROBLEMS FOR YOUR REVIEW

PROBLEM ONE

Do you agree with the following statements? Explain.

1. To charge an account means to credit it.
2. One person's debit is another person's credit.
3. A charge account may be credited.
4. My credit is my most valuable asset.
5. When I give credit, I debit my customer's account.

SOLUTION TO PROBLEM ONE

Remember that in accounting, debit means left side and credit means right side.

1. No. Charge and debit and left side are synonyms.
2. Yes, in certain situations. The clearest example is probably the sale of merchandise on open account. The buyer's account payable would have a credit (right) balance, and the seller's account receivable would have a debit (left) balance.
3. Yes. When collections are received, Accounts Receivable is credited (right).
4. Note that "charge" as used in "charge account" is not a synonym for debit. As used in this statement, "my credit" refers to "my ability to borrow," not which side of a balance sheet is affected. "My ability to borrow" may indeed be a valuable right, but the accountant does not recognize that ability (as such) as an asset to be measured and reported in the balance sheet. When borrowing occurs, the borrower's assets are increased (debited, increased on the left side) and the liabilities are increased (credited, increased on the right side).
5. Yes. Accounts Receivable is debited (left). "Give credit" in this context means that the seller is allowing the customer to defer payment. The corresponding account payable on the customer's accounting records will be increased (credited, right).

PROBLEM TWO

The trial balance of Hassan Used Auto Co. on March 31, 19X1, follows:

| | Balance | |
Account Title	Debit	Credit
Cash	$ 10,000	
Accounts receivable	20,000	
Automobile inventory	100,000	
Accounts payable		$ 3,000
Notes payable		70,000
Hassan, owner's equity		57,000
Total	$130,000	$130,000

The Hassan business is only a proprietorship, thus the equity account used here is Hassan, Owner's Equity. In practice, it is often called Hassan, Capital.

Hassan rented operating space and equipment on a month-to-month basis. During April, the business had the following summarized transactions:

a. Invested an additional $20,000 cash in the business.
b. Collected $10,000 on accounts receivable.

c. Paid $2,000 on accounts payable.

d. Sold autos for $120,000 cash.

e. Cost of autos sold was $70,000.

f. Replenished inventory for $60,000 cash.

g. Paid rent expense in cash, $14,000.

h. Paid utilities in cash, $1,000.

i. Paid selling expense in cash, $30,000.

j. Paid interest expense in cash, $1,000.

Required

1. Journalize transactions a–j and post the entries to the ledger. Key entries by transaction letter.

2. Open the following T-accounts in the general ledger: cash; accounts receivable; automobile inventory; accounts payable; notes payable; Hassan, owners' equity; sales; cost of goods sold; rent expense; utilities expense; selling expense; and interest expense. Enter the March 31 balances in the appropriate accounts.

3. Prepare the trial balance at April 30, 19X1.

4. Prepare an income statement for April. Ignore income taxes.

SOLUTION TO PROBLEM TWO

The solutions to requirements 1 through 4 are in Exhibits 3-8 through 3-11. The journal entries are prepared in Exhibit 3-8 and posted to the ledger in Exhibit 3-9. Opening balances are placed in the appropriate accounts in Exhibit 3-9. A trial balance is prepared in Exhibit 3-10, and the income statement is shown in Exhibit 3-11.

PROBLEM THREE

An annual report of Kobe Steel, Ltd., one of the world's largest producers of iron and steel, showed (in billions of Japanese yen):

Property, plant, and equipment, at cost	¥2,062	
Accumulated depreciation	1,051	¥1,011

1. Open T-accounts for (a) Property, Plant, and Equipment, (b) Accumulated Depreciation, and (c) Depreciation Expense. Enter the above amounts therein.

2. Assume that during the ensuing month no additional property, plant, and equipment were acquired, but depreciation expense of ¥80 billion was incurred. Prepare the journal entry, and post to the T-accounts.

3. Show how Kobe Steel would present its property, plant, and equipment accounts in its balance sheet after the journal entry in requirement 2.

SOLUTION TO PROBLEM THREE

1. Amounts are in billions of Japanese yen.

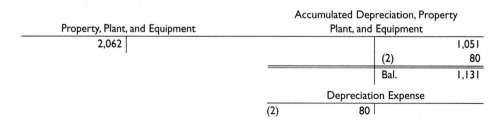

2. Depreciation expense   80

    Accumulated depreciation, property, plant, and equipment   80

3. The plant and equipment section would appear as follows:

    Property, plant, and equipment, at cost   ¥2,062

    Accumulated depreciation   1,131   ¥931

Exhibit 3-8

Hassan Used Auto Co.

General Journal

ENTRY	ACCOUNTS AND EXPLANATION	POST REF.*	DEBIT	CREDIT
a.	Cash	✓	20,000	
	Hassan, owners' equity	✓		20,000
	Investment in business by Hassan.			
b.	Cash	✓	10,000	
	Accounts receivable	✓		10,000
	Collected cash on accounts.			
c.	Accounts payable	✓	2,000	
	Cash	✓		2,000
	Disbursed cash on accounts owed to others.			
d.	Cash	✓	120,000	
	Sales (or Sales Revenue)	✓		120,000
	Sales for cash.			
e.	Cost of goods sold	✓	70,000	
	Automobile inventory	✓		70,000
	Cost of inventory that was sold to customers.			
f.	Automobile inventory	✓	60,000	
	Cash	✓		60,000
	Replenished inventory.			
g.	Rent expense	✓	14,000	
	Cash	✓		14,000
	Paid April rent.			
h.	Utilities expense	✓	1,000	
	Cash	✓		1,000
	Paid April utilities.			
i.	Selling expense	✓	30,000	
	Cash	✓		30,000
	Paid April selling expenses.			
j.	Interest expense	✓	1,000	
	Cash	✓		1,000
	Paid April interest expense.			

* Ordinarily, account numbers are used to denote specific posting references. Otherwise check marks are used to indicate that the entry has been posted to the general ledger.

Highlights to Remember

Two very important steps in the accountant's recording process involve the journal and the general ledger. The journal provides a chronological record of transactions, whereas the general ledger provides a dated summary of the effects of the transactions on all accounts, account by account. This book uses a simplified version of general ledger accounts called T-accounts. Accountants at all levels use T-accounts to help think through complex transactions.

Accountants use the terms *debit* and *credit* repeatedly. Remember that debit simply means "left side" and credit means "right side."

Journal entries are a convenient, simple way to analyze a transaction. Journal entries are always posted to the general ledger.

Exhibit 3-9

Hassan Used Auto Co.
General Ledger

Cash					Accounts Payable					Hassan, Owners' Equity		
Bal.*	10,000	(c)	2,000	(c)	2,000	Bal.*	3,000			Bal.*	57,000
(a)	20,000	(f)	60,000			Bal.	1,000			(a)	20,000
(b)	10,000	(g)	14,000							Bal.	77,000
(d)	120,000	(h)	1,000		Notes Payable							
	160,000	(i)	30,000			Bal.*	70,000			Sales		
		(j)	1,000							(d)	120,000
			108,000†		Cost of Goods Sold							
Bal.	52,000			(e)	70,000					Rent Expense		

Accounts Receivable					Selling Expense			(g)	14,000		
Bal.*	20,000	(b)	10,000	(i)	30,000						
Bal.	10,000				Utilities Expense				Interest Expense		
				(h)	1,000			(j)	1,000		

Automobile Inventory			
Bal.*	100,000	(e)	70,000
(f)	60,000		
Bal.	90,000		

*Balances denoted with an asterisk are as of March 31; balances without asterisks are as of April 30. A lone number in any account also serves as an ending balance.

†Subtotals are included in the Cash account. They are not an essential part of T-accounts. However, when an account contains many postings, subtotals ease the checking of arithmetic.

Exhibit 3-10

Hassan Used Auto Co.
Trial Balance April 30, 19X1

Account Title	Balance	
	Debit	Credit
Cash	$ 52,000	
Accounts receivable	10,000	
Automobile inventory	90,000	
Accounts payable		$ 1,000
Notes payable		70,000
Hassan, owners' equity		77,000
Sales		120,000
Cost of goods sold	70,000	
Rent expense	14,000	
Utilities expense	1,000	
Selling expense	30,000	
Interest expense	1,000	
Total	$268,000	$268,000

Exhibit 3-11

Hassan Used Auto Co.
Income Statement For the Month Ended April 30, 19X1

Sales		$120,000
Deduct expenses:		
Cost of goods sold	$70,000	
Rent expense	14,000	
Utilities expense	1,000	
Selling expense	30,000	
Interest expense	1,000	116,000
Net Income		$ 4,000

Trial balances are internal reports that are used for detecting errors in the accounts and to aid in preparing financial statements. Trial balances that fail to balance are inevitably the result of careless or rushed journalizing or posting. The good news is that the out-of-balance condition lets you know that an error has been made.

Despite precautions, errors sometimes occur in accounting entries. Such errors should be corrected when discovered, adjusting account balances so that they equal the amounts that would have existed if the correct entry had been made.

T-accounts help organize thinking and aid in the discovery of unknown amounts. The key idea is to fill in the related accounts with all known debits, credits, and balances, and then solve for the unknown amounts.

Accounting Vocabulary

accumulated depreciation, p. 94

allowance for depreciation, p. 94

balance, p. 83

book of original entry, p. 85

book value, p. 94

carrying amount, p. 94

carrying value, p. 94

charge, p. 84

chart of accounts, p. 86

compound entry, p. 89

contra account, p. 94

contra asset, p. 94

credit, p. 84

cross-referencing, p. 86

data processing, p. 102

debit, p. 84

double-entry system, p. 82

general journal, p. 85

general ledger, p. 83

journal entry, p. 86

journalizing, p. 86

keying of entries, p. 88

ledger, p. 83

net book value, p. 94

posting, p. 88

simple entry, p. 89

source documents, p. 85

T-account, p. 83

trial balance, p. 85

Assignment Material

QUESTIONS

3-1. "Double entry means that amounts are shown in the journal and ledger." Do you agree? Explain.

3-2. "Increases in cash and stockholders' equity are shown on the right side of their respective accounts." Do you agree? Explain.

3-3. "Debit and credit are used as verbs, adjectives, or nouns." Give examples of how debit may be used in these three meanings.

3-4. Name three source documents for transactions.

3-5. "The ledger is the major book of original entry because it is more essential than the journal." Do you agree? Explain.

3-6. "Revenue and expense accounts are really little stockholders' equity accounts." Explain.

3-7. "Accumulated depreciation is the total depreciation expense for the year." Do you agree? Explain.

3-8. Give two synonyms for book value.

3-9. "A trial balance assumes that the amounts in the financial statements are correct." Do you agree? Explain.

3-10. "If debits equal credits in a trial balance, you can be assured that no errors were made." Do you agree? Explain.

3-11. "In double-entry accounting, errors are not a problem because they are self-correcting." Do you agree? Explain.

3-12. Are all data processing systems computerized? Explain.

EXERCISES

3-13 Debits and Credits

For each of the following accounts, indicate whether it normally possesses a debit or a credit balance. Use *Dr.* or *Cr.*:

1. Sales
2. Accounts payable
3. Accounts receivable
4. Supplies expense
5. Supplies inventory
6. Retained income
7. Depreciation expense
8. Dividends payable
9. Paid-in capital
10. Subscription revenue

3-14 Debits and Credits

Indicate for each of the following transactions whether the account *named in parentheses* is to be debited or credited:

1. Bought merchandise on account (Merchandise Inventory), $4,000.
2. Paid Napoli Associates $3,000 owed them (Accounts Payable).
3. Received cash from customers on accounts due (Accounts Receivable), $2,000.
4. Bought merchandise on open account (Accounts Payable), $5,000.
5. Sold merchandise (Merchandise Inventory), $1,500.
6. Borrowed money from a bank (Notes Payable), $10,000.

3-15 Debits and Credits

For the following transactions, indicate whether the accounts *in parentheses* are to be debited or credited. Use *Dr.* or *Cr.:*

1. Merchandise was sold on credit (Accounts Receivable).
2. Dividends were declared and paid in cash (Retained Income).
3. A county government received property taxes (Tax Revenue).
4. Wages were paid to employees (Wages Expense).
5. A newsstand sold magazines (Sales Revenue).
6. A three-year fire insurance policy was acquired (Prepaid Expenses).

3-16 True or False

Use *T* or *F* to indicate whether each of the following statements is true or false:

1. Repayments of bank loans should be charged to Notes Payable and credited to Cash.
2. Asset debits should be on the right and liability debits should be on the left .
3. Inventory purchases on account should be credited to Accounts Payable and debited to an expense account.
4. In general, all debit entries are recorded on the left side of accounts and represent decreases in the account balances.
5. Cash collections of accounts receivable should be recorded as debits to Cash and credits to Accounts Receivable.
6. Credit purchases of equipment should be debited to Equipment and charged to Accounts Payable.
7. In general, entries on the right side of asset accounts represent decreases in the account balances.
8. Increases in liability and revenue accounts should be recorded on the left side of the accounts.
9. Decreases in retained income are recorded as debits.
10. Both increases in assets and decreases in liabilities are recorded on the debit sides of accounts.
11. In some cases, increases in account balances are recorded on the right sides of accounts.

3-17 Matching Transaction Accounts

Listed here are a series of accounts that are numbered for identification. Accompanying this problem are columns in which you are to write the identification numbers of the accounts affected by the transactions described. The same account may be used in several answers. For each transaction, indicate which account(s) are to be debited and which are to be credited.

1. Cash
2. Accounts receivable
3. Inventory
4. Equipment

5. Accumulated depreciation, equipment
6. Prepaid insurance
7. Accounts payable
8. Notes payable
9. Paid-in capital
10. Retained earnings
11. Sales revenues
12. Costs of goods sold
13. Operating expense

	Debit	Credit
(a) Purchased new equipment for cash plus a short-term note.	4	1,8
(b) Bought regular merchandise on credit.		
(c) Made sales on credit. Inventory is accounted for as each sale is made.		
(d) Paid cash for salaries and wages for work done during the current fiscal period.		
(e) Collected cash from customers on account.		
(f) Paid some old trade bills with cash.		
(g) Purchased three-year insurance policy on credit.		
(h) Sold for cash some old equipment at cost.		
(i) Paid off note owed to bank.		
(j) Paid cash for inventory that arrived today.		
(k) In order to secure additional funds, 400 new shares of common stock were sold for cash.		
(l) Recorded the entry for depreciation on equipment for the current fiscal period.		
(m) Paid cash for ad in today's *Chicago Tribune*.		
(n) Some insurance premiums have expired.		

3-18 Prepaid Expenses

Continental Aktiengesellschaft is a large German supplier of auto parts. Continental has DM35.6 million of prepaid expenses on its balance sheet on January 1, 1997. (DM stands for German deutsch marks.) A footnote to the company's financial statements indicates that this is "primarily rental, leasing, and interest prepayments." Assume that all these prepayments were for services that were used in 1997. In addition, DM150 million was spent in cash during 1997 for rent, leasing, and interest, of which DM38 million was a prepayment of expenses for 1998.

Required

1. Prepare a journal entry recognizing the use of the DM35.6 million of prepaid assets during 1997.

2. Prepare a compound journal entry for the cash payment of DM150 million for rent, leasing, and interest during 1997 with the proper amounts going to expense and prepaid expenses.

3-19 Journalizing and Posting

(Alternate is 3-20.) Prepare journal entries and post to T-accounts the following transactions of Eduardo's Catering Company:

a. Cash sales, $9,000.

b. Collections on accounts, $7,000.

c. Paid cash for wages, $3,000.

d. Acquired inventory on open account, $5,000.

e. Paid cash for janitorial services, $600.

3-20 Journalizing and Posting

(Alternate is 3-19.) Prepare journal entries and post to T-accounts the following transactions of Joie Leonhardt, Realtor:

a. Acquired office supplies of $800 on open account. Use a Supplies Inventory account.

b. Sold a house and collected a $9,000 commission on the sale. Use a Commissions Revenue account.

c. Paid cash of $700 to a local newspaper for current advertisements.

d. Paid $800 for a previous credit purchase of a desk.

e. Recorded office supplies used of $300.

3-21 Reconstruct Journal Entries

(Alternate is 3-22.) Reconstruct the journal entries (omit explanations) that resulted in the postings to the following T-accounts of a consulting firm:

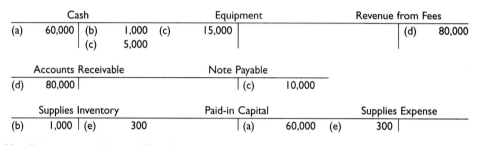

Cash				Equipment		Revenue from Fees	
(a) 60,000	(b)	1,000	(c)	15,000		(d)	80,000
	(c)	5,000					

Accounts Receivable		Note Payable	
(d) 80,000		(c)	10,000

Supplies Inventory		Paid-in Capital		Supplies Expense	
(b) 1,000	(e) 300		(a) 60,000	(e) 300	

3-22 Reconstruct Journal Entries

(Alternate is 3-21.) Reconstruct the journal entries (omit explanations) that resulted in the postings to the following T-accounts of a small computer retailer:

Cash		Accounts Payable		Paid-in Capital	
(a) 40,000	(e) 25,000	(e) 25,000	(b) 90,000		(a) 40,000

Accounts Receivable	
(c) 100,000	

Inventory		Cost of Goods Sold		Sales	
(b) 90,000	(d) 57,000	(d) 57,000			(c) 100,000

3-23 Effects of Errors

The bookkeeper of Beenair Dunnit Legal Services included the cost of a new computer, purchased on December 30 for $9,000 and to be paid in January, as an operating expense instead of as an addition to the proper asset account. What was the effect of this error ("no effect," "overstated," or "understated"?—use symbols *n,o,* or *u,* respectively) on:

1. Operating expenses for the year ended December 31   _____
2. Profit from operations for the year   _____
3. Retained earnings as of December 31 after the books are closed   _____
4. Total assets as of December 31   _____
5. Total liabilities as of December 31   _____

3-24 Effects of Errors

Analyze the effect of the following errors on the net profit figures of EuroPac Trading Company for 19X7 and 19X8. Choose one of three answers: understated (*u*), overstated (*o*), or no effect (*n*). Problem *a* has been answered as an illustration.

a. EXAMPLE: Failure to adjust at end of 19X7 for prepaid rent that had expired during December 19X7. The remaining prepaid rent was charged in 19X8. 19X7: *o;* 19X8: *u.* (*Explanation:* In 19X7, expenses would be understated and profits overstated. This error would carry forward so that expenses in 19X8 would be overstated and profits understated.)

b. Omission of Depreciation on Office Machines in 19X7 only. Correct depreciation was taken in 19X8.

c. During 19X8 $300 of office supplies were purchased and debited to Office Supplies, an asset account. At the end of 19X8 only $100 worth of office supplies were left. No entry had recognized the use of $200 of office supplies during 19X8.

d. Machinery, cost price $500, bought in 19X7, was not entered in the books until paid for in 19X8. Ignore depreciation; answer in terms of the specific error described.

e. Three months' rent, paid in advance in December 19X7, for the first quarter of 19X8 was debited directly to Rent Expense in 19X7. No prepaid rent was on the books at the end of 19X7.

PROBLEMS

3-25 Account Numbers, Journal, Ledger, Trial Balance

Journalize and post the entries required by the following transactions for Lombardi Construction Company. Prepare a trial balance, April 30, 19X6. Ignore interest. Use dates, posting references, and the following account numbers:

Cash	100	Note payable	130
Accounts receivable	101	Paid-in capital	140
Equipment	111	Retained income	150
Accumulated depreciation,		Revenues	200
equipment	111A	Expenses	300, 301, etc.
Accounts payable	120		

- April 1, 19X6. The Lombardi Construction Company was formed with $100,000 cash upon the issuance of common stock.
- April 2. Equipment was acquired for $75,000. A cash down payment of $25,000 was made. In addition, a note for $50,000 was signed.
- April 3. Sales on credit to a local hotel, $2,200.
- April 3. Supplies acquired (and used) on open account, $200.
- April 3. Wages paid in cash, $700.
- April 30. Depreciation expense for April, $1,000.

3-26 Account Numbers, T-Accounts, and Transaction Analysis

Consider the following (in thousands):

Ontario Computing
Trial Balance December 31, 19X7

Account Number	Account Titles	Balance	
		Debit	*Credit*
10	Cash	$ 50	
20	Accounts receivable	115	
21	Note receivable	100	
30	Inventory	130	
40	Prepaid insurance	12	
70	Equipment	120	
		(continued)	

Account Number	Account Titles	Balance Debit	Balance Credit
70A	Accumulated depreciation, equipment		$ 30
80	Accounts payable		135
100	Paid-in capital		60
110	Retained income		182
130	Sales		950
150	Cost of goods sold	550	
160	Wages expense	200	
170	Miscellaneous expense	80	
		$1,357	$1,357

The following information had not been considered before preparing the trial balance:

1. The note receivable was signed by a major customer. It is a three-month note dated November 1, 19X7. Interest earned during November and December was collected at 4 p.m. on December 31. The interest rate is 12% per year.

2. The Prepaid Insurance account reflects a one-year fire insurance policy acquired for cash on August 1, 19X7.

3. Depreciation for 19X7 was $15,000.

4. Wages of $13,000 were paid in cash at 5 p.m. on December 31.

Required

1. Enter the December 31 balances in a general ledger. Number the accounts. Allow room for additional T-accounts.

2. Prepare the journal entries prompted by the additional information. Show amounts in thousands.

3. Post the journal entries to the ledger. Key your postings. Create logical new account numbers as necessary.

4. Prepare a new trial balance, December 31, 19X7.

3-27 Trial Balance Errors

Consider the following trial balance (in thousands of dollars):

Winslow Auto Parts Store
Trial Balance for the Year Ended December 31, 19X7

Cash	$ 16	
Equipment	33	
Accumulated depreciation, equipment	15	
Accounts payable	42	
Accounts receivable	14	
Prepaid insurance	1	
Prepaid rent		$ 4
Inventory	129	
Paid-in capital		12
Retained income		10
Cost of goods sold	500	
Wages expense	100	
Miscellaneous expenses	80	
Advertising expense		30
Sales		788
Note payable	40	
	$970	$844

List and describe all the errors in the above trial balance. Be specific. On the basis of the available data, prepare a corrected trial balance. Required

3-28 Journal, Ledger, and Trial Balance

(Alternates are 3-30 through 3-35.) The Clothes Hanger is a retailer. The entity's balance sheet accounts had the following balances on October 31, 19X5:

Cash	$ 39,000	
Accounts receivable	90,000	
Inventory	70,000	
Prepaid rent	2,000	
Accounts payable		$ 25,000
Paid-in capital		160,000
Retained income		16,000
	$201,000	$201,000

Following is a summary of the transactions that occurred during November:

a. Collections of accounts receivable, $85,000.

b. Payments of accounts payable, $19,000.

c. Acquisitions of inventory on open account, $80,000.

d. Merchandise carried in inventory at a cost of $70,000 was sold on open account for $86,000.

e. Recognition of rent expense for November, $1,000.

f. Wages paid in cash for November, $8,000.

g. Cash dividends declared and disbursed to stockholders on November 29, $15,000.

1. Prepare journal entries (in thousands of dollars). Required

2. Enter beginning balances in T-accounts. Post the journal entries to T-accounts. Use the transaction letters to key your postings.

3. Prepare a trial balance, November 30, 19X5.

4. Explain why accounts payable increased by so much during November.

3-29 Financial Statements

Refer to problem 3-28. Prepare a balance sheet as of November 30, 19X5, and an income statement for the month of November. Prepare a statement of retained income. Prepare the income statement first.

3-30 Journal, Ledger, and Trial Balance

(Alternates are 3-28, and 3-31 through 3-35.) The final trial balance of Solvang Appliance Co. on December 31, 19X8, follows:

	Balance	
Account Title	*Debit*	*Credit*
Cash	$35,000	
Accounts receivable	30,000	
Merchandise inventory	120,000	
Accounts payable		$ 35,000
Notes payable		80,000
Paid-in capital		39,000
Retained income		31,000
Total	$185,000	$185,000

Operating space and equipment are rented on a month-to-month basis. A summary of January transactions follows:

   a. Collected $26,000 on accounts receivable.

   b. Sold appliances for $70,000 cash and $40,000 on open account.

   c. Cost of appliances sold was $60,000.

   d. Paid $19,000 on accounts payable.

   e. Replenished inventory for $63,000 on open account.

   f. Paid selling expense in cash, $33,000.

   g. Paid rent expense in cash, $7,000.

   h. Paid interest expense in cash, $1,000.

Required

   1. Open the appropriate T-accounts in the general ledger. In addition to the seven accounts listed in the trial balance of December 31, open accounts for Sales, Cost of Goods Sold, Selling Expense, Rent Expense, and Interest Expense. Enter the December 31 balances in the accounts.

   2. Journalize transactions *a–h*. Post the entries to the ledger, keying by transaction letter.

   3. Prepare a trial balance, January 31, 19X9.

3-31 Journal, Ledger, and Trial Balance
(Alternates are 3-28, 3-30, 3-32, 3-33, 3-34, and 3-35.) Norma Nielsen owned and managed a franchise of Seattle Expresso, Inc. The accompanying trial balance existed on September 1, 19X8, the beginning of a fiscal year.

Norma's Seattle Expresso
Trial Balance September 1, 19X8

Cash	$ 2,600	
Accounts receivable	25,200	
Merchandise inventory	77,800	
Prepaid rent	4,000	
Store equipment	21,000	
Accumulated depreciation, store equipment		$ 5,750
Accounts payable		45,000
Paid-in capital		30,000
Retained income		49,850
	$130,600	$130,600

Summarized transactions for September were:

   1. Acquisitions of merchandise inventory on account, $52,000.

   2. Sales for cash, $39,400.

   3. Payments to creditors, $29,000.

   4. Sales on account, $38,000.

   5. Advertising in newspapers, paid in cash, $3,000.

   6. Cost of goods sold, $40,000.

   7. Collections on account, $33,000.

   8. Miscellaneous expenses paid in cash, $8,000.

   9. Wages paid in cash, $9,000.

10. Entry for rent expense. (Rent was paid quarterly in advance, $6,000 per quarter. Payments were due on February 1, May 1, August 1, and November 1.)

11. Depreciation of store equipment, $250.

Required

1. Enter the September 1 balances in a general ledger.

2. Prepare journal entries for each transaction.

3. Post the journal entries to the ledger. Key your postings.

4. Prepare an income statement for September and a balance sheet as of September 30, 19X8.

3-32 Journalizing, Posting, Trial Balance

(Alternates are 3-28, 3-30, 3-31, 3-33, 3-34, and 3-35.) Canseco Gardens, a retailer of garden supplies and equipment, had the accompanying balance sheet accounts, December 31, 19X7:

Assets			Liabilities and Stockholders' Equity	
Cash		$ 22,000	Accounts payable*	$111,000
Accounts receivable		37,000	Paid-in capital	40,000
Inventory		131,000	Retained income	79,000
Prepaid rent		4,000		
Store equipment	$60,000			
Less: Accumulated depreciation	24,000	36,000		
Total		$230,000	Total	$230,000

*For merchandise only.

Following is a summary of transactions that occurred during 19X8:

a. Purchases of merchandise inventory on open account, $550,000.

b. Sales, all on credit, $800,000.

c. Cost of merchandise sold to customers, $440,000.

d. On June 1, 19X4, borrowed $80,000 from a supplier. The note is payable at the end of 19X8. Interest is payable yearly on December 31 at a rate of 15% per annum.

e. Disbursed $25,000 for the rent of the store. Add to Prepaid Rent.

f. Disbursed $165,000 for wages through November.

g. Disbursed $76,000 for miscellaneous expenses such as utilities, advertising, and legal help. (Combined here to save space. Debit Miscellaneous expenses.)

h. On July 1, 19X8, lent $20,000 to the office manager. He signed a note that will mature on July 1, 19X9, together with interest at 10% per annum. Interest for 19X8 is due on December 31, 19X8.

i. Collections on accounts receivable, $690,000.

j. Payments on accounts payable $470,000.

The following entries were made on December 31, 19X8:

k. Previous rent payments applicable to 19X9 amounted to $3,000.

l. Depreciation for 19X8 was $6,000.

m. Wages earned by employees during December were paid on December 31, $5,000.

n. Interest on the loan from the supplier was disbursed.

o. Interest on the loan made to the office manager was received.

1. Prepare journal entries in thousands of dollars.
2. Post the entries to the ledger, keying your postings by transaction letter.
3. Prepare a trial balance, December 31, 19X8.

3-33 Transaction Analysis, Trial Balance

(Alternates are 3-28, 3-30, 3-31, 3-32, 3-34 and 3-35.) Hawkeye Appliance Repair Service, Incorporated, had the accompanying trial balance on January 1, 19X8.

Hawkeye Appliance Repair Service, Inc.
Trial Balance January 1, 19X8

Cash	$ 5,000	
Accounts receivable	4,000	
Parts inventory	2,000	
Prepaid rent	2,000	
Trucks	36,000	
Equipment	8,000	
Accumulated depreciation, trucks		$15,000
Accumulated depreciation, equipment		5,000
Accounts payable		2,900
Paid-in capital		17,000
Retained income		17,100
Total	$57,000	$57,000

During January, the following summarized transactions occurred:

Jan 2 Collected accounts receivable, $3,000.

3 Rendered services to customers for cash, $2,200 ($700 collected for parts, $1,500 for labor). Use two accounts, Parts Revenue and Labor Revenue.

3 Cost of parts used for services rendered, $300.

7 Paid legal expenses, $500 cash.

9 Acquired parts on open account, $900.

11 Paid cash for wages, $1,000.

13 Paid cash for truck repairs, $500.

15 Paid cash for utilities, $400.

19 Billed customer for services, $4,000 ($1,200 for parts and $2,800 for labor).

19 Cost of parts used for services rendered, $500.

24 Paid cash for wages, $1,300.

27 Paid cash on accounts payable, $1,500.

31 Rent expense for January, $1,000 (reduce Prepaid Rent).

31 Depreciation for January: trucks, $600; equipment, $200.

31 Paid cash to local gas station for gasoline for trucks for January, $300.

31 Paid cash for wages, $900.

Required

1. Enter the January 1 balances in T-accounts. Leave room for additional accounts.
2. Record the transactions in the journal.
3. Post the journal entries to the T-accounts. Key your entries by date. (Note how keying by date is not as precise as by transaction number or letter. Why? Because there is usually more than one transaction on any given date.)
4. Prepare a trial balance, January 31, 19X8.

3-34 Transaction Analysis, Trial Balance

(Alternates are 3-28, 3-30 through 3-33, and 3-35.) McDonald's Corporation is a well-known fast-foods restaurant company. Examine the accompanying condensed trial balance, which is based on McDonald's annual report and actual terminology.

McDonald's Corporation
Trial Balance January 1, 1997 (in millions)

Cash	$ 330	
Accounts and notes receivable	495	
Inventories	70	
Prepaid expenses	208	
Property and equipment, at cost	19,134	
Other assets	1,931	
Accumulated depreciation		$ 4,782
Notes and accounts payable		1,236
Other liabilities		7,432
Paid-in capital		940
Retained earnings		7,778
Total	$22,168	$22,168

Consider the following assumed partial summary of transactions for 1997 (in millions):

a. Revenues in cash, company-owned restaurants, $2,100.

b. Revenues, on open account from franchised restaurants, $500. Set up a separate revenue account for these sales.

c. Inventories acquired on open account, $827.

d. Cost of the inventories sold, $820.

e. Depreciation, $226. (Debit Depreciation Expense.)

f. Paid rents and insurance premiums in cash in advance, $42. (Debit Prepaid Expenses.)

g. Prepaid expenses expired, $37. (Debit Operating Expenses.)

h. Paid other liabilities, $148.

i. Cash collections on receivables, $590.

j. Cash disbursements on notes and accounts payable, $747.

k. Paid interest expense in cash, $100.

l. Paid other expenses in cash, mostly payroll and advertising, $1,510. (Debit Operating Expenses.)

Required

1. Record the transactions in the journal.
2. Enter beginning balances in T-accounts. Post the journal entries to the T-accounts. Key your entries with the transaction letters used here.
3. Prepare a trial balance, December 31, 1997.

3-35 Transaction Analysis, Trial Balance

(Alternates are 3-28, and 3-30 through 3-34.) Kellogg Company's major product line is ready-to-eat breakfast cereals. Examine the following condensed trial balance, which is based on Kellogg's annual report:

Kellogg Company Trial Balance
January 1, 1997 (in millions)

Cash	$ 243.8	
Accounts receivable	592.3	
Inventories	424.9	
Prepaid expenses	267.6	
Property and equipment	5,020.1	
Other assets	588.5	
Accumulated depreciation		$2,087.2
Accounts payable		335.2
Other liabilities		3,432.4
Paid-in capital		201.8
Retained earnings		1,080.6
Total	$7,137.2	$7,137.2

Consider the following assumed partial summary of transactions for 1997 (in millions):

a. Acquired inventories for $1,750 on open account.

b. Sold inventories that cost $1,600 for $2,500 on open account.

c. Collected $2,550 on open account.

d. Disbursed $1,650 on open accounts payable.

e. Paid cash of $300 for advertising expenses. (Use an Operating Expenses account.)

f. Paid rent and insurance premiums in cash in advance, $20. (Use a Prepaid Expenses account.)

g. Prepaid expenses expired, $18. (Use an Operating Expenses account.)

h. Other liabilities paid in cash, $110.

i. Interest expense of $13 was paid in cash. (Use an Interest Expense account.)

j. Depreciation of $50 was recognized. (Use an Operating Expenses account.)

Required

1. Record the transactions in the journal.

2. Enter beginning balances in T-accounts. Post the journal entries to the T-accounts. Key your entries with the transaction letters used here.

3. Prepare a trial balance, December 31, 1997.

4. Explain why cash increased more than five-fold during 1997.

3-36 Preparation of Financial Statements from Trial Balance

Pepsico produces snack foods such as Fritos and Lay's Potato Chips as well as beverages such as Pepsi and Mug Root Beer. The company had the following trial balance for the year ended December 28, 1996 (in millions):

	Debits	Credits
Current assets	$ 5,139	
Property and equipment, net	10,191	
Intangible assets, net	7,136	
Other assets	2,046	
Current liabilities		$ 5,139
Long-term debt and other liabilities		12,750
Stockholders' equity*		6,169
Net sales		31,645
Cost of sales	15,383	
Selling, general, and administrative expenses	12,593	
Other expenses	2,621	
Interest income		101
Cash dividends	695	
Total	$55,804	$55,804

*Includes *beginning* retained earnings.

1. Prepare Pepsico's income statement for the year ended December 28, 1996.

2. Prepare Pepsico's balance sheet as of December 28, 1996.

Required

3-37 Accumulated Depreciation

Michelin, the French tire company, had the following balances on its January 1, 1997 balance sheet (in thousands, where FF stands for French franc):

Tangible fixed assets, at cost	FF 20,121
Accumulated depreciation	15,812
Net tangible fixed assets	FF 4,309

Michelin depreciates most of its tangible fixed assets over 10 years.

1. What is the approximate average age of Michelin's tangible fixed assets?

2. Michelin invested FF 620,000 in tangible fixed assets in 1996. Is this surprising, given your answer in requirement 1? Explain.

Required

3-38 Reconstructing Journal Entries, Posting

Sony Corporation is a leading international supplier of audio and video equipment. The Sony annual report at the end of the 1997 fiscal year included the following balance sheet items (in millions of Japanese yen):

Cash	¥ 428,518
Receivables	1,066,314
Prepaid expenses	240,195
Land	179,011
Accounts payable, trade	653,826

Consider the following assumed transactions that occurred immediately subsequent to the balance sheet date (in millions of yen):

a. Collections from customers	¥820,000
b. Purchase of land for cash	20,000
c. Purchase of insurance policies on account	12,000
d. Disbursements to trade creditors	590,000

1. Enter the five account balances in T-accounts.

2. Journalize each transaction.

3. Post the journal entries to T-accounts. Key each posting by transaction letter.

Required

3-39 Reconstructing Journal Entries, Posting

(Alternate is 3-40.) Dayton Hudson owns department stores and discount stores, including Target stores. A partial income statement from its annual report for the 1996 fiscal year showed the following actual numbers, nomenclature, and format (in millions):

Net sales	$25,025
Interest and other income	346
	25,371
Costs and expenses:	
Cost of retail sales, buying, and occupancy	18,628
Selling, publicity, and administrative	4,289
Interest expense, net	442
Other expenses	1,229
	24,588
Earnings before income taxes	$ 783

1. Prepare six summary journal entries for the given data. Label your entries *a* through *f.* Omit explanations. For simplicity, assume that all transactions (except for cost of products sold) were for cash. One fourth of the cost of retail sales, buying, and occupancy was paid in cash. The other three-fourths represented a decrease in inventories.

2. Post to a ledger for all affected accounts. Key your postings by transaction letter.

3-40 Reconstructing Journal Entries, Posting

(Alternate is 3-39.) Linens 'n Things is a specialty retailer with more than 170 stores throughout the United States. A partial income statement from its annual report for the 1996 fiscal year showed the following actual numbers and nomenclature (in millions):

Net sales		$ 696
Cost and expenses:		
Cost of sales	$ 426	
Selling, general, and administrative expenses	239	
Interest expense	5	
Total costs and expenses		670
Earnings before income taxes		$ 26

1. Prepare four summary journal entries for the given data. Label your entries *a* through *d.* Omit explanations. For simplicity, assume that all transactions except for cost of sales were for cash.

2. Post to a ledger for all affected accounts. Key your postings by transaction letter.

3-41 Plant Assets and Accumulated Depreciation

Georgia-Pacific, the pulp, paper, and building products company, had the following in its 1996 annual report (in millions):

Total property, plant, and equipment, at cost	$13,733
Accumulated Depreciation	7,173
Property, Plant, and Equipment, Net	$ 6,560

1. Open T-accounts for (a) Property, Plant, and Equipment; (b) Accumulated Depreciation, Property, Plant, and Equipment; and (c) Depreciation Expense. Enter the above amounts into the T-accounts.

2. Assume that in 1997 no assets were purchased or sold. Depreciation expense for 1997 was $600 million. Prepare the journal entry, and post to the T-accounts.

3. Prepare the property, plant, and equipment section of Georgia-Pacific's balance sheet at the end of 1997.

4. Land comprises $408 million of Georgia-Pacific's property, plant, and equipment, and land is not depreciated. Comment on the age of the company's depreciable assets (that is, all property, plant, and equipment except land) at the end of 1996.

3-42 Management Incentives, Financial Statements, and Ethics

Juanita Reynolds was controller of the San Leandro Electronic Components (SLEC) division of a major medical instruments company. On December 30, 1998, Reynolds prepared a preliminary income statement and compared it with the 1998 budget:

San Leandro Electronic Components Division
Income Statement for the Year Ended
December 31, 1998 (in thousands)

	Budget	Preliminary Actual
Sales revenues	$1,200	$1,600
Cost of goods sold	600	800
Gross margin	600	800
Other operating expenses	450	500
Operating income	$ 150	$ 300

The top managers of each division had a bonus plan that paid each a 10% bonus if operating income exceeded budgeted income by more than 20%. It was obvious to Reynolds that the SLEC division had easily exceeded the $180,000 of operating income needed for a bonus. In fact, she wondered if it wouldn't be desirable to reduce operating income this year—after all, the higher the income this year, the higher top management is likely to set the budget next year. Besides, if some of December's sales could just be held back and recorded in January, the division would have a running start on next year.

Reynolds had always been a team player, and she saw holding back sales as the best strategy for her team of managers. Therefore, she recorded only $1,500,000 of sales in 1995—the other $100,000 was recorded as January 1999 sales. Operating income for 1995 then became $250,000 and there was a head start of $50,000 on 1999's operating income.

Comment on the ethical implications of Reynold's decision.

Required

3-43 The Gap Annual Report

This problem helps to develop skill in recording transactions by using an actual company's account titles. Refer to the financial statements of The Gap in Appendix A at the end of the book. Note the following summarized items from the income statement for the year ended February 1, 1997 (in millions):

Net sales		$5,284
Cost of goods sold and occupancy expenses	$3,285	
Operating expenses	1,270	
Net interest income	(19)	4,536
Earnings before income taxes		$ 748

Required

1. Prepare four summary journal entries for the given data. Use The Gap account titles and label your entries *a* through *d*. Omit explanations. For simplicity, assume that all transactions (except for cost of goods sold) were for cash. Assume that 60% of the $3,285 million cost of goods sold and occupancy expenses was for cost of goods sold and 40% was for occupancy expenses.

2. Post to a ledger for all affected accounts. Key your postings by transaction letter.

3-44 Financial Statement Research

Select the financial statements of any company.

1. Prepare an income statement in the following format:

   Total sales (or revenues)
   Cost of goods sold
   Gross margin
   Other expenses
   Income before income taxes

   Be sure that all revenues are included in the first line and that all expenses (except income taxes) are included in either Cost of goods sold or Other expenses.

2. Prepare three summary journal entries for the income statement data you prepared. Use the given account titles and label your entries *a, b,* and *c.* Omit explanations. For simplicity, assume that all "Other expenses" were paid in cash.

3. Post to a ledger for all affected accounts. Key your postings by transaction letter.

COLLABORATIVE LEARNING EXERCISE

3-45 Income Statement and Balance Sheet Accounts

Form teams of two persons each. Each person should make a list of 10 account names, with approximately half being income statement accounts and half being balance sheet accounts. Give the list to the other member of the team, who is to write beside each account name the financial statement (*I* for income statement or *B* for balance sheet) on which it belongs. If there are errors or disagreements in classification, discuss the account and come to an agreement about which financial statement it belongs to.

3-46 Internet Case

Go to **http://www.sbaonline.sba.gov/** to find the U.S. Small Business Administration's home page.

Answer the following questions about the services provided by this government entity to anyone interested in starting or running a small business:

1. Select *Starting* from the main menu, then *Your First Steps.* Starting a new business goes beyond just the ability to create and sell a product or service. What are the four steps of a business plan? How does accounting fit in?

2. Select *Business Plans* from the *Starting Your Business* menu. A business plan involves projections of amounts that will later appear on financial statements. What three financial statements are projected? How could this information be helpful?

3. Select *Business Plans* from the *Starting Your Business* menu. Is it necessary for a business to plan the type of accounting system before operations begin? Why or why not?

4. Select *Business Plans* from the *Starting Your Business* menu. Go to *Appendix 2.* Where does a company find the accounts used on the balance sheet in its accounting records? What accounts given for the balance sheet have normal credit balances? What does the account name, "net worth," mean?

5. Select *Shareware Programs* from the *Starting Your Business* menu. Over 500 free, public-domain software programs are available for starting, running, or expanding a business. Select *Table of Contents,* then select the listing of programs called,

Files for Financing Your Business. Write the titles/names of three programs that would probably contain a general ledger.

6. Download and install one of the programs you selected in part 5 above. Open the program and make sure it does contain a general ledger system. Enter two or three transactions from your text. How does this software program refine your data processing as compared to a manual system? How will the output of data from the journals and ledgers in the software program differ from a manual system? (Note: If you are using a networked computer lab, consult your instructor prior to doing this.)

Chapter

4

USING FINANCIAL STATEMENTS

Lands' End rugby shirts symbolize comfortable fashion and fit, by mail order, at a profit.

Learning Objectives

After studying this chapter, you should be able to

1 Make adjustments for the expiration or consumption of assets.

2 Make adjustments for the earning of unearned revenues.

3 Make adjustments for the accrual of unrecorded expenses.

4 Make adjustments for the accrual of unrecorded revenues.

5 Describe the sequence of the final steps in the recording process and relate cash flows to adjusting entries.

6 Prepare a classified balance sheet and use it to assess solvency.

7 Prepare single- and multiple-step income statements and use ratios to assess profitability.

8 Relate Generally Accepted Accounting Principles (GAAP) to the accounting practices we have learned.

Chances are you or someone you know is one of the eight million customers who have purchased something from Lands' End, the Wisconsin-based mail-order company. Selling clothes from socks to winter coats, from business suits and dresses to rain boots, Lands' End has built up a great reputation based on quality, affordable prices, and excellent customer service—factors that concern, and have won over, discerning shoppers. Lands' End managers are also concerned about these factors, and they take pride in their high ratings for customer satisfaction. But customer satisfaction alone doesn't pay their salaries, so managers also want to know whether the company is making a profit. Do managers have to turn to complicated equations and formulas to figure out the company's profit? No, they can turn to Lands' End's financial statements—just as we can.

Information in Lands' End financial statements comes straight from the company's financial accounting system. Lands' End has a financial accounting system that provides information about the company's financial success. And most important to managers, it also provides detailed information about the financial results of each product. As Don Hughes, Lands' End Vice President of Finance, says, "We record all the activities [of Lands' End] in the financial statements. We make decisions primarily from the financial information about individual products."

Suppose you want to buy Lands' End stock instead of their clothes. Then you, too, would be interested in the company's financial statements. You would want to know the company's financial position and prospects to judge whether it is wise to invest in Lands' End stock. You need to understand the fundamentals of financial accounting if you want to read and understand Lands' End financial statements and compare them to the statements of other companies.

Entities as large as IBM or Exxon and as small as Rosa Mexicana use accrual accounting and must make adjusting entries before preparing financial statements. Accountants in nonprofit as well as for-profit organizations, and accountants in France, Kenya, China, and every other country in the world, must be able to apply the adjustment procedures and techniques discussed in this chapter.

ADJUSTMENTS TO THE ACCOUNTS

Objective 1
Make adjustments for the expiration or consumption of assets.

explicit transactions Events such as cash receipts and disbursements, credit purchases, and credit sales that trigger nearly all day-to-day routine entries.

implicit transactions Events (such as the passage of time) that are temporarily ignored in day-to-day recording procedures and are recognized via end-of-period adjustments.

adjustments (adjusting entries) End of period entries that assign the financial effects of implicit transactions to the appropriate time periods.

accrue To accumulate a receivable or payable during a given period even though no explicit transaction occurs.

We have already seen how most transactions are normally recorded in journals and ledgers. The majority of a company's transactions are recorded when they occur. However, some transactions are just a little trickier to handle. In fact, they might not even seem like transactions at all and are recognized only at the end of an accounting period. The difference between these transactions and normal transactions stems from how obvious or explicit they are.

Explicit transactions are obvious events, such as cash receipts and disbursements, credit purchases, and credit sales. For every explicit transaction, you can easily show that something has happened and must be recorded in a routine day-to-day entry. Recording explicit transactions is straightforward. Entries for such transactions are supported by source documents (for example, sales slips, purchase invoices, and employee payroll checks) or other tangible evidence. Note that some explicit transactions do not involve actual exchanges of goods and services between the entity and another party. For instance, the losses of assets from fire or theft are also explicit transactions even though no market exchange occurs. In all cases, though, explicit transactions involve events that you know have happened.

Conversely, the events that trigger implicit transactions are not so obvious. **Implicit transactions** are events (such as the passage of time) that do not generate source documents or any visible evidence that the event actually happened. Because bookkeepers do not receive specific notification to record such events they are not formally recognized in the accounting records until the end of an accounting period. For example, entries for depreciation expense and expiration of prepaid rent are prepared at the end of an accounting period from special schedules or memorandums, not because an explicit event occurred. You cannot point to an actual event that used up part of the rent asset, yet at the end of the month you must make an entry showing the expiration of a month's worth of rent.

The end-of-period entries used to acknowledge these implicit events are known as adjustments. These **adjustments** (also called **adjusting entries,**) help assign the financial effects of implicit transactions to the appropriate time periods. Thus, adjustments are made at periodic intervals, usually when the financial statements are about to be prepared. The adjustments are made in the form of journal entries that are recorded in the general journal and then posted to the general ledger. After recognizing these adjustments for implicit transactions, the balances in the general ledger accounts will be updated through the end of the period and can be used for preparing financial statements.

Adjusting entries are at the heart of accrual accounting. **Accrue** means to accumulate a receivable (asset) or payable (liability) during a given period even though no explicit transaction occurs. The receivables or payables grow as the clock ticks, but nothing changes hands and no events are causing changes. Examples of accruals are the wages earned by employees for partial payroll periods and the interest earned on borrowed money before the interest payment date. Usually wage expense is recognized when wages are paid. But if wages are paid every Friday and the accounting period ends on Wednesday, a problem arises. Three days of wages have been earned but not recorded. The accrual adjusting entry for wages payable corrects this. Because accruals are not based on explicit transactions, they are not recorded on a day-to-day basis. Thus adjusting entries need to be made at the end of each period to recognize unrecorded, but relevant accruals.

Adjustments are essential for understanding the logic behind accounts because they help in the matching of revenues and expenses to a particular period. For example, consider the $5 million annual contract of a baseball star, such as Ken Griffey, Jr., or Barry Bonds, for the 1999 season. If all $5 million is paid in cash in 1999, it is an obvious explicit transaction. But suppose only $2 million is paid in cash and $3 million is deferred until 2000 or later. The $2 million cash payment is an explicit transaction and is recorded as an expense when the payment is made. Because no explicit transaction for the $3 million occurs during the period, it is not routinely entered into the accounting record. However, the entire $5 million contract was incurred for the benefit of the 1999 season, so the $3 million deferred payment is an expense for 1999 that arises because of an implicit transaction for the period. Thus, at the end of the period, when the 1999 financial statements are being prepared, an adjustment is necessary to record the deferred $3 million payment as an expense and to record a $3 million liability for its payment.

The principal adjustments arise from four basic types of implicit transactions:

I. Expiration of unexpired costs
II. Earning of revenues received in advance
III. Accrual of unrecorded expenses
IV. Accrual of unrecorded revenues

Let us now examine each of these categories in detail.

I. EXPIRATION OF UNEXPIRED COSTS

As you should recall from previous chapters, some costs expire because of the passage of time. For example, prepaid rent is used up in increments at the end of every month, until it is completely used (expires). As we have already seen, adjustments are made at the end of each month to mark the gradual expiration of these costs. Other examples of adjusting for asset expirations include the write-offs to expense of such assets as Office Supplies Inventory, Prepaid Fire Insurance, and even Depreciation Expense. Originally cash is paid and an asset is created. The adjustment recognizes an expense (debit an expense account) and reduces the corresponding asset (credits the account). The key characteristic of unexpired items is that an explicit transaction in the past has created an asset, and a subsequent implicit transaction serves to adjust the value of this asset.

Objective 2
Make adjustments for the earning of unearned revenues.

II. EARNING OF REVENUES RECEIVED IN ADVANCE

Just as some assets are acquired and then expire over time, some revenue is received and then earned over time. **Unearned revenue** (also called **revenue received in advance, deferred revenue** or **deferred credit**) is revenue that is received and recorded before it is earned. That is, payment is received in exchange for a commitment to provide services (or goods) at a later date.

The analysis of adjusting entries for unearned revenue is easier to understand if we visualize the financial positions of both parties to a contract. For example, recall the

unearned revenue (revenue received in advance, deferred revenue, deferred credit) Revenue received and recorded before it is earned.

Biwheels Company's January advance payment of $6,000 for three months' rent. Compare the financial impact on Biwheels Company with the impact on the owner of the property, who received the rental payment:

	Owner of Property (Landlord, Lessor)			Biwheels Company (Tenant, Lessee)		
	A =	L +	SE	A	= L +	SE
	Cash	Unearned Rent Revenue	Rent Revenue	Cash	Prepaid Rent	Rent Expense
(a) Explicit transaction (advance payment of three months' rent)	+6,000 =	+6,000		−6,000	+6,000 =	
(b) January adjustment (for one month's rent)	=	−2,000	+2,000		−2,000 =	−2,000
(c) February adjustment (for one month's rent)	=	−2,000	+2,000		−2,000 =	−2,000
(d) March adjustment (for one month's rent)	=	−2,000	+2,000		−2,000 =	−2,000

The journal entries for (a) and (b) follow:

OWNER (LANDLORD)

(a) Cash...	6,000	
Unearned rent revenue		6,000
(b) Unearned rent revenue..	2,000	
Rent revenue		2,000

BIWHEELS CO. (TENANT)

(a) Prepaid rent	6,000	
Cash..		6,000
(b) Rent expense...	2,000	
Prepaid rent...		2,000

(Entries for (c) and (d) are the same as for (b).)

We are already familiar with the analysis from Biwheels' point of view. The $2,000 monthly entries for Biwheels are examples of the first type of adjustments, the expiration of a prepaid asset. From the viewpoint of the owner of the rental property, though, transaction (a) recognizes the receipt of unearned revenue. The balancing amount for the increase in cash is recorded in a liability account because the lessor is now obligated to deliver the rental services (or to refund the money if the services are not delivered). Sometimes this account is called Rent Collected in Advance rather than Unearned Rent Revenue, as in our example. Regardless of its title, it is an unearned revenue type of liability account. That is, it is revenue collected in advance that has not yet been earned.

Notice that transaction (a) does not affect stockholders' equity because it does not recognize any revenue. The revenue is recognized (earned) only when the adjusting entries are made in transactions (b), (c), and (d). That is, as the liability Unearned Rent Revenue is decreased (debited), the stockholders' equity account Rent Revenue is increased (credited). The net effect is an increase in stockholders' equity at the time the revenue is recognized.

By looking at both sides of the Biwheels rent contract, you should see that adjustment categories I and II are really mirror images of each other. If a contract causes one party to have a prepaid expense, it must cause the other party to have an unearned revenue. This basic relationship holds for any prepayment situation, from a three-year fire insurance policy to a three-year magazine subscription. The buyer—we will use the mag-

Franchises and Revenue Recognition

In a franchise arrangement, a central organization, such as McDonald's or the National Basketball Association, sells the right to use the company name and company products to a franchisee. The franchisee also receives the benefit of advertising through the larger company, along with management assistance and product development. There are more than 500,000 franchise outlets of various types in the United States, with sales totaling more than $700 billion.

Franchising raises an interesting accounting problem. How does the central organization account for the franchise fees? At first glance, it might seem clear that such fees should be recorded as revenue. However, under accrual accounting, revenue should be recorded only after two conditions have been satisfied: (1) The "work" has been completed (that is, it has been earned), and (2) there is reasonable assurance the fee can be collected (it is realized in cash or will be collectible).

Jiffy Lube, a subsidiary of Pennzoil Company, is a franchisor of fast oil-change centers and provides an example of receipt of franchise fees before the related work is performed. Jiffy Lube sells its franchisees area development rights, which grant the franchisee the exclusive right to develop Jiffy Lube outlets in a certain area. In return for these rights, Jiffy Lube receives an upfront fee. Should Jiffy Lube record the fee as revenue? No, because Jiffy Lube's work is not done until the franchisee actually opens the outlets. In the interim, Jiffy Lube must report the fees as unearned revenue.

Porta-John, which acquires chemical toilets and sells the right to service the toilets to franchisees, illustrates the second condition. The franchisees agree to pay Porta-John an upfront fee. However, only 10% of the fee is collected in cash, and historically, franchisees have taken up to 10 years to pay the remainder of the fee. The fact is that many of the franchisees don't stick with the portable toilet business for very long (their money goes down the toilet, as it were), so there is no assurance that the total fee can be collected. Accordingly, Porta-John is required to account for the fees using the cash basis, reporting revenue only as the franchise fees are actually received in cash.

---

azine buyer here—recognizes a prepaid expense (asset) and uses adjustments to spread the initial cost to an expense account over the useful life of the subscription. In turn, the seller, the magazine publisher, must initially record its liability, Unearned Subscription Revenue, on receipt of payment for the three-year subscription. For example, the publisher of *Time* magazine showed a liability of more than $670 million as of January 1, 1998, calling it Unearned Portion of Paid Subscriptions. The unearned revenue of this liability is then systematically recognized as earned revenue when magazines are delivered throughout the life of the subscription. The following diagrams show that the initial explicit cash transactions in such situations are recorded as balance sheet items but, thanks to periodic adjustments for the implicit transactions, are later transformed into income statement items:

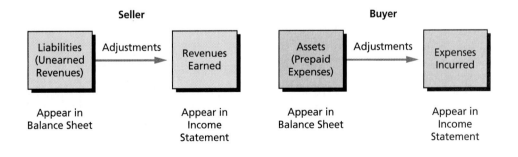

Unearned revenues are essentially advances from customers who have paid for goods or services to be delivered at a future date. For instance, airlines often require advance payments for special-fare tickets. American Airlines showed a recent balance of more than $2.0 billion in an unearned revenue account labeled Air Traffic Liability.

III. ACCRUAL OF UNRECORDED EXPENSES

It is awkward and unnecessary to make hourly, daily, or even weekly formal recordings in the accounts for many accrued expenses. Remember, these expenses continually grow over the length of a given period, so the cost of such frequent recording would certainly exceed the benefits. This is true, even though computers can perform these tasks somewhat effortlessly. The costs of computing may be small, but the benefits are even smaller. These balances are only important when we prepare financial statements and this rarely needs to be done hourly or daily. Consequently, adjustments are made to bring each accrued expense (and corresponding liability) account up to date at the end of the period, just before the formal financial statements are prepared in order to match the expense to the period.

ACCOUNTING FOR PAYMENT OF WAGES

Consider wages. Most companies pay their employees at predetermined times. Here is a sample calendar for January:

January						
S	M	T	W	T	F	S
	1	2	3	4	5	6
7	8	9	10	11	12	13
14	15	16	17	18	19	20
21	22	23	24	25	26	27
28	29	30	31			

The Calvin Corporation, for example, pays its employees each Friday for services rendered during that week. Thus, wages paid on January 26 are compensation for the week ended January 26 and wage expense accrues for an entire week before it is finally paid. The cumulative total wages paid on the four Fridays during January amount to $20,000, or $5,000 per five-day workweek, or $1,000 per day. Calvin Corp. would make routine entries for wage payments at the end of each week in January. As wages were paid, wage expense would be recorded while cash was decreased. During the January shown in the preceding calendar, wages would be paid on the 5th, 12th, 19th, and 26th. These events were explicit transactions, driven by writing a payroll check. At the end of January, the balance sheet shows the summarized amounts and their effect on the accounting equation:

	Assets A	=	Liabilities L	+	Stockholders' Equity SE
	Cash				Wages Expense
(a) Routine entries for explicit transactions	−20,000	=			−20,000

ACCOUNTING FOR ACCRUAL OF WAGES

Suppose that Calvin's accountant wishes to prepare financial statements at the end of January. In addition to the $20,000 actually paid to employees during the month, Calvin owes $3,000 for employee services rendered during the last three days of the month. The employees will not be paid for these services until Friday, February 2. To ensure an accurate accounting of wage expenses for the month of January, adjustments must be made to account for the accrual of these unrecorded wages, which are owed but not paid in January. Transaction (a) shows the total of the routine entries in the journal for the explicit wage payments made to employees, and transaction (b) shows the entries for the accrued wages.

```
(a) Wages expense ...........................   20,000
        Cash ..................................              20,000
(b) Wages expense ...........................    3,000
        Accrued wages payable ...................            3,000
```

The total effect of wages on the balance sheet equation for the month of January, including transactions (a) and (b), are as follows:

	A	=	L	+	SE
			Accrued Wages		Wages
	Cash		Payable		Expense
(a) Routine entries for explicit transactions	−20,000	=			−20,000
(b) Adjustment for implicit transaction, the accrual of unrecorded wages		=	+3,000		− 3,000
Total effects	−20,000	=	+3,000		−23,000

The adjustment in entry (b) is the first adjusting entry we have examined that shows an expense that is offset by an increase in a liability instead of a decrease in an asset. You can see that the accountant's problem is different for this type of accrual than for prepaid rent for example. With prepaid rent, there is a record in the accounts of an asset and the accountant might recognize the necessity for an adjustment by asking, is the balance shown on the books correct or is an adjustment required to reduce it? With accrued wages, the accountant's question is a little harder. Is there something that does not appear in the records at all that should appear there? Of course, most adjustments at the end of the period are routine. We know to check for used up rent and for accrued wages because we experience these items every period.

On February 2, the liability will be paid off, together with the wages expense for February 1 and 2:

```
Wages expense (February 1 and 2) ................   2,000
Accrued wages payable.........................   3,000
        Cash.....................................              5,000
(To record wages expense for February 1 and 2
and to pay wages for the week ended February 2.)
```

These entries clearly demonstrate the matching principle. The routine entries and the adjusting entries match the wage expenses to the periods in which they help generate revenues.

ACCRUAL OF INTEREST

Other examples of accrued expenses include sales commissions, property taxes, income taxes, and interest paid on borrowed money. You can think of interest as "rent" paid for the use of money, just as rent is paid for the use of buildings. The interest accumulates (accrues) as time unfolds, regardless of when the actual cash for interest is paid.

Suppose Calvin Corporation borrowed $100,000 on December 31, 19X1. The loan is for one year with interest at 9%. This means that on December 31, 19X2, Calvin must repay the lender the $100,000 that was borrowed plus interest. Interest for one year is calculated as follows:

$$\text{Principal} \times \text{interest rate} \times \text{fraction of a year} = \text{interest}$$
$$\$100,000 \times .09 \quad\quad \times 1 = \$9,000$$

Principal is the amount borrowed ($100,000). The interest rate is expressed as an annual percentage (.09). The time is recorded as the fraction of a year (1 for a full year).

As of January 31, Calvin has had the benefit of a $100,000 bank loan for one month. Calvin owes the bank for the use of this money, and the amount owed has been accruing for the entire month of January. The amount owed is $1/12 \times 0.09 \times \$100,000 = \$750$. (Note: We multiply the interest rate and the principal by 1/12 because the interest rate is for an entire year, and here we are calculating the interest paid for one month, or 1/12 of a year.) The monthly benefit from the loan, is $750. Because it has already been acquired and used up for January, an adjusting entry is required for the month of January. The interest is not actually due to be paid until December 31, 19X1, but at the end of January, there is a liability for one month of Accrued Interest Payable. The adjustment is analyzed and recorded in a fashion similar to the adjustment for accrued wages:

	A	=	L	+	SE
			Accrued Interest Payable		*Interest Expense*
Adjustment to accrue January interest not yet recorded		=	+750		−750

The adjusting journal entry is:

Interest expense	750	
Accrued interest payable		750

At the end of January, Calvin Corporation owes the bank $100,750, not $100,000. The adjusting entry matches the $750 interest expense with the period in which it occurred. If the adjusting entry is omitted, liabilities will be understated for January.

ACCRUAL OF INCOME TAXES

As income is generated, income tax expense is accrued. Income taxes exist worldwide, although rates and details differ from country to country and from state to state. Corporations in the United States are subject to federal and state corporate income taxes. For many corporations, the federal-plus-state income tax rates hover around 40%. Thus, for every dollar of income a company makes, it accrues forty cents worth of income tax expense. Of course, this forty cents is not paid out as each dollar comes in. Instead, it accrues over the period, and an adjustment is made at the end of the period when the financial statements are prepared.

Companies use various labels to denote income taxes on their income statements: income tax expense, provision for income taxes, and just plain income taxes are found most frequently. For multinational firms, income tax expense may include tax obligations in every country in which they operate. In preparing their income statements, about 85% of publicly held U.S. companies calculate a subtotal called income before taxes and then show income taxes as a separate income statement item just before net income. This arrangement is logical because income tax expense is based on income before taxes. **Pretax income** is a synonym for income before taxes. In contrast, the other 15% list income taxes along with other operating expenses such as wages. The 1996 McDonald's annual report contains the format adopted by the vast majority of companies:

pretax income Income before income taxes.

Income before provision for income taxes	$2,251,000,000
Provision for income taxes	678,400,000
Net income	$1,572,600,000

IV. ACCRUAL OF UNRECORDED REVENUES

Just as the realization of unearned revenues was the mirror image of the expiration of unexpired costs, the accrual of unrecorded revenues is the mirror image of the accrual of unrecorded expenses. The adjusting entries show the recognition of revenues that have been earned but not yet received. Because no payment has occurred, nothing has been entered in the accounts. According to the revenue recognition principle, revenues affect stockholders' equity in the period they are earned, not the period in which they are received. Thus an adjustment is required.

Objective 4
Make adjustments for
the accrual of
unrecorded revenues.

Suppose First National Bank had loaned the $100,000 to Calvin. As of January 31, First National Bank has earned $750 on the loan. The following tabulations show the mirror-image effect:

	First National Bank, as a Lender				Calvin, as a Borrower			
	A	= L +	SE	A	=	L	+	SE
	Accrued Interest Receivable		Interest Revenue			Accrued Interest Payable		Interest Expense
January interest	+750	=	+750		=	+750		−750

Other examples of accrued revenues and receivables include "unbilled" fees. For example, attorneys, public accountants, physicians, and advertising agencies may earn hourly fees during a particular month but not send out bills to their clients until the completion of an entire contract or engagement. Under the accrual basis of accounting, such revenues should be recorded in the month in which they were earned rather than at a later time. Suppose an attorney renders $10,000 of services during January, but will not bill for these services until March 31. Before the attorney's financial statements can be prepared for January, an adjustment for unrecorded revenue for the month must be made:

	A	=	L	+	SE
	Accrued (Unbilled) Fees Receivable				Fee Revenue
Adjustment for fees earned	+10,000	=			+10,000

Utility companies often recognize unbilled revenues for services provided but not yet billed. In fact, American Water Works Company, a utility that provides water supply services to more than 1.6 million customers in 20 states, includes more unbilled revenues than accounts receivable among its current assets:

Customer accounts receivable	$46,795,000
Unbilled revenues	57,298,000

THE ADJUSTING PROCESS IN PERSPECTIVE

Chapter 3 presented the various steps in the recording process as follows:

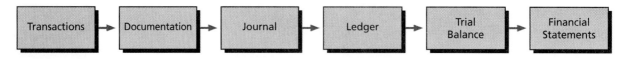

This process has a final aim: the preparation of accurate financial statements prepared on the accrual basis. To accomplish this goal, the process must include adjusting entries to record implicit transactions. When we consider the adjustments, the final steps in the recording process can be divided further as follows:

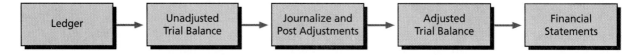

Objective 5
Describe the sequence of the final steps in the recording process and relate cash flows to adjusting entries.

Each adjusting entry affects at least one income statement account—a revenue or an expense—and one balance sheet account—an asset or a liability. No adjusting entry debits or credits cash. Why? Because cash transactions are explicit transactions that are routinely recorded as they happen. The end-of-period adjustment process is reserved for the implicit transactions that must be recognized by the accrual basis of accounting. Exhibit 4-1 summarizes the major adjusting entries.

Cash flows (that is, explicit transactions of cash receipts or disbursements) may precede or follow the adjusting entry that recognizes the related revenue or expense. The accompanying diagrams underscore the basic differences between the cash flows and the accrual accounting entries.

Entries for adjustments I and II, expiration of unexpired costs and realization of unearned revenues, are usually made subsequent to the cash flows. For example, the cash received or disbursed for rent had an initial impact on the balance sheet. The adjustment process was used to show the later impact on the income statement.

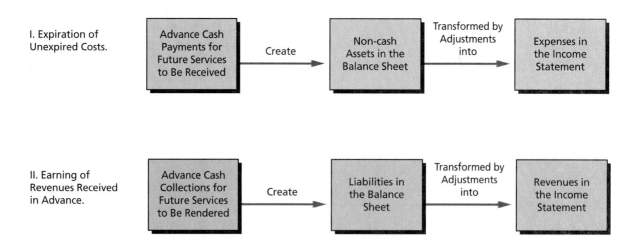

Entries for adjustments III and IV, accrual of unrecorded expenses and accrual of unrecorded revenues, are made before the related cash flows. The income statement is affected before the cash receipts and disbursements occur. The accounting entity must compute the amount of goods or services provided or received prior to any cash receipt or payment.

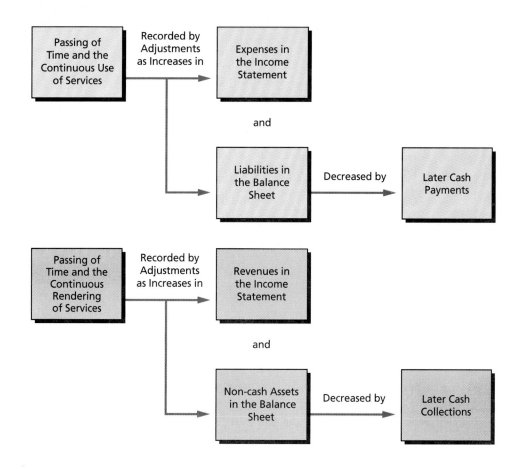

Exhibit 4-1

Summary of Adjusting Entries

Adjusting Entry	Type of Account Debited	Type of Account Credited
I. Expiration of unexpired costs	Expense	Prepaid Expense, Accumulated Depreciation
II. Earning of revenues received in advance	Unearned Revenue	Revenue
III. Accrual of unrecorded expenses	Expense	Payable
IV. Accrual of unrecorded revenues	Receivable	Revenue

SUMMARY PROBLEM FOR YOUR REVIEW

PROBLEM ONE

Chan Audio Co. is a retailer of stereo equipment. Chan Audio has been in business one month. The company's unadjusted trial balance, January 31, 19X2, has the following accounts:

Cash	$ 71,700	
Accounts receivable	160,300	
Note receivable	40,000	
Merchandise inventory	250,200	
Prepaid rent	15,000	
Store equipment	114,900	
Note payable		$100,000
Accounts payable		117,100
Unearned rent revenue		3,000
Paid-in capital		400,000
Sales		160,000
Cost of goods sold	100,000	
Wages expense	28,000	
Total	$780,100	$780,100

Consider the following adjustments on January 31:

a. January depreciation, $1,000.

b. On January 2, rent of $15,000 was paid in advance for the first quarter of 19X2, as shown by the debit balance in the Prepaid Rent account. Adjust for January rent.

c. Wages earned by employees during January but not paid as of January 31 were $3,750.

d. Chan borrowed $100,000 from the bank on January 1. This explicit transaction was recorded when the business began, as shown by the credit balance in the Note Payable account. The principal and 9% interest are to be paid one year later (January 1, 19X3). However, an adjustment is necessary now for the interest expense of $1/12 \times 0.09 \times \$100,000 = \$750$ for January.

e. On January 1, a cash loan of $40,000 was made to a local supplier, as shown by the debit balance in the Note Receivable account. The promissory note stated that the loan is to be repaid one year later (January 1, 19X3), together with interest at 12% per annum. On January 31, an adjustment is needed to recognize the interest earned on the note receivable.

f. On January 15, a nearby corporation paid $3,000 cash to Chan Audio Co. as an advance rental for Chan's storage space and equipment to be used temporarily from January 15 to April 15 (three months). This $3,000 is the credit balance in the Unearned Revenue account. On January 31, an adjustment is needed to recognize the rent revenue earned for one-half month.

g. Income tax expense was accrued on January income at a rate of 50% of income before taxes.

1. Enter the trial-balance amounts in the general ledger. Set up the new asset account, Accrued Interest Receivable, and the new asset-reduction account, the contra account, Accumulated Depreciation, Store Equipment. Set up the following new liability accounts: Accrued Wages Payable, Accrued Interest Payable, and Accrued Income Taxes Payable. Set up the following new expense and revenue accounts: Depreciation Expense, Rent Expense, Interest Expense, Interest Revenue, Rent Revenue, and Income Tax Expense.

2. Journalize adjustments a–g and post the entries to the ledger. Key entries by transaction letter.

3. Prepare an adjusted trial balance as of January 31, 19X2.

Exhibit 4-2

Chan Audio Co.

Journal Entries

(a)	Depreciation expense	1,000	
	Accumulated depreciation, store equipment		1,000
	Depreciation for January.		
(b)	Rent expense	5,000	
	Prepaid rent		5,000
	Rent expense for January.		
(c)	Wages expense	3,750	
	Accrued wages payable		3,750
	Wages earned but not paid.		
(d)	Interest expense	750	
	Accrued interest payable		750
	Interest for January.		
(e)	Accrued interest receivable	400	
	Interest revenue		400
	Interest earned for January:		
	$\frac{1}{12} \times \$40,000 \times .12 = \$400$.		
(f)	Unearned rent revenue	500	
	Rent revenue		500
	Rent earned for January. Rent per month is		
	$\$3,000 \div 3 = \$1,000$; for one-half month, $\$500$.		
(g)	Income tax expense	11,200	
	Accrued income taxes payable		11,200
	Income tax on January income:		
	$.50 \times [160,000 + 400 + 500 - 100,000 - 31,750 - 1,000 - 5,000 - 750]$		

SOLUTION TO PROBLEM ONE

The solutions to requirements 1 through 3 are in Exhibits 4-2, 4-3, and 4-4. Accountants often refer to the final trial balance, Exhibit 4-4, as the adjusted trial balance. Why? Because all the necessary adjustments have been made, thus the trial balance provides the data necessary for creating the formal financial statements.

CLASSIFIED BALANCE SHEET

Objective 6
Prepare a classified balance sheet and use it to assess solvency.

As we have seen throughout this book thus far, accounts are listed on the balance sheet according to the major categories of assets, liabilities, and owners' equity. A **classified balance sheet** further groups the accounts into subcategories to help readers quickly gain a perspective on the company's financial position. The classifications help to draw attention to certain amounts or groups of accounts. Assets are frequently classified into two groupings: current assets and long-term assets. Liabilities are similarly classified into current liabilities and long-term liabilities. This distinction is useful in assessing the company's ability to meet obligations as they fall due. For the most part, current assets will give rise to the cash needed to pay current liabilities, so the relationship between these categories is important. In this section we concentrate on these current elements and on a ratio that is useful in analyzing them.

classified balance sheet A balance sheet that groups the accounts into subcategories to help readers quickly gain a perspective on the company's financial position.

CURRENT ASSETS AND LIABILITIES

Current assets are cash and those other assets that are expected to be converted to cash, sold, or consumed during the next twelve months (or within the normal operating cycle if longer than a year). Similarly, **current liabilities** are those liabilities that fall due within the coming year (or within the normal operating cycle if longer than a year).

Exhibit 4-3

Chan Audio Co.

General Ledger

Assets	=	Liabilities + Stockholders' Equity
(Increases Left, Decreases Right)		(Decreases Left, Increases Right)

Cash

Bal. 71,700	

Accounts Receivable

Bal. 160,300	

Note Receivable

Bal. 40,000	

Merchandise Inventory

Bal. 250,200	

Prepaid Rent

Bal. 15,000	(b) 5,000
Bal. 10,000	

Store Equipment

Bal. 114,900	

Accumulated Depreciation, Store Equipment

	(a) 1,000

Accrued Interest Receivable

(e) 400	

Note Payable

	Bal. 100,000

Accounts Payable

	Bal. 117,100

Unearned Rent Revenue

(f) 500	Bal. 3,000
	Bal. 2,500

Accrued Wages Payable

	(c) 3,750

Accrued Interest Payable

	(d) 750

Accrued Income Tax Payable

	(g) 11,200

Paid-in Capital

	Bal. 400,000

Sales

	Bal. 160,000

Cost of Goods Sold

Bal. 100,000	

Wages Expense

Bal. 28,000	
(c) 3,750	
Bal. 31,750	

Depreciation Expense

(a) 1,000	

Rent Expense

(b) 5,000	

Interest Expense

(d) 750	

Interest Revenue

	(e) 400

Rent Revenue

	(f) 500

Income Tax Expense

(g) 11,200	

current assets Cash plus assets that are expected to be converted to cash or sold or consumed during the next twelve months or within the normal operating cycle if longer than a year.

current liabilities Liabilities that fall due within the coming year or within the normal operating cycle if longer than a year.

Exhibit 4-5 shows the classified balance sheet for Chan Audio Company, which is prepared from the adjusted trial balance for the company (shown in Exhibit 4-4). On the classified balance sheet, the current asset accounts are generally listed in the order in which they will be converted to cash during the coming year. Cash is thus listed first because it is, obviously, already in the form of cash. Accounts Receivable are listed next because cash payments for these accounts should be received within weeks or months. Note Receivable and Accrued Interest Receivable, which are listed as the third and fourth accounts, will be converted to cash by the end of the year. Nonmonetary assets, such as inventories and prepaid expenses (in this case, Merchandise Inventory and Prepaid Rent) are usually listed last in the current assets section of the balance sheet. Prepaid Rent is never expected to be converted to cash, but it is a current asset in the sense that it reduces the obligation to pay cash within the next year.

Exhibit 4-4

Chan Audio Co.

Adjusted Trial Balance January 31, 19X2

Account Title	Balance		
	Debit	*Credit*	
Cash	$ 71,700		
Accounts receivable	160,300		
Note receivable	40,000		
Merchandise inventory	250,200		
Prepaid rent	10,000		
Store equipment	114,900		
Accumulated depreciation, store equipment		$ 1,000	Balance
Accrued interest receivable	400		Sheet
Note payable		100,000	Exhibit 4-5
Accounts payable		117,100	
Unearned rent revenue		2,500	
Accrued wages payable		3,750	
Accrued interest payable		750	
Accrued income taxes payable		11,200	
Paid-in capital		400,000	
Sales		160,000	
Cost of goods sold	100,000		
Wages expense	31,750		
Depreciation expense	1,000		
Rent expense	5,000		Income
Interest expense	750		Statement,
Interest revenue		400	Exhibit 4-8
Rent revenue		500	
Income tax expense	11,200		
Total	$797,200	$797,200	

As shown in Exhibit 4-5, current liability accounts are also listed in the approximate order in which they will draw on, or decrease, cash during the coming year. Wages tend to be paid weekly or monthly, while interest tends to be paid monthly, quarterly or annually and taxes are also paid monthly, quarterly or annually.

The excess of current assets over current liabilities is known as **working capital.** In the case of the Chan Audio Company, the working capital on January 31, 19X2, is $297,300 ($532,600 − $235,300). The number is important because it connects assets and liabilities. Working capital should be proportional to the size of the firm and is normally evaluated with the current ratio.

working capital The excess of current assets over current liabilities.

CURRENT RATIO

Current assets tell you how much cash a company will have on hand in the near future, current liabilities tell you how much debt the company will have to pay off with that cash in the near future. Comparing the two amounts can help readers of financial statements assess a business entity's **solvency,** which is its ability to meet its immediate financial obligations with cash and near-cash assets as those obligations become due. The **current ratio** (also called the **working capital ratio**), which is calculated by dividing current assets by current liabilities, is widely used to evaluate solvency. Chan Audio's current ratio, for example, is:

solvency An entity's ability to meet its immediate financial obligations as they become due.

current ratio (working capital ratio) Current assets divided by current liabilities.

$$\text{Current ratio} = \frac{\text{Current assets}}{\text{Current liabilities}} = \frac{\$532,600}{\$235,300} = 2.3$$

Exhibit 4-5

Chan Audio Co.

Balance Sheet, January 31, 19X2

Assets			Liabilities and Owners' Equity		
Current assets:			Current liabilities:		
Cash		$ 71,700	Note payable		$100,000
Accounts receivable		160,300	Accounts payable		117,100
Note receivable		40,000	Unearned rent revenue		2,500
Accrued interest receivable		400	Accrued wages payable		3,750
Merchandise inventory		250,200	Accrued interest payable		750
Prepaid rent		10,000	Accrued income taxes payable		11,200
Total current assets		$532,600	Total current liabilities		$235,300
Long-term asset:			Stockholders' equity:		
Store equipment	$114,900		Paid-in capital	$400,000	
Accumulated			Retained income	11,200	411,200
depreciation	1,000	113,900			
Total		$646,500	Total		$646,500

Other things being equal, the higher the current ratio, the more assurance creditors have about being paid in full and on time. Conversely, a current ratio that is too high may indicate excessive holdings of cash, accounts receivable, or inventories. Excessive holdings of this nature are bad for a company because it ties up money that could be more effectively used elsewhere. Analysts will compare a company's current ratio with those of past years and with those of similar companies to make judgments about the company's solvency.

An old rule of thumb was that the current ratio should be greater than 2.0. However, today current ratios are more commonly close to one. One useful assessment can be made by comparing a company's current ratio with the average in its industry. For example, recently IBM's ratio was 1.2, compared with an industry average of 1.7. While below the average, IBM's ratio is certainly not a cause for concern. Microsoft's current ratio of 5.1 was more than four times as large as IBM's. Microsoft is a rapidly growing firm that continues to use cash to fund acquisitions of other firms. This high current ratio in Microsoft's case just emphasizes the fact that Microsoft generates high volumes of cash and tends to use it to grow the business by investing in new technology and buying other companies. Utilities often have low current ratios because of low inventories and stable cash flows. For example, NYNEX, the telephone company in New York and New England, has a current ratio of only 0.6.

Although the current ratio is widely used as a measure of short-term debt-paying ability, a budget (prediction) of cash receipts and disbursements is more useful. Whether a company's level of cash is too low or too high really depends on the predictions of operating requirements over the coming months. For example, a company such as a small comic book and baseball card retailer might need very little cash on hand because upcoming debts and operating needs will be small in the next few months. Conversely, Marvel Comics, the corporation that produces the comic books sold at the small retailer, might need hundreds of thousands of dollars worth of cash to meet upcoming debt and short-term operating needs. As a rule, companies should try to keep as little cash as possible on hand because intelligent management calls for trying to invest any temporary excess cash to generate additional income.

FORMATS OF BALANCE SHEETS

The particular details and formats of balance sheets and other financial statements vary among companies. Yet, all balance sheets contain the same basic information, regardless

Managing Working Capital

The traditional view is that large amounts of working capital and high current ratios are good—they show that a company is likely to remain solvent. However, maintaining solvency is not as big a problem for most companies as is generating profits. Large amounts of working capital may needlessly tie up funds that could profitably be used elsewhere in the company.

The main components of working capital for the typical company are accounts receivable plus inventories less accounts payable. In the 1990s, building inventories and accounts receivable fell out of fashion. Each dollar not invested in working capital is a dollar of free cash available for investing in value-adding activities—activities that actually create and deliver products or services to customers. In addition, there is another downside to large accounts receivable or inventories. Receivables may grow because of increasing sales, but they can also zoom upward when collection of receivables slows down. Soaring inventories may mean increased ability to deliver orders on time. They may also mean that sales are not keeping up with production or that the company is incurring excessive storage and handling costs for inventory. Companies with large inventories may also lack the ability to adapt products quickly to customers' wishes.

You can see that there are mixed signals in measures such as working capital and current ratio. In the 1990s many companies have made a concerted effort to reduce working capital and hence lower their current ratios. For example, in the fiscal year ending February 1, 1997 The Gap reduced its working capital by $174 million. This meant that The Gap had an extra $174 million to invest in new products, corporate acquisitions, or whatever other opportunity presented itself. A food company, Quaker Oats, reduced its working capital by $200 million, primarily by smoothing out its production

runs. Instead of building inventories and then offering huge discounts to entice customers to take delivery, Quaker now produces its cereals and other products just in time to ship them. Each product is produced once a week instead of once every six weeks or so. Of course, this requires more time resetting machines to produce a different product. By streamlining its procedures, one Quaker Oats factory spent only $20,000 a year on the extra machine setups compared with the annual savings of $500,000 from lowering inventories.

A measure of working capital that is increasingly popular is working capital per dollar of sales. The Fortune 500 firms have an average ratio of $.20 for every dollar of sales. Recent figures for Quaker Oats and The Gap are $.07 and $.10, respectively.

Reduction of working capital is not just a U.S. phenomenon. Consider Wabco UK, the British auto products manufacturer. In the 1990's, its working capital has gone from $13 million to a negative $154,000. Currently, payables exceed receivables by $2.35 million and inventories are only $2.2 million. How did it accomplish this? Partly by cutting cycle time—the time from receipt of an order to delivery of the product. For example, a vacuum pump that formerly took three weeks to build can now be built in six minutes. Wabco is also collecting receivables more quickly—42 days compared with 54 days five years ago.

Many companies have set a target of zero working capital and therefore a current ratio of 1.0. As these efforts prove to be successful, the rule of thumb of a desirable current ratio of 2.0 is being revised. Companies with twice as many current assets as current liabilities may be solvent but may lose out in the long run. Why? Because they may not be using their capital as profitably as possible.

---

of format. For example, consider the reproduction of the balance sheet of Walgreen Co., the drugstore chain, as shown in Exhibit 4-6. The format and classifications are those actually used by Walgreen. Note the "non-current" terminology used to denote long-term items. Headings such as long-term assets and long-term liabilities might be used instead of non-current assets and non-current liabilities, respectively. Some accountants prefer to omit a general heading for noncurrent items when there are only one or two items within a specific class.

Exhibit 4-6 presents a classified balance sheet in the **report format** (assets at top) in contrast to the **account format** (assets at left) that has previously been illustrated (Exhibit 4-5). Either format is acceptable. A recent survey of six hundred U.S. companies indicated that 70% use the report format and 30% use the account format.

Non-U.S. companies may use other formats than those presented in Exhibits 4-5 and 4-6. Exhibit 4-7 shows a condensed balance sheet for British Petroleum Company. Notice

report format A classified balance sheet with the assets at the top.

account format A classified balance sheet with the assets at the left.

Exhibit 4-6

Walgreen Co.

At August 31, 1997 and 1996 (Dollars in Millions)

Assets	1997	1996
Current Assets:		
Cash and cash equivalents	$ 73	$ 9
Accounts receivable	376	288
Inventories	1,733	1,632
Other current assets	144	90
Total Current Assets	2,326	2,019
Non-Current Assets		
Property and equipment, at cost, less accumulated depreciation and amortization	1,754	1,449
Other non-current assets	127	166
Total Assets	$4,207	$3,634

Liabilities and Shareholders' Equity		
Current Liabilities:		
Trade accounts payable	$ 813	$ 692
Accrued expenses and other liabilities	554	467
Income taxes	72	23
Total Current Liabilities	1,439	1,182
Non-Current Liabilities		
Deferred income taxes	113	145
Other non-current liabilities	282	264
Total Non-Current Liabilities	395	409
Shareholders' Equity		
Preferred stock, $.125 par value; authorized 16 million shares; none issued		
Common stock, $.15625 par value; authorized 1.6 billion shares; issued and outstanding 493, 789, 966 in 1997 and 492, 282, 144 in 1996	77	77
Paid-in capital	30	
Retained earnings	2,266	1,966
Total Shareholders' Equity	2,373	2,043
Total Liabilities and Shareholders' Equity	$4,207	$3,634

Exhibit 4-7

British Petroleum Company Balance Sheet
December 31, 1996 (in millions)

Fixed assets		£21,820
Current assets	£10,752	
Current liabilities	10,617	
Net current assets		135
Total assets less current liabilities		£21,955
Long-term liabilities		9,160
Shareholders' interests		£12,795

that fixed assets (that is, long-term assets) are listed before current assets. Current liabilities are deducted from current assets to give a direct measure of working capital (called net current assets by British Petroleum). Again, regardless of the format, balance sheets will always contain the same basic information. Note that British Petroleum has working capital of £135 million. Current assets and current liabilities are essentially equal. As suggested in the preceding boxed example, Managing Working Capital, zero or negative working capital is becoming more common as companies reduce their inventories and accounts receivable.

INCOME STATEMENT

As we have just seen, balance sheets can provide decision makers with information about a company's ability to meet its short-term operating and debt needs. However, most investors are much more concerned about a company's ability to produce long-run earnings and dividends—information that can be gleaned from the income statement. In this regard, income statements are often considered to be much more important than are balance sheets. To be most informative, income statements, like balance sheets, may be prepared with subcategories that help focus attention on certain accounts or groups of accounts.

SINGLE- AND MULTIPLE-STEP INCOME STATEMENTS

The adjusted trial balance for Chan Audio Company (Exhibit 4-4) provides the data for the two formats of income statements shown in Exhibit 4-8. The statement in Part A of the exhibit is called a **single-step income statement** because it groups all revenues together (sales plus interest and rent revenues) and then lists and deducts all expenses together without drawing any intermediate subtotals.

Another major form of income statement is the **multiple-step income statement.** It contains one or more subtotals that highlight significant relationships. For example, Exhibit 4-8, Part B, shows a gross profit figure. **Gross profit** (also called **gross margin**) is the excess of sales revenue over the cost of the inventory that was sold. Most multiple-step income statements start with this section.

The next section of a multiple-step income statement usually contains the operating expenses, which is a group of recurring expenses that pertain to the firm's routine, ongoing operations. Examples of such expenses are wages, rent, depreciation, and various other operation-oriented expenses, such as telephone, heat, and advertising. These operating expenses are deducted from the gross profit to obtain **operating income,** which is also called **operating profit.**

The next grouping in the multiple-step income statement is usually called other revenue and expense (or other income or other expense, or nonoperating items, or some similar catchall title). These categories are not directly related to the mainstream of a firm's operations. The revenues are usually minor in relation to the revenues shown at the top of the income statement. The expenses are also minor, with one likely exception—interest expense. There is no theoretical or practical reason to prefer one of these alternatives over another. Experienced readers of financial statements can easily adjust from one to another. For the newcomer to accounting it can seem confusing. As you begin to read and evaluate actual statements, do not let the superficial differences between one structure and the other confuse you.

Accountants have usually regarded interest revenue and interest expense as "other" items because they arise from lending and borrowing money—activities that are distinct from most companies' ordinary operations of selling of goods or services. Of course, the exceptions are companies in the business of lending and borrowing money; banks, credit unions, insurance companies and other financial intermediaries. Some operating companies make heavy use of debt, which causes high interest expenses, whereas other companies incur little debt and have low interest expenses. Because interest revenue and expense appear in a separate category, comparisons of operating income between years and between companies can be made easily. Comparisons of operating income focus attention on selling the product and controlling the costs of doing so. Success in this arena is the ultimate test of a company. Recently many analysts have noted that corporate earnings are significantly

single-step income statement An income statement that groups all revenues together and then lists and deducts all expenses together without drawing any intermediate subtotals.

multiple-step income statement An income statement that contains one or more subtotals that highlight significant relationships.

gross profit (gross margin) The excess of sales revenue over the cost of the inventory that was sold.

operating income (operating profit) Gross profit less all operating expenses.

Exhibit 4-8, Part A

Chan Audio Co.

Single-Step Income Statement
Income Statement for the Month Ended January 31, 19X2

Sales		$160,000
Rent revenue		500
Interest revenue		400
Total sales and other revenues		$160,900
Expenses:		
Cost of goods sold	$100,000	
Wages	31,750	
Depreciation	1,000	
Rent	5,000	
Interest	750	
Income taxes	11,200	
Total expenses		149,700
Net income		$ 11,200

Exhibit 4-8, Part B

Chan Audio Co.

Multiple-Step Income Statement
Income Statement for the Month Ended January 31, 19X2

Sales		$160,000
Cost of goods sold		100,000
Gross profit		$ 60,000
Operating expenses:		
Wages	$31,750	
Depreciation	1,000	
Rent	5,000	37,750
Operating income		$ 22,250
Other revenues and expenses:		
Rent revenue	$ 500	
Interest revenue	400	
Total other revenue	$ 900	
Deduct: Interest expense	750	150
Income before income taxes		$ 22,400
Income taxes (at 50%)		11,200
Net income		$ 11,200

improving. But these analysts make a major distinction between those whose earnings are growing because interest cost is falling or because production costs are being aggressively reduced and those whose earnings are growing because sales are soaring. The first two sources of earnings growth depend on outside forces or one-time changes. But when more and more people want to buy your product, the long-term potential for growth is better.

EXAMPLES OF ACTUAL INCOME STATEMENTS

Exhibits 4-9 and 4-10 demonstrate how two different companies use assorted terminology and formats for their individual income statements. Note that extremely condensed income statement information is provided in both of these published reports. This level of detail is appropriate for external analysts and investors. In contrast, firms also prepare income statements to be used by managers inside the firm. Suppose you were the person responsible for managing inventory at a Gap store. You would want a very detailed financial statement for your store. You would want to know what the inventory was for spring

Exhibit 4-9

H. J. Heinz Co.

Statement of Income (in thousands) for the Year Ended April 30, 1996

Sales	$9,357,007
Cost of products sold	6,385,091
Gross profit	2,971,916
Selling, general and administrative expenses	2,215,645
Operating income	756,271
Interest income	39,359
Interest expense	274,746
Other expenses, net	41,820
Income before income taxes	479,064
Provision for income taxes	177,193
Net income	$ 301,871

Exhibit 4-10

Wm. Wrigley Jr. Company

Consolidated Statement of Earnings for the Year Ended December 31, 1996

	(in thousands)
Revenues:	
Net sales	$1,835,987
Investment and other income	14,614
Total revenues	1,850,601
Costs and expenses:	
Cost of sales	814,483
Factory closure and related costs	19,436
Selling, distribution and general administrative	656,473
Interest	1,097
Total costs and expenses	1,491,489
Earnings before income taxes	359,112
Income taxes	128,840
Net earnings	$ 230,272

merchandise and for summer merchandise, for men's wear and ladies' wear, and for clothing and accessories. You would need detail about the balance sheet. And the same is true for the income statement. You would want sales and cost information for all of those categories. You need this detail to manage your operation and to evaluate your performance against that of other Gap stores. But outside investors are more concerned with the overall performance of Gap as a whole relative to competing retailers, so summarized companywide information is sufficient.

The H. J. Heinz income statement in Exhibit 4-9 uses a multiple-step format, as do 65% of all corporate external reports in the United States. The multiple-step format highlights significant relationships, especially two key measures of performance, gross profit and operating income. In all financial statements, accountants use the label net to denote that some amounts have been deducted in computing the final result. Thus "other expenses, net" in the Heinz statement, means that some revenue items and some expense items have been combined into one number. Wm. Wrigley Jr. Company, maker of chewing gum, uses a single-step format for its income statement in Exhibit 4-10, as do 35% of corporate external reports in the United States. Wrigley follows the single-step model and groups all revenues together and all expenses together without drawing subtotals within revenue and expense categories.

Note where income taxes appear in both of these income statements. Most companies follow this practice of showing income taxes as a separate item immediately above net income regardless of the grouping of other items on the income statement.

As the Wrigley income statement shows, the term costs and expenses is sometimes used in statements instead of just the phrase expenses. Of course, expenses would be an adequate description here. Why? Because the "costs" listed on the income statement are expired costs, such as cost of sales, and thus are really expenses of the current period.

PROFITABILITY EVALUATION RATIOS

We have learned to construct an income statement and a balance sheet. But they may seem a bit like tables of numbers without much meaning. In fact, for managers who work with them all of the time these statements are the "language of business." These managers know what last month and last year looked like; they know their competitors' financial statements inside and out, and they know that earnings of $2 million will cause them to earn a big bonus. How can we create meaning in these financial statements for individuals who do not have this deep company and industry knowledge? How can we use the data in these statements to enhance our understanding of these companies? What creates a context for interpreting them.

profitability The ability of a company to provide investors with a particular rate of return on their investment.

Earlier in this chapter, we saw that ratios can help give meaning to the numbers in the balance sheet. The same is true for the income statement. Income statements are most useful in evaluating a company's profitability. In its ultimate sense, **profitability** is the ability of a company to provide its investors with a particular rate of return on their investment. Return on investment refers to the amount of money an investor receives because of a prior investment. If Mary invests $100 in Calvin Corporation and receives $10 every year as a result, $10 is her return on investment. But absolute amounts are hard to evaluate. Had Mary given Calvin Corporation $200, a return of $10 would not be nearly as attractive. Thus it is common to express the return as a rate of return, a return per dollar invested. In this case for a $100 investment, a $10 return is a 10% rate of return ($10 ÷ $100). For a $200 investment, a $10 return is a 5% rate of return ($10 ÷ $200).

Profitability measures are useful decision-making tools for company managers. Investors use profitability measures to distinguish between different investment opportunities they are considering. Managers know that the profitability measures on their company will affect investors and that good profitability makes it easier to raise capital by selling stock or issuing debt securities. Managers are also often faced with a decision to buy another company, a division of a company, or a machine that makes a new product. In every such case, the manager will evaluate the profitability of the project as part of making the decision.

Profitability comparisons through time and within and among industries are thus used as a basis for predictions and decisions by both external and internal users of financial statements. By far, the easiest way to analyze a company's profitability is through three popular ratios:

1. A ratio based on gross profit (sales revenues minus cost of goods sold) is particularly useful to a retailer in choosing a pricing strategy and in judging its results. This measure, the **gross profit percentage**, or **gross margin percentage**, is defined as gross profit divided by sales. The Chan Audio gross profit percentage for January was:

gross profit percentage (gross margin percentage) Gross profit divided by sales.

$$\text{Gross profit percentage} = \text{Gross profit} \div \text{Sales}$$
$$= \$60,000 \div \$160,000$$
$$= 37.5\%$$

These relationships can also be presented as follows:

	Amount	Percentage
Sales	$160,000	100.0%
Cost of goods sold	100,000	62.5
Gross profit	$ 60,000	37.5%

Gross profit percentages vary greatly by industry. Software companies have high gross profit percentages (Microsoft's is 90%). Why? Because most costs in that industry are in research and development and sales and marketing, not in cost of goods sold. In contrast, retail companies have lower gross margin percentages because product costs are their main expense. For example, the gross profit percentage for Safeway is 27%. Other gross margin percentages fall between the extremes, such as General Mills at 47% and Nike at 39%.

2. A ratio based on a comparison of expenses and sales will be carefully followed by managers from month to month. The **return on sales ratio** shows the relationship of net income to sales revenue. Chan Audio's return on sales ratio is computed as follows:

return on sales ratio Net income divided by sales.

$$\text{Return on sales} = \text{Net income} \div \text{sales}$$
$$= \$11,200 \div \$160,000$$
$$= 7\%$$

3. The **return on stockholders' equity ratio** also uses net income but compares it with invested capital (as measured by average stockholders' equity) instead of sales. This ratio is widely regarded as the ultimate measure of overall accomplishment. The return on stockholders' equity calculation for Chan Audio is:

return on stockholders' equity ratio Net income divided by invested capital (measured by average stockholders' equity).

$$\text{Return on stockholders' equity} = \text{Net income} \div \text{Average stockholders' equity}$$
$$= \$11,200 \div 1/2 \text{ (January 1 balance,}$$
$$\$400,000 + \text{January 31 balance, } \$411,200)$$
$$= \$11,200 \div \$405,600$$
$$= 2.8\% \text{ (for one month)}$$

Some recent examples of actual annual return on sales and return on stockholders' equity ratios are:

	Return on Sales	Return on Stockholders' Equity
Microsoft	30%	32%
Nike	9%	25%
McDonald's	15%	18%
Bell Atlantic	14%	26%
Walgreens	3%	18%
British Petroleum (United Kingdom)	5%	21%
Nordstrom	9%	22%
Kobe Steel (Japan)	1%	1%

Chan Audio's 37.5% gross profit is relatively low compared with the usual 40% to 45% for the retail stereo industry. However, Chan Audio has maintained excellent expense control because its 7% return on sales and its 33.6% return on stockholders' equity (a monthly rate of 2.8% × 12 = 33.6% as an annual rate) are higher than the 6% and 18% annual returns usually earned by the industry.

GENERALLY ACCEPTED ACCOUNTING PRINCIPLES AND BASIC CONCEPTS

Objective 8
Relate Generally
Accepted Accounting
Principles (GAAP) to
the accounting practices
we have learned.

**generally accepted
accounting principles
(GAAP)** A term that
applies to the broad
concepts or guidelines and
detailed practices in
accounting, including all
the conventions, rules, and
procedures that make up
accepted accounting
practice at a given time.

**Financial Accounting
Standards Board (FASB)**
A private-sector body that
determines generally
accepted accounting
standards in the United
States.

AICPA American
Institute of Certified Public
Accountants, the leading
organization of the
auditors of corporate
financial reports.

FASB Statements The
FASB's rulings on
generally accepted
accounting principles
(GAAP).

**Accounting Principles
Board (APB)** The
predecessor to the
Financial Accounting
Standards Board.

APB Opinions A series
of thirty-one opinions of
the Accounting Principles
Board, many of which are
still the "accounting law of
the land."

Financial statements are the result of a measurement process that rests on a set of principles. If every accountant used a different set of measurement rules, decision makers would find it difficult to use and compare financial statements. For example, consider the recording of an asset such as a machine on the balance sheet. If one accountant listed the purchase cost, another the amount for which the used machine could be sold, and others listed various other amounts, the readers of financial statements would be confused. It would be as if each accountant were speaking a different language. Therefore, accountants have agreed to apply a common set of measurement principles—that is, a common language—to record information on financial statements.

Generally accepted accounting principles (GAAP) is the term that applies to all of the broad concepts and detailed practices in accounting. It includes all the conventions, rules, and procedures that together make up accepted accounting practice. We will concentrate on the GAAP that exists today in the United States. However, we will frequently use practices from other countries and financial reports for non-U.S. firms to illustrate the extent of global diversity in practice. Although there is no single, perfect method for measuring an organization's performance, each country has found it useful to narrow the range of practices to a few acceptable ones.

Accounting principles become "generally accepted" by agreement. Such agreement is not influenced only by formal logical analysis. Experience, custom, usage, and practical necessity contribute to a set of principles. Therefore, it might be better to call them conventions. Why? Because "principles" erroneously connotes that GAAP is the product of airtight logic. Nevertheless, accountants use the term "principles" rather than "conventions" to describe the entire framework that guides their work.

STANDARD SETTING BODIES

The existence of generally accepted accounting principles (GAAP) implies that someone must decide which principles are generally accepted and which are not. This decision is made by regulatory agencies or professional associations. In the United States, GAAP is set primarily in the private sector (with government oversight), but in many countries, such as France, the government sets the standards directly.

The **Financial Accounting Standards Board (FASB)** is responsible for establishing GAAP in the United States. The FASB is an independent creature of the private sector consisting of seven qualified individuals who work full-time. The board is supported by a large staff and an annual $16 million budget provided by various professional accounting associations (such as the leading organization of auditors, the American Institute of Certified Public Accountants, also known as the **AICPA**). The FASB's rulings on GAAP are called **FASB Statements.**

The FASB, established in 1973, replaced the **Accounting Principles Board (APB),** a group of eighteen accountants (mostly partners in large accounting firms) who worked part-time. The APB issued a series of 31 **APB Opinions** during 1962 to 1973, many of which are still the "accounting law of the land."

The U.S. Congress has charged the **Securities and Exchange Commission (SEC)** with the ultimate responsibility for authorizing the generally accepted accounting principles for companies whose stock is held by the general investing public. However, the SEC has informally delegated much rule-making power to the FASB. This public sector/private sector authority relationship can be sketched as follows:

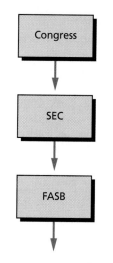

Issues pronouncements on various accounting issues. These pronouncements govern the
preparation of typical financial statements.

Take a careful look at the preceding three-tiered structure. Note that Congress can overrule both the SEC and the FASB, and the SEC can overrule the FASB. Such undermining of the FASB occurs rarely, but pressure is exerted on all three tiers by corporations if they think an impending pronouncement is "wrong." Thus the setting of accounting principles is a complex process involving heavy interactions among the affected parties: public regulators (Congress and the SEC), private regulators (FASB), companies, the public accounting profession, representatives of investors, and other interested groups.

Recent years have seen a growing interest in developing a common set of accounting principles throughout the world. Often called harmonization of accounting standards, the movement seeks to eliminate differences in accounting principles that are not caused by cultural or environmental differences between countries. Leading the way is the **International Accounting Standards Committee (IASC),** which represents more than 100 accountancy bodies from 82 countries. Like the FASB, the IASC is a private-sector body that issues standards—so far more than 30 of them. Although compliance with IASC standards is voluntary, a growing number of countries and multinational companies are adopting the methods advocated by the IASC.

Also affecting international accounting standards is the European Union (EU). Via a series of Directives, which have the force of law, the EU is reducing the variations in financial statements of companies in its 15 member nations.

Securities and Exchange Commission (SEC) The agency designated by the U.S. Congress to hold the ultimate responsibility for authorizing the generally accepted accounting principles for companies whose stock is held by the general investing public.

International Accounting Standards Committee (IASC) An organization representing over one hundred accountancy boards from over seventy-five countries that is developing a common set of accounting standards to be used throughout the world.

CONCEPTS AND CONVENTIONS OF GAAP

The FASB sets some fairly detailed rules in place, and they are part of GAAP. Some of the most difficult issues in accounting center on when an unexpired cost expires and becomes an expense. For example, some accountants believe that research and development costs should be accounted for as unexpired costs, shown on balance sheets among the assets, and written off to expense in some systematic manner over a period of years. After all, companies engage in research and product development activities because they expect them to create future benefits. But the FASB in the United States and regulators in many other countries have ruled that such costs have vague future benefits that are difficult to measure reliably. Therefore, research and development costs are treated as expenses. In such cases, research costs are not found on balance sheets. In contrast, Italy and Spain allow research and development costs to be recognized initially as an asset and to be shown on the balance sheet. In addition to such a specific pronouncement by regulators such as the FASB, there are a number of concepts and conventions that guide our accounting process.

THE ENTITY CONCEPT   The first basic concept or principle in accounting is the entity concept. An accounting entity is an organization or a section of an organization that stands apart from other organizations and individuals as a separate economic unit. Accounting draws sharp boundaries around each entity to avoid confusing its affairs with those of other entities.

An example of an entity is General Motors Corporation, an enormous entity that encompasses many smaller entities such as the Chevrolet Division and the Buick Division. In turn, Chevrolet encompasses many smaller entities such as a Michigan assembly plant and an Ohio assembly plant. Managers want accounting reports that are confined to their particular entities.

The key point here is that the entity concept helps the accountant relate events to a clearly defined area of accountability. For example, business entities should not be confused with personal entities. A purchase of groceries for merchandise inventory is an accounting transaction of a grocery store (the business entity), but the store owner's purchase of a stereo set with a personal check is a transaction of the owner (the personal entity).

THE RELIABILITY CONCEPT   Users of financial statements want assurance that the numbers are not fabricated by management. Consequently, accountants regard reliability as an essential characteristic of measurement. **Reliability** is a quality of information that assures decision makers that the information captures the conditions or events it purports to represent. Reliable data are supported by convincing evidence that can be verified by independent accountants.

reliability The quality of information that assures decision makers that the information captures the conditions or events it purports to represent.

The accounting process focuses on reliable recording of events that affect an organization. Although many events may affect a company—including wars, elections, and general economic booms or depressions—the accountant recognizes only specified types of events as being reliably recorded as accounting transactions.

Suppose the president of Exxon is killed in an airplane crash, and the company carries no life insurance for him or her. The accountant would not record this event. Suppose further that Exxon discovers that an employee has embezzled $1,000 in cash, and the company carries no employee theft insurance. The accountant would record this event. The death of the president may have considerably more economic or financial significance for Exxon than does the embezzlement, but the monetary effect is hard to measure in any objective way. Accountants measure the impact of events in a systematic, reliable manner.

going concern convention (continuity convention) The assumption that in all ordinary situations an entity persists indefinitely.

GOING CONCERN CONVENTION   The **going concern convention (continuity convention)** is the assumption that ordinarily an entity persists indefinitely. This notion implies that a company's existing resources, such as plant assets, will be used to fulfill the general business needs of the company rather than be sold in tomorrow's real estate or equipment markets. For a going concern it is reasonable to use historical cost to record long-lived assets. Also, for a going concern it is reasonable to report liabilities at the amount to be paid at maturity.

The opposite view of this going concern convention is an immediate-liquidation assumption whereby all items on a balance sheet are valued at the amounts appropriate if the entity were to be liquidated in piecemeal fashion within a few days or months. This liquidation approach to valuation is usually used only when the probability is high that the company will be liquidated.

MATERIALITY CONVENTION   How does an accountant know what to include on financial statements? Well, there are a lot of rules and regulations about what must appear in those statements. But what about items that aren't covered by the rules? The **materiality convention** asserts that an item should be included in a financial statement if its omission or misstatement would tend to mislead the reader of the financial statements under consideration.

materiality convention The concept that states that a financial statement item is material if its omission or misstatement would tend to mislead the reader of the financial statements under consideration.

Most large items, such as cars and machinery, are clearly material. Smaller items, though, may not be so clear cut. Many acquisitions that should theoretically be recorded as assets are immediately written off as expenses because of their insignificance. For example, coat hangers may last indefinitely but never appear in the balance sheet as assets. Many corporations require the immediate write-off to expense of all outlays under a specified minimum, such as $100, regardless of the useful life of the asset acquired. The resulting $100 understatement of assets and stockholders' equity is considered too trivial to worry about. In general, GAAP need not be applied to immaterial items. The FASB regularly includes the following statement in its standards: "The provisions of this statement need not be applied to immaterial items."

When is an item material? There will probably never be a universal, clear-cut answer. What is trivial to General Motors may be material to Evelyn's Boutique. A working rule is that an item is material if its proper accounting would probably affect the decision of a knowledgeable party. In sum, materiality is an important convention. But it is difficult to use anything other than prudent judgment to tell whether an item is material.

COST-BENEFIT CRITERION   Accounting systems vary in complexity—from the minimum crude records kept by a small business to satisfy government authorities, to the sophisticated budgeting and feedback schemes that are required to manage a huge, multinational corporation. Of course, a system can start out small and get much bigger as is necessary. But when are changes to an accounting system necessary? The **cost-benefit criterion** states that a system should be changed when the expected additional benefits of the change exceed its expected additional costs. Often the benefits are difficult to measure, but this criterion should always underlie the decisions about the design and change of accounting systems. In fact, the FASB uses a cost-benefit criterion in judging new standards. It safeguards the cost-effectiveness of its standards by (1) assuring that a standard does not "impose costs on the many for the benefit of a few," and (2) seeking alternative ways of handling an issue that are "less costly and only slightly less efficient."

cost-benefit criterion   As a system is changed, its expected additional benefits should exceed its expected additional costs.

STABLE MONETARY UNIT   The monetary unit (called the dollar in the United States, Canada, Australia, New Zealand, and elsewhere) is the principal means for measuring assets and equities. It is the common denominator for quantifying the effects of a wide variety of transactions. Accountants record, classify, summarize, and report in terms of the monetary unit. The ability to use historical cost accounting depends on a stable monetary unit. A stable monetary unit is simply one that is not expected to change in value significantly over time.

ACCOUNTING FOR NONPROFIT ORGANIZATIONS

Most examples thus far have focused on profit-seeking organizations, but balance sheets and income statements are also used by nonprofit organizations. For example, hospitals and universities have income statements, although they are called statements of revenue and expense. The "bottom line" is frequently called "excess of revenue over expense" or "net financial result" rather than "net income."

The basic concepts of assets, liabilities, revenue, expense, and operating statements are applicable to all organizations, whether they be utilities, symphony orchestras, private, public, American, or Asian. However, some nonprofit organizations have been slow to adopt some ideas that are widely used in progressive companies. For example, many government organizations used only the cash basis of accounting, not the accrual basis. This practice hampered the evaluation of the performance of such organizations. A recent annual report of the New York Metropolitan Museum of Art stated: "As the Museum's financial operations have begun to resemble in complexity those of a corporation, it has become necessary to make certain changes in our accounting. . . . Operating results are reported on an accrual rather than the previously followed cash basis. Thus, revenue and expenses are recorded in the proper time period."

An article in *Forbes* commented:

> *Shoddy, misleading accounting has not been the cause of our cities' problems but it has prevented us from finding solutions. Or even looking for solutions until it's too late. Chicago's schools, for example, suddenly found themselves unable to pay their teachers. Had the books been kept like any decent corporation's, that could never have happened. The most basic difference is in the common use of cash accounting rather than the accrual method that nearly all businesses use.*

In response to concerns such as these, regulators are bringing greater discipline to reporting by not-for-profit entities and governmental entities. The FASB now requires that financial statements for large not-for-profit firms include essentially equivalent financial statements to those required for businesses. A parallel organization that regulates governmental reporting is considering a requirement that governmental units such as cities and states use accrual-based accounting and the basic financial statements that businesses use.

SUMMARY PROBLEM FOR YOUR REVIEW

PROBLEM TWO

Johnson & Johnson (maker of Tylenol, Band-Aids, and other health care and personal use products) uses a statement of earnings and retained earnings, as follows:

Johnson & Johnson
Statement of Earnings as of December 31, 1996

(dollars in millions except per share figures)	
Sales to customers	$21,620
Cost of products sold	7,018
Selling, marketing, and administrative expenses	8,394
Research expense	1,905
Interest income	(139)
Interest expense	125
Other expense, net	284
	17,587
Earnings before provision for taxes on income	4,033
Provision for taxes on income	1,146
Net earnings	2,887
Net earnings per share	$ 2.17

1. Is this a single-step or a multiple-step income statement? Explain your answer.
2. What term would Wm. Wrigley Jr. use as a label for the line in Johnson and Johnson's statements having the $17,587 figure? (Refer to the Wrigley income statement in Exhibit 4-10.)
3. Suggest an alternative term for interest income.
4. Compute the gross profit.
5. What is the amount of the famous "bottom line" that is so often referred to by managers?

6. Net earnings per share is defined as net earnings divided by the average number of common shares outstanding. Compute the average number of common shares outstanding during the year.

Solution to Problem Two

1. As is often the case, Johnson & Johnson uses a hybrid of single-step and multiple-step income statements. However, it is closer to a single-step than a multiple-step statement. A purebred single-step statement would place interest income with sales to obtain total revenues.

2. Wrigley would use "total costs and expenses" to describe the $17,587 figure.

3. Interest revenue is preferable to interest income.

4.
Sales to customers	$21,620	100%
Cost of products sold	7,018	32
Gross profit	$14,602	68%

5. The bottom line in total is net earnings of $2,887 million. The bottom line per average common share outstanding is $2.17.

6. As Chapter 2 explains, net earnings per share is required to be shown on the face of the income statement.

$$\text{Earnings per share (EPS)} = \frac{\text{Net earnings}}{\text{Average number of common shares outstanding}}$$

$$2.17 = \frac{\$2,887,000,000}{\text{Average shares}}$$

Average shares = $2,887,000,000 ÷ 2.17
Average shares = 1,330,414,747

Highlights to Remember

At the end of each accounting period, adjustments must be made so that financial statements can be presented on a full-fledged accrual basis. The major adjustments are for (1) the expiration of unexpired costs, (2) the earning of unearned revenues, (3) the accrual of unrecorded expenses, and (4) the accrual of unrecorded revenues. Frequently, accounting adjustments are clarified when they are seen as mirror images by looking at both sides of the adjustment simultaneously. For example, (a) the expiration of unexpired costs (the tenant's rent expense) is accompanied by (b) the earning of unearned revenues (the landlord's rent revenue). Similarly, (a) the accrual of unrecorded expenses (a borrower's interest expense) is accompanied by (b) the accrual of unrecorded revenues (a lender's interest revenue).

The adjusting entries can either precede or follow the related cash flows. Entries for the expiration of unexpired costs and the recognition (earning) of unearned revenues follow the cash flows, while entries for the accrual of unrecorded expenses and the accrual of unrecorded revenues precede the cash flows.

Classified balance sheets divide various items into subcategories. For example, assets and liabilities are separated into current and long-term. These subcategories are used in analysis. For example, current assets minus current liabilities is called working capital. The current ratio, defined as current assets divided by current liabilities, is used to help assess solvency.

Income statements may appear in single-step or multiple-step form. Regardless of the format, published income statements are highly condensed and summarized compared with reports used within an organization.

Income statement ratios are used to assess profitability. Among the most useful are gross margin (or gross profit), return on sales, and return on stockholders' equity.

Generally accepted accounting principles (GAAP) are based on many concepts including the entity concept, the going concern assumption, materiality, and a stable monetary unit. GAAP in the United States is generally determined by the Financial Accounting Standards Board (FASB), with oversight by the Securities and Exchange Commission (SEC). Growing interest in a common international GAAP has moved the International Accounting Standards Committee (IASC) into the forefront of standard setting.

Accounting Vocabulary

account format, p. 141	Financial Accounting Standards Board (FASB), p. 148	operating profit, p. 143
Accounting Principles Board (APB), p. 148	generally accepted accounting principles (GAAP), p. 148	pretax income, p. 132
accrue, p. 126	going concern convention, p. 150	profitability, p. 146
adjusting entries, p. 126		reliability, p. 150
adjustments, p. 126	gross margin, p. 143	report format, p. 141
AICPA, p. 148	gross margin percentage, p. 146	return on sales ratio, p. 147
APB Opinions, p. 148	gross profit, p. 143	return on stockholders' equity ratio, p. 147
classified balance sheet, p. 137	gross profit percentage, p. 146	revenue received in advance, p. 127
continuity convention, p. 150	implicit transactions, p. 126	
cost-benefit criterion, p. 151	International Accounting Standards Committee (IASC), p. 149	Securities and Exchange Commission (SEC), p. 149
current assets, p. 138		single-step income statement, p. 143
current liabilities, p. 138		
current ratio, p. 139	materiality convention, p. 151	solvency, p. 139
deferred credit, p. 127	multiple-step income statement, p. 143	unearned revenue, p. 127
deferred revenue, p. 127		working capital, p. 139
explicit transactions, p. 126	operating income, p. 143	working capital ratio, p. 139
FASB Statements, p. 148		

Assignment Material

QUESTIONS

4-1. Give two examples of an explicit transaction.

4-2. Give two examples of an implicit transaction.

4-3. Give two synonyms for *unearned revenue.*

4-4. Distinguish between the accrual of wages and the payment of wages.

4-5. Give a synonym for *income tax expense.*

4-6. Explain why income tax expense is usually the final deduction on both single-step and multiple-step income statements.

4-7. "The accrual of previously unrecorded revenues is the mirror image of the accrual of previously unrecorded expenses." Explain, using an illustration.

4-8. What types of adjusting entries are made before the related cash flows? What types after the related cash flows?

4-9. Why are current assets and current liabilities grouped separately from long-term assets and long-term liabilities?

4-10. "Microsoft is much more profitable than IBM because its current ratio is more than four times larger than IBM's." Do you agree? Explain.

4-11. "Companies should always strive to avoid negative working capital." Do you agree? Explain.

4-12. Explain the difference between a *single-step* and a *multiple-step* income statement.

4-13. Why does interest expense appear below operating income on a multiple-step income statement?

4-14. The term "costs and expenses" is sometimes found instead of just "expenses" on the income statement. Would "expenses" be an adequate description? Why?

4-15. Name three popular ratios for measuring profitability, and indicate how to compute each of the three.

4-16. "Computer software companies are generally more profitable than grocery stores because their gross profit percentages are usually at least twice as large." Do you agree? Explain.

4.17 Distinguish between GAAP, FASB, SEC, and APB.

4.18 What functions does the International Accounting Standards Committee (IASC) have in setting GAAP?

4.19 "This idea implies that existing equipment will be used rather than sold in tomorrow's equipment markets." What is the name of this idea?

4.20 "What is trivial to General Electric may be significant to Don's Hobby Shop." What idea is being described?

EXERCISES

4-21 True or False
Use *T* or *F* to indicate whether each of the following statements is true or false:

1. Retained Earnings should be accounted for as a current asset item.
2. Cash should be classified as a stockholders' equity item.
3. Machinery used in the business should be recorded as a noncurrent asset item.
4. The cash balance is the best evidence of stockholders' equity.
5. From a single balance sheet you can find stockholders' equity for a period of time but not for a specific day.
6. It is not possible to determine changes in the condition of a business from a single balance sheet.

4-22 Tenant and Landlord
The Trucano Company, a retail hardware store, pays quarterly rent on its store at the beginning of each quarter. The rent per quarter is $15,000. The owner of the building in which the store is located is the Resing Corporation.

Using the balance sheet equation format, analyze the effects of the following on the tenant's and the landlord's financial position:

1. Trucano pays $15,000 rent on July 1.
2. Adjustment for July.
3. Adjustment for August.
4. Adjustment for September. Also prepare the journal entries for Trucano and Resing for September.

4-23 Customer and Airline
The Scott Paper Company decided to hold a managers' meeting in Hawaii in February. To take advantage of special fares, Scott purchased airline tickets in advance from United Airlines at a total cost of $80,000. These were acquired on December 1 for cash.

Using the balance sheet equation format, analyze the impact of the December payment and the February travel on the financial position of both Scott and United. Also prepare journal entries for February.

4-24 Accruals of Wages
Consider the following calendar:

		September				
S	M	T	W	T	F	S
		1	2	3	4	5
6	7	8	9	10	11	12
13	14	15	16	17	18	19
20	21	22	23	24	25	26
27	28	29	30			

The Montlake Department Store commenced business on September 1. It is open every day except Sunday. Its total payroll for all employees is $6,000 per day. Payments are made each Tuesday for the preceding week's work through Saturday.

Required Using the balance sheet equation format, analyze the financial impact on Montlake of the following:

1. Disbursements for wages on September 8, 15, 22, and 29.
2. Adjustments for wages on September 30. Also prepare the journal entry.

4-25 Accrued Vacation Pay

Delta Airlines had the following as a current liability on its balance sheet, March 31, 1997:

Accrued vacation pay	$471,000,000

Under the accrual basis of accounting, vacation pay is ordinarily accrued throughout the year as workers are regularly paid. For example, suppose a Delta baggage handler earns $750 per week for fifty weeks and also gets paid $1,500 for two weeks' vacation. Accrual accounting requires that the obligation for the $1,500 be recognized as it is earned rather than when the payment is disbursed. Thus, in each of the fifty weeks Delta would recognize a wage expense (or vacation pay expense) of $1,500 ÷ 50 = $30.

Required

1. Prepare the weekly Delta adjusting journal entry called for by the $30 example.
2. Prepare the entry for the $1,500 payment of vacation pay.

4-26 Placement of Interest in Income Statement

Two companies have the following balance sheets as of December 31, 19X8:

Jupiter Company

debt

Cash	$ 50,000	Note payable*	$100,000
Other assets	150,000	Stockholders' equity	100,000
Total	$200,000	Total	$200,000

* 12% interest.

Saturn Company

Cash	$ 50,000	Stockholders' equity	$200,000
Other assets	150,000		
Total	$200,000		

In 19X9, each company had sales of $550,000 and expenses (excluding interest) of $500,000. Ignore income taxes.

Required Did the two companies earn the same net income? The same operating income? Explain, showing computations of operating income and net income.

4-27 Effects of Interest on Lenders and Borrowers

Prudential lent Dayglo Paint Company $800,000 on March 1, 19X1. The loan plus interest of 12% is payable on March 1, 19X2.

Required

1. Using the balance sheet equation format, prepare an analysis of the impact of the transactions on both Prudential's and Dayglo's financial position on March 1,

19X1. Show the summary adjustments on December 31, 19X1, for the period March 1–December 31.

2. Prepare adjusting journal entries for Prudential and Dayglo on December 31, 19X1.

4-28 Identification of Transactions

Valenzuela Corporation's financial position is represented by the nine balances shown on the first line of the following schedule (in thousands of dollars). Assume that a single transaction took place for each of the following lines, and describe what you think happened, using one short sentence for each line.

	Cash	Accounts Receivable	Inventory	Equipment	Accounts Payable	Accrued Wages Payable	Unearned Rent Revenue	Paid-in Capital	Retained Income
Bal.	19	32	54	0	29	0	0	55	21
(1)	29	32	54	0	29	0	0	65	21
(2)	29	32	54	20	29	0	0	85	21
(3)	29	32	66	20	41	0	0	85	21
(4a)	29	47	66	20	41	0	0	85	36
(4b)	29	47	58	20	41	0	0	85	28
(5)	34	42	58	20	41	0	0	85	28
(6)	14	42	58	20	21	0	0	85	28
(7)	19	42	58	20	21	0	5	85	28
(8)	19	42	58	20	21	2	5	85	26
(9)	19	42	58	19	21	2	5	85	25
(10)	19	42	58	19	21	2	3	85	27

4-29 Effects on Balance Sheet Equation

Following is a list of effects of accounting transactions on the basic accounting equation: Assets equal Liabilities plus Stockholders' Equity.

a. Increase in assets, increase in liabilities

b. Increase in assets, decrease in liabilities

c. Increase in assets, increase in stockholders' equity

d. Increase in assets, decrease in assets

e. Decrease in assets, decrease in liabilities

f. Increase in liabilities, decrease in stockholders' equity

g. Decrease in assets, increase in liabilities

h. Decrease in liabilities, increase in stockholders' equity

i. Decrease in assets, decrease in stockholders' equity

j. None of these

Which of the foregoing relationships defines the accounting effect of each of the following?

1. The adjusting entry to recognize periodic depreciation.

2. The adjusting entry to record accrued salaries.

3. The adjusting entry to record accrued interest receivable.

4. The collection of interest previously accrued.

5. The settlement of an account payable by the issuance of a note payable.

6. The recognition of an expense that had been paid for previously. A "prepaid" account was increased upon payment.

7. The earning of income previously collected. Unearned Revenue was increased when collection was made in advance.

4-30 Effects of Errors in Adjustments

What will be the effect—understated (*u*), overstated (*o*), or no effect (*n*)—upon the income of the present and future periods if the following errors were made. In all cases assume that amounts carried over into 19X7 would affect 19X7 operations via the routine accounting entries of 19X7.

	Period	
	19X6	**19X7**
1. Revenue has been collected in advance, but earned amounts have not been recognized at the end of 19X6. Instead, all revenue was recognized as earned in 19X7.	_____	_____
2. Revenue for services rendered has been earned, but the unbilled amounts have not been recognized at the end of 19X6.	_____	_____
3. Accrued wages payable have not been recognized at the end of 19X6.	_____	_____
4. Prepaid items like rent have been paid (in late 19X6) through half of 19X7, but not adjusted at the end of 19X6. The payments have been debited to Prepaid Rent. They were written off in mid-19X7.	_____	_____

4-31 Effects of Adjustments and Corrections

Listed below are a series of accounts that are numbered for identification. All accounts needed to answer the parts of this question are included. Prepare an answer sheet with columns in which you are to write the identification numbers of the accounts affected by your answers. The same account may be used in several answers.

1. Cash
2. Accounts receivable
3. Notes receivable
4. Inventory
5. Accrued interest receivable
6. Accrued rent receivable
7. Fuel on hand
8. Unexpired rent
9. Unexpired insurance
10. Unexpired repairs and maintenance
11. Land
12. Buildings
13. Machinery and equipment
14. Accounts payable
15. Notes payable
16. Accrued wages and salaries payable
17. Accrued interest payable
18. Unearned subscription revenue
19. Capital stock
20. Sales
21. Fuel expense
22. Sales and wages
23. Insurance expense
24. Repairs and maintenance expense
25. Rent expense
26. Rent revenue
27. Subscription revenue
28. Interest revenue
29. Interest expense

Required

Prepare any necessary adjusting or correcting entries called for by the following situations, *which were discovered at the end of the calendar year.* With respect to each situation, assume that no entries have been made regarding the situation other than those specifically described (i.e., no monthly adjustments have been made during the year). *Consider each situation separately.* These transactions were not necessarily conducted by one business firm. Amounts are in thousands of dollars. *Illustration:* Purchased new equipment for $100 cash, plus a $300 short-term note. The bookkeeper failed to record the transaction. The answer would appear as follows:

	Account		Amount	
	Debit	*Credit*	*Debit*	*Credit*
Illustration	13	1 & 15	400	100 & 300
a.	—	———	—	———
b.	—	———	—	———
c.	—	———	—	———
etc.	—	———	—	———

a. A $400 purchase of equipment on December 5 was erroneously debited to Accounts Payable. The credit was correctly made to Cash.

b. A business made several purchases of fuel oil. Some purchases ($800) were debited to Fuel Expense, while others ($1,100) were charged to an assets account. An oil gauge revealed $400 of fuel on hand at the end of the year. There was no fuel on hand at the beginning of the year.

c. On April 1, a business took out a fire insurance policy. The policy was for two years, and the premium paid was $400. It was debited to Insurance Expense on April 1.

d. On December 1, $400 was paid in advance to the landlord for four months' rent. The tenant debited Unexpired Rent for $400 on December 1. What adjustment is necessary on December 31 on the tenant's books?

e. Machinery is repaired and maintained by an outside maintenance company on an annual fee basis, payable in advance. The $240 fee was paid in advance on September 1 and charged to Repairs and Maintenance Expense. What adjustment is necessary on December 31?

f. On November 16, $800 of machinery was purchased. $200 cash was paid down and a 90-day, 5% note payable was signed for the balance. The November 16 transaction was properly recorded. Prepare the adjustment for the interest.

g. A publisher sells subscriptions to magazines. Customers pay in advance. Receipts are originally credited to Unearned Subscription Revenue. On August 1, many one-year subscriptions were collected and recorded, amounting to $12,000.

h. On December 30, certain merchandise was purchased for $1,000 on open account. The bookkeeper debited Machinery and Equipment and credited Accounts Payable for $1,000. Prepare a correcting entry.

i. A 120-day, 9%, $7,500 cash loan was made to a customer on November 1. The November 1 transaction was recorded correctly.

4-32 Working Capital and Current Ratio

The Royal Dutch/Shell Group of Companies operates the Shell Oil Company. Headquartered in both The Netherlands and the United Kingdom, the company's financial statements are in British Pounds (£). On January 1, 1997 Royal Dutch/Shell had current assets of £25,452 million and current liabilities of £19,525 million.

Compute Royal Dutch/Shell's working capital and current ratio on January 1, 1997.

Required

4-33 Profitability Ratios

Nestlé S.A., the Swiss Chocolate company, sells many other food items in addition to various types of chocolates. Sales in 1996 were SF 60,490 million (where SF means Swiss francs), cost of goods sold was SF 31,495 million, net income was SF 3,401 million, and average stockholders' equity was SF 19,964 million.

Compute Nestle's gross profit percentage, return on sales, and return on stockholders' equity.

Required

PROBLEMS

4-34 Adjusting Entries

(Alternates are 4-36, 4-37, and 4-38.) Christy Blair, certified public accountant, had the following transactions (among others) during 19X8:

a. For accurate measurement of performance and position, Blair uses the accrual basis of accounting. On August 1, she acquired office supplies for $2,000. Office Supplies Inventory was increased, and Cash was decreased by $2,000 on Blair's books. On December 31, her inventory was $800.

b. On September 1, a client gave Blair a retainer fee of $36,000 cash for monthly services to be rendered over the following twelve months. Blair increased Cash and Unearned Fee Revenue.

c. Blair accepted an $8,000 note receivable from a client on October 1 for tax services. The note plus interest of 12% per year were due in six months. Blair increased Note Receivable and Fee Revenue by $8,000.

d. As of December 31, Blair had not recorded $400 of unpaid wages earned by her secretary during late December.

Required For the year ended December 31, 19X8, prepare all adjustments called for by the above transactions. Assume that appropriate entries were routinely made for the explicit transactions described above. However, no adjustments have been made before December 31. For each adjustment, prepare an analysis in the same format used when the adjustment process was explained in the chapter (i.e., the balance sheet equation format). Also prepare the adjusting journal entry.

4-35 Multiple-Step Income Statement

(Alternate is 4-39.) From the following data, prepare a multiple-step income statement for the Ortonville Company for the fiscal year ended May 31, 19X6 (in thousands except for percentage).

Sales	$900	Cost of goods sold	$450
Interest expense	72	Depreciation	30
Rent expense	52	Rent revenue	10
Interest revenue	14	Wages	200
Income tax rate	40%		

4-36 Four Major Adjustments

(Alternates are 4-34, 4-37, and 4-38.) Jocelyn Noller, an attorney, had the following transactions (among others) during 19X8, her initial year in practicing law:

a. On August 1, Noller leased office space for one year. The landlord (lessor) insisted on full payment in advance. Prepaid Rent was increased and Cash was decreased by $24,000 on Noller's books. Similarly, the landlord increased Cash and increased Unearned Rent Revenue.

b. On October 1, Noller received a retainer fee of $15,000 cash for services to be rendered to her client, a local trucking company, over the succeeding twelve months. Noller increased Cash and Unearned Fee Revenue. The trucking company increased Prepaid Expenses and decreased Cash.

c. As of December 31, Noller had not recorded $400 of unpaid wages earned by her secretary during late December.

d. During November and December, Noller rendered services to another client, a utility company. She had intended to bill the company for $5,400 services through

December 31, but she decided to delay formal billing until late January when the case would probably be settled.

Required

1. For the year ended December 31, 19X8, prepare all adjustments called for by the above transactions. Assume that appropriate entries were routinely made for the explicit transactions described above. However, no adjustments have been made before December 31. For each adjustment, prepare an analysis in the same format used when the adjustment process was explained in the chapter (i.e., the balance sheet equation format). Prepare two adjustments for each transaction, one for Noller and one for the other party to the transaction. In part *c*, assume that the secretary uses the accrual basis for his personal entity.

2. For each transaction, prepare the journal entries for Jocelyn Noller *and* the other entities involved.

4-37 Four Major Adjustments
(Alternates are 4-34, 4-36, and 4-38.) The Goodyear Tire and Rubber Company included the following items in its January 1, 1997 balance sheet (in millions):

Prepaid expenses (a current asset)	$306.3
United States and foreign taxes (a current liability)	382.1

Required

1. Analyze the impact of the following transactions on the financial position of Goodyear. Prepare your analysis in the same format used when the adjustment process was explained in the chapter. Also show adjusting journal entries.

   a. On January 31, an adjustment of $3 million was made for the rentals of various retail outlets that had originally increased Prepaid Expenses but had expired.

   b. During December 1997, Goodyear sold tires for $2 million cash to U-Haul, but delivery was not made until January 28. Unearned Revenue had been increased in December. No other adjustments had been made since. Prepare the adjustment on January 31.

   c. Goodyear had loaned cash to several of its independent retail dealers. As of January 31, the dealers owed $4 million of interest that had been unrecorded.

   d. On January 31, Goodyear increased its accrual of federal income taxes by $21 million.

2. Compute the ending balances on January 31, 1997 in prepaid expenses and in United States and foreign taxes.

4-38 Four Major Adjustments
(Alternates are 4-34, 4-36, and 4-37.) Alaska Airlines had the following items in its balance sheet, December 31, 1996, the end of the fiscal year (in millions):

Inventories and supplies	$ 29.0
Prepaid expenses and other current assets	65.9
Air traffic liability	123.7
Accrued wages, vacation, and payroll taxes	36.6

A footnote stated: "Passenger revenues are considered earned at the time service is provided. Tickets sold but not yet used are reported as Air Traffic Liability."
The 1996 income statement included (in millions):

Passenger revenues	$925.9
Wages and benefits expense	323.1

1. Analyze the impact of the following assumed 1997 transactions on the financial position of Alaska. Prepare your analysis in the same format used when the adjustment process was explained in the chapter. Also show adjusting journal entries.

   a. Rented a sales office in a Transamerica office building for one year, beginning December 1, 1997, for $18,000 cash.

   b. On December 31, 1997, an adjustment was made for the rent in requirement 1.

   c. Sold two charter flights to Apple Computer for $100,000 each. Cash of $200,000 was received in advance on November 20, 1997. The flights were for transporting marketing personnel to two business conventions in New York.

   d. As the financial statements were being prepared on December 31, 1997, accountants for both Alaska and Apple Computer independently noted that the first charter flight had occurred in late December. The second would occur in early February. An adjustment was made on December 31.

   e. Alaska had lent $2 million to Boeing. Interest of $160,000 was accrued on December 31.

   f. Additional wages of $140,000 were accrued on December 31.

2. Compute the balance in the Air Traffic Liability account after the recording of these transactions.

4-39 Budweiser Financial Statements

(Alternate is 4-31.) Anheuser-Busch (maker of Budweiser beer) is the largest beer producer in the United States. Some actual financial data and nomenclature from its 1996 annual report were (in millions):

Anheuser-Busch, Inc.

Interest expense, net	$ 187.9	Cash dividends declared	$?
Sales	10,883.7	Other income	30.8
Gross profit	3,919.1	Net income	1,189.9
Operating income	2,083.8	Retained earnings:	
Other operating income	54.7	Beginning of year	6,193.5
Marketing, distribution, and		End of year	6,924.5
administrative expenses	?	Provision for income taxes	
Cost of products sold	?	(income tax expense)	736.8

1. Prepare a combined multiple-step statement of income and retained earnings for the year ended December 31, 1996. *Hint:* see page 144.

2. Compute the percentage of gross profit on sales and the percentage of net income on sales.

3. The average stockholders' equity for the year was $4,231.5 million. What was the percentage of net income on average stockholders' equity?

4-40 Accounting for Dues

(Alternate is 4-41.) The Stone Beach Golf Club provided the following data from its comparative balance sheets:

	December 31	
	19X8	*19X7*
Dues receivable	$90,000	$75,000
Unearned dues revenue	—	$30,000

The income statement for 19X8, which was prepared on the accrual basis, showed dues revenue earned of $720,000. No dues were collected in advance during 19X8.

Required

Prepare journal entries and post to T-accounts for the following:

1. Earning of dues collected in advance.
2. Billing of dues revenue during 19X8.
3. Collection of dues receivable in 19X8.

4-41 Accounting for Subscriptions

(Alternate is 4-40.) A French magazine company collects subscriptions in advance of delivery of its magazines. However, many magazines are delivered to magazine distributors (for newsstand sales), and these distributors are billed and pay later. The subscription revenue earned for the month of March on the accrual basis was FF200,000 (FF refers to the French franc). Other pertinent data were:

	March	
	31	*1*
Unearned subscription revenue	FF190,000	FF140,000
Accounts receivable	7,000	9,000

Required

Reconstruct the entries for March. Prepare journal entries and post to T-accounts for the following:

1. Collections of unearned subscription revenue of FF140,000 prior to March 1.
2. Billing of accounts receivable (a) of FF9,000 prior to March 1, and (b) of FF80,000 during March. (Credit Revenue Earned)
3. Collections of cash during March and any other entries that are indicated by the given data.

4-42 Financial Statements and Adjustments

Marcella Wholesalers, Inc., has just completed its fourth year of business, 19X3. A set of financial statements was prepared by the principal stockholder's eldest child, a college student who is beginning the third week of an accounting course. Following is a list (in no systematic order) of the items appearing in the student's balance sheet, income statement, and statement of retained income:

Accounts receivable	$183,100	Advertising expense	$ 98,300
Note receivable	36,000	Merchandise inventory	201,900
Cash	99,300	Cost of goods sold	590,000
Paid-in capital	620,000	Unearned rent revenue	4,800
Building	300,000	Insurance expense	2,500
Accumulated depreciation,		Unexpired insurance	2,300
building	20,000	Accounts payable	52,500
Land	169,200	Interest expense	600
Sales	936,800	Telephone expense	2,900
Salary expense	124,300	Notes payable	20,000
Retained income:		Net income	110,500
December 31,19X2	164,000	Miscellaneous expense	3,400
December 31,19X3	274,500	Maintenance expense	4,300

Assume that the statements in which these items appear are current and complete except for the following matters not taken into consideration by the student:

a. Salaries of $5,200 have been earned by employees for the last half of December 19X3. Payment by the company will be made on the next payday, January 2, 19X4.

b. Interest at 10% per annum on the note receivable has accrued for two months and is expected to be collected by the company when the note is due on January 31, 19X4.

c. Part of the building owned by the company was rented to a tenant on November 1, 19X3, for six months, payable in advance. This rent was collected in cash and is represented by the item labeled Unearned Rent Revenue.

d. Depreciation on the building for 19X3 is $6,100.

e. Cash dividends of $60,000 were declared in December 19X3, payable in January 19X4.

f. Income tax at 40% applies to 19X3, all of which is to be paid in the early part of 19X4.

Required Prepare the following corrected financial statements:

1. Multiple-step income statement for 19X3.
2. Statement of retained income for 19X3.
3. Classified balance sheet at December 31, 19X3. (Show appropriate support for the dollar amounts you compute.)

4-43 Mirror Side of Adjustments
Problem 4-34 described some Blair adjustments. Repeat the requirement for each adjustment as it would be made by the client in transactions *b* and *c* and by the secretary in transaction *d*. For our purposes here, assume that the secretary keeps personal books on the accrual basis.

4-44 Mirror Side of Adjustments
Problem 4-37 described some Goodyear adjustments. Repeat the requirements for each adjustment as it would be made by (a) landlords, (b) U-Haul, (c) retail dealers, and (d) U.S. and foreign governments. Assume that all use accrual accounting.

4-45 Mirror Side of Adjustments
Problem 4-38 described some Alaska Airlines adjustments lettered a through f. Repeat the requirements for each adjustment as it would be made by the other party in the transaction. Specifically, (a) and (b) Transamerica, (c) and (d) Apple Computer, (e) Boeing, and (f) employees. Assume that all use accrual accounting.

4-46 Journal Entries and Posting

Nike, Inc., has many well-known products, including footwear. The company's balance sheet included (in thousands):

	May 31	
	1997	*1996*
Prepaid expenses	$152,058	$94,427
Income taxes payable	53,923	79,253

Suppose that during the fiscal year ended May 31, 1997, $210,000,000 cash was disbursed and charged to Prepaid Expenses. Similarly, $254,772,000 was disbursed for income taxes and charged to Income Taxes Payable.

1. Assume that the Prepaid Expenses account relates to outlays for miscellaneous operating expenses (for example, supplies, insurance, and short-term rentals). Prepare summary journal entries for (a) the disbursements and (b) the expenses for fiscal 1997. Post the entries to the T-accounts.

2. Assume that there were no other accounts related to income taxes. Prepare summary journal entries for (a) the disbursements and (b) the expenses for fiscal 1997. Post the entries to T-accounts.

4-47 Advance Service Contracts

Diebold, Incorporated, a manufacturer of automated teller machines (ATMs), showed the following balance sheet account:

	January 2	
	1997	*1996*
Deferred income	$69,094,000	$62,687,000

A footnote to the financial statements stated: "Deferred income is recognized for customer billings in advance of the period in which the service will be performed and is recognized in income on a straight-line basis over the contract period."

1. Prepare summary journal entries for the creation in 1996 and subsequent earning in 1997 of the deferred income of $62,687,000. Use the following accounts: Accounts Receivable, Deferred Income, and Income from Advance Billings.

2. A one-year job contract was billed to Keystone Bank on January 2, 1997, for $36,000. Work began on January 2. The full amount was collected on February 15. Prepare all pertinent journal entries through February 28, 1997. ("Straight-line" means an equal amount per month.)

4-48 Journal Entries and Adjustments

Northern States Power Company is a public utility in Minnesota. An annual report included the following footnote:

Revenues—Because utility customer meters are read and billed on a cycle basis, unbilled revenues are estimated and recorded for services provided from the monthly meter-reading dates to month-end.

The income statements showed:

	1996	1995
Operating revenues	$2,654,206,000	$2,568,584,000
Operating income	366,044,000	345,879,000

The balance sheet showed as part of current assets:

	December 31	
	1996	*1995*
Customer accounts receivable	$288,330,000	$281,584,000
Unbilled utility revenues	147,366,000	112,650,000

Prepare the adjusting journal entry for (a) the unbilled revenues at the end of 1996 and (b) the eventual billing and collection of the unbilled revenues. Ignore income taxes.

4-49 Classified Balance Sheet and Current Ratio

Intel is the world's leading producer of microprocessors. The company's balance sheet for December 28, 1996 contained the following items (in millions of dollars):

Property and equipment, net	$ 8,487
Accrued compensation and benefits	1,128
Cash	4,165
Other assets	1,564
Other noncurrent liabilities	1,272
Short-term debt	389
Inventories	1,293
Other current liabilities	1,391
Income taxes payable	986
Other current assets	761
Accounts payable	969
Short-term investments	3,742
Accounts receivable	3,723
Long-term debt	?
Stockholders' equity	16,872

Required

1. Prepare a December 28, 1996 classified balance sheet for Intel. Include the correct amount for long-term debt.

2. Compute the company's working capital and current ratio.

3. Comment on the company's current ratio. In 1995 the ratio was 2.2. The industry average is 2.0.

4. During 1996 Intel increased its short-term investments by $2,747,000. Suppose the company had not increased its short-term investments but had instead increased its long-term investments by $2,747,000. How would this have affected Intel's current ratio? How would it have affected the company's solvency?

4-50 Multiple-Step Income Statement

Kimberly-Clark Corporation has many well-known products, including Kleenex and Huggies. Its 1996 annual report contained the following data and actual terms (in milions):

Cost of products sold	$8,241	Advertising, promotion,	
Research expense	208	and selling expense	$2,030
Interest expense	187	Provision for income taxes	
Interest and other income	135	(income tax expense)	701
Gross profit	4,908	General and other expense	616

Required Prepare a multiple-step statement of income.

4-51 Single-Step Income Statement

A. T. Cross Company's best-known products are writing instruments such as ballpoint pens. The Cross 1996 annual report contained the following items (in thousands):

Interest and other income	$ 2,091	Selling, general, and	
Cost of goods sold	94,093	administrative expenses	$ 70,627
		Other expenses	7,196
Provision for income taxes		Retained earnings at end	
(income tax expense)	2,772	of year	106,781
Sales	179,203	Cash dividends	10,568

1. Prepare a combined single-step statement of income and retained earnings for the year. Required

2. Compute the percentage of gross profit on sales and the percentage of net income on sales.

3. The average stockholders' equity for the year was about $129 million. What was the percentage of net income on average stockholders' equity?

4. In 1992 the gross profit percentage was 47.0%, the percentage of net income to sales was 5.8%, and the return on average stockholders' equity was 6.9%. Comment on the changes between 1992 and 1996.

4-52 Retail Company Financial Statements

Kmart Corporation is one of the world's largest retailers. The annual report for the year ended January 29, 1997 included the data shown below (in millions of dollars). Unless otherwise specified, the balance sheet amounts are the balances at the end on January 29, 1997.

Sales	$31,437	Interest expense	$ 453
Cash dividends	0	Long-term debt	2,121
Merchandise inventories	6,354	Cash	406
Cost of sales, buying,		Selling, general, & administrative	
and occupancy	24,390	expenses	6,274
Paid-in capital	3,074	Accrued taxes payable	139
Accounts receivable	973	Accrued payroll and other current	
Other expenses	472	liabilities	1,298
Retained earnings:			
Beginning of year	3,218	Provision for income taxes	68
End of year	2,998	Property & equipment, net	5,740
Notes payable	156	Other noncurrent assets	813
Accounts payable	2,009	Other noncurrent liabilities	2,491

1. Prepare a combined multiple-step statement of income and retained earnings. Required

2. Prepare a classified balance sheet.

3. The average stockholders' equity for the year was about $5,671 million. What was the percentage of net income (loss) on average stockholders' equity?

4. Compute (a) gross profit percentage and (b) percentage of net income to sales.

5. Optional: Why might stockholders want to invest in a company with a loss?

4-53   Preparation of Financial Statements from Trial Balance

ConAgra, the Omaha company that produces consumer foods such as Armour and Swift meats, Banquet and Morton frozen foods, and Healthy Choice brands, prepared the following (slightly modified) trial balance as of May 31, 1997, the end of the company's fiscal year:

ConAgra, Inc.
Trial Balance May 31, 1997 (in millions)

	Debits	Credits
Cash and cash equivalents	$ 105.8	
Receivables	1,367.6	
Inventories	3,342.9	
Prepaid expenses	388.7	
Property, plant, and equipment, at cost	5,274.3	

continued

Accumulated depreciation, property, plant, and equipment		$ 2,031.8
Brands, trademarks, and goodwill, net	$ 2,434.0	
Other assets	395.6	
Notes payable		529.0
Accounts payable		1,894.7
Accrued payroll		283.3
Advances on sales (deferred revenues)		766.5
Other current liabilities		1,516.1
Long-term debt		2,355.7
Other noncurrent liabilities		935.1
Preferred stock		525.0
Common stock, $5 par value		1,265.4
Retained earnings (May 31, 1996)		1,683.5
Additional paid-in capital		643.3
Treasury stock*	1,498.2	
Net sales		24,002.1
Cost of goods sold	20,441.8	
Selling, administrative, and general expenses	2,265.4	
Interest expense	277.2	
Income taxes	402.7	
Cash dividends	237.3	
Total	$38,437.5	$38,437.5

*Part of stockholders' equity.

Required

1. Prepare ConAgra's income statement for the year ended May 31, 1997, using a multiple-step format.

2. Prepare ConAgra's income statement for the year ended May 31, 1997, using a single-step format. Which format for the income statement is more informative? Why?

3. Prepare ConAgra's classified balance sheet as of May 31, 1997.

4-54 Professional Football Income

Examine the accompanying condensed income statement of the Green Bay Packers, Inc.

Income:		
Regular season:		
Net receipts from home games	$ 3,223,803	
Out-of-town games	2,288,967	
Television and radio programs	14,322,244	$19,835,014
Preseason:		
Net receipts from preseason games	1,356,751	
Television and radio programs	355,032	1,711,783
Miscellaneous:		
Club allocation of league receipts	784,988	
Other income	511,516	1,296,504
Total income		22,843,301
Expenses:		
Salaries and other season expenses	16,243,729	
Training expense	725,079	
Overhead expense	4,744,336	
Severance pay	656,250	22,369,394
Income from operations		473,907
Interest income		1,203,281
Income before taxes		1,677,188
Provision for income taxes		167,000
Net income		$ 1,510,188

1. Do you agree with the choice of terms in this statement? If not, suggest where a preferable label should be used.
2. Is this a single-step income statement? If not, which items would you shift to prepare a single-step statement?
3. Identify the major factors that affect the Packers' net income.

4-55 Adjusting Entries and Ethics

By definition, adjusting entries are not triggered by an explicit event. Therefore, accountants must initiate adjusting entries. For each of the following adjusting entries, discuss a potential unethical behavior that an accountant or manager might undertake:

a. Recognition of expenses from the prepaid supplies account.
b. Recognition of revenue from the unearned revenue account.
c. Accrual of interest payable.
d. Accrual of fees receivable.

4-56 The Gap Annual Report

This problem uses an actual company's accounts to develop skill in preparing adjusting journal entries. Refer to the financial statements of The Gap (Appendix A at the end of the book). Note the following balance sheet items:

	February 1	
	1997	*1996*
Prepaid expenses and other current assets	$129,214,000	$128,398,000
Accrued expenses	282,494,000	194,426,000

Suppose that during the year ended February 1, 1997, $1,200,000,000 cash was disbursed and charged to Prepaid Expenses and $1,600,000,000 of accrued liabilities were paid.

1. Assume that the Prepaid Expenses account relates to outlays for miscellaneous Operating Expenses (for example, supplies, insurance, and short-term rentals). Prepare summary journal entries for (a) the disbursements and (b) the expenses (for our purposes, debit Operating Expenses) for the year ended February 1, 1997. Post the entries to the T-accounts.
2. Prepare summary journal entries for (a) the disbursements and (b) the expenses related to the accrued liabilities for the year ended February 1, 1997. (For our purposes, debit Operating Expenses.) Post the entries to the T-accounts.

4-57 Financial Statement Research

Select any two companies.

1. For each company, determine the amount of working capital and the current ratio.
2. Compare the current ratios. Which company has the larger ratio, and what do the ratios tell you about the solvency of the companies?
3. Compute the gross margin percentage, the return on sales, and the return on stockholders' equity.
4. Compare the profitability of the two companies.

COLLABORATIVE LEARNING EXERCISE

4-58 Implicit Transactions

Form groups of from three to six "players." Each group should have a die and a paper (or board) with four columns labeled:

1. Expiration of unexpired costs
2. Realization of unearned revenues
3. Accrual of unrecorded expenses
4. Accrual of unrecorded revenues

The players should select an order in which they wish to play. Then, the first player rolls the die. If he or she rolls a 5 or 6, the die passes to the next player. If he or she rolls a 1, 2, 3, or 4, he or she must, within 20 seconds, name an example of a transaction that fits in the corresponding category; for example, if a 2 is rolled, the player must give an example of realization of unearned revenues. Each time a correct example is given, the player receives one point. If someone doubts the correctness of a given example, he or she can challenge it. If the remaining players unanimously agree that the example is incorrect, the challenger gets a point and the player giving the example does not get a point for a correct example and is out of the game. If the remaining players do not unanimously agree that the answer is incorrect, the challenger loses a point and the player giving the example gets a point for a correct example. If a player fails to give an example within the time limit or gives an incorrect example, he or she is out of the game (except for voting when an example is challenged), and the remaining players continue until everyone has failed to give a correct example within the time limit. Each correct answer should be listed under the appropriate column. The player with the most points is the group winner.

When all groups have finished a round of play, a second level of play can begin. All the groups can get together and list all the examples for each of the four categories by group. Discussion can establish the correctness of each entry; the faculty member or an appointed discussion leader will be the final arbitrator of the correctness of each entry. Each group gets one point for each correct example and loses one point for each incorrect entry. The group with the most points is the overall winner.

4-59 Internet Case

Go to **http://www.landsend.com** to find Lands' End's home page. Select *About Us* from the menu, and choose the most recent annual report.

Answer the following questions about Lands' End:

1. Name two items on Lands' End's balance sheet that most likely represent unexpired (prepaid) costs. Name two items that most likely represent accruals of unrecorded expenses.
2. Does Lands' End prepare a single- or multiple-step income statement? How do you know?
3. Determine Lands' End's gross profit percentage for the two most recent years. Is the change favorable or not? Does management of Lands' End comment on the reason for this change? (Hint: Try the *Management's Discussion and Analysis* section.) If so, what comments do they make? If not, why do you think management did not feel the need to justify the change? How do you think management determines the *reason* that gross profit changed given the extremely condensed nature of the income statement?
4. Calculate Lands' End's current ratio for the two most recent years. Did this ratio improve or decline? Does management comment about any particular problems

that could have affected this ratio? (Try the *Shareholders' Letter.*) Should management be concerned with the change in its current ratio?

5. Where can you find evidence in Lands' End's annual report that the financial statements were prepared using GAAP?

6. Examine the amount of income tax expense (income tax provision) and the amount of taxes actually paid during the year. (Use the *Statement of Cash Flows.*). Are you able to tell if any income taxes were accrued during the year? Explain. You do not need to calculate a number.

7. Explain how Lands' End's financial statements illustrate one of the basic concepts or principles that are presented in this chapter of your text.

5

ACCOUNTING FOR SALES

The odds are high that these are the chips inside your personal computer. "Intel inside" is a slogan and a practice that has transformed the company and the industry.

Learning Objectives

After studying this chapter, you should be able to

1 Recognize revenue items at the proper time on the income statement.

2 Account for cash and credit sales.

3 Record sales returns and allowances, sales discounts, and bank credit card sales.

4 Manage cash and explain its importance to the company.

5 Estimate and interpret uncollectible accounts receivable balances.

6 Assess the level of accounts receivable.

7 Develop and explain internal control procedures.

Would you like to invest in a stock whose price increases tenfold in just four years? Anyone who bought Intel's stock in 1993 already has. Intel stock purchased for $100 in 1993 sold for more than $1,000 before the end of 1997.

If you had been able to read and understand Intel's financial statements in 1993, could you have predicted this large increased in stock price? Unfortunately, probably not. If understanding financial statements were sufficient for making good investment decisions, there would be a lot of rich accountants in this world. But looking at Intel's financial statement from 1993 through 1996 will help explain why the company did so well over that period. And understanding what made Intel successful will help you predict whether that success will continue.

Intel's revenues increased from $8,782 million in 1993 to $20,847 million in 1996, a rate of growth of more than 33% per year. Meanwhile, income rose $2,277 million to $5,157 million. To support this growth in sales and profits, Intel's total assets increased from $11,384 million in 1993 to $23,735 million in 1996. Because of profitable operations, retained earnings soared from $5,306 million to $13,975 million between 1993 and 1996.

Will Intel continue to be this successful? No one knows for sure. But there are some clues in the company's 1997 balance sheet. For one thing, Intel has more than $4 billion in cash. That much cash can help Intel fund its expansion plans. Or it can provide a shot in the arm in case sales drop. The microprocessor industry is cyclical, which means that sales throughout the industry will rise and fall. Sales, of course, is the driving force behind any company's success. If Intel's sales remain strong, the company will continue to be successful. Even if the industry stumbles and Intel's sales fall, $4 billion makes a nice cushion.

When sales are recognized in the income statement, the firm receives either cash or the promise of cash, which is classified under accounts receivable. Both cash and accounts receivable are considered assets, so the recognition of sales directly affects the balance sheet. In this chapter we will examine sales revenue issues and explain their direct impact on both the income statement and balance sheet.

RECOGNITION OF SALES REVENUE

Objective 1
Recognize revenue items at the proper time on the income statement.

Why is the timing of revenue recognition important? Because it is critical to the measurement of net income. The revenue itself affects net income, both directly and indirectly. Under the matching principle, the cost of the items sold is reported in the same period in which revenue is recognized. Thus, not only does the recording of revenue affect net income directly, but it also determines the recognition of certain related expenses.

The timing of changes in net income might not seem so important until you realize that managers often receive higher salaries or greater bonuses for increasing sales and net income. Therefore, they prefer to recognize sales revenue as soon as possible. Owners and potential investors, however, want to be sure the economic benefits of the sale are guaranteed before recognizing revenue. In other words, they want to be sure that the company will actually receive payment before they recognize the accounting effects of a completed sale. Because of these different perspectives, accountants must carefully assess when revenue should be recognized.

A key feature of accrual-basis accounting is that recognition of revenue requires a two-pronged test: (1) goods or services must be delivered to the customers (that is, the revenue is *earned*), and (2) cash or an asset virtually assured of being converted into cash must be received (that is, the revenue is *realized*). Most revenue is recognized at the point of sale. Suppose you buy a compact disc at a local music store. Both revenue recognition tests are generally met at the time of purchase. You receive the merchandise, and the store receives cash, a check, or a credit card slip. Because both checks and credit card slips are readily converted to cash, the store can recognize revenue at the point of sale regardless of which of these three methods of payment you use.

Of course, the two revenue recognition tests are not always met at the same time. In such cases, revenue is generally recognized only when both tests are met. Consider magazine subscriptions. The realization test is met when the publisher receives cash. However, revenues are not earned until magazines are delivered. Therefore revenue recognition is delayed until the time of delivery.

Sometimes accountants must make a judgment call on when the recognition criteria are met. A classic example is accounting for long-term contracts. Suppose Lockheed signs a $40 million contract with the U.S. government to produce a part for the space shuttle. The contract is signed, and work begins on January 2, 19X1. The completion date is December 31, 19X4. Payment will be made upon delivery of the part. Lockheed expects to complete one-fourth of the project each year. When should the $40 million of revenue be recorded on the company's income statement?

The most common answer is that one-fourth of the revenue is earned each year, so $10 million of the revenue should be recognized annually. Generally, the government and major corporations can be counted on to make payments on their contracts. Therefore, revenues on such contracts are recognized as the work is performed. Because payment is virtually certain, revenues can be realized as they are gradually earned. Once the decision is made to recognize the revenue as production occurs, the matching principle requires that corresponding recognition be given to the associated expenses. When one-quarter of the revenue is recognized, one-quarter of the expected expenses are recorded as well.

After deciding when revenue is to be recognized, the accountant must determine how much revenue to record. In other words, how should accountants measure revenue?

A cash sale increases Sales Revenue, an income statement account, and increases Cash, a balance sheet account. A credit sale on open account is recorded much like a cash sale except that the balance sheet account Accounts Receivable is increased instead of Cash. Note that cash and accounts receivable represent the two accounts that both can be affected by sales and that both represent assets. To measure revenue, accountants approximate the net realizable value of the asset inflow from the customer. That is, the revenue is measured in terms of the cash equivalent value of the asset (either cash or accounts receivable) received.

Revenue is recorded equal to the asset received:

```
Cash  ..............................  xxx
        Sales revenue  .....................        xxx
OR
Accounts receivable  ....................  xxx
        Sales revenue  .....................        xxx
```

Objective 2
Account for cash and credit sales.

In fact, there are many ways in which prices are not what they appear and ultimately the revenue earned may not be equal to the original sales price. Merchants give discounts for prompt payment, or discounts for high volume purchases. Sometimes, the customer is unable or unwilling to pay the full amount owed. The accounting system must deal with all of these issues and the manager must have information to determine how company policy is affecting the relationship with the customer.

MERCHANDISE RETURNS AND ALLOWANCES

Suppose revenue for a given sale is recognized at the point of that sale, but later the customer decides to return the merchandise. He or she may be unhappy with the product's color, size, style, or quality, or simply may have a change of heart. The supplier (vendor) calls these **sales returns;** the customer calls them **purchase returns.** Such merchandise returns are minor for manufacturers and wholesalers but are major for retail department stores. For instance, returns of 12% of gross sales are not abnormal for stores such as Marshall Field's or Macy's.

Sometimes, instead of returning merchandise, the customer demands a reduction of the selling price (the original price previously agreed upon). For example, a customer may complain about finding scratches on a household appliance or about buying a cordless phone for $40 on Wednesday and seeing the same item for sale in the same store or elsewhere for $35 on Thursday. Such complaints are often settled by the seller's granting a **sales allowance** (or **purchase allowance**), which is essentially a reduction of the original selling price.

Naturally, sales allowances and returns are going to have an effect on **net sales,** but not on gross sales. **Gross sales** are equal to the initial revenues or asset inflows based on the sales price, and they must be decreased by the amount of the returns and allowances to give the net sales. But instead of directly reducing the revenue (or sales) account, managers of retail stores typically use a contra account, Sales Returns and Allowances, which combines both returns and allowances in a single account. Managers use a contra account so they can watch changes in the level of returns and allowances. For instance, a change in the percentage of returns in fashion merchandise may give early signals about changes in customer tastes. Similarly, a buyer of fashion or fad merchandise may want to keep track of purchase returns to help assess the quality of products and services of various suppliers. Also, it is useful to track sales and returns separately so that sales figures for commissions or bonuses are properly interpreted. Another reason managers use separate accounts for sales and returns is that the returns happen after the sales, and separate tracking avoids going back and changing the original entries for the sale, a messy and unreliable process. Let's take a look at how a real retailer might adjust gross sales by accounting for sales returns and allowances. Suppose your

Objective 3
Record sales returns and allowances, sales discounts, and bank credit card sales.

sales returns (purchase returns) Products returned by the customer.

sales allowance (purchase allowance) Reduction of the original selling price.

net sales Total sales revenue reduced by sales returns and allowances.

gross sales Total sales revenue before deducting sales returns and allowances.

local outlet of The Disney Store has $900,000 gross sales on credit and $80,000 sales returns and allowances. The analysis of transactions would show:

	A	=	L +		SE
Credit sales on open account	+900,000 Increase Accounts Receivable	=			+900,000 Increase Sales
Returns and allowances	−80,000 Decrease Accounts Receivable	=			−80,000 Increase Sales Returns and Allowances

The journal entries (without explanations) are:

```
Accounts receivable  . . . . . . . . . . . . . . . . . 900,000
        Sales  . . . . . . . . . . . . . . . . . . . . . . . . .          900,000
Sales returns and allowances  . . . . . . . . . . .  80,000
        Accounts receivable  . . . . . . . . . . . . .           80,000
```

The income statement would begin:

Gross sales	$900,000
Deduct: Sales returns and allowances	80,000
Net sales	$820,000
or	
Sales, net of $80,000 returns and allowances	$820,000

Returns and allowances are not the only factors that affect gross and net sales figures. Discounts also affect the reported sales. There are two major types of sales discounts: trade and cash. **Trade discounts** offer one or more reductions to the gross selling price for a particular class of customers. These discounts are generally price concessions or purchase incentives. An example is a discount for large-volume purchases. The seller might offer no discount on the first $10,000 of merchandise purchased per year but a 2% discount on the next $10,000 worth of purchases and a discount of 3% to a customer on all sales in excess of $20,000.

trade discounts
Reductions to the gross selling price for a particular class of customers.

Companies set trade discount terms for various reasons. If such discounts are offered by competing firms, the seller may offer trade discounts to be competitive. Discounts may also be used to encourage certain customer behavior. For example, manufacturers with seasonal products (gardening supplies, snow shovels, fans, Christmas gifts, and so on) might offer price discounts on early orders and deliveries to smooth out production throughout the year and minimize the manufacturer's cost of storing the inventory. In deciding to accept early delivery, the buyer must weigh the storage costs it will incur against the reduced price the discount provides. The gross sales revenue recognized from a trade discount sale is the price received after deducting the discount.

cash discounts
Reductions of invoice prices awarded for prompt payment.

In contrast to trade discounts, **cash discounts** are rewards for prompt payment. The terms of the discount may be quoted in various ways on the invoice:

Credit Terms	Meaning
n/30	The full billed price (net price) is due on the thirtieth day after the invoice date.
1/5, n/30	A 1% discount can be taken for payment within five days of the invoice date; otherwise the full billed price is due in thirty days.
15 E.O.M.	The full price is due within fifteen days after the end-of-the-month of sale. An invoice dated December 20 is due January 15.

For example, a manufacturer sells $30,000 of computer games to Toys "Я" Us, a retailer, on terms 2/10, n/60. Therefore, Toys "Я" Us may remit $30,000 less a cash discount of 0.02 × $30,000, or $30,000 − $600 = $29,400, if payment is made within 10 days after the invoice date. Otherwise the full $30,000 is due in 60 days.

Cash discounts entice prompt payment and reduce the manufacturer's need for cash. Early collection also reduces the risk of bad debts. Favorable credit terms with attractive cash discounts are also a way to compete with other sellers. That is, if one seller grants such terms, competitors tend to do likewise.

Should cash discounts be taken by purchasers? The answer is usually yes, but the decision depends on the relative costs of interest. Suppose Toys " Я " Us decides not to pay the $30,000 invoice for 60 days. It has the use of $29,400 for an extra 50 days (60 − 10) for an "interest" payment of $600. Think of this as if Toys " Я " Us had two choices. They could borrow the money from the bank and pay 10% interest per year. Interest for 50 days on $29,400 would be $402 ($29,400 × 10% × 50 ÷ 365). Alternatively, they could delay payment for 50 days and pay the higher invoice price. Notice that it is much cheaper to borrow the money, and that is what most companies should do. The total invoice is $600 higher than the discount price and the interest is only $402.

You could also calculate the annual interest rate equivalent of the discount using the following logic. If you pay $600 to use the money for 50 days, you are paying 2.04% for the 50 days ($600 ÷ $29,400). During a year there are 7.3 periods of 50 days (365 days ÷ 50 days). If the interest rate is 2.04% for 50 days, it will be 14.9% for the year (2.04% per period × 7.3 periods per year). Most well-managed companies, such as Toys " Я " Us, can obtain funds for less than 14.9% interest per year, so their accounting systems are designed to take advantage of all cash discounts automatically. However, some retailers pass up the discounts. Why? Because they have trouble getting loans or other financing at interest rates lower than the annual rates implied by the cash discount terms offered by their suppliers. Usage of cash discounts varies through time and from one industry to another. You may be familiar with some gas stations that offer a lower price for cash payment, while other stations do not.

RECORDING CHARGE CARD TRANSACTIONS

Cash discounts also occur when retailers accept charge cards such as Visa, MasterCard, American Express, Carte Blanche, or Diner's Club. Retailers accept these cards for three major reasons: (1) to attract credit customers who would otherwise shop elsewhere, (2) to get cash immediately rather than wait for customers to pay in due course, and (3) to avoid the cost of keeping track of many customers' accounts.

Retailers can deposit VISA slips in their bank accounts daily (just like cash). But this service costs money (in the form of service charges on every credit sale), and this cost must be included in the calculations to determine net sales revenue. Card companies impose a service charge for card sales of anywhere from 1% to 3% of gross sales, although large-volume retailers bear less cost as a percentage of sales. For example, JC Penney had an arrangement where it accepted charge cards other than its own branded card. It paid 4.3 cents per transaction plus only 1.08% of the gross sales using charge cards.

With the 3% rate, credit sales of $10,000 will result in cash of only $10,000 − 0.03 ($10,000), or $10,000 − $300, or $9,700. The $300 amount may be separately tabulated for management control purposes:

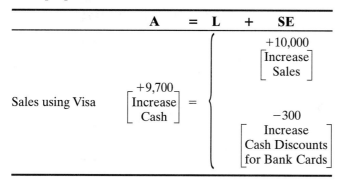

```
Cash ............................. 9,700
Cash discounts for bank cards ........... 300
         Sales ......................... 10,000
```

ACCOUNTING FOR NET SALES REVENUE

Cash discounts and sales returns and allowances are recorded as deductions from Gross Sales. Consequently, a detailed income statement will often contain:

Gross sales		XXX
Deduct:		
Sales returns and allowances	X	
Cash discounts on sales	X	XX
Net sales		XXX

Reports to shareholders often omit details and show only net revenues. For example, when Nike shows "Revenues . . . $3,789,668,000" on its income statement, the number refers to its net revenues. Note also that in many countries outside the United States, the word **turnover** is used as a synonym for sales or revenues. Thus British Petroleum began its income statement with "Turnover . . . £34,950,000,000."

An important feature of the income statement is the fact that returns, allowances, and most discounts are offsets to gross sales. Management may design an accounting system to use one account, Sales, or several accounts, as shown in the preceding sample income statement. If only one account is used, all returns, allowances, and cash discounts are direct decreases to the sales account. If a separate account is used for cash discounts on sales, the following analysis would be made for our Toys "Я" Us example:

turnover A synonym for sales or revenues in many countries outside the United States.

	A	= L +	SE
1. Sell at terms of 2/10, n/60	+30,000 [Increase Accounts Receivable]	=	+30,000 [Increase Sales]

Followed by either 2 or 3

	A	= L +	SE
2. Either collect $29,400 ($30,000 less 2%)	+29,400 [Increase Cash] −30,000 [Decrease Accounts Receivable]	=	−600 [Increase Cash Discounts on Sales]
or 3. collect $30,000	+30,000 [Increase Cash] −30,000 [Decrease Accounts Receivable]	=	(no effect)

The journal entries follow:

```
1. Accounts receivable ........................  30,000
     Sales ...................................          30,000
2. Cash  ................................... 29,400
     Cash discounts on sales ...................    600
       Accounts receivable ......................          30,000
   OR
3. Cash  ................................... 30,000
     Accounts receivable ......................          30,000
```

Many companies combine cash and cash equivalents on their balance sheets. **Cash equivalents** are highly liquid short-term investments that can easily and quickly be converted into cash. For example, the 1996 balance sheet of Chrysler begins with "Cash and equivalents . . . $5,158 million." Chrysler describes its cash equivalents as "highly liquid investments with a maturity of three months or less at the date of purchase."

Cash has essentially the same meaning to organizations that it does to individuals. It isn't just paper money and coins, though. Instead, cash encompasses all the items that are accepted for deposit by a bank, notably paper money and coins, money orders, and checks. Banks do not accept postage stamps, IOUs, or postdated checks as cash. Of course, not all of the items a bank does accept for deposit are treated the same. For example, although all deposits may be credited to the accounts of bank customers on the date received, the bank may not provide the depositor with access to the funds from a deposited check until the check "clears" through the banking system (until payment is actually made from the check writer's account). If the check fails to clear because its writer has insufficient funds, its amount is deducted from the depositor's account.

COMPENSATING BALANCES

There are other reasons that the entire cash balance in a bank account may not be available for unrestricted use. Banks frequently require companies to maintain **compensating balances,** which are required minimum balances on deposit to compensate the bank for providing loans. The size of the minimum balance may depend on the amount borrowed, the amount of credit available, or both.

Compensating balances increase the effective interest rate paid by the borrower. When borrowing $100,000 at 10% per year, annual interest will be $10,000. With a 10% compensating balance, the borrower can use only $90,000 of the loan, raising the effective interest rate on the usable funds to 11.1% ($10,000 ÷ $90,000).

To prevent any misleading information regarding cash, annual reports must disclose the state of any significant compensating balances. For example, a footnote in the annual report of North Carolina Natural Gas Corporation disclosed a requirement for keeping a compensating balance "of 10% of the annual average loan outstanding" in its bank account. Without such a disclosure, financial statement readers might think that a company has more cash available than it really does.

MANAGEMENT OF CASH

Cash is usually a small portion of the total assets of a company. Yet, managers spend much time managing cash. Why? For many reasons. First, although the cash balance may be small at any one time, the flow of cash can be enormous. Weekly receipts and disbursements of cash may be many times as large as the cash balance. Second, because cash is the most liquid asset, it is enticing to thieves and embezzlers. If companies do not watch their cash, someone might walk off with it. Third, adequate cash is essential to the smooth functioning of operations. Companies need it for everything from routine purchases to major investments, from purchasing lunch for a visiting business partner to purchasing another

Objective 4
Manage cash and explain its importance to the company.

cash equivalents Highly liquid short-term investments that can easily be converted into cash.

compensating balances Required minimum cash balances on deposit when money is borrowed from banks.

company. Finally, because cash itself does not earn income, it is important not to hold excess cash. The treasury department will be responsible for managing the levels of cash efficiently and for assuring that unneeded cash is deposited in income generating accounts.

Most organizations have detailed, well-specified procedures for receiving, recording, and disbursing cash. It is usually placed in a bank account, and the company's books are periodically reconciled with the bank's records. To **reconcile a bank statement** means to verify that the bank balance and the accounting records are consistent. The two balances are rarely identical. A company accountant records a deposit when made and a payment when the check is written. The bank, however, may receive or record the deposit several days after the accountant recorded it because of postal delay, deposit on a bank holiday or weekend, and so on. The bank may also process a check days, weeks, or even months after it was issued.

reconcile a bank statement
To verify that the bank balance for cash is consistent with the accounting records.

In addition to reconciling the bank balance, other internal control procedures are set up to safeguard cash. Briefly, the major procedures include the following:

1. The individuals who receive cash do not also disburse cash.
2. The individuals who handle cash cannot access accounting records.
3. Cash receipts are immediately recorded and deposited and are not used directly to make payments.
4. Disbursements are made by serially numbered checks, only upon proper authorization by someone other than the person writing the check.
5. Bank accounts are reconciled monthly.

Why are such internal controls necessary? Consider a person who handles cash and makes entries into the accounting records. That person could take cash and cover it up by making the following entry in the books:

```
Operating expenses . . . . . . . . . . . . . . . xxx
     Cash . . . . . . . . . . . . . . . . . . . . . . .        xxx
```

Besides guarding against dishonest actions, the listed procedures help ensure accurate accounting records. For example, suppose a check is written but not recorded in the books. Without serially numbered checks, there would be no way of discovering the error before receiving a bank statement showing that the check was paid. But if checks are numbered, an unrecorded check can be identified, and such errors can be discovered early.

CREDIT SALES AND ACCOUNTS RECEIVABLE

accounts receivable (trade receivables, receivables)
Amounts owed to a company by customers as a result of delivering goods or services and extending credit in the ordinary course of business.

Credit sales on open account increase **accounts receivable,** which are amounts owed to the company by its customers as a result of delivering goods or services. Accounts receivable, sometimes called **trade receivables** or simply **receivables,** arise when the company grants credit to its customer on an ongoing basis. This means the company agrees to accept payment in the future for goods or services delivered today.

UNCOLLECTIBLE ACCOUNTS

uncollectible accounts (bad debts) Receivables determined to be uncollectible because debtors are unable or unwilling to pay their debts.

Granting credit entails cost and benefits. The main benefit is the boost in sales and profit that would otherwise be lost if credit were not extended. Many potential customers would not buy if credit were unavailable or they would buy from a competitor that offered credit. One cost is administration and collection of the credit amount. Another cost is the delay in receiving payment. The seller must finance its activities in other ways while awaiting payment. Perhaps the most significant cost is **uncollectible accounts** or **bad debts**—receivables that some credit customers are either unable or unwilling to pay. Accountants often label this major cost of granting credit that arises from uncollectible accounts as **bad debts expense.**

The extent of nonpayment of debts varies. It often depends on the credit risks that managers are willing to accept. For instance, many smaller, local establishments, will accept a higher level of risk than will larger, national stores, such as Sears. The small stores know their customers personally. The extent of a nonpayment can also depend on the industry. For example, the problem of uncollectible accounts is especially difficult in the health-care field. The Bayfront Medical Center of St. Petersburg, Florida, suffered bad debts equal to 21% of gross revenue.

bad debts expense The cost of granting credit that arises from uncollectible accounts.

DECIDING WHEN AND HOW TO GRANT CREDIT

Competition and industry practice affect whether and how companies offer credit, and the final decision is based on cost-benefit trade-offs. In other words, companies offer credit only when the additional earnings on credit sales exceed the costs of offering credit. Suppose 5% of credit sales are bad debts, administrative costs of a credit department are $5,000 per year, and $20,000 of credit sales (with earnings of $8,000 before credit costs) are achieved. Assume that none of the credit sales would have been made without granting credit. Offering credit is worthwhile because the earnings of $8,000 exceeds the credit costs of $6,000 ((5% × $20,000) + $5,000).

MEASUREMENT OF UNCOLLECTIBLE ACCOUNTS

Uncollectible accounts require special accounting procedures and thus deserve special attention here. Consider an example. Suppose Compuport has credit sales of $100,000 (two hundred customers averaging $500 each) during 19X1. Collections during 19X1 were $60,000. The December 31, 19X1, accounts receivable of $40,000 includes the accounts of 80 different customers who have not yet paid for their 19X1 purchases. During 19X1 there was no bad debt, but it turns out that 40% of the year's sales are still unpaid at year end and some may never be paid. The outstanding balances are:

Objective 5
Estimate and interpret uncollectible accounts receivable balances.

Customer	Amount Owed
1. Jones	$ 1,400
2. Slade	125
⋮	⋮
42. Monterro	600
⋮	⋮
79. Weinberg	700
80. Porras	11
Total receivables	$40,000

How should Compuport account for these receivables? Should we assume they will all be collected? Should we assume some will not be? If the latter, how do we decide which are collectible and which are not? Of course we would never have initially made a credit sale to someone we really believed would not pay us.

There are two basic ways to record uncollectibles: by waiting to see which ones are unpaid or by making estimates today of the portion that will not be collected. The methods are called the *specific write-off method* and the *allowance method*.

SPECIFIC WRITE-OFF METHOD

A company that rarely experiences a bad debt might use the **specific write-off method,** which assumes that all sales are fully collectible until proved otherwise. If uncollectibles are small and very infrequent, this practice will not misstate the economic situation in a

specific write-off method
This method of accounting for bad debt losses assumes all sales are fully collectible until proved otherwise.

material way. When a specific customer account is later identified as uncollectible, the Account Receivable is reduced. Because no specific customer's account is deemed to be uncollectible at the end of 19X1, the December 31, 19X1, Compuport balance sheet would simply show an Account Receivable of $40,000.

Now assume that during the next year, 19X2, the retailer identifies Jones and Monterro as customers who are not expected to pay. When the chances of collection from specific customers become dim, the amounts in the particular accounts are recognized as bad debts expense:

Specific Write-Off Method	A	= L +	SE
19X1 Sales	+100,000 [Increase Accounts Receivable]	=	+100,000 [Increase Sales]
19X2 Write-off	−2,000 [Decrease Accounts Receivable]	=	−2,000 [Increase Bad Debts Expense]

Unfortunately, the specific write-off method has been criticized justifiably because it fails to apply the matching principle of accrual accounting. The $2,000 bad debts expense in 19X2 is related to (or caused by) the $100,000 of 19X1 sales. Matching requires recognition of the bad debts expense at the same time as the related revenue, that is, in 19X1, not 19X2. As a result of not matching expenses to revenues, the specific write-off method produces two errors. First, 19X1 income is overstated by $2,000 because no bad debts expense is charged to that year. Second, 19X2 income is understated by $2,000. Why? Because 19X1's bad debts expense of $2,000 is charged in 19X2. Compare the specific write-off method with a correct matching of revenue and expense:

	Specific Write-off Method: Matching Violated		Matching Applied Correctly	
	19X1	19X2	19X1	19X2
Sales revenue	100,000	0	100,000	0
Bad debts expense	0	2,000	2,000	0

allowance method
Method of accounting for bad debt losses using estimates of the amount of sales that will ultimately be uncollectible and a contra asset account, allowance for doubtful accounts.

The principal arguments in favor of the specific write-off method are based on cost-benefit concerns and materiality. Basically, the method is simple and extremely inexpensive to use. Moreover, no great error in measurement of income occurs if amounts of bad debts are small and similar from one year to the next.

ALLOWANCE METHOD

allowance for uncollectible accounts (allowance for doubtful accounts, allowance for bad debts, reserve for doubtful accounts) A contra asset account that measures the amount of receivables estimated to be uncollectible.

Most accountants do not use the specific write-off method because it violates the matching principle. Instead, they use an alternate method that estimates the amount of uncollectible accounts to be matched to the related revenue. This method, known as the **allowance method,** has two basic elements: (1) an estimate of the amount of sales that will ultimately be uncollectible and (2) a contra account, which records the estimate and is deducted from the accounts receivable. The contra account is usually called **allowance for uncollectible accounts** (or **allowance for doubtful accounts, allowance for bad debts,** or **reserve for doubtful accounts**). It measures the amount of receivables estimated to be uncollectible from as yet unidentified customers. In other words, it allows accountants to recognize bad debts in general during the proper period, before specific uncollectible accounts are identified in the following period.

Returning to our example, suppose that Compuport knows from experience that 2% of sales is never collected. Therefore 2% $\times$ $100,000 = $2,000 of the 19X1 sales can be estimated to be uncollectible. However, the exact customer accounts that will not be collected are unknown at December 31, 19X1. (Of course, all $2,000 must be among the $40,000 of accounts receivable because the other $60,000 has already been collected.) Compuport can still acknowledge the $2,000 worth of bad debt in 19X1, before the specific accounts of Jones and Monterro are identified in 19X2. The effects of the allowance method on the balance sheet equation in the Compuport example follow:

	A	= L +	SE
Allowance Method:			
19X1 Sales	+100,000 [Increase Accounts Receivable]	=	+100,000 [Increase Sales]
19X1 Allowance	−2,000 [Increase Allowance for Uncollectible Accounts]	=	−2,000 [Increase Bad Debts Expense]
19X2 Write-off	+2,000 [Decrease Allowance for Uncollectible Accounts]		
	−2,000 [Decrease Accounts Receivable]	=	(No effect)

The associated journal entries are:

```
19X1
Sales       Accounts receivable ....................  100,000
                 Sales ...........................              100,000
19X1
Allowances  Bad debts expense ......................    2,000
                 Allowance for uncollectible accounts .....          2,000
19X2
Write-offs  Allowance for uncollectible accounts ........    2,000
                 Accounts receivable, Jones .............          1,400
                 Accounts receivable, Monterro .........            600
```

Note in the 19X2 journal entry that two credit entries are made, one for $1,400 due to Jones and one for $600 due to Monterro. For accounts receivable, records must be maintained for each individual customer. In a similar manner, the 19X1 increase of $100,000 to accounts receivable would actually be recorded as many (200 in this example) individual sales to specific customers.

The principal argument in favor of the allowance method is its superiority in measuring accrual accounting income in any given year. That is, under this method the $2,000 of 19X1 sales that is estimated never to be collected is recorded in 19X1, the period in which the $100,000 sales revenue is recognized.

The allowance method results in the following presentation in the Compuport balance sheet, December 31, 19X1:

Accounts receivable	$40,000
Less: Allowance for uncollectible accounts	2,000
Net accounts receivable	$38,000

Other formats for presenting the allowance method on recent balance sheets of actual companies include:

	1997
IBM (in millions):	
Notes and accounts receivable,	
trade, net of allowances	$ 16,850
Dow Jones & Company (in thousands):	
Accounts receivable—trade,	
net of allowance for doubtful accounts of $16,445	$295,250

The various approaches to the allowance method are based on historical experience and assume the current year is similar to prior years in terms of economic circumstances (growth versus recession, interest rate levels, and so on) and in terms of customer composition. Of course, estimates are revised when conditions change. For example, if a local employer closed or drastically reduced employment and many local customers were thus suddenly unemployed, Compuport might increase expected bad debts.

APPLYING THE ALLOWANCE METHOD USING A PERCENTAGE OF SALES

How do managers and accountants estimate the percentage of bad debt in the allowance method? In our example, Compuport managers determined a 2% rate of bad debt, for a total of $2,000 (2% × $100,000), based on experience. Expressing the amount of bad debt as a percentage of total sales is known as the **percentage of sales method,** which relies on historical relationships between credit sales and uncollectible debts.

percentage of sales method An approach to estimating bad debts expense and uncollectible accounts based on the historical relations between credit sales and uncollectibles.

The percentage of sales method is easier to understand if we look at the relationship between the general ledger item Accounts Receivable and its supporting detail. Each time a sale is made on account we record the amount in the general ledger but we also record it in a separate, supporting ledger called a subsidiary ledger. In the subsidiary ledger a separate page is maintained for each customer, recording both sales and payments. On December 31, 19X1, the sum of the balances of all the customer accounts in the subsidiary ledger must equal the accounts receivable balance in the general ledger.

Compuport General Ledger, December 31, 19X1

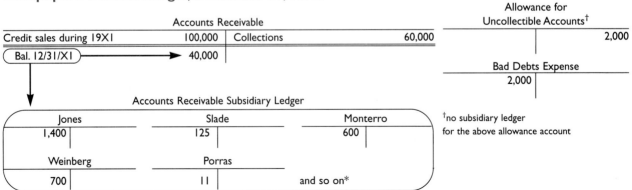

*Total of these individual customer accounts must equal $40,000.

Note that the use of the allowance account enables us to record bad debt expense without identifying specific accounts that will be uncollectible. In 19X2, after exhausting all practical means of collection, the retailer decides the Jones and Monterro accounts are uncollectible. Recording the $2,000 write-off for Jones and Monterro in 19X2 has the following effect:

Compuport General Ledger, December 31, 19X1

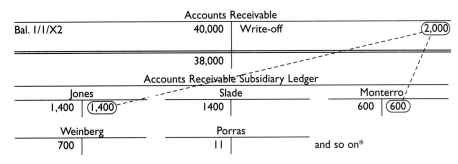

Convince yourself that the ultimate write-off has no effect on total assets:

	Before Write-off	After Write-off
Accounts receivable	$40,000	$38,000
Allowance for uncollectible accounts	2,000	—
Book value (net realized value)	$38,000	$38,000

APPLYING THE ALLOWANCE METHOD USING A PERCENTAGE OF ACCOUNTS RECEIVABLE

Like the percentage of sales method, the **percentage of accounts receivable method** uses historical experience, but the estimate of uncollectible accounts is based on the historical relations of uncollectibles to year-end gross accounts receivable, not to total sales made during the year.

The amount added to the Allowance for Bad Debts contra account is the approximate amount of bad debts contained in the end-of-period accounts receivable. Under the percentage of accounts receivable method, additions to the Allowance for Bad Debts are calculated to achieve a desired ending balance in the Allowance account. Consider the historical experience in the following table:

percentage of accounts receivable method An approach to estimating bad debts expense and uncollectible accounts at year end using the historical relations of uncollectibles to accounts receivable.

	Accounts Receivable at End of Year	Bad Debts Deemed Uncollectible and Written Off
19X1	$100,000	$ 3,500
19X2	80,000	2,450
19X3	90,000	2,550
19X4	110,000	4,100
19X5	120,000	5,600
19X6	112,000	2,200
Six-year total	$612,000	$20,400
Average (divide by 6)	$102,000	$ 3,400
Average percentage not collected = 3,400 ÷ 102,000 = 3.33%		

At the end of 19X7, assume the accounts receivable balance is $115,000. The 19X7 addition to the Allowance for Bad Debts is computed as follows:

1. Divide average bad debt losses of $3,400 by average ending accounts receivable of $102,000 to calculate the historical average uncollectible percentage of 3.33%.

2. Apply the percentage from step 1 to the ending Accounts Receivable balance for 19X7 to determine the ending balance that should be in the Allowance account at the end of the year: 3.33% × $115,000 receivables at the end of 19X7 is $3,830.

3. Prepare an adjusting entry to bring the Allowance to the appropriate amount determined in step 2. Suppose the books show a $700 credit balance in the Allowance account at the end of 19X7. Then the adjusting entry for 19X7 is $3,830 − $700, or $3,130 to record the Bad Debts expense. The journal entry is:

```
Bad debts expense  . . . . . . . . . . . . . .   3,130
      Allowance for bad debts  . . . . . . .            3,130
To bring the Allowance to the level
justified by bad debt experience during
the past six years.
```

The percentage of accounts receivable method differs from the percentage of sales method in two ways: (1) the percentage is based on the ending accounts receivable balance rather than on sales, and (2) the dollar amount calculated using the percentage is the appropriate ending balance in the allowance account, not the amount added to the account for the year.

APPLYING THE ALLOWANCE METHOD USING THE AGING OF ACCOUNTS RECEIVABLE

aging of accounts receivable An analysis that considers the composition of year-end accounts receivable based on the age of the debt.

A refinement on the percentage of accounts receivable approach is the **aging of accounts receivable method,** which considers the composition of the end-of-year accounts receivable based on the age of the debt. This method directly incorporates the customers' payment histories. The more time that elapses after the sale, the less likely collection becomes. The seller may send the buyer a late notice 30 days after the sale and a second reminder after 60 days, make a phone call after 90 days, and place the account with a collection agency after 120 days. Companies that analyze the age of their accounts receivable for credit management purposes naturally incorporate this information into estimates of the allowance for uncollectibles. For example, the $115,000 balance in Accounts Receivable on December 31, 19X7, for Compuport might be aged as follows:

Name	Total		1–30 Days		31–60 Days		61–90 Days		Over 90 Days
Oxwall Tools	$ 20,000		$20,000						
Chicago Castings	10,000		10,000						
Estee	20,000		15,000		$ 5,000				
Sarasota Pipe	22,000				12,000		$10,000		
Ceilcote	4,000						3,000		$1,000
Other accounts (each detailed)	39,000		27,000		8,000		2,000		2,000
Total	$115,000		$72,000		$25,000		$15,000		$3,000
Historical bad debt percentages			0.1%		1%		5%		90%
Bad debt allowance to be provided	$3,772	=	$ 72	+	$ 250	+	$ 750	+	$2,700

This aging schedule produces a different target balance for the Allowance account than the percentage of accounts receivable method did: $3,772 versus $3,830. Similarly, the journal entry is slightly different. Given the same $700 credit balance in the Allowance account, the journal entry to record the Bad Debts Expense is $3,772 − $700, or $3,072:

```
Bad debts expense  ....................  $3,072
        Allowance for uncollectible accounts  ...          $3,072
    To bring the Allowance to the level justified by
    prior experience using the aging method.
```

Whether the percentage of sales, percentage of accounts receivable, or aging method is used to estimate bad debts expense and the Allowance for Uncollectible Accounts, the subsequent accounting for write-offs is the same—a decrease in Accounts Receivable and a decrease in the allowance for Uncollectible Accounts.

BAD DEBT RECOVERIES

A few accounts will be written off as uncollectible, but then collection will occur at a later date. When such **bad debt recoveries** occur, the write-off should be reversed, and the collection handled as a normal receipt on account. In this way, a company will be better able to keep track of the customer's true payment history. Return to the Compuport example and assume that Monterro's account for $600 is written off in February 19X2 and collected in October 19X2. The following journal entries produce a complete record of the transactions in Monterro's individual accounts receivable account.

bad debt recoveries
Accounts receivable that were written off as uncollectible but then collected at a later date.

```
Feb. 19X2   Allowance for uncollectible accounts  ..............   600
                 Accounts receivable ........................          600
            To write off uncollectible account of
            Monterro, a specific customer.
Oct. 19X2   Accounts receivable  ..........................   600
                 Allowance for uncollectible accounts ...........          600
            To reverse February 19X2 write-off of
            account of Monterro.
            Cash .........................................   600
                 Accounts receivable ........................          600
            To record the collection on account.
```

Note that these 19X2 entries have no effect on the level of bad debt expense estimated for 19X1. At the end of 19X1, using one of the three estimation methods we just examined, Compuport estimated bad debt expense based on the expected level of uncollectibles. These estimates are not changed whether future uncollectibles are greater or less than expected. The errors in estimate affect future periods but do not produce adjustments of prior periods. Briefly, in 19X2 Compuport thought that Monterro would be a nonpaying customer. This was not ultimately the case, and the records now reflect Monterro's payment.

ASSESSING THE LEVEL OF ACCOUNTS RECEIVABLE

You now know how to account for bad debts, but you should realize that the management issue is how to control bad debts at the proper level. The more credit a company provides, the greater the chances of bad debts occurring. Management and financial analysts like to monitor the firm's ability to control accounts receivable. Can the firm generate increasing sales without excessive growth in receivables? Do bad debt expenses rise sharply when sales grow, indicating a reduction in the credit quality of the store's customers? One measure of the ability to control receivables is the **accounts receivable turnover,** which is calculated by dividing the credit sales by the average accounts receivable for the period during which the sales were made:

Objective 6
Assess the level of accounts receivable.

accounts receivable turnover Credit sales divided by average accounts receivable.

$$\text{Accounts receivable turnover} = \frac{\text{Credit sales}}{\text{Average accounts receivable}}$$

This ratio indicates how rapidly collections occur. If the turnover were 12, it would indicate that receivables are collected after one month on average. Higher turnovers indicate that receivables are collected quickly—lower turnovers indicate slower collection cycles. The level of the ratio is often driven by competitive conditions in the industry. But changes in the ratio provide important guidance regarding changes in the company's policies, changes in the industry, or changes in the general economic environment. For example, a decline in the general level of economic activity will slow collections across the board and this turnover measure will tend to rise for all firms.

Suppose credit sales (or sales on account) for Compuport in 19X2 were $1 million, and beginning and ending accounts receivable were $115,000 and $112,000 respectively.

$$\text{Accounts receivable turnover} = \frac{1,000,000}{0.5\,(115,000\,+\,112,000)} = 8.81$$

Receivables levels are also assessed in terms of how long it takes to collect them. This ratio is simply an alternative way to express the turnover ratio but it has an appealing direct interpretation. How long does it take to get my money after I make a sale? The **days to collect accounts receivable,** or **average collection period,** is calculated by dividing 365 by the accounts receivable turnover. For our example:

$$\begin{aligned}\text{Days to collect}\atop\text{accounts receivable} &= \frac{365 \text{ days}}{\text{Accounts receivable turnover}}\\ &= \frac{365 \text{ days}}{8.81}\\ &= 41.4 \text{ days}\end{aligned}$$

The following illustrates the variability in accounts receivable turnover levels among industries.

Industry	Median Levels	
	Accounts Receivable Turnover	Days to Collect Accounts Receivable
Automobile Retailer	58.2	6.3
Department Stores	38.7	9.4
Furniture Retailer	60.5	6.0
Jewelry Retailer	3.4	107.4
Management Consulting Firms	4.5	81.1

Source: RMA, *Annual Statement Studies for 1996.*

The high accounts receivable turnovers for automobile retailers and department stores are a result of the way customers finance their purchases. For automobiles, customers generally finance through banks or through the credit arms of the automobile manufacturer. For department stores, credit is often provided by national credit cards, such as Visa and MasterCard. In both industries the seller receives cash quickly. The other three industries more frequently involve direct granting of credit by the selling firm. In other words, outside credit providers tend to pay off the sellers quickly, but when the sellers themselves provide the credit, payments come in much more slowly. In fact, if department stores provided their own credit to customers, as used to be the case, their accounts receivable turnover would drop sharply.

OVERVIEW OF INTERNAL CONTROL

Bank reconciliations and cash controls were discussed earlier, but internal control is broader than a focus on cash. The essence of **internal control** is the creation of a system of checks and balances that assures that all actions occurring within the company are in

days to collect accounts receivable (average collection period) 365 divided by accounts receivable turnover.

accord with organizational objectives and have the general approval of top management. At one level, this means that a highly placed manager should not expose the company to unauthorized, speculative losses from, for example, trading exotic derivatives securities. Here internal control seeks to tie daily decisions to corporate strategy. At another level, it means that a salesperson at the clothing-store giant, The Gap, should not be able to walk out of the store with holiday gifts for the family without paying for them. Here internal control refers to the protection of firm assets from theft and loss. Therefore, an electronic tag on a leather coat is an internal control device and so is the requirement that checks over $200 have the approval of two people.

In its broadest sense, internal control refers to both administrative control and accounting control:

1. **Administrative controls** include the plan of organization (for example, the formal organizational chart concerning who reports to whom) and all methods and procedures that facilitate management planning and control of operations. Examples are departmental budgeting procedures, reports on performance, and procedures for granting credit to customers.

2. **Accounting controls** include the methods and procedures for authorizing transactions, safeguarding assets, and ensuring the accuracy of the financial records. Good accounting controls help maximize efficiency, and they help minimize waste, unintentional errors, and fraud.

Our focus is on internal accounting controls, which should provide reasonable assurance concerning:

1. *Authorization.* Transactions are executed in accordance with management's general or specific intentions.

2. *Recording.* All authorized transactions are recorded in the correct amounts, periods, and accounts. No fictitious transactions are recorded.

3. *Safeguarding.* Precautions and procedures appropriately restrict access to assets.

4. *Reconciliation.* Records are compared with other independently kept records and physical counts. Such comparisons help ensure that other control objectives are attained.

5. *Valuation.* Recorded amounts are periodically reviewed for impairment of values and necessary write-downs.

The first three general objectives–authorization, recording, and safeguarding—relate to establishing the system of accountability and are aimed at the prevention of errors and irregularities. The final two objectives—reconciliation and valuation—are aimed at detecting errors and irregularities. A sixth objective of an internal control system should be added—promoting operating efficiency. Management should recognize that an internal control system's purpose is as much a positive one (promoting efficiency) as a negative one (preventing errors and fraud).

THE ACCOUNTING SYSTEM

An entity's **accounting system** is a set of records, procedures, and equipment that routinely deals with the events affecting the entity's financial performance and position. The system maintains accountability for the firm's assets and liabilities.

Chapters 3 and 4 provided an overview of the heart of the accounting system—source documents, journal entries, postings to ledgers, trial balances, adjustments, and financial reports. The focus of the system is on repetitive, voluminous transactions, which almost always fall into four categories:

1. Cash disbursements
2. Cash receipts

Objective 7
Develop and explain internal control procedures.

internal control System of checks and balances that assures that all actions occurring within the company are in accordance with organizational objectives.

administrative controls All methods and procedures that facilitate management planning and control of operations.

accounting controls The methods and procedures for authorizing transactions, safeguarding assets, and ensuring the accuracy of the financial records.

accounting system A set of records, procedures, and equipment that routinely deals with the events affecting the financial performance and position of the entity.

3. Purchase of goods and services, including employee payroll
4. Sales or other rendering of goods and services

The magnitude of the physical handling of records is often staggering. For example, telephone companies and credit card companies process millions of transactions daily. Without computers and data-processing systems, most modern organizations would be forced to halt operations.

Well-designed and well-run accounting systems are positive contributions to organizations and the economy. Credit card companies use sophisticated systems to evaluate transactions on your credit card and may refuse credit transactions that seem likely to be fraudulent use of your card by an unauthorized party. While such refusals sometimes inconvenience a legitimate card-holder, they more frequently foil criminal use. Federal Express created a dominant position in the overnight delivery market by developing an efficient system for continuous tracking of an item from pickup to delivery. Wal-Mart's extraordinary success as a low-price retailer is partly due to their development of an integrated inventory control and ordering system that allows its computer to interact automatically with suppliers such as Procter & Gamble to generate orders and reduce delivery times.

MANAGEMENT'S RESPONSIBILITY

Although outside auditors attest to the financial reports of an entity, management bears the primary responsibility for a company's financial statements. Most annual reports of publicly held companies in the United States contain an explicit statement of management responsibility for its financial statements. These **management reports** state that management is responsible for all audited and unaudited information in the annual report, and they include a statement on the adequacy of internal control. They also include a description of the composition and duties of the audit committee as well as the duties of the independent auditor. You can review an example for the Gap in the appendix to the text.

THE AUDIT COMMITTEE

Management's primary responsibility for the entity's financial statements extends upward to the board of directors. Most boards have an **audit committee,** which oversees the internal accounting controls, financial statements, and financial affairs of the corporation.

Audit committees typically have many "outside" board members who are not managers of the company. They are considered to be more independent than the "inside" directors—employees who serve as part of the corporation's management. Mobil Corporation, the oil company, has a typical board composition. Of fourteen directors in 1997, three are also members of management and eleven are "outside" directors. Five of the outside directors form the audit committee. The committee provides contact and communication among the board, the external auditors, the internal auditors, the financial executives, and the operating executives.

CHECKLIST OF INTERNAL CONTROL

All good systems of internal control have certain features in common. These features can be summarized in a checklist of internal control, which may be used to appraise any specific procedures for cash, purchases, sales, payroll, and the like. The following checklist summarizes the guidance that is found in much of the systems and auditing literature.

1. Reliable Personnel with Clear Responsibilities

   The most important element of successful control is personnel. Incompetent or dishonest individuals can undermine a system, no matter how well it meets the other items on the checklist. Procedures to hire, train, motivate, and supervise employees are essential. Individuals must be given authority, responsibility, and duties commensurate with their abilities, interests, experience, and reliability. Yet, many employers use low-cost talent that may prove exceedingly expensive in the long run, not only because of fraud but because of poor productivity.

   Assessing responsibility means tracking actions as far down in the organization as is feasible, so that results can be related to individuals. It means having salesclerks sign sales slips, inspectors initial packing slips, and workers sign time cards and requisitions. Grocery stores often assign each cashier a separate money tray; therefore, shortages can easily be traced to the person responsible. The psychological impact of fixing responsibility tends to promote care and efficiency.

   The National Mass Retailing Institute estimates that retailers lose about 2% of sales to theft and mistakes. Shoplifting accounts for part of this, but employee theft causes much larger losses than shoplifting. The institute estimates that an average retail store loses $10 per shift per clerk.

2. Separation of Duties

   The separation of duties not only helps ensure accurate compilation of data but also limits the chances for fraud. Separation of duties makes it hard for one person, acting alone, to defraud the company. It is difficult, although not impossible, for two or more employees to collude in a fraud. This is why movie theaters have a cashier selling tickets and an usher taking them. The cashier takes in cash, the usher keeps the ticket stubs, and in an audit step performed by a third person, the cash is compared with the number of stubs. But suppose they do collude. The ticket seller pockets the cash and issues a fake ticket. The usher accepts the fake ticket and allows entry. Separation of duties alone will not prevent collusive theft. Consider three additional examples where failure to separate duties allows easy theft.

   In a computer system, a person with custody of assets should not have access to programming or any input of records. In a classic example, a programmer in a bank rounded transactions to the next lower cent rather than the nearest cent and had the computer put the fraction of a cent into his account. For example, a customer amount of $10.057 became $10.05, and the programmer's account received $.007. With millions of transactions, the programmers' account became very large.

   The same individual should not authorize the payment of a supplier's invoice and also sign the check in payment of the bill. Nor should an individual who handles cash receipts have the authority to indicate which accounts receivable should be written off as uncollectible.

   The latter separation of powers prevents such embezzlement as the following: A bookkeeper opens the mail, removes a $1,000 check from a customer, and somehow cashes it. To hide the theft, the bookkeeper prepares the following journal entry to write off an amount owed by a customer:

Allowance for bad debts	1,000	
Accounts receivable		1,000

   An accounts payable clerk at a pharmaceuticals company embezzled $25,000 by writing checks to companies that he created. Following a standard practice, his employer had an executive authorize payments by initialing invoices. The resulting checks, for small amounts, were created by the clerk, mechanically signed, and mailed. The extra payments to the clerk's companies were detected one day when the clerk called in sick and his coworker noted checks written to an unfamiliar vendor. In another case, a bookkeeper wrote fraudulent paychecks to seasonal employees and cashed them himself. The theft was revealed when a seasonal employee objected that the W-2 form, sent to the government at year end to report his annual earnings for income tax purposes, reported too much income. Good systems of internal control would reduce such losses.

3. Proper Authorization

Authorization can be either general or specific. General authorization is usually found in writing. It often sets definite limits on what price to pay (whether to fly economy or first class), on what price to receive (whether to offer a sales discount), on what credit limits to grant to customers, and so forth. There may also be complete prohibitions (against paying extra fees or bribes or overtime premiums). Specific authorization usually means that a superior manager must permit (typically in writing) any particular deviations from the limits set by general authorization. For example, a manager may have to approve any overtime. The board of directors may have to approve expenditures for capital assets in excess of a specific limit.

4. Adequate Documents

Documents and records vary considerably, from source documents such as sales invoices and purchase orders to journals and ledgers. Immediate, complete, and tamper-proof recording is the aim. It is encouraged by optical scanning of bar-coded data, by having all source documents prenumbered and accounted for, by using devices such as cash registers, and by designing forms for ease of recording. Immediate recording is especially important for handling cash sales. Devices used to ensure immediate recording include "rewards" to customers if they are not offered a receipt at the time of sale and forcing clerks to make change by pricing items at $1.99, $2.99, and $3.99 rather than at $2, $3, and $4. (Historically, such pricing was originally adopted to force clerks to make change as well as for its psychological impact on potential customers.) The need to access the change drawer forces the clerk to ring up the sale so the drawer will open.

5. Proper Procedures

Most organizations use procedures manuals to specify the flow of documents and provide information and instructions to facilitate adequate recordkeeping. Routine and automatic checks are major ways of attaining proper procedures. In a phrase, this means doing things "by the numbers." The use of general routines permits specialization of effort, division of duties, and automatic checks on previous steps in the routine.

6. Physical Safeguards

Obviously, losses of cash, inventories, and records are minimized by safes, locks, guards, and limited access. For example, many companies (such as Boeing and Hewlett-Packard) require all visitors to sign a register and wear a name tag. Often, employees will also wear name tags that are coded to show the facilities to which they have access. Doors to research areas or computer rooms often may be opened only with special keys or by use of a specific code.

Sometimes small businesses are especially vulnerable to theft of physical assets. For example, retail stores use alarm systems, guard dogs, security guards, special lighting, and many other safeguards to protect their property.

7. Bonding, Vacations, and Rotation of Duties

Key people may be subject to excessive temptation. Thus, top executives, branch managers, and individuals who handle cash or inventories should have understudies, be required to take vacations, and be bonded.

Rotating employees and requiring them to take vacations ensures that at least two employees know how to do each job so that an absence due to illness or a sudden resignation does not create major problems. Further, the practice of having another employee periodically perform their duties discourages employees from engaging in fraudulent activities that might be discovered when someone else has access to their records.

Rotation of duties is illustrated by the common practice of having employees such as receivables and payables clerks periodically exchange duties. A receivables clerk may handle accounts from A to C for three months, and then be rotated to accounts M to P for three months, and so forth.

Bonding or buying insurance against embezzlement is not a substitute for vacations, rotation of duties, and similar precautions. Insurance companies will pay only when a loss is proved; establishing proof is often difficult and costly in itself. Prevention of the loss is far better.

8. Independent Check

All phases of the system should be subjected to periodic review by outsiders (for example, by independent public accountants) and by internal auditors. Auditors have independence and a degree of objectivity that allows them to spot weaknesses overlooked by managers immersed in day-to-day operations. It is too costly for external auditors to examine all transactions, so they inspect a sample of the transactions. By first evaluating the system of internal control and testing the extent to which it is being followed, the auditor decides on the likelihood of undetected errors. If internal controls are weak, there is a greater probability of significant errors in the accounting records. Then the auditor must examine many transactions to provide reasonable assurance that existing errors will be found. If internal controls are strong, the auditor can use a smaller sample to develop confidence in the accuracy of the accounting records.

Internal auditors are company employees who help design control systems and assess the degree of compliance with the existing systems. Their main goal is to enhance efficiency of operations by promoting adherence to both administrative and accounting controls and to continuously improve the system.

9. Cost-Benefit Analysis

Highly complex systems tend to strangle people in red tape, impeding rather than promoting efficiency. Besides, the "cost of keeping the costs" sometimes gets out of hand. Investments in more costly systems must be compared with the expected benefits. Unfortunately, it is easier to relate new lathes or production methods to cost savings in manufacturing than to link a new computer to cost savings in inventory control, yet efforts must be made. For example, the accounting firm of KPMG Peat Marwick completed a study of office automation for a client. After examining the jobs of 2,600 white-collar workers, KPMG Peat Marwick quantified a cost-benefit relationship: "A single investment of $10 million would result in a productivity savings equal to $8.4 million every year."

Although many companies implement more complex procedures to improve internal control, a few have taken a reverse course. They have decided that the increased costs of additional scrutiny are not worth the expected savings from catching mistakes or crooks. For example, an aerospace manufacturer routinely pays the invoice amounts without checking supporting documentation except on a random-sampling basis. An aluminum company sends out a blank check with its purchase orders, and then the supplier fills out the check and deposits it.

No framework for internal control is perfect in the sense that it can prevent some shrewd individual from "beating the system" either by outright embezzlement or by producing inaccurate records. The task is not total prevention of fraud, nor is it implementation of operating perfection; rather, the task is the designing of a cost-effective tool that will help achieve efficient operations and reduce temptation.

SUMMARY PROBLEMS FOR YOUR REVIEW

PROBLEM ONE

Hector Lopez, marketing manager for Fireplace Distributors, sold 12 wood stoves to Woodside Condominiums, Inc. The sales contract was signed on April 27, 19X1. The list price of each wood stove was $1,200, but a 5% quantity discount was allowed. The wood stoves were to be delivered on May 10, and a cash discount of 2% of the amount owed was offered if payment was made by June 10. Fireplace Distributors delivered the wood stoves as promised and received the proper payment on June 9.

1. How much revenue should be recognized in April? in May? in June? Explain.
2. Suppose Fireplace Distributors has a separate account titled "Cash Discounts on Sales." What journal entries would be made on June 9 when the cash payment is received?
3. Suppose Fireplace Distributors has another account titled "Sales Returns and Allowances." Suppose further that one of the wood stoves had a scratch, and Fireplace Distributors allowed Woodside to deduct $100 from the total amount due. What journal entries would be made on June 9 when the cash payment is received?

SOLUTION TO PROBLEM ONE

1. Revenue of $13,680 (12 × $1,200 less a 5% quantity discount of $720) would be recognized in May and none in April or June. The key to recognizing revenue is whether the revenue is earned and the asset received from the buyer is realized. The revenue is not earned until the merchandise is delivered. Therefore, revenue cannot be recognized in April because nothing was delivered then. Provided that Woodside Condominiums has a good credit rating, the receipt of cash is reasonably ensured before the cash is actually received. Therefore recognition of revenue need not be delayed until June. On May 10 both revenue recognition tests were met, and the revenue would be recorded on May's income statement. However, if Woodside had a poor credit rating, the revenue would not be recognized and recorded until it was received in June.

2. The original revenue recorded was $13,680. The 2% cash discount is 2% × $13,680 = $273.60. Therefore the cash payment is $13,680 − $273.60 = $13,406.40:

Cash	13,406.40	
Cash discounts on sales	273.60	
Accounts receivable		13,680.00

3. The only difference from requirement 2 is a $100 smaller cash payment and a $100 debit to sales returns and allowances:

Cash	13,306.40	
Cash discounts on sales	273.60	
Sales returns and allowances	100.00	
Accounts receivable		13,680.00

PROBLEM TWO

H.J. Heinz Company sells many popular food products, including its best-selling Heinz ketchup. Its balance sheet showed the following (in thousands):

	April 30, 1997	May 1, 1996
Receivables	$1,137,808	$1,225,172
Less allowance for doubtful accounts	18,934	17,298
	$1,118,874	$1,207,874

Suppose a large grocery chain that owed Heinz $2 million announced bankruptcy on May 1, 1997. Heinz decided that chances for collection were virtually zero. The account was immediately written off. Show the balances as of May 1, 1997, after the write-off. Explain the effect of the write-off on income for the year beginning May 1, 1997.

SOLUTION TO PROBLEM TWO

Receivables ($1,137,808 − $2,000)	$1,135,808
Less allowance for doubtful accounts ($18,934 − $2,000)	16,934
	$1,118,874

Because Heinz has an account labeled allowance for doubtful accounts, it must use the allowance method. The write-off will not affect the net carrying amount of the receivables, which is still $1,118,874. Moreover, the income will be unaffected. Why? Because the estimated expense has already been recognized in prior periods. Under the allowance method, net assets and income are affected when the estimation process occurs, not when the write-off happens.

Highlights to Remember

Revenue is generally recognized when two tests are met: (1) the revenue is earned, and (2) the asset received in return is realized. Most often, revenue is recognized at the point of sale, when the product is delivered to the customer. In offering products for sale, many special practices produce differences between the price at which a product is offered and the final price that a customer is charged. The term net sales represents the final proceeds to the seller—gross sales less offsetting amounts for returns, allowances, and cash discounts.

Sales made for cash are the most easily recorded and valued. However, cash creates a number of procedural problems for the firm. Protecting cash from theft or loss, adequately planning for the availability of cash as needed, and reconciling the firm's accounting records with the bank's records are just some of these problems.

Potential uncollectible accounts reduce the amount of accounts receivable reported on the balance sheet. Reporting the uncollectible portion of credit sales requires estimates that may be based on a percentage of sales, a percentage of accounts receivable, or an aging of accounts receivable. These estimates permit the financial statements to (1) properly reflect asset levels on the balance sheet, and (2) properly match bad debts expense with revenue on the income statement.

Companies and analysts use ratios to assess the level of accounts receivable. The accounts receivable turnover ratio and the days to collect accounts receivable ratio both relate the average dollar value of accounts receivable to the level of sales activity during the year. Comparisons with other companies in the same industry or examination of a particular company over time draw attention to unusual circumstances and possible problems.

It is tempting to delegate internal control decisions to accountants. However, managers at all levels have a major responsibility for the success of internal controls. To help monitor internal control, boards of directors appoint audit committees, which oversee accounting controls, the financial statements, and general financial affairs of the company.

The following general characteristics form a checklist that can be used as a starting point for judging the effectiveness of internal control:

1. Reliable personnel with clear responsibilities
2. Separation of duties
3. Proper authorization

4. Adequate documents
5. Proper procedures
6. Physical safeguards
7. Bonding, vacations, and rotation of duties
8. Independent check
9. Cost-benefit analysis

Managers and accountants should recognize that the role of an internal control system is as much a positive one (enhancing efficiency) as a negative one (reducing errors and fraud).

Appendix 5A: Bank Reconciliations

Exhibit 5-1 displays a bank statement for account number 96848602, one of thousands of the bank's deposits. Together, these accounts form the subsidiary ledger that supports the bank's general ledger account *Deposits,* a liability.

The supporting documents for the detailed checks on the statement are canceled checks; for additional deposits, deposit slips. Notice that the minimum balance, -33.39, is negative. This indicates an *overdraft,* which is a negative account balance arising from the bank's paying a check even though the depositor had insufficient funds available at the instant the check was presented. Overdrafts are permitted as an occasional courtesy by the bank, although the bank may levy a fee (e.g., $10 or $30) for each overdraft.

Exhibit 5-2 shows selected records for the depositor and the bank. The bank balance on December 31 is an asset (Cash) on the depositor's books and a liability (Deposits) on the bank's books. The terms *debit* and *credit* as used by banks may seem strange. Banks *credit* the depositor's account for additional deposits because the bank has a liability to the depositor. Banks *debit* the account for checks written by the depositor and paid by the bank. When the $2,000 check drawn by the depositor on January 5 is paid by the bank on January 8, the bank's journal entry would be:

Jan. 8 Deposits	$2,000	
Cash		$2,000
To decrease the depositor's account.		

A monthly *bank reconciliation* (see p. 000) is conducted by the depositor to make sure that all cash receipts and disbursements are accounted for. Bank reconciliations take many forms, but the objective is to explain all differences in the cash balances shown on the bank statement and in the depositor's general ledger at a given date. Using the data in Exhibit 5-2:

Bank Reconciliation, January 31, 19X2

Balance per books (also called *balance per check register, register balance*)	$ 8,000
Deduct: Bank service charges for January not recorded on the books (also include any other charges by the bank not yet deducted)*	20
Adjusted (corrected) balance per books	$ 7,980
Balance per bank (also called *bank statement balance, statement balance*)	$10,980
Add: Deposits not recorded by bank (also called *unrecorded deposits, deposits in transit*), deposit of 1/31	7,000
Total	$17,980
Deduct: Outstanding checks, check of 1/29	10,000
Adjusted (corrected) balance per bank	$ 7,980

*Note that new entries on the depositor's books are required for all previously unrecorded additions and deductions made to achieve the adjusted balance per books.

Exhibit 5-1

An Actual Bank Statement

SEAFIRST BANK
University Branch
4701 University Way NE
Seattle WA 98145

		Account Number
Richard B. Sandstrom	777	96848602
2420 Highline Rd.		Statement Period
Redmond WA 98110		11-21-98 to 12-20-98

SUMMARY OF YOUR ACCOUNTS
CHECKING

First Choice Minimum Balance	96848602
Beginning Balance	368.56
Deposits	5,074.00
Withdrawals	3,232.92
Service Charges/Fees	16.00
Ending Balance	2,193.64
Minimum Balance on 12-9-98	**−33.39**

CHECKING ACTIVITY

Deposits

Posted	Amount	Description
11-21	700.00	Deposit
11-25	1,810.00	Payroll Deposit
12-10	1,810.00	Payroll Deposit
12-16	754.00	Deposit

Withdrawals

Ck No.	Paid	Amount
1606	12-02	1134.00
1607	11-28	561.00
1609*	12-09	12.00
1617*	12-05	7.00
1629*	11-26	10.00
1630	11-25	16.95
1639*	12-02	96.00
1641*	12-09	1025.00
1642	12-05	50.00
1643	12-15	236.25
1644	12-17	84.72

* = Gap in check sequence
Total number of checks = 11

The bank reconciliation indicates that an adjustment is necessary on the books of the depositor:

Jan. 31	Bank service charge expense	. . . .	20	
	Cash	. . . .		20
	To record bank charges for printing checks.			

Exhibit 5-2

Comparative Cash Balances, January 19X2

Depositor's Records			
Cash in Bank			
(receivable from bank)			
1/1/X2 Bal.	11,000	1/5	2,000
		1/15	3,000
1/10	4,000		
		1/19	5,000
1/24	6,000		
1/31	7,000	1/29	10,000
	28,000		20,000
1/31/X2 Bal.	8,000		

Bank's Records			
Deposits			
(payable to depositor)			
1/8	2,000	1/1/X2 Bal.	11,000
1/20	3,000		
		1/11	4,000
1/28	5,000	1/26	6,000
1/31	20*		
	10,020		21,000
		1/31/X2 Bal.	10,980

* Service charge for printing checks.

Date	Depositor's General Journal	Debit	Credit
1/5	Accounts payable	2,000	
	Cash		2,000
	Check No. 1.		
1/10	Cash	4,000	
	Accounts receivable		4,000
	Deposit slip No. 1.		
1/15	Income taxes payable	3,000	
	Cash		3,000
	Check No. 2.		
1/19	Accounts payable	5,000	
	Cash		5,000
	Check No. 3.		
1/24	Cash	6,000	
	Accounts receivable		6,000
	Deposit No. 2.		
1/29	Accounts payable	10,000	
	Cash		10,000
	Check No. 4.		
1/31	Cash	7,000	
	Accounts receivable		7,000
	Deposit No. 3.		

The popular reconciliation format on page 196 has two major sections. The first section begins with the balance per books (that is, the balance in the Cash T-account). Adjustments are made for items not entered on the books but already entered by the *bank,* such as deduction of the $20 service charge. These adjustments are then recorded in the records of the company. No additions are shown in the illustrated section, but an illustrative addition would be the bank's collection of a customer receivable on behalf of the company. The second section begins with the balance per bank. Adjustments are made for items not entered by the *bank* but already entered in the company's books. These items will normally adjust automatically as deposits and checks reach the bank for processing. After adjustments, each section should end with identical adjusted cash balances. This is the amount that should appear as cash in bank on the depositor's balance sheet.

Accounting Vocabulary

accounting controls, p. 189
accounting system, p. 189
accounts receivable, p. 180
accounts receivable turnover,
  p. 187
administrative controls, p. 189
aging of accounts receivable,
  p. 186
allowance for bad debts, p. 182
allowance for doubtful
  accounts, p. 182
allowance for uncollectible
  accounts, p. 182
allowance method, p. 182
audit committee, p. 190
average collection period, p. 188

bad debt recoveries, p. 187
bad debts, p. 180
bad debts expense, p. 181
cash discounts, p. 176
cash equivalents, p. 179
compensating balances, p. 179
days to collect accounts receivable, p. 188
gross sales, p. 175
internal control, p.189
management reports, p. 190
net sales, p. 175
percentage of accounts receivable method, p. 185
percentage of sales method,
   p. 184

purchase allowance, p. 175
purchase returns, p. 175
receivables, p. 180
reconcile a bank statement,
  p. 180
reserve for doubtful accounts,
  p. 182
sales allowance, p. 175
sales returns, p. 175
specific write-off method,
  p. 181
trade discounts, p. 176
trade receivables, p. 180
turnover, p. 178
uncollectible accounts, p. 180

Assignment Material

QUESTIONS

5-1. Describe the timing of revenue recognition for a defense contractor on a $50 million long-term government contract with work spread evenly over five years.

5-2. Why is the realizable value of a credit sale often less than that of a cash sale?

5-3. Distinguish between a *sales* and a *purchase return.*

5-4. Distinguish between a *cash discount* and a *trade discount.*

5-5. "Trade discounts should not be recorded by the accountant." Do you agree? Explain.

5-6. "Retailers who accept Visa or MasterCard are foolish because they do not receive the full price for merchandise they sell." Comment.

5-7. Describe and give two examples of *cash equivalents.*

5-8. "A compensating balance essentially increases the interest rate on money borrowed." Explain.

5-9. "Cash is only 3% of our total assets. Therefore we should not waste time designing systems to manage cash. We should use our time on matters that have a better chance of affecting our profits." Do you agree? Explain.

5-10. It is common in sub shops and pizza parlors around the Cornell University campus to find signs that say "Your purchase is free if the clerk does not give you a receipt" or "Two free lunches if your receipt has a red star." What is management trying to accomplish with these free offers?

5-11. "The cash balance on a company's books should always equal the cash balance shown by its bank." Do you agree? Explain.

5-12. List 5 internal control procedures used to safeguard cash.

5-13. "If everyone were honest, there would be no need for internal controls to safeguard cash." Do you agree? Explain.

5-14. What is the cost-benefit relationship in deciding whether to offer credit to customers? Whether to accept bank credit cards?

5-15. If a company accepts bank credit cards, why might they accept specific cards rather than all of them? For example, some retailers accept Visa and Master-Card, but not American Express or Diner's Club, while the exact opposite is true for some restaurants.

5-16. Distinguish between the allowance method and the specific write-off method for bad debts.

5-17. The El Camino Hospital uses the allowance method in accounting for bad debts. A journal entry was made for writing off the accounts of Jane Jensen, Eunice Belmont, and Samuel Maze: Do you agree with this entry? If not, show the correct entry and the correcting entry.

Bad debts expense 14,321
   Accounts receivable   14,321

5-18. "The Allowance for Uncollectible Accounts account has no subsidiary ledger, but the Accounts Receivable account does." Explain.

5-19. "Under the allowance method, there are three popular ways to estimate the bad debts expense for a particular year." Name the three.

5-20. What is meant by "aging of accounts"?

5-21. Describe why a write-off of a bad debt should be reversed if collection occurs at a later date.

5-22. What is the relationship between the average collection period and the accounts receivable turnover?

5-23. Distinguish between the percentage of sales approach to applying the allowance method and the aging of accounts receivable approach.

5-24. Distinguish between *internal accounting control* and *internal administrative control*.

5-25. "The primary responsibility for internal controls rests with the outside auditors." Do you agree? Explain.

5-26. What is the primary responsibility of the audit committee?

5-27. Prepare a checklist of important factors to consider in judging an internal control system.

5-28. "The most important element of successful control is personnel." Explain.

5-29. What is the essential idea of separation of duties?

EXERCISES

5-30 Revenue Recognition, Cash Discounts, and Returns.

University Bookstore ordered 500 copies of an introductory economics textbook from Prentice Hall on July 17, 19X0. The books were delivered on August 12, at which time a bill was sent requesting payment of $40 per book. However, a 2% discount was allowed if Prentice Hall received payment by September 12. University Bookstore sent the proper payment, which was received by Prentice Hall on September 10. On December 18 University Bookstore returned 60 books to Prentice Hall for a full cash refund.

Required

1. Prepare the journal entries (if any) for Prentice Hall on (a) July 17, (b) August 12, (c) September 10, and (d) December 18. Include appropriate explanations.

2. Suppose this was the only sales transaction in 19X0. Prepare the revenue section of Prentice Hall's income statement.

5-31 Revenue Recognition

Cascade Logging Company hired Dmitri Construction Co. to build a new bridge across the Logan River. The bridge would extend a logging road into a new stand of timber. The contract called for a payment of $10 million upon completion of the bridge. Work was begun in 19X0 and completed in 19X2. Total costs were:

19X0	$2 million
19X1	2 million
19X2	3 million
Total	$7 million

Required

1. Suppose the accountant for Dmitri Construction Co. judged that Cascade Logging might not be able to pay the $10 million. Still, the chance of a $3 million profit makes the contract attractive enough to sign. How much revenue would you recognize each year?

2. Suppose Cascade Logging is a subsidiary of a major wood-products company. Therefore, receipt of payment on the contract is reasonably certain. How much revenue would you recognize each year?

5-32 Sales in Britain

The first line of the income statement of Cadbury Schweppes, the British candy and beverage company, showed:

Turnover	£5,115,000,000

The current assets on the company's balance sheet were shown as follows:

CURRENT ASSETS:

Stocks [inventories]		£ 436,000,000
Debtors:		
Trade debtors	£643,000,000	
Other debtors	248,000,000	
Total		891,000,000
Investments		75,000,000
Cash at bank and in hand		91,000,000
Total current assets		£1,493,000,000

Required

1. What term is used in the United States for the item called "trade debtors" on the Cadbury Schweppes balance sheet?
2. Using the account titles given in this exercise, make a journal entry for the sale of £150,000 of chocolates to Harrod's Department Store. The cost of the chocolates was £100,000.

5-33 Compensating Balances

Gemini Company borrowed $100,000 from First Bank at 9% interest. The loan agreement stated that a compensating balance of $10,000 must be kept in the Gemini checking account at First Bank. The total Gemini cash balance at the end of the year was $45,000.

Required

1. How much usable cash did Gemini Company receive for its $100,000 loan?
2. What was the real interest paid by Gemini?
3. Prepare a footnote for the annual report of Gemini Company explaining the compensating balance.

5-34 Sales Returns and Discounts

San Jose Electronics Wholesalers had gross sales of $800,000 during the month of March. Sales returns and allowances were $50,000. Cash discounts granted were $22,000.

Required

Prepare an analysis of the impact of these transactions on the balance sheet equation. Also show the journal entries. Prepare a detailed presentation of the revenue section of the income statement.

5-35 Gross and Net Sales

Midwest Metal Products, Inc., reported the following in 19X8 (in thousands):

Net sales	$610
Cash discounts on sales	20
Sales returns and allowances	35

Required

1. Prepare the revenue section of the 19X8 income statement.
2. Prepare journal entries for (a) initial revenue recognition for 19X8 sales, (b) sales returns and allowances, and (c) collection of accounts receivable. Assume that all sales were on credit and all accounts receivable for 19X8 sales were collected in 19X8. Omit explanations

5-36 Cash Discounts Transactions

Video Specialties is a wholesaler that sells on terms of 2/10, n/30. It sold video equipment to Video City for $300,000 on open account on January 10. Payment (net of cash discount) was received on January 19. Using the equation framework, analyze the two transactions for Video Specialties. Also prepare journal entries.

5-37 Entries for Cash Discounts and Returns on Sales

The Sonoma Wine Company is a wholesaler of California wine that sells on credit terms of 2/10, n/30. Consider the following transactions:

June 9 Sales on credit to Sierra Wines, $20,000.

June 11 Sales on credit to Marty's Liquors, $12,000.

June 18 Collected from Sierra Wines.

June 26 Accepted the return of six cases from Marty's, $1,000.

July 10 Collected from Marty's.

July 12 Sierra returned some defective wine that it had acquired on June 9 for $100. Sonoma issued a cash refund immediately.

Required Prepare journal entries for these transactions. Omit explanations. Assume that the full appropriate amounts were exchanged.

5-38 Credit Terms, Discounts, and Annual Interest Rates

As the struggling owner of a new Korean restaurant, you suffer from a habitual shortage of cash. Yesterday the following invoices arrived:

Vender	Face Amount	Terms
Cornation Produce	$ 600	n/30
Rose Exterminators	90	EOM
Nebraska Meat Supply	900	15, EOM
John's Fisheries	1,000	1/10, n/30
Garcia Equipment	2,000	2/10, n/30

most important

Required
1. Write out the exact meaning of each of the terms.
2. You can borrow cash from the local bank on a ten-, twenty-, or thirty-day note bearing an annual interest rate of 16%. Should you borrow to take advantage of the cash discounts offered by the last two vendors? Why? Show computations. For interest rate computations, assume a 360-day year.

5-39 Accounting for Credit Cards

La Roux Designer Clothing Store has extended credit to customers on open account. Its average experience for each of the past three years has been:

	Cash	Credit	Total
Sales	$500,000	$300,000	$800,000
Bad debts expense	—	6,000	6,000
Administrative expense	—	10,000	10,000

Edith La Roux is considering whether to accept bank cards (e.g., Visa, MasterCard). She has resisted because she does not want to bear the cost of the service, which would be 5% of gross sales.

The representative of Visa claims that the availability of bank cards would have increased overall sales by at least 10%. However, regardless of the level of sales, the new mix of the sales would be 50% bank card and 50% cash.

Required
1. How would a bank card sale of $200 affect the accounting equation? Where would the discount appear on the income statement?
2. Should La Roux adopt the bank card if sales do not increase? Base your answer solely on the sparse facts given here.
3. Repeat requirement 2, but assume that total sales would increase 10%.

5-40 Trade-Ins Versus Discounts

Many states base their sales tax on gross sales less any discount. Trade-in allowances are not discounts, so they are not deducted from the sales price for sales tax purposes. Suppose Michio Nagata had decided to trade in his old car for a new one with a list price of $20,000. He will pay cash of $12,000 plus sales tax. If he had not traded in a car, the dealer would have offered a discount of 15% of the list price. The sales tax is 8%.

How much of the $8,000 price reduction should be called a discount? How much a trade-in? Mr. Nagata wants to pay as little sales tax as legally possible.

Required

5-41 Uncollectible Accounts

During 19X8, the Rainbow Paint Store had credit sales of $600,000. The store manager expects that 2% of the credit sales will never be collected, although no accounts are written off until ten assorted steps have been taken to attain collection. The ten steps require a minimum of fourteen months.

Assume that during 19X9, specific customers are identified who are never expected to pay $10,000 that they owe from the sales of 19X8. All ten collection steps have been completed.

Required

1. Show the impact on the balance sheet equation of the above transactions in 19X8 and 19X9 under (a) the specific write-off method and (b) the allowance method. Which method do you prefer? Why?

2. Prepare journal entries for both methods. Omit explanations.

5-42 Specific Write-Off Versus Allowance Methods

AirTouch Communications, the cellular phone company, uses the allowance method for recognizing uncollectible accounts. The company had the following on its January 1, 1997 balance sheet (in millions):

Accounts receivable, net of allowance for uncollectibles of $61.1	$415.5

Required

1. Suppose AirTouch wrote off a specific uncollectible account for $1 million on January 2, 1997. Assume that this was the only transaction affecting the accounts receivable or allowance accounts on that day. Show the balance sheet entry for accounts receivable at the end of the day on January 2.

2. Suppose AirTouch used the specific write-off method instead of the allowance method for recognizing uncollectible accounts. Compute the accounts receivable balance that would be shown on the January 1, 1997, balance sheet.

5-43 Bad Debts

Prepare all journal entries regarding the following data. Consider the following balances of a medical clinic on December 31, 19X1: Receivables from patients, $200,000; and Allowance for Doubtful Receivables, $50,000. During 19X2, total billings to individual patients, excluding the billings to third-party payers such as Blue Cross and Medicare, were $2.5 million. Past experience indicated that 20% of such individual billings would ultimately be uncollectible. Write-offs of receivables during 19X2 were $490,000.

5-44 Bad Debt Allowance

Myrick Appliance had sales of $1,000,000 during 19X8, including $600,000 of sales on credit. Balances on December 31, 19X7, were Accounts Receivable, $45,000; and Allowance for Bad Debts, $4,000. Data for 19X8: Collections on accounts receivable were $530,000. Bad debts expense was estimated at 2% of credit sales, as in previous years. Write-offs of bad debts during 19X8 were $11,000.

1. Prepare journal entries regarding the above information for 19X8.
2. Show the ending balances of the balance sheet accounts, December 31, 19X8.
3. Based on the given data, what questions seem worth raising with Alice Myrick, the president of the store?

5-45   Bad Debt Recoveries

Seneca Department Store has many accounts receivable. The Seneca balance sheet, December 31, 19X1, showed Accounts Receivable, $950,000 and Allowance for Uncollectible Accounts, $40,000. In early 19X2, write-offs of customer accounts of $30,000 were made. In late 19X2, a customer, whose $4,000 debt had been written off earlier, won a $1 million sweepstakes cash prize. She immediately remitted $4,000 to Seneca. The store welcomed her money and her return to high credit standing. Prepare the journal entries for the $30,000 write-off in early 19X2 and the $4,000 receipt in late 19X2.

5-46   Subsidiary Ledger

An appliance store made credit sales of $800,000 in 19X4 to a thousand customers: Schumacher, $5,000; Cerruti, $7,000; others, $789,000. Total collections during 19X4 were $700,000 including $5,000 from Cerruti, but nothing was collected from Schumacher. At the end of 19X4, an allowance for uncollectible accounts was provided of 3% of credit sales.

Required

1. Set up appropriate general ledger accounts plus a subsidiary ledger for Accounts Receivable. The subsidiary ledger should consist of two individual accounts plus a third account called Others. Post the entries for 19X4. Prepare a statement of the ending balances of the individual accounts receivable to show that they reconcile with the general ledger account.
2. On March 24, 19X5, the Schumacher account was written off. Post the entries.

5-47   Accounts Receivable Turnover and Average Collection Period

Honda Motor Company had sales in fiscal 1997 of ¥5,293,302 million. Beginning and ending accounts receivable for fiscal 1997 were ¥337,848 and ¥381,774, respectively.

Required

Compute Honda's accounts receivable turnover and average collection period for fiscal 1997. Assume that all sales are on open account.

5-48   Internal Control Weaknesses

Identify the internal control weaknesses in each of the following situations and indicate what change or changes you would recommend to eliminate the weaknesses.

a. The internal audit staff of MacDougall Aerospace, Inc., reports to the controller. However, internal audits are undertaken only when a department manager requests one, and audit reports are confidential documents prepared exclusively for the manager. Internal auditors are not allowed to talk to the external auditors.

b. Alice Walker, president of Northwestern State Bank, a small-town midwestern bank, wants to expand the size of her bank. She hired Fred Howell to begin a foreign-loan department. Howell had previously worked in the international department of a London bank. The president told him to consult with her on any large loans, but she never specified exactly what was meant by "large." At the end of Howell's first year, the president was surprised and pleased by his results. Although he had made several loans larger than any made by other sections of the bank and had not consulted with her on any of them, the president hesitated to say anything because the financial results were so good. Walker certainly did not want to upset the person most responsible for the bank's excellent growth in earnings.

c. Michael Grant is in charge of purchasing and receiving watches for Blumberg, Inc., a chain of jewelry stores. Grant places orders, fills out receiving documents when the watches are delivered, and authorizes payment to suppliers. According to Blumberg's procedures manual, Grant's activities should be reviewed by a purchasing supervisor. But to save money, the supervisor was not replaced when she resigned three years ago. No one seems to miss the supervisor.

5-49 Assignment of Duties

Music Supplies, Inc., is a distributor of several popular lines of musical instruments and supplies. It purchases merchandise from several suppliers and sells to hundreds of retail stores. Here is a *partial list* of the company's necessary office routines:

1. Verifying and comparing related purchase documents: purchase orders, purchase invoices, receiving reports, etc.
2. Preparing vouchers for cash disbursements and attaching supporting purchase documents.
3. Signing above vouchers to authorize payment (after examining vouchers with attached documents).
4. Preparing checks for above.
5. Signing checks (after examining voucher authorization and supporting documents).
6. Mailing checks.
7. Daily sorting of incoming mail into items that contain money and items that do not.
8. Distributing the above mail: money to cashier, reports of money received to accounting department, and remainder to various appropriate offices.
9. Making daily bank deposits.
10. Reconciling monthly bank statements.

The company's chief financial officer has decided that no more than five people will handle all of these routines, including himself as necessary.

Prepare a chart to show how these operations should be assigned to the five employees, including the chief financial officer. Use a row for each of the numbered routines and a column for each employee: Financial Officer, A, B, C, D. Place a check mark for each row in one or more of the columns. Observe the rules of the textbook checklist for internal control, especially separation of duties.

Required

5-50 Simple Bank Reconciliation

Study Appendix 5A. St. Luke's Hospital has a bank account. Consider the following information:

a. Balances as of July 31: per books, $48,000; per bank statement, $28,880.
b. Cash receipts of July 31 amounting to $10,000 were recorded and then deposited in the bank's night depository. The bank did not include this deposit on its July statement.
c. The bank statement included service charges of $120.
d. Patients had given the hospital some bad checks amounting to $13,000. The bank marked them NSF and returned them with the bank statement after charging the hospital for the $13,000. The hospital had made no entry for the return of these checks.
e. The hospital's outstanding checks amounted to $4,000.

1. Prepare a bank reconciliation as of July 31.
2. Prepare the hospital journal entries required by the given information.

Required

5-51 Allowance for Credit Losses

A major U.S. bank included the following in the footnotes to its 1996 annual report:

The following is a summary of changes in the allowance for loan losses (in millions):

	1996
Balance, beginning of year	$505
Loans charged off	(209)
Recoveries	55
Provision expense	155
Other additions (deductions)	(29)
Balance, end of year	$477

Required

1. Terminology in bank financial statements sometimes differs slightly from that in statements of industrial companies. Explain what is meant by "allowance for loan losses," "provision expense," and "loans charged off" in the footnote.

2. Prepare the 1996 journal entries to record the writing off of specific credit losses, the recovery of previously written off credit losses, and the charge for credit losses against 1996 income. Omit explanations.

3. Suppose the bank analyzed its loans at the end of 1996 and decided that an allowance for credit losses equal to the 1995 amount ($505 million) was required. Compute the provision for credit losses that would be charged in 1996. In other words, instead of a provision for credit losses of $155 million, what provision would have been charged?

4. The bank had income before income taxes of $908 million in 1996. Compute the income before income taxes if the allowance for loan losses at the end of 1996 had been the same as at the end of 1995?

5-52 Aging of Accounts

Consider the following analysis of Accounts Receivable, February 28, 19X9:

Name of Customer	Total	Remarks
Ng Nurseries	$ 20,000	50% over 90 days, 50% 61–90 days
Michael's Landscaping	8,000	75% 31–60 days, 25% under 30 days
Shoven Garden Supply	12,000	60% 61–90 day, 40% 31–60 days
Bonner Perennial Farm	16,000	all under 30 days
Hjortshoj Florists	4,000	25% 61–90 days, 75% 1–30 days
Other accounts (each detailed)	80,000	50% 1–30 days, 30% 31–60 days, 15% 61–90 days, 5% over 90 days
Total	$140,000	

Required

Prepare an aging schedule, classifying ages into four categories: 1–30 days, 31–60 days, 61–90 days, and over 90 days. Assume that the prospective bad debt percentages for each category are 0.2%, 0.8%, 10%, and 80%, respectively. What is the ending balance in the Allowance for Uncollectible Accounts?

5-53 Percentage of Ending Accounts Receivable

Consider the following data.

	Accounts Receivable at End of Year	Accounts Receivable Deemed Uncollectible and Written Off During Subsequent Years
19X1	$210,000	$ 8,000
19X2	170,000	6,000
19X3	180,000	6,400
19X4	230,000	9,000
19X5	250,000	12,000
19X6	220,000	9,000

Required

The unadjusted credit balance in Allowance for Uncollectible Accounts at December 31, 19X7, is $600. Using the percentage of ending accounts receivable method, prepare an adjusting entry to bring the Allowance to the appropriate amount at December 31, 19X7 when the Accounts Receivable balance is $230,000.

5-54 Estimates of Uncollectible Accounts

Rashid Company has made an analysis of its sales and accounts receivable for the past five years. Assume that all accounts written off in a year related to sales of the preceding year and were part of the accounts receivable at the end of that year. That is, no account is written off before the end of the year of the sale, and all accounts remaining unpaid are written off before the end of the year following the sale. The analysis showed:

	Sales	Ending Accounts Receivable	Bad Debts Written Off During the Year
19X1	$680,000	$ 90,000	$12,000
19X2	750,000	97,000	12,500
19X3	750,000	103,000	14,000
19X4	850,000	114,000	16,500
19X5	850,000	110,000	17,600

The balance in Allowance for Uncollectible Accounts on December 31, 19X4, was $16,000.

Required

1. Determine the bad debts expense for 19X5 and the balance of the Allowance for Uncollectible Accounts for December 31, 19X5, using the percentage of sales method.

2. Repeat requirement 1 using the percentage of ending accounts receivable method.

5-55 Percentage of Sales and Percentage of Ending Accounts Receivable

Teton Equipment Company had credit sales of $6 million during 19X7. Most customers paid promptly (within 30 days), but a few took longer; an average of 1.5% of credit sales were never paid. On December 31, 19X7, accounts receivable were $450,000. The Allowance for Bad Debts account, before any recognition of 19X7 bad debts, had a $1,200 debit balance.

Teton produces and sells mountaineering equipment and other outdoor gear. Most of the sales (about 80%) come in the period of March through August; the other 20% is spread almost evenly over the other six months. Over the last six years, an average of 18% of the December 31 accounts receivable has not been collected.

1. Suppose Teton Equipment uses the percentage of sales method to calculate an allowance for bad debts. Present the accounts receivable and allowance accounts as they should appear on the December 31, 19X7, balance sheet. Give the journal entry required to recognize the bad debts expense for 19X7.

2. Repeat requirement 1 except assume that Teton Equipment uses the percentage of ending accounts receivable method.

3. Which method do you prefer? Why?

5-56 Average Collection Period
Consider the following:

	19X8	19X7	19X6
Sales	$2,000,000	$2,500,000	$2,400,000

	December 31		
	19X8	*19X7*	*19X6*
Accounts receivable	$ 195,000	$ 190,000	$ 185,000

Eighty percent of the sales are on account.

Compute the average collection period for the years 19X7 and 19X8. Comment on the results.

5-57 Bank Cards
Visa and MasterCard are used to pay for a large percentage of retail purchases. The financial arrangements are similar for both bank cards. A news story said:

> If a cardholder charges a pair of $60 shoes, for instance, the merchant deposits the sales draft with his bank, which immediately credits $60 less a small transaction fee (usually 2% of the sale) to the merchant's account. The bank that issued the customer his card then pays the shoe merchant's bank $60 less a 1.5% transaction fee, allowing the merchant's bank a 0.5% profit on the transaction.

1. Prepare the journal entry for the sale by the merchant.

2. Prepare the journal entries for the merchant's bank regarding (a) the merchant's deposit and (b) the collection from the customer's bank that issued the card.

3. Prepare the journal entry for the customer's bank that issued the card.

4. The national losses from bad debts for bank cards are about 1.8% of the total billings to cardholders. If so, how can the banks justify providing this service if their revenue from processing is typically 1.5% to 2.0%?

5-58 Student Loans
An annual report of the University of Washington includes information about its receivables from student loans in a footnote to the financial statements (in thousands):

	Year 1		Year 2	
Student Loans:				
Federal programs	$30,905		$33,109	
Less—allowances	2,793	$28,112	2,378	$30,731
University funds	$ 4,748		$ 4,999	
Less—allowances	337	4,411	271	4,728
Total, net		$32,523		$35,459

1. Compare the quality of the loans under federal programs with the quality of those using university funds. Compare the quality of the loans outstanding at the end of Year 2 with the quality of those outstanding at the end of Year 1. **Required**

2. Using the allowance method, which accounts would be affected by an allowance for bad debts of an appropriate percentage of $200,000 of new loans in Year 2 from university funds? Choose a percentage.

5-59 Hospital Bad Debts

EquiMed, Inc., a medical management company based in State College, Pennsylvania, owns, operates, and manages 35 radiation oncology centers. Notes to the 1996 earnings statement reported the following about net revenue (in thousands):

Gross revenues	$159,944
Less provision for contractual adjustments	60,829
Net revenues	$ 99,115

1. Prepare a reasonable footnote to accompany the above presentation. What do you think is the purpose of contractual adjustments? **Required**

2. Prepare the summary journal entries for the $159,944 and the $60,829.

5-60 Discounts and Doubtful Items

Bristol-Myers Squibb Company, the major pharmaceutical company, includes the following in the notes to the financial statements (in millions):

	December 31, 1996
Customer receivables	$2,758
Allowance for discounts and doubtful accounts	(107)
	$2,651

1. Compute the ratio of the allowance for discounts and doubtful items to gross accounts receivable for December 31, 1996. In 1995 this ratio was 4.1%. What are some possible reasons for the change in this ratio? **Required**

2. Assume that all discounts are cash discounts, not trade discounts. Why does the allowance for cash discounts exist?

3. Independent of Bristol-Myers Squibb's actual balances, prepare a journal entry to write off an uncollectible account of $100,000 on January 2, 1997.

5-61 Uncollectible Accounts

Nike, Inc., is a worldwide supplier of athletic products. Its balance sheet on May 31, 1997, included the following data (in thousands):

Accounts receivable, less allowance for doubtful accounts of $57,233	$1,754,137

1. The company uses the allowance method for accounting for bad debts. Suppose the company added $20 million to the allowance during the year ending May 31, 1997. Write-offs of uncollectible accounts were $19 million. Show (a) the impact on the balance sheet equation of these transactions and (b) the journal entries. **Required**

2. Suppose Nike had used the specific write-off method for accounting for bad debts. Using the same information as in requirement 1, show (a) the impact on the balance sheet equation and (b) the journal entry.

3. How would the Nike balance sheet amounts above have been affected if the specific write-off method had been used up to that date? Be specific.

5-62   Uncollectible Accounts

Exxon Corporation is the world's largest producer of oil and gas. Its balance sheet included the following actual presentation:

	December 31	
	1996	*1995*
	(millions of dollars)	
Notes and accounts receivable less estimated doubtful accounts	$10,499	$8,925

Required

1. Footnote 4 to Exxon's financial statements revealed that estimated doubtful notes and accounts receivable were $98 million at the end of 1996 and $104 million at the end of 1995. Suppose that during 1996 Exxon had added $300 million to its allowance for estimated doubtful accounts. (a) Calculate the write-offs of uncollectible accounts and show (b) the impact on the balance sheet equation of these transactions and (c) the journal entries.

2. Assume that Exxon had used the specific write-off method for accounting for bad debts. Using the same information as in requirement 1, show (a) the impact on the balance sheet equation and (b) the journal entry.

3. How would the Exxon balance sheet amounts have been affected if the specific write-off method had been used? Be specific.

5-63   Allowance for Doubtful Accounts and 10-K Disclosures

The following is schedule II, taken from the 10-K filing of Dayton Hudson Corporation for the year ending December 31, 1996. Dayton Hudson runs department stores such as Dayton's and discount stores such as Target. The 10-K is a required filing that companies must make with the Securities and Exchange Commission each year in order for their common stock to be traded publicly in the United States. It includes more detail than is often found in the annual report that is sent to all shareholders. This schedule describes exactly what occurred in the allowance for doubtful accounts. Use the information in schedule II to reproduce the journal entries affecting the allowance for doubtful accounts during the year ending December 31, 1996.

Dayton Hudson Corporation
Schedule II—Valuation and Qualifying Accounts (in millions)

Column A	Column B	Column C	Column D	Column E
		Additions		
	Balance at	*Charged to*		*Balance at*
	Beginning	*Cost and*		*End*
Descriptions	*of Period*	*Expenses*	*Deductions*	*of Period*
Allowance for doubtful accounts:				
1996	$69	$124	$74	$119
1995	$46	$ 93	$70	$ 69

5-64   Sales, Accounts Receivable, and Ethics

Writing in *Corporate Cashflow*, Howard Schillit described how the market value of Comptronix fell from $238 million to $67 million in a few hours when it was revealed that management had "cooked the books." Comptronix provides contract manufacturing services to makers of electronic equipment. Its 1991 financial results looked strong:

	1991	1990	Change
Sales	$102.0 million	$70.2 million	+45%
Accounts receivable	12.6 million	12.0 million	+5%
Accounts receivable turnover	8.1	5.9	

However, the relationship between sales and accounts receivable sent signals to knowledgeable analysts.

Required

1. Discuss the relationship that you would expect between sales and accounts receivable in a normal situation.
2. What unethical actions might cause sales to grow so much faster than accounts receivable? What unethical actions might cause the opposite, that is, for accounts receivable to grow faster than sales?
3. What is the most likely type of "cooking the books" that occurred at Comptronix?

5-65 Audit Committee Role

In a recent court decision, a U.S. corporation was required to delegate certain responsibilities to its audit committee. Management was required to

1. Consult with its independent auditors before deciding any significant or material accounting question or policy.
2. Retain independent auditors to perform quarterly reviews of all financial statements prior to public issuance.
3. Conduct internal audits, with personnel reporting directly to the audit committee (internal auditors must report quarterly to the audit committee).
4. Retain or dismiss independent and internal auditors.
5. Consult with the independent auditors on their quarterly reviews of financial statements.
6. Review all monthly corporate and division financial statements and the auditor's management letter.
7. Receive quarterly reports from independent auditors on internal control deficiencies.
8. Review and approve all reports to shareholders and the SEC before dissemination.

The court also ruled that the audit committee must be composed of at least three outside directors who have no business dealings with the firm other than directors' fees and expense reimbursements.

Required

a. Prepare a partial corporation organization chart to depict these requirements. Use boxes only for Audit Committee, Independent Auditors, Internal Auditing, Finance Vice-President, and Board of Directors. Connect the appropriate boxes with lines: solid lines for direct responsibility, dashed lines for information and communications. Place numbers on these lines to correspond to the eight items specified by the court decision.
b. Identify the main elements of the chapter checklist of internal control that seem most relevant to this system design.

5-66 Embezzlement of Cash Receipts

Braxton Company is a small wholesaler of pet supplies. It has only a few employees.

The owner of Braxton Company, who is also its president and general manager, makes daily deposits of customers' checks in the company bank account and writes all checks issued by the company. The president also reconciles the monthly bank statement with the books when the bank statement is received in the mail.

The assistant to Braxton Company's president renders secretarial services, which include taking dictation, typing letters, and processing all mail, both incoming and outgoing. Each day the assistant opens the incoming mail and gives the president the checks received from customers. The vouchers attached to the checks are separated by the assistant and sent to the bookkeeper, along with any other remittance advices that have been enclosed with the checks.

The bookkeeper makes prompt entries to credit customers' accounts for their remittances. From these accounts, the bookkeeper prepares monthly statements for mailing to customers.

Other employees include marketing and warehouse personnel.

Required For the thefts described below, explain briefly how each could have been concealed and what precautions you would recommend for forestalling the theft and its concealment:

1. The president's assistant takes some customers' checks, forges the company's endorsements, deposits the checks in a personal bank account, and destroys the check vouchers and any other remittance advices that have accompanied these checks.

2. The same action is taken as above, except that the vouchers and other remittance advices are sent intact to the bookkeeper.

5-67 Film Processing
Write not more than one page about the possible areas where internal controls should be instituted in the business described briefly below. Keep in mind the size of the business and do not suggest controls of a type impossible to set up in a firm of this sort. Make any reasonable assumptions about management duties and polices not expressly set forth below.

You have a film-developing service on Long Island, with ten employees driving their own cars six days a week to contact about forty places each, where film is left to be picked up and developed. Drivers bring film in one day and return the processed film the second or third day later. Stores pay the driver for his charges made on film picked up at their store, less a percentage for their work as an agency. The driver then turns this cash in to the Long Island office, where all film is developed and books are kept. Six to ten employees work at the office in Long Island, depending on the volume of work. You run the office and have one full-time accounting-clerical employee. Route drivers are paid monthly by miles of route covered.

5-68 Appraisal of Internal Control System
From the *San Francisco Chronicle:*

> The flap over missing ferry fares was peacefully—and openly—resolved at a meeting of the Golden Gate Bridge District finance committee yesterday.
>
> Only a week ago, the subject was a matter of furious dispute in which bridge manager Dale W. Luehring was twice called a liar and there were prospects of a closed meeting on personnel matters.
>
> But yesterday, after a week of investigation, the meeting turned out to be public after all, and attorney Thomas M. Jenkins revealed the full total of stolen ferry tickets equaled $26.20.
>
> The controversy began when auditor Gordon Dahlgren complained that there was an auditing "problem" and that he had not been informed when four children swiped $13.75 worth of tickets February 28. Committee chairman Ben K. Lerer, of San Francisco, ordered a full investigation.
>
> Jenkins said the situation was complicated because children under 5 have been allowed to ride the ferry without a ticket, but after May 1 everyone will have to have a ticket, allowing for a closer audit.

Secondly, Jenkins explained, the "vault" in which tickets are deposited was proved insecure (resulting in two thefts totaling $26.20 worth of tickets) but has been replaced.

In the future, it was decided, all thefts of cash or tickets must be reported immediately to the California Highway Patrol or the local police, the bridge lieutenant on duty, the general manager, the security officer, the auditor-controller, and the transit manager.

In addition, employees must make a full written report within 24 hours to the president of the district board, the chairman of the finance-auditing committee, the auditor-controller, the attorney, the bus transit manager, the water transit manager, the toll captain, and the chief of administration and security.

What is your reaction to the new system? Explain, giving particular attention to applicable criteria for appraising an internal control system.

5-69 Casino Skimming

An article in the *Wall Street Journal* reported that about $7 million in quarters disappeared from the slot machines of four casinos of Argent Corporation in an 18-month period. The coins weighed nearly 150 tons, and the odds against such a payout to players of the slot machines is one in 3,875,000,000,000,000,000,000,000,000,000,000,000,000,000,000,000,000,000—an extremely unlikely event, to say the least. The disappearance was part of the biggest known skim operation ever. *Skimming* is taking a portion of gambling revenues before they can be counted for tax purposes.

Internal control is especially important in casinos. Meters in the slot machines record the winnings paid to customers. Coins are taken immediately to the slot counting room when machines are emptied. In the counting rooms, coins are weighed, and a portion is returned to the change booths.

What items in the chapter checklist of internal control seem especially important regarding slot machine operations? How could the money from slot machine operations have been stolen in such large amounts?

5-70 Employee Dishonesty

Consider the following true newspaper reports of dishonesty:

a. At a small manufacturer, supervisors had access to time cards and gave out W-2 forms each year. The supervisors pocketed $80,000 a year in the paychecks for phantom workers.

b. A manager at a busy branch office of a copying service had a receipt book of his own. Jobs of $200 and $300 were common. The manager stole cash by simply giving customers a receipt from his book instead of one of the company's numbered forms.

c. A purchasing agent received tiny kickbacks on buttons, zippers, and other trims used at a successful dress company. The agent got rich, and the company was overcharged $10 million.

Specify what control or controls would have helped avoid each of the listed situations.

5-71 Internal Control Weaknesses

Identify the internal control weaknesses in each of the following situations.

a. Rodney Williams, a football star at the local university, was hired by D.A. Mount to work in the accounting department of Mount Electronics during summer vacation. Providing summer jobs is one way that Mount supports the team. After a week of training, Williams opened the mail containing checks from customers, recorded the payment in the books, and prepared the bank deposit slip.

b. Jim Sanchez manages a local franchise of a major twenty-four-hour convenience store. Sanchez brags that he keeps labor costs well below the average for such stores by operating with only one clerk. He has not granted a pay increase in four years. He loses a lot of clerks, but he can find replacements.

c. Martha McGuire operates an Exxon service station. Because it takes much extra time for attendants to walk from the gas pumps to the inside cash register, McGuire placed a locked cash box next to the pumps and gave each attendant a key. Cash and credit card slips are placed in the cash box. Each day the amounts are counted and entered in total into the cash register.

d. Lazlo Perconte trusts his employees. The former manager purchased fidelity bonds on employees who handle cash. Perconte decided that such bonds showed a lack of trust, so he ceased purchasing them. Besides, the money saved helped Perconte meet his budget for the year.

5-72 Cooking the Books

In *The Accounting Wars* (MacMillan, 1985), author Mark Stevens presents a chapter on "Book Cooking, Number Juggling, and Other Tricks of the Trade." He quotes Glen Perry, a former chief accountant of the SEC's Enforcement Division: "Companies play games with their financial reports for any number of reasons, the most common being the intense pressure on corporate management to produce an unbroken stream of increasing earnings reports." Stevens then lists Perry's "terrible ten of accounting frauds—ploys used to misrepresent corporate financial statements":

1. Recognition of revenues before they are realized.
2. Recognition of rentals to customers as sales.
3. Inclusion of fictitious amounts in inventories.
4. Improper cutoffs at year end.
5. Improper application of LIFO.
6. Creation of fraudulent year-end transactions to boost earnings.
7. Failure to recognize losses through write-offs and allowances.
8. Inconsistent accounting practices without disclosures.
9. Capitalization or improper deferral of expenses.
10. Inclusion of unusual gains in operating income.

Required

Suppose you were a division manager in a major corporation. Give a brief specific example of each of the ten methods.

5-73 Straightforward Bank Reconciliation

Study Appendix 5A. The City of Royalton has a checking account with First National Bank. The city's cash balance on February 28, 19X1, was $30,000. The deposit balance on the bank's books on February 28, 19X1, was also $30,000. The following transactions occurred during March.

Date	Check Number	Amount	Explanation
3/1	261	$11,000	Payment of previously billed consulting fee
3/6	262	8,000	Payment of accounts payable
3/10		12,000	Collection of taxes receivable
3/14	263	14,000	Acquisition of equipment for cash
3/17		16,000	Collection of license fees receivable
3/28	264	9,000	Payment of accounts payable
3/30	265	21,000	Payment of interest on municipal bonds
3/31		25,000	Collection of taxes receivable

All cash receipts are deposited via a night depository system after the close of the municipal business day. Therefore the receipts are not recorded by the bank until the succeeding day.

On March 31, the bank charged the City of Royalton $95 for miscellaneous bank services.

Required

1. Prepare the journal entries on the bank's books for check 262 and the deposit of March 10.

2. Prepare the journal entries for all March transactions on the books of the City of Royalton.

3. Post all transactions for March to T-accounts for the City's Cash in Bank account and the bank's Deposit account. Assume that only checks 261–263 have been presented to the bank in March, each taking four days to clear the bank's records.

4. Prepare a bank reconciliation for the City of Royalton, March 31, 19X1. The final three City of Royalton transactions of March had not affected the bank's records as of March 31. What adjusting entry in the books of the City of Royalton is required on March 31?

5. What would be the cash balance shown on the balance sheet of the City of Royalton on March 31, 19X1?

5-74   Semicomplex Bank Reconciliation

Study Appendix 5A. An employee, Sylvia Nelson, has a personal bank account. Her employer deposits her weekly paycheck automatically each Friday. The employee's check register (checkbook) for October is summarized as follows:

Reconciled cash balance, September 30, 19X1			$ 100
Additions:			
Weekly payroll deposits:	October		
	3		800
	10		800
	17		800
	24		800
Deposit of check received for gambling debt	25		500
Deposit of check received as winner of cereal contest	31		400
Subtotal			$4,200
Deductions:			
Checks written #325-#339	1-23	$3,300	
Check #340	26	70	
Check #341	30	90	
Check #342	31	340	3,800
Cash in bank, October 31, 19X1			$ 400

The bank statement is summarized in Exhibit 5-3. Note that NSF means "not sufficient funds." The check deposited on October 25 bounced; by prearrangement with Nelson, the bank automatically lends sufficient amounts (in multiples of $100) to ensure that her balance is never less than $100.

Required

1. Prepare Nelson's bank reconciliation, October 31, 19X1.

2. Assume that Nelson keeps a personal set of books on the accrual basis. Prepare the compound journal entry called for by the bank reconciliation.

5-75   Bank Versus Book Records

Study Appendix 5A. The Mead Corporation, primarily a forest products company, lists the following among its current assets and current liabilities (in millions):

	December 31,	
	1996	*1995*
As part of current assets:		
Cash and cash equivalents	$ 20.6	$292.6
As part of current liabilities:		
Accounts payable:		
Trade	271.1	242.3
Affiliated companies	34.9	52.1
Outstanding checks	52.9	86.1

It is unusual to find a liability account labeled "Outstanding Checks."

Required

1. Most companies have checks outstanding at any balance sheet date. Why is it unusual to have a liability for outstanding checks?

2. Suppose you examined the "Cash and Cash Equivalents" account in Mead's general ledger. What balance would you find for December 31, 1996? for December 31, 1995?

3. Why do you suppose Mead reported outstanding checks as a liability?

Exhibit 5-3

Bank Statement of Sylvia Nelson

SUMMARY OF YOUR CHECKING ACCOUNTS	
Beginning Balance	100.00
Deposits	4,600.00
Withdrawals	3,870.00
Service Charges/Fees	25.00*
Ending Balance	805.00
Minimum Balance on 10-28	**−80.00**

*$10.00 for returned check;
$15.00 monthly service charge

CHECKING ACTIVITY

Deposits

Posted	Amount	Description
10-03	800.00	Payroll Deposit
10-10	800.00	Payroll Deposit
10-17	800.00	Payroll Deposit
10-24	800.00	Payroll Deposit
10-25	500.00	Deposit
10-28	100.00	Automatic loan
10-31	800.00	Payroll Deposit

Withdrawals

Ck No	Paid	Amount
325-339 Various dates in October. These would be shown by specific amounts, but are shown here as a total.		3,300.00
340	10-27	70.00
NSF	10-28	500.00

Total Number of checks = 16

5-76 Ethics and Bank Reconciliations

The Springfield Chamber of Commerce recently hired you as an accounting assistant. Upon assuming your position on September 15, one of your first tasks was to reconcile the August bank statement. Your immediate supervisor, Ms. Ratelli, had been in charge of nearly all accounting tasks, including paying bills, preparing the payroll, and recording all transactions in the books. She has been very helpful to you, providing assistance on all the tasks she has asked you to do. The reconciliation was no different. Without assistance, you were able to locate the following information from the bank statement and the Chamber's books:

Balance per books	$16,710
Balance per bank statement	16,500
Bank service charges	30
NSF check returned	3,000
Deposit in transit	4,600
Outstanding checks	9,750

You also found a deposit on the bank statement of $3,300 that was incorrectly recorded as $3,030 on the Chamber's books.

When you could not reconcile the book and bank balances, you asked Ms. Ratelli for help. She responded that an additional $2,600 deposit was in transit. By coincidence, you noticed a $2,600 check, signed by Ms. Ratelli, to an individual whose name you did not recognize.

Required

1. Assume that all the information given is accurate and complete. Prepare the August bank reconciliation with the original information, showing that the book and the bank balances do not reconcile.

2. Prepare a reconciliation using the new number, $7,200, for deposits in transit.

3. Why might Ms. Ratelli have instructed you to add $2,600 to the deposits in transit? What might she be trying to hide? If there were deceit, when might it be discovered?

4. What actions would you take if you were the accounting assistant?

5-77 The Gap Annual Report

Refer to The Gap financial statements (Appendix A).

Required

1. The Gap combines cash and cash equivalents on the balance sheet. Define cash equivalents and give an example.

2. Assume the "other current assets" includes $75 million of accounts receivable on February 1, 1997 and $77 million on February 3, 1996. Calculate the average collection period for the year ended February 1, 1997, assuming all sales were on account.

3. Assume that The Gap's average collection period was 45 days. What percentage of sales would this imply were on credit?

5-78 Financial Statement Research

Select an industry and choose two companies within that industry.

Required

Calculate the accounts receivable turnover and days to collect accounts receivable for the two companies for two years and comment on the results.

COLLABORATIVE LEARNING EXERCISE

5-79 Revenue Recognition

Form groups of three to six students. Each student should pick one of the six industries listed below. The Standard Industrial Classification (SIC) number is provided for each industry. This number may be helpful in locating companies in that industry, especially if using search routines in electronic media.

Each group member should learn as much as possible about the revenue recognition issues in his or her industry. Select at least two companies in the industry, and examine the description of each company's revenue recognition policies in the footnotes (usually in footnote 1 or 2) to the financial statements. Two possible companies are listed for each industry, but do not feel restricted to using the companies listed.

After the individual research on a particular industry, get together as a team and report on what each member has learned. Compare and contrast the issues relating to when revenue is earned and realized in each industry. Discuss why issues that are important in one industry are unimportant in another.

- 2721—Periodicals Publishing and Printing
  Marvel Entertainment Group
  Readers Digest Association
- 4512—Air Transportation, Scheduled
  Alaska Air Group
  Southwest Airlines Company
- 4911—Electric Services
  Duke Power
  Puget Sound Energy
- 6311—Life Insurance
  Allstate Corp.
  USLIFE, Inc.
- 7811—Motion Picture, Video Tape Production
  Dick Clark Productions
  Walt Disney Company
- 8062—General Medical and Surgical Hospitals
  Columbia/HCA Healthcare
  Regency Health Services

5-80 Internet Case

Go to **http://www.mci/com/** to find MCI Communications Corporation home page. Select *About Us* from the menu, then select *Investor Relations.* Choose *Annual Reports,* and select the most recent year.

Answer the following questions about the company:

1. From the company's *Letter to Shareholders* and *Note 1* of *Notes to Consolidated Financial Statements,* what services are provided by MCI that contribute to its revenue? What primary industry is this?

2. What amounts are deducted from gross sales by MCI in reporting net sales for the year? (Hint: See the *Notes to Consolidated Financial Statements.*)

3. Examine MCI's balance sheet. What method of accounting for uncollectible accounts does MCI use? How do you know this without reading the notes to the financial statements?

4. What items are included in MCI's, "cash and cash equivalents"? Does the company have a compensating balance agreement with its bank? How do you know this?

5. Compare the amount of cash collected from customers with the amount of sales reported on the income statement. Why do you think these two amounts are different? What conclusions can you draw?

6. MCI participates with American Airlines Advantage frequent flyer miles program in conjunction with the Advantage Citibank charge cards. The program allows MCI customers to earn air miles with American Airlines by charging the long distance services on a customers' Advantage Citibank card. Citibank has a fee equal to about 2% of the amount charged. Where would you expect to find this 2% fee reported on MCI's financial statements? Why do you think this amount is not obvious from examining the financial statements?

6

INVENTORIES AND COST OF GOODS SOLD

These men, Bernie Marcus (left) and Arthur Blank (right), founded Home Depot and drove its success by managing its inventory to assure customers would find what they wanted.

Learning Objectives

After studying this chapter, you should be able to

1 Link inventory valuation to gross profit.

2 Use both perpetual and periodic inventory systems.

3 Calculate the cost of merchandise acquired.

4 Choose one of the four principal inventory valuation methods.

5 Calculate the impact on net income of LIFO liquidations.

6 Use the lower-of-cost-or-market method to value inventories.

7 Show the effects of inventory errors on financial statements.

8 Evaluate the gross profit percentage and inventory turnover.

Have you ever gone to your local hardware store and been frustrated because they did not have what you wanted? A goal of Home Depot is to help you avoid this frustration. They do it by keeping a large inventory—40,000 to 50,000 different items, more than three times the number at a typical hardware store. As CEO and Chairman Bernie Marcus says, one of the three main values at Home Depot is assortment— "everything a do-it-yourselfer needs to complete a project."

Inventory requires a large investment by retail companies—$2.7 billion at Home Depot, about 30% of the company's total assets—and accounting for this inventory is important. By carefully monitoring inventory levels, Home Depot makes sure it does not lose sales by having too little inventory and does not lose money by investing in too much inventory.

In Chapter 5, we learned how to account for sales revenues. Of course, when a company sells a product, it also incurs costs. For example, Home Depot must buy the tools it sells. Similarly, a Toyota dealership has to pay for every car it sells. The cost of tools or Toyotas sold must be recognized when the related revenues are.

Determining the cost of the Toyota sold is easy enough—you look up the cost on the invoice for the specific car you sold. Unfortunately, the calculations are not always that simple. Because products such as tools sold by Home Depot are often purchased in quantity and held in inventory, tracing the precise cost of a single product can be difficult. As a result, companies must develop procedures to determine the value of their inventories and the cost of goods sold.

This chapter will examine methods for valuing and accounting for inventories. Different inventory accounting practices are found around the globe, and multiple methods exist even in the same country or in the same industry. These differences make it hard to compare one firm to another. By understanding these differences, you will be better able to evaluate the profitability of different companies. You will be able to distinguish between apparent differences that arise solely from different accounting practices and real economic differences that distinguish two firms based on their profitability.

GROSS PROFIT AND COST OF GOODS SOLD

Gross profit = profit margin gross margin

Objective 1
Link inventory valuation to gross profit.

For merchandising firms, an initial step in assessing profitability is gross profit (also called profit margin or gross margin), which is the difference between sales revenues and the costs of the goods sold. Sales revenue must cover the cost of goods sold and provide a gross profit sufficient to cover all other costs, including research and development, selling and marketing, administration, and so on. As illustrated in Exhibit 6-1, products being held prior to sale are reported as inventory, a current asset in the balance sheet. When the goods are sold, the costs of the inventory become an expense, Cost of Goods Sold, in the income statement. This expense is deducted from Net Sales to determine Gross Profit, and additional expenses are deducted from Gross Profit to determine Net Income.

THE BASIC CONCEPT OF INVENTORY ACCOUNTING

In theory, the accounting for inventory and cost of goods sold is very simple. Suppose Christina sells T-shirts. Periodically, she orders many shirts of various sizes and colors. They sell, she orders more, and her business operating cycle continues on in this way.

Exhibit 6-1

Merchandising Company (Retailer or Wholesaler)

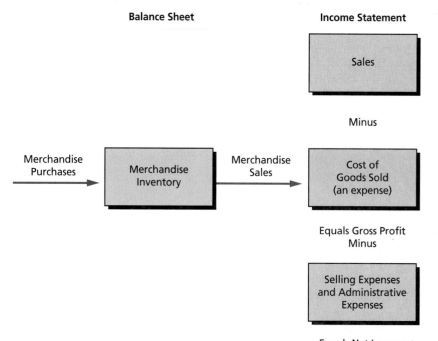

After a year, to evaluate her success, Christina prepares financial statements. To calculate the value of inventory on hand, she counts up all the inventory items remaining at year end (known as a physical count). She then develops a **cost valuation** by assigning a specific value from the historical cost records to each item in ending inventory. If the shirts cost $5.00 each and there are 100 shirts remaining in inventory, Christina's total ending inventory is $500. Suppose she had no shirts at the beginning of the year, and total purchases for the year were $26,000. Her cost of goods sold would thus be $25,500 ($26,000 of available shirts minus $500 of unsold shirts). Notice that the key to calculating the cost of goods sold is accounting for the remaining inventory.

Unfortunately, determining the cost of goods sold and accounting for inventory are not this simple in practice. In the following sections, we will show you some of the problems that can arise as well as how to deal with these problems. We will also show you the major techniques for measuring inventories that various companies use.

cost valuation Process of assigning specific historical costs to items counted in the physical inventory.

PERPETUAL AND PERIODIC INVENTORY SYSTEMS

There are two main systems for keeping merchandise inventory records: *perpetual* and *periodic*. The **perpetual inventory system** has been used in prior examples in this text. It keeps a continuous record that tracks inventories and the cost of goods sold on a day-to-day basis. Such a record helps managers control inventory levels and prepare interim financial statements. The perpetual system does not eliminate the need for a physical count and valuation of the inventory. A **physical count** of the inventory should be conducted at least once a year to check on the accuracy of the continuous records. The perpetual system was developed to provide managers with information to aid in pricing or ordering. At first it was extremely cumbersome and expensive to maintain constant records, but computerized inventory systems and optical scanning equipment at checkout counters have made implementation of perpetual inventory systems much less costly in many industries.

Previous chapters have used the perpetual system to record inventory transactions without referring to it by name. It can be illustrated as follows:

Objective 2
Use both perpetual and periodic inventory systems.

perpetual inventory system A system that keeps a running, continuous record that tracks inventories and the cost of goods sold on a day-to-day basis.

physical count The process of counting all the items in inventory at a moment in time.

		A	=	L	+	SE
a. Purchase	+	Increase Merchandise Inventory	= +	Increase Accounts Payable		
b. Sale	+	Increase Accounts Receivable	=		+	Increase Sales Revenue
Cost of inventory sold	−	Decrease Inventory	=		−	Increase Cost of Goods Sold

In the perpetual inventory system, the journal entries are:

a. When inventory is purchased:
   Merchandise inventory   xxx
      Accounts payable   xxx
b. When inventory is sold:
   Accounts receivable (or cash)   xxx
      Sales revenue   xxx
   Cost of goods sold   xxx
      Inventory   xxx

Thus, in the perpetual inventory system, the sale of an item and the accompanying inventory reduction are recorded simultaneously.

periodic inventory system
The system in which the cost of goods sold is computed periodically by relying solely on physical counts without keeping day-to-day records of units sold or on hand.

inventory shrinkage
Inventory reductions from theft, breakage, or losses of inventory.

cost of goods available for sale Sum of beginning inventory plus current year purchases.

In contrast, the **periodic inventory system** does not involve a day-to-day record of inventories or of the cost of goods sold. Instead the cost of goods sold and an updated inventory balance are computed only at the end of an accounting period, when a physical count of inventory is taken. The physical count allows management to delete from inventory goods that are damaged or obsolete and thus helps reveal **inventory shrinkage,** which refers to losses from theft, breakage, and loss. Inventory shrinkage can be quite large in some businesses. This periodic inventory system was illustrated in the example of Christina's T-shirt business.

Under the periodic system, calculations for the cost of goods sold start with the **cost of the goods available for sale.** This is the sum of the opening inventory for the period plus purchases during the period. The accountant computes the cost of goods sold by subtracting the ending inventories from this sum. Thus the periodic system computes cost of goods sold as a residual amount.

Although the cost of goods sold under the perpetual system is computed instantaneously as goods are sold, under the periodic system, the computation is delayed until a physical count is made:

$$\underbrace{\text{Beginning inventory} + \text{Purchases}}_{\text{Goods available for sale}} - \underbrace{\text{Ending inventory}}_{\text{Inventory left over}} = \underbrace{\text{Cost of goods sold}}_{\text{Cost of goods sold}}$$

Exhibit 6-2 compares the perpetual and periodic inventory systems. Note that for annual financial statements, the two methods produce the same cost of goods sold figure. The perpetual system is more timely but it is also more costly to administer. While the periodic system is less costly because there is no day-to-day processing regarding cost of goods sold, it is not always the best system. The perpetual system often provides managers with better assessments of levels of inventory and helps them order more appropriately to restock the shelves with the right merchandise.

PHYSICAL INVENTORY

Good inventory control procedures require a physical count of each item being held in inventory at least annually in both periodic and perpetual inventory systems. The physical count is an imposing, time-consuming, and expensive process. You may have seen "closed for inventory" signs. To simplify counting and valuation, firms often choose fiscal accounting periods so that the year ends when inventories are low. For example, Kmart and JC Penney have late January year ends, which follow the holiday season.

The physical inventory is so important to income determination that external auditors usually observe the client's physical count and confirm the accuracy of the subsequent valuation. Some audit firms hire outside experts to assist them. For example, assess-

Exhibit 6-2

Inventory Systems

Periodic System		Perpetual System
Beginning inventories		Cost of goods sold (kept on a
(by physical count)	xxx	day-to-day basis rather than
Add: Purchases	xxx	being determined periodically)*
Cost of goods available for sale	xxx	
Less: Ending inventories		
(by physical count)	xxx	
Cost of goods sold	xxx	

* Such a condensed figure does not preclude the presentation of a supplementary schedule similar to that on the left.

ing a jeweler's inventory might require an expert to test the color, size, clarity, and imperfections in the diamonds on hand. Similarly, the client and auditor might rely on an engineer to measure the physical dimensions of an electric utility's coal pile so the volume and weight could be estimated without actually weighing the coal itself.

Inventory fraud is well illustrated by the Classic Salad Oil Swindle. On Thursday, November 21, 1963, reports linked the suspension of two Wall Street brokerage firms to uncollectible loans made to an obscure company named Allied Crude Vegetable Oil and Refining. Collateral for the loans had been $175 million worth of vegetable oil supposedly stored in 40 converted gasoline storage tanks in Bayonne, New Jersey. Investigation revealed that, instead of being filled with vegetable oil, the tanks contained sea water, soap stock, and "sludge."

Allied used some ingenious techniques to hide their shortfall from the watchful auditors. Because the 40 storage tanks were connected by pipes, the vegetable oil was pumped from tank to tank during the week required to complete the inventory count. The same vegetable oil was counted over and over. Moreover, no one tank was ever completely filled with the oil. Allied welded shut all but one opening to the tank. Beneath this working opening the company then welded a pipe, which was filled with a few hundred pounds of real oil. When the auditors took samples, they were actually testing what was in this pipe, not what was in the tank. The tank itself was filled with sea water. After the fraud was uncovered, a faucet on one tank was opened, and water poured out for 12 days.

Thanks largely to Allied's scam and the accompanying brokerage suspensions, the Dow Jones Industrial Average experienced its largest decline in more than a year. However, news of the unfolding "Great Salad Oil Swindle" was rapidly overshadowed when, on the following day, President John F. Kennedy was assassinated in Dallas.

COST OF MERCHANDISE ACQUIRED

Objective 3
Calculate the cost of merchandise acquired.

Regardless of whether you use the periodic or perpetual system, the basis of inventory accounting is the cost of the merchandise a company purchases to then sell. But what makes up that cost? To be more specific, does that cost include all or part of the following: invoice price, transportation charges, trade and cash discounts, cost of handling and placing in stock, storage, purchasing department, receiving department, and other indirect charges? In practice, accountants usually consider the cost of merchandise to include only the invoice price plus the directly identifiable transportation charges less any offsetting discounts. The costs of the purchasing and receiving departments are treated as period costs and appear on the income statement as they are incurred.

TRANSPORTATION CHARGES

The major cost of transporting merchandise is typically the freight charges from the shipping point of the seller to the receiving point of the buyer. When the seller bears this cost, the terms are stated on the sales invoice as **F.O.B. (free on board) destination.** When the buyer bears this cost, the terms are stated as **F.O.B. shipping point.**

In theory, any transportation costs borne by the buyer should be added to the cost of the inventory acquired. In practice, though, transportation costs are not always easy to trace to specific inventory items. Companies tend to order several different items and have them shipped at the same time. Therefore it is often difficult to allocate freight costs among the items. In addition, management may want to compile freight costs separately to see how they change over time and to compare costs using rail service to costs using trucks. Consequently, accountants frequently use a separate transportation cost account, labeled as Freight In, Transportation In, Inbound Transportation, or Inward Transportation.

Freight in (or **inward transportation**) appears in the purchases section of an income statement as an additional cost of the goods acquired during the period. **Freight out**

F.O.B. destination Seller pays freight costs from the shipping point of the seller to the receiving point of the buyer.

F.O.B. shipping point Buyer pays freight costs from the shipping point of the seller to the receiving point of the buyer.

freight in (inward transportation) An additional cost of the goods acquired during the period, which is often shown in the purchases section of an income statement.

freight out The transportation costs borne by the seller of merchandise and often shown as a "shipping expense."

represents the costs borne by the seller and is shown as a "shipping expense," which is a form of selling expense. Thus Freight In affects the gross profit section of an income statement for the *buyer,* and Freight Out appears below the gross profit line on the *seller's* income statement.

RETURNS, ALLOWANCES AND DISCOUNTS

The accounting for purchase returns, purchase allowances, and cash discounts on purchases is just the opposite of their sales counterparts. Using the periodic inventory system, suppose gross purchases are $960,000 and purchase returns and allowances are $75,000. The summary journal entries are:

Purchases	960,000	
Accounts payable		960,000
Accounts payable	75,000	
Purchase returns and allowances		75,000

Suppose also that cash discounts of $5,000 are taken upon payment of the remaining $960,000 − $75,000 = $885,000 of payables. The summary journal entry is:

Accounts payable	885,000	
Cash discounts on purchases		5,000
Cash		880,000

The accounts Cash Discounts on Purchases and Purchase Returns and Allowances are deducted from Purchases in calculating cost of goods sold.

Car dealers sometimes sell cars "below cost" or "$100 below invoice." Do dealers lose money on such sales? Probably not, because gross invoice cost to the dealer and final cost of goods sold may differ. Dealers receive incentives from the manufacturers such as volume discounts or special discounts to push particular models. The dealer's invoice shows the list price before discounts and allowances, not the final net dealer cost.

A detailed gross profit section in the income statement is often arranged as in Exhibit 6-3 (figures in thousands are assumed).

Exhibit 6-3

Detailed Gross Profit Calculation

Gross sales			$1,740
Deduct: Sales returns and allowances		$ 70	
Cash discounts on sales		100	170
Net sales			$1,570
Deduct: Cost of goods sold:			
Merchandise inventory, December 31, 19X1		$ 100	
Purchases (gross)	$960		
Deduct: Purchase returns and allowances	$75		
Cash discounts on purchases	5	80	
Net purchases		$880	
Add: Freight in		30	
Total cost of merchandise acquired		910	
Cost of goods available for sale		$1,010	
Deduct: Merchandise inventory,			
December 31, 19X2		140	
Cost of goods sold			870
Gross profit			$ 700

Although management may find such detail valuable, summary information is much more common in the annual report to shareholders:

Net Sales	$1,570
Cost of Goods Sold	870
Gross Profit	$ 700

COMPARING ACCOUNTING PROCEDURES FOR PERIODIC AND PERPETUAL INVENTORY SYSTEMS

GoodEarth Products, Inc., has a balance of $100,000 in merchandise inventory at the beginning of 19X2 (December 31, 19X1). A summary of transactions for 19X2 follows:

a. Purchases	$990,000
b. Purchase returns and allowances	80,000

Net purchases were therefore $990,000 less $80,000, or $910,000. The physical count of the ending inventory for 19X2 led to a cost valuation of $140,000. Note how these figures can be used to compute the $870,000 cost of goods sold:

$$\frac{\text{Beginning}}{\text{inventory}} + \text{Net purchases} - \frac{\text{Ending}}{\text{inventory}} = \frac{\text{Cost of}}{\text{goods sold}}$$

$$\$100,000 + \$910,000 \quad - \$140,000 \quad = \$870,000$$

$$\underbrace{\begin{array}{c}\text{Cost of goods}\\ \text{available for sale}\end{array}} \quad \begin{array}{c}- \text{Cost of goods} =\\ \text{left over}\end{array} \quad \begin{array}{c}\text{Cost of}\\ \text{goods sold}\end{array}$$

$$\$1,010,000 \quad - \$140,000 \quad = \$870,000$$

The periodic and perpetual procedures would record these transactions differently. As Exhibit 6-4 shows, the perpetual system entails directly increasing the Inventory account by the $990,000 purchases (entry a) and decreasing it by the $80,000 in returns and allowances (entry b) and the $870,000 cost of goods sold (entry c). The Cost of Goods Sold account would be increased daily as sales are made.

Before proceeding, reflect on how the perpetual system in Exhibit 6-4 creates the ending inventory of $140,000 in the general ledger account for Inventory. But recall that a physical count will also be conducted to verify the number. The $870,000 debit to cost of goods sold represents the sum of many daily entries that are made as sales occur.

GoodEarth Products, Inc.
General Ledger at December 31, 19X2
(amounts in thousands) Perpetual Inventory

Inventory				Cost of Goods Sold	
Balance 12/31/X1	100	(b)	80	(c)	870
(a)	990	(c)	870		
Balance 12/31/X2	140			Balance 12/31/X2	870

Under the periodic system, Purchases and Purchase Returns and Allowances are each accounted for in a separate account, as entries a and b indicate. The periodic system is called "periodic" because neither the Cost of Goods Sold account nor the Inventory account is

Exhibit 6-4

Comparison of Perpetual and Periodic Inventory Entries
(amounts in thousands)

	Perpetual Records			Periodic Records		
a. Gross purchases:	Inventory	990		Purchases	990	
	Accounts payable		990	Accounts payable		990
b. Returns and allowances:	Accounts payable	80		Accounts payable	80	
	Inventory		80	Purchase returns and allowances.		80
c. As goods are sold:	Cost of goods sold	870		No entry		
	Inventory		870			
d. At the end of the accounting period:	d1. } No entry d2. }			d1. Cost of goods sold	1,010	
				Purchase returns and allowances	80	
				Purchases		990
				Inventory		100
				d2. Inventory	140	
				Cost of goods sold		140

computed on a daily basis. Entries d1 and d2 at the bottom of Exhibit 6-4 show how these accounts are updated during the eventual periodic calculation of cost of goods sold.

Entry d1 transfers the beginning inventory balance, purchases, and purchase returns and allowances, totaling $1,010,000, to cost of goods sold, which provides the cost of goods available for sale. Next, the ending inventory is physically counted, and its cost is computed. Entry d2 recognizes the $140,000 ending inventory and reduces the $1,010,000 cost of goods available for sale by $140,000 to obtain a final cost of goods sold of $870,000.

GoodEarth Products, Inc.
General Ledger at December 31, 19X2
(amounts in thousands) Periodic Inventory

Inventory				Cost of Goods Sold			
Balance 12/31/X1	100	(d1)	100	(d1)	1,010	(d2)	140
(d2)	140						
Balance 12/31/X2	140			Balance 12/31/X2	870		

PRINCIPAL INVENTORY VALUATION METHODS

Objective 4
Choose one of the four principal inventory valuation methods.

Each period, accountants must divide the cost of beginning inventory and merchandise acquired between cost of goods sold and cost of items remaining in ending inventory. Under a perpetual system, we must determine a cost for each item sold. Under a periodic system, we instead must determine the costs of the items remaining in ending inventory. Regardless of the inventory system, costs of individual items must be determined by some inventory valuation method. Four principal inventory valuation methods have been generally accepted in the United States: specific identification, FIFO, LIFO, and weighted-average. Each will be explained and compared in this section.

If unit prices and costs did not fluctuate, all four inventory methods would show identical results. But prices change, and these changes raise central issues regarding cost of goods sold (income measurement) and inventories (asset measurement). As a simple example of the valuation method choices facing management, consider Emilio, a new vendor of a cola drink at the fairgrounds, who begins the week with no inventory. He buys one can on Monday for 30 cents; a second can on Tuesday for 40

Exhibit 6-5

Emilio's Cola Sales

Comparison of Inventory Methods (all monetary amounts are in cents)

	(1) Specific Identification			(2) FIFO	(3) LIFO	(4) Weighted Average
	(1A)	(1B)	(1C)			
Panel I						
Income Statement for the Period Monday through Thursday						
Sales	90	90	90	90	90	90
Deduct cost of goods sold:						
1 30¢ (Monday) unit	30			30		
1 40¢ (Tuesday) unit		40				
1 56¢ (Wednesday) unit			56		56	
1 weighted-average unit [(30 + 40 + 56) ÷ 3 = 42]						42
Gross profit for Monday through Thursday	60	50	34	60	34	48
Thursday's ending inventory, 2 units:						
Monday unit @ 30¢		30	30		30	
Tuesday unit @ 40¢	40		40	40	40	
Wednesday unit @ 56¢	56	56		56		
Weighted-average units @ 42¢						84
Total ending inventory on Thursday	96	86	70	96	70	84
Panel II						
Income Statement for Friday						
Sales, 2 units @ 90¢	180	180	180	180	180	180
Cost of goods sold (Thursday ending inventory from above)	96	86	70	96	70	84
Gross profit, Friday only	84	94	110	84	110	96
Panel III						
Gross profit for full week						
Monday through Thursday (Panel 1)	60	50	34	60	34	48
Friday (Panel II)	84	94	110	84	110	96
Total gross profit	144	144	144	144	144	144

cents; and a third can on Wednesday for 56 cents. He then sells one can on Thursday for 90 cents.

As Panel I of Exhibit 6-5 shows, Emilio's choice of an inventory method can significantly affect the amount reported as cost of goods sold (and hence gross profit and net income) and ending inventory. The gross profit for Monday through Thursday ranges from 34 cents to 60 cents, depending on the method chosen. Using Exhibit 6-5 as a guide, let us now examine each of the four methods in detail.

SPECIFIC IDENTIFICATION

The **specific identification method** concentrates on the physical linking of the particular items sold. Suppose Emilio could tell which can of cola was purchased on each day. He could mark each can with its cost and record that cost as cost of goods sold when the can was handed to a customer. If he reached for the Monday can instead of the Wednesday can, the specific identification method would show different results. Thus Panel I of Exhibit 6-5 indicates that gross profit for operations of Monday through Thursday could be 60 cents, 50 cents, or 34 cents, depending on the particular can handed to the customer. Emilio could choose which can to sell and affect reported results by doing so.

Because the cost of goods sold is determined by the specific item handed to the customer, the specific identification method permits managers to manipulate income and inventory values by filling a sales order from a number of physically equivalent items with differ-

specific identification method This inventory method concentrates on the physical linking of the particular items sold.

ent historical costs. Overall, this method is easy to use, but it works best for relatively expensive low-volume merchandise, such as custom artwork, diamond jewelry, and automobiles. However, most organizations have vast segments of inventories that have too many items that are insufficiently valuable per unit to warrant such individualized attention.

FIFO

first-in, first-out (FIFO)
This method of accounting for inventory assigns the cost of the earliest acquired units to cost of goods sold.

FIFO refers to **First-in, First-out.** The method is a cost assignment method and does not track the actual physical flow of individual items except by coincidence. For identical units, it assigns the cost of the earliest acquired units to cost of goods sold. Picture Emilio putting each new can of cola at the back of the cooler to chill and the oldest, coldest can being sold first. Thus under FIFO, Emilio's Monday can of cola is deemed to have been sold—regardless of the actual can delivered. The costs of the newer stock are assigned to the units in ending inventory. This fact leads some to label this method LISH (Last-in, Still-here).

By using the more recent costs to measure the ending inventory, FIFO tends to provide inventory valuations that closely approximate the actual market value of the inventory at the balance sheet date. In addition, in periods of rising prices, FIFO leads to higher net income. Note that gross profit is 60 cents in Panel I of Exhibit 6-5 under FIFO because the oldest, cheapest unit is used in the calculation of cost of goods sold. Higher reported incomes may favorably affect investor attitudes toward the company. Similarly, higher reported incomes may lead to higher salaries, higher bonuses, or higher status for the management of the company. Unlike specific identification, FIFO specifies the order in which acquisition costs will become cost of goods sold, so management cannot affect income by choosing to sell one identical item rather than another.

LIFO

last-in, first-out (LIFO)
This inventory method assigns the most recent costs to cost of goods sold.

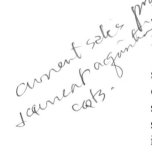

LIFO refers to **Last-in, First-out.** Whereas FIFO associates the most recent costs with ending inventories, LIFO assigns the most recent costs to costs of goods sold. The LIFO method assumes that the stock acquired most recently is sold first. Picture Emilio putting each new can, as it is acquired, into the top of a cooler. At each customer purchase, the top can is the one sold. This is the physical flow that corresponds to the LIFO cost system. Thus under LIFO, Emilio's Wednesday can of cola is deemed to have been sold—regardless of the actual can delivered from the cooler.

LIFO provides an income statement perspective in the sense that net income measured using LIFO combines current sales prices and current acquisition costs. In a period of rising prices and constant or growing inventories, LIFO yields lower net income as shown by the 34 cents of gross margin in Panel I of Exhibit 6-5. Why is lower net income such an important feature of LIFO? Because in the United States LIFO is an acceptable inventory accounting method for income tax purposes. When lower income is reported to the tax authorities, lower taxes are paid, so it is not surprising that almost two-thirds of U.S. corporations use LIFO for at least some of their inventories. However, the Internal Revenue Code requires that if LIFO is used for tax purposes, it must also be used for financial reporting purposes.

You might think of LIFO as the good news/bad news method. Lower income taxes provide the good news but the accompanying bad news is lower reported profits. During a recent period of higher inflation, the *Wall Street Journal* reported that many small firms changed from FIFO to LIFO. As an example, Chicago Heights Steel Co. "boosted cash by 5% to 10% by lowering income taxes when it switched to LIFO." When Becton, Dickinson and Company changed to LIFO, its annual report stated that its "change to the LIFO method . . . for both financial reporting and income tax purposes resulted in improved cash flow due to lower income taxes paid." Indeed, some observers maintain that executives are guilty of serious mismanagement by not adopting LIFO when FIFO produces significantly higher taxable income.

The whole issue with respect to LIFO is driven by inflation. When inflation is low, as it is in the late 1990s, the tax and income differences are small as well, and which inventory method is chosen matters little. Low inflation has been the norm in the United States during most of the twentieth century, but in 1974, the inflation rate in the United States reached double digits for the first time. In response, more than 40 U.S. corporations switched from FIFO to LIFO, apparently deciding the benefit of lower income taxes exceeded the cost of reporting lower profits. These tax savings were not trivial. For example, by switching from FIFO to LIFO, DuPont saved more than $200 million in taxes in 1974, and could anticipate greater savings in the future.

Why did some firms remain on FIFO? Possible reasons include the high bookkeeping costs of implementing the switch, reluctance by management to make an accounting switch reducing reported income and possibly reducing management bonuses, fear that banks would view the reduction in income unfavorably in loan negotiations, and belief that lower reported income would result in a lower stock price. But some firms should choose FIFO because for them it lowers taxes. Even when prices were rising in general, some industries, such as computers, faced declining costs and prices, so FIFO minimized reported income and taxes.

LIFO permits management to influence reported income by the timing of purchases of inventory items. Consider Emilio's case. Suppose that acquisition prices increase from 56 cents on Wednesday to 68 cents on Thursday, the day of the sale of the one unit. How is net income affected if one more unit is acquired on Thursday? Under LIFO, cost of goods sold would change to 68 cents, and profit would fall by 12 cents. In contrast, under FIFO, cost of goods sold and gross profit would be unchanged.

	LIFO		FIFO	
	As in Exhibit 6-5	If One More Unit Acquired	As in Exhibit 6-5	If One More Unit Acquired
Sales	90¢	90¢	90¢	90¢
Cost of goods sold	56¢	68¢	30¢	30¢
Gross profit	34¢	22¢	60¢	60¢
Ending inventory:				
First purchase, Monday	30¢	30¢		
Second purchase, Tuesday	40¢	40¢	40¢	40¢
Third purchase, Wednesday		56¢	56¢	56¢
Fourth purchase, Thursday				68¢
	70¢	126¢	96¢	164¢

WEIGHTED AVERAGE

The **weighted-average method** computes a unit cost by dividing the total acquisition cost of all items available for sale by the number of units available for sale. Picture Emilio dropping his cooler and not knowing which can was on top. He would have to average out everything he knows about the costs of all the cans in the cooler. Exhibit 6-5 shows the calculations Emilio would make. The average cost is 42 cents [(30 + 40 + 56) ÷ 3].

The averaging in the *weighted-average* method can be better understood by assuming Emilio bought two cans rather than one on Monday at 30 cents each. To get the weighted average, we must consider not only the price paid, but also the number of units purchased as follows:

Weighted average = Cost of goods available for sale ÷ Units available for sale
Weighted average = [(2 × 30¢) + (1 × 40¢) + (1 × 56¢)] ÷ 4
= 156¢ ÷ 4
= 39¢

weighted-average method
This inventory method computes a unit cost by dividing the total acquisition cost of all items available for sale by the number of units available for sale.

The weighted-average method produces a gross profit somewhere between that obtained under FIFO and that under LIFO (48 cents as compared with 60 cents and 34 cents in Panel I of Exhibit 6-5).

COST FLOW ASSUMPTIONS

Because the actual physical flow of identical products is less important to the financial success of most businesses than is the flow of the units' costs, the accounting profession has concluded that companies may choose any of the four methods to record cost of goods sold. Basically, the units are all the same, but their costs differ, so tracing the flow or assignment of those costs is more important than is tracing where each specific unit goes. Because three out of the four methods are not linked to the physical flow of merchandise, inventory methods are often referred to as *cost flow assumptions*. For example, when we decide that the cost of the first inventory item purchased will be matched with the sales revenue from the first item sold to calculate the gross profit from the sale, we are adopting the FIFO cost flow assumption.

It is interesting to note that no matter what cost flow assumptions we use, the cumulative gross profit over the life of a company remains the same. Suppose Emilio sells his remaining inventory on Friday and enters a more attractive business. Panel II of Exhibit 6-5 shows Friday's gross profit. As you can see, the gross profit for this one period, Friday, varies with the cost flow assumption used. However, Panel III of Exhibit 6-5 shows that the cumulative gross profit over the life of Emilio's business would be the same $1.44 under any of the inventory methods. What makes the choice of method important is the need to match particular costs to particular periods during the life of the business in order to prepare financial statements and evaluate performance.

INVENTORY COST RELATIONSHIPS

Note that all four methods work with the same basic numbers. Nothing in our choice of methods affects accounts payable. We record inventory purchases at cost and recognize a liability in the same way under all of these methods. All that changes is how those costs are dealt with.

Recall that during a period of rising prices, FIFO yields higher inventory and higher gross profit than does LIFO. This result is consistent with the accounting equation that requires that A = L + OE. If inventory is higher under FIFO (higher assets) and the equation is to balance, either liabilities or owners' equity must also be higher. Higher gross profit under FIFO implies higher net income and higher owners' equity (OE in the equation).

There are, of course, relationships other than those of the accounting equation that come into play in the various inventory methods. Consider also the link between cost of goods sold and the valuation of ending inventory. Emilio's three cola cans had a total cost of goods available for sale of $1.26. At the end of the period, this $1.26 must be allocated either to cans sold or to cans in ending inventory. The higher the cost of goods sold, the lower the ending inventory. Exhibit 6-6 illustrates that interdependence. At one extreme, FIFO treats the 30 cent cost of the first can acquired as cost of goods sold and 96 cents as ending inventory. At the other extreme, LIFO treats the 56 cent cost of the last can acquired as cost of goods sold and 70 cents as ending inventory.

THE CONSISTENCY CONVENTION

consistency Conformity from period to period with unchanging policies and procedures.

Although companies can choose just about any inventory cost flow assumption they want, they have to be consistent over time and stick with whatever they choose. The FASB has referred to **consistency** as "conformity from period to period with unchanging policies and procedures." Interpreting financial performance over time involves compar-

Exhibit 6-6

Emilio's Cola Sales

Diagram of Inventory Methods (data are from Panel I,
Exhibit 6-5; monetary amounts are in cents)

Beginning inventory	+	Merchandise purchases	=	Cost of goods available for sale
0	+	126	=	126
Cost of goods available for sale	−	Cost of goods sold	=	Ending inventory

$$
\begin{Bmatrix} 1\ @\ 30 \\ 1\ @\ 40 \\ 1\ @\ 56 \end{Bmatrix}
\quad 126 \quad - \quad
\begin{Bmatrix} 30 \\ \text{or} \\ 40 \\ \text{or} \\ 56 \end{Bmatrix}
\quad = \quad
\begin{Bmatrix} 96 \\ \text{or} \\ 86 \\ \text{or} \\ 70 \end{Bmatrix}
\quad \text{Specific identification}
$$

126	−	30	=	96	FIFO
126	−	56	=	70	LIFO
126	−	42	=	84	Weighted average

ing the results of different periods. If accounting methods for inventory were changed often, meaningful comparisons over time would be impossible.

Occasionally a change in market conditions or other circumstances may justify a change in inventory method. With its auditor's approval, a firm may change method. But the firm is required to note the change in its financial statements, and the auditor will also refer to the change in the audit opinion. Therefore, financial statement readers will be alerted to the possible effects of the change on their analysis.

CHARACTERISTICS AND CONSEQUENCES OF LIFO

LIFO is just another method, but it is very widely used in the United States, has strong tax benefits for certain companies, and has some unusual features in application. Because of its dominant role in inventory accounting in the United States, LIFO will get a little extra attention from us in this section. Actually, LIFO is a fairly uncommon method in most countries. For example, in Brazil and Australia it is not permitted at all, and in Canada it is disallowed for tax purposes. The most popular method worldwide is the average cost method, and the next most common choice is FIFO.

HOLDING GAINS AND INVENTORY PROFITS

LIFO's income statement orientation provides a particular economic interpretation of operating performance in inflationary periods, based on replacement of inventory. A merchant such as Emilio is in the business of buying and selling on a daily basis. To continue in business, he must be able to maintain his stock of cola and must make sufficient profit on each transaction to make it worth his while to run his soda stand. So, before he can feel he has really made a profit, he will need to restock his inventory and be ready for the next day. If he must spend 56 cents to replace the can that was sold, we might call 56 cents the **replacement cost** of the inventory. Under LIFO we calculate his profit to be 34 cents, because we use that recent inventory acquisition cost of 56 cents to measure cost of goods sold. So LIFO approximates a replacement cost view of the transaction.

replacement cost The cost at which an inventory item could be acquired today.

In contrast, FIFO measures profit relative to the 30-cent can acquired on Monday and reports a profit of 60 cents. The difference between the 60 cents FIFO profit and the 34 cents LIFO profit is 26 cents, which is also the difference between the historical cost of 30 cents under FIFO and 56 cents under LIFO. This 26 cents difference that occurs because prices are rising, is called a **holding gain** or an **inventory profit.** The idea is that between Monday and Thursday, Emilio's first can of cola acquired for 30 cents became more valuable as prices rose, and because he held it during those days he experienced a 26 cents gain.

Because LIFO matches the most recent acquisition costs with sales revenue, LIFO cost of goods sold typically offers a close approximation to replacement cost, and reported net income rarely contains significant holding gains. In contrast, FIFO reports a profit of 60 cents including the economic profit of 34 cents calculated as sales price less replacement costs, plus the inventory profit or holding gain of 26 cents that arose because the value of the inventory item rose with the passage of time.

This issue is more than an accounting complexity of academic interest. Whenever government begins to reconsider the tax law, this issue takes center stage. For example, a recent reduction in U.S. capital gains taxes relies on the notion that holding gains are economically different from true economic profit and should be taxed less.

LIFO Layers

The ending inventory under LIFO will have one total value, but it may contain prices from many different periods. For example, Emilio's ending inventory contained two cans, one acquired on Monday at 30 cents and one acquired on Tuesday at 40 cents. Each distinct cost element of inventory might be called a **LIFO layer** (also called **LIFO increment**)—an addition to inventory at an identifiable cost level. As a company grows, the LIFO layers tend to pile on top of one another over the years. Suppose Emilio's business grew for years, ending each year with two more cans in inventory than were there the year before. Each year would have an identifiable LIFO layer, much like the annual rings on a tree. After five years of inventory growth and rising prices, his ending inventory might be structured as follows:

Year 1	layer 1——1 can @ .30	
	layer 2——1 can @ .40	.70
Year 2	layer 3——2 cans @.45	.90
Year 3	layer 4——2 cans @.50	1.00
Year 4	layer 5——2 cans @.55	1.10
Total inventory		$3.70

Many LIFO companies show inventories that have ancient layers going back as far as 1940, when LIFO was first used. Reported LIFO inventory values may therefore be far below what the true market value or current replacement value of the inventory might be. From a balance sheet perspective, this means that the book values being reported will have little relevance to investors interested in assessing the assets of the company. While LIFO presents the economic reality on the income statement well, FIFO provides more up to date valuations on the balance sheet.

LIFO Inventory Liquidations

The existence of old LIFO layers can cause problems in income measurement when inventory decreases. Examine Exhibit 6-7. Suppose Harbor Electronics bought an inventory of 100 units at $10 per unit on December 31, 19X0. The company bought and sold 100 units each year, 19X1 through 19X4, at the purchase and selling prices shown. The exam-

holding gain (inventory profit) Increase in the replacement cost or other measure of current value of the inventory held during the current period.

LIFO layer (LIFO increment) A separately identifiable additional segment of LIFO inventory.

Objective 5
Calculate the impact on net income of LIFO liquidations.

Exhibit 6-7

Harbor Electronics

Effect of Inventory Liquidations under LIFO (Purchases and sales of 100 units in 19X1–19X4.
Purchases but no sales in 19X0; sales but no purchases in 19X5.)

Year	Purchase Price Per Unit	Selling Price Per Unit	Revenue	FIFO Cost of Goods Sold	FIFO Gross Profit	FIFO Ending Inventory	LIFO Cost of Goods Sold	LIFO Gross Profit	LIFO Ending Inventory
19X0	$10	—	—	—	—	$1,000	—	—	$1,000
19X1	12	$15	$1,500	$1,000	$ 500	1,200	$1,200	$ 300	1,000
19X2	14	17	1,700	1,200	500	1,400	1,400	300	1,000
19X3	16	19	1,900	1,400	500	1,600	1,600	300	1,000
19X4	18	21	2,100	1,600	500	1,800	1,800	300	1,000
19X5		23	2,300	1,800	500	0	1,000	1,300	0
Total			$9,500	$7,000	$2,500		$7,000	$2,500	

ple assumes replacement costs and sales prices rise by the same amount, with a difference between the two of $3 per unit. In 19X5, 100 units were sold but none were purchased.

Compare the gross profit each year under LIFO with that under FIFO in Exhibit 6-7. LIFO gross profit was generally less than FIFO gross profit because prices were rising, and LIFO's cost of goods sold reflected the latest prices, while FIFO's did not. But what happened in 19X5? The old 19X0 inventory became the cost of goods sold under LIFO because inventory was depleted. As a result, gross profit under LIFO soared to $1,300, well above the FIFO gross profit, which was stable at $500. In general, when the physical amount of inventory decreases, under LIFO old, low inventory acquisition costs associated with old LIFO layers are used to calculate cost of goods sold. This is called a LIFO liquidation. This treatment can create a very low cost of goods sold and high gross profit. For example, LIFO inventory liquidations by Amoco, an international oil company, increased its 1993 net income by $50 million, about 3% of its $1.8 billion income before tax. In a sense, a LIFO liquidation means that the cumulative inventory profit from years of increasing prices is reflected in the income statement in one year. An analyst tracking Amoco's profitability would want to know that its profit increase that year was not due solely to opening new stations and selling more gasoline. It was partly due to the company's inventory accounting process.

The effect of LIFO liquidations is potentially large and security analysts like to remain aware of the effect of the choice between LIFO and FIFO on net income. The difference between a company's LIFO inventory level and what they would be under FIFO is helpful in tracking these relations. This difference is called the **LIFO reserve.** Most companies that use LIFO explicitly measure and report this LIFO reserve on the front of the balance sheet or in the footnotes.

Refer to Exhibit 6-7. What is Harbor Electronics' LIFO reserve at the end of 19X1? It is $1,200 − $1,000 = $200, the difference in the LIFO and FIFO ending inventories. Note that it is the same as the difference in gross profit of $200 in the first year of the example. What about year 19X2? The LIFO reserve is $400 (FIFO ending inventory of $1,400 less LIFO ending inventory of $1,000). This difference represents the cumulative effect on earnings (or gross profit) over the first two years the company was in business. The specific effect on earnings during 19X2 is the change in the LIFO reserve, or $200. Exhibit 6-8 summarizes these effects.

From Exhibit 6-8 note that the annual difference between gross profit using FIFO and that using LIFO is the yearly change in the LIFO reserve. Finally, when all of the inventory is sold in 19X5, the liquidation of the LIFO inventory leads to recognition of higher earnings than under FIFO by the amount of the LIFO reserve. LIFO recognizes inventory profits

LIFO reserve The difference between a company's inventory valued at LIFO and what it would be under FIFO.

Exhibit 6-8

	Ending Inventory		LIFO	Change	Gross Profit Effect	
Year	FIFO	LIFO	Reserve	in Reserve	Current	Cumulative
X0	$1,000	$1,000	$ 0	$ 0	$ 0	$ 0
X1	1,200	1,000	200	200	200	200
X2	1,400	1,000	400	200	200	400
X3	1,600	1,000	600	200	200	600
X4	1,800	1,000	800	200	200	800
X5	0	0	0	(800)	(800)	0

when inventory levels are reduced. The balance of the LIFO reserve at any point in time indicates the cumulative effect on gross profit over all prior years due to LIFO.

How significant are the effects of LIFO? Ford Motor Company reported 1996 inventory of $6.7 billion. LIFO was used for the U.S. inventories. If FIFO had been used for all inventories, the total inventory would have been $1.4 billion higher (over a 20% difference). This means that over time, Ford has reported lower income on its tax returns by $1.4 billion and paid lower taxes of approximately $560 million ($1.4 billion times approximately a 40% tax rate) as a result of its decision to use LIFO rather than FIFO.

This savings amounts to an interest-free loan from the government. If Ford ever goes out of business, the sale of old inventory items will create a large LIFO liquidation and all of these delayed taxes will become due. In the meantime, Ford has the use of some $560 million it has not yet had to pay in taxes.

ADJUSTING FROM LIFO TO FIFO

As just mentioned, Ford Motor Company uses LIFO and therefore reports higher cost of goods sold and lower inventory levels than it would if FIFO were used. Ford reported the following in 1996:

Ford Motor Company ($ in Millions)

	1996 Inventory			Cost of Goods Sold
	Beginning	Ending	Average	
LIFO	$7,162	$6,656	$6,909.0	$108,882
LIFO Reserve	1,406	1,445		39*
FIFO	$8,568	$8,101	8,334.5	$108,843

*Change in LIFO reserve is $39 ($1,406 − $1,445).

Note that Ford's LIFO reserve increased from $1,406 million to $1,445 million during the year. This increase of $39 million in the LIFO reserve is exactly the amount by which the cost of goods sold for the year under LIFO exceeds the cost of goods sold under FIFO ($108,882 million − $108,843 million = $39 million, see above).

Why is the LIFO cost of goods sold higher? Because costs are rising and under LIFO the new higher costs flow directly to the cost of goods sold reported in the earnings statement. In contrast, under FIFO the new higher costs flow into ending inventory, while older lower costs are used to calculate cost of goods sold. Cumulatively, this process has happened year after year for Ford. We can use the LIFO reserve to answer two questions. The *change* in the LIFO reserve from one year to the next answers the question "How much did this year's LIFO cost of goods sold differ from what the cost of goods sold would have been if FIFO were used?" In contrast, the end of year *level* of the LIFO reserve is the answer to the question "During the years that Ford has used LIFO, what has the total, cumulative effect been on cost of goods sold over all those years?" To see this, do the mental experiment of having Ford sell all of its 1996 year-end inventory for $10,000 million. This complete *liquidation* would produce *higher* profits under LIFO. These higher profits in the final liquidation year are equal to the cumulative amount by which gross profits were lower under LIFO in past years. The hypothetical liquidation of Ford inventories would show:

	LIFO	FIFO	Difference
Sales	$10,000	$10,000	—
Cost of goods sold	6,656	8,101	(1,445)
Gross profit	$ 3,344	$ 1,899	1,445

LOWER-OF-COST-OR-MARKET METHOD

Sometimes obsolete or damaged inventory items cannot be easily sold at amounts equal to their historical cost. Investors want to know if the inventory can be sold to at least recover its cost. Under the **lower-of-cost-or-market method (LCM),** a market-price test is run on an inventory costing method. The current market price is compared with historical cost derived under one of the four primary methods: specific identification, FIFO, LIFO, or weighted average. The lower of the two—current market value or historical cost—is conservatively selected as the basis for the valuation of goods at a specific inventory date. When market value is lower and is used for valuing the ending inventory, the effect is to increase the amount reported as cost of goods sold.

LCM is an example of conservatism. **Conservatism** means selecting methods of measurement that yield lower net income, lower assets, and lower stockholders' equity. Conservatism was illustrated in accounts receivable with the use of an allowance for bad debts. We estimated and recorded losses on uncollectible accounts before they were certain. With inventories, conservatism dictates the use of the LCM method.

Accountants feel that erring in the direction of conservatism is better than erring in the direction of overstating assets and net income. The accountant's conservatism balances management's optimism. Management prepares the financial statements, but the conservatism principle moderates management's human tendency to hope for, and expect, the best.

Objective 6
Use the lower-of-cost-or-market method to value inventories.

lower-of-cost-or-market method (LCM) The superimposition of a market-price test on an inventory cost method.

conservatism Selecting the methods of measurement that yield lower net income, lower assets, and lower stockholders' equity.

ROLE OF REPLACEMENT COST

Under GAAP, the definition of market price is complex. For our purposes we will think of it as the replacement cost of the inventory item—that is, what it would cost to buy the inventory item today. Keep in mind, though, that this method assumes that when replacement costs decline in the wholesale market, so do the retail selling prices. Consider the following example. The Ripley Company has 100 units in its ending FIFO inventory on December 31, 19X1. Its gross profit of $990 for 19X1 has been tentatively computed as follows:

Sales	$2,180
Cost of goods available for sale	$1,980
Ending inventory of 100 units, at cost	$ 790
Cost of goods sold	$1,190
Gross profit	$ 990

Assume a sudden decline in market prices during the final week of December from $7.90 per unit to $4 per unit. If we assume that the sales price will drop along with the market price, an inventory write-down of ($7.90 − $4.00) × 100 units, or $390, is in order. A **write-down** reduces the assumed cost of an item in response to a decline in value. When a write-down occurs, the new $4 per unit replacement cost becomes, for accounting purposes, the unexpired cost of the inventory. Thus, if replacement prices subsequently rise to $8 per unit in January 19X2, the assigned cost of each unit will remain $4. In short, the lower-of-cost-or-market method would regard the December 31 $4 cost as the "new historical cost" of the inventory. The required journal entry is:

Loss on write-down of inventory (or cost of goods sold)	390	
Inventory		390
To write down inventory from $790 cost to $400 market value.		

The write-down of inventories increases cost of goods sold by $390. Therefore reported income for 19X1 would be lowered by $390:

	Before $390 Write-Down	After $390 Write-Down	Difference
Sales	$2,180	$2,180	
Cost of goods available	$1,980	$1,980	
Ending inventory	790	400	−$390
Cost of goods sold	$1,190	$1,580	+$390
Gross profit	$ 990	$ 600	−$390

Why is $390 written down? LCM holds that of the $790 historical cost, $390 is considered to have expired during 19X1 because that cost cannot be justifiably carried forward to the future as an asset. Of course, if the market replacement cost falls but selling prices remain the same, items still have their original earnings power. No loss has occurred and no reduction in the book value of the inventory is necessary.

CONSERVATISM IN ACTION

Compared with a pure cost method, the lower-of-cost-or-market method reports less net income in the period of decline in the market value of the inventory and more net income in the period of sale. More generally, cumulative net income (the sum of all net income amounts from the inception of the firm to the present date) is never lower and is usually higher under the strict cost method. The lower-of-cost-or-market method affects how much income is reported in each year but not the total income over the company's life. Exhibit 6-9 underscores this point. Suppose the Ripley Company goes out of business in early 19X2. That is, no more units are acquired. There are no sales in 19X2 except for the disposal of the inventory in question at $8 per unit (100 × $8 = $800). Neither combined gross profit nor combined net income for the two periods will be affected by the LCM method, as the bottom of Exhibit 6-9 reveals.

A full-blown lower-of-cost-or-market method is rarely encountered in practice. Why? Because it is expensive to get the correct replacement costs of hundreds or thousands of different products in inventory. Further, the benefit from doing so does not justify the cost. Auditors do watch for price trends in the industry that might indicate a serious concern. In particular, they watch for subclasses of inventory that are obsolete, shopworn, or otherwise of only nominal value and apply LCM to such inventory.

Exhibit 6-9

The Ripley Company
Effects of Lower-of-Cost-or-Market

| | Cost Method | | Lower-of-Cost-or-Market Method | |
	19X1	19X2	19X1	19X2
Sales	$2,180	$800	$2,180	$800
Cost of goods available	$1,980	$790	$1,980	$400
Ending inventory	790	—	400*	—
Cost of goods sold	$1,190	$790	$1,580	$400
Gross profit	$ 990	$10	$ 600	$400

Combined gross profit for two years:
  Cost method: $990 + $10 = $1,000
  Lower-of-cost-or-market method: $600 + $400 = $1,000

---

* The inventory is shown here after being written down by $390, from $790 to $400. For internal purposes, many accountants prefer to show the write-down separately, presenting a gross profit before write-down of inventory, the write-down, and a gross profit after write-down.

EFFECTS OF INVENTORY ERRORS

Objective 7
Show the effects of inventory errors on financial statements.

Inventory errors can arise from many sources. For example, incorrect physical counts might be taken because goods that were in receiving or shipping areas instead of in the inventory stockroom were not counted. A clerk might hit a 5 on the keyboard instead of a 6.

An undiscovered inventory error usually affects two reporting periods. Amounts will be misstated in the period in which the error occurred, but the effects will then be counterbalanced by identical offsetting amounts in the following period. Consider the income statements in Exhibit 6-10 (all numbers are in thousands), which assume ending 19X7 inventory shown in Panel A is reported to be $10,000 too low.

Think about the effects of the uncorrected error on the following year, 19X8, shown in Panel B. The beginning inventory will be $60,000 rather than the correct $70,000. Therefore all the errors in 19X7 will be offset by counterbalancing errors in 19X8. Thus the retained income at the end of 19X8 would show a cumulative effect of zero. Why? Because the net income in 19X7 would be understated by $6,000, but the net income in 19X8 would be overstated by $6,000.

The point here is that the ending inventory of one period is also the beginning inventory of the succeeding period. The example assumes that the operations during 19X8 are a duplication of those of 19X7 except that the ending inventory is correctly counted as $40,000.

The complete analyses for 19X7 and 19X8 show the full detail of the inventory error, and they provide us with a handy rule of thumb. If ending inventory is understated, retained income is understated. If ending inventory is overstated, retained income is overstated. These relations are clear from the accounting equation. Including taxes in this rule of thumb is really just adding another piece of the accounting equation. Why? Because understated inventory implies overstated cost of goods sold

Exhibit 6-10

Effects of Inventory Errors

Panel A

19X7	Correct Reporting		Incorrect Reporting*		Effects of Errors
Sales		$980		$980	
Deduct: Cost of goods sold:					
Beginning inventory	$100		$100		
Purchases	500		500		
Cost of goods available for sale	$600		$600		
Deduct: Ending inventory	70		60		Understated by $10
Cost of goods sold		530		540	Overstated by $10
Gross profit		$450		$440	Understated by $10
Other expenses		250		250	
Income before income taxes		$200		$190	Understated by $10
Income tax expense at 40%		80		76	Understated by $4
Net income		$120		$114	**Understated by $6**
Ending balance sheet items:					
Inventory		$ 70		$ 60	Understated by $10
Retained income includes					
current net income of		120		114	Understated by $6
Income tax liability†		80		76	Understated by $4

* Because of error in ending inventory.

† For simplicity, assume that the entire income tax expense for the year will not be paid until the succeeding year. Therefore the ending liability will equal the income tax expense.

Panel B

19X8	Correct Reporting		Incorrect Reporting*		Effects of Errors
Sales		$980		$980	
Deduct: Cost of goods sold:					
Beginning inventory	$ 70		$ 60		Understated by $10
Purchases	500		500		
Cost of goods available for sale	$570		$560		Understated by $10
Deduct: Ending inventory	40		40		
Cost of goods sold		530		520	Understated by $10
Gross profit		$450		$460	Overstated by $10
Other expenses		250		250	
Income before income taxes		$200		$210	Overstated by $10
Income tax expense at 40%		80		84	Overstated by $4
Net income		$120		$126	**Overstated by $6**
Ending balance sheet items:					
Inventory		$ 40		$ 40	Correct
Retained income includes:					
Net income of previous year		120		114	Counterbalanced and
Net income of current year		120		126	thus now correct in total
Two-year total		240		240	
Income tax liability:					
End of previous year		80		76	Counterbalanced and
End of current year		80		84	thus now correct in total†
Two-year total		160		160	

* Because of error in beginning inventory.

† The $84 really consists of the $4 that pertains to income of the previous year plus $80 that pertains to income of the current year.

and therefore lower current-year income and lower tax liability. The shortcut analysis including taxes follows:

	A	=	L	+	SE
	Inventory		Income Tax Liability		Retained Income
Effects of error	$10,000 understated	=	$4,000 understated	+	$6,000 understated*

* Cost of goods overstated	$10,000
Pretax income understated	$10,000
Income taxes understated	4,000
Net income, which is included in ending retained income, understated	$ 6,000

In the second year, the income and taxes will be affected in the opposite direction and the total taxes over both years will be right.

CUTOFF ERRORS AND INVENTORY VALUATION

The accrual basis of accounting should include the physical counting and careful valuation of inventory at least once yearly. Auditors routinely search for **cutoff errors,** which are failures to record transactions in the correct time period. For example, assume a periodic inventory system. Suppose a physical inventory is conducted on December 31. Inventory purchases of $100,000 arrive in the receiving room during the afternoon of December 31. The acquisition is included in Purchases and Accounts Payable but excluded from the ending inventory valuation. Such an error would understate ending inventory, thereby overstating cost of goods sold and understating gross profit. On the other hand, if the acquisition were not recorded until January 2, the error would understate both the ending inventory and Accounts Payable as of December 31. However, cost of goods sold and gross profit would be correct because Purchases and the ending inventory would be understated by the same amount.

cutoff error Failure to record transactions in the correct time period.

The general approach to recording purchases and sales is keyed to the legal transfer of ownership. Auditors are especially careful about cutoff tests because the pressure for profits sometimes causes managers to postpone the recording of bona fide purchases of goods and services. Similarly, the same managers may deliberately include sales *orders* near year end (rather than bona fide completed sales) in revenues. For example, consider the case of Datapoint, a maker of small computers and telecommunications equipment. A news story reported: "Datapoint's hard-pressed sales force was still logging orders that might not hold up after shipment." In the wake of an accounting scandal, Datapoint's president declared a three-week "amnesty period" during which scheduled shipments could be removed from the sales account, no questions asked.

A similar news story referred to difficulties at McCormick & Co., a firm known for its spices; "The investigation also found that improprieties included the company's accounting for sales. In a longstanding practice, the company recorded as sales, goods that had been selected and prepared for shipment rather than waiting until after they had been shipped as is the customary accounting practice."

THE IMPORTANCE OF GROSS PROFITS

We began this chapter by discussing gross profits, which are the result of sales revenue less the cost of goods sold. Management and investors are intensely interested in gross profit and how it changes over time. In comparing the gross profits of two firms, it is sometimes important to examine which inventory method they have used to calculate their gross profit.

Objective 8
Evaluate the gross profit percentage and inventory turnover.

GROSS PROFIT PERCENTAGE

Gross profit is often expressed as a percentage of sales. Consider the following information on a past year for a typical Safeway grocery store:

	Amount	**Percentage**
Sales	$10,000,000	100%
Net cost of goods sold	7,500,000	75%
Gross profit	$ 2,500,000	25%

gross profit percentage
Gross profit as a percentage of sales.

The **gross profit percentage**—gross profit divided by sales—here is 25%. It is worth noting that financial analysts define the gross profit percentage this way, as a percent of sales. In marketing the profit percentage is sometimes expressed as a markup on cost. In this example, the markup on cost is $2,500,000 ÷ $7,500,000 = 33%.

The following table illustrates the extent to which gross profit percentages vary among industries.

Industry	**Gross Profit (%)**
Auto retailers	15.7
Auto manufacturers	18.9
Jewelry retailers	46.1
Grocery retailers	25.9
Grocery wholesalers	12.9
Drug manufacturers	57.2

Source: RMA, *Annual Statement Studies for 1996.*

wholesaler An intermediary that sells inventory items to retailers.

retailer A company that sells items directly to the final users, individuals.

What accounts for this wide variation in gross profit percentage? The nature of the business has a lot to do with it. **Wholesalers** sell in larger quantity and incur fewer selling costs because they sell to other companies rather than to individuals. As a result of competition and high volumes, they have smaller gross profit percentages than do retailers. **Retailers** sell directly to the public—to individual buyers. Among retailers, jewelers have twice the gross profits of grocers because of extensive personal selling. Drug manufacturers earn high gross profits because of high drug prices, caused by the need for substantial research and development outlays (up to 15% of sales) and allowed by patent protection on specific drugs. In contrast, auto manufacturers face more direct competition and earn lower gross profit percentages.

ESTIMATING INTRAPERIOD GROSS PROFIT AND INVENTORY

The gross profit percentage can be extremely useful, especially when related information is unavailable. For example, exact ending inventory balances are not usually available for monthly or quarterly reports. To avoid costly physical counts, interim reports often rely on estimates derived from percentage or ratio methods.

For example, assume that past sales of Tip Top Variety Store have usually resulted in a gross profit percentage of 25%. The accountant would estimate gross profit to be 25% of sales. If the monthly sales are $800,000, the cost of goods sold can be estimated as follows:

$$\text{Sales} - \text{Cost of goods sold} = \text{Gross profit}$$
$$\text{S} - \text{CGS} = \text{GP}$$
$$\$800,000 - \text{CGS} = 0.25 \times \$800,000 = \$200,000$$
$$\text{CGS} = \$600,000$$

If we know Tip Top's beginning inventory is $30,000 and purchases are $605,000, we can then estimate ending inventory to be $35,000 as follows:

$$\text{Beginning inventory} + \text{Purchases} - \text{Ending inventory} = \text{CGS}$$
$$\text{BI} + \text{P} - \text{EI} = \text{CGS}$$
$$\$30{,}000 + \$605{,}000 - \text{EI} = \$600{,}000$$
$$\text{EI} = \$35{,}000$$

GROSS PROFIT PERCENTAGE AND TURNOVER

Retailers often attempt to increase total profits by increasing sales levels. They may lower prices and hope to increase their total gross profits by selling their inventories more quickly, replenishing, selling again, and so forth. In essence they are accepting a lower gross profit per unit but expecting to increase total sales more than enough to compensate. A high volume of sales activity allows a smaller gross margin per unit sold while providing high total profits. This is one of the reasons that a store such as Wal-Mart can do well.

A way to measure sales levels is in terms of **inventory turnover,** which is defined as cost of goods sold divided by the average inventory held during a given period. Average inventory is usually the sum of beginning inventory and ending inventory divided by 2. For the Tip Top Variety Store, the average inventory is ($30,000 + $35,000) ÷ 2 = $32,500. The inventory turnover is computed as follows:

inventory turnover The cost of goods sold divided by the average inventory held during the period.

$$\text{Turnover} = \text{Cost of goods sold} \div \text{Average inventory}$$
$$= \$600{,}000 \div \$32{,}500 = 18.5$$

Suppose the inventory sells twice as quickly if prices are lowered. With a 5% reduction in sales price, sales revenue on the current level of business drops from $800,000 to (0.95 × $800,000), or $760,000. But twice as many units are sold, so total revenue becomes 2 × $760,000, or $1,520,000. How profitable is Tip Top? Cost of goods sold doubles from $600,000 to $1,200,000. Total gross profit is $320,000. The inventory turnover doubles: $1,200,000 divided by $32,500 (the unchanged average inventory) is 36.9. However, the gross profit percentage falls from 25% to 21% ($320,000 divided by $1,520,000).

Is the company better off? Maybe. Certainly, in the current month gross profit has risen. Long-term strategic concerns, though, raise the question: Is this new sales level maintainable? For some products, when prices fall, consumers sharply increase purchases and stockpile the extras for later consumption. There is little increase in underlying demand, just a shift of future purchases to the present. Therefore, the current good sales could result in terrible future sales.

Another strategic question is: What will the competition do? If Tip Top's increased sales came at a competitor's expense, the competitor's response may be a similar decrease in prices. The competition might recover most of its old customers, with each buying a little more at the new price than they did at the old. Assuming all competitors decrease prices similarly, the whole market would see, not a doubling of sales, but perhaps a 20% sales growth. In that case, Tip Top would be worse off overall because the 20% growth would not cover the 5% price reduction.

Exhibit 6-11 illustrates two principles. Panel A shows that if a firm can increase inventory turnover while maintaining a constant gross profit percentage, it should do so. However, as shown in Panel B, if the increased inventory turnover results from a decrease in sales price, the gross margin percentage may fall. The desirability of the change depends on whether the sales gain could offset the decreased margin. In the Tip Top Variety Store example, when a 5% price reduction produces only a 20% increase in units sold, the new gross margin of $192,000 is less than the initial margin of $200,000. Dropping the price is not justified even though the inventory turnover rises to 22.2 from 18.5. However, at a 50% increase in sales volume, the new gross margin of $240,000 would exceed the original $200,000. Basically, the lesson of Exhibit 6-11 is that you cannot focus on only one number or measure of company performance. Paying too much attention to one measure could cause you to miss the fact that another was falling fast.

Exhibit 6-11

Tip Top Variety Store

Effects of Increased Inventory Turnover (in thousands)

		Unit Sales Increase		
Panel A	**Original**	*20%*	*50%*	*100%*
No change in sales price				
Sales	$800	$960	$1,200	$1,600
Cost of goods sold (75%)	600	720	900	1,200
Gross margin (25%)	$200	$240	$ 300	$ 400
Inventory turnover	18.5	22.2	27.7	36.9
Panel B				
5% reduction in sales price				
Sales (95% of above)	$760	$912	$1,140	$1,520
Cost of goods sold (as above)	600	720	900	1,200
Gross margin (21% of sales)	$160	$192	$ 240	$ 320
Inventory turnover (as above)	18.5	22.2	27.7	36.9

The industry variability in gross margin percentages referred to earlier is also reflected in inventory turnover percentages.

Industry	Gross Profit (%)	Inventory Turnover
Grocery wholesalers	12.9	14.1
Grocery retailers	25.9	15.6
Drug manufacturers	57.2	3.4
Jewelry retailers	46.1	1.8

Source: RMA, *Annual Statement Studies for 1996.*

As you can see, the industries with the highest gross profit percentages tend to have the lowest inventory turnover. This reflects the observation earlier that firms must have gross margins high enough to cover other selling and administrative costs. The lower turnover for jewelers and pharmaceuticals relates to high costs of selling or research that must be covered by high margins.

Thus the inventory turnover measure is especially effective for assessing companies in the same industry. If one industry member has a higher turnover than another, it is probably more efficient. That is, the higher turnover indicates an ability to use smaller inventory levels to attain a high sales level. This is good, because it reduces the investment in inventory. Fewer products are sitting on display shelves in warehouses and less capital is tied up in maintaining, moving and displaying inventory items.

When ratios are being calculated it is important to keep the accounting methods in mind. Consider the data for Ford Motor Company given earlier on page 236. Using LIFO and FIFO results for Ford Motor Company, we can calculate the inventory turnover and gross profit percentages (sales of $118,023 million) to be:

LIFO

Gross profit percentage: ($118,023 − $108,882) ÷ $118,023 = 7.75%

Inventory turnover: $108,882 ÷ $6,909.0 = 15.76

FIFO

Gross profit percentage: ($118,023 − $108,843) ÷ $118,023 = 7.78%

Inventory turnover: $108,843 ÷ $8,334.5 = 13.06

LIFO tends to *decrease* the gross profit percentage and to *increase* the inventory turnover relative to FIFO. Why? Because, under LIFO, cost of goods sold is usually greater and inventory values are lower.

GROSS PROFIT PERCENTAGES AND ACCURACY OF RECORDS

Auditors, including those from the Internal Revenue Service (IRS), use the gross profit percentage to help satisfy themselves about the accuracy of records. For example, the IRS compiles gross profit percentages by types of retail establishment. If a company shows an unusually low percentage compared with similar companies, IRS auditors may suspect that the company has failed to record all cash sales in order to avoid taxes. Similarly, managers watch changes in gross profit percentages to judge operating profitability and to monitor how well employee theft and shoplifting are being controlled.

Suppose an internal revenue agent, a manager, or an outside auditor had gathered the following data for a particular jewelry company for the past three years (in millions):

	19X3	19X2	19X1
Net sales	$350	$325	$300
Cost of goods sold	210	165	150
Gross profit	$140	$160	$150
Gross profit percentage	40%	49%	50%

Comparing these data is a good acid test to see if there are any changes worth investigating. As you can see, the percentage for the jewelry company has been fairly steady, for two years. However, the decline in the percentage in year 3 could be a sign of trouble. Obviously, a decline in the percentage might be attributable to many factors, and not all of them are cause for concern. Possible explanations include the following:

1. Competition has intensified, resulting in intensive price wars that reduced selling prices.
2. The mix of goods sold has shifted so that, for instance, the $350 million of sales in 19X3 is composed of relatively more products bearing lower gross margins (for example, more costume jewelry bearing low margins and less diamond jewelry bearing high margins).
3. Shoplifting or embezzling has soared out of control. For example, a manager may be pocketing and not recording cash sales of $70 million. After all, sales in 19X3 would have been $210 × 2 = $420 million if the past 50% margin had been maintained.

REPORTS TO SHAREHOLDERS

The importance of gross profits to investors is demonstrated in the following example based on a quarterly report to shareholders of Superscope, Inc., a manufacturer and distributor of stereophonic equipment that encountered rocky times. The following condensed income statement was presented for a three-month period (in thousands):

	Current Year	Previous Year
Net sales	$40,000	$40,200
Cost and expenses:		
Cost of sales	33,100	28,200
Selling, general, and administrative	11,200	9,900
Interest	2,000	1,200
Total costs and expenses	46,300	39,300
Income (loss) before income tax		
provision (benefit)	(6,300)	900
Income tax provision (benefit)	(3,000)	200
Net income (loss)	$(3,300)	$ 700

Although the statement does not show the amount of gross profit, the gross profit percentages can readily be computed as ($40,000 − $33,100) ÷ $40,000 = 17% and ($40,200 − $28,200) ÷ $40,200 = 30%. To show how seriously these percentages are considered, the chairman's letter to shareholders began as follows:

> *I shall attempt herein to provide you with a candid analysis of the Company's present condition, the steps we have instituted to overcome current adversities, and the potential which we believe can, in due course, be realized by the Company's realistic positive determination to regain profitability.*
>
> *In the second quarter the Company's gross profit margins decreased to 17% compared to 30% in the corresponding quarter of a year ago. For the first six months gross profit margins were 22%, down from 31% for the corresponding period of a year ago.*
>
> *Essentially, the gross profits and consequential operating losses in the second quarter, as reflected in the condensed financial statements appearing in this report, resulted from lower than anticipated sales volume and from the following second quarter factors: liquidation of our entire citizens band inventory; increases in dealer cash discounts and sales incentive expenses; gross margin reductions resulting from sales of slow moving models at less than normal prices; and markdown of slow moving inventory on hand to a realistic net realizable market value.*

INTERNAL CONTROL OF INVENTORIES

In many organizations, inventories are more easily accessible than cash. Therefore they become a favorite target for thieves.

Retail merchants must contend with inventory shrinkage, a polite term for shoplifting by customers and embezzling by employees. Consider the following footnote from a recent annual report of Associated Dry Goods, one of the largest operators of department and discount stores in the country: "Physical inventories are taken twice each year. Department store inventory shrinkage at retail, as a percent of retail sales, was 2.4% this year compared with 2.1% last year. Discount store inventory shrinkage as a percent of retail sales was 0.4% and 0.3%, respectively." Some department stores have suffered shrinkage losses of 4% to 5% of their sales volume. Compare this with the typical net profit margin of 5% to 6%.

A management consulting firm has demonstrated how widespread shoplifting has become. The firm concentrated on a midtown New York City department store. Five hundred shoppers, picked at random, were followed from the moment they entered the store to the time they departed. Forty-two shoppers, or one out of every twelve, took something. They stole $300 worth of merchandise, an average of $7.15 each. Similar experiments were conducted in Boston (1 of 20 shoplifted), Philadelphia (1 of 10), and again in New York (1 of 12).

Experts on controlling inventory shrinkage generally agree that the best deterrent is an alert employee at the point of sale. Retail stores use sensitized tags on merchandise; if not detached or neutralized by a salesclerk, these miniature transmitters trip an alarm as the culprit begins to leave the store. Many libraries use a similar system to safeguard their books. Macy's in New York has continuous surveillance with over fifty television cameras.

Retailers must also scrutinize their own personnel, because they account for at least 30% to 40% of inventory shortages. Some stores have actors pose as shoplifters, who are then subjected to fake arrests. If potential thieves see the arrests, they may be deterred. Such ploys have helped reduce thefts by employees at major retail chains.

The imposing magnitude of retail inventory shrinkage demonstrates how management objectives may differ among industries. For example, consider the grocery business, where net income is about 1% of sales. You can readily see why a prime responsibility of the store manager is to control inventory shrinkage rather than boost gross sales volume. The trade-off is clear: If the operating profit is 2% of sales, to offset a $1,000 increase in shrinkage requires a $50,000 boost in gross sales.

SHRINKAGE IN PERPETUAL AND PERIODIC INVENTORY SYSTEMS

Measuring inventory shrinkage is straightforward for companies that use a perpetual inventory system. Shrinkage is simply the difference between the cost of inventory identified by a physical count and the clerical inventory balance. Consider the following example:

Sales	$100,000
Cost of goods sold (perpetual inventory system)	$ 80,000
Beginning inventory	$ 15,000
Purchases	$ 85,000
Ending inventory, per clerical records	$ 20,000
Ending inventory, per physical count	$ 18,000

Shrinkage is $20,000 − $18,000 = $2,000. The journal entries under a perpetual inventory system would be:

Inventory shrinkage	2,000	
Inventory		2,000

To adjust ending inventory to its balance per physical count.

Cost of goods sold	2,000	
Inventory shrinkage		2,000

The transfer inventory shrinkage to cost of goods sold.
The total cost of goods sold would be $80,000 + $2,000 = $82,000.

By definition, a periodic inventory system has no continuing balance of the inventory account. Inventory shrinkage is automatically included in cost of goods sold. Why? Because beginning inventory plus purchases less ending inventory measures all inventory that has flowed out, whether it went to customers, shoplifters, or embezzlers, or was simply lost or broken. Our example would show:

Beginning inventory	$ 15,000
Plus: Purchases	85,000
Goods available for sale	$100,000
Less: Ending inventory, per physical count	18,000
Cost of goods sold	$ 82,000

SUMMARY PROBLEMS FOR YOUR REVIEW

PROBLEM ONE

Examine Exhibit 6-12. The company uses the periodic inventory system. Using these facts, prepare a columnar comparison of income statements for the year ended December 31, 19X2. Compare the FIFO, LIFO, and weighted-average inventory methods. Assume that other expenses are $1,000. The income tax rate is 40%.

Exhibit 6-12

Facts for Summary Problem One

	Purchases	Sales	Inventory
December 31, 19X1			200 @ $5 = $1,000
January 25	170@ $6 = $1,020		
January 29		150*	
May 28	190@ $7 = $1,330		
June 7		230*	
November 20	150@ $8 = $1,200		
December 15		100*	
Total	510	$3,550	480*
December 31, 19X2			230 @ ?

* Selling prices were $9, $11, and $13, respectively, providing total sales of:

	150 @ $ 9 = $1,350	Summary of costs:
	230 @ $11 = $2,530	Beginning inventory $1,000
	100 @ $13 = $1,300	Purchases $3,550
Total sales	480 $5,180	Cost of goods available for sale $4,550

SOLUTION TO PROBLEM ONE

See Exhibit 6-13.

PROBLEM TWO

"When prices are rising, FIFO produces profits that confuse economic profit and holding profits because more resources are needed to maintain operations than previously." Do you agree? Explain.

SOLUTION TO PROBLEM TWO

The merit of this position depends on the concept of income favored. LIFO gives a better measure of "distributable" income than FIFO. Recall Emilio's Cola Sales example in Exhibit 6-5. The gross profit under FIFO was 60 cents, and under LIFO it was 34 cents. The 60¢ − 34¢ = 26¢ difference is a fool's profit because it must be reinvested to maintain the same inventory level as previously. It arises from a profit on holding inventory as prices change rather than from buying at wholesale and selling at retail. Therefore the 26 cents cannot be distributed as a cash dividend without reducing the current level of operations.

PROBLEM THREE

Hewlett-Packard (HP) designs, manufactures and services a broad array of products including perhaps your calculator or printer. Some results for the year ended October 31, 1997 were (in millions):

Sales of products	$36,672
Cost of merchandise sold	24,217
Net earnings	3,119
Beginning merchandise inventory	3,956
Ending merchandise inventory	4,136

Exhibit 6-13

Comparison of Inventory Methods for the Year Ended December 31, 19X2

	FIFO	LIFO	Weighted Average
Sales, 480 units	$5,180	$5,180	$5,180
Deduct cost of goods sold:			
Beginning inventory, 200 @ $5	$1,000	$1,000	$1,000
Purchases, 510 units (from Exhibit 6-12)*	3,550	3,550	3,550
Available for sale, 710 units †	$4,550 *available*	$4,550	$4,550
Ending inventory, 230 units ‡			
150 @ $8	$1,200		
80 @ $7	560 1,760		
or			
200 @ $5		$1,000	
30 @ $6		180 1,180	
or			
230 @ $6.408			1,474
Cost of goods sold, 480 units	—— 2,790	—— 3,370	3,076
Gross profit	$2,390	$1,810	$2,104
Other expenses	1,000	1,000	1,000
Income before income taxes	$1,390	$ 810	$1,104
Income taxes at 40%	556	324 *lower*	442
Net income	$ 834	$ 486	$ 662

* Always equal across all three methods.
† These amounts will not be equal in general across the three methods because beginning inventories will generally be different. They are equal here only because beginning inventories were assumed to be equal.
‡ Under FIFO, the ending inventory is composed of the last purchases plus the second-last purchases, and so forth, until the costs of 230 units are compiled. Under LIFO, the ending inventory is composed of the beginning inventory plus the earliest purchases of the current year until the costs of 230 units are compiled. Under weighted average, the ending inventory and cost of goods sold are accumulations based on a unit cost. The latter is the cost of goods available for sale divided by the number of units available for sale: $4,550 ÷ 710 = $6.408.

1. Calculate the 1997 gross profit and gross profit percentage for Hewlett-Packard.

2. Calculate the inventory turnover ratio.

3. What gross profit would have been reported if inventory turnover in 1997 had been 7, the gross profit percentage remained the same as that calculated in requirement 1, and the level of inventory was unchanged?

SOLUTION TO PROBLEM THREE

1. Gross profit = Sales − Cost of merchandise sold
   = $36,672 − $24,217
   = $12,455

   Gross profit percentage = Gross profit ÷ Sales
   = $12,455 ÷ $36,672
   = 34%

2. Inventory turnover = Cost of merchandise sold ÷ Average merchandise inventory
   = $24,217 ÷ [($3,956 + $4,136) ÷ 2]
   = $24,217 ÷ $4,046
   = 6.0

3. Cost of merchandise sold = Inventory turnover × Average merchandise inventory

$$= 7 \times \$4{,}046$$
$$= \$28{,}322$$

Gross profit percentage = (Sales − Cost of merchandise sold) ÷ Sales

$$34\% = (S - \$28{,}322) \div S$$
$$.34 \times S = S - \$28{,}322$$
$$S - (0.34 \times S) = \$28{,}322$$
$$S \times (1 - 0.34) = \$28{,}322$$
$$S = \$28{,}322 \div (1 - 0.34)$$
$$S = \$42{,}912$$

Gross profit = Sales − Cost of merchandise sold

$$= \$42{,}912 - \$28{,}322$$
$$= \$14{,}590$$

The increase in inventory turnover from 6.0 to 7.0 would raise gross profit from $12,455 to $14,590.

PROBLEM FOUR

At the end of 19X1, a $1,000 error was made in the physical inventory so the inventory value was understated. The error went undetected. The subsequent inventory at the end of 19X2 was done correctly. Assess the effect of this error on income before tax, taxes, net income, and retained earnings for 19X1 and 19X2, assuming a 40% tax rate.

SOLUTION TO PROBLEM FOUR

	19X1	19X2
Beginning Inventory	ok	too low
Purchases	ok	ok
Goods available for sale	ok	too low
Ending Inventory	too low	ok
Cost of goods sold	too high	too low

Note that 19X1 Ending Inventory becomes 19X2 Beginning Inventory, reversing the effects on Cost of Goods Sold. The 19X1 Cost of Goods Sold being too high causes 19X1 income before tax to be too low by $1,000. Therefore taxes will be too low by .40 × $1,000 = $400 and net income will be too low by $600, causing retained income to be too low by $600 also. In 19X2 the effects reverse and by year's end retained income is correctly stated.

Highlights to Remember

Inventory accounting involves allocating the cost of goods available for sale between cost of goods sold and ending inventory as of the balance sheet date. Under the perpetual inventory system, this allocation occurs continually, and cost of goods sold is recorded for each sale. Under the periodic inventory system, the allocation occurs via an adjusting entry at year end. A physical inventory is conducted at the end of each period under either system. The goods on hand are counted, and a cost is calculated for each item from purchase records. The cost of an item of inventory includes not only the purchase price but also inward transportation costs.

Under the periodic system, the physical inventory is the basis for the year-end adjusting entry to recognize cost of goods sold. Under the perpetual system, the physical inventory is used to confirm the accounting records. Differences, if any, lead to adjustments to cost of goods sold and ending inventory.

Valuation of inventories involves the assignment of specific historical costs of acquisition either to units sold or to units remaining in ending inventory. Four major inventory valuation methods are in use in the United States: specific identification, weighted average, FIFO, and LIFO. When prices are rising and inventories are constant or growing, less income is shown by LIFO than by FIFO. LIFO liquidation refers to the relatively higher profits generated under LIFO when reductions in inventory levels cause older, lower inventory costs to be used in calculating cost of goods sold. Notice that even with declining inventories, with rising costs the cumulative taxable income is always less under LIFO than it is under FIFO because the inventory valuation is less and the cumulative cost of goods sold is higher.

LIFO is popular in the United States among companies who face rising prices, for whom lower profits under LIFO mean lower taxes. The U.S. tax law contains a conformity requirement that allows companies to use LIFO for tax purposes only if they use it also for financial reporting purposes.

Conservatism leads to the lower-of-cost-or-market method, which treats cost as the maximum value of inventory. Inventory is reduced to replacement cost (with a corresponding increase in cost of goods sold) when acquisition prices fall below historical cost levels.

The nature of accrual accounting for inventories creates a self-correcting quality about errors in counting or valuing the ending inventory. This occurs because the ending inventory in one period becomes the beginning inventory of the subsequent period.

Financial analysts and managers use gross profit percentages as a measure of profitability and inventory turnover as a measure of efficient asset use. These measures are compared with prior levels to examine trends and with current levels of other industry members to assess relative performance.

Appendix 6: Inventory in a Manufacturing Environment

In this chapter, inventory accounting is covered from the viewpoint of a merchandiser. When a company manufactures products, the cost of inventory is a combination of the acquisition cost of raw material, the wages paid to workers who combine the raw materials into finished products, and an allocation of the costs of space, energy, and equipment used by the workers as they transform the various elements into a finished product.

Consider how costs are accumulated in a manufacturing environment for Packit, a company that makes backpacks. The raw materials are heavy fabric, glue, and thread. The transformation occurs when workers use cutters to make the panels that other workers sew and glue together. The costs of manufacture include depreciation on the manufacturing building, depreciation on the sewing machines and cutters, and utilities to support the effort in the form of heat, power, and light. The finished goods are backpacks.

The accounting process is easiest to understand when calculating the cost of a complete year of production. In the example below, 100,000 backpacks are produced during Packit's first year at a total cost of $800,000, providing a cost per backpack of $8.00 each ($800,000 ÷ 100,000 units). At year end, if all have been sold, the financial statements would include $800,000 in cost of goods sold.

Beginning inventory	—
Fabric purchased and used	$200,000
Wages paid to workers	300,000
Thread and glue used	50,000
Depreciation on building and equipment	220,000
Utilities	30,000
Total Costs to Manufacture	$800,000
Cost per backpack ($800,000 ÷ 100,000)	$8.00

raw material inventory Includes the cost of materials held for use in the manufacturing of a product.

work in process inventory Includes the cost incurred for partially completed items, including raw materials, labor, and other costs.

finished goods inventory The accumulated costs of manufacture for goods that are complete and ready for sale.

In the above example, all of the materials acquired during the year are transformed into finished products before year end and sold. In reality, if we take a snapshot of the typical backpack manufacturer at year end we would observe bolts of fabric, spools of thread, and gallons of glue waiting to be put into production. We call these items held for use in the manufacturing of a product **raw material inventory.** In addition we would also observe fabric already cut but not assembled and some partially completed backpacks. We refer to the material, labor, and other costs accumulated for partially completed items as **work in process inventory.** When manufacture is complete and the goods are ready to deliver to customers, the inventory is called **finished goods inventory.** The accounting system for managing these costs for the second year of production of our backpack manufacturer is illustrated in Exhibit 6-14. During this second year 120,000 backpacks are completed and 110,000 are sold. Some remain in the assembly process at year end, and unused fabric, thread, and glue are held in preparation for future production.

Exhibit 6-14

Packit Company Accounting for Manufacturing Costs

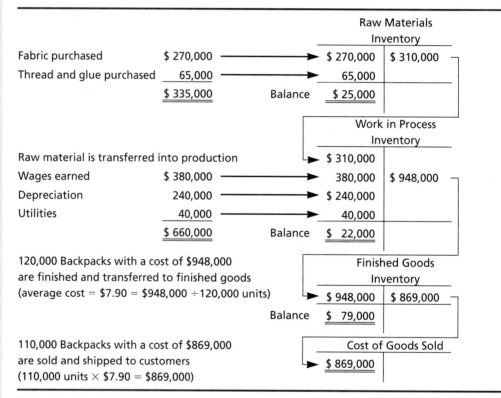

The summary journal entries to record these events for year 2 would be:

PURCHASE OF RAW MATERIAL:

Raw material inventory 335,000
    Accounts payable 335,000

PRODUCTION ACTIVITY:

Work in process inventory 310,000
    Raw materials inventory. 310,000
Work in process inventory 660,000
    Wages payable 380,000
    Accumulated depreciation 240,000
    Utilities payable 40,000

COMPLETION OF PRODUCTION:

Finished goods inventory. 869,000
    Work in process inventory 869,000

The schematic in Exhibit 6-14 captures the production process. You might think of each of the accounts as corresponding to a physical reality. The raw material is stored in a locked room, ready for use. The work-in-process is located in the production room and as it is finished it is physically transferred to a storage site. When goods are sold they are removed from that storage site and are given to the customer in exchange for cash or an account receivable. Raw materials, work-in-process, and finished goods are all forms of inventory and appear on the balance sheet as current assets. They are simply in different stages of completion. The act of sale converts the asset into an expense to be reported on the income statement. At year end, Packit will show total inventory on its year 2 balance sheet of $126,000, as follows:

Raw Materials Inventory	$ 25,000
Work in Process Inventory	22,000
Finished Goods Inventory	79,000
Total Inventory	$126,000

Accounting Vocabulary

conservatism, p. 237

consistency, p. 232

cost of goods available for sale, p. 224

cost valuation, p. 223

cutoff error, p. 241

finished goods inventory, p. 252

first-in, first-out (FIFO), p. 230

F.O.B. destination, p. 225

F.O.B. shipping point, p. 225

freight in, p. 226

freight out, p. 226

gross profit percentage, p. 242

holding gain, p. 234

inventory profit, p. 234

inventory shrinkage, p. 224

inventory turnover, p. 243

inward transportation, p. 226

last-in, first-out (LIFO), p. 230

LIFO increment, p. 234

LIFO layer, p. 234

LIFO reserve, p. 235

lower-of-cost-or-market method (LCM), p. 237

periodic inventory system, p. 224

perpetual inventory system, p. 223

physical count, p. 223

raw material inventory, p. 252

replacement cost, p. 233

retailer, p. 242

specific identification method, p. 229

weighted-average method, p. 231

wholesaler, p. 242

work in process inventory, p. 252

write-down, p. 238

Assignment Material

QUESTIONS

6-1. When a company records a sales transaction, it also records another related transaction. Explain the related transaction.

6-2. "There are two steps in the periodic system of accounting for inventories." What are they?

6-3. Distinguish between the *perpetual* and *periodic* inventory systems.

6-4. "An advantage of the perpetual inventory system is that a physical count of inventory is unnecessary. The periodic method requires a physical count to compute cost of goods sold." Do you agree? Explain.

6-5. Distinguish between *F.O.B. destination* and *F.O.B. shipping point.*

6-6. "Freight out should be classified as a direct offset to sales, not as an expense." Do you agree? Explain.

6-7. Name the four inventory cost flow assumptions or valuation methods that are generally accepted in the United States. Give a brief phrase describing each.

6-8. Which of the following items would a company be likely to account for using the specific identification inventory method?

a. Corporate jet aircraft   e. Timex watches

b. Large sailboats   f. Automobiles

c. Pencils   g. Books

d. Diamond rings   h. Compact discs

6-9. If a company uses a FIFO cost flow assumption, will it report the same cost of goods sold using the periodic inventory method that it reports using the perpetual method? Why or why not?

6-10. Why is LIFO a good news/bad news inventory method?

6-11. "Purchases of inventory at the end of a fiscal period can have a direct effect on income under LIFO." Do you agree? Explain.

6-12. "Gamma Company has five units of inventory, two purchased for $4 each and three purchased for $5 each. Thus, the weighted-average cost of the inventory is ($4 + $5) ÷ 2 = $4.50 per unit." Do you agree? Explain.

6-13. Assume that the physical level of inventory is constant at the beginning and end of year and that the cost of inventory items is rising. Which will produce a higher ending inventory value, LIFO or FIFO?

6-14. Will LIFO or FIFO produce higher cost of goods sold during a period of *falling* prices? Explain.

6-15. What is *consistency,* and why is it an important accounting principle?

6-16. "There is a single dominant reason why more and more U.S. companies have adopted LIFO." What is the reason?

6-17. "An inventory profit is a fictitious profit." Do you agree? Explain.

6-18. LIFO produces absurd inventory valuations. Why?

6-19. "Conservatism always results in lower reported profits." Do you agree? Explain.

6-20. "Accountants have traditionally favored taking some losses but no gains before an asset is exchanged." What is this tradition or convention called?

6-21. What does *market* mean in inventory accounting?

6-22. "The lower-of-cost-or-market method is inherently inconsistent." Do you agree? Explain.

6-23. "Inventory errors are counterbalancing." Explain.

6-24. Express the cost of goods sold section of the income statement as an equation.

6-25. "Gross profit percentages help in the preparation of interim financial statements." Explain.

6-26. The branch manager of a national retail grocery chain has stated: "My managers are judged more heavily on the basis of their merchandise-shrinkage control than on their overall sales volume." Why? Explain.

EXERCISES

6-27 Gross Profit Section
Given the following, prepare a detailed gross profit section for Prag's Jewelry Wholesalers for the year ended December 31, 19X8 (in thousands):

Cash discounts on purchases	$ 6	Cash discounts on sales	$ 5
Sales returns and allowances	35	Purchase returns and allowances	27
Gross purchases	650		
Merchandise inventory,		Merchandise inventory,	
December 31, 19X7	103	December 31, 19X8	180
Gross profit	365	Freight in	50

6-28 Gross Margin Computations and Inventory Costs
On January 15, 19X4, Malia Mayes valued her inventory at cost, $40,000. Her statements are based on the calendar year, so you find it necessary to establish an inventory figure as of January 1, 19X4. You find that from January 2 to January 15, sales were $71,200; sales returns, $2,300; goods purchased and placed in stock, $54,000; goods removed from stock and returned to suppliers, $2,000; freight in, $500. Calculate the inventory cost as of January 1, assuming that goods are priced to provide a 23% gross profit.

6-29 Journal Entries
Vadim Company had sales of $24 million during the year. The goods cost Vadim $16 million. Give the journal entry or entries at the time of sale under the perpetual and the periodic inventory systems.

6-30 Valuing Inventory and Cost of Goods Sold
Glasgow Metals Ltd. had the following inventory transactions during the month of January.

1/1 beginning inventory,	4,000 units @ £2.00	£8,000
week 1, purchases	2,000 units @ £2.10	4,200
week 2, purchases	3,000 units @ £2.20	6,600
week 3, purchases	1,000 units @ £2.30	2,300
week 4, purchases	1,000 units @ £2.40	2,400

On January 31, a count of the ending inventory was completed, and 5,500 units were on hand. Using the periodic inventory system, calculate the cost of goods sold and ending inventory using LIFO, FIFO, and weighted-average inventory methods.

6-31 Entries for Purchase Transactions

The Volkert Company is a Swiss wholesaler of office supplies. Its unit of currency is the Swiss franc (CHF). Volkert uses a periodic inventory system. Prepare journal entries for the following summarized transactions (omit explanations):

Aug. 2 Purchased merchandise, CHF 300,000, terms 2/10, n/45.

Aug. 3 Paid cash for freight in, CHF 10,000.

Aug. 7 Volkert complained about some defects in the merchandise acquired on August 2. The supplier hand-delivered a credit memo granting an allowance of CHF 20,000.

Aug. 11 Cash disbursement to settle purchase of August 2.

6-32 Cost of Inventory Acquired

On July 5, Solanski Company purchased on account a shipment of sheet steel from Northwest Steel Co. The invoice price was $160,000, F.O.B. shipping point. Shipping cost from the steel mill to Solanski's plant was $12,000. When inspecting the shipment, the Solanski receiving clerk found several flaws in the steel. She informed Northwest's sales representative of the flaws, and after some negotiation, Northwest granted an allowance of $15,000.

To encourage prompt payment, Northwest grants a 2% cash discount to customers who pay their accounts within 30 days of billing. Solanski paid the proper amount on August 1.

Required

1. Compute the total cost of the sheet steel acquired.
2. Prepare the journal entries for the transaction. Omit explanations.

6-33 Entries for Periodic and Perpetual Systems

Gulick Co. had an inventory of $220,000, December 31, 19X7. Data for 19X8 follow:

Gross purchases	$960,000
Cost of goods sold	890,000
Inventory, December 31, 19X8	200,000
Purchase returns and allowances	90,000

Required

Using the data, prepare comparative journal entries, including closing entries, for a perpetual and a periodic inventory system.

6-34 Entries for Purchase Transactions

Pier Four Imports uses a periodic inventory system. Prepare journal entries for the following summarized transactions for 19X8 (omit explanations). For simplicity, assume that the beginning and ending balances in accounts payable were zero.

1. Purchases (all using trade credit), $900,000.
2. Purchase returns and allowances, $60,000.

3. Freight in, $72,000 paid in cash.

4. Cash discounts on purchases, $18,000.

6-35 Journal Entries, Periodic Inventory System

 Refer to the data in the preceding problem. Inventories were: December 31, 19X7, $81,000; December 31, 19X8, $130,000. Sales were $1,250,000. Prepare summary journal entries for 19X8. Omit explanations.

6-36 Journal Entries, Periodic Inventory System

 Consider the following data taken from the adjusted trial balance of the Emerald Bay Boat Company, December 31, 19X3 (in millions):

Purchases	$125	Sales	239
Sales returns and allowances	5	Purchase returns and	
Freight in	14	allowances	6
Cash discounts on purchases	1	Cash discounts on sales	8
Inventory (beginning of year)	25	Other expenses	80

Required   Prepare summary journal entries. The ending inventory was $30 million.

6-37 Reconstruction of Transaction

Apple Computer, Inc. produces the well-known Macintosh computer. Consider the following account balances (in millions):

	June 27, 1997	September 27, 1996
Inventories	$534	$662

Required   The purchases of inventories during the nine months between September 27, 1996 and June 27, 1997 were $1,261,000,000. The income statement for that nine-month period had an item "cost of sales." Compute its amount.

6-38 Reconstruction of Records

An earthquake caused heavy damage to the Modern Jazz Record Store on May 3, 19X8. All the merchandise was destroyed. Some accounting data are missing. In conjunction with an insurance investigation, you have been asked to estimate the cost of the inventory destroyed. The following data for 19X8 are available:

Cash discounts on purchases	$ 1,000	Inventory, December 31, 19X7	$19,000
Gross sales	140,000	Purchase returns and allowances	4,000
Sales returns and allowances	12,000	Inward transportation	3,000
Gross purchases	80,000	Gross profit percentage on net sales	45%

6-39 Cost of Inventory Destroyed by Fire

Liao Company's insurance agent requires an estimate of the cost of merchandise lost by fire on March 9. Merchandise inventory on January 1 was $65,000. Purchases since January 1 were $195,000; freight in, $28,000; purchase returns and allowances, $10,000. Sales are made at a gross margin of 20% of *sales* and totaled $200,000 up to March 9. What was the cost of the merchandise destroyed?

6-40 Inventory Shortage

An accounting clerk of the Ayers Company absconded with cash and a truck full of the entire electronic merchandise on May 14, 19X8. The following data have been compiled:

Beginning inventory, January 1	$ 60,000
Sales to May 14, 19X8	280,000
Average gross profit rate	25%
Purchases to May 14, 19X8	200,000

Compute the estimated cost of the missing merchandise.

Required

6-41 Inventory Errors

At the end of his first business year, Cal Stokes counted and priced the inventory. A few very high-value items were hidden in a dark corner of the storage shelves and Cal understated his 1998 inventory by $10,000. His business financial statements and his tax return were affected. Assume a 40% tax rate.

Required

1. Calculate the effect on taxable income, taxes, net income, and retained earnings for 1998.

2. Repeat requirement 1 for 1999, assuming the 1999 ending inventory is correctly calculated.

6-42 Decision about Pricing

Genuine Gems, Inc., a retail jewelry store, had gross profits of $880,000 on sales of $1,600,000 in 19X3. Average inventory was $720,000.

Required

1. Compute inventory turnover.

2. Aaron Siegl, owner of Genuine Gems, is considering whether to become a "discount" jeweler. For example, Aaron believes that a cut of 20% in average selling prices would have increased turnover to 1.5 times per year. Beginning and ending inventory would be unchanged. Suppose Aaron's beliefs are valid. Would the gross profit in 19X3 have improved? Show computations.

6-43 LIFO and FIFO

The inventory of the Alcon Gravel Company on June 30 shows 1,000 tons at $9 per ton. A physical inventory on July 31 shows a total of 1,200 tons on hand. Revenue from sales of gravel for July totals $98,000. The following purchases were made during July:

July 8	5,000 tons @ $10 per ton
July 13	1,000 tons @ $11 per ton
July 22	900 tons @ $12 per ton

1. Compute the inventory cost as of July 31 using (a) LIFO and (b) FIFO.

Required

2. Compute the gross profit using each method.

6-44 Lower-of-Cost-or-Market

(Alternate is 6-70.) Matsushita Company uses the inventory method "cost or market, whichever is lower." There were no sales or purchases during the periods indicated, although selling prices generally fluctuated in the same directions as replacement costs. At what amount would you value merchandise on the dates listed below?

	Invoice Cost	Replacement Cost
December 31, 19X1	$200,000	$180,000
April 30, 19X2	200,000	190,000
August 31, 19X2	200,000	220,000
December 31, 19X2	200,000	175,000

6-45   Reconstruction of Transactions

Consider the following account balances of Converse, Inc., maker of athletic shoes (in thousands):

	June 28	
	1997	**1996**
Inventories	$98,406	$97,209

Required The income statement for the fiscal year included the item "cost of sales" of $307,392. Compute the net cost of the acquisition of inventory for the 1997 fiscal year.

6-46   Gross Profit Percentage

Toys " Я " Us operates nearly 1,500 stores in the United States and abroad. Like most retailers, the managers of Toys " Я " Us monitor the company's gross margin percentage. The following information is from the company's income statement:

	For the Year Ended		
	February 1, 1997	*February 3, 1996*	*January 28, 1995*
Sales	$9,932.4	$9,426.9	$8,745.6
Cost of sales	6,892.5	6,592.3	6,008.0

Required Compute the gross profit percentage for each of the three years. Comment on the changes in gross profit percentage.

6-47   Profitability and Turnover

Zeke's Building Supply began 19X1 with inventory of $160,000. Zeke's 19X1 sales were $800,000, purchases of inventory totaled $690,000, and ending inventory was $230,000.

Required
1. Prepare a statement of gross profit for 19X1.
2. What was Zeke's inventory turnover?

PROBLEMS

6-48   Detailed Income Statement

(Alternate is 6-51.) Following are accounts taken from the adjusted trial balance of the Marchesi Kitchen Supply Company, December 31, 19X5. The company uses the periodic inventory system.

Required Prepare a detailed income statement for 19X5. All amounts are in thousands:

Sales salaries and		Freight in	$ 50
commissions	$160	Miscellaneous expenses	13
Inventory, December 31, 19X4	200	Sales	1,085
Allowance for bad debts	14	Bad debts expense	8
Rent expense, office space	10	Cash discounts on purchases	15
Gross purchases	600	Inventory, December 31, 19X5	325
Depreciation expense, office		Office salaries	60
equipment	3	Rent expense, selling space	90
Cash discounts on sales	10	Income tax expense	44
Advertising expense	45	Sales returns and allowances	50
Purchase returns and		Office supplies used	6
allowances	40	Depreciation expenses, trucks	
Delivery expense	20	and store fixtures	29

6-49   Perpetual Inventory Calculations

Lincoln Electric is a wholesaler for commercial builders. The company uses a perpetual inventory system and a FIFO cost-flow assumption. The data concerning Lincoln Electric for the year 19X8 follows:

	Purchased	Sold	Balance
December 31, 19X7			110 @ $5 = $550
February 10, 19X8	80 @ $6 = $480		
April 14		60	
May 9	110 @ $7 = $770		
July 14		120	
October 21	100 @ $8 = $800		
November 12		75	
Total	290 $2,050	255	

Required

Calculate the ending balance in units and dollars.

6-50 Gross Profit and Turnover

Retailers closely watch a number of financial ratios, including the gross profit (gross margin) percentage and inventory turnover. Suppose the results for the furniture department in a large store in a given year were:

Sales	$3,000,000
Cost of goods sold	1,800,000
Gross profit	$1,200,000
Beginning inventory	$ 650,000
Ending inventory	550,000

Required

1. Compute the gross profit percentage and the inventory turnover.
2. Suppose the retailer is able to maintain a reduced inventory of $450,000 throughout the succeeding year. What inventory turnover would have to be obtained to achieve the same $1,200,000 gross profit? Assume that the gross profit percentage is unchanged.
3. Suppose the retailer maintains inventory at the $450,000 level throughout the succeeding year but cannot increase the inventory turnover from the level in requirement 1. What gross profit percentage would have to be obtained to achieve the same total gross profit?
4. Suppose the average inventory of $600,000 is maintained. Compute the total gross profit in the succeeding year if there is
   a. A 10% increase of the gross profit *percentage* (that is, 10% of the percentage, not an additional ten percentage points) and a 10% decrease of the inventory turnover; or
   b. A 10% decrease of the gross profit percentage and a 10% increase of the inventory turnover.
5. Why do retailers find the above types of ratios helpful?

6-51 Detailed Income Statement

(Alternate is 6-48.) Hartmarx Corporation is a clothing company with many retail outlets, including Country Miss and Kuppenheimer. The company's annual report contained the following actual data for the year ended November 30, 1996 (in thousands):

Net sales	$610,180
Cost of goods sold	463,533
Selling, general, and	
administrative expenses	127,699
Other expenses (net)	12,418
Profit before tax	$ 6,530

The balance sheets included the following actual data (in thousands of dollars):

	November 30	
	1996	*1995*
Allowance for doubtful accounts	$ 9,983	$ 7,920
Inventories	165,913	154,898

Consider the following additional assumed data (in thousands of dollars):

Bad debts expense	$ 5,000	Freight in	$14,000
Gross purchases	473,548	Advertising expense	16,000
Cash discounts on sales	10,000	Sales returns and allowances	35,000
Sales salaries and compensation	49,699	Depreciation expense	15,000
Purchase returns and		Cash discounts on purchases	2,000
allowances	11,000	Rent expense	30,000
Freight out	12,000	Miscellaneous other	
		expenses (net)	12,418

Required Prepare a detailed multistep income statement that ends with profit (or loss) before tax. You need not subclassify the selling, general, and administrative expenses into three separate categories.

6-52   Comparison of Inventory Methods

(Alternates are 6-63 and 6-65.) The Hauck Co. is a wholesaler for commercial builders. The company uses a periodic inventory system. The data concerning Zelton cooktops for the year 19X8 follow:

	Purchases	**Sold**	**Balance**
December 31, 19X7			110 @ $50 = $5,500
February 10, 19X8	80 @ $60 = $4,800		
April 14		60	
May 9	120 @ $70 = $8,400		
July 14		120	
October 21	100 @ $80 = $8,000		
November 12		80	
Total	300 $21,200	260	
December 31, 19X8			150 @ ?

The sales during 19X8 were made at the following selling prices:

60 @ $ 80 =	$ 4,800
120 @ 100 =	12,000
80 @ 110 =	8,800
260	$25,600

Required

1. Prepare a comparative statement of gross profit for the year ended December 31, 19X8, using FIFO, LIFO, and weighted-average inventory methods.

2. By how much would income taxes differ if Hauck used LIFO instead of FIFO for Zelton cooktops? Assume a 40% income tax rate.

6-53   Effects of Late Purchases

(Alternates are 6-64 and 6-66.) Refer to the preceding problem. Suppose 100 extra units had been acquired on December 30 for $80 each, a total of $8,000. How would net income and income taxes have been affected under FIFO? under LIFO? Show a tabulated comparison.

6-54 LIFO, FIFO, and Lower-of-Cost-or-Market

ASR Company began business on March 15, 19X0. The following are ASR's purchases of inventory.

March 17	100 units @ $10	$1,000
April 19	50 units @ $12	600
May 14	100 units @ $13	1,300
Total		$2,900

On May 25, 140 units were sold, leaving inventory of 110 units. ASR Company's accountant was preparing a balance sheet for June 1, at which time the replacement cost of the inventory was $12 per unit.

Required

1. Suppose ASR Company uses LIFO, without applying lower-of-cost-or-market. Compute the June 1 inventory amount.

2. Suppose ASR Company uses lower-of-LIFO-cost-or-market. Compute the June 1 inventory amount.

3. Suppose ASR Company uses FIFO, without applying lower-of-cost-or-market. Compute the June 1 inventory amount.

4. Suppose ASR Company uses lower-of-FIFO-cost-or-market. Compute the June 1 inventory amount.

6-55 Inventory Errors

(Alternate is 6-62.) The following data are from the 19X1 income statement of the Oriental Rug Emporium (in thousands):

Sales		$1,700
Deduct cost of goods sold:		
Beginning inventory	$ 390	
Purchases	820	
Cost of goods available for sale	$1,210	
Deduct: Ending inventory	370	
Cost of goods sold		840
Gross profit		$ 860
Other expenses		610
Income before income taxes		$ 250
Income tax expense at 40%		100
Net income		$ 150

The ending inventory was overstated by $30,000 because of errors in the physical count. The income tax rate was 40% in 19X1 and 19X2.

Required

1. Which items in the income statement are incorrect? By how much? Use *O* for overstated, *U* for understated, and *N* for not affected. Complete the following tabulation:

	19X1	19X2
Beginning inventory	N	0 $30
Ending inventory	?	?
Cost of goods sold	?	?
Gross margin	?	?
Income before income taxes	?	?
Income tax expense	?	?
Net income	?	?

2. What is the dollar effect of the inventory error on retained income at the end of 19X1? at the end of 19X2?

6-56 LIFO, FIFO, Prices Rising and Falling

The Fasano Company has a periodic inventory system. Inventory on December 31, 19X1, consisted of 10,000 units @ $10 = $100,000. Purchases during 19X2 were 13,000 units. Sales were 12,000 units for sales revenue of $20 per unit.

Required Prepare a four-column comparative statement of gross margin for 19X2:

1. Assume purchases were at $12 per unit. Assume FIFO and then LIFO.
2. Assume purchases were at $8 per unit. Assume FIFO and then LIFO.
3. Assume an income tax rate of 40%. Suppose all transactions were for cash. Which inventory method in requirement 1 would result in more cash for Fasano Company? by how much?
4. Repeat requirement 3. Which inventory method in requirement 2 would result in more cash for Fasano Company? by how much?

6-57 LIFO, FIFO, Cash Effects

In 19X8, MacGregor Company had sales revenue of £360,000 for a line of woolen scarves. The company uses a periodic inventory system. Pertinent data for 19X8 included:

Inventory, December 31, 19X7	14,000 units @ £ 6	£ 84,000
January purchases	20,000 units @ £ 7	140,000
July purchases	32,000 units @ £ 8	256,000
Sales for the year	30,000 units	

Required
1. Prepare a statement of gross margin for 19X8. Use two columns, one assuming LIFO and one assuming FIFO.
2. Assume a 40% income tax rate. Suppose all transactions were for cash. Which inventory method would result in more cash for MacGregor Company? by how much?

6-58 FIFO and LIFO

Two companies, the LIFO Company and the FIFO Company, are in the scrap metal warehousing business as arch competitors. They are about the same size and in 19X1 coincidentally encountered seemingly identical operating situations. Only their inventory accounting systems differed.

Their beginning inventory was 10,000 tons; it cost $50 per ton. During the year, each company purchased 50,000 tons at the following prices:

- 20,000 @ $60 on March 17
- 30,000 @ $70 on October 5

Each company sold 45,000 tons at average prices of $100 per ton. Other expenses in addition to cost of goods sold but excluding income taxes were $650,000. The income tax rate is 40%.

Required
1. Compute net income for the year for both companies. Show your calculations.
2. As a manager, which method would you prefer? Why? Explain fully. Include your estimate of the overall effect of these events on the cash balances of each company, assuming that all transactions during 19X1 were direct receipts or disbursements of cash.

6-59 Effects of LIFO and FIFO

The Karas Company is starting in business on December 31, 19X0. In each *half year,* from 19X1 through 19X4, it expects to purchase 1,000 units and sell 50 units for the amounts listed below. In 19X5, it expects to purchase no units and sell 4,000 units for the amount indicated in the following table:

	19X1	19X2	19X3	19X4	19X5
Purchases:					
First 6 months	$ 2,000	$ 4,000	$ 6,000	$ 6,000	0
Second 6 months	4,000	9,000	6,000	8,000	0
Total	$ 6,000	$13,000	$12,000	$14,000	0
Sales (at selling price)	$10,000	$10,000	$10,000	$10,000	$40,000

Assume that there are no costs or expenses other than those shown above. The tax rate is 40%, and taxes for each year are payable on December 31 of each year. Karas Company is trying to decide whether to use periodic FIFO or LIFO throughout the five-year period.

Required

1. What was net income under FIFO for each of the five years? under LIFO? Show calculations.
2. Explain briefly which method, LIFO or FIFO, seems more advantageous, and why.

6-60 Effects of LIFO on Purchase Decisions

The Ramayya Corporation is nearing the end of its first year in business. The following purchases of its single product have been made:

	Units	Unit Price	Total Cost
January	1,000	$10	$ 10,000
March	1,000	10	10,000
May	1,000	11	11,000
July	1,000	13	13,000
September	1,000	14	14,000
December	4,000	15	60,000
	9,000		$118,000

Sales for the year will be 5,000 units for $120,000. Expenses other than cost of goods sold will be $20,000.

The president is undecided about whether to adopt FIFO or LIFO for income tax purposes. The company has ample storage space for up to 7,000 units of inventory. Inventory prices are expected to stay at $15 per unit for the next few months.

Required

1. What would be the net income before taxes, the income taxes, and the net income after taxes for the year under (a) FIFO or (b) LIFO? Income tax rates are 30% on the first $25,000 of net taxable income and 50% on the excess.
2. If the company sells its year-end inventory in Year 2 @ $24 per unit and goes out of business, what would be the net income before taxes, the income taxes, and the net income after taxes under (a) FIFO and (b) LIFO? Assume that other expenses in Year 2 are $20,000.
3. Repeat requirements 1 and 2, assuming that the 4,000 units @ $15 purchased in December were not purchased until January of the second year. Generalize on the effect on net income of the timing of purchases under FIFO and LIFO.

6-61 Changing Quantities and LIFO Reserve

Consider the following data for the year 19X8:

	Units	Unit Cost
Beginning inventory	4	*
Purchases:	6	24
	6	28
Ending inventory	4	†

*FIFO, $20; LIFO, $16.

†To be computed.

1. Prepare a comparative table computing the cost of goods sold, using columns for FIFO and LIFO. In a final column, show (a) the difference between FIFO and LIFO inventories (the LIFO reserve) at the beginning of the year and at the end of the year, and (b) how the *change* in this amount explains the difference in cost of goods sold.

2. Repeat requirement 1, except assume that the ending inventory consisted of (a) six units, (b) zero units.

3. In your own words, explain why, for a given year, the increase in the LIFO reserve measures the amount by which cost of goods sold is higher under LIFO than FIFO.

6-62 Inventory Errors, Three Years

(Alternate is 6-55.) The Janoski Company had the accompanying data for three successive years (in millions):

	19X3	19X2	19X1
Sales	$200	$160	$170
Deduct: Cost of goods sold:			
Beginning inventory	15	25	40
Purchases	135	100	90
Cost of goods available for sale	150	125	130
Ending inventory	30	15	25
Cost of goods sold	120	110	105
Gross profit	80	50	65
Other expenses	70	30	30
Income before income taxes	10	20	35
Income tax expense at 40%	4	8	14
Net income	$ 6	$ 12	$ 21

In early 19X4, a team of internal auditors discovered that the ending inventory for 19X1 had been overstated by $15 million. Furthermore, the ending inventory for 19X3 had been understated by $10 million. The ending inventory for December 31, 19X2, was correct.

1. Which items in the income statement are incorrect? by how much? Prepare a tabulation covering each of the three years.

2. Is the amount of retained income correct at the end of 19X1, 19X2, and 19X3? If it is erroneous, indicate the amount and whether it is overstated (*O*) or understated (*U*).

6-63 Comparison of Inventory Methods

(Alternates are 6-52 and 6-65.) Cray Research is a leading producer of supercomputers. The following actual data and descriptions are from the company's fiscal 1995 annual report (in millions):

	December 31	
	1995	*1994*
Inventories	$177,359	$207,496

A footnote states: "Inventories are stated at the lower of cost (determined principally on the first-in, first-out method) or market."

The income statement for the fiscal year ended December 31, 1995, included (in thousands):

	Units	Total
Total revenue from sales, lease, and service fees		$676,244
Cost of sales, lease, and services		436,569

Assume that Cray used the periodic inventory system. Suppose a division of Cray had the accompanying data regarding the use of its computer parts that it acquires and resells to customers for maintaining equipment (dollars are *not* in millions):

	Units	Total
Inventory (December 31, 1995)	100	$ 400
Purchase (February 20, 1996)	200	1,000
Sales, March 17, 1996 (at $9 per unit)	150	
Purchase (June 25, 1996)	160	960
Sales, November 7, 1996 (at $10 per unit)	160	

1. For these computer parts only, prepare a tabulation of the cost of goods sold section of the income statement for the year ended December 31, 1996. Support your computations. Round totals to the nearest dollar. Show your tabulation for four different inventory methods: (a) FIFO, (b) LIFO, (c) weighted-average, and (d)specific identification.

   For requirement *d,* assume that the purchase of February 20 was identified with the sale of March 17. Also assume that the purchase of June 25 was identified with the sale of November 7.

2. By how much would income taxes differ if Cray used (a) LIFO instead of FIFO for this inventory item? (b) LIFO instead of weighted-average? Assume a 40% tax rate.

Required

6-64   Effects of Late Purchases

(Alternates are 6-53 and 6-66.) Refer to the preceding problem. Suppose Cray acquired 60 extra units @ $7 each on December 29, 1996, a total of $420. How would gross profit and income taxes be affected under FIFO? That is, compare FIFO results before and after the purchase of 60 extra units. Under LIFO? That is, compare LIFO results before and after the purchase of 60 extra units. Show computations and explain.

6-65   Comparison of Inventory Methods

(Alternates are 6-52 and 6-63.) Texas Instruments is a major producer of semiconductors and other electrical and electronic products. Semiconductors are especially vulnerable to price fluctuations. The following actual data and descriptions are from the company's annual report (in millions):

	December 31	
	1996	1995
Inventories	$703	$978

Texas Instruments uses a variety of inventory methods, but for this problem assume that only FIFO is used.

Net revenues for the fiscal year ended December 31, 1996, were $9,940 million. Cost of revenues was $7,146 million.

Assume that Texas Instruments had the accompanying data regarding one of its semiconductors. Assume a periodic inventory system.

	In	Out	Balance
December 31, 1995			80 @ $5 = 400
February 25, 1996	50 @ $6 = $ 300		
March 29		60* @ ?	
May 28	80 @ $7 = $ 560		
June 7		90* @ ?	
November 20	90 @ $8 = $ 720		
December 15		50* @ ?	
Total	220 $1,580	200	
December 31, 1996			100 @ ?

* Selling prices were $9, $11, and $13, respectively:

	60 @ $9 = $ 540	
	90 @ 11 = 990	
	50 @ 13 = 650	
Total sales	200 $2,180	

Summary of costs to account for:

Beginning inventory	$ 400
Purchases	1,580
Cost of goods available for sale	$1,980
Other expenses for this product	$ 500
Income tax rate, 40%	

Required

1. Prepare a comparative income statement for the 1996 fiscal year for the product in question. Use the FIFO, LIFO, and weighted-average inventory methods.

2. By how much would income taxes have differed if Texas Instruments had used LIFO instead of FIFO for this product?

3. Suppose Texas Instruments had used the specific identification method. Compute the gross margin (or gross profit) if the ending inventory had consisted of (a) 90 units @ $8, and 10 units @ $7; and (b) 60 units @ $5, and 40 units @ $8.

6-66 Effects of Late Purchases
(Alternates are 6-53 and 6-64.) Refer to the preceding problem. Suppose Texas Instruments had acquired 50 extra units @ $8 each on December 30, 1996, a total of $400. How would income before income taxes have been affected under FIFO? That is, compare FIFO results before and after the purchase of 50 extra units. Under LIFO? That is, compare LIFO results before and after the purchase of 50 extra units. Show computations and explain.

6-67 Classic Switch from LIFO to FIFO
Effective January 1, 1970, Chrysler Corporation adopted the FIFO method for inventories previously valued by the LIFO method. The 1970 annual report stated: "This . . . makes the financial statements with respect to inventory valuation comparable with those of the other United States automobile manufacturers."

The *Wall Street Journal* reported:

> *The change improved Chrysler's 1970 financial results several ways. Besides narrowing the 1970 loss by $20 million it improved Chrysler's working capital. The change also made the comparison with 1969 earnings*

look somewhat more favorable because, upon restatement, Chrysler's 1969 profit was raised by only $10.2 million from the original figures.

Finally, the change helped Chrysler's balance sheet by boosting inventories, and thus current assets, by $150 million at the end of 1970 over what they would have been under LIFO. As Chrysler's profit has collapsed over the last two years and its financial position tightened, auto analysts have eyed warily Chrysler's shrinking ratio of current assets to current liabilities.

To get the improvements in its balance sheet and results, however, Chrysler paid a price. Roger Helder, vice president and comptroller, said Chrysler owed the government $53 million in tax savings it accumulated by using the LIFO method since it switched from FIFO in 1957. The major advantage of LIFO is that it holds down profit and thus tax liabilities. The other three major auto makers stayed on the FIFO method. Mr. Helder said Chrysler now has to pay back that $53 million to the government over 20 years, which will boost Chrysler's tax bills about $3 million a year.

Required

Given the content of this text chapter, do you think the Chrysler decision to switch from LIFO to FIFO was beneficial to its stockholders? Explain, being as specific as you can.

6-68   LIFO, FIFO, Purchase Decisions, and Earnings Per Share

Hollywood Pet Supplies, a company with one million shares of common stock outstanding, had the following transactions during 19X1, its first year in business:

Sales:	1,100,000 units @ $5
Purchases:	900,000 units @ $2
	300,000 units @ $3

The current income tax rate is a flat 50%; the rate next year is expected to be 40%.

It is December 20 and Lane Braxton, the president, is trying to decide whether to buy the 600,000 units he needs for inventory now or early next year. The current price is $4 per unit. Prices on inventory are expected to remain stable; in any event, no decline in prices is anticipated.

Braxton has not chosen an inventory method as yet, but will pick either LIFO or FIFO. Other expenses for the year will be $1.4 million.

Required

1. Using LIFO, prepare a comparative income statement assuming the 600,000 units (a) are not purchased, (b) are purchased. The statement should end with reported earnings per share.

2. Repeat requirement 1, using FIFO.

3. Comment on the above results. Which method should Braxton choose? Why? Be specific.

4. Suppose that in Year 2 the tax rate drops to 40%, prices remain stable, 1.1 million units are sold @ $5, enough units are purchased at $4 so that the ending inventory will be 700,000 units, and other expenses are reduced to $800,000.
   a. Prepare a comparative income statement for the second year showing the impact of each of the four alternatives on net income and earnings per share for the second year.
   b. Explain any differences in net income that you encounter among the four alternatives.
   c. Why is there a difference in ending inventory values under LIFO even though the same amount of physical inventory is in stock?

d. What is the total cash outflow for income taxes for the two years together under the four alternatives?

e. Would you change your answer in requirement 3 now that you have completed requirement 4? Why?

6-69 Eroding the LIFO Base

Many companies on LIFO are occasionally faced with strikes or material shortages that necessitate a reduction in their normal inventory levels in order to satisfy current sales demands. A few years ago several large steel companies requested special legislative relief from the additional taxes that ensued from such events.

A news story stated:

> *As steelworkers slowly streamed back to the mills this week, most steel companies began adding up the tremendous losses imposed by the longest strike in history. At a significant number of plants across the country, however, the worry wasn't losses but profits—"windfall" bookkeeping profits that for some companies may mean painful increases in corporate income taxes.*
>
> *These outfits have been caught in the backfire of a special mechanism for figuring up inventory costs on tax returns. It's known to accountants as LIFO, or last in, first out. Ironically, it's designed to slice the corporate tax bill in a time of rising prices.*
>
> *Biggest Bite—Most of the big steel companies—16 out of the top 20— as well as 40 percent of all steel warehousers, use LIFO accounting in figuring their taxes. But the tax squeeze from paper LIFO profits won't affect them all equally. It will put the biggest bite on warehousers that kept going during the strike—and as a result, the American Steel Warehouse Assn. may ask Congress for a special tax exemption on these paper profits. . . .*
>
> *Companies such as Ryerson and Castle have been caught because they have had to strip their shelves bare in order to satisfy customer demands during the strike. And they probably won't be able to rebuild their stocks by the time they close their books for tax purposes.*

To see how this situation can happen, consider the following example. Suppose a company adopted LIFO in 1976. At December 31, 1997, its LIFO inventory consisted of three "layers":

From 1976:	100,000 units @ $1.00	$100,000
From 1977:	50,000 units @ 1.10	55,000
From 1978:	30,000 units @ 1.20	36,000
		$191,000

In 1998, prices rose enormously. Data follow:

Sales	500,000 units @ $3.00 = $1,500,000
Purchases	340,000 units @ $2.00 = $ 680,000
Operating expenses	500,000

A prolonged strike near the end of the year resulted in a severe depletion of the normal inventory stock of 180,000 units. The strike was settled on December 28, 1998. The company intended to replenish the inventory as soon as possible.
The applicable income tax rate is 60%.

1. Compute the income taxes for 1998.
2. Suppose the company had been able to meet the 500,000-unit demand out of current purchases. Compute the income taxes for 1998 under those circumstances.

Required

6-70 Lower-of-Cost-or-Market

(Alternate is 6-44.) Polaroid Corporation's annual report stated: "Inventories are valued on a first-in, first-out basis at the lower of cost or market value." Assume that severe price competition in 1997 necessitated a write-down on December 31 for a class of camera inventories with a cost of $12 million. The appropriate valuation at market was deemed to be $8 million.

Suppose the product line was terminated in early 1998 and the remaining inventory was sold for $8 million.

Required

1. Assume that sales of this line of camera for 1997 were $19 million and cost of goods sold was $14 million. Prepare a statement of gross margin for 1997 and 1998. Show the results under a strict FIFO cost method in the first two columns and under a lower-of-FIFO-cost-or-market method in the next two columns.
2. Assume that Polaroid did not discontinue the product line. Instead a new marketing campaign spurred market demand. Replacement cost of the cameras in the December 31 inventory was $9 million on January 31, 1998. What inventory valuation would be appropriate if the inventory of December 31, 1997, was still held on January 31, 1998?

6-71 LIFO Liquidation

Maytag Corporation reported 1996 pretax operating income of $269,079,000. Footnotes to Maytag's financial statements read: "Inventories are stated at the lower of cost or market. Inventory costs are determined by the last-in, first-out (LIFO) method for 91% of the company's inventory. . . . If the FIFO method of inventory accounting, which approximates current cost, had been used for all inventories, they would have been $79.5 million and $82.1 million higher than reported at December 31, 1996 and 1995, respectively."

Required

1. Calculate the pretax income that Maytag would have reported if the FIFO inventory method had been used.
2. Suppose Maytag's income tax rate is 34%. What were Maytag's income taxes using LIFO? What would they have been if Maytag had used FIFO?
3. How could Maytag have avoided the extra taxes?

6-72 LIFO Reserve

Brunswick Corporation reported LIFO inventories of $444.9 million on its 1996 balance sheet. A footnote to the financial statements indicated that the "LIFO cost was $83.6 million lower than the FIFO cost of inventories at December 31, 1996."

1. Has the cost of Brunswick's inventory generally been increasing or decreasing? Explain.
2. Suppose Brunswick sold its entire inventory for $600 million in 1997 and did not replace it. Compute the gross profit from the sale of this inventory (a) as Brunswick would report it using LIFO and (b) as it would have been reported if Brunswick had always used FIFO instead of LIFO. Which inventory method creates higher 1997 gross profit? Explain.

6-73 Inventory Errors

IBM had inventories of $5.9 billion at December 31, 1996, and $6.3 billion one year earlier.

1. Suppose the beginning inventory for fiscal 1996 had been overstated by $40 million because of errors in physical counts. Which items in the financial statements would be incorrect? By how much? Use *O* for overstated, *U* for understated, and *N* for not affected. Assume a 40% tax rate.

	Effect on Fiscal Year	
	1996	*1995*
Beginning inventory	O by $40	N
Ending inventory	?	?
Cost of sales	?	?
Gross profit	?	?
Income before taxes on income	?	?
Taxes on income	?	?
Net income	?	?

2. What is the dollar effect of the inventory error on retained earnings at the end of fiscal 1995? 1996?

6-74 LIFO Liquidation

The inventory footnote taken from the 1996 annual report of Monsanto is printed below. Monsanto reported Income Before Income Taxes of $33 million in 1996.

	Inventories	
(in millions)	*1996*	*1995*
Inventories at FIFO cost:		
Finished goods	$258	$266
Goods in process	47	53
Raw materials and supplies	126	145
Inventories, at FIFO cost	431	464
Excess of FIFO over LIFO cost	(140)	(153)
Total	$291	$311

In 1996 and 1995, inventory quantities were reduced, resulting in liquidations of LIFO inventory quantities carried at the lower costs prevailing in prior years. The effects of these liquidations increased pretax income by $5 million in 1996 and were immaterial in 1995.

1. What would Monsanto have reported as Income Before Income Taxes for 1996 had they used FIFO to account for all their inventories?

2. How does the change in the LIFO reserve relate to the effect of the LIFO liquidation?

6-75 Year-End Purchases and LIFO

A company engaged in the manufacture and sale of dental supplies maintained an inventory of gold for use in its business. The company used LIFO for the gold content of its products.

On the final day of its fiscal year, the company bought 10,000 ounces of gold at $380 per ounce. Had the purchase not been made, the company would have penetrated its LIFO layers for 8,000 ounces of gold acquired at $260 per ounce.

The applicable income tax rate is 40%.

1. Compute the effect of the year-end purchase on the income taxes of the fiscal year.

2. On the second day of the next fiscal year, the company resold the 10,000 ounces of gold to its suppliers. What do you think the Internal Revenue Service should do if it discovers this resale? Explain.

6-76 Comparison of Gross Profit Percentages and Inventory Turnover

JC Penney and Kmart are competitors in the retail business, although they target slightly different markets. The gross margin for each company and average inventory appear below for the indicated years (both have January year ends; 1997 refers to the year ending in January of 1997).

JC Penney

	1997	1995
	(in millions)	
Retail sales	22,653	20,380
Cost of goods sold*	16,043	13,970
Gross profit	6,610	6,410
Average inventory	4,829	3,711

Kmart

	1997	1995
	(millions)	
Retail sales	31,437	34,025
Cost of goods sold*	24,390	25,992
Gross profit	7,047	8,033
Average inventory	6,188	7,317

*Both companies classify costs of occupancy, buying, and warehousing with cost of goods sold.

Calculate gross profit percentages and inventory turnovers for 1995 and 1997 for each company and compare them. What trends do you observe? Which company appears to perform better? To what extent do their different performances seem to relate to their relative positions in the retail market?

Required

6-77 Gross Profit on German Income Statement

Most German companies use an income statement format called a "type-of-cost" format. Consider a slightly simplified version of the 1996 and 1995 income statements of Mannesman AG, the large engineering and manufacturing firm (in millions of German Marks):

	1996	1995
Net sales	DM34,683	DM32,094
Increase in inventories	746	830
Total operating output	35,429	32,924
Cost of goods manufactured	31,204	29,351
Other operating expenses (net)	3,215	2,662
Operating income	DM 1,010	DM 911

Note that the cost of goods manufactured includes the cost of the additional units produced to increase the inventories.

Compute the gross profit and gross profit percentage for Mannesman in 1995 and 1996. Comment on the change in gross profit percentage between 1995 and 1996.

Required

6-78   LIFO and Ethical Issues

Yamaha Instrument Distributors is a wholesaler of electronic instruments. Yamaha has used the LIFO inventory method since 1971. Near the end of 1998 the company's inventory of a particular instrument listed three LIFO layers, two of which were from earlier years and one from 1998 purchases:

	No. of Units	Unit Cost
Layer One	4,000	$40
Layer Two	2,500	50
1998 Purchases	30,000	60
Total available	36,500	

In 1998, Yamaha sold 32,500 units, leaving 4,000 units in inventory.

On December 27, 1998, Yamaha had a chance to buy a minimum of 15,000 units of the instrument at a unit cost of $70. The offer was good for ten days, and delivery would be immediate upon placing the order.

Suki Yamaguchi, chief purchasing manager of Yamaha, was trying to decide whether to make the purchase, and, if it is made, whether to make it in 1998 or 1999. The controller had told her that she should buy immediately, because the company would save $70,000 in taxes. The tax rate is 40%.

Required

1. Explain why $70,000 of taxes would be saved.

2. Are there any ethical considerations that would influence this decision? Explain.

6-79   Inventory Shrinkage

Jim Rivera, owner of Village Hardware Company, was concerned about his control of inventory. In December 19X7, he installed a computerized perpetual inventory system. In April, his accountant brought him the following information for the first three months of 19X8:

Sales	$700,000
Cost of goods sold	590,000
Beginning inventory (per physical count)	130,000
Merchandise purchases	630,000

Rivera had asked his public accounting firm to conduct a physical count of inventory on April 1. The CPAs reported inventory of $140,000.

Required

1. Compute the ending inventory shown in the books by the new perpetual inventory system.

2. Provide the journal entry to reconcile the book inventory with the physical count. What is the corrected cost of goods sold for the first three months of 19X8?

3. Do your calculations point out areas about which Rivera should be concerned? Why?

6-80   Cheating on Inventories

The *Wall Street Journal* reported: "Cheating on inventories is a common way for small businesses to chisel on their income taxes. . . . A New York garment maker, for example, evades a sizable amount of income tax by undervaluing his firm's inventory by 20 percent on his tax return. He hides about $500,000 out of a $2.5 million inventory."

The news story concluded: "When it's time to borrow, business owners generally want profits and assets to look fat." The garment maker uses a different fiscal period for financial statements to his bank: "After writing down the inventory as of Dec. 31, he writes it up six months later when the fiscal year ends. In this way, he underpays the IRS and impresses his banker. Some describe that kind of inventory accounting as WIFL—Whatever I Feel Like."

1. At a 40% income tax rate, what amount of federal income taxes would the owner evade according to the news story?

2. Consider the next year. By how much would the ending inventory have to be understated to evade the same amount of income taxes?

Use the following table and fill in the blanks:

	(in dollars)			
	Honest Reporting		**Dishonest Reporting**	
	First Year	*Second Year*	*First Year*	*Second Year*
Beginning inventory	$ 3,000,000	$?	$ 3,000,000	$?
Purchases	10,000,000	10,000,000	10,000,000	10,000,000
Available for sale	13,000,000	?	13,000,000	?
Ending inventory	2,500,000	2,500,000	2,000,000	?
Cost of goods sold	$10,500,000	$?	$11,000,000	$?
Income tax savings @ 40%*	$ 3,150,000	$?	$?	$?
Income tax savings for two years together	$?		$?	

*This is the income tax effect of only the cost of goods sold. To shorten and simplify the analysis, sales and operating expenses are assumed to be the same each year.

6-81 Manufacturing Costs

Study Appendix 6. Sean O'Neal made custom T-shirts for himself and his friends for years before trying to treat it seriously as a business. January 1, 19X1, he decided to become more serious. He bought some screening equipment for $4,000 that he figured was good for 8,000 screenings. He decided to use units of production depreciation. He acquired 2,000 shirts for $4,000 and rented a studio for $500 per month. During the month he paid an assistant $1,600 and together they created three designs, screened 1,500 shirts, and sold 1,200 at $8 each. At month end, there were 500 shirts unused, 300 finished shirts ready for sale, and Sean was trying to figure out how he was doing.

1. Calculate the cost of goods sold and the value of ending inventory (including raw material and finished goods).

2. Prepare an income statement for Sean's first month of operations. Assume a 30% tax rate.

6-82 The Gap Annual Report

Refer to the financial statements for The Gap in Appendix A. Assume that The Gap uses the periodic inventory procedure and that all "cost of goods sold and occupancy expense" is cost of goods sold.

1. Compute the amount of merchandise inventory purchased during the year ended February 1, 1997. (Hint: Use the inventory T-account.)

2. Suppose The Gap used LIFO instead of FIFO and therefore had inventory at February 1, 1997 of $538,765,000. How would this choice have affected the balance in retained earnings on February 1, 1997?

3. Compute the inventory turnover for The Gap for the year ended February 1, 1997.

4. The Gap has opened more than 200 new stores in each of the last two years. Does the opening of new stores tend to increase or decrease the inventory turnover?

5. Calculate the gross margin percentage for each of the last three years. Comment on any changes.

6-83   Financial Reporting Research

Select an industry and identify two firms within that industry.

Required

1. Identify the inventory accounting method used by each.

2. Calculate gross profit percentages and inventory turnovers for 2 years for each firm. Comment on the comparison and any trends.

COLLABORATIVE LEARNING EXERCISE

6-84   Understanding Inventory Methods

Form groups of three students each. (If there are more than three students in a group, extras can be paired up.) Each student should select or be assigned one of these three inventory methods:

1. Specific identification

2. FIFO

3. LIFO

Consider the following information from the fiscal 1997 annual report of Levitz Corporation, one of the largest specialty retailers of furniture in the United States. Levitz uses the LIFO method to account for its inventories. Amounts are in thousands.

For the Year Ended March 31, 1997:	
Sales	$966,855
Cost of goods sold (using LIFO)	533,555
Other operating expenses	417,283
Operating income	$ 16,017
Purchases of inventory	$562,125
At March 31, 1997:	
Inventories @ LIFO	$169,488
Inventories @ FIFO	180,688
At March 31, 1996:	
Inventories @ LIFO	$140,918
Inventories @ FIFO	151,918

Assume that in fiscal 1998 Levitz had exactly the same physical sales as in fiscal 1997, but prices were 5% higher. Thus, 1998 sales were 1.05 × $966,855 = $1,015,198. Assume that other operating expenses in 1998 were exactly the same as in 1997. Further assume that the physical level of inventories at the end of fiscal 1998 were the same as at the end of fiscal 1997, but because of a 5% price increase on April 1, 1997, purchases of inventories in fiscal 1998 were $560,233. (Note that if there had been no price increase, the purchases of inventories in 1998 would have been $533,555.)

Required

1. Compute both fiscal 1997 and fiscal 1998 operating income for Levitz using the inventory method to which you were assigned. Those using the LIFO and FIFO methods have all the information needed for the calculations. Those using specific identification must make some assumptions, and their operating income numbers will depend on the assumptions made.

2. Explain to the other members of the group how you computed the operating income, including an explanation of how you chose the assumptions you made.

6-85   Internet Case

Go to **http://www.homedepot.com/** to find The Home Depot's home page. From the menu, select *Financial Information,* then select the most recent annual report.

Answer the following questions about The Home Depot:

1. Read the *Summary of Significant Accounting Policies* section of the *Notes to Consolidated Financial Statements*. How are inventories valued and accounted for? Why do you think the company applies its particular costing method?

2. Select *Management's Discussion and Analysis*. What is the amount of gross profit reported for the current year? Has this amount increased or decreased compared to the previous year? What does management believe is the cause of this change?

3. Examine the *Ten Year Financial and Operating Highlights* and *Management's Discussion and Analysis*. What is the amount of the company's inventory turnover that is reported for The Home Depot's most recent fiscal year? Explain its meaning. What could The Home Depot do to increase the turnover even more?

4. Given what you have learned concerning The Home Depot's inventory, how often should the company take a physical inventory? When do you think is an appropriate time for its physical inventory?

LONG-LIVED
ASSETS AND
DEPRECIATION

More than 2,000 Gap stores, and every one has tables, shelves, doors, and walls; expensive assets to support the sales effort.

Learning Objectives

After studying this chapter, you should be able to

1. Measure the acquisition cost of tangible assets such as land, buildings, and equipment.

2. Compute depreciation for buildings and equipment using various depreciation methods.

3. Differentiate financial statement depreciation from income tax depreciation.

4. Explain depreciation's effects on cash flow.

5. Distinguish expenses from expenditures that should be capitalized.

6. Compute gains and losses on disposal of fixed assets.

7. Interpret depletion of natural resources.

8. Account for various intangible assets.

It was the late 1960s, and Don Fisher, like most people of his generation, liked blue jeans and music. Also like many of his peers, he was annoyed that existing clothing stores had disorganized and poorly stocked jeans departments, so he decided to do something about it. He opened a store that sold only blue jeans and music, and called it "Gap" in reference to the generation gap that was the buzz of the times.

That was 1969. Nearly 30 years later, the number of stores operated by The Gap exceeds 2,000. Although the music is now gone, The Gap still offers a wide selection of blue jeans to a market that never seems to tire of their appeal. Keeping more than 2,000 stores, though, costs money. Virtually all stores run by The Gap are leased, but the company still must make a tremendous investment in long-lived assets such as fixtures in order to operate each location. For example, under the balance sheet asset category for "Property and Equipment," leasehold improvements, and furniture and equipment are listed at $836.6 million and $960.5 million, respectively. These assets have useful lives that vary, but they all last longer than the average pair of blue jeans.

By now you should understand how to account for short-lived assets, such as those in inventory. Their costs are easily matched to the single periods in which the associated revenues are recognized. What about assets that are not used up quickly? Many long-lived assets, such as buildings and heavy machinery, produce revenues in numerous periods and their costs must be spread across all of those periods.

How important are long-lived assets? Depending on the industry, they can be the most important assets a company owns. For example, consider the plant and equipment accounts (the main long-lived asset accounts) in the 1996 balance sheets of the following companies (in millions):

Company	Total Assets	Plant and Equipment	
		Total	Percentage
Bethlehem Steel	$ 5,109	$2,420	47%
Sears	36,167	5,878	16
Bankers Trust	120,235	976	1

Why do these numbers vary so greatly? Because different types of businesses require different types of assets. Bethlehem Steel has significant manufacturing facilities. Conversely, Sears has $26 billion in receivables and inventory and only $6 billion in plant, property and equipment. Finally, banks and other financial services companies such as Bankers Trust have primarily financial assets and relatively minor plant and equipment investments in comparison.

As you can imagine, accounting for long-lived assets presents some interesting and unique concerns. The main issue is when to charge the cost of a long-lived asset as an expense on the income statement. For example, if an asset lasts 10 years, how much of its cost should be assigned to each of the 10 years it is used? The answer to this question relies on the method chosen for recording depreciation.

This chapter shows how to account for long-lived assets. Much of our time in this chapter will be spent focusing on depreciation—both understanding the nature of depreciation and learning about the various depreciation methods. We start off, though, with a look at long-lived assets in general.

OVERVIEW OF LONG-LIVED ASSETS

long-lived assets
Resources that are held for an extended time, such as land, buildings, equipment, natural resources, and patents.

tangible assets (fixed assets, plant assets)
Physical items that can be seen and touched, such as land, natural resources, buildings, and equipment.

intangible assets Rights or economic benefits, such as franchises, patents, trademarks, copyrights, and goodwill, that are not physical in nature.

Most business entities hold such major assets as land, buildings, equipment, natural resources, and patents. These **long-lived assets** help produce revenues over many periods by facilitating the production and sale of goods or services to customers. Because these assets are necessary in a company's day-to-day operations, companies do not sell them in the ordinary course of business. Keep in mind, though, that one company's long-lived asset might be another company's short-lived asset. For example, a delivery truck is a long-lived asset for nearly all companies, but a truck dealer would regard a delivery truck as short-lived merchandise inventory.

Not all long-lived assets are the same. They are often divided into tangible and intangible categories. **Tangible assets** (also called **fixed assets** or **plant assets**) are physical items that can be seen and touched. Examples are land, natural resources, buildings, and equipment. In contrast, **intangible assets** are not physical in nature. They generally consist of rights or economic benefits, such as, patents, trademarks, and copyrights.

As you might have guessed, different types of long-lived assets are accounted for differently. In fact, there are a few different methods used just for the various types of tangible assets. Land is unique in that it does not wear out or become obsolete. Therefore it is reported in the financial records at its historical cost. It is not depreciated. Other long-lived assets are used up or worn out, or become obsolete. As these assets expire over time, accountants convert their historical cost to expense.

Exhibit 7-1
Summary of Accounting for Long-Lived Assets

Balance Sheet	Income Statement
Land ⟶	—
Buildings and equipment ⟶	Depreciation
Natural resources ⟶	Depletion
Intangible assets (for example, franchises or patents) ⟶	Amortization

depletion The process of allocating the cost of natural resources to the periods in which the resources are used.

In practice, different words are used to describe the allocation of costs over time. For tangible assets such as buildings, machinery, and equipment, the allocation is called *depreciation*. For natural resources the allocation is called **depletion.** Although it has a broader meaning, **amortization** is typically used specifically to refer to the allocation of the costs of intangible assets to the periods that benefit from these assets. These terms are summarized in Exhibit 7-1.

amortization When referring to long-lived assets, it usually means the allocation of the costs of intangible assets to the periods that benefit from these assets.

ACQUISITION COST OF TANGIBLE ASSETS

The acquisition cost of long-lived assets is the cash-equivalent purchase price, including incidental costs required to complete the purchase, to transport the asset, and to prepare it for use.

LAND

The acquisition cost of land includes charges to the purchaser for the cost of land surveys, legal fees, title fees, realtors' commissions, transfer taxes, and even the demolition costs of old structures that might be torn down to get the land ready for its intended use. Under historical-cost accounting, land is reported in the balance sheet at its original cost.

Of course, after years of rising real estate values and inflation, the carrying amount of land is likely to be far below its current market value. Should land acquired and held since 1936 be placed on a 1998 balance sheet at the 1936 cost? Accountants do exactly that. For example, Weyerhaeuser lists on its balance sheet 5.9 million acres of land at $125 million (only $21 per acre). The current value of the land is in the billions of dollars. In some countries, periodic revaluation of assets is permitted, but in the United States the conservative bias using historical costs is firmly rooted in accounting for land and other long-lived assets.

Objective 1
Measure the acquisition cost of tangible assets such as land, buildings, and equipment.

BUILDINGS AND EQUIPMENT

The cost of buildings, plant, and equipment should include all costs of acquisition and preparation for use. Consider the following example for some used packaging equipment:

Invoice price, gross	$100,000
Deduct 2% cash discount for payment within 30 days	2,000
Invoice price, net	$ 98,000
State sales tax at 8% of $98,000	7,840
Transportation costs	3,000
Installation costs	8,000
Repair costs prior to use	7,000
Total acquisition cost	$123,840

As you can see, total acquisition cost is made up of several individual costs, but the $123,840 would be the total capitalized cost added to the Equipment account. A cost is described as being **capitalized** when it is added to an asset account, as distinguished from

capitalized A cost that is added to an asset account, as distinguished from being expensed immediately.

being "expensed" immediately. In the example above, repair costs are included in the amount that we capitalize, the amount recorded as the cost of the asset. Normally repair costs are expensed in the income statement as incurred. The difference is that repair costs prior to first use are part of getting the asset ready to produce and belong in acquisition cost on the balance sheet. Repair costs to maintain the productive ability of the machine belong in expense in the income statement.

DEPRECIATION OF BUILDINGS AND EQUIPMENT

Objective 2
Compute depreciation for buildings and equipment using various depreciation methods.

depreciable value The amount of the acquisition cost to be allocated as depreciation over the total useful life of an asset. It is the difference between the total acquisition cost and the predicted residual value.

residual value (terminal value, disposal value, salvage value, scrap value) The amount received from disposal of a long-lived asset at the end of its useful life.

useful life (economic life) The time period over which an asset is depreciated.

depreciation schedule The listing of depreciation amounts for each year of an asset's useful life.

Depreciation is frequently misunderstood. It is not a process of valuation. In everyday use, we might say that an auto depreciates in value, meaning that its current market value declines. But to an accountant, depreciation is not a technique for approximating current values such as replacement costs or resale values. It is simply a system for cost allocation. Companies in the United States freely select the depreciation method they believe best portrays their economic circumstance. Thus we will discuss several alternatives. In contrast, in countries such as Japan, Germany, and France, depreciation methods are specified by government (tax) authorities.

Depreciation is one of the key factors distinguishing accrual accounting from cash-basis accounting. If a long-lived asset is purchased for cash, cash-basis accounting would treat the entire cost of the asset as an expense immediately. In contrast, accrual accounting allocates the cost in the form of depreciation over the periods the asset is used, thereby matching expenses with the revenues produced.

The amount of the acquisition cost to be depreciated or allocated over the total useful life of the asset is the **depreciable value.** It is the difference between the total acquisition cost and the predicted residual value. The **residual value,** also known as **terminal value, disposal value, salvage value,** and **scrap value,** is the amount predicted to be received from sale or disposal of a long-lived asset at the end of its useful life. The **useful (or economic) life** of an asset is determined as the shorter of the physical life of the asset before it wears out or the economic life of the asset before it is obsolete.

Given the rapidly increasing speed and decreasing cost of computers in recent times, most companies replace them long before they wear out. That is, their economic life is shorter than their physical life. Sometimes an asset's life is measured directly in terms of the benefit it provides rather than the time period over which it is used. For example, the useful life of a truck might be measured as the total miles to be driven, perhaps 100,000 or 200,000 miles. If a truck were purchased for $50,000, the depreciation would be $.50 per mile if the truck were expected to last 100,000 miles with no salvage value.

Depreciation methods differ primarily in the amount of cost allocated to each period. A list of depreciation amounts for each year of an asset's useful life is called a **depreciation schedule.** We will use the following symbols and amounts to compare the various depreciation schedules for a hypothetical $41,000 company truck:

Symbols	Amounts for Illustration
Let	
C = total acquisition cost on December 31, 19X2	$41,000
R = residual value	$ 1,000
n = useful life (in years or miles)	4 years; 200,000 miles
D = amount of depreciation	Various

Exhibit 7-2

Straight-Line Depreciation Schedule

	Balances at End of Year			
	1	*2*	*3*	*4*
Plant and equipment (at original acquisition cost)	$41,000	$41,000	$41,000	$41,000
Less: Accumulated depreciation (the portion of original cost that has already been charged to operations as expense)	10,000	20,000	30,000	40,000
Net book value (the portion of original cost that will be charged to future operations as expense)	$31,000	$21,000	$11,000	$ 1,000

STRAIGHT-LINE DEPRECIATION

Straight-line depreciation spreads the depreciable value evenly over the useful life of an asset. It is by far the most popular method for corporate reporting to shareholders. In fact, it is used by almost 95% of major companies for at least part of their fixed assets, and 70% use it exclusively.

Exhibit 7-2 shows how our company truck would be displayed in the balance sheet if a straight-line method of depreciation were used. The annual depreciation expense that would appear on the income statement is:

$$Depreciation\ expense = \frac{Acquisition\ cost - Residual\ value}{Years\ of\ useful\ life}$$

$$= \frac{C - R}{n}$$

$$= \frac{\$41,000 - \$1,000}{4} = \$10,000\ per\ year$$

> **straight-line depreciation** A method that spreads the depreciable value evenly over the useful life of an asset.

DEPRECIATION BASED ON UNITS

In some cases, time is not the limiting factor on the useful life of an asset. When physical wear and tear determines the useful life of the asset, accountants often base depreciation on units of service or units of production rather than on the units of time (years) so commonly used. Depreciation based on units of service is called **unit depreciation.** Note that the shipping truck in our example has a useful life of 200,000 miles. Depreciation computed on a mileage basis is:

$$D = \frac{C - R}{n}$$

$$= \frac{\$41,000 - \$1,000}{200,000\ miles}$$

$$= \$.20\ per\ mile$$

> **unit depreciation** A depreciation method based on units of service when physical wear and tear is the dominating influence on the useful life of the asset.

For some assets, such as transportation equipment, this depreciation pattern may have more logical appeal than the straight-line method. However, the unit depreciation method is not widely used, probably for two major reasons:

1. Unit-based depreciation frequently produces approximately the same yearly depreciation amounts as does straight-line depreciation.

2. Straight-line depreciation is easier. Under straight-line, the entire depreciation schedule can be set at the time of acquisition, but under unit depreciation, detailed records of units of service must be kept to determine the amount depreciated each year.

DECLINING-BALANCE DEPRECIATION

accelerated depreciation
Any depreciation method that writes off depreciable costs more quickly than the ordinary straight-line method based on expected useful life.

double-declining-balance depreciation (DDB) The most popular form of accelerated depreciation. It is computed by doubling the straight-line rate and multiplying the resulting DDB rate by the beginning book value.

Any pattern of depreciation that writes off depreciable costs more quickly than does the ordinary straight-line method based on expected useful life is called **accelerated depreciation.** Although an infinite number of accelerated depreciation methods are possible, the most popular form of accelerated depreciation is the **double-declining-balance (DDB) method.** DDB is computed as follows:

1. Compute a rate by dividing 100% by the years of useful life. This result is the straight-line rate. You then double the rate. In our example, the straight-line rate is 100% ÷ 4 years = 25%. The DDB rate would be 2 × 25%, or 50%.
2. To compute the depreciation on an asset for any year, ignore the residual value and multiply the asset's book value at the beginning of the year by the DDB rate. Cease depreciation when the book value reaches the residual value.

The DDB method can be illustrated as follows:

$$\text{DDB rate} = 2 \times (100\% \div n)$$
$$\text{DDB rate, 4-year life} = 2 \times (100\% \div 4) = 50\%$$
$$\text{DDB depreciation} = \text{DDB rate} \times \text{Beginning book value}$$

For year 1: D = .50 ($41,000)
          = $20,500
For year 2: D = .50 ($41,000 − $20,500)
          = $10,250
For year 3: D = .50 [$41,000 − ($20,500 + $10,250)]
          = $5,125
For year 4: D = .50 [$41,000 − ($35,875)]
          = $2,563

Cumulative 3-year total = $35,875

In this example, by coincidence, the depreciation amount for each year happens to be half the preceding year's depreciation. However, this halving is a special case that happens only with a four-year life. Remember, the basic approach of DDB is to apply the depreciation rate to the beginning book value. About 20% of U.S. companies use accelerated depreciation for part of their long-lived assets. While we have illustrated the declining balance method with DDB, other versions use different multiples. For example, the 150% declining balance method simply multiples the straight-line rate by 1.5.

COMPARING AND CHOOSING DEPRECIATION METHODS

Exhibit 7-3 compares the results of straight-line and DDB depreciation for our shipping truck example. Note that the DDB method provides $38,438 of total depreciation and does not allocate the full $40,000 cost to expense. To compensate for this fact, some companies that use DDB change to the straight-line method part way through the asset's depreciable life. This is illustrated in the right-most columns of Exhibit 7-3.

To decide when to change, calculate the straight-line depreciation over the remaining life of the asset given the undepreciated cost. Change methods when the next year's straight-line depreciation first equals or exceeds the amount in the original DDB schedule. During year three DDB gives depreciation of $5,125. Switching to straight-line would give depreciation of $4,625 for the remaining two years. [($10,250 − $1,000) ÷ 2]. DDB is used because it gives a higher depreciation amount. After year three, the undepreciated book value is $5,125. With one year remaining and a $1,000 salvage this gives $4,125 to be

Exhibit 7-3

Depreciation: Two Popular Methods
(assume equipment costs $41,000, four-year life, predicted residual value of $1,000)

	Straight-Line*		Declining Balance at Twice the Straight-Line Rate (DDB)[†]		Modified DDB Switch to Straight-Line in Year 4[‡]	
	Annual Depreciation	*Book Value*	*Annual Depreciation*	*Book Value*	*Annual Depreciation*	*Book Value*
At acquisition		$41,000		$41,000		$41,000
Year 1	$10,000	31,000	$20,500	20,500	$20,500	20,500
Year 2	10,000	21,000	10,250	10,250	10,250	10,250
Year 3	10,000	11,000	5,125	5,125	5,125	5,125
Year 4	10,000	1,000	2,563	2,562	4,125	1,000
Total	$40,000		$38,438		$40,000	

*Depreciation is the same each year, 25% of ($41,000 − $1,000).

[†]100%/4 = 25%. The double rate is 50%. Then 50% of $41,000; 50% of ($41,000 − $20,500); 50% of [$41,000 − ($20,500 + $10,250)]; etc. Unmodified, this method will never fully depreciate the existing book value.

[‡]The switch to straight-line occurs in year 4 and the depreciation amount is the amount required to reduce the book value to the final salvage value.

recorded as straight-line depreciation for year four [($5,125 − $1,000) ÷ 1 year] as shown in the far right-hand column of Exhibit 7-3. Because $4,125 exceeds 2,563, the switch occurs for year four.

Companies do not necessarily use the same depreciation methods for all types of depreciable assets. For example, consider the annual report of Kobe Steel, Ltd., a major Japanese company: "Buildings and structures in all locations and machinery and equipment located in the Kakogawa Works, the Kobe Works, the Takasago Works, the Mooka Plant, and the Chofu Plant are depreciated using the straight-line method, and all other machinery and equipment are depreciated using the declining balance method over estimated useful lives." How does a company choose among the alternatives? In some cases tradition leads one company to select the method used by other companies in its industry to enhance comparability. Sometimes one method provides far superior matching of expense and revenue as units of production would for certain types of equipment and manufacturing processes. Sometimes the method is chosen to present the life-cycle cost of the asset. Suppose a type of equipment requires little maintenance in the first years of its life but increasing maintenance later. Accelerated depreciation with decreasing depreciation charges each year, plus rising maintenance costs each year would provide a somewhat constant cost per year of use and production. Thus the choice depends on the nature of the industry and the equipment and the goals of management.

CONTRASTING INCOME TAX AND SHAREHOLDER REPORTING

In accounting for long-lived assets, reporting to stockholders and reporting to the income tax authorities may differ. Reports to stockholders must abide by GAAP. In contrast, reports to income tax authorities must abide by the income tax rules and regulations. These rules are often consistent with GAAP, but the two sometimes vary. Therefore, there is nothing immoral or unethical, as some might suggest, about keeping two sets of records. In fact, it is necessary.

Objective 3
Differentiate financial statement depreciation from income tax depreciation.

DEPRECIATION ON TAX REPORTS

Congress changes the U.S. tax rules in some way almost every year. However, since 1986 the tax authorities have required the use of the Modified Accelerated Cost Recovery System (MACRS) for computing accelerated depreciation. MACRS approximates declining-balance depreciation over very short lives. MACRS often provides lives for tax purposes much shorter than the real economic life of the depreciable asset.

The short useful lives are a key factor in MACRS. Why? Because under an accelerated method, the shorter the life, the earlier depreciation expense is realized. The earlier the depreciation expense is recognized, the earlier the company gets a reduction in income taxes (remember that higher expenses mean lower net income, which means lower income taxes). MACRS allows for higher depreciation in the early years of an asset's service life than does the straight-line method. When implementing MACRS, Congress purposely included accelerated depreciation with short lives as a means of lowering taxes to encourage companies to invest in long-lived assets.

SHAREHOLDER REPORTING

Although they use MACRS for tax purposes, most companies use straight-line depreciation for shareholder reporting. Tax authorities may use special rates, very short lives, or immediate write-off to increase the tax benefits of investing in long-lived assets, but shareholder reporting is driven by efforts to use depreciation to match the costs of an asset to all the periods in which that asset generates revenues.

There are several practical reasons for adopting straight-line depreciation, namely simplicity, convenience, and the reporting of higher earnings in early years than would be reported under accelerated depreciation. Managers tend not to choose accounting methods that hurt reported earnings in the early years of long-lived assets. Previously we noted that many firms choose LIFO which reduces earnings in a period of rising prices. But they did so because they were required to use LIFO for financial reporting in order to do so on the tax return. That conformity feature does not exist for depreciation, so firms normally use straight-line for financial reporting and MACRS for tax.

DEPRECIATION AND CASH FLOW

Objective 4
Explain depreciation's effects on cash flow.

Too often, the relationships between depreciation expense, income tax expense, cash, and accumulated depreciation are confused. For example, the business press frequently contains misleading quotations such as ". . . we're looking for financing $3.75 billion. Of that, about 60% will be recovered in depreciation and amortization." As another example, consider a *Business Week* news report concerning an airline company: "And with a hefty boost from depreciation and the sale of $6 million worth of property, its cash balance rose by $10 million in the year's first quarter."

These statements imply that depreciation somehow generates cash. It does not. Depreciation simply allocates the original cost of an asset to the periods in which the asset is used—nothing more and nothing less. Furthermore, accumulated depreciation is merely the portion of an asset's original cost that has already been written off to expense in prior periods—not a pile of cash waiting to be used.

EFFECTS OF DEPRECIATION ON CASH

To illustrate depreciation's relationship to cash, consider Acme Service Company, which began business with cash and common stock equity of $100,000. On the same day, equipment was acquired for $40,000 cash. The equipment had an expected four-year life and a predicted residual value of zero. The first year's operations generated cash sales of

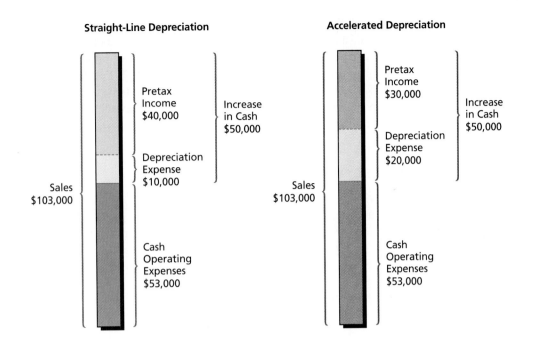

Straight-Line Depreciation

Sales $103,000

Pretax Income $40,000

Depreciation Expense $10,000

Cash Operating Expenses $53,000

Increase in Cash $50,000

Accelerated Depreciation

Sales $103,000

Pretax Income $30,000

Depreciation Expense $20,000

Cash Operating Expenses $53,000

Increase in Cash $50,000

$103,000 and cash operating expenses of $53,000. These facts are depicted visually in the following illustration. Notice that the increase in cash is $50,000 for both straight-line and accelerated depreciation, although the two depreciation methods lead to different amounts of pretax income.

Assume straight-line depreciation of $10,000 and accelerated depreciation of $20,000. Note that the reported before-tax income in Exhibit 7-4 differs as a result of the depreciation method chosen, but cash flow from operations is the same. Comparing the before-tax amounts stresses the role of depreciation expense most vividly. Why? Because before taxes, changes in the depreciation method affect only the accumulated depreciation and retained earnings accounts. The before-tax ending cash balances are completely unaffected.

Exhibit 7-4

Acme Service Company

Income Statement and Statement of Cash Flows for the Year Ended December 31, 19X1 (in thousands)

	Before Taxes		After Taxes	
	Straight-Line Depreciation	*Accelerated Depreciation*	*Straight-Line Depreciation*	*Accelerated Depreciation*
Panel I. INCOME STATEMENT				
Sales	$103	$103	$103	$103
Operating expenses	53	53	53	53
Depreciation expense	10	20	10	20
Pretax income	40	30	40	30
Income tax expense (40%)	—	—	16	12
Net income	$ 40	$ 30	$ 24	$ 18
Panel II. STATEMENT OF CASH FLOWS				
Cash collections	$103	$103	$103	$103
Cash operating expenses	53	53	53	53
Cash tax payments	—	—	16	12
Cash provided by operations*	$ 50	$ 50	$ 34	$ 38

*Sometimes called cash flow from operations or just cash flow. But it is usually simply called cash provided by operations, which is typically defined as cash collected on sales (a) less all operating expenses requiring cash and (b) less income taxes.

One final set of calculations should finish proving that the level of depreciation does not generate cash. Assume depreciation at Acme to now be $40,000, and compute the pretax income and increase in cash. You should have obtained pretax income of only $10,000. However, the increase in cash remains at $50,000. Why? Because cash received from sales is $103,000, and cash expenses are $53,000, leaving $50,000 cash provided by operations regardless of how much depreciation exists, so long as we ignore taxes.

EFFECTS OF DEPRECIATION ON INCOME TAXES

Now consider the after-tax portions of Exhibit 7-4 in the two right-most columns. Depreciation is a deductible noncash expense for income tax purposes. Thus, the higher the depreciation allowed to be deducted in any given year, the lower the taxable income, and therefore the lower the cash paid for income taxes. In short, if depreciation expense is higher, taxes are lower and more cash is conserved and kept for use in the business.

To emphasize the relationship between depreciation and cash and to simplify the comparison, we assume the depreciation method used for financial reporting is the same as for tax purposes. From the last two columns of Exhibit 7-4, you can see that Acme would pay $16,000 of income taxes using straight-line depreciation but only $12,000 using accelerated depreciation. Therefore, compared with the straight-line depreciation method, the accelerated method conserves $4,000 in cash. Depreciation, then, does not generate cash, but it does have a cash benefit if it results in lower taxes.

CONTRASTING LONG-LIVED ASSET EXPENDITURES WITH EXPENSES

Objective 5
Distinguish expenses from expenditures that should be capitalized.

expenditures The purchases of goods or services, whether for cash or on credit.

Expenditures are purchases of goods or services, whether for cash or on credit. Asset-related expenditures that will benefit more than the current accounting year are capitalized (that is, added to an asset account). Such capital expenditures add new fixed assets or increase the capacity, efficiency, or useful life of an existing fixed asset. In contrast, expenditures that provide a benefit lasting one year or less are charged as expenses in the current year.

THE DECISION TO CAPITALIZE

There are no hard and fast rules about which expenditures can be capitalized, but the topic tends to get the attention of both the public accounting firms and the income tax authorities. Consider whether an engine repair is properly classified as an asset or an expense. The public accountant might want to call it an expense, while an income tax auditor might want to call it an asset. Why? Because public accountants are usually on the alert for any tendencies to understate current expenses through the unjustified charging of a repair to an asset account. In contrast, the income tax auditor is looking for the unjustified charging to an expense account because it provides an immediate income tax deduction.

Wherever doubt exists, there is a tendency in practice to charge an expense rather than an asset account for repairs, parts, and similar items. First, many of these expenditures are minor, so the cost-benefit test of record keeping and the concept of materiality justifies this choice. For instance, many companies have a policy of charging to expense all expenditures that are less than a specified minimum such as $100, $500, or $1,000.

REPAIRS AND MAINTENANCE VERSUS CAPITAL IMPROVEMENTS

Repairs and maintenance costs are necessary to maintain a fixed asset in operating condition. The costs of repairs and maintenance are usually compiled in a single account and are regarded as expenses of the current period. Repairs are sometimes distinguished from maintenance as follows. Repairs include the occasional costs of restoring a fixed asset to its ordinary operating condition after breakdowns, accidents, or damage. Maintenance includes the routine recurring costs of oiling, polishing, painting, and adjusting. However, accountants spend little effort distinguishing between repairs and maintenance expenditures because both are period costs.

However, an **improvement** (sometimes called a **betterment** or a **capital improvement**) is an expenditure that is intended to add to the future benefits from an existing fixed asset by decreasing its operating cost, increasing its rate of output, or prolonging its useful life. Repairs and maintenance maintain the level of an asset's future benefits, while improvements increase those benefits. Improvements are generally capitalized. Examples of capital improvements or betterments include the rehabilitation of an apartment house that will allow increased rents and the rebuilding of a packaging machine that increases its speed or extends its useful life.

Suppose the $40,000 truck with a four-year life and $1,000 salvage value presented earlier in the chapter experiences a major overhaul costing $7,000 at the start of year 3. If this overhaul is judged to extend the useful life of our shipping truck from four to five years, the required accounting would be:

1. Increase the book value of the asset (now $41,000 − $20,000 = $21,000) by $7,000. This increase is usually done by adding the $7,000 to Equipment.

2. Revise the depreciation schedule so that the new unexpired cost is spread over the remaining three years, as follows (assume straight-line depreciation):

	Original Depreciation Schedule		Revised Depreciation Schedule	
	Year	*Amount*	*Year*	*Amount*
	1	$10,000	1	$10,000
	2	10,000	2	10,000
	3	10,000	3	9,000*
	4	10,000	4	9,000
			5	9,000
Accumulated depreciation		$40,000		$47,000†

*New depreciable amount is [($41,000 − $20,000 + $7,000) − $1,000 residual value] = $27,000. New depreciation expense is $27,000 divided by remaining useful life of 3 years, or $9,000 per year.

†Recapitulation:

Original cost	$41,000
Major overhaul	7,000
	48,000
Less residual	1,000
Depreciable cost	$47,000

GAINS AND LOSSES ON SALES OF TANGIBLE ASSETS

So far we have seen how to account for property, plant, and equipment assets, from calculating acquisitions cost to depreciating this cost up to the end of the asset's useful life. Not all assets are retained throughout their life, and when they are sold, gains or losses are inevitable.

improvement (betterment, capital improvement) An expenditure that is intended to add to the future benefits from an existing fixed asset.

Objective 6
Compute gains and losses on disposal of fixed assets.

These gains or losses are usually measured in a cash sale by the difference between the cash received and the net book value (net carrying amount) of the asset given up.

RECORDING GAINS AND LOSSES

Suppose the shipping truck in our earlier example was sold at the end of year 2 for $27,000 when its book value was $21,000. The sale would have the following effects:

A				=	L + SE
+$27,000 [Increase Cash]	−	$41,000 [Decrease Equipment]	+ $20,000 [Decrease Accumulated Depreciation]	=	+ $6,000 [Increase Gain on Sale of Equipment]

Note that the disposal of the equipment requires the removal of its carrying amount or book value, which appears in two accounts, not one. Therefore both the Accumulated Depreciation account and the Equipment account are affected when dispositions occur.

If the selling price were $17,000 rather than $27,000:

+$17,000 [Increase Cash]	−	$41,000 [Decrease Equipment]	+ $20,000 [Decrease Accumulated Depreciation]	=	− $4,000 [Decrease Loss on Sale of Equipment]

The T-account presentations and journal entries for these transactions are in Exhibit 7-5. Note again that both the original cost of the equipment and the accompanying accumulated depreciation must be eliminated when the asset is sold. Of course, the net effect is to eliminate the $21,000 carrying amount of the equipment (cost of $41,000 less accumulated depreciation of $20,000).

INCOME STATEMENT PRESENTATION

In most instances, gains or losses on disposition of plant assets are not significant, so they are buried as a part of "other income" on the income statement and are not separately identified as shown in the following three lines from DuPont's 1996 financial statements.

Sales	$43,810
Other Income	1,340
Total	45,150

Footnote 2 revealed that other income includes $279 million arising from the sales of assets. The $279 million is "not significant" in the sense that it is not a material thing for analysts to understand in evaluating the company. The focus is on ongoing selling activity of chemicals and other products produced to be sold. Occasionally, even large sales of plant, property, and equipment may be immaterial to understanding the company. To put things in perspective, remember that DuPont had $38 billion in assets in 1996.

Other income, including gains from sales of assets, may be included with sales at the very top of the income statement, which is the choice DuPont made. Alternatively, the gain (or loss) may be excluded from the computation of major profit categories such as gross profit or operating profit. Coca-Cola did this in its 1996 income statement in which other income is subtracted after calculating gross profit and operating income.

Exhibit 7-5

Journal and Ledger Entries
Gain or Loss on Sale of Equipment (in thousands of dollars)

Sale at $27,000:

Cash	27		
Accumulated depreciation	20		
Equipment		41	
Gain on sale of equipment		6	

Cash		
27		

Equipment		
* 41	41	

Gain on Sale of Equipment	
	6

Accumulated Depreciation, Equipment	
20	* 20

Sale at $17,000:

Cash	17	
Accumulated depreciation	20	
Loss on sale of equipment	4	
Equipment		41

Cash		
17		

Equipment		
* 41	41	

Loss on Sale of Equipment	
4	

Accumulated Depreciation, Equipment	
20	* 20

*Beginning balance

DEPLETION OF NATURAL RESOURCES

We now turn our attention to another group of long-lived assets—natural resources, such as minerals, oil, and timber (sometimes called wasting assets). Depletion is the accounting measure used to allocate the acquisition cost of natural resources. Depletion differs from depreciation because depletion focuses specifically on the physical use and exhaustion of the natural resources, while depreciation focuses more broadly on any reduction of the economic value of a fixed asset, including physical deterioration and obsolescence.

The costs of natural resources are usually classified as fixed assets. However, buying natural resources is actually like buying massive quantities of inventories under the ground (iron ore) or above the ground (timber). Depletion expense is the measure of that portion of this "long-term inventory" that is used up in a particular period. For example, a coal mine may cost $20 million and originally contain an estimated one million tons of usable coal. The depletion rate would be $20 million ÷ 1 million tons = $20 per ton. If 100,000 tons were mined during the first year, the depletion would be 100,000 × $20, or $2 million for that year. Each year the amount of coal extracted would be measured, and the amount of depletion recorded would be based on that usage.

As our coal mine example shows, depletion is measured on a units-of-production basis. The annual depletion may be accounted for as a direct reduction of the mining asset, or it may be accumulated in a separate contra account similar to accumulated depreciation.

Objective 7
Interpret depletion of natural resources.

AMORTIZATION OF INTANGIBLE ASSETS

Our final category of long-lived assets is intangibles. These assets are not physical in nature. Instead they are rights or claims to expected benefits that tend to be contractual in nature. Examples of intangible assets are patents, copyrights, and franchises.

Intangible assets are accounted for in the same manner as plant and equipment. That is, their acquisition costs are capitalized as assets and are then gradually expensed [amortized] over the estimated useful lives of the assets. Because of obsolescence, the useful lives of intangible assets tend to be shorter than their legal lives.

Objective 8
Account for various intangible assets.

An intangible asset is shown on a company's balance sheet only if the rights to some benefit are purchased. Equally valuable assets may be created by internal expenditures, but they are not recognized as assets in the accounting records. For example, suppose Pfizer paid $5 million to another company for that company's patent on a drug. Pfizer would record the $5 million as an intangible asset and amortize the cost over the useful life of the patent. In contrast, suppose Pfizer spent $5 million to internally develop and patent a new drug. Pfizer would charge the $5 million for this research and development to expense, and the patent would not be recognized as an asset.

Why does this discrepancy exist between external and internal items? The difference arises because it is difficult for management to honestly and objectively value the results of its internal research and development efforts. However, when another company purchases the results of those efforts, the purchase price that is negotiated more realistically measures the value. As a result, GAAP requires that the costs of internal research, advertising, and employee training be immediately expensed, although they surely have expected future benefits.

To gain a better understanding of exactly what constitutes an intangible asset, we will now examine some of those assets in detail.

EXAMPLES OF INTANGIBLE ASSETS

patents Grants by the federal government to an inventor, bestowing (in the United States) the exclusive right for 17 years to produce and sell the invention.

Patents are grants by the federal government to an inventor, bestowing (in the United States) the exclusive right to produce and sell a given invention for 17 years. After that, others can produce and sell the invention themselves. Suppose a company acquires such a patent from the inventor for $170,000. Suppose further that because of fast-changing technology, the economic life of the patent is only five years. The amortization would be over the shorter of the economic or legal life—$170,000 ÷ 5 = $34,000 per year, rather than $170,000 ÷ 17 = $10,000 per year.

copyrights Exclusive rights to reproduce and sell a book, musical composition, film, and similar items.

Copyrights are exclusive rights to reproduce and sell a book, musical composition, film, or similar creative items. These rights are issued (in the United States) by the federal government and provide protection to a company or individual for 75 years. The original costs of obtaining copyrights from the government are nominal, but a company may pay a large sum to purchase an existing asset from the owner. For example, a publisher of paperback books will pay the author of a popular novel in excess of a million dollars for his or her copyright. Although copyrights last for 75 years, their economic lives may be no longer than two or three years, so amortization occurs accordingly.

trademarks Distinctive identifications of a manufactured product or of a service taking the form of a name, a sign, a slogan, a logo, or an emblem.

Trademarks are distinctive identifications of a manufactured product or of a service, taking the form of a name, a sign, a slogan, a logo, or an emblem. An example is an emblem for Coca-Cola or the Prentice Hall logo on the spine of this book. Trademarks, trade names, trade brands, secret formulas, and similar items are property rights with economic lives depending on their length of use. Of course, if you look on Coca-Cola's balance sheet you will see no accounting recognition of its secret formula. It is internally developed, not purchased, so it is not recorded. In fact, the story is that they chose to keep it a secret rather than to patent it because they did not want patent protection to expire and leave others free to produce their product. Similarly, the Coca-Cola balance sheet does not report an intangible asset for its trademark, although Coke has spent millions of advertising dollars creating public awareness of the brand.

If a company has trademarks or other intangible assets that cease to have value, they should be immediately written off as an expense. For example, Brown-Forman Corporation had $60 million of intangible assets associated with the brand California Cooler when it decided the assets no longer provided future benefits. The $60 million expense reduced the company's income before taxes from $218 million to $158 million.

Franchises and **licenses** are legal contracts that grant the buyer the right to sell a product or service. An example is a local McDonald's franchise. The buyer obtains the right to use the McDonald's name, to acquire branded products such as cups and bags, and to share in advertising and special promotions. In exchange, the franchisee promises to follow McDonald's procedures and maintain standards of quality, cleanliness, and pricing. The lengths of the franchises vary from one year to perpetuity. Again, the acquisition costs of franchises and licenses are amortized over their economic lives rather than their legal lives.

franchises (licenses) Privileges granted by a government, manufacturer, or distributor to sell a product or service in accordance with specified conditions.

AMORTIZATION OF LEASEHOLDS AND LEASEHOLD IMPROVEMENTS

A **leasehold** is the right to use a fixed asset (such as a building or some portion thereof) for a specified period of time beyond one year. Leaseholds are frequently classified with plant assets although they are technically intangible assets. A company that owns its own plant clearly counts that plant as a tangible asset. However, if a company has a leasehold or leases its plant, then that company owns only the right to use the leased plant, not the plant itself. Because the leasehold allows for the recognition of future benefits (in this case, the use of the plant) but does not provide for the ownership of a tangible asset, it is an intangible asset.

leasehold The right to use a fixed asset for a specified period of time, typically beyond one year.

Related to a leasehold is a **leasehold improvement,** which occurs when a lessee (tenant) spends money to add new materials to a leased property. These new materials then become part of the leased property and are no longer owned by the lessee. A leasehold improvement can take various forms. Examples are the installation of new fixtures, panels, walls, and air-conditioning equipment that are not permitted to be removed from the premises when a lease expires.

leasehold improvement Investments by a lessee in items that are not permitted to be removed from the premises when a lease expires, such as installation of new fixtures, panels, walls, and air-conditioning equipment.

The costs of leases and leasehold improvements are amortized over the life of the lease, even if the physical life of the leasehold improvement is longer. The straight-line method is used almost exclusively, probably because accelerated methods have not been permitted for income tax purposes.

AMORTIZATION OF DEFERRED CHARGES

Deferred charges are like prepaid expenses—in fact, the two often appear lumped together on a single line of the balance sheet—but deferred charges have longer-term benefits. For example, the costs of relocating a mass of employees to a different geographical area, or the costs of rearranging an assembly line or developing new markets, must be paid before any benefit from these actions is realized. Of course, relocating and developing new markets are not done unless they will provide years worth of benefits. As a result, their costs may be carried forward as deferred charges and written off as expense over a three- to five-year period. This procedure is often described as the amortization of deferred charges.

deferred charges Similar to prepaid expenses, but they have longer-term benefits.

BASKET PURCHASES

Frequently, companies acquire more than one type of long-lived asset for a single overall purchase price. The acquisition of two or more types of assets for a lump-sum cost is sometimes called a **basket purchase.** The acquisitions cost of a basket purchase is always split among assets according to some estimate of relative sales value for the assets. For instance, suppose a company acquires land and a building for $1 million. How much of the $1 million should the company allocate to land and how much to the building? If an appraiser indicates that the market values of the land and the building are $480,000 and $720,000 respectively, the cost would be allocated as follows:

basket purchase The acquisition of two or more types of assets for a lump-sum cost.

	(1)	(2)	(3)	(2) × (3)
	Appraised Value	*Weighting*	*Total Cost to Allocate*	*Allocated Costs*
Land	$ 480,000	480/1,200 (or 40%)	$1,000,000	$ 400,000
Building	720,000	720/1,200 (or 60%)	1,000,000	600,000
Total	$1,200,000			$1,000,000

Allocating a basket purchase cost to the individual assets can significantly affect future reported income if the useful lives of various assets differ. In our example, if less cost is allocated to the land, more cost is allocated to the building, which is depreciable. In turn, depreciation expenses are higher, operating income is lower, and fewer income taxes are paid. Within the bounds of the law, tax-conscious managers load as much cost as possible on depreciable assets rather than on land.

SUMMARY PROBLEMS FOR YOUR REVIEW

PROBLEM ONE

"The net book value of plant assets that appears on the balance sheet is the amount that would be spent today for their replacement." Do you agree? Explain.

SOLUTION TO PROBLEM ONE

Net book value of the plant assets on the balance sheet is the result of deducting accumulated depreciation from original cost. It is a result of cost allocation, not valuation. This process does not attempt to reflect all the technological and economic events that may affect replacement value. Consequently, there is little assurance that net book value will approximate replacement cost.

PROBLEM TWO

"Accumulated depreciation provides cash for the replacement of fixed assets." Do you agree with this quotation from a business magazine? Explain.

SOLUTION TO PROBLEM TWO

Accumulated depreciation does not generate cash. It is the amount of the asset already used up and in no way represents a direct stockpile of cash for replacement.

PROBLEM THREE

Refer to Exhibit 7-3, page 283. Suppose the predicted residual value had been $5,000 instead of $1,000.

Required

1. Compute depreciation for each of the first two years using straight-line and double-declining-balance methods.
2. Assume that DDB depreciation is used and that the equipment is sold for $20,000 cash at the end of the second year. Compute the gain or loss on the sale. Show the

effects of the sale in T-accounts for the equipment and accumulated depreciation. Where and how would the sale appear in the income statement?

3. Assume that straight-line depreciation is used and that the equipment is sold for $20,000 cash at the end of the second year. Compute the gain or loss on the sale. Compare this amount to the gain or loss computed in the previous question.

SOLUTION TO PROBLEM THREE

1.

	Straight-Line Depreciation $= \dfrac{C - R}{n}$	DDB Depreciation = Rate* × (Beginning Book Value)
Year 1	$36,000/4 = $9,000	.50 ($41,000) = $20,500
Year 2	$36,000/4 = $9,000	.50 ($41,000 − $20,500) = $10,250

*Rate = 2(100% ÷ n) = 2(100% ÷ 4) = 50%

2.

Revenue	$20,000
Expense: Net book value of equipment sold is $41,000 − ($20,500 + $10,250), or $41,000 − $30,750 =	10,250
Gain on sale of equipment	$ 9,750

The effect of removing the book value is a $10,250 decrease in assets. Note that the effect of a decrease in Accumulated Depreciation (by itself) is an increase in assets:

Equipment			
Acquisition cost	41,000	Cost of equipment sold	41,000

Accumulated Depreciation, Equipment			
Accumulated depreciation on equipment sold	30,750	Depreciation for:	
		Year 1	20,500
		Year 2	10,250
			30,750

The $9,750 gain is usually shown as a separate item on the income statement as Gain on Sale of Equipment or Gain on Disposal of Equipment or combined with similar transactions as "Other Gains and Losses."

3.

Revenue	$20,000
Expense: $41,000 − ($9,000 + $9,000)	23,000
Loss on sale of equipment	$ 3,000

There is a loss of $3,000 instead of a gain of $9,750 because the book value is $12,750 higher. The amount of gains or losses on disposed-of equipment depends on the depreciation method used.

PROBLEM FOUR

Review the important chapter illustration in the section "Depreciation and Cash Flow" on page 284. Suppose the equipment had been acquired for $80,000 instead of $40,000. The predicted residual value remains zero and the useful life remains four years.

Exhibit 7-6

Acme Service Company
Income Statement and Statement of Cash Flows for the Year Ended December 31, 19X1 (in thousands)

| | Before Taxes | | After Taxes | |
	Straight-Line Depreciation	Accelerated Depreciation	Straight-Line Depreciation	Accelerated Depreciation
Panel I. INCOME STATEMENT				
Sales	$103	$103	$103	$103
Operating expenses	53	53	53	53
Depreciation expense	20	40	20	40
Pretax income	30	10	30	10
Income tax expense (40%)	—	—	12	4
Net income	$ 30	$ 10	$ 18	$ 6
Panel II. STATEMENT OF CASH FLOWS				
Cash collections	$103	$103	$103	$103
Cash operating expenses	53	53	53	53
Cash tax payments	—	—	12	4
	$ 50	$ 50	$ 38	$ 46

1. Prepare a revised Exhibit 7-4. Assume an income tax rate of 40%; round all income tax computations to the nearest thousand.

2. Indicate all items affected by these changes. Also tabulate all differences between the final two columns in your revised exhibit as compared with Exhibit 7-4.

SOLUTION TO PROBLEM FOUR

1. The revised income statements are in Exhibit 7-6.

2. The following comparisons of Exhibits 7-6 and 7-4 are noteworthy. Sales, operating expenses, and cash provided by operations before income taxes are unaffected by the change in depreciation. Because of higher depreciation, net income would be lower in all four columns of Exhibit 7-6 than it would be in Exhibit 7-4. Comparison of the final two columns of the exhibits follows:

| | As Shown in | | |
	Exhibit 7-6	Exhibit 7-4	Difference
Straight-line depreciation	20	10	10 higher
Accelerated depreciation	40	20	20 higher
Income tax expense based on :			
Straight-line depreciation	12	16	4 lower
Accelerated depreciation	4	12	8 lower
Net income based on:			
Straight-line depreciation	18	24	6 lower
Accelerated depreciation	6	18	12 lower
Cash provided by operations based on:			
Straight-line depreciation	38	34	4 higher
Accelerated depreciation	46	38	8 higher

Especially noteworthy is the phenomenon that higher depreciation decreases net income but also decreases cash outflows for income taxes. As a result, cash provided by operations increases.

Highlights to Remember

Long-lived assets are either tangible—physical in nature—or intangible—rights or benefits that are not physical. Depreciation, depletion, and amortization are similar concepts, providing for systematic write-offs of the acquisition costs of long-lived assets over their useful lives. Depletion usually refers to natural resources, depreciation to other tangible assets, and amortization to intangible assets. The acquisition cost includes both the purchase price and all incidental costs necessary to get the asset ready for use.

Land is not depreciated. It remains on the books at acquisition cost. Buildings and equipment can be depreciated using the straight-line method, units of production method, or an accelerated method, such as the double-declining-balance method.

Financial reports to shareholders often differ from the reports to tax authorities. Keeping two sets of records to satisfy these two purposes is necessary, not illegal or immoral.

By itself, depreciation does not provide cash. Customers provide cash. However, depreciation is deductible for income tax purposes. Therefore the larger the depreciation reported on the tax return in any given year, the lower the annual pretax income and subsequent income taxes, and the greater the amount of cash from customers that may be kept by the business instead of being disbursed to the income tax authorities.

Expenditures can be capitalized or expensed. Expenditures with benefits extending beyond the current year should be capitalized—other expenditures should be expensed. When fixed assets are sold, the difference between the amount received from the sale and the book value of the asset is a gain or loss, which is generally included with "other income" on the income statement.

Intangible assets, such as patents, trademarks, or copyrights, are shown on the balance sheet if they were purchased. However, equally valuable items that were generated by internal expenditures are not recorded as assets.

Accounting Vocabulary

accelerated depreciation, p. 282

amortization, p. 279

basket purchase, p. 291

betterment, p. 287

capital improvement, p. 287

capitalized, p. 279

copyrights, p. 290

deferred charges, p. 291

depletion, p. 279

depreciable value, p. 280

depreciation schedule, p. 280

disposal value, p. 280

double-declining-balance depreciation (DDB), p. 282

economic life, p. 280

expenditures, p. 286

fixed assets, p. 278

franchises, p. 290

improvement, p. 287

intangible assets, p. 278

long-lived assets, p. 278

leasehold, p. 291

leasehold improvement, p. 291

licenses, p. 291

patents, p. 290

plant assets, p. 278

residual value, p. 280

salvage value, p. 280

scrap value, p. 280

straight-line depreciation, p. 280

tangible assets, p. 278

terminal value, p. 280

trademarks, p. 290

unit depreciation, p. 281

useful life, p. 280

Assignment Material

QUESTIONS

7-1. Distinguish between *tangible* and *intangible* assets.

7-2. Distinguish between *amortization, depreciation,* and *depletion.*

7-3. "The cash discount on the purchase of equipment is income to the buyer during the year of acquisition." Do you agree? Explain.

7-4. "When an expenditure is capitalized, stockholders' equity is credited." Do you agree? Explain.

7-5. "Accumulated depreciation is a sum of cash being accumulated for the replacement of fixed assets." Do you agree? Explain.

7-6. "The accounting process of depreciation is allocation, not valuation." Explain.

7-7. Criticize: "Depreciation is the loss in value of a fixed asset over a given span of time."

7-8. "Keeping two sets of books is immoral." Do you agree? Explain.

7-9. Compare the choice between straight-line and accelerated depreciation with the choice between FIFO and LIFO. Give at least one similarity and one difference.

7-10. "Most of the money we'll spend this year for replacing our equipment will be generated by depreciation." Do you agree? Explain.

7-11. "Accelerated depreciation saves cash but shows lower net income." Explain.

7-12. Contrast repairs and maintenance expenditures with expenditures for capital improvements or betterments.

7-13. The manager of a division reported to the president of the company: "Now that our major capital improvements are finished, the division's expenses will be much lower." Is this really what he means to say? Explain.

7-14. "The gain on sale of equipment should be reported fully on the income statement." Explain what the complete reporting would include.

7-15. Name and describe four kinds of intangible assets.

7-16. "Internally acquired patents are accounted for differently than externally acquired patents." Explain the difference.

7-17. "Accountants sometimes are too concerned with physical objects." Explain.

7-18. "Improvements by a tenant to leased property cannot be capitalized because they become part of the leased property and therefore belong to the lessor." Do you agree? Explain.

7-19. Promotion expenditures incurred before the opening of a new hotel are often capitalized and amortized over approximately three years. What are such assets called on the balance sheet?

7-20. "In a basket purchase, all assets that are part of the purchase must be depreciated over the same useful lives." Do you agree? Explain.

EXERCISES

7-21 Computing Acquisition Costs

From the following data, calculate the cost to be added to the Land account and the Building account of Edmonton University.

On January 1, 19X9, the university acquired a twenty-acre parcel of land immediately adjacent to its existing facilities. The land included a warehouse, parking lots, and driveways. The university paid $500,000 cash and also gave a note for $2 million, payable at $200,000 per year plus interest of 10% on the outstanding balance.

The warehouse was demolished at a cash cost of $250,000 so that it could be replaced by a new classroom building. The construction of the building required a cash down payment of $3 million plus a mortgage note of $8 million. The mortgage was payable at $250,000 per year plus interest of 10% on the outstanding balance.

Required Prepare journal entries (without explanations) to record the above transactions.

7-22 Government Equipment

An office of the Internal Revenue Service acquired some used computer equipment. Installation costs were $7,000. Repair costs prior to use were $8,000. The purchasing manager's salary is $54,000 per annum and he spent one month evaluating equipment and completing the transaction. The invoice price was $400,000. The seller paid its salesman a commission of 4% and offered the buyer a cash discount of 2% if the invoice was paid within sixty days. Freight costs were $4,400, paid by the agency. Repairs during the first year of use were $9,000.

Required Compute the total capitalized cost to be added to the Equipment account. The seller was paid within 60 days.

7-23 Journal Entries for Depreciation

(Alternates are 7-24 and 7-25.) On January 1, 19X1, the Dayton Auto Parts Company acquired 10 assembly robots for a total of $660,000 cash. The robots had an expected useful life of 10 years and an expected terminal scrap value of $60,000. Dayton uses straight-line depreciation.

Required 1. Set up T-accounts and prepare the journal entries for the acquisition and for the first annual depreciation charge. Post to T-accounts.

2. One of the robots with an original cost of $66,000 on January 1, 19X1, and an expected terminal scrap value of $6,000 was sold for $42,000 cash on December 31, 19X3. Prepare the journal entry for the sale.

3. Refer to requirement 2. Suppose the robot had been sold for $55,000 cash instead of $42,000. Prepare the journal entry for the sale.

7-24 Journal Entries for Depreciation

(Alternates are 7-23 and 7-25.) The USAirways. balance sheet, December 31, 1997, included the following (in millions):

Property and Equipment	
Flight equipment	$5,221
Ground property and equipment	877
Less accumulated depreciation and amortization	(2,527)
	$3,571

Assume that on January 1, 1998, some new maintenance equipment was acquired for $880,000 cash. The equipment had an expected useful life of five years and an expected terminal scrap value of $80,000. Straight-line depreciation was used.

Required 1. Prepare the journal entry that would be made annually for depreciation on the new equipment.

2. Suppose some of the equipment with an original cost of $220,000 on January 1, 1998, and an expected terminal scrap value of $20,000 was sold for $150,000 cash two years later. Prepare the journal entry for the sale.

3. Refer to requirement 2. Suppose the equipment had been sold for $120,000 cash instead of $150,000. Prepare the journal entry for the sale.

7-25 Journal Entries for Depreciation

(Alternates are 7-23 and 7-24.) The Coca-Cola Company balance sheet, December 31, 1996, included the following:

Property, plant, and equipment	$5,581,000,000
Less allowances for depreciation	2,031,000,000
	$3,550,000,000

Note that the company uses "allowances for" rather than "accumulated" depreciation. Assume that on January 1, 1997, some new bottling equipment was acquired for $2.2 million cash. The equipment had an expected useful life of five years and an expected terminal scrap value of $200,000. Straight-line depreciation was used.

Required 1. Prepare the journal entry that would be made annually for depreciation.

2. Suppose some of the equipment with an original cost of $55,000 on January 1, 1997, and an expected terminal scrap value of $5,000 was sold for $30,000 cash two years later. Prepare the journal entry for the sale.

3. Refer to requirement 2. Suppose the equipment had been sold for $45,000 cash instead of $30,000. Prepare the journal entry for the sale.

7-26 Simple Depreciation Computations

A company acquired the following assets:

    a. Conveyor, five-year useful life, $38,000 cost, straight-line method, $5,000 residual value.

    b. Truck, three-year useful life, $18,000 cost, DDB method, $1,500 residual value.

Required Compute the first three years of depreciation.

7-27 Units-of-Production Method

The Rockland Transport Company has many trucks that are kept for a useful life of 300,000 miles. Depreciation is computed on a mileage basis. Suppose a new truck is purchased for $65,000 cash. Its expected residual value is $5,000. Its mileage during Year 1 is 60,000 and during Year 2 is 90,000.

Required
1. What is the depreciation expense for each of the two years?
2. Compute the gain or loss if the truck is sold for $40,000 at the end of Year 2.

7-28 Fundamental Depreciation Approaches

(Alternates are 7-30 and 7-31.) U-Haul acquired some new trucks for $1 million. Their predicted useful life is five years, and predicted residual value is $100,000.

Required Prepare a depreciation schedule similar to Exhibit 7-3, page 283, comparing straight-line and double-declining-balance.

7-29 Units-of-Production, Straight-Line, and DDB

Yukon Mining Company buys special drills for $440,000 each. Each drill can extract about 100,000 tons of ore, after which it has a $40,000 residual value. One such drill was bought in early January, 19X1. Projected tonnage figures for the drill are 30,000 tons in 19X1, 30,000 tons in 19X2, and 15,000 tons in 19X3. Yukon is considering units-of-production, straight-line, or double-declining-balance depreciation for the drill.

Required Compute depreciation for each year under each of the three methods.

7-30 Comparison of Popular Depreciation Methods

(Alternates are 7-28 and 7-31.) Port Angeles Cedar Company acquired a saw for $32,000 with an expected useful life of five years and a $2,000 expected residual value. Prepare a tabular comparison (similar to Exhibit 7-3, p. 283) of the annual depreciation and book value for each year under straight-line and double-declining-balance depreciation. (Note that this is a comparison of methods used for reporting to shareholders. Such methods may differ from those used for reporting to the income tax authorities.)

7-31 Fundamental Depreciation Policies

(Alternates are 7-28 and 7-30.) Suppose the Printing department of Safeco Insurance acquired a new press for $190,000. The equipment's predicted useful life is eight years and predicted residual value is $14,000.

Required Prepare a depreciation schedule similar to Exhibit 7-3 (p. 283), comparing straight-line and double-declining-balance. Show all amounts in thousands of dollars (rounded to the nearest tenth). Limit the schedule to each of the first three years of useful life. Show the depreciation for each year and the book value at the end of each year. (Note that this is a comparison of methods used for reporting to shareholders. Such methods may differ from those used for reporting to the income tax authorities.)

7-32   Balance Sheet Presentation of PPE
Boeing, the world's largest maker of commercial airplanes, had the following items under property, plant, and equipment on its 1996 balance sheet (in millions):

Construction in progress	$ 367
Land	431
Total property, plant, and equipment	6,813
Machines and equipment	7,688
Buildings	6,165
Accumulated depreciation	?

Required

Prepare the property, plant, and equipment section of Boeing's balance sheet in proper form. Include the appropriate amount for accumulated depreciation.

7-33   Accumulated Depreciation
Bethlehem Steel Company reported the following line on its January 1, 1997 balance sheet (in millions):

Buildings, Machinery, and Equipment, net	$2,211.4

A footnote revealed that the original cost of the buildings, machinery, and equipment was $6,135.6 million.

Required

1. Compute Bethlehem Steel's accumulated depreciation on buildings, machinery, and equipment on January 1, 1997.

2. Bethlehem Steel uses an 18-year economic life for computing straight-line depreciation on most of its assets. Are most of their assets more than or less than nine years old? Explain how you can determine this.

7-34   Depreciation, Income Taxes, and Cash Flow
Fleck Company began business with cash and common stock equity of $150,000. The same day, December 31, 19X1, the company acquired equipment for $50,000 cash. The equipment had an expected useful life of five years and a predicted residual value of $5,000. The first year's operations generated cash sales of $160,000 and cash operating expenses of $85,000.

Required

1. Prepare an analysis of income and cash flow for the year 19X2, using the format illustrated in Exhibit 7-4 (p. 285). Assume (a) straight-line depreciation and (b) DDB depreciation. Assume an income tax rate of 40%. Income taxes are paid in cash. The company uses the same depreciation method for reporting to shareholders and to income tax authorities.

2. Examine your answer to requirement 1. Does depreciation provide cash? Explain as precisely as possible.

3. Suppose depreciation were tripled under straight-line and DDB methods. How would before-tax cash flow be affected? Be specific.

7-35   MACRS Versus Straight-Line
Chicago Machinery bought special tooling equipment for $1.5 million. The useful life is five years, with no residual value. For tax purposes, assume MACRS specifies a three-

year, DDB depreciation schedule. Chicago Machinery uses the straight-line depreciation method for reporting to shareholders.

Required
1. Explain the two factors that account for acceleration of depreciation for tax purposes.
2. Compute the first year's depreciation (a) for shareholder reporting and (b) for tax purposes. (Ignore complications in the tax law that are not introduced in this chapter.)

7-36 Leasehold Improvements

Pizza Hut has a 10-year lease on space in a suburban shopping center. Near the end of the sixth year of the lease, Pizza Hut exercised its rights under the lease, removing walls and replacing floor coverings and lighting fixtures. The cost was $150,000. The useful life of the redesigned facilities was predicted to be twelve years.

Required
What accounts would be affected by the $150,000 expenditure? What would be the annual amortization?

7-37 Classic Case from the Business Press

A news story regarding Chrysler Corporation stated:

> Yet the $7.5 billion that John J. Riccardo, its money man, estimates the company will need to finance a recovery over the next five years is huge by any standard. But, says Riccardo, "half is charged to the P&L [profit and loss] as incurred, so we're looking for $3.75 billion. Of that, about 60% will be recovered in depreciation and amortization. That leaves a balance of $1.5 billion over the five years, to be financed through earnings, borrowings, and divestitures. Over the period, that overall number is manageable."

Required
Explain or comment on the following:

1. "Half is charged to the P&L as incurred, so we're looking for $3.75 billion."
2. "Of that, about 60% will be recovered in depreciation and amortization."

7-38 Capital Expenditures

Consider the following transactions:

   a. Acquired building for a down payment plus a mortgage payable.
   b. Paid interest on building mortgage.
   c. Paid principal on building mortgage.
   d. Paid cash dividends.
   e. Paid plumbers for repair of leaky faucets.
   f. Acquired new air-conditioning system for the building.
   g. Replaced smashed front door (not covered by insurance).
   h. Paid travel expenses of sales personnel.
   i. Paid janitorial wages.
   j. Paid security guard wages.

Required
Answer by letter:

1. Indicate which transactions are capital expenditures.
2. Indicate which transactions are expenses in the current year.

7-39 Capital Expenditures

Consider each of the following transactions. For each one, indicate whether it is a capital expenditure (C) or an expense in the current year (E).

a. Paid organization costs to incorporate a new company.

b. Paid a consultant to advise on marketing strategy.

c. Installed new lighting fixtures in a leased building.

d. Paid for routine maintenance on equipment.

e. Acquired a patent for $50,000.

f. Paid for overhaul of machinery that extends its useful life.

g. Developed a patentable product by paying for research and development.

h. Paid for a tune-up on one of the autos in the company's fleet.

7-40 Repairs and Improvements

Yakima Wheat Company acquired harvesting equipment for $90,000 with an expected useful life of five years and an $10,000 expected residual value. Straight-line depreciation was used. During its fourth year of service, expenditures related to the equipment were as follows:

1. Oiling and greasing, $200.

2. Replacing belts and hoses, $450.

3. Major overhaul during the final week of the year, including the replacement of an engine. The useful life of the equipment was extended from five to seven years. The cost was $20,000. The residual value is now expected to be $13,000 instead of $10,000.

Required

Indicate in words how each of the three items would affect the income statement and the balance sheet. Prepare a tabulation that compares the original depreciation schedule with the revised depreciation schedule.

7-41 Disposal of Equipment

The Outpatient Clinic of Eastside Hospital acquired x-ray equipment for $29,000 with an expected useful life of five years and a $4,000 expected residual value. Straight-line depreciation was used. The equipment was sold at the end of the fourth year for $14,000 cash.

Required

1. Compute the gain or loss on the sale. Show the effects of the sale on the balance sheet equation, identifying all specific accounts by name. Where and how would the sale appear on the income statement?

2. (a) Show the journal entries for the transaction in requirement 1. (b) Repeat 2a, assuming that the cash sales price was $5,000 instead of $14,000.

7-42 Gain or Loss on Sales of Fixed Assets

Luigi's Pizza Company purchased a delivery van in early 19X1 for $30,000. It was being depreciated on a straight-line basis over its useful life of five years. Estimated residual value was $5,000. The van was sold in early 19X3 after two years of depreciation had been recognized.

Required

1. Suppose Luigi's Pizza received $22,000 for the van. Compute the gain or loss on the sale. Prepare the journal entries for the sale of the van.

2. Suppose Luigi's Pizza received $16,000 for the van. Compute the gain or loss on the sale. Prepare the journal entries for the sale of the van.

7-43 Depletion

A zinc mine contains an estimated 900,000 tons of zinc ore. The mine cost $13.5 million. The tonnage mined during 19X4, the first year of operations, was 120,000 tons.

1. What was the depletion for 19X4?
2. Suppose that in 19X5 100,000 tons were mined. What depletion expense would be charged for 19X5?

7-44 Various Intangible Assets
Consider the following:

1. On December 29, 19X1, a publisher acquires the paperback copyright for a book by Steven King for $2 million. Most sales of this book are expected to take place uniformly during 19X2 and 19X3. What will be the amortization for 19X2?
2. In 19X1, Company C spent $6 million in its research department, which resulted in new valuable patents. In December 19X1, Company D paid $6 million to an outside inventor for some valuable new patents. How would the income statements for 19X1 for each company be affected? How would the balance sheets as of December 31, 19X1, be affected?
3. On December 28, 19X8, Black Electronics Company purchased a patent for a calculator for $420,000. The patent has ten years of its legal life remaining. Technology changes fast, so Black Electronics expects the patent to be worthless in five years. What will be the amortization for 19X9?

7-45 Various Intangible Assets

1. On December 29, 1998, Sony Corporation purchased a patent on some broadcasting equipment for $600,000. The patent has sixteen years of its legal life remaining. Because technology moves rapidly, Sony expects the patent to be worthless at the end of five years. What is the amortization for 1999?
2. An annual report of Associated Hosts, owner and operator of many restaurants and hotels, including the Beverly Hillcrest Hotel, stated: "It is the company's policy to defer preopening costs during periods of construction of new units or remodeling of existing units and to amortize such costs over a period of 12 to 24 months commencing on the opening date."
   During the year, preopening costs of $582,000 were capitalized. The beginning-of-the-year asset balance for preopening costs was $779,000, and the end-of-the-year balance was $617,000. Compute the amortization for the year.
3. (a) Amgen, a biotech firm with more than $2 billion in revenues, spent more than $500 million in its research departments in 1997, and this resulted in valuable new patents. (b) Suppose that in December 1997, Amgen had paid $500 million to various outside companies for the same new patents. How would the income statement for 1997 have been affected under a and b? How would the balance sheet on December 31, 1997, be affected?

7-46 Various Intangible Assets

1. (a) Dow Chemical Company's annual report indicated that research and development expenditures for the year were $761 million. How did this amount affect operating income, which was $3,087 million? (b) Suppose the entire $761 million arose from outlays for patents acquired from various outside parties on December 30. What would be the operating income for the year? (c) How would Dow's December 31 balance sheet be affected by b?
2. On January 1, American Telephone and Telegraph Company (AT&T) acquired new patents on some communications equipment for $5 million. Technology changes quickly. The equipment's useful life is expected to be five years rather than the seventeen-year life of the patent. What will be the amortization for the first year?

3. Hilton Hotels has an account classified under assets in its balance sheet called preopening costs. A footnote said that these costs "are charged to income over a three-year period after the opening date." Suppose expenditures for preopening costs in 1998 were $2,000,000 and the preopening costs account balance on December 31, 1998, was $1,840,000 and on December 31, 1997, was $2,390,000. What amount was amortized for 1998?

7-47 Basket Purchase

On February 21, 19X2, Speed-Tune, an auto service chain, acquired an existing building and land for $720,000 from a local gas station that had failed. The tax assessor had placed an assessed valuation on January 1, 19X2, as follows:

Land	$220,000
Building	380,000
Total	$600,000

How much of the $720,000 purchase price should be attributed to the building? Why?   **Required**

7-48 Basket Purchase of Sports Franchise

Paul Allen, co-founder of Microsoft, recently purchased the Seattle Seahawks, an NFL football team. Assume a total purchase price of $200 million. The largest assets are the franchise and the contracts. Assume that for reporting to the IRS, the franchise has an indefinite useful life while the contracts have a five-year useful life. Other assets are relatively minor. Suppose the seller shows the following book values of the assets (in millions):

Player contracts	$30
Franchise	50
Total book value	$80

As Allen, if you have complete discretion for tax purposes, how much of the $200 million price would you allocate to the contracts? Explain.   **Required**

PROBLEMS

7-49 Popular Depreciation Methods

(Problem 7-63 is an extension of this problem.) The annual report of Alaska Airlines contained the following footnote:

> *PROPERTY, EQUIPMENT, AND DEPRECIATION—Property and equipment are recorded at cost and depreciated using the straight-line method over the estimated useful lives, which are as follows:*

Aircraft and other flight equipment	14–20 years
Buildings	10–30 years
Capitalized leases and leasehold improvements	Term of lease
Other equipment	3–15 years

Consider a Boeing 727-100 airplane, which was acquired for $26 million. Its useful life is 20 years, and its expected residual value is $4 million. Prepare a tabular comparison of the   **Required** annual depreciation and book value for each of the first three years of service life under straight-line and double-declining-balance depreciation. Show all amounts in thousands of dollars (rounded to the nearest thousand). (Note that this is a comparison of methods used for reporting to shareholders. Such methods may differ from those used for reporting to the income tax authorities.) *Hint:* See Exhibit 7-3, p. 283.

7-50 Depreciation Practices

The 1997 annual report of General Mills, maker of *Wheaties, Cheerios,* and *Betty Crocker* baking products, contained the following (in millions):

	1997	1996
Total land, buildings, and equipment	$2,571.6	$2,508.0
Less accumulated depreciation	1,292.2	1,195.6
Net land, buildings, and equipment	$1,279.4	$1,312.4

During 1997, depreciation expense was $182.8 million, and General Mills acquired land, buildings, and equipment worth $162.5 million. Assume that no gain or loss arose from the disposition of land, buildings, and equipment and that cash of $12.7 million was received from such disposals.

Required

Compute (1) the gross amount of assets written off (sold or retired), (2) the amount of accumulated depreciation written off, and (3) the book value of the assets written off. *Hint:* The use of T-accounts may help your analysis.

7-51 Depreciation

Asahi Chemical Industry Co. Ltd., has sales greater than the equivalent of $11 billion U.S. dollars. The company included the following in its 1996 balance sheet (in millions of yen):

Property, plant and equipment, net of accumulated depreciation (Note 7):	
Buildings	¥ 135,337
Machinery and equipment	188,428
Land	64,817
Construction in progress	20,929
Other	17,233
Total property, plant and equipment	¥ 426,744

Footnote 7 contains the following:

Accumulated depreciation comprises the following (in millions of yen):	
Buildings	¥ 182,957
Machinery and equipment	745,911
Other	72,498
Total accumulated depreciation	¥ 1,001,366

Footnote 2 says: "Depreciation is provided under a declining-balance method at rates based on estimated useful lives of the assets."

Required

1. Compute the original acquisition cost of each of the five assets listed under property, plant, and equipment.
2. Explain why no accumulated depreciation is shown for land or construction in progress.

3. Suppose Asahi had used straight-line instead of declining-balance depreciation. How do you suppose this would affect the values shown above for property, plant, and equipment? How would this influence your estimate of the average age of Asahi's assets?

7-52 Reconstruction of Plant Asset Transactions

The Ford Motor Company's balance sheets included (in millions of dollars):

Ford Motor Company

	December 31	
	1996	*1995*
Property:		
Land, plant, and equipment	$51,698	$48,483
Less accumulated depreciation	(26,176)	(25,313)
Net land, plant, and equipment	25,522	23,170
Unamortized special tools	8,005	8,103
Net property	$33,527	$31,273

The following additional information was available from the notes to the income statement for 1996 (in millions):

Depreciation	$2,644
Amortization	3,272

The account Unamortized Special Tools is increased by new investments in tools, dies, jigs, and fixtures necessary for new models and production processes. These investments are then amortized over various periods. Hence the account is called "unamortized" because its amount will become amortized during future periods.

Hint: Analyze with the help of T-accounts.

Required

1. There were no disposals of special tools during 1996. Compute the cost of new acquisitions of special tools.
2. Suppose the proceeds from the sales of land, plant, and equipment during 1996 were $92 million, and the loss on sale of land, plant, and equipment was $25 million. Compute the original cost *and* the accumulated depreciation of the land, plant, and equipment that was sold.
3. Compute the cost of the new acquisitions of land, plant, and equipment.

7-53 Average Age of Assets

Southwestern Bell Telephone Company provides phone services in Texas and surrounding states. The company had the following on its January 1, 1997, balance sheet (in millions):

Total property, plant, and equipment	$29,347
Less: Accumulated depreciation	17,588
	$11,759

A footnote states that "property, plant, and equipment is depreciated using straight-line method." Annual depreciation expense is approximately $1,800 million.

Required

1. Estimate the average useful life of Southwestern Bell's depreciable assets.
2. Estimate the average age of Southwestern Bell's depreciable assets on January 1, 1997.

7-54 Depreciation, Income Tax, and Cash Flow

(Alternates are 7-55, 7-56, and 7-73.) Sanchez Metal Products Co. had the following balances, among others, at the end of December 19X1: Cash, $300,000; Equipment, $400,000; Accumulated Depreciation, $100,000. Total revenues (all in cash) were $850,000. Cash operating expenses were $550,000. Straight-line depreciation expense was $50,000. If accelerated depreciation had been used, depreciation expense would have been $80,000.

Required

1. Assume zero income taxes. Fill in the blanks in the accompanying table. Show the amounts in thousands.
2. Repeat requirement 1, but assume an income tax rate of 40%. Assume also that Sanchez uses the same depreciation method for reporting to shareholders and to income tax authorities.
3. Compare your answers to requirements 1 and 2. Does depreciation provide cash? Explain as precisely as possible.
4. Assume that Sanchez had used straight-line depreciation for reporting to shareholders and to income tax authorities. Indicate the change (increase or decrease and amount) in the following balances if Sanchez had used accelerated depreciation instead of straight-line: Cash, Accumulated Depreciation, Operating Income, Income Tax Expense, and Retained Income.
5. Refer to requirement 1. Suppose depreciation were tripled under both straight-line and accelerated methods. How would cash be affected? Be specific.

Table for Problem 7-54
(amounts in thousands)

	1. Zero Income Taxes		2. 40% Income Taxes	
	Straight-Line Depreciation	*Accelerated Depreciation*	*Straight-Line Depreciation*	*Accelerated Depreciation*
Revenues	$	$	$	$
Cash operating expenses				
Cash provided by operations before income taxes				
Depreciation expense				
Operating income				
Income tax expense				
Net income	$	$	$	$
Supplementary analysis:				
Cash provided by operations before income taxes	$	$	$	$
Income tax payments				
Net cash provided by operations	$	$	$	$

7-55 Depreciation, Income Taxes, and Cash Flow

(Alternates are 7-54, 7-56, and 7-72.) The 1996 annual report of Kmart, a major retailing company, listed the following property and equipment (in millions):

Property and equipment, at cost	$10,768
Less: Accumulated depreciation	5,028
Property and equipment, net	$ 5,740

The cash balance was $406,000,000.

Depreciation expense during the year was $654,000,000. The condensed income statement follows (in millions):

Revenues	$31,437
Expenses	30,654
Operating income	$ 783

For purposes of this problem, assume that all revenues and expenses, excluding depreciation, are for cash. Thus, cash operating expenses were $30,654,000,000 − $654,000,000 = $30,000,000,000.

Required

1. Kmart uses straight-line depreciation. Suppose accelerated depreciation had been $754,000,000 instead of $654,000,000. Assume zero income taxes. Fill in the blanks in the accompanying table (in millions of dollars).

2. Repeat requirement 1, but assume an income tax rate of 40%. Assume also that Kmart uses the same depreciation method for reporting to shareholders and to income tax authorities.

3. Compare your answers to requirements 1 and 2. Does depreciation provide cash? Explain as precisely as possible.

4. Assume that Kmart had used straight-line depreciation for reporting to shareholders and to income tax authorities. Indicate the change (increase or decrease and amount) in the following balances if Kmart had used accelerated depreciation instead of straight-line during that year: Cash, Accumulated Depreciation, Operating Income, Income Tax Expense, and Retained Income. What would be the new balances in Cash and Accumulated Depreciation?

5. Refer to requirement 1. Suppose depreciation were increased by an extra $300,000,000 under both straight-line and accelerated methods. How would cash be affected? Be specific.

Table for Problem 7-55
(amounts in millions)

	1. Zero Income Taxes		2. 40% Income Taxes	
	Straight-Line Depreciation	Accelerated Depreciation	Straight-Line Depreciation	Accelerated Depreciation
Revenues	$	$	$	$
Cash operating expenses				
Cash provided by operations before income taxes				
Depreciation expense				
Operating income				
Income tax expense				
Net income	$	$	$	$
Supplementary analysis:				
Cash provided by operations before income taxes	$	$	$	$
Income tax payments				
Net cash provided by operations	$	$	$	$

7-56   Depreciation, Income Taxes, and Cash Flow

(Alternates are 7-54, 7-55, and 7-72.) The French auto company, PSA Peugeot Citroen, sells the majority of its cars outside of France. The company's annual report showed the following balances (in millions of French francs):

Revenues	FF173,516	
Operating expenses	171,841	
Operating income	FF 1,675	

PSA Peugeot Citroen had depreciation expense of FF7,089,000,000 (included in operating expenses). The company's ending cash balance was FF2,886,000,000.

PSA Peugeot Citroen reported its property and equipment in the following way (in millions):

Property, plant, and equipment, at cost	FF107,044
Less: Accumulated depreciation	56,835
Net property and equipment	FF 50,209

For purposes of this problem, assume that all revenues and expenses, excluding depreciation, are for cash.

Required

1. PSA Peugeot Citroen used straight-line depreciation. Suppose accelerated depreciation had been FF7,589 million instead of FF7,089 million. Assume zero income taxes. Fill in the blanks in the accompanying table (in thousands of dollars).

2. Repeat requirement 1, but assume an income tax rate of 60%. Assume also that PSA Peugeot Citroen uses the same depreciation method for reporting to shareholders and to income tax authorities.

3. Compare your answers to requirements 1 and 2. Does depreciation provide cash? Explain as precisely as possible.

4. PSA Peugeot Citroen used straight-line depreciation for reporting to shareholders and to income tax authorities. Indicate the change (increase or decrease and amount) in the following balances if PSA Peugeot Citroen had used accelerated depreciation rather than straight-line: Cash, Accumulated Depreciation, Operating Income, Income Tax Expense, and Retained Income. What would be the new balances in Cash and Accumulated Depreciation?

5. Refer to requirement 1. Suppose depreciation were doubled under both straight-line and declining-balance methods. How would cash be affected? Be specific.

Table for Problem 7-56
(amounts in thousands)

	1. Zero Income Taxes		2. 60% Income Taxes	
	Straight-Line Depreciation	*Declining-Balance Depreciation*	*Straight-Line Depreciation*	*Declining-Balance Depreciation*
Revenues	$	$	$	$
Cash operating expenses				
Cash provided by operations before income taxes				
Depreciation expense				
Operating income				
Income tax expense				
Net income	$	$	$	$
Supplementary analysis:				
Cash provided by operations before income taxes	$	$	$	$
Income tax expense				
Net cash provided by operations	$	$	$	$

7-57 Depreciation, Income Taxes, and Cash Flow

Mr. Brandt, president of the Bremen Shipping Company, had read a newspaper story that stated: "The Frankfurt Steel Company had a cash flow last year of 1,500,000 DM, consisting of 1,000,000 DM of net income plus 500,000 DM of depreciation. New plant facilities helped the cash flow, because depreciation was 25 percent higher than in the preceding year." "Cash flow" is frequently used as a synonym for "cash provided by operations," which, in turn, is cash revenue less cash operating expenses and income taxes. (DM stands for Deutschmark, the German unit of currency.)

Brandt was encouraged by the quotation because Bremen Shipping Company had just acquired a vast amount of new transportation equipment. These acquisitions had placed a severe financial strain on the company. Brandt was heartened because he thought that the added cash flow from the depreciation of the new equipment should ease the financial pressures on the company.

The income before income taxes of the Bremen Shipping Company last year (19X8) was 200,000 DM. Depreciation was 200,000 DM; it will also be 200,000 DM on the old equipment in 19X9.

Revenue in 19X8 was 2.1 million DM (all in cash), and operating expenses other than depreciation were 1.7 million DM (all in cash).

In 19X9, the new equipment is expected to help increase revenue by 1 million DM. Operating expenses other than depreciation will increase by 800,000 DM.

1. Suppose depreciation on the new equipment for financial reporting purposes is 100,000 DM. What would be the "cash flow" from operations (cash provided by operations) for 19X9? Show computations. Ignore income taxes.

2. Repeat requirement 1, assuming that the depreciation on the new equipment is 50,000 DM. Ignore income taxes.

3. Assume an income tax rate of 40%. (a) Repeat requirement 1; (b) repeat requirement 2. Assume that the same amount of depreciation is shown for tax purposes and for financial reporting purposes.

4. In your own words, state as accurately as possible the effects on "cash flow" of depreciation. Comment on requirements 1, 2, and 3 above in order to bring out your points. This is a more important requirement than requirements 1, 2, and 3.

7-58 Rental Cars

An annual report of the Hertz rental car company contained the following footnote:

> *Depreciable assets—the provisions for depreciation and amortization are computed on a straight-line basis over the estimated useful lives of the respective assets. . . . Hertz follows the practice of charging maintenance and repairs, including the costs of minor replacements, to maintenance expense accounts. Costs of major replacement of units of property are charged to property and equipment accounts and depreciated. . . . Upon disposal of revenue earning equipment, depreciation expense is adjusted for the difference between the net proceeds from sale and the remaining book value.*

1. Assume that some new cars are acquired on October 1, 1998, for $60 million. The useful life is one year. Expected residual values are $42 million. Prepare a summary journal entry for depreciation for 1998. The fiscal year ends on December 31.

2. Prepare a summary journal entry for depreciation for the first six months of 1999.

3. Assume that the automobiles are sold for $48 million cash on September 30, 1999. Prepare the journal entry for the sale. Automobiles are considered "revenue earning equipment."

4. What is the total depreciation expense for 1999? If the $48 million proceeds could have been predicted exactly when the cars were originally acquired, what would depreciation expense have been in 1998? In 1999? Explain.

7-59 Nature of Research Costs

Katherine Mori, a distinguished scientist of international repute, had developed many successful drugs for a well-established pharmaceutical company. Having an entrepreneurial spirit, she persuaded the board of directors that she should resign her position as vice-president of research and launch a subsidiary company to produce and market some powerful new drugs for treating arthritis. However, she did not predict overnight success. Instead, she expected to gather a first-rate research team that might take three to five years to generate any marketable products. Furthermore, she admitted that the risks were so high that conceivably no commercial success might result. Nevertheless, she had little trouble obtaining an initial investment of $5 million. The Mori Pharmaceuticals Company was 80% owned by the parent and 20% by Katherine.

Katherine acquired a team of researchers and began operations. By the end of the first year of the life of the new subsidiary, $2 million had been expended on research activities, mostly for researchers' salaries, but also for related research costs.

No marketable products had been developed, but Katherine and other top executives were extremely pleased about overall progress and were very optimistic about getting such products within the next three or four years.

Required

How would you account for the $2 million? Would you write it off as an expense in Year 1? Could it be capitalized as an intangible asset? If so, would you carry it indefinitely? Write it off systematically over three years or some longer span? Why? Explain, giving particular attention to the idea of an asset as an unexpired cost.

7-60 Meaning of Book Value

Chavez Company purchased an office building twenty years ago for $1.3 million, $500,000 of which was attributable to land. The mortgage has been fully paid. The current balance sheet follows:

Cash		$300,000	Stockholders'	
Land		500,000	equity	$950,000
Building at cost	$800,000			
Accumulated depreciation	650,000			
Net book value		150,000		
Total assets		$950,000		

The company is about to borrow $1.8 million on a first mortgage to modernize and expand the building. This amounts to 60% of the combined appraised value of the land and building before the modernization and expansion.

Required

Prepare a balance sheet after the loan is made and the building is expanded and modernized. Comment on its significance.

7-61 Capital Expenditures

Disputes sometimes arise between the taxpayer and the Internal Revenue Service regarding whether legal costs should be deductible as expenses in the year incurred or be considered as capital expenditures because they relate to defining or perfecting title to business property.

Consider three examples from court cases:

Example 1

Several years after Rock set up his stone-quarrying business, Smalltown passed an ordinance banning it. Rock spent $1,000 to invalidate the ordinance.

Example 2

Now suppose Rock decided to expand his business. He applied to Smalltown for a permit to build an additional crusher. It was denied because an ordinance prohibited the expansion of nonconforming uses, including quarrying. Rock sued to invalidate the ordinance and won after spending $2,000. He then built the crusher.

Example 3

Smalltown's zoning board established a restrictive building (setback) line across Rock's business property. The line lowered the property's value. Rock spent $3,000 trying unsuccessfully to challenge it.

Indicate whether each example should be deemed (a) an expense or (b) a capital expenditure. Briefly explain your answer.

> **Required**

7-62 Change in Service Life

An annual report of TWA contained the following footnote:

> *Note 2, Change in accounting estimate. TWA extended the estimated useful lives of Boeing 727-100 aircraft from principally sixteen years to principally twenty years. As a result, depreciation and amortization expense was decreased by $9,000,000.*

The TWA annual report also contained the following data: depreciation, $235,518,000; net income, $42,233,000.

The cost of the 727-100 aircraft subject to depreciation was $800 million. Residual values were predicted to be 10% of acquisition cost.

Assume a combined federal and state income tax rate of 46% throughout all parts of these requirements.

> **Required**

1. Was the effect of the change in estimated useful life a material difference? Explain, including computations.

2. The same year's annual report of Delta Air Lines contained the following footnote:

   > *Depreciation—Substantially all of the flight equipment is being depreciated on a straight-line basis to residual values (10% of cost) over a 10-year period from dates placed in service.*

   The Delta annual report also contained the following data: depreciation, $220,979,000; net income, $146,474,000. Suppose Delta had used a 20-year life instead of a 10-year life. Assume a 46% applicable income tax rate. Compute the new depreciation and net income.

3. Suppose TWA had used a 10-year life instead of a 20-year life on its 727-100 equipment. Compute the new depreciation and net income. For purposes of this requirement, assume that the equipment cost $800 million and has been in service one year and that reported net income based on a 20-year life was $42,233,000.

7-63 Disposal of Equipment

(Alternate is 7-64.) Alaska Airlines acquired a new Boeing 727-100 airplane for $26 million. Its expected residual value was $6 million. The company's annual report indicated that straight-line depreciation was used based on an estimated service life of 20 years. In addition, the company stated: "The cost and related accumulated depreciation of assets sold or retired are removed from the appropriate accounts, and gain or loss, if any, is recognized in Other Income (Expense)."

Required Show all amounts in millions of dollars.

1. Assume that the equipment is sold at the end of the sixth year for $22 million cash. Compute the gain or loss on the sale. Show the effects of the sale on the balance sheet equation, identifying all specific accounts by name. Where and how would the sale appear on the income statement?

2. (a) Show the journal entries for the transaction in requirement 1. (b) Repeat 2a, assuming that the cash sales price was $19 million instead of $22 million.

7-64 Disposal of Property and Equipment

(Alternate is 7-63.) Rockwell International is an advanced technology company operating primarily in aerospace and electronics. The company's annual report indicted that both accelerated and straight-line depreciation were used for its property and equipment. In addition, the annual report said: "Gains or losses on property transactions are recorded in income in the period of sale or retirement."

Rockwell received $27.9 million for property that it sold.

Required 1. Assume that the total property in question was originally acquired for $150 million and the $27.9 million was received in cash. There was a gain of $8.5 million on the sale. Compute the accumulated depreciation on the property and equipment sold. Show the effects of the sale on the balance sheet equation, identifying all specific accounts by name.

2. For this requirement, round your entries to the nearest tenth of a million dollars. (a) Show the journal entries and postings to T-accounts for the transaction in requirement 1. (b) Repeat 2a, assuming that the cash sales price was $17.9 million cash instead of $27.9 million.

7-65 Gain on Airplane Crash

A few years ago, a Delta Air Lines 727 crashed in Dallas. The crash resulted in a gain of $.11 per share for Delta. How could this happen? Consider the accounting for airplanes. Airlines insure their craft at market value, $6.5 million for Delta's 727. However, the planes' book values are often much less because of large accumulated depreciation amounts. The book value of Delta's 727 was only $962,000.

Required 1. Suppose Delta received the insurance payment and immediately purchased another 727 for $6.5 million. Compute the effect of the crash on pretax income. Also compute the effect on Delta's total assets.

2. Do you think a casualty should generate a reported gain? Why?

7-66 Disposal of Equipment

Airline Executive reported on an airline as follows:

> *Lufthansa's highly successful policy of rolling over entire fleets in roughly ten years—before the aircrafts have outlived their usefulness—got started in a "spectacular" way when seven first-generation 747s were sold.*
>
> *The 747s were bought six to nine years earlier for $22–28 million each and sold for about the same price.*

Required 1. Assume an average original cost of $25 million each, an average original expected useful life of ten years, a $2.5 million expected residual value, and an average actual life of eight years before disposal. Use straight-line depreciation. Compute the total gain or loss on the sale of the seven planes.

2. Prepare a summary journal entry for the sale.

7-67 Depreciation of Professional Sports Contracts

"Accounting Professor Says the Owners Lost $27 Million" read the headline. Major league baseball players and owners were engaged in contract negotiations. The owners claimed to have lost $43 million in the last year, and the Players Association maintained that the owners had made a profit of as much as $10 million. George Sorter, Professor of Accounting at New York University, fixed the loss at $27 million, primarily because he added back "initial roster depreciation" to adjust the owners' figure. "That depreciation, an amount that arises when a team is purchased and a portion of the purchase price that makes up player contracts is paid off [amortized] over several years, should not be treated as an operating expense," Sorter said. When a team is sold, an amount representing the value of current player contracts is put into an intangible asset account and amortized (or depreciated) over several years.

Required

Explain why such an intangible asset account is created. Should this asset be amortized (or depreciated), thereby reducing income? Why would Professor Sorter eliminate this expense when assessing the financial operating performance of the major league teams?

7-68 Valuation of Intangible Assets of Basketball Team

Suppose that new owners acquired a National Basketball Association team for $72 million. They valued the contracts of their fifteen players at a total of $35 million, the franchise at $36 million, and other assets at $1 million. For income tax purposes, the team amortized the $35 million over five years; therefore they took a tax deduction of $7 million annually.

The Internal Revenue Service challenged the deductions. It maintained that only $3 million of the $72 million purchase price was attributable to the player contracts, and that $32 million of the $35 million in dispute should be attributed to the league franchise rights. Such franchise rights are regarded by the Internal Revenue Service as a valuable asset with an indefinite future life; therefore no amortization is permitted for tax-reporting purposes.

Suppose the operating income for each of the five years (before any amortization) was $10 million.

Required

1. Consider the reporting to the Internal Revenue Service. Tabulate a comparison of annual operating income (after amortization) according to two approaches, (a) the NBA team's and (b) the IRS's. What is the difference in annual operating income?

2. Consider the reporting to shareholders. Reports to shareholders by American companies amortize franchise fees. The NBA team had been using a five-year life for player contracts and a forty-year life for the league franchise rights. Tabulate a comparison of operating income (after amortization) using (a) this initial approach and (b) the approach whereby only $3 million would have been attributed to player contracts. What is the difference in annual operating income?

3. Comment on the results in requirements 1 and 2. Which alternative do you think provides the more informative report of operating results? Why?

7-69 Deferred Charges

Four Seasons Hotels, Inc., the Ontario-based operator of luxury hotels and resorts throughout the world, had the following items under assets in its 1996 balance sheet:

	1996	1995
Deferred Charges	$ 1,969,000	$ 1,991,000
Investment in management contracts	98,437,000	92,615,000

A footnote to the financial statements stated: "The corporation defers development costs directly relating to the negotiation, structuring and execution of new hotel contracts. When the hotel is opened, these deferred charges are reclassified to "Investment in management contracts." The deferred charges associated with new management contracts developed by the Corporation are amortized on a straight-line basis over a 10-year period commencing when the hotel is opened."

Required

1. In 1996 Four Seasons amortized $6,769,000 of investment in management contracts. Compute the amount transferred from deferred charges to investment in management contracts during 1996.

2. Compute the amount of deferred charges capitalized during 1996.

3. Prepare journal entries for amortization of investment in management contracts, for the recognition of deferred charges (assume the expenditures are paid in cash), and for the transfer from deferred charges to investment in management contracts.

4. Explain why investment in management contracts is a legitimate asset to be included on the balance sheet. Also explain why some accountants would not consider it an asset.

7-70 Software Development Costs

Microsoft, Incorporated, is one of the largest producers of software for personal computers. Special rules apply to accounting for the costs of developing software for sale or lease. Such costs are expensed until the technological feasibility of the product is established. Thereafter, they should be capitalized and amortized over the life of the product.

One of Microsoft's divisions began working on some special business applications software for Apple MacIntosh computers. Suppose $800,000 had been spent on the project by the end of 19X1, but it was not yet clear whether the software was technologically feasible.

On about July 1, 19X2, after spending another $400,000, management decided that the software was technologically feasible. During the second half of 19X2, the division spent another $1 million on this project. In December 19X2 the product was announced, with deliveries to begin in March 19X3. No research and development costs for the software were incurred after December 19X2. Projected sales were: 19X3, $800,000; 19X4, $1.4 million; 19X5, $1.2 million; 19X6, $400,000; and 19X7, $200,000.

Required

1. Prepare journal entries to account for the research and development expenses for the software for 19X1 and 19X2. Assume that all expenditures were paid in cash.

2. Would any research and development expenses affect income in 19X3? If so, prepare the appropriate journal entry. Actual 19X3 sales were $800,000.

7-71 Basket Purchase and Intangibles

A tax newsletter stated: "When a business is sold, part of the sales price may be allocated to tangible assets and part to a 'covenant not to compete.' How this allocation is made can have important tax consequences to both the buyer and seller."

A large law firm, organized as a professional services corporation, purchased a successful local firm for $100,000. The purchase included both tangible assets, which have an average remaining useful life of 10 years, and a three-year covenant not to compete. Suppose the buyer has legally supportable latitude concerning how to allocate this amount, as follows:

	Allocation One	Allocation Two
Covenant	$ 66,000	$ 48,000
Tangible assets	34,000	52,000
Total for two assets	$100,000	$100,000

Required

1. For income tax purposes, which allocation would the buyer favor? Why?
2. For shareholder reporting purposes, which allocation would the buyer favor? Why?

7-72 Depreciation Policies and Ethics

Some companies have depreciation policies that differ substantially from the norm of their industry. For example, Cineplex Odeon depreciates its theater seats, carpets, and related equipment over 27 years, much longer than most of its competitors. Another example is Blockbuster Entertainment, which depreciates the videotapes it rents over 36 months. Others depreciate them over a period as short as nine months.

Growing companies can increase their current income by depreciating fixed assets over a longer period of time. Sometimes companies lengthen the depreciable lives of their fixed assets when a boost in income is desired. Comment on the ethical implications of choosing an economic life for depreciation purposes, with special reference to the policies of Cineplex Odeon and Blockbuster.

7-73 The Gap Annual Report

Refer to the financial statements of The Gap in Appendix A. The Gap uses straight-line depreciation for all assets, as explained in Note A. Depreciation and amortization expense was $214,905,000 for the year ended February 1, 1997. For purposes of this problem, assume that all revenues and expenses, except depreciation and amortization, are for cash. Therefore cash expenses for the year ended February 1, 1997 were $4,535,854,000 − $214,905,000 = $4,320,949,000.

Required

1. Suppose The Gap had used DDB instead of straight-line depreciation, and therefore depreciation and amortization expense was $314,905,000 instead of $214,905,000. Assume zero income taxes. Fill in the blanks in the following table (in thousands of dollars).
2. Repeat requirement 1, but assume an income tax rate of 39.5%. Assume also that The Gap uses the same depreciation method for reporting to shareholders and to the IRS.
3. Compare your answers to requirements 1 and 2. Does depreciation provide cash? Explain as precisely as possible.

	1. Zero Income Taxes		2.39.5% Income Taxes	
	Straight-Line Depreciation	*DDB Depreciation*	*Straight-Line Depreciation*	*DDB Depreciation*
Revenues	$	$	$	$
Cash expenses				
Cash provided before income taxes				
Depreciation expense				
Income before income taxes				
Income taxes				
Net income	$	$	$	$
Supplementary analysis:				
Cash provided before income taxes	$	$	$	$
Income taxes				
Net cash provided	$	$	$	$

7-74   Financial Statement Research

Select two distinct industries and identify two companies in each industry.

Required

1. Identify the depreciation methods used by each company.

2. Calculate gross and net plant, property, and equipment as a percentage of total assets for each company. What differences do you observe between industries? Within industries?

3. Do the notes disclose any unusual practices with regard to long-lived assets?

COLLABORATIVE LEARNING EXERCISE

7-75   Accumulated Depreciation

Form groups of at least four students (this exercise can be done as an entire class, if desired). Each student, on his or her own, should select a company and find the fixed asset section of its most recent balance sheet. From the balance sheet (and possibly the footnotes) find the original acquisition cost of property, plant, and equipment (the account title will vary slightly by company) and the accumulated depreciation on property, plant, and equipment. Compute the ratio of accumulated depreciation to original acquisition cost. Also note the depreciation method used and the average economic life of the assets, if given. (For an extra bonus, find a company that uses accelerated depreciation for reporting to shareholders; such companies are harder to find.)

When everyone gets together, make four columns on the board or on a piece of paper. Find the 25% of the companies with the highest ratios and list them in the first column. Then list the 25% with the next highest ratios in the second column, and so on. As a group, make a list of explanations for the rankings of the companies. What characteristics of the company, its industry, or its depreciation methods distinguish the companies with high ratios from those with low ratios?

7-76   Internet Case

Go to **http://www.gap.com/** to find The Gap's home page. Select *Financial Information* from the menu. Choose its most recent annual report.

Answer the following questions about The Gap:

1. Read the *Notes to Consolidated Financial Statements*. What is the nature of The Gap's operations? What type of plant and equipment would you expect would be included in The Gap's plant and equipment section of the balance sheet?

2. In which section of its financial statements does The Gap provide information on the method of depreciation and amortization? What other disclosures concerning depreciable assets are available in this same location?

3. Does The Gap have any intangible assets? What type of intangibles assets are these? Over what period of time are these costs allocated?

4. What does the amount reported on the balance sheet for property and equipment represent—the cost, market value, or other amount? If no additional property and equipment assets are purchased, what will happen to the book value over time?

5. The Gap uses a different method of depreciation for tax purposes. Why do you suppose management decided to do this? What method would The Gap most likely use for tax purposes?

6. How much depreciation and amortization expense did The Gap report as shown on its most recent annual report? Why is this amount not obvious from looking at the income statement? Which financial statement provides this amount?

8

LIABILITIES AND INTEREST

America West Airlines is smaller than some of its competitors but nonetheless has major liabilities for airplanes and frequent flyer miles.

Learning Objectives

After studying this chapter, you should be able to

1 Account for current liabilities.

2 Design an internal control system for cash disbursements.

3 Explain simple long-term liabilities.

4 Understand restructurings and the liabilities they create.

5 Interpret deferred tax liabilities.

6 Locate and understand the contingent liabilities information in a company's financial statements.

7 Use ratio analysis to assess a company's debt levels.

From a marketing perspective, the idea is a simple one. On most of today's major air carriers, you'll earn one mile of free travel credit for every paid mile you fly. Earn enough miles and you can travel to any number of dream destinations. What better way to reward loyal air travelers than with free tickets in the future? Yet the accounting behind the scenes for all this activity is quite a complex matter.

America West Airlines, based in Phoenix, Arizona, began offering its frequent flyer miles in 1987. Its program is called "Flight Fund" and has over one million active members. The miles accrued by members are a liability to the airline because they represent an obligation to provide air travel at some point in the future. This obligation is called "Air Traffic Liability" and appears as a current liability on America West's balance sheet. In fact, the program is now the company's single largest current liability.

The financial impact of this liability is estimated by considering how many people are eligible for free travel, how many will redeem mileage during the current period, and their possible destinations. Historical redemption patterns are factored into the estimation. Once the probable "free" travel is estimated as to the number of people and routes traveled, this free travel must be expressed in financial terms. The valuation technique is referred to as the "incremental cost method" and requires a charge to operations for the accumulated miles. Under this valuation method, the incremental costs reflect the additional gas and other cash costs incurred to serve additional passengers on existing flights. At the end of its most recent fiscal year, America West's air traffic liability amounted to $191.7 million, or 44% of current liabilities.

When individuals seek to buy a car or a house, lenders assess the buyer's financial position carefully and pay special attention to the size of the down payment the buyer will make. The larger the down payment, the more "equity" the borrower has in the purchase, and the more comfortable the lender is in making the loan. Similarly, potential investors in the common stock or bonds of a company carefully evaluate the amount of debt the company has relative to the amount of stockholders' equity to assess the potential risk of their investment. Thus a major element of generally accepted accounting principles in the United States is the careful definition of what constitutes a liability and how best to disclose the liability to readers of financial statements.

LIABILITIES IN PERSPECTIVE

As stated in previous chapters, liabilities are one company's obligations to pay cash or to provide goods and services to other companies or individuals. Liabilities include wages due to employees, payables to suppliers, taxes to the government, interest and principal due to lenders, the loss of a lawsuit and so on. Such obligations usually stem from a transaction with an outside party such as a supplier, a lending institution, or an employee. Accrual accounting recognizes expenses as they occur, not necessarily when they are paid in cash. Whenever an expense is recognized before it is paid, a liability is created.

Investors, financial analysts, management, and creditors consider existing liabilities of the firm when valuing the firm's common stock, when evaluating a new loan to the company, and in making many other decisions. Problems arise when companies appear to have excessive debt or seem to be unable to meet existing obligations. For example, suppliers who normally sell on credit may evaluate a customer's debt level; after concluding that it is excessive, they would refuse to ship new items or may ship only C.O.D. (collect on delivery). Also, lenders may refuse to provide new loans, and customers, worried that the company will not be around long enough to honor warranties, may prefer to buy elsewhere. Of course, once creditors and customers go, a company is not long for this world. Debt problems can snowball quickly.

Once a debt problem gets so bad that the company cannot pay, the creditors can take legal action to collect the debt. Depending on the type of obligation, creditors may be able to force the sale of specific assets, take over the board of directors, or force the company out of business. Because poorly managed debt can cause such problems, financial statements users tend to be very concerned about debt levels. Accountants preparing financial statements are thus careful to disclose fully the company's liabilities.

To get a better understanding of the reporting of liabilities, consider a real example. Exhibit 8-1 shows the balance sheet presentation of liabilities from the annual report of The Timberland Company, a footwear and apparel company known mainly for its boots.

As is common practice, Timberland classifies its liabilities as either current or long-term, which helps financial statement readers interpret the immediacy of the company's obligations. **Long-term liabilities** are those that fall due more than one year beyond the balance sheet date. Conversely, current liabilities fall due within the coming year or within the company's normal operating cycle (if that cycle is longer than a year). Some long-term obligations are paid gradually, in yearly or monthly installments. As the Timberland example illustrates, the current portion of these long-term obligations ($17,778) is included as a part of the company's current liabilities.

long-term liabilities
Obligations that fall due beyond one year from the balance sheet date.

In the general ledger, separate accounts are kept for different liabilities, such as wages, salaries, commissions, interest, and similar items. In the annual report, though, these liabilities may be combined and shown as a single current liability labeled accrued liabilities or accrued expenses payable. Sometimes the adjective accrued is deleted so that these liabilities are labeled simply taxes payable, wages payable, and so on. Similarly, the term accrued may be used, and payable may be deleted.

Exhibit 8-1

The Timberland Company

Consolidated Balance Sheets As of December 31, 1996 and 1995

(Dollars in Thousands, Except Per Share Data)

	1996	1995
Current liabilities		
Current maturities of long-term debt	$ 17,778	$ 7,733
Accounts payable	21,348	25,207
Accrued expenses		
Payroll and related	15,173	7,882
Interest and other	35,753	28,001
Income taxes payable	11,813	892
Total current liabilities	$101,865	$69,715

Liabilities can be measured in different ways. Basically, though, they are best measured in terms of the amount of cash needed to meet or pay off an obligation. For current liabilities, measurement is relatively easy, and the accounting process is straightforward.

ACCOUNTING FOR CURRENT LIABILITIES

Objective 1
Account for current liabilities.

Not all current liabilities are recorded the same way. Some are recorded as a result of a transaction with an outside entity, such as a lender or supplier. Other liabilities are recorded with an adjusting journal entry to acknowledge an obligation arising over time, such as interest or wages. Let's take a look at the accounting procedures for different types of current liabilities.

ACCOUNTS PAYABLE

Accounts payable (or trade accounts payable) are amounts owed to suppliers. Over 90% of major U.S. companies show accounts payable as a separate line under current liabilities on their balance sheet. However, a few combine accounts payable with accrued liabilities. Payments on these amounts tend to be made frequently to the same suppliers. Large sums of money flow through these account payable systems. Therefore, data-processing and internal control systems are carefully designed for these transactions. The key is to assure that checks are only written for legitimate obligations of the company. The internal control system includes checks and balances to assure that products have been ordered, have been received in good condition, and that they are billed at agreed upon prices.

NOTES PAYABLE

When companies take out loans, they must sign promissory notes. A **promissory note** is a written promise to repay the loan principal plus interest at specific future dates. Most promissory notes are payable to banks and are called notes payable.

Balance sheet presentation of notes payable varies. Notes that are payable within one year are shown as current liabilities; others are long-term liabilities. Chevron reports the current portion of long-term debt with notes payable with the descriptive caption, "short-term debt." Merck, a pharmaceutical company included in the Dow, calls a similar account "loans payable and current portion of long-term debt."

Rather than having to apply for small loans one at a time, many companies will create lines of credit with a bank or other lender. A **line of credit** sets up a predetermined maximum amount that a company can borrow from a given lender without significant additional credit checking or other time-consuming procedures. Lines of credit benefit

promissory note A written promise to repay principal plus interest at specific future dates.

line of credit An agreement with a bank to provide automatically short-term loans up to some preestablished maximum.

lenders and borrowers. The lender gets the advantage of not having to run credit checks and extensive paperwork every time the borrower wants a loan. The borrower gets the advantage of having a preset amount of borrowing available.

Companies do not always take out loans from banks to meet short-term needs for credit. **Commercial paper** is a debt contract issued by prominent companies that borrow directly from investors. They may work with financial intermediaries or dealers who match borrowers and lenders. The liability created by commercial paper always falls due in nine months or less, usually in 60 days after issuance.

commercial paper A short-term debt contract issued by prominent companies that borrow directly from investors.

Coca-Cola showed $3.4 billion of loans and notes payable on its 1996 balance sheet, and the accompanying footnotes explained this amount as follows: "On December 31, 1996, we had $3.2 billion outstanding in commercial paper borrowings. In addition, we had $1.1 billion in lines of credit . . . available, under which $0.2 billion was outstanding. Our . . . interest rates for commercial paper were approximately 5.6 and 5.7 percent on December 31, 1996 and 1995, respectively." Coca-Cola borrows more in the commercial paper market than it does from banks because the interest rates are lower in the commercial paper market. However, only companies with the sort of visibility and credit-worthiness of Coca-Cola can issue commercial paper.

ACCRUED EMPLOYEE COMPENSATION

Expenses that have been incurred and recognized on the income statement but not yet paid are accrued liabilities. Some accrued liabilities are obligations to employees for payment of wages. In fact, most companies have a separate current-liability account for such items, with a label such as salaries, wages, and commissions payable. Timberland follows this practice by separately stating "Payroll and Related" accrued liabilities.

In earlier chapters, we assumed that an employee earned, say, $100 per week and, in turn, received $100 in cash on payday. In reality, however, payroll accounting is never that easy. For one, employers must withhold some employee earnings and pay them instead to the government, insurance companies, labor unions, charitable organizations, and so forth.

For example, consider the withholding of income taxes and social security taxes (also called FICA taxes). Assume a company has a $100,000 monthly payroll and, for simplicity, assume that the only amounts withheld are $15,000 for income taxes and $7,000 for social security taxes. The withholdings are not additional employer costs. They are simply part of the employee wages and salaries that are paid instead to third parties. The journal entry for this $100,000 payroll is:

Compensation expense	100,000	
Salaries and wages payable		78,000
Income tax withholding payable		15,000
Social security withholding payable		7,000

A second complication companies must deal with is payroll taxes and fringe benefits. These are employee-related costs in addition to salaries and wages. Payroll taxes are amounts paid to the government for items such as the employer's portion of social security, federal and state unemployment taxes, and workers' compensation taxes. Fringe benefits include employee pensions, life and health insurance, and vacation pay. At many organizations the fringe benefits exceed 30% of salary. Thus a person who earns $30,000 per year in salary, effectively costs the company $39,000 ($30,000 + 30% of $30,000). Liabilities are accrued for each of these costs. If they have not yet been paid at the balance sheet date, they are included among the current liabilities.

Note that the social security taxes are paid in two parts. About half is withheld directly from the employee and a similar amount represents an additional amount paid by the employer. If employers pay an additional FICA tax equal to the $7,000 withheld from the employee and also pay 10% of gross wages into a retirement account, the following journal entry should be made:

Employee Benefit Expense	17,000		
Employer Social Security Payable ...		7,000	
Pension Liability Payable		10,000	

INCOME TAXES PAYABLE

A corporation must pay income taxes as a percentage of its earnings. Instead of paying one lump sum at tax time, corporations make periodic installment payments based on their estimated tax for the year. Therefore the accrued liability for income taxes at year-end is generally much smaller than the annual income tax expense.

To illustrate, suppose a corporation has an estimated taxable income of $100 million for the calendar year 19X0. At a 40% tax rate, the company's estimated taxes for the year are $40 million. Payments must be made as follows:

	April 15	June 15	September 15	December 15
Estimated taxes (in millions)	$10	$10	$10	$10

The final income tax return must be filed, and payment must be made by March 15, 19X1. Suppose the actual taxable income for the year turned out to be $110 million instead of the estimated $100 million. Total tax would then be calculated as $44 million. On March 15, the corporation must pay the $4 million additional tax on the additional $10 million of taxable income. The accrued liability on December 31, 19X0, would appear in the current liability section of the balance sheet as:

Income taxes payable	$4,000,000

For simplicity, the illustration assumed equal quarterly payments. However, the estimated taxable income for a calendar year may change as the year unfolds. The corporation must change its quarterly payments accordingly. Regardless of how a company changes its estimates, there will nearly always be a tax payment or refund due on March 15 and there will be an accrual adjustment at year-end.

CURRENT PORTION OF LONG-TERM DEBT

A company's long-term debt often includes some payments due within a year that should be reclassified as current liabilities. The journal entry for recognizing the current portion of long-term debt reclassifies a noncurrent liability as a current liability. Using the Timberland illustration in Exhibit 8-1, the reclassification journal entry for 1996 would be:

Long-term obligations	17,778	
Current portion of long-term obligations		17,778

SALES TAX

When retailers collect sales taxes, they are collecting on behalf of the state or local government. For example, suppose a 7% sales tax is levied on sales of $10,000. The total collected from the customer must be $10,000 + $700, or $10,700. The transaction would affect the balance sheet as follows:

A	=	L	+	SE
+ 10,700	=	+ 700		+ 10,000
[Increase Cash or Accounts Receivable]		[Increase Sales Tax Payable]		[Increase Sales]

The sales shown on the income statement would be $10,000, not $10,700. The sales tax never affects the income statement. The $700 received for taxes affects the current liability account Sales Tax Payable and is shown on the balance sheet until it is paid to the government. The journal entries (without explanations) are:

Cash or accounts receivable	10,700	
Sales		10,000
Sales tax payable		700
Sales tax payable	700	
Cash		700

Product Warranties

Not all current liabilities can be measured exactly. For example, a sales warranty creates a liability, but warranty claims will arise in the future and cannot be estimated precisely. If warranty obligations are material, they must be accrued when products are sold because the obligation arises then, not when the actual repair services are performed. Ford describes its warranty accounting as follows: "Anticipated costs related to product warranty are accrued at the time of sale."

The estimated warranty expenses are typically based on past experience for replacing or remedying defective products. Although estimates should be close, they are rarely precisely correct. Differences between the estimated and actual results are usually added to or subtracted from the current warranty expense account as additional information unfolds. The accounting entry at the time of sale is:

Warranty expense	600,000	
Liability for warranties (or some similar title)		600,000

To record the estimated liability for warranties arising from current sales. The provision is 3% of current sales of $20 million, or $600,000.

When a warranty claim arises, an entry such as the following is made:

Liability for warranties	1,000	
Cash, accounts payable, accrued wages payable, and similar accounts		1,000

To record the acquisition of supplies, outside services, and employee services to satisfy claims for repairs.

If the estimate for warranty expense is accurate, the entries for all claims will total about $600,000.

Returnable Deposits

Customers occasionally must make money deposits that are to be returned in full, sometimes with interest and sometimes not. Well-known examples of returnable deposits are those for returnable containers such as soft-drink bottles, oil drums, or beer kegs. Also, many landlords require security deposits that are to be returned in full at the end of a lease, as long as the tenants do not cause any damage to the property. These examples are actual exchanges of cash between the user and the seller. The credit-card imprint that your local Blockbuster video store takes serves the same purpose; it assures that videos will be returned. However, because cash only changes hands if Blockbuster charges the credit card because the video is not returned, the act of taking the imprint does not lead to the recording of an item on Blockbuster's financial statements.

Companies that receive deposits record them as a form of payable, although the word payable may not be a part of their specific labeling. The accounting entries by the recipients of deposits have the following basic pattern (numbers assumed in thousands of dollars):

	Interest-Bearing			Non-Interest-Bearing		
1. Deposit	Cash	100		Cash	100	
	Deposits (payable)		100	Deposits (payable)		100
2. Interest recognized	Interest expense	9		No entry		
	Deposits		9			
3. Deposit returned	Deposits	109		Deposits	100	
	Cash		109	Cash		100

The account Deposits is a current liability of the company receiving the deposit. Ordinarily the recipient of the cash deposit may use the cash for investment purposes from the date of deposit to the date of its return to the depositor. For example, landlords may deposit security deposits in interest bearing accounts. In some states the interest earned is kept by the landlord, in others the interest must be paid to the tenant.

UNEARNED REVENUE

Revenues that are collected before services or goods are delivered are called unearned revenue under accrual accounting. These unearned revenues are usually considered current liabilities because they require a company either to deliver the product or service or to make a full refund. Examples include lease rentals, magazine subscriptions, insurance premiums, advance airline or theater ticket sales, and advance repair service contracts. The journal entries to record $100,000 of prepayments for services and the subsequent performance of those services and appropriate revenue recognition would be as follows:

```
Cash ...................................   100,000
    Unearned sales revenue ....................           100,000
To record advance collections from customers.
Unearned sales revenue .....................   100,000
    Sales ...................................           100,000
To record sales revenue when products are
delivered to customers who paid in advance.
```

Unearned revenues are also called revenues collected in advance, but more specific titles may also be used. For example, Dow Jones & Company lists "Unexpired subscriptions," and Wang Laboratories shows "Unearned service revenue." These advance collections are also frequently referred to as deferred credits. Why? Because, as the second entry shows, the ultimate accounting entry is a "credit" to revenue, but such an entry has been deferred to a later accounting period.

INTERNAL CONTROL OVER PAYABLES

Objective 2
Design an internal control system for cash disbursements.

Huge sums flow through corporate bank accounts as sales are collected and payments for goods and services are made. It is important to create internal controls over cash disbursements to assure that all payments involve properly approved and valid obligations of the company. Thus, most disbursement systems require that all payments are made by check. Why? Because prenumbered checks make record keeping easy, and companies can thus trace exactly how much of their money is going where.

Under most payables systems, all checks issued must be supported by source documents. This means that before a check is written a series of steps are completed to document the obligation. One document is the **purchase order** which specifies that the items were ordered by the company at specific prices. A second document is the **receiving report** which indicates that the shipment was received and verifies the number of items and their condition upon receipt. The company does not want to pay for unordered merchandise or merchandise received in damaged condition. Once the purchase order, receiving report, and the invoice from the seller are matched and found to

purchase order A document that specifies the items ordered and the price to be paid by the ordering company.

receiving report A document that specifies the items received by the company and the condition of the items.

invoice A bill from the seller to a buyer indicating the number of items shipped, their price, and any additional costs (such as shipping) along with payment terms, if any.

be in agreement, the check can be issued. The **invoice** is a bill from the seller specifying number of units and price per unit along with freight charges the buyer is responsible to pay, plus any payment terms such as cash discounts for prompt payment or quantity discounts.

Checks in excess of a specified amount typically require additional authorization and must be signed by two people (usually by a supervisor, manager, or accountant). This process leaves a paper trail that is easy to follow in case anything should go wrong. It permits periodic, systematic reviews to assure that nothing does go wrong. Because multiple people are involved, errors should be avoided or detected early before their consequences are large.

What can go wrong? An employee could create a bank account for a fictitious company (Fred's Fraud Inc.) and write checks to it. By requiring different employees to create the source documents, keep purchase records, and cut the checks, companies make it harder to succeed with such frauds. More people see the transactions and begin to wonder exactly what sort of business the company does with Fred's Fraud Inc.

With computer automation, a file of approved vendors can be maintained. Checks can be written only to approved vendors, and a high-level employee must approve all additions to the vendor list. Some corporations have created computer networks with their suppliers that generate automatic payments when the proper source information is provided electronically by the supplier.

Even with the best control system, mistakes can and do occur. The most common mistake is overpayment, which is usually caused by multiple billings. For various reasons, such as late payment, suppliers will sometimes send out two or more bills for the same goods. Companies can then mistakenly overpay by paying both bills instead of just one. Fortunately, most companies strive to provide honest and efficient service to both their customers and suppliers. Generally the overpayment is detected by the supplier's internal control system over cash receipts and receivables. The supplier then either refunds the money or provides a credit on the payer's account with the supplier.

LONG-TERM LIABILITIES

Objective 3
Explain simple long-term liabilities.

We have seen how companies report short-term liabilities and will now turn to long-term liabilities. Some long-term liabilities are similar to short-term liabilities except for the time frame. For example, long-term loans such as car loans or home mortgage loans are similar to notes payable. In these circumstances, money is borrowed and a contract is signed that defines the terms under which the borrower will repay the lender. The accounting for these contracts involves reporting the liability on the balance sheet and recording interest expense in the income statement. As time passes, interest and principal payments eliminate the loan obligation.

Consider Michelle Young's loan to purchase a $14,000 car on January 1, 19X0. She has only $4,000 cash, so she borrows $10,000 at 10% interest, agreeing to pay $3,154.71 each December 31 from 19X0 through 19X3. (Normally payments would be made monthly, but for simplicity we assume annual payments.) The loan is illustrated in Exhibit 8-2.

Michelle's total payments are $12,618.83, which consists of interest of $2,618.83 and her repayment of the $10,000 principal. These amounts are the totals of columns 2, 3 and 4 in Exhibit 8-2. Notice that her payments are $3,154.71 for three years and one cent less in the final year. In the first year the payment includes $1,000 in interest (10% × $10,000 of principal). The remainder of the payment, $2,154.71, is applied to reduce the principal amount to $7,845.29 as shown in column 5. That new balance then becomes the basis for interest calculation in year two. The journal entry to record the first year payment would be:

```
Interest expense  . . . . . . .    1,000.00
Principal  . . . . . . . . . . . . .    2,154.71
        Cash  . . . . . . . . . . . .              3,154.71
```

BONDS AND NOTES

Notes and bonds are common financial contracts that businesses use to raise money. Both are legal contracts that specify how much is to be borrowed as well as the dates and amounts for repayment by the borrower. Notes and bonds are often called **negotiable** financial instruments or securities because they can be transferred from one lender to another (thus the term negotiable). Sometimes these securities are created to borrow directly from a financial institution such as a pension plan or insurance company. Notes and bonds issued for these purposes are known as **private placements** because they are not held or traded among the general public. Private placements provide over half the capital borrowed by corporations in the United States. They are popular because they are generally easy to arrange and because they allow the lender to evaluate the creditworthiness of the borrower very carefully and directly.

Corporations have heavy demands for borrowed capital, so they often borrow from the general public by issuing bonds in the financial markets. **Bonds** are formal certificates of debt that include (1) a promise to pay interest in cash at a specified annual rate (often called the **nominal interest rate, contractual rate, coupon rate,** or **stated rate**) plus (2) a promise to pay the **principal** (often called the **face amount**) of the loan amount at a specific maturity date. The interest is usually paid every six months. Fundamentally, bonds are individual promissory notes issued to many lenders.

The **interest rate** on the bond represents the return the lender earns for loaning the money. A basic principle about interest is that lenders charge higher interest rates for riskier loans. Compare a $1,000 bond issued by the U.S. government and a $1,000 bond issued by Apple Computer. In 1998, the U.S. government bond might pay interest of 6% per year while the Apple Computer bond might pay interest of 12% per year.

BOND ACCOUNTING

Suppose that on December 31, 2000, a company issued 10,000 two-year, 10% debentures, at par. Par means that the company received exactly the amount of the bond principal. Bonds typically have a principal or face value of $1,000 each. Thus, in this case the total issue is for $10 million (10,000 × $1,000). Exhibit 8-3 shows how the issuer would account for the bonds throughout their life, assuming that they are held to maturity. The interest expense equals the amount of the interest payments, 5% × $10 million = $500,000 each six months. The interest expense (and the cash payments for interest) totals $2,000,000 over the four semiannual periods. The journal entries for the issue follow:

negotiable Legal financial contracts that can be transferred from one lender to another.

private placement A process whereby notes are issued by corporations when money is borrowed from a few sources, not from the general public.

bonds Formal certificates of indebtedness that are typically accompanied by (1) a promise to pay interest in cash at a specified annual rate plus (2) a promise to pay the principal at a specific maturity date.

nominal interest rate (contractual rate, coupon rate, stated rate) A contractual rate of interest paid on bonds.

principal (face amount) The loan amount that a borrower promises to repay at a specific maturity date.

interest rate The percentage applied to a principal amount to calculate the interest charged.

Exhibit 8-2

Analysis of Car Loan

Year	(1) Beginning Liability	(2) End-of-Year Cash Payment	(3) Interest @ 10% (1) × 0.10	(4) Reduction of Principal (2) − (3)	(5) Ending Liability (1) − (4)
19X0	$10,000.00	$ 3,154.71	$1,000.00	$ 2,154.71	$7,845.29
19X1	7,845.29	3,154.71	784.53	2,370.18	5,475.11
19X2	5,475.11	3,154.71	547.51	2,607.20	2,867.91
19X3	2,867.91	3,154.70	286.79	2,867.91	0.00
		$12,618.83	$2,618.83	$10,000.00	

```
1. Cash ................................  10,000,000
        Bonds payable ....................                    10,000,000
        To record proceeds upon issuance of 10%
        bonds maturing on December 31, 2002.
2. Interest expense .....................     500,000
        Cash ...........................                         500,000
        To record payment of interest each six-
        month period.
3. Bonds payable .......................  10,000,000
        Cash ...........................                      10,000,000
        To record payment of maturity value of
        bonds and their retirement.
```

The issuer's balance sheet at December 31, 2001 (at the end of the first year, after paying semiannual interest) shows:

Bonds payable, 10% due December 31, 2002	$10,000,000

MORTGAGE BONDS AND DEBENTURES

mortgage bond A form of long-term debt that is secured by the pledge of specific property.

Different lenders have different priority claims in collecting their money. For example, **mortgage bonds** are a form of long-term debt that is secured by the pledge of specific property. In case of default, these bondholders can sell the pledged property to satisfy their claims. Moreover, the holders of mortgage bonds have a further unsecured claim on the corporation if the proceeds from the pledged property are not enough to cover the debt.

debenture A debt security with a general claim against all assets rather than a specific claim against particular assets.

In contrast, debenture holders have a lower-priority claim to recover their loan amount. A **debenture** is a debt security with a general claim against the company's total assets, rather than against a particular asset. To see how a debenture bond claim works, suppose a company defaults and is liquidated to repay the creditors. An example of a default would be when a borrower does not make an interest or principal payment at the required time. **Liquidation** means converting assets to cash and terminating or paying off outside claims. After liquidation, a debenture bondholder shares the available assets with other general creditors, such as trade creditors who seek to recover their accounts payable claims.

liquidation Converting assets to cash and terminating or paying off outside claims.

If all claims were of equal priority, each claimant would receive a share in the liquidated assets proportional to his or her percentage of the total claim. But, as we have just seen, not all claims are equal. Mortgage bonds take priority over debenture bonds because they set aside certain assets for the claimants. Interestingly enough, not all general claims are equal, either. Some debenture bonds are **subordinated,** which means that their holders have claims against only the assets that remain after the claims of general creditors are satisfied.

subordinated debentures Debt securities whose holders have claims against only the assets that remain after the claims of general creditors are satisfied.

Exhibit 8-3

Analysis of Bond Transactions: Issued at Par
(in thousands of dollars)

	A	=	L	+	SE
	Cash		Bonds Payable		Retained Income
Issuer's records					
1. Issuance	+10,000	=	+10,000		
2. Semiannual interest (repeated twice a year for two years)	− 500	=			−500 [Increase Interest Expense]
3. Maturity value (final payment)	−10,000	=	−10,000		

To clarify these ideas, suppose a liquidated company had a single asset, a building, that was sold for $110,000 cash. The liabilities total $160,000 as follows:

Liabilities:	
Accounts Payable	$ 50,000
First-Mortgage Bonds	80,000
Subordinated Bonds	30,000
Total Liabilities	$160,000

The mortgage bondholders, having a direct claim on the building, will be paid in full ($80,000). The trade creditors (the company's suppliers, to whom the company owes money) will be paid the remaining $30,000 for their $50,000 claim ($0.60 on the dollar). The subordinated debenture claimants will get what is left over—nothing. Suppose their $30,000 of bonds were not subordinated. The bondholders would have a general claim on assets equivalent to that of the company suppliers. The $30,000 of cash remaining after paying $80,000 to the mortgage holders would then be used to settle the remaining $80,000 claims of the suppliers and bondholders proportionally as follows:

Liabilities:		Payments:	
Accounts Payable	$ 50,000	5/8 × 30,000 =	18,750
First-Mortgage Bonds	80,000		80,000
Unsubordinated Bonds	30,000	3/8 × 30,000 =	11,250
	$160,000		$110,000

In order of priority, we have the mortgage bond, then the debenture and accounts payable, and finally the subordinated debenture. If the interest rate is higher for riskier bonds, you can see that mortgage bonds would have the lowest interest rate, then debentures. Subordinated debentures would carry the highest interest rate.

BOND PROVISIONS

An issue of bonds is usually accompanied by a **trust indenture,** in which the issuing corporation promises a trustee (someone who will look after the interests of the lenders—usually a bank or trust company) that it will abide by stated provisions, often called **protective covenants** or simply **covenants.** The covenant provisions pertain to payments of principal and interest, sales of pledged property, restrictions on dividends, and like matters. In general, the indenture's purpose is to protect the bondholders' interests. Based on our concept of less risky bonds paying lower interest, you can see that these covenants have the ability to make the bond safer and to lower the interest rate.

For example, The Gap, Inc. indicated "Borrowings under the Company's loan and credit agreements are subject to the Company maintaining certain levels of tangible net worth and financial ratios." If The Gap failed to do so, the principal amount of the loans would become due immediately. Timberland's 1996 annual report discloses a credit agreement that "places limitations on the payment of dividends and the incurrence of additional debt, and contains certain other financial and operating covenants." In general, the more covenants there are, the more restricted the borrower is, and the more attractive the security is to the lender.

trust indenture A contract whereby the issuing corporation of a bond promises a trustee that it will abide by stated provisions.

protective covenant (covenant) A provision stated in a bond, usually to protect the bondholders' interests.

CALLABLE, SINKING FUND, AND CONVERTIBLE BONDS

Most companies have an assortment of long-term debt, including a variety of bonds payable. There are too many types of bonds to discuss them all here. However, we can focus on some of the more important and popular types.

callable bonds Bonds subject to redemption before maturity at the option of the issuer.

call premium The amount by which the redemption price of a callable bond exceeds par.

sinking fund bonds Bonds with indentures that require the issuer to make annual payments to a sinking fund.

sinking fund A pool of cash or securities set aside for meeting certain obligations.

convertible bonds Bonds that may, at the holder's option, be exchanged for other securities.

Some bonds are **callable,** which means that they are subject to redemption before maturity at the option of the issuer. Typically the call is at a redemption price in excess of par. The excess over par is referred to as a **call premium.** To illustrate, consider a bond issued in 1995 with a 2015 maturity date, which might be callable any time after 2010. Then it may be subject to call for an initial price in 2010 of 105 (105% of par), in 2011 of 104, in 2012 of 103, and so on. The call premium declines from $50 per $1,000 bond to $40 in 2011 and so on. This feature is good for the borrower because the borrower has a choice to redeem the bond early or wait to maturity. The feature creates uncertainty for the lender who might therefore require a slightly higher interest rate on callable bonds.

Sinking fund bonds require the issuer to make annual payments into a sinking fund. A **sinking fund** is a pool of cash or securities set aside solely for meeting certain obligations. It is an asset that is usually classified as part of a balance sheet category called "investments" or "other assets." The sinking fund helps assure the bondholders that enough cash will be on hand to repay the bond's principal at maturity. These provisions increase the attractiveness of the bond to lenders and lower the interest rate.

Convertible bonds are those bonds that may, at the lenders' option, be exchanged for other securities. The conversion is usually for a preset number of shares of the issuing company's common stock. Because of the conversion feature, convertible bondholders are willing to accept a lower interest rate than on a similar bond without the conversion privilege.

The body of the balance sheet usually summarizes the various types of bonds and other long-term debt on one line with details in the footnotes. Coca-Cola recently listed nine specific bonds and notes totaling $1.1 billion. Most were payable in U.S. dollars, but Coca-Cola is an international company that earns only about one-third of its $18.5 billion in revenues from its U.S. activity. Given Coca-Cola's international focus, it is not surprising that one of the company's bond series is payable in yen and another is payable in German marks.

RESTRUCTURING

Objective 4
Understand restructurings and the liabilities they create.

restructuring A significant makeover of part of the company typically involving the closing of plants, firing of employees, and relocation of activities.

During the 1990's many companies recorded restructuring charges, and some recognized significant liabilities for future costs. A **restructuring** is a significant makeover of part of the company. It typically involves the closing of one or more plants, firing of a significant number of employees, and termination or relocation of various activities. For example, Timberland reported a $16 million restructuring in 1995 and described it as follows in the footnotes (amonts in thousands): "... the Company closed its manufacturing facilities in Boone, North Carolina, and Mountain City, Tennessee, reduced its manufacturing operations in the Dominican Republic and downsized its corporate office workforce due to a reorganized management structure.... Of the total charge for restructuring, $9,914 related to anticipated losses associated with the disposal of assets and was a non-cash item; $3,891 related to payments for contractual lease obligations and expenditures to close idle facilities; and $2,195 related to payments for severance and other employee liabilities." In Timberland's case, most of these actions were actually completed in 1995. Liabilities were recognized for leases and employee terminations at the end of the second quarter of 1995. In the quarterly financial statements these liabilities would have appeared, but they were paid by the end of that year.

Bethlehem Steel recorded a restructuring loss in 1996 equal to 10% of sales. The $465 million restructuring loss involved closing, relocating, and selling various activities. Assets were reduced by $250 million while most of the remainder involved employee related costs. Over 2,000 employees were facing loss of jobs as a result of the decision.

DEFERRED TAXES

We have previously seen that delays in payment of taxes between the time that income is earned and taxes are due leads to short term taxes payable. There is another source of difference between when income is recognized in the financial statements and when it is reported to the tax authorities that arises because of differences between U.S. income tax rules and the GAAP requirements for financial reporting. Sometimes the difference between GAAP reporting and tax laws forces some income tax expense to be recorded long before it is paid and thus creates a deferred income tax liability. For example, GE reported income tax expense of $3.5 billion in its 1996 financial statements. However, GE paid only $1.4 billion in income taxes and deferred the remainder to future years.

Objective 5
Interpret deferred tax liabilities.

The differences arise because GAAP is designed to provide useful information to investors, while the tax code is written to generate revenue for the government. Revenue recognition and expense recognition rules for tax purposes can differ from GAAP rules on two dimensions: (1) *whether* an item is recognized (permanent differences) and (2) *when* it is recognized (temporary differences).

To save their companies money, good managers struggle to pay the least amount of income tax at the latest possible moment permitted within the law. As a result, they delay the reporting of taxable revenue as long as possible, while deducting tax-deductible expense items as quickly as possible. This leads the tax return to report the smallest taxable income consistent with the law and the firm's financial results. Taxes paid to the government are calculated as a percentage of the taxable income that results from subtracting tax deductible expenses from taxable revenue. The percentage is called the **tax rate.** U.S. corporations face graduated tax rates ranging from 15% on incomes under $50,000 to 35% on incomes over $335,000. Many states also levy an income tax, with tax rates varying from state to state. To simplify our illustrations, we will generally assume a flat tax rate of 40%. This is a reasonable approximation of the combination of the federal 35% statutory (legally set) rate plus a state tax rate.

tax rate The percentage of taxable income paid to the government.

Net income before taxes for financial reporting may differ from taxable income because differences in rules create the difference or because managers make different choices of accounting treatment for financial reporting than for tax. Although the company tries to minimize taxable income to minimize taxes, it does not have the same incentive for financial reporting purposes. Reporting higher net income may often be desirable for financial reporting purposes, to increase bonuses or to make the company appear more profitable. For simplicity we will illustrate these issues with one permanent difference, municipal bond interest, and two timing differences, depreciation and warranty expense.

PERMANENT DIFFERENCES

Permanent differences involve either revenue and expense items that are recognized for tax purposes but not recognized under GAAP, or items that are not recognized for tax purposes but are recognized under GAAP. For example, suppose a company owns a bond issued by the city of Seattle and periodically receives interest income on it. Under GAAP, this interest income is reported on the income statement. Under federal law, interest on municipal bonds issued by cities, states, and towns is not taxed. Dealing with this permanent difference is straightforward. It is included as income for financial reporting but no income tax expense is recognized because no income tax will ever be paid. Thus permanent differences do not have a tax effect.

permanent differences
Revenue or expense items that are recognized for tax purposes but not recognized under GAAP, or vice versa.

TEMPORARY DIFFERENCES

Temporary or **timing differences** arise because some revenue and expense items are recognized at different times for tax purposes than for financial reporting purposes. A common temporary difference arises when firms use a special accelerated depreciation (MACRS) for tax purposes, while using straight-line depreciation for financial reporting. Suppose a small company earns $40,000 per year before deducting depreciation and taxes and pays taxes at a rate of 40% of taxable income. The company acquires a $10,000 asset with a two-year useful life. It can deduct the $10,000 immediately for tax purposes and will depreciate it at $5,000 per year for book purposes.

timing differences (temporary differences)
Differences between net income and taxable income that arise because some revenue and expense items are recognized at different times for tax purposes than for reporting purposes.

	Financial Reporting		Income Tax Return	
	Year 1	Year 2	Year 1	Year 2
Income before depreciation and taxes	$40,000	$40,000	$40,000	$40,000
Depreciation	5,000	5,000	10,000	0
Pretax income	$35,000	$35,000	$30,000	$40,000
Taxes payable at 40%			$12,000	$16,000

The total tax paid to the government over the two years will be $12,000 + $16,000 = $28,000, which is 40% of the two years of combined taxable income $30,000 + $40,000 = $70,000. How should this fact be shown for financial reporting purposes? One approach is to report the amount actually paid to the government each year, but the FASB does not permit this alternative. When timing differences arise, GAAP requires a hypothetical tax expense number. It is the tax that would have been paid if the pretax income used for shareholder reporting had also been reported to the tax authorities. Both approaches are illustrated in the following table.

	Tax Expense Based on Financial Reporting (Required)		Tax Expense Based on Tax Return (Not Allowed)	
	Year 1	Year 2	Year 1	Year 2
Pretax income	$35,000	$35,000	$35,000	$35,000
Tax Expense	14,000*	14,000*	12,000†	16,000†
Net Income	$21,000	$21,000	$23,000	$19,000

*$14,000 is 40% of $35,000.

†From the tax return columns in the prior example: 40% × $30,000 = $12,000; 40% × $40,000 = $16,000.

In our example, the company has a stable economic earnings pattern. When the tax expense is based on the financial reporting numbers, that stable pattern is evident in a constant $21,000 net income over the two years. However, if the actual tax paid is used to measure tax expense, the apparent pattern of net income is a declining one, from $23,000 to $19,000. Because the use of the actual tax amount paid to the government tends to distort the level and pattern of reported earnings, the FASB requires companies to calculate tax expense based on the accounting methods used for financial reporting purposes. This requirement correctly matches the income tax expense with the income to which it relates.

How is this hypothetical income tax expense number to be recorded? The payable to the government in year 1 is $12,000, but tax expense of $14,000 is being recorded. Think of it as a current payable for the $12,000 currently owed to the government and a $2,000 liability that arises because of predictable future taxes. This $2,000 liability is called a deferred tax liability, because it will be paid only when a future tax return is filed. The journal entry would be:

```
Income tax expense  . . . . . . . . . . . . . . . .   14,000
      Deferred tax liability  . . . . . . . . . . . .              2,000
      Cash (or taxes payable)  . . . . . . . . . .              12,000
```

Note that the deferred tax liability of $2,000 will be shown on the balance sheet. It is equal to the tax rate of 40% times the $5,000 timing difference in depreciation expense ($5,000 on the books versus $10,000 on the tax return). Not only can this be seen as a difference in depreciation, but also as a difference in the book values of the assets. The undepreciated cost for financial reporting at the end of year one is $5,000 (cost of $10,000 less depreciation of $5,000). The undepreciated cost for tax purposes at the end of year 1 is $0.00 (cost of $10,000 less depreciation of $10,000). The deferred tax liability is the tax rate times the difference in undepreciated cost (40% of ($5,000 less $0)). In this example we are assuming that tax rates are always constant at 40% and details about how to treat changing tax rates are deferred to future courses.

Remember that differences between reported income and taxable income result in *deferral* of taxes, not cancellation of taxes. For almost a decade, General Dynamics Corporation, a large defense contractor took advantage of tax deferral. From 1973 through 1984, General Dynamics reported total pretax income of $2.7 billion and total federal income tax expense of $1 billion for financial reporting purposes. How much income tax did General Dynamics pay during this period? Zero! Thanks to a quirk in the tax law regarding revenue recognition on very long-term government contracts (that has since been changed), the company managed to defer income taxes completely. Eventually, in the years 1987 through 1992, the company paid income taxes totaling $1.6 billion. This amount exceeded income tax expense during these periods as the timing differences between tax and financial reporting reversed. General Dynamics' shareholders were happy, though. The decade of delayed taxes was equivalent to an interest-free loan from the government.

Not all temporary differences result in early deduction for tax purposes and later deduction for financial reporting. Unlike depreciation expenses, expenses for warranty costs are typically deducted earlier for financial reporting purposes than they are for tax purposes. In such cases, a deferred tax asset is recorded to acknowledge that the taxes being paid now are higher than the tax expense provided, based on pretax income reported for financial purposes.

Deferred tax liabilities are found on the balance sheets of nearly every company. The following schedule illustrates the magnitude of the deferred tax liability as reported by various companies in 1996. The deferred tax liability is reported along with the total stockholders' equity and total assets to provide perspective (in millions):

Company	Deferred Tax	Stockholders' Equity	Total Assets
CSX Corporation	$ 2,720	$ 4,995	$16,965
DuPont	2,133	10,709	37,987
Exxon	13,475	43,542	95,527
McDonald's	976	8,718	17,386
Merck	2,872	11,971	24,293
Timberland	11	165	450

The deferred tax liability, expressed as a percentage of total assets, varies for these firms from 13% for Exxon to 2% for Timberland. For most companies the primary source of deferred taxes is timing differences related to depreciation. In a recent survey of international practice, 60% of the countries surveyed required the use of deferred taxes when financial reporting of expenses differed from the timing of reporting of corresponding tax deductions.

CONTINGENT LIABILITIES

A **contingent liability** is a potential (possible) liability that depends on a future event arising out of a past transaction. Sometimes it has a definite amount. For instance, Company X may guarantee the payment on a related Company Y's note payable. In other words, Company X will pay if, and only if, Company Y fails to pay. Such a note payable is the liability (either current or long-term) of the primary borrower (Company Y) and the contingent liability of the guarantor (Company X). More often, a contingent liability has an

contingent liability A potential liability that depends on a future event arising out of a past transaction.

indefinite amount. A common example is a lawsuit. Many companies have lawsuits pending against them. These are possible obligations of indefinite amounts. Why? Because if a judge rules against the company, it will be obligated to pay an amount that is currently unknown. However, the judge may rule in the company's favor, in which case there is no obligation and may even be a receivable because the company has made counterclaims.

Some companies show contingent liabilities on the balance sheet. Most often they are listed after long-term liabilities but before stockholders' equity. United Technologies has sales of more than $18 billion in providing "high-technology products to customers in the aerospace, building systems and automotive industries throughout the world." The 1996 balance sheet has a line labeled "Commitments and contingent liabilities (Notes 3 and 14)" at the end of the liabilities. As is usually the case, no amount is shown in the body of the balance sheet. The item is listed solely to direct readers to the details in the footnotes. The United Technologies footnotes are lengthy. Note 3 describes the commitments that the company often makes to customers to provide relatively long-term financing for future purchases. Note 14 describes potential and actual liability for environmental contamination at various waste disposal sites (and other risks). It reveals that some amounts have already been accrued for some sites where responsibility has been established or clean-up is underway. These would be included in expenses when accrued and carried as part of "other liabilities" until paid.

Footnote disclosure of lawsuits is very common. Most companies have some lawsuits pending regarding the environment, product liability, or employment issues. The result of such litigation is extremely hard to estimate. Some years ago IBM lost a multimillion-dollar lawsuit for patent violation. On appeal, the verdict was reversed, and IBM ended up collecting damages from the plaintiff. The uncertainty involved in law suits does not always center on whether the verdict will be overturned. Sometimes the uncertainty concerns just how big the settlement will be. For example, Eagle Picher is a company that most recently makes auto parts but years ago did contracts for the federal government that required the use of asbestos for insulation. When the company became subject to extensive product liability claims over asbestos, it had trouble estimating the ultimate costs. The company initially estimated its costs to settle existing and future claims at $270 million and recorded them in the financial statements as an expense, with a related liability. The company later realized that its earlier estimate was low, and the asbestos liability was increased by $544 million.

The best-known recent case of uncertainty from product liability lawsuits involved Dow Corning, Inc. In the 1980s the company began facing many accusations from patients who were unhappy with silicone breast implants made by the company and surgically installed for reconstructive or cosmetic purposes. The accusations became lawsuits over time, and the company was confronted with a major product liability. Throughout the 1980s, Dow Corning regularly reported on its ongoing litigation. However, the lawsuits being heard in court were still fairly few, and no one knew how they might be resolved. So for several years the financial statements disclosed the litigation in some detail, but the balance sheet and income statement did not show specific numbers.

In 1991, the company recorded $25 million of pretax costs, and in 1992 it recorded another $69 million. Remember that each of these amounts was intended to be a best estimate of future costs to be incurred. The product from which the claims stemmed had been produced and delivered years before. In fact, production of all silicone implants ceased in 1992. But the liability estimates provided through 1992 were woefully inadequate. In 1993, Dow Corning recorded another pretax charge of $640 million. Combined with expected insurance coverage exceeding $600 million, the total cost of litigation exceeded $1.2 billion. Dow Corning and other manufacturers joined together to structure a settlement that would properly compensate plaintiffs, minimize legal costs, and allow the companies to survive. The deal required an agreement between the plaintiffs, the companies, and the insurance carriers. In late 1994 agreement seemed close. Dow Corning provided another pretax charge of $241 million. Combined with additional expected insurance costs, the amounts set aside for injured parties approached $2 billion from Dow Corning and another similar amount from other manufacturers. There were over 19,000 pending lawsuits on this product.

In May of 1995, Dow Corning declared bankruptcy. They claimed that too many plaintiffs were unwilling to agree to the settlement. Bankruptcy changes the company's whole litigation situation and leaves the final outcome very much in doubt. Throughout 1996 and 1997 legal proceedings continued. Reorganization plans emerged in 1998. As this book is printed and used, the final outcome of the case will develop. However, the facts to date show the difficulty of predicting the cost of litigation. Any time your initial estimate of $25 million is so far off, you know your prediction methods have a problem or two.

There are significant philosophical issues about responsibility for the safety of products. There are equally important questions about how to determine scientifically what is safe. Although these are important social questions, our immediate concern is: how should companies measure their obligations, disclose the nature of the obligations, and record these amounts in financial statements? For contingent liabilities, the answer is often that footnote disclosure is the best we can do.

DEBT RATIOS AND INTEREST-COVERAGE RATIOS

We have emphasized the link between the interest rate paid to lenders and the risk associated with the loan. When people take out loans to buy a car or a house, the interest on the loan is often smaller if the down payment is larger. For example, with 5% down the interest rate might be 8%, whereas it would be 7½% with a 20% down payment. Lenders feel that the higher a down payment, the less risk they have. Why? Their assumption is that a buyer who puts down more of his or her own cash (equity) will be more likely to take care of and pay off the car or house. How does this concept work for corporations? Debt ratios are used to measure the extent to which a company has used borrowing to finance its activity. The more the borrowing, and the less the equity, the riskier it is to lend money to the firm.

Objective 7
Use ratio analysis to assess a company's debt levels.

$$\text{Debt-to-equity ratio} = \frac{\text{Total liabilities}}{\text{Total shareholders' equity}}$$

$$\text{Long-term-debt-to-total-capital ratio} = \frac{\text{Total long-term debt}}{\text{Total shareholders' equity} + \text{long-term debt}}$$

$$\text{Debt-to-total-assets ratio} = \frac{\text{Total liabilities}}{\text{Total assets}}$$

$$\text{Interest-coverage ratio} = \frac{\text{Pretax income} + \text{interest expense}}{\text{Interest expense}}$$

debt-to-equity ratio Total liabilities divided by total shareholders' equity.

long-term-debt-to-total-capital ratio Total long-term debt divided by total shareholders' equity plus long-term debt.

debt-to-total-assets ratio Total liabilities divided by total assets.

interest-coverage ratio Pretax income plus interest expense divided by interest expense.

Note that the first three ratios are alternate ways of expressing what part of the firm's resources is obtained by borrowing and what part is invested by the owners. The interest-coverage ratio more directly measures the firm's ability to meet its interest obligation.

The debt burden varies greatly from firm to firm and industry to industry. For example, retailing companies, utilities, and transportation companies tend to have debt of more than 60% of their assets. Computer companies and textile firms have debt levels of about 45% of assets.

Debt-to-equity ratios that were thought to be too high a few years ago are becoming commonplace today. The average debt-to-total-assets ratio for major U.S. industrial companies grew from about 35% in 1960 to nearly 60% today.

The following ratios demonstrate the variation among industries and among countries:

Company	Industry	Country	Debt-Total Capital	Interest-Coverage
RJR Nabisco	Tobacco	USA	48%	3
IBM	Computers	USA	37%	7
Eli Lilly	Drugs	USA	35%	17
Merck	Drugs	USA	12%	52
Glaxo Holdings	Drugs	UK	20%	14
Exxon	Oil	USA	14%	18
Royal Dutch	Oil	Holland	9%	15
Repsol	Oil	Spain	44%	6
Ford	Autos	USA	73%	2
Volvo	Autos	Sweden	22%	4
Toyota	Autos	Japan	15%	16

Source: *VALUE LINE* 1997

SUMMARY PROBLEMS FOR YOUR REVIEW

PROBLEM ONE

Suppose that on December 31, 1999, Exxon issued $12 million of 10-year, 10% debentures at par.

Required

1. Prepare an analysis of the following items: (a) issuance of the debentures; (b) the first two semiannual interest payments; and (c) the payment of the maturity value. Use the balance sheet equation (similar to Exhibit 8-3). Round to the nearest thousand dollars.

2. Prepare journal entries for the items in requirement 1.

SOLUTION TO PROBLEM ONE

1. See Exhibit 8-4.

2.
12/31/99:	Cash	12,000,000	
	Bonds payable		12,000,000
6/30/00:	Interest expense	600,000	
	Cash		600,000
12/31/00:	Interest expense	600,000	
	Cash		600,000
12/31/09:	Bonds payable	12,000,000	
	Cash		12,000,000

PROBLEM TWO

Suppose that you are preparing financial statements for Liz Claiborne, Inc., a fashion company that designs and markets many types of clothing and accessories, including the Liz Claiborne and Dana Buchman brands. You notice that there are several lawsuits pending against the company. How would you assess the nature of accounting disclosures required? What choices do you have?

SOLUTION TO PROBLEM TWO

The first step would be to determine the details of the lawsuits and the size of potential losses. The second step would be to get expert legal opinions with respect to the status of the suits. How far along in the process are they? How likely are they to cause changes in

Exhibit 8-4

Analysis of Exxon's Bond Transactions: Problem One
(rounded to thousands of dollars)

	A	=	L	+	SE
			Bonds		
	Cash		*Payable*		*Retained Income*
Exxon's records:					
1. Issuance	12,000		12,000		
2. Semiannual interest					
Six months ended:					[Increase]
6/30/00	−600				−600 Interest
12/31/00	−600				−600 [Expense]
3. Maturity value					
(final payment)	−12,000		−12,000		
Bond-related totals*	−12,000		0		−12,000

*Totals after all 20 interest payments (20 × 600) and payment at maturity.

the financial statements? The possible actions include (1) recording a liability and recognizing an expense in the income statement, (2) providing a footnote that describes the issue without explicitly recording an amount, or (3) not saying anything because the materiality of the possible loss is small and /or the likelihood of the loss is small.

Not all companies face problems such as those discussed in the text regarding asbestos or medical products liabilities. Liz Claiborne is not the kind of company that typically faces large legal risks. In the 1996 financial statements, the balance sheet includes a line labeled Commitments and Contingencies with no number recorded. The notes describe two risks. Forty-six percent of sales are with three customers. This is not a liability, but is disclosed to help alert readers to the fact that Liz Claiborne's sales and the collectibility of its receivables are linked to a few large accounts. The other reference is to legal proceedings and says: "The Company is party to several pending legal proceedings and claims. Although the outcome of such actions cannot be determined with certainty, management is of the opinion that the final outcome should not have a material adverse effect on the Company's results of operations or financial position."

PROBLEM THREE

The Solar Kitchen Corporation manufactures and sells energy-efficient additions to provide solar-heated eating areas next to existing kitchens. Because of good styling and marketing to an energy-conscious public, sales have grown briskly. Solar Kitchen has no pre-existing deferred tax liability. During 19X0 the following transactions occurred.

1. On January 1, 10,000 new shares of common stock were sold at $100 per share.
2. Half of the proceeds from the stock sale were immediately invested in tax-free bonds yielding 6% per annum. The bonds were held throughout the year, resulting in interest revenue of $500,000 × .06 = $30,000.
3. Sales for the year were $4,500,000, with expenses of $3,800,000 reported under GAAP (exclusive of income tax expense).
4. Tax depreciation exceeded depreciation included in item 3 above by $300,000.
5. For financial reporting purposes, warranty costs are calculated at 1% of sales, and the resulting $45,000 is included in the $3,800,000 of expenses. Actual expenditures under warranty were $22,000. The difference is $23,000.

Required

1. Calculate earnings before tax for shareholder reporting.
2. Calculate income tax payable to the tax authorities and income tax expense for shareholder reporting using a 40% tax rate.
3. Make the appropriate journal entry. Assume the 40% tax rate is expected to be maintained.

SOLUTION TO PROBLEM THREE

1. Earnings before taxes for shareholder reporting are:

Sales revenue	$4,500,000
Interest revenue	30,000
Less operating expenses	(3,800,000)
Pretax income	$ 730,000

2.

	Reporting to Tax Authorities	Reporting to Shareholders
Earnings before tax	$730,000	$730,000
Permanent differences:		
Nontaxable interest	(30,000)	(30,000)
Subtotal	700,000	700,000
Timing differences:		
Depreciation	(300,000)	—
Warranty expenses	23,000	—
Earnings on which tax is based:	423,000	700,000
Tax rate	.40	.40
Income tax payable	$169,200	
Income tax expense reported to shareholders		$280,000

3.

```
Income tax expense .......................  280,000
    Income tax payable ....................          169,200
    Deferred tax liability ................          110,800
```

Highlights to Remember

Liabilities are obligations to pay money or to provide goods or services. An entity's liability level is important to analysts because unpaid liabilities may produce difficulties ranging from an inability to raise additional capital to forced liquidation. To help assess debt levels, financial statements typically separate liabilities requiring payment within one year as current liabilities. Accounting for current liabilities is a straightforward extension of procedures covered in earlier chapters. Transactions are recorded as they occur, and accruals at the end of a period capture incomplete transactions such as accruing interest, wages, utilities, or taxes.

Long-term liabilities are more complex contracts that convey many rights and responsibilities over long periods of time. Bonds, a common long-term liability, are originally recorded at the amount received from investors at issue. During the life of the bond, interest expense is recognized each period.

Deferred tax liabilities arise because the timing of tax deductions such as depreciation expense on the company's tax return is often earlier than on the company's books. When this happens, the tax payable immediately is less than it would appear to be if one examined the financial reports. To help investors understand the long-run tax obligations of the company, tax expense is reported as if taxes were paid on the net income reported to shareholders. A deferred tax liability is recognized to reflect predictable higher taxes in the future, when these timing differences will reverse.

Contingent liabilities are uncertain in amount and timing of payment. Examples include lawsuits, contract disputes, possible losses on multiyear contracts, and environmental liabilities. Footnote disclosure is used to alert interested parties to the uncertain, unmeasurable future possibilities.

Debt ratios and interest-coverage ratios are two measures used to evaluate the level of a company's indebtedness. The more debt a company has, the more problems it will face if cash flow is inadequate to meet liabilities as they fall due.

Accounting Vocabulary

bonds, p. 327
callable bonds, p. 330
call premium, p. 330
commercial paper, p. 322
contingent liability, p. 333
contractual rate, p. 327
convertible bonds, p. 330
coupon rate, p. 327
covenant, p. 329
debenture, p. 328
debt-to-equity ratio, p. 335
debt-to-total-assets ratio, p. 335
face amount, p. 327
interest-coverage ratio, p. 335

interest rate, p. 327
invoice, p. 326
line of credit, p.321
liquidation, p. 328
long-term-debt-to-total-capital ratio, p. 335
long-term liabilities, p. 320
mortgage bond, p. 328
negotiable, p. 327
nominal interest rate, p. 327
par value, p. 327
permanent differences, p. 331
principal, p. 327
private placement, p. 327
promissory note, p. 321

protective covenant, p. 329
purchase order, p. 325
receiving report, p. 326
restructuring, p. 330
sinking fund, p. 330
sinking fund bonds, p. 330
stated rate, p. 327
subordinated debentures, p. 328
tax rate, p. 331
temporary differences, p. 331
timing differences, p. 331
trust indenture, p. 329
unsubordinated debentures, p. 329

Assignment Material

QUESTIONS

8-1. Distinguish between *current liabilities* and *long-term liabilities.*

8-2. Name and briefly describe five items that are often classified as current liabilities.

8-3. "Withholding taxes really add to employer payroll costs." Do you agree? Explain.

8-4. Distinguish between *employee* payroll taxes and *employer* payroll taxes.

8-5. "Product warranties expense should not be recognized until the actual services are performed.

Until then you don't know which products might require warranty repairs." Do you agree? Explain.

8-6. Why do companies require source documents before they will issue a check?

8-7. "If companies pay a bill twice, they are out of luck. No company is going to return the money after receiving it." Do you agree? Explain.

8-8. Distinguish between a *mortgage bond* and a *debenture.* Which is safer?

8-9. Distinguish between *subordinated* and *unsubordinated* debentures.

8-10. "The face amount of a bond is what you can sell it for." Do you agree? Explain.

8-11. "Protective covenants protect the shareholders' interests in cases of liquidation of assets." Do you agree? Explain.

8-12. Bond covenants usually restrict the borrower's rights in various ways. An example might be a restriction that no additional long-term debt could be issued unless the debt-to-total assets ratio was below 0.5. Who benefits from such a covenant? How?

8-13. Many callable bonds have a call premium for "early" calls. Who does the call premium benefit, the issuer or the purchaser of the bond? How?

8-14. "Restructuring charges recognize today expenses that will be incurred in the future." Explain.

8-15. Compare and contrast permanent differences and temporary differences between GAAP and tax reporting.

8-16. "Differences in tax and GAAP rules lead to more depreciation being charged on tax statements than on financial reports to the public." Do you agree? Explain.

8-17. "It is unethical for big companies to recognize a large income tax expense on their income statements reported to the public but to pay a smaller amount to the government." Do you agree? Explain.

8-18. "A contingent liability is a liability having an estimated amount." Do you agree? Explain.

8-19. "At the balance sheet date, a private high school has lost a court case for an uninsured football injury. The amount of damages has not been set. A reasonable estimate is between $800,000 and $2 million." How should this information be presented in the financial statements?

8-20. Suppose IBM won a lawsuit for $1 million against Innovative Software, a young company with assets of $20 million. Innovative has appealed the suit. How would each company disclose this event in financial statements prepared while the appeal was under way.

8-21. We observe higher debt levels in the automobile industry than in the pharmaceutical industry. Why?

EXERCISES

8-22 Current Liabilities

Chrysler, one of the big-three automakers, had the following items on its June 30, 1997 balance sheet (in millions):

Cash and cash equivalents	$5,623
Accounts payable	9,564
Inventories	6,079
Additional paid-in capital	5,169
Accrued liabilities and expenses	9,410
Payments due within one year on long-term debt	3,538
Short-term debt	3,903
Long-term debt	9,729

Required Prepare the current liabilities section of Chrysler's balance sheet. Include only the items that are properly included in current liabilities. Compute the total current liabilities.

8-23 Accrued Employee Compensation

Weitz Company had total compensation expense for March of $23,000. The company paid $18,000 to employees during March. The remainder will be paid in April.

Required
1. Prepare the journal entry for recording the compensation expense for March.
2. Suppose salaries and wages payable were $2,000 at the beginning of March. Compute salaries and wages payable at the end of March.

8-24 Sales Taxes

(Alternate is 8-25.) The Long Lake Store is in a midwestern state where the sales tax is 7%. Total sales for the month of September were $400,000, of which $325,000 was subject to sales tax.

1. Prepare a journal entry that summarizes sales (all in cash) for the month.
2. Prepare a journal entry regarding the disbursement for the sales tax.

8-25 Sales Taxes

(Alternate is 8-24.) Most of the food sold in retail stores in California is not subject to sales taxes (for example, candy), but some items are (for example, soft drinks). Apparently, the candy lobbyists were more effective than soft drinks lobbyists when dealing with the state legislature. Most cash registers are designed to record taxable sales and nontaxable sales and automatically add the appropriate sales tax.

The sales for the past week in the local Safeway store were $130,000, $20,000 of which was taxable at a rate of 7%. Using the $A = L + SE$ equation, show the impact on the entity, both now and when the sales taxes are paid at a later date. Also prepare corresponding journal entries.

8-26 Product Warranties

During 19X9, the Perez Appliance Company had sales of $800,000. The company estimates that the cost of servicing products under warranty will average 2% of sales.

1. Prepare journal entries for sales revenue and the related warranty expense for 19X9. Assume all sales are for cash.
2. The liability for warranties was $11,400 at the beginning of 19X9. Expenditures (all in cash) to satisfy warranty claims during 19X9 were $17,400, of which $4,500 was for products sold in 19X9. Prepare the journal entry for the warranty expenditures.
3. Compute the end-of-19X9 balance in the Liability for Warranties account.

8-27 Unearned Revenues

The Reader's Digest Association, Inc., one of the largest publishers of magazines in the world, had unearned revenues of $399 million on its March 31, 1997 balance sheet. Suppose that during April, Reader's Digest delivered magazines with a sales value of $30 million to prepaid subscribers and sold subscriptions for $37 million.

1. Prepare journal entries for the new subscriptions and the deliveries to prepaid subscribers.
2. Compute the amount in the unearned revenue account at the end of April.

8-28 Priorities of Claims

Ashton Real Estate Corporation is being liquidated. It has one major asset, an office building, which was converted into $19 million cash. The stockholders' equity has been wiped out by past losses. The following claims exist: accounts payable, $3 million; debentures payable, $5 million; first mortgage payable, $13 million.

1. Assume the debentures are not subordinated. How much will each class of claimants receive?
2. If the debentures are subordinated, how much will each class of claimants receive? How much will each class receive if the cash proceeds from the sale of the building amount to only $14.5 million?

8-29 Deferred Taxes

Monsanto Company produces chemicals and pharmaceuticals. Its net sales in 1996 exceeded $9 billion. On its income statement in 1996, Monsanto reported the following (in millions):

Income before taxes	$540
Income tax expense	155
Net income	$385

Payments to the government for income taxes related to operations in 1996 were $200 million. Assume that the income tax expense and these income tax payments were the only tax-related transactions during 1996.

Required

1. Prepare the journal entry that recognizes the $155 million income tax expense and the $200 million income tax payment.
2. Compute the change in the deferred income tax liability account for 1996.

8-30 Various Liabilities

(Alternate is 8-31.)

1. Suki Du made a $12,000 savings deposit on August 1. On September 30, the bank recognized two months' interest thereon at an annual rate of 10%. On October 1, Du closed her account with the bank. Interest is payable from the date of deposit through the date before withdrawal. Prepare the bank's journal entries.

2. On August 31 the Manchester Opera sold season tickets for £4.8 million cash in advance of the opera season, which begins on September 10. These tickets are for eight performance dates.

   a. What is the effect on the balance sheet, August 31? Prepare the appropriate journal entry for the sale of the tickets.

   b. Assume that seven dates remain after September 30. What is the effect on the balance sheet, September 30? Prepare the related summary journal entry for September.

3. AV Corporation sells audio and video equipment. Experience has shown that warranty costs average 4% of sales. Sales for June were $9 million. Cash disbursements for rendering warranty service during June were $320,000. Prepare the journal entries for these transactions.

4. A wholesale distributor gets cash deposits for its returnable bottles. In November, the distributor received $160,000 cash and disbursed $130,000 for bottles returned. Prepare the journal entries for these transactions.

5. The county hospital has lost a lawsuit. Damages were set at $2 million. The hospital plans to appeal the decision to a higher court. The hospital's attorneys are 80% confident of a reversal of the lower court's decision. What liability, if any, should appear on the hospital's balance sheet?

8-31 Various Liabilities

(Alternate is 8-30.)

1. Maytag Corporation sells electric appliances, including automatic washing machines. Experience in recent years has indicated that warranty costs average 3.0% of sales. Sales of washing machines for April were $2.5 million. Cash

disbursements and obligations for warranty service on washing machines during April totaled $71,000. Prepare the journal entries prompted by these facts.

2. Pepsi-Cola Company of New York gets cash deposits for its returnable bottles. In November it received $100,000 cash and disbursed $92,000 for bottles returned. Prepare the journal entries regarding the receipts and returns of deposits.

3. Citibank received a $4,000 savings deposit on April 1. On June 30, it recognized interest thereon at an annual rate of 5%. On July 1, the depositor closed her account with the bank. Prepare the bank's necessary journal entries.

4. The Paramount Theater sold for $150,000 cash a "season's series" of tickets in advance of December 31 for four plays, each to be held in successive months, beginning in January.

    a. What is the effect on the balance sheet, December 31? What is the appropriate journal entry for the sale of the tickets?

    b. What is the effect on the balance sheet, January 31? What is the related journal entry for January?

5. Suppose a tabloid newspaper has lost a lawsuit. Damages were set at $500,000. The newspaper plans to appeal the decision to a higher court. The newspaper's attorneys are 90% confident of a reversal of the lower court's decision. What liability, if any, should be shown on the newspaper's balance sheet?

PROBLEMS

8-32 Accounting for Payroll

For the week ended January 27, the Adirondak Manufacturing Company had a total payroll of $200,000. Three items were withheld from employees' paychecks: (1) social security (FICA) tax of 7.1% of the payroll; (2) income taxes, which average 21% of the payroll; and (3) employees' savings that are deposited in their Credit Union, which are $9,500. All three items were paid on January 30.

1. Use the balance sheet equation to analyze the transactions on January 27 and January 30.

2. Prepare journal entries for the recording of the items in requirement 1.

3. In addition to the payroll, Adirondak pays (1) payroll taxes of 9% of the payroll, (2) health insurance premiums of $13,000, and (3) contributions to the employees' pension fund of $16,000. Prepare journal entries for the recognition of these additional expenses.

8-33 Analysis of Payroll and Interest

Consider a bank loan of $800,000 to a church on August 31, 19X8. The loan bears interest at 9%. Principal and interest are due in one year. The church reports on a calendar-year basis.

1. Prepare an analysis of transactions, using the balance sheet equation. Indicate the entries for the church for August 31, 19X8, December 31, 19X8, and August 31, 19X9. Allocate interest within the year on a straight-line basis. Show all amounts in thousands of dollars.

2. Prepare all the corresponding journal entries keyed as above.

8-34 Bonds Issued at Par

On December 31, 1998, Key Computers issued $10 million of 10-year, 12% debentures at par.

Required

1. Compute the proceeds from issuing the debentures.
2. Using the balance sheet equation format, prepare an analysis of this bond transaction. Show entries for the issuer regarding (a) issuance, (b) the first semiannual interest payment, and (c) payment of maturity value.
3. Show all the corresponding journal entries keyed as in requirement 2.
4. Show how the bond-related accounts would appear on the balance sheet as of December 31, 1998, and June 30, 1999. Assume that the semiannual interest payment and amortization due on the balance sheet date have been recorded.

8-35 Bonds Issued at Par

On January 1, 1998, Chen Electronics issued $2 million of five-year, 11% debentures at par.

Required

1. Compute the proceeds from issuing the debentures.
2. Using the balance sheet equation format, prepare an analysis of this bond transaction. Show entries for the issuer regarding (a) issuance, (b) the first semiannual interest payment, and (c) payment of maturity value.
3. Show all the corresponding journal entries keyed as in requirement 2.
4. Show how the bond-related accounts would appear on the balance sheets as of January 1, 1999, and July 1, 1999. Assume that the semiannual interest payment and amortization due on the balance sheet dates have been recorded.

8-36 Convertible Bonds

Sometimes a small company finds it necessary to include a convertibility option in order to sell bonds at a reasonable interest rate. Commodore Applied Technologies is a young company in the business of separating, destroying, and neutralizing hazardous wastes. In 1993 and 1994 the company issued $4 million of convertible bonds, with each $1 face value of bonds being convertible into 1 common share of Commodore. The interest rate on the bonds is 8.5%, which is less than the rate the company would have paid to issue bonds without the conversion option.

In 1996 Commodore had revenues of $5.1 million and a net loss of $8.3 million. The company pays no dividends. The market price of Commodore's common shares is below $1.

Required

1. Compute the annual interest received by the holders of the convertible bonds.
2. Suppose the price of one share of Commodore common stock rose to $1.25. If you held some of Commodore's convertible bonds, would you immediately convert your bonds to common stock? Why or why not?
3. Suppose the maturity date of the convertible bonds was rapidly approaching. Would you convert your holdings of the convertible bonds if the price of Commodore stock were $1.25 per share? If the price were $.75 per share? Explain.

8-37 Restructuring

Many well-known companies have incurred restructuring charges in recent years. Consider H. J. Heinz Company, maker of ketchup and many other products. In fiscal 1997, Heinz recorded a $647.2 million pretax restructuring charge. At the end of fiscal 1997, the balance in the accrued restructuring costs account was $210,804,000. The account had a zero balance at the beginning of the year. After the charge, Heinz's fiscal 1997 income before income taxes was $479,064,000. The company's income before income taxes was $1,023,661,000 in 1996.

Required

1. Prepare the journal entry to record the restructuring charge.

2. Prepare a summary journal entry for the decreases in the accrued restructuring costs account during fiscal 1997. Assume that all the restructuring costs actually incurred in fiscal 1997 were paid in cash.

3. Compute the amount of income before income taxes Heinz would have reported for fiscal 1997 if there had been no restructuring charges. Compare this to the income before income taxes reported in fiscal 1996.

4. Which number, the reported income before income taxes reported in Heinz's income statement or the number you computed in requirement 3, would be most useful in predicting Heinz's income before income taxes for fiscal 1998? Explain.

8-38   Deferred Taxes

Cadbury Schweppes is a major global company in beverages and confectionery based in London. Sales in 1996 were more than £5 billion (where £ is the British pound). The company's 1996 income statement included the following, using Cadbury Schweppes' terminology (in millions):

Profit on ordinary activities before taxation	£ 592
Tax on profit on ordinary activities	(180)
Profit on ordinary activities after taxation	£ 412

As a result of 1996's operations, the deferred tax liability account increased by £32 million. There was no change in taxes payable.

Required

1. Compute the income taxes paid to the government in 1996.

2. Prepare the journal entry to record taxes on ordinary activities for 1996.

3. Explain why the amount of income taxes paid to the government was not the same as the amount of income taxes recorded on the income statement in 1996.

8-39   The Income Tax Footnote

Norfolk Southern Corporation is a railway and motor carrier with 1996 operating revenues of approximately $4.8 billion and income before income taxes of $1,196.9 million. Footnote 3 to the financial statements provided the following:

The provision for income taxes consists of the following:

	1996	1995
	(In millions of dollars)	
Current:		
Federal	$287.8	$282.6
State	41.6	52.7
Total current	329.4	335.3
Deferred:		
Federal	79.2	57.8
State	17.9	8.9
Total deferred	97.1	66.7
Total	$426.5	$402.0

1. Provide the journal entries to record income tax expense for 1996.
2. Compute net income for 1996.

8-40 Debt-to-Equity Ratios

The total debt and stockholders' equity for four companies follows (in thousands). The companies are described as follows:

- AT&T provides long-distance phone service and is a large, well-established company.
- Bell Atlantic is a regional phone company that is diversifying into a variety of telecommunications and information systems areas.
- Micron Technology is a fast-growing producer of memory products for electronic systems.
- Amgen is a biotechnology company pioneering the development of products based on advances in recombinant DNA.

(in millions)	Total Debt		Stockholders' Equity	
	1996	*1992*	*1996*	*1992*
AT&T	$10,343	$17,122	$20,295	$20,313
Bell Atlantic	17,288	20,283	7,423	7,816
Micron Technology	1,196	213	2,502	511
Amgen	859	440	1,906	934

1. Compute debt-to-equity ratios for each company for 1992 and 1996.
2. Discuss the differences in the ratios across firms.
3. Discuss the changes in individual company ratios from 1992 to 1996.

8-41 Review of Chapters 7 and 8

Albertson's, Inc., based in Boise, Idaho, operates more than 800 food and drug stores in 20 states. The company's annual report for fiscal 1997 contained the following (in millions):

Albertson's Inc.

	January 30	
	1997	*1996*
Property, plant, and equipment, at cost	$4,623	$4,063
Less accumulated depreciation	1,568	1,366
Net property, plant, and equipment	$3,055	$2,697
Long-term debt due within one year	$ 1	$ 78
Long-term debt	922	603

Purchases of buildings, machinery, and equipment during fiscal 1997 were $673 million and depreciation expense was $294 million.

Proceeds from issuance of *long-term debt* were $322 million during fiscal 1997.

(The use of T-accounts should help your analysis.)

1. Compute the dollar amounts of
   a. Accumulated depreciation relating to properties and plants disposed of during fiscal 1997.
   b. Original acquisition cost of properties and plants disposed of during fiscal 1997.
2. Compute the dollar amounts of
   a. Long-term debt reductions
   b. The *net increase or decrease* in long-term debt.

8-42 Liabilities for Frequent Flier Miles and Ethics

Most airlines in the United States have frequent flier programs that grant free flights if a customer accumulates enough flight miles on the airline. For example, United Airlines offers a free domestic flight for every 25,000 miles flown on United. Delta Air Lines describes its program as follows in a footnote to the financial statements:

> *The Company sponsors a travel incentive program whereby frequent travelers accumulate mileage credits that entitle them to certain awards including free travel. The company accrues the estimated incremental cost of providing free travel awards under its frequent flyer program when free travel award levels are achieved. The accrued incremental cost is recorded in current liabilities.*

In a recent annual report, American Airlines reported a liability of $270 million for free flights, representing approximately 4 billion flight miles owed to customers. Assuming the average free flight is 2,000 miles, there is a $270 million liability for 2 million flights, an average of $135 per flight. However, some airlines maintain that the true liability is closer to $10 per flight, including the cost of food, insurance, and other miscellaneous expenses. They argue that all other costs would be incurred even in the absence of the person traveling free.

Suppose airlines use one estimate of the cost of these "free" flights for their internal decision making and another for computing the liability for their publicly reported balance sheet. Comment on the ethical issues.

8-43 The Gap Annual Report

Refer to The Gap's financial statements in Appendix A. Focus on the liabilities section of the balance sheet and footnote B.

1. Compute the following three ratios at February 3, 1996 and February 1, 1997. Assess the changes in these ratios. Required
   a. Debt-to-equity ratio
   b. Debt-to-total-assets ratio
   c. Interest-coverage ratio
2. There are covenants related to The Gap's lines of credit that restrict the payment of dividends. What is the total amount of retained earnings that The Gap must have before dividends can be paid, according to the most restrictive of the covenants? Is this likely to constrain The Gap's ability to pay dividends? Explain.

8-44 Financial Statement Research

Identify an industry and select two companies within the industry.

Calculate and compare the following ratios between the companies and through time.

1. Debt-to-equity ratio
2. Debt-to-total-assets ratio
3. Interest-coverage ratio

COLLABORATIVE LEARNING EXERCISE

8-45 Characteristics of Bonds

Form groups of three to six persons each. Each person should select a company that has long-term debt in the form of bonds (or debentures). Pick one of the company's bonds, and note the interest rate on the bond. If the company does not list bonds individually, you may need to select one of the groups of bonds that it presents.

Find out as much as you can about the factors that might explain the bond's interest rate. Among the items to look for are characteristics of the bond, such as the size of the issue, the length of the term, and any special features such as subordination, convertibility, and covenants, and characteristics of the company, such as its industry, its debt-equity ratio, and its interest-coverage ratio. Also, try to find out when the bond was issued and the level of prevailing interest rates at the time. (Companies do not usually show the issue date in the footnotes to their financial statements. You might try looking at past annual reports to see when the bonds first appeared on the financial statement.) Prevailing interest rates may be represented by the rates on U.S. Treasury securities. Note the amount by which the interest rate of the bond exceeds the rate of a U.S. Treasury security of the same duration.

After each student has done his or her independent research, get together and compare results. Do the factors you have identified explain the differences in rates across the companies? How do the factors relate to the riskiness of the bonds? Is the amount by which the bond interest rate exceeds the U.S. Treasury rate related to the bond's riskiness?

8-46 Internet Case

Go to **http://www.jnj.com/** to find the home page of Johnson & Johnson, a consolidated group of more than 170 operating companies in 50 countries. Select *News and Finance* from the bottom of the page. Then choose its most recent annual report.

Answer the following questions about Johnson & Johnson:

1. Which of Johnson & Johnson's liabilities would you expect to be measured in terms of the amount of cash needed to meet or pay off an obligation? Estimate within which of the following periods you would expect each of the company's current liabilities to be repaid:

   1 to 15 days, 16 to 45 days, 46 to 90 days, 91 to 365 days

2. Examine *Note 5* on borrowings. What are the items that are referred to as "debentures"? What is meant by "Medium Term Notes"?

3. Where are amounts related to income taxes reported in Johnson & Johnson's financial statements? Why do deferred taxes exist?

4. Read *Management Discussion and Analysis of Results.* Does the company anticipate any liabilities relating to environmental liabilities? Explain. Where will these items be reported if they do exist?

5. Which of the *Notes to the Consolidated Financial Statements* primarily address *liabilities?* Why do you suppose so much disclosure is necessary for liabilities?

VALUING AND ACCOUNTING FOR BONDS AND LEASES

This colorful annual report contains the consolidated financial results of the May Company, the parent company of many department stores including Hecht's, Filene's, and Lord & Taylor.

Learning Objectives

After studying this chapter, you should be able to

1 Compute and interpret present and future values.

2 Use present value techniques to value long-term liabilities.

3 Account for bond issues over their entire life.

4 Value and account for long-term lease transactions.

5 Evaluate pensions and other postretirement benefits.

Maybe you have never heard of May Department Stores, but you've probably shopped in one of its stores. The company operates department stores under the names of Foley's, Hecht's, Robinsons-May, Filene's, Lord & Taylor, Kaufmann's, and others. The company owns more than 350 stores across the United States and has plans to open 100 more over the next five years. To accomplish this feat, May will invest $2.1 billion to add 19 million square feet of selling space. That's a lot of money—too much to come from just the results of May's normal operations. How will the company pay for it? In part, through the issuance of long-term debt in the form of bonds and notes.

May's latest annual report reveals the issuance this fiscal year of a total of $475 million in bonds, with interest rates ranging from 7.5% to 8.125%. They will come due between the years 2013 and 2035. During this same fiscal year, $125 million, 7.15% notes due in 2004 were issued. The proceeds were added to May Department Stores' general funds to cover capital expenditures, acquisitions, working capital needs, and other general corporate purposes.

Why would May want to run up this much debt? From management's perspective, the growth plans and resulting financing needs are a competitive requirement. May has achieved over 20 consecutive years of record sales and earnings per share from continuing operations, a fact not lost on investors. Management is taking aggressive measures to maintain this record.

Measuring and reporting long-term liabilities uses fundamental concepts of compound interest, especially present-value techniques. In Chapter 8 we focused on the accounting process for simple securities and situations. We did not worry about where the values came from. Now we will use present-value techniques to value and account for bond issues, and for leases, and to interpret disclosures about pensions and other postretirement employee benefits.

You may think that bonds are boring investments that provide semiannual interest payments until they mature and the original principal is repaid. Think again. The resale value of a bond may rise and fall greatly over its life as market conditions change. Large changes in value may accompany general changes in interest rates or changes in the specific circumstances of the issuing firm.

For example, during October 1973, the American car maker Chrysler issued 8% bonds with principal value of $1,000 maturing in 1998. The bonds were sold at $1,000 because the market rate of interest was also 8% per year.

What was the market price of Chrysler's bonds 9 years after issuance, (that is, in October 1982)? The listing in the *Wall Street Journal* revealed a price of $491.24. At that time, Chrysler's bond had 16 years (or 32 half-yearly interest payments) until maturity. The market value of the bonds was based on the value of the $40 interest payments made every half year ($1,000 × 8% × ½ = $40) and the $1,000 principal payment at maturity. In this chapter we will learn why the value of Chrysler's bonds was only $491.24, not $2,280, the total of the 32 $40 payments and the $1,000 payment at maturity.

The historical market value of Chrysler's bonds can be found in past issues of *Moody's Bond Record*. Moody's provides bond ratings that measure the likelihood that the issuer will be able to pay back the debt. They range from Aaa (highest) to Baa (middle) to C (lowest). When the Chrysler bonds were issued in 1973, Moody's assigned them an A rating. The table below shows the market value and bond rating in October for 1973 and 1982–1993. Why did the price of the bonds fall to $491.24? One reason is that Chrysler bonds became riskier, as indicated by the fall in Moody's rating from A to Caa. During the next year Chrysler's condition improved significantly, its bond rating rose, and owners of these bonds earned a return of 50% including interest and appreciation.

Market Value of Chrysler Bond That Was Issued at Par for $1,000 in October 1973

October	Market Value	Moody's Rating
1973	$ 1,000	A
.	.	.
.	.	.
1982	491.24	Caa
1983	665.00	B 2
1984	621.25	Ba 2
1985	753.75	Baa 3
1986	922.50	Baa 3
1987	840.00	Baa 1
1988	912.50	Baa 1
1989	932.50	Baa 1
1990	750.00	Baa 3
1991	680.00	Ba 3
1992	968.75	B 1
1993	1,021.25	Baa 3

Chrysler's accounting for these bonds was completely unaffected by these wide swings in value and the associated gains and losses being realized by investors. Chrysler issued the bonds at par and continued to record interest expense and interest payable of $40 per bond every six months until the bonds were repaid.

VALUING LONG-TERM LIABILITIES

We have already seen how to value and account for current liabilities. Long-term liabilities are more difficult to value because they involve long time frames. How exactly do accountants measure the value of obligations that are not due for at least a year? They use the time value of money, which refers to the fact that a dollar you expect to pay or receive in the future is not worth as much as a dollar you have today. For example, suppose a company owes $105, due in one year. It can put $100 in a savings account that pays 5% interest. In one year, the original $100 plus the $5 interest earned can be used to pay the $105 obligation. Satisfying the $105 obligation took only 100 of today's dollars. Therefore a current balance sheet could include an obligation of only $100, rather than $105. As you will see, accounting has embraced present value approaches in valuing bonds, leases, and pensions.

COMPOUND INTEREST, FUTURE VALUE, AND PRESENT VALUE

Depending on your prior background, these topics may be familiar, in which case skip directly to the heading "Accounting for Bond Transactions", p. 361. This discussion uses values from interest tables to solve problems, however, many of you will be using either Excel or another spreadsheet or financial calculators to make these calculations. The mechanism is not important, but the principles are paramount to understanding these liabilities completely.

Objective 1
Compute and interpret present and future values.

When you borrow money, the amount borrowed is known as the loan principal. For the borrower, interest is the cost of using the principal. It is the rental charge for cash, just as rental charges are often made to use an automobile or hotel room. Investing money is basically the same as making a loan. The investor gives money to a company, and that company acts as a borrower. For the investor, then, interest is the return on investment or the fee for lending money. Contracts that bear interest have many forms, from simple short-term promissory notes to multimillion-dollar issues of bonds.

Calculating the amount of interest depends on the interest rate—a specified percentage of the principal—and the interest period—the time period over which this interest rate is applied.

Simple interest is calculated by multiplying an interest rate by an unchanging principal amount. Because principal amounts increase when you add interest onto them as interest is earned, simple interest is rare in U.S. financial practice. Instead, we see **compound interest,** which is calculated by multiplying an interest rate by a principal amount that increases each time interest is earned. The accumulated interest is added to the principal to become the new principal for the next period.

simple interest For any period, interest rate multiplied by an unchanging principal amount.

compound interest For any period, interest rate multiplied by a changing principal amount. The unpaid interest is added to the principal to become the principal for the new period.

FUTURE VALUE

Consider an example. Suppose Christina's T-shirt business has $10,000 in cash that is not needed at this moment. Rather than hold the $10,000 in her business checking account, which does not pay interest, she can deposit $10,000 in an account that pays 10% yearly interest, compounded annually. She plans to let the $10,000 remain in the account and earn interest for three years. After three years, she will withdraw all of the money. The amount that will be accumulated in the account, including principal and interest, is called the **future value.**

Compound interest provides interest on interest. That is, interest payments are added to the principal each period, and interest is then earned on the original principal amount

future value The amount accumulated, including principal and interest.

and on the amount of added interest. In our Christina example, interest in year 1 is paid on $10,000: 10% × $10,000 = $1,000. If the interest is not withdrawn, the principal for year 2 includes the initial $10,000 deposit plus the $1,000 of interest earned in the first year, $11,000. Interest in year 2 is paid on the $11,000: 10% × $11,000 = $1,100. And in the third year interest will thus be earned on $12,100: $12,100 × 10% = 1,210. The future value of the deposit at the end of three years with compound interest would be $13,310:

	Principal	Compound Interest	Balance End of Year
Year 1	$10,000	$10,000 × 10 = $1,000	$11,000
Year 2	11,000	11,000 × 10 = 1,100	12,100
Year 3	12,100	12,100 × 10 = 1,210	13,310

More generally, suppose you invest S dollars for two periods and earn interest at an interest rate i. After one period, the investment would be increased by the interest earned, Si. You would have $S + $Si = $S(1 + i)$. In the second period you would again earn interest ($i[S(1 + i)]$). After two periods you would have :

$$[S(1 + i)] + (i[S(1 + i)]) = S(1 + i)(1 + i) = S(1 + i)^2$$

The general formula for computing the future value (FV) of S dollars in n years at interest rate i is

$$FV = S(1 + i)^n$$

In general, n refers to the number of periods the funds are invested. Periods can be years, months, days, or any other time period. However, the interest rate must be consistent with the time period. That is, if n refers to days, i must be expressed as X% per day.

The "force" of compound interest can be staggering. For example:

Compound Interest	Future Values at End of		
	10 Years	*20 Years*	*40 Years*
$10,000 × (1.10)^{10}$ = $10,000 × 2.5937 =	$25,937		
$10,000 × (1.10)^{20}$ = $10,000 × 6.7275 =		$67,275	
$10,000 × (1.10)^{40}$ = $10,000 × 45.2593 =			$452,593

Calculating future values and compound interest by hand can be tedious and time consuming. Fortunately, there are tables that do much of the work for you. For example, Table 9-1, page 355, shows the future values of $1 for various periods and interest rates. In the table each number is the solution to the expression $(1 + i)^n$. The value of i is given in the column heading. The value of n is given in the row label for number of periods. Notice that the three-year, 10% future value factor is 1.3310 (the third row, seventh column). This number is calculated as $(1 + 0.10)^3$. This is consistent with our calculation above where we show that $10,000 grows to $13,310 over three years ($10,000 × 1.3310 = $13,310).

Suppose you want to know how much $800 will grow to if left in the bank for nine years at 8% interest. Multiply $800 by $(1 + 0.08)^9$. The value for $(1 + .08)^9$ is found in the nine-year row and 8% column of Table 9-1.

$$\$800 \times 1.9990 = \$1,599.20$$

The examples in this text use the factors from Table 9-1 and similar tables in this chapter, which are rounded to four decimal places. If you use tables with different rounding, or if you use a hand calculator or personal computer, your answers may differ slightly from those given because of a small rounding error.

Table 9-1
Future Value of $1

$$FV = 1(1 + i)^n$$

Periods	3%	4%	5%	6%	7%	8%	10%	12%	14%	16%	18%	20%	22%	24%	25%
1	1.0300	1.0400	1.0500	1.0600	1.0700	1.0800	1.1000	1.1200	1.1400	1.1600	1.1800	1.2000	1.2200	1.2400	1.2500
2	1.0609	1.0816	1.1025	1.1236	1.1449	1.1664	1.2100	1.2544	1.2996	1.3456	1.3924	1.4400	1.4884	1.5376	1.5625
3	1.0927	1.1249	1.1576	1.1910	1.2250	1.2597	1.3310	1.4049	1.4815	1.5609	1.6430	1.7280	1.8158	1.9066	1.9531
4	1.1255	1.1699	1.2155	1.2625	1.3108	1.3605	1.4641	1.5735	1.6890	1.8106	1.9388	2.0736	2.2153	2.3642	2.4414
5	1.1593	1.2167	1.2763	1.3382	1.4026	1.4693	1.6105	1.7623	1.9254	2.1003	2.2878	2.4883	2.7027	2.9316	3.0518
6	1.1941	1.2653	1.3401	1.4185	1.5007	1.5869	1.7716	1.9738	2.1950	2.4364	2.6996	2.9860	3.2973	3.6352	3.8147
7	1.2299	1.3159	1.4071	1.5036	1.6058	1.7138	1.9487	2.2107	2.5023	2.8262	3.1855	3.5832	4.0227	4.5077	4.7684
8	1.2668	1.3686	1.4775	1.5938	1.7182	1.8509	2.1436	2.4760	2.8526	3.2784	3.7589	4.2998	4.9077	5.5895	5.9605
9	1.3048	1.4233	1.5513	1.6895	1.8385	1.9990	2.3579	2.7731	3.2519	3.8030	4.4355	5.1598	5.9874	6.9310	7.4506
10	1.3439	1.4802	1.6289	1.7908	1.9672	2.1589	2.5937	3.1058	3.7072	4.4114	5.2338	6.1917	7.3046	8.5944	9.3132
11	1.3842	1.5395	1.7103	1.8983	2.1049	2.3316	2.8531	3.4785	4.2262	5.1173	6.1759	7.4301	8.9117	10.6571	11.6415
12	1.4258	1.6010	1.7959	2.0122	2.2522	2.5182	3.1384	3.8960	4.8179	5.9360	7.2876	8.9161	10.8722	13.2148	14.5519
13	1.4685	1.6651	1.8856	2.1329	2.4098	2.7196	3.4523	4.3635	5.4924	6.8858	8.5994	10.6993	13.2641	16.3863	18.1899
14	1.5126	1.7317	1.9799	2.2609	2.5785	2.9372	3.7975	4.8871	6.2613	7.9875	10.1472	12.8392	16.1822	20.3191	22.7374
15	1.5580	1.8009	2.0789	2.3966	2.7590	3.1772	4.1772	5.4736	7.1379	9.2655	11.9737	15.4070	19.7423	25.1956	28.4217
16	1.6047	1.8730	2.1829	2.5404	2.9522	3.4259	4.5950	6.1304	8.1372	10.7480	14.1290	18.4884	24.0856	31.2426	35.5271
17	1.6528	1.9479	2.2920	2.6928	3.1588	3.7000	5.0545	6.8660	9.2765	12.4677	16.6722	22.1861	29.3844	38.7408	44.4089
18	1.7024	2.0258	2.4066	2.8543	3.3799	3.9960	5.5599	7.6900	10.5752	14.4625	19.6733	26.6233	35.8490	48.0386	55.5112
19	1.7535	2.1068	2.5270	3.0256	3.6165	4.3157	6.1159	8.6128	12.0557	16.7765	23.2144	31.9480	43.7358	59.5679	69.3889
20	1.8061	2.1911	2.6533	3.2071	3.8697	4.6610	6.7275	9.6463	13.7435	19.4608	27.3930	38.3376	53.3576	73.8641	86.7362
21	1.8603	2.2788	2.7860	3.3996	4.1406	5.0338	7.4002	10.8038	15.6676	22.5745	32.3238	46.0051	65.0963	91.5915	108.4202
22	1.9161	2.3699	2.9253	3.6035	4.4304	5.4365	8.1403	12.1003	17.8610	26.1864	38.1421	55.2061	79.4175	113.5735	135.5253
23	1.9736	2.4647	3.0715	3.8197	4.7405	5.8715	8.9543	13.5523	20.3616	30.3762	45.0076	66.2474	96.8894	140.8312	169.4066
24	2.0328	2.5633	3.2251	4.0489	5.0724	6.3412	9.8497	15.1786	23.2122	35.2364	53.1090	79.4968	118.2050	174.6306	211.7582
25	2.0938	2.6658	3.3864	4.2919	5.4274	6.8485	10.8347	17.0001	26.4619	40.8742	62.6686	95.3962	144.2101	216.5420	264.6978
26	2.1566	2.7725	3.5557	4.5494	5.8074	7.3964	11.9182	19.0401	30.1666	47.4141	73.9490	114.4755	175.9364	268.5121	330.8722
27	2.2213	2.8834	3.7335	4.8223	6.2139	7.9881	13.1100	21.3249	34.3899	55.0004	87.2598	137.3706	214.6424	332.9550	413.5903
28	2.2879	2.9987	3.9201	5.1117	6.6488	8.6271	14.4210	23.8839	39.2045	63.8004	102.9666	164.8447	261.8637	412.8642	516.9879
29	2.3566	3.1187	4.1161	5.4184	7.1143	9.3173	15.8631	26.7499	44.6931	74.0085	121.5005	197.8136	319.4737	511.9516	646.2349
30	2.4273	3.2434	4.3219	5.7435	7.6123	10.0627	17.4494	29.9599	50.9502	85.8499	143.3706	237.3763	389.7579	634.8199	807.7936

PRESENT VALUE

Accountants generally use present values rather than future values to record long-term liabilities. The **present value** is the value today of a future cash inflow or outflow.

Suppose you invest $1.00 today. As shown in the discussion of future values, the $1.00 will grow to $1.06 in one year at 6% interest—that is, $1 \times 1.06 = \$1.06$. At the end of the second year its value is $(\$1 \times 1.06) \times 1.06 = \$1 \times (1.06)^2 = \$1.124$.

present value The value today of a future cash inflow or outflow.

We know how to calculate the future value (FV) of S dollars invested at a known interest rate i for n periods. We can reverse the process to calculate the present value when we know the future value. If

$$FV = S\,(1 + i)^n$$

then the present value (PV) is S, or

$$S = \frac{FV}{(1 + i)^n}$$

If $1.00 is to be received in one year, it is worth $\$1 \div 1.06 = \$0.9434$ today. Suppose you invest $0.9434 today. In one year you will have $\$0.9434 \times 1.06 = \$1.00$. Thus $0.9434 is the present value of $1.00 a year hence at 6%. If the dollar will be received in two years, its present value is $\$1.00 \div (1.06)^2 = \$0.8900$. If $0.89 is invested today, it will grow to $1.00 at the end of two years. The general formula for the present value (PV) of a future value (FV) to be received or paid in n periods at an interest rate of $i\%$ per period is:

$$PV = \frac{FV}{(1 + i)^n} = FV \times \frac{1}{(1 + i)^n}$$

discount rates The interest rates used in determining present values.

Table 9-2 gives factors for $1/(1 + i)^n$ (which is the present value of $1.00) at various interest rates (often called **discount rates**) over several different periods. Present values are also called *discounted values,* and the process of finding the present value is *discounting.* You can think of present values as discounting (decreasing) the value of a future cash inflow or outflow. Why is the value discounted? Because the cash is to be received or paid in the future, not today.

Assume that a prominent city is issuing a three-year non-interest-bearing note payable that promises to pay a lump sum of $1,000 exactly three years from now. You desire an interest rate of return of exactly 6%, compounded annually. The interest rate is being earned by the investor and we use the phrase **rate of return** to refer to the amount earned by the investor expressed as a percentage of the amount invested. How much should you be willing to pay now for the three-year note? The situation is sketched as follows:

rate of return The amount earned by an investor expressed as a percentage of the amount invested.

End of Year	0	1	2	3
	Present Value			Future Value
	? ⟵			$1,000

The factor in the Period 3 row and 6% column of Table 9-2 is 0.8396. The present value of the $1,000 payment is $\$1{,}000 \times 0.8396 = \$839.60$. You should be willing to pay $839.60 for the $1,000 to be received in three years.

Suppose interest is compounded semiannually rather than annually. How much should you be willing to pay now? Remember to pay attention to the number of periods involved, not just the number of years. The three years become six interest payment periods. The rate per period is half the annual rate, or $6\% \div 2 = 3\%$. The factor in the Period 6 row and 3% column of Table 2 is 0.8375. You should now be willing to pay $\$1{,}000 \times 0.8375$, or only $837.50 rather than $839.60. Why do you pay less? Because with more frequent compounding the original investment will grow faster.

Table 9-2
Present Value of $1

$$PV = \frac{1}{(1 + i)^n}$$

Periods	3%	4%	5%	6%	7%	8%	10%	12%	14%	16%	18%	20%	22%	24%	25%
1	.9709	.9615	.9524	.9434	.9346	.9259	.9091	.8929	.8772	.8621	.8475	.8333	.8197	.8065	.8000
2	.9426	.9246	.9070	.8900	.8734	.8573	.8264	.7972	.7695	.7432	.7182	.6944	.6719	.6504	.6400
3	.9151	.8890	.8638	.8396	.8163	.7938	.7513	.7118	.6750	.6407	.6086	.5787	.5507	.5245	.5120
4	.8885	.8548	.8227	.7921	.7629	.7350	.6830	.6355	.5921	.5523	.5158	.4823	.4514	.4230	.4096
5	.8626	.8219	.7835	.7473	.7130	.6806	.6209	.5674	.5194	.4761	.4371	.4019	.3700	.3411	.3277
6	.8375	.7903	.7462	.7050	.6663	.6302	.5645	.5066	.4556	.4104	.3704	.3349	.3033	.2751	.2621
7	.8131	.7599	.7107	.6651	.6227	.5835	.5132	.4523	.3996	.3538	.3139	.2791	.2486	.2218	.2097
8	.7894	.7307	.6768	.6274	.5820	.5403	.4665	.4039	.3506	.3050	.2660	.2326	.2038	.1789	.1678
9	.7664	.7026	.6446	.5919	.5439	.5002	.4241	.3606	.3075	.2630	.2255	.1938	.1670	.1443	.1342
10	.7441	.6756	.6139	.5584	.5083	.4632	.3855	.3220	.2697	.2267	.1911	.1615	.1369	.1164	.1074
11	.7224	.6496	.5847	.5268	.4751	.4289	.3505	.2875	.2366	.1954	.1619	.1346	.1122	.0938	.0859
12	.7014	.6246	.5568	.4970	.4440	.3971	.3186	.2567	.2076	.1685	.1372	.1122	.0920	.0757	.0687
13	.6810	.6006	.5303	.4688	.4150	.3677	.2897	.2292	.1821	.1452	.1163	.0935	.0754	.0610	.0550
14	.6611	.5775	.5051	.4423	.3878	.3405	.2633	.2046	.1597	.1252	.0985	.0779	.0618	.0492	.0440
15	.6419	.5553	.4810	.4173	.3624	.3152	.2394	.1827	.1401	.1079	.0835	.0649	.0507	.0397	.0352
16	.6232	.5339	.4581	.3936	.3387	.2919	.2176	.1631	.1229	.0930	.0708	.0541	.0415	.0320	.0281
17	.6050	.5134	.4363	.3714	.3166	.2703	.1978	.1456	.1078	.0802	.0600	.0451	.0340	.0258	.0225
18	.5874	.4936	.4155	.3503	.2959	.2502	.1799	.1300	.0946	.0691	.0508	.0376	.0279	.0208	.0180
19	.5703	.4746	.3957	.3305	.2765	.2317	.1635	.1161	.0829	.0596	.0431	.0313	.0229	.0168	.0144
20	.5537	.4564	.3769	.3118	.2584	.2145	.1486	.1037	.0728	.0514	.0365	.0261	.0187	.0135	.0115
21	.5375	.4388	.3589	.2942	.2415	.1987	.1351	.0926	.0638	.0443	.0309	.0217	.0154	.0109	.0092
22	.5219	.4220	.3418	.2775	.2257	.1839	.1228	.0826	.0560	.0382	.0262	.0181	.0126	.0088	.0074
23	.5067	.4057	.3256	.2618	.2109	.1703	.1117	.0738	.0491	.0329	.0222	.0151	.0103	.0071	.0059
24	.4919	.3901	.3101	.2470	.1971	.1577	.1015	.0659	.0431	.0284	.0188	.0126	.0085	.0057	.0047
25	.4776	.3751	.2953	.2330	.1842	.1460	.0923	.0588	.0378	.0245	.0160	.0105	.0069	.0046	.0038
26	.4637	.3607	.2812	.2198	.1722	.1352	.0839	.0525	.0331	.0211	.0135	.0087	.0057	.0037	.0030
27	.4502	.3468	.2678	.2074	.1609	.1252	.0763	.0469	.0291	.0182	.0115	.0073	.0047	.0030	.0024
28	.4371	.3335	.2551	.1956	.1504	.1159	.0693	.0419	.0255	.0157	.0097	.0061	.0038	.0024	.0019
29	.4243	.3207	.2429	.1846	.1406	.1073	.0630	.0374	.0224	.0135	.0082	.0051	.0031	.0020	.0015
30	.4120	.3083	.2314	.1741	.1314	.0994	.0573	.0334	.0196	.0116	.0070	.0042	.0026	.0016	.0012
40	.3066	.2083	.1420	.0972	.0668	.0460	.0221	.0107	.0053	.0026	.0013	.0007	.0004	.0002	.0001

(handwritten annotations) Compound

Semi annual → Multiply years by 2 + divide interest rate by 2

To see how present values work in conjunction with future values, let's return to our Christina example. Suppose Christina's financial institution promised to pay her a lump sum of $13,310 at the end of three years for her investment. How much does Christina need to deposit to earn a 10% rate of return, compounded annually? Using Table 9-2, the Period 3 row and the 10% column show a factor of 0.7513. Multiply this factor by the future amount and round to the nearest dollar:

$$PV = 0.7513 \times \$13,310 = \$10,000$$

To make sure you have the hang of present values, use Table 9-2 to obtain the present values of

1. $1,600, @ 20%, to be received at the end of 20 years.
2. $8,300, @ 10%, to be received at the end of 12 years.
3. $8,000, @ 4%, to be received at the end of 4 years.

Answers:

1. $1,600 (0.0261) = $41.76.
2. $8,300 (0.3186) = $2,644.38.
3. $8,000 (0.8548) = $6,838.40.

PRESENT VALUE OF AN ORDINARY ANNUITY

annuity Equal cash flows to take place during successive periods of equal length.

An ordinary **annuity** is a series of equal cash flows to take place at the end of successive periods of equal length. In other words, an annuity pays you the same amount at the end of each period for a set period of time. Its present value is denoted PV_A. Assume that you buy a note from a municipality that promises to pay $1,000 at the end of each of three years. How much should you be willing to pay for this note if you desire a rate of return of 6%, compounded annually?

You could solve this problem using Table 9-2. First, find the present value of each payment you will receive, and then add the present values as in Exhibit 9-1. You should be willing to pay $943.40 for the first payment, $890.00 for the second, and $839.60 for the third, a total of $2,673.00.

Table 9-3 provides a shortcut method for calculating the present value of an annuity. The present value in Exhibit 9-1 can be expressed as:

$$
\begin{aligned}
PV_A &= (\$1,000 \times .9434) + (\$1,000 \times .8900) + (\$1,000 \times .8396) \\
&= \$1,000 \,(.9434 + .8900 + .8396) \\
&= \$1,000 \,(2.6730) \\
&= \$2,673.00
\end{aligned}
$$

The three terms in parentheses are the first three numbers from the 6% column of Table 9-2, and their sum is in the third row of the 6% column of Table 3: 0.9434 + 0.8900 +

Exhibit 9-1

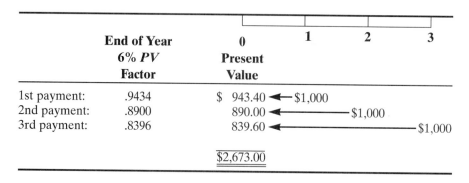

End of Year 6% *PV* Factor	Present Value			
	0	1	2	3
1st payment: .9434	$ 943.40 ◄—$1,000			
2nd payment: .8900	890.00 ◄————$1,000			
3rd payment: .8396	839.60 ◄—————————$1,000			
	$2,673.00			

Table 9-3
Present Value of Ordinary Annuity of $1

$$PV_A = 1\left[\frac{1 - \frac{1}{(1+i)^n}}{i}\right]$$

Periods	3%	4%	5%	6%	7%	8%	10%	12%	14%	16%	18%	20%	22%	24%	25%
1	.9709	.9615	.9524	.9434	.9346	.9259	.9091	.8929	.8772	.8621	.8475	.8333	.8197	.8065	.8000
2	1.9135	1.8861	1.8594	1.8334	1.8080	1.7833	1.7355	1.6901	1.6467	1.6052	1.5656	1.5278	1.4915	1.4568	1.4400
3	2.8286	2.7751	2.7232	2.6730	2.6243	2.5771	2.4869	2.4018	2.3216	2.2459	2.1743	2.1065	2.0422	1.9813	1.9520
4	3.7171	3.6299	3.5460	3.4651	3.3872	3.3121	3.1699	3.0373	2.9137	2.7982	2.6901	2.5887	2.4936	2.4043	2.3616
5	4.5797	4.4518	4.3295	4.2124	4.1002	3.9927	3.7908	3.6048	3.4331	3.2743	3.1272	2.9906	2.8636	2.7454	2.6893
6	5.4172	5.2421	5.0757	4.9173	4.7665	4.6229	4.3553	4.1114	3.8887	3.6847	3.4976	3.3255	3.1669	3.0205	2.9514
7	6.2303	6.0021	5.7864	5.5824	5.3893	5.2064	4.8684	4.5638	4.2883	4.0386	3.8115	3.6046	3.4155	3.2423	3.1611
8	7.0197	6.7327	6.4632	6.2098	5.9713	5.7466	5.3349	4.9676	4.6389	4.3436	4.0776	3.8372	3.6193	3.4212	3.3289
9	7.7861	7.4353	7.1078	6.8017	6.5152	6.2469	5.7590	5.3282	4.9464	4.6065	4.3030	4.0310	3.7863	3.5655	3.4631
10	8.5302	8.1109	7.7217	7.3601	7.0236	6.7101	6.1446	5.6502	5.2161	4.8332	4.4941	4.1925	3.9232	3.6819	3.5705
11	9.2526	8.7605	8.3064	7.8869	7.4987	7.1390	6.4951	5.9377	5.4527	5.0286	4.6560	4.3271	4.0354	3.7757	3.6564
12	9.9540	9.3851	8.8633	8.3838	7.9427	7.5361	6.8137	6.1944	5.6603	5.1971	4.7932	4.4392	4.1274	3.8514	3.7251
13	10.6350	9.9856	9.3936	8.8527	8.3577	7.9038	7.1034	6.4235	5.8424	5.3423	4.9095	4.5327	4.2028	3.9124	3.7801
14	11.2961	10.5631	9.8986	9.2950	8.7455	8.2442	7.3677	6.6282	6.0021	5.4675	5.0081	4.6106	4.2646	3.9616	3.8241
15	11.9379	11.1184	10.3797	9.7122	9.1079	8.5595	7.6061	6.8109	6.1422	5.5755	5.0916	4.6755	4.3152	4.0013	3.8593
16	12.5611	11.6523	10.8378	10.1059	9.4466	8.8514	7.8237	6.9740	6.2651	5.6685	5.1624	4.7296	4.3567	4.0333	3.8874
17	13.1661	12.1657	11.2741	10.4773	9.7632	9.1216	8.0216	7.1196	6.3729	5.7487	5.2223	4.7746	4.3908	4.0591	3.9099
18	13.7535	12.6593	11.6896	10.8276	10.0591	9.3719	8.2014	7.2497	6.4674	5.8178	5.2732	4.8122	4.4187	4.0799	3.9279
19	14.3238	13.1339	12.0853	11.1581	10.3356	9.6036	8.3649	7.3658	6.5504	5.8775	5.3162	4.8435	4.4415	4.0967	3.9424
20	14.8775	13.5903	12.4622	11.4699	10.5940	9.8181	8.5136	7.4694	6.6231	5.9288	5.3527	4.8696	4.4603	4.1103	3.9539
21	15.4150	14.0292	12.8212	11.7641	10.8355	10.0168	8.6487	7.5620	6.6870	5.9731	5.3837	4.8913	4.4756	4.1212	3.9631
22	15.9369	14.4511	13.1630	12.0416	11.0612	10.2007	8.7715	7.6446	6.7429	6.0113	5.4099	4.9094	4.4882	4.1300	3.9705
23	16.4436	14.8568	13.4886	12.3034	11.2722	10.3711	8.8832	7.7184	6.7921	6.0442	5.4321	4.9245	4.4985	4.1371	3.9764
24	16.9355	15.2470	13.7986	12.5504	11.4693	10.5288	8.9847	7.7843	6.8351	6.0726	5.4509	4.9371	4.5070	4.1428	3.9811
25	17.4131	15.6221	14.0939	12.7834	11.6526	10.6748	9.0770	7.8431	6.8729	6.0971	5.4669	4.9476	4.5139	4.1474	3.9849
26	17.8768	15.9828	14.3752	13.0032	11.8258	10.8100	9.1609	7.8957	6.9061	6.1182	5.4804	4.9563	4.5196	4.1511	3.9879
27	18.3270	16.3296	14.6430	13.2105	11.9867	10.9352	9.2372	7.9426	6.9352	6.1364	5.4919	4.9636	4.5243	4.1542	3.9903
28	18.7641	16.6631	14.8981	13.4062	12.1371	11.0511	9.3066	7.9844	6.9607	6.1520	5.5016	4.9697	4.5281	4.1566	3.9923
29	19.1885	16.9837	15.1411	13.5907	12.2777	11.1584	9.3696	8.0218	6.9830	6.1656	5.5098	4.9747	4.5312	4.1585	3.9938
30	19.6004	17.2920	15.3725	13.7648	12.4090	11.2578	9.4269	8.0552	7.0027	6.1772	5.5168	4.9789	4.5338	4.1601	3.9950
40	23.1148	19.7928	17.1591	15.0463	13.3317	11.9246	9.7791	8.2438	7.1050	6.2335	5.5482	4.9966	4.5439	4.1659	3.9995

0.8396 = 2.6730. This shortcut is especially valuable if the cash payments or receipts extend over many periods. Consider an annual cash payment of $1,000 for 20 years at 6%. The present value, calculated from Table 9-3, is $1,000 × 11.4699 = $11,469.90. To use Table 9-2 for this calculation, you would have to perform twenty calculations and then add up the twenty products.

The factors in Table 9-3 can be calculated using the following general formula:

$$PV_A = \frac{1}{i}\left[1 - \frac{1}{(1 + i)^n}\right]$$

Applied to our illustration:

$$PV_A = \frac{1}{0.06}(1 - 0.83962) = \frac{0.16038}{0.06} = 2.6730$$

To make sure you understand present values of annuities, use Table 9-3 to obtain the present values of the following ordinary annuities:

1. $1,600 to be received at the end of each year for 20 years, assuming interest at 20%.
2. $8,300 to be received at the end of each year for 12 years, assuming interest at 10%.
3. $8,000 to be received at the end of each year for 4 years, assuming interest at 4%.

Answers

1. $1,600 (4.8696) = $7,791.36.
2. $8,300 (6.8137) = $56,553.71.
3. $8,000 (3.6299) = $29,039.20.

In particular, note that the higher the interest rate, the lower the present value. Why? Because, at a higher interest rate, you would need to invest less now to obtain the same future value.

VALUING BONDS

Bonds create cash flows in many future periods. As a result, bonds are recorded at the present value of all those future payments, discounted at the market interest rate in effect when the liability was incurred. In Chapter 8 we dealt with cases where the coupon rate paid by the bond and the market rate when it was issued were identical and therefore the bond sold at par value. We did not explain the valuation.

A typical bond consists of a promise to pay interest every six months until maturity and a promise to pay a lump sum at maturity. Suppose a two-year $1,000 bond is issued that pays interest of 10%, that is to say the coupon rate is 10%.

Exhibit 9-2 shows how the bond would be valued, using the tables on pages 357 and 359 and three different effective market interest rates. Note that:

1. Although the quoted bond rates state an annual rate, interest is actually paid semiannually. Thus a 10% bond really pays 5% interest each semiannual period. A two-year bond has four periods, a ten-year bond has twenty periods, and so on.
2. The higher the effective (or market) rate of interest, the lower the present value.

discount on bonds The excess of face amount over the proceeds upon issuance of a bond.

3. When the market interest rate equals the coupon rate of 10%, the bond is worth $1,000. We say such a bond is issued at par. We described the accounting for such a bond in Chapter 8.
4. When the market interest rate of 12% exceeds the 10% coupon rate, the bond sells at a **discount** (that is, for less than par).

premium on bonds The excess of the proceeds over the face amount of a bond.

5. When the market interest rate of 8% is less than the 10% coupon rate, the bond sells at a **premium** (that is, for more than par).

Exhibit 9-2

Computation of Market Value of Bonds
(in dollars)

	Present Value Factor	Total Present Value	Sketch of Cash Flows by Period				
			0	1	2	3	4
Valuation at 10% per year, or 5% per half-year:							
Principal,							
4-period line, Table 9-2							
.8227 × $1,000 = $822.70	.8227	822.70					1,000
Interest,							
4-period line, Table 9-3							
3.5460 × $50 = $177.30	3.5460	177.30	50	50	50	50	
Total		1,000.00					
Valuation at 12% per year, or 6% per half-year:							
Principal	.7921	792.10					1,000
Interest	3.4651	173.25	50	50	50	50	
Total		965.35					
Valuation at 8% per year, or 4% per half-year:							
Principal	.8548	854.80					1,000
Interest	3.6299	181.50	50	50	50	50	
Total		1,036.30					

ACCOUNTING FOR BOND TRANSACTIONS

ISSUING AND TRADING BONDS

Bonds are typically sold through a syndicate (special group) of investment bankers called **underwriters.** That is, the syndicate buys the entire issue of bonds from the corporation, thus guaranteeing that the company will obtain the funds it needs. The syndicate then sells the bonds to the general investing public.

The company sets the terms of the bond contract with the advice of the investment banker who manages the underwriting syndicate. The terms include the time to maturity, interest payment dates, interest amounts, and the size of the bond issue. The rate of interest to be paid by the bond (**coupon rate** or **nominal interest rate**) is usually set as close to the current **market rate** as possible. The market rate is the rate available on investments in similar bonds at a moment in time. Many factors affecting the market rate are discussed here and in Chapter 8, notably general economic conditions, industry conditions, risks of the use of the proceeds, and specific features of the bonds (examples include callability, sinking fund, convertibility).

On the day of issuance, the proceeds to the issuer may be above par or below par, depending on market conditions. If the proceeds are above par, the bonds have been sold at a premium; if the proceeds are below par, the bonds are sold at a discount. When a bond sells at a discount or premium, the **yield to maturity** (market rate, **effective interest rate**)—the rate of interest demanded by investors in a bond—differs from the nominal interest rate. The interest paid in cash, usually semiannually, is determined by the nominal rate, not the effective rate. The yield to maturity is the interest rate at which all contractual cash flows for interest and principal have a present value equal to the proceeds at issue.

Objective 3
Account for bond issues over their entire life.

underwriters A group of investment bankers that buys an entire bond or stock issue from a corporation and then sells the bonds to the general investing public.

coupon rate The rate of interest to be paid on a bond.

nominal interest rate Synonym for coupon rate.

market rate The rate available on investments in similar bonds at a moment in time.

yield to maturity (effective interest rate) The interest rate that equates market price at issue to the present value of principal and interest.

Note that premiums and discounts do not reflect the creditworthiness of the issuer. Instead, they simply reflect differences in the nominal rate and the market rate. These differences often result from the delay between the time a company sets the terms of the bond and when the bond is actually issued.

Bonds typically have a par value of $1,000, but they are usually expressed in terms of percentages of par. When bonds are traded in markets or on exchanges such as the New York Stock Exchange, you can find quotations of their prices in newspaper business sections. A daily quotation for an IBM bond from the February 23, 1998 issue of *Barron's* follows:

| Description | Current Yield | Sales (000) | Weekly | | | Net Change | 52-Weeks | |
			High	Low	Last		High	Low
IBM 7S25	6.8	26	105½	102½	102½	−1⅛	105⅞	90

* The ending price of one $1,000 bond is 102½% of $1,000 = $1,025.00.

current yield Annual interest payments divided by the current price of a bond.

IBM's bonds carrying a 7% coupon rate and maturing in 2025 closed at a price of $1,025.00 (102-½% of $1,000) at the end of the day. The **current yield** is calculated as the annual interest divided by the current price, or 6.8%. Twenty-six thousand bonds were traded, each having a face, or par, value of $1,000. The closing price was down 1⅛ from that of the week earlier. During the last 52 weeks the bonds have varied between 90 and 105⅞. *Barron's* is a weekly publication. Similar daily reporting occurs in *The Wall Street Journal* and *The New York Times*.

The Chrysler example presented earlier showed a sharp drop in value from 1973 to 1982 due to sharply higher interest rates. Extreme increases in general interest rates coincided with increases in Chrysler's firm-specific risk during the period. Interest rates and market values change constantly. Consider the IBM 8⅜ coupon bond maturing in 2019. In 1990 it was rated an Aaa bond, Moody's highest rating, and sold for $928.75 (92⅞) to yield 9.07% if held to maturity. By the end of 1997 it was lower rated on quality (A1). However, its price had risen sharply to $1,168.75 (116⅞) and its yield to maturity had fallen to 6.87%. For IBM bonds, the general fall in interest rates had a bigger effect than the firm-specific increase in risk.

ASSESSING THE RISKINESS OF BONDS

A key feature in deciding the market rate of interest, and therefore the value of a bond, is a risk assessment of the bond. The higher the risk, the higher the interest rate investors will require before making the investment. An individual investor typically cannot spend the time to do in-depth analysis of each bond offering, so commercial services have developed to offer this service. Moody's and Standard & Poor's Corporation (S&P) are perhaps the best known.

They rate bonds issued by corporations according to their creditworthiness. Higher ratings are safer and therefore companies with better ratings pay lower interest rates. Issuers with high proportions of debt and low interest-coverage ratios usually receive lower bond ratings and therefore pay higher interest rates. Why? Because high debt levels and low interest-coverage imply less ability to meet bond obligations and thus place more risk on bondholders. Lower ratings lead to lower prices and therefore higher yields on the bond. As of 1984, 1990, and 1997, the average yields for industrial bonds rated by Moody's were as follows, by rating category:

Rating	Aaa	Aa	A	Baa
Yield 1984	11.76	12.23	12.72	13.34
Yield 1990	9.16	9.58	9.84	11.12
Yield 1997	6.54	6.90	6.95	7.24

Note going across from left to right that in each year the yields rise uniformly as the ratings decrease. Comparing 1990 to 1997 shows that interest rates have fallen significantly during the 1990s. To assign the ratings, S&P often interviews management in addition to analyzing financial data. AAA bonds have the lowest debt ratios and the highest interest-coverage ratios, as you would expect. Investors will accept a lower yield for debt issued by the least risky companies.

In assessing the riskiness of a company's securities, U.S. analysts rely heavily on the debt level. In the United States debt obligations are legally enforceable, and many examples exist where creditors have forced a company to liquidate in order to pay interest or to repay principal. A recent example is Montgomery Ward.

Financial analysts must adapt to the realities facing the specific companies. In Japan, for example, debt ratios tend to be much higher than they are in the United States. This difference partly reflects banking practices. Japanese banks lend very large sums to the biggest and most creditworthy corporations. Although the transaction has the form of debt, it tends to be part of a very long-term relationship between bank and customer. The banks end up with long-term rights that look somewhat like the rights of a U.S. shareholder.

A mortgage bond, which has a specific lien on particular assets, is an inherently safer investment than the company's debentures, which have no specific lien on any asset. If you consider interest payments to be the return the lender earns for making the loan, it would be reasonable for the interest rate on a mortgage bond to be less than the interest rate on a subordinated debenture bond. It will be useful as we consider various characteristics of bond contracts and other lending arrangements, to think about whether the feature would make the contract more or less attractive to the lender. The more attractive to the lender, the lower the interest rate. Here we might think of attractiveness in terms of risk. The less risk of default or nonpayment, the more attractive it is to the lender.

Regardless of a particular lien on an asset, or other feature, the relative attractiveness of specific bonds depends primarily on the creditworthiness of the issuer. Thus IBM can issue billions of dollars of unsecured debentures at relatively low interest rates when compared with the secured mortgage bonds that might be issued by riskier real estate companies.

BONDS ISSUED AT A DISCOUNT

Suppose the 10,000 bonds described in Exhibit 9-2, page 361, are issued at a discount on December 31, 1999 when annual market interest rates are 12%. Proceeds of the sale are $10,000 \times \$965.35 = \$9,653,500$, which reflects an effective interest rate of 6% per semiannual period, as shown in Exhibit 9-2. Therefore the company recognizes a discount of $10,000,000 - \$9,653,500 = \$346,500$ at issuance. The discount results from the fact that the company has use of only $9,653,500, not $10,000,000. The journal entry at issue is:

Cash	9,653,500	
Discount on bonds payable	346,500	
Bonds payable		10,000,000

The discount on bonds payable is a *contra* account. It is deducted from bonds payable. The bonds payable account usually shows the face amount, and the difference between bonds payable and discount on bonds payable is the amount shown on the balance sheet, often referred to as the net carrying amount, the net liability, or simply the book value:

Issuer's Balance Sheet	December 31, 1999
Bonds payable, 10% due December 31, 2001	$10,000,000
Deduct: Discount on bonds payable	346,500
Net liability	$ 9,653,500

For bonds issued at a discount, interest takes two forms—semiannual cash outlays of $5\% \times \$10$ million = $500,000 plus an "extra" lump-sum cash payment of $346,500 at maturity (total payment of $10,000,000 at maturity when only $9,653,500 was actually borrowed). For the issuer, the extra $346,500 is another cost of using the borrowed funds over the four semiannual periods. For the investor, the extra amount represents extra interest in addition to the coupon payments. The issuer should spread the extra $346,500 over all four periods, not simply charge it at maturity. The spreading of the discount over the life of the bonds is called **discount amortization.**

discount amortization
The spreading of bond discount over the life of the bonds as expense.

How much of the $346,500 should be amortized each semiannual period? A simple alternative is straight-line amortization:

Cash interest payment, 0.05 × $10,000,000	$500,000
Amortization of discount, $346,500 ÷ 4 periods	86,625
Total semiannual interest expense	$586,625

Notice that the amortization of a bond discount increases the interest expense of the issuer. The straight-line amortization is simple to use, but it has the drawback of implying a different effective interest rate each period. During the first six months of the life of the bonds, the implied interest rate would be 6.08% ($586,625 interest expense divided by proceeds or carrying value of $9,653,500). The $86,625 of amortized discount would increase the carrying value or book value of the debt to $9,740,125 in the second six months, yielding an implied interest rate of 6.02% ($586,625 ÷ $9,740,125).

effective-interest amortization (compound interest method) An amortization method that uses a constant interest rate.

A preferred amortization method that uses a constant interest rate is **effective-interest amortization,** also called the **compound interest method.** The FASB requires its use for bond discounts and premiums. The key to effective-interest amortization is that each period bears an interest expense equal to the carrying value of the debt (the net liability or the face amount less unamortized discount) multiplied by the market interest rate in effect when the bond was issued. The product is the effective-interest amount. The difference between the effective-interest amount and the cash interest payment is the amount of discount amortized for the period.

Consider our example with a market rate of 12% (or 6% each semiannual period) when the bond was issued. The effective-interest amortization schedule is shown in Exhibit 9-3. Notice that the discount amortized is not the same amount each period. The balance sheet disclosure of the bond payable is the ending net liability, calculated as the difference between the face or par value and the unamortized discount. Thus at June 30, 2000, the balance sheet would reflect a liability of $9,732,707. The calculation might be shown on the balance sheet or in the footnotes as:

Issuer's Balance Sheets	12/31/99	6/30/00	12/31/00	6/30/01	12/31/01*
Bonds payable, 10% due 12/31/01	$10,000,000	$10,000,000	$10,000,000	$10,000,000	$10,000,000
Deduct: Unamortized discount	346,500	267,293	183,334	94,337	—
Net liability	$ 9,653,500	$ 9,732,707	$ 9,816,666	$ 9,905,663	$10,000,000

*Before payment at maturity.

Exhibit 9-3 shows the worksheet and journal entries for the effective-interest method of amortizing the bond discount. The journal entries are presented in the left column using a discount account and in the right column using only a bonds payable account. Note that the interest expense each period is the market rate of interest at issue times the carrying value or book value of the bond (see column (2) of Exhibit 9-3). This value changes each semiannual period. The cash payment is a constant $500,000, calculated as one-half the coupon rate (10% ÷ 2) times the par value ($10,000,000). Exhibit 9-4 illustrates this information in the context of the accounting equation.

Exhibit 9-3

Effective-Interest Amortization of Bond Discount

For Six Months Ended	(1) Beginning Net Liability	(2) Effective Interest* @ 6%**	(3) Nominal Interest† @ 5%	(4) Discount Amortized (2) − (3)	Ending Liability Face Amount	Ending Liability Unamortized Discount	Ending Net Liability
12/31/99	—	—	—	—	$10,000,000	$346,500	$ 9,653,500
6/30/00	$9,653,500	$579,207	$500,000	$79,207	10,000,000	267,293++	9,732,707
12/31/00	9,732,707	583,959	500,000	83,959	10,000,000	183,334	9,816,666
6/30/01	9,816,666	588,997	500,000	88,997	10,000,000	94,337	9,905,663
12/31/01	9,905,663	594,337	500,000	94,337	10,000,000	0	10,000,000

*Market interest rate when issued times beginning net liability, column (1).

**To avoid rounding errors, an unrounded actual effective rate slightly under 6% was used. The table used to calculate the proceeds of the issue has too few significant digits to calculate the exact present value of a number as large as $10 million. The more exact issue price would be $9,653,489.

†Nominal (coupon interest) rate times par value (face value), for six months.

++$346,500 − $79,207 = $267,293; $267,293 − $83,959 = $183,334; etc.

JOURNAL ENTRIES: USING A DISCOUNT ACCOUNT OR USING BONDS PAYABLE DIRECTLY

12/31/99	1.	Cash 9,653,500			Cash	9,653,500	
		Discount on bonds payable	346,500		Bonds payable		9,653,500
		Bonds payable		10,000,000			
6/30/00	2.	Interest expense	579,207		Interest expense	579,207	
		Discount on bonds payable ..		79,207	Bonds payable		79,207
		Cash		500,000	Cash		500,000
12/31/00		Interest expense	583,959		Interest expense	583,959	
		Discount on bonds payable ..		83,959	Bonds payable		83,959
		Cash		500,000	Cash		500,000
6/30/01		Interest expense	588,997		Interest expense	588,997	
		Discount on bonds payable ..		88,997	Bonds payable		88,997
		Cash		500,000	Cash		500,000
12/31/01		Interest expense	594,337		Interest expense	594,337	
		Discount on bonds payable ..		94,337	Bonds payable		94,337
		Cash		500,000	Cash		500,000
12/31/01	3.	Bonds payable	10,000,000		Bonds payable	10,000,000	
		Cash		10,000,000	Cash		10,000,000

Exhibit 9-4

Balance Sheet Equation Effects of Effective-Interest Amortization of Bond Discount (rounded to thousands of dollars)

	A	=	L		+	SE
	Cash		Bonds Payable	Discount on Bonds Payable		Retained Income
Issuer's records:						
1. Issuance	+9,654	=	+10,000	−346 [Increase Discount]		
2. Semiannual interest Six months ended:						
6/30/00	−500	=		+ 79		−579
12/31/00	−500	=		+ 84 [Decrease		−584 [Increase
6/30/01	−500	=		+ 89 Discount]		−584 Interest
12/31/01	−500	=		+ 94		−594 Expense]
3. Maturity value (final payment)	−10,000	=	−10,000	0		
Bond-related totals	− 2,346	=	+ 0	+0	+	−2,346

BONDS ISSUED AT A PREMIUM

Accounting for bonds issued at a premium is not difficult after you have mastered bond discounts. The differences are reversed from discount bonds:

1. The cash proceeds exceed the face amount.
2. The amount of the contra account Premium on Bonds Payable is added to the face amount to determine the net liability reported in the balance sheet.
3. The amortization of bond premium decreases the interest expense.

To illustrate, suppose the 10,000 bonds described earlier were issued when annual market interest rates were 8% (and semiannual rates 4%). Proceeds would be 10,000 × $1,036.30 = $10,363,000 as shown in Exhibit 9-2. Exhibits 9-5 and 9-6 show how the effective-interest method is applied to the bond premium. The key concept remains the same as that for amortization of a bond discount. The interest expense equals the net liability each period multiplied by the market interest rate in effect when the bond was issued. Balance sheets show the net liability calculated as the face amount plus unamortized premium. The premium reduces to zero over the life of the bond:

Issuer's Balance Sheets	12/31/99	6/30/00	12/31/00	6/30/01	12/31/01*
Bonds payable, 10% due 12/31/01	$10,000,000	$10,000,000	$10,000,000	$10,000,000	$10,000,000
Add: Premium on bonds payable	363,000	277,517	188,615	96,157	0
Net liability	$10,363,000	$10,277,517	$10,188,615	$10,096,157	$10,000,000

*Before payment at maturity.

EARLY EXTINGUISHMENT

Investors do not always hold bonds until maturity. Often they sell the bonds to other investors. Such a sale does not affect the issuer's books unless the issuer is the one doing the buying. Companies do redeem or pay off their own bonds either by purchases on the open market or by exercising a call option. When a company chooses to redeem its own bonds before maturity, the transaction is known as an early extinguishment. Gains or losses on these early extinguishments of debt are computed in the usual manner. That is, the difference between the cash paid and the net carrying amount of the bonds (face less unamortized discount or plus unamortized premium) is the gain or loss.

Consider the bonds issued at a discount and described in Exhibit 9-3. Suppose the issuer purchases all of its bonds on the open market for 96 on December 31, 2000 (after all interest payments and amortization were recorded for 2000):

Carrying amount:		
Face or par value	$10,000,000	
Deduct: Unamortized discount on bonds*	183,334	$9,816,666
Cash required, 96% of $10,000,000		9,600,000
Difference, gain on early extinguishment of debt		$ 216,666

*See Exhibit 9-3. Of the original $346,500 discount, $79,207 + $83,959 = $163,166 has been amortized, leaving $183,334 of the discount unamortized.

Exhibit 9-5

Effective-Interest Amortization of Bond Premium

For Six Months Ended	(1) Beginning Net Liability	(2) Effective Interest* @ 4%**	(3) Nominal Interest† @ 5%	(4) Premium Amortized (3) − (2)	Ending Liability		
					Face Amount	Unamortized Premium	Ending Net Liability
12/31/99	—	—	—	—	$10,000,000	$363,000	$10,363,000
6/30/00	$10,363,000	$414,517	$500,000	$85,483	10,000,000	277,517‡	10,277,517
12/31/00	10,277,517	411,098	500,000	88,902	10,000,000	188,615	10,188,615
6/30/01	10,188,615	407,542	500,000	92,458	10,000,000	96,157	10,096,157
12/31/01	10,096,157	403,843	500,000	96,157	10,000,000	0	10,000,000

*Market interest rate when issued times beginning net liability, column (1).
**To avoid rounding errors, an unrounded actual effective rate slightly under 4% was used.
†Nominal (coupon interest) rate times par value (face values), for six months.
‡$363,000 − $85,483 = $277,517; $277,517 − $88,902 = $188,615; etc.

JOURNAL ENTRIES: PREMIUM AMORTIZATION (WITHOUT EXPLANATIONS)

```
12/31/99   1.  Cash .........................    10,363,000
                   Premium on bonds payable ...                   363,000
                   Bonds payable ..............               $10,000,000
6/30/00    2.  Interest expense .................      414,517
               Premium on bonds payable ........       85,483
                   Cash .......................                   500,000
12/31/00       Interest expense .................      411,098
               Premium on bonds payable ........       88,902
                   Cash .......................                   500,000
6/30/01        Interest expense .................      407,542
               Premium on bonds payable ........       92,458
                   Cash .......................                   500,000
12/31/01       Interest expense .................      403,843
               Premium on bonds payable ........       96,157
                   Cash .......................                   500,000
12/31/01   3.  Bonds payable ...................    10,000,000
                   Cash .......................                10,000,000
```

Exhibit 9-6

Balance Sheet Equation Effects of Effective-Interest Amortization of Bond Premium

(rounded to thousands of dollars)

	A	=	L		+	SE
	Cash		Bonds Payable	Premium on Bonds Payable		Retained Income
Issuer's records:						
1. Issuance	+10,363	=	+10,000	+363 [Increase Premium]		
2. Semiannual interest						
Six months ended:						
6/30/00	−500	=		−85		−415 [Increase Interest Expense]
12/31/00	−500	=		−89 [Decrease Premium]		−411
6/30/01	−500	=		−92		−408
12/31/01	−500	=		−96		−404
3. Maturity value (final payment)	−10,000	=	−10,000			
Bond-related totals	− 1,637	=	+ 0	+ 1*		+ −1,638*

*Rounding error; should equal 0 and 1637.

Exhibit 9-7

Analysis of Early Extinguishment of Debt on Issuer's Records
(in thousands of dollars)

	A	=	L			+	SE
	Cash		Bonds Payable	Discount on Bonds Payable			Retained Income
Redemption, December 31, 2000	−9,600	=	−10,000	+183	[Decrease] [Discount]	+217	[Gain on Early Extinguishment]

Exhibit 9-7 presents an analysis of the transaction (rounded to thousands of dollars). The $216,666 gain on extinguishment of debt would be shown on an income statement below operating income as a separate classification called an extraordinary item. The journal entry on December 31, 2000, is:

Bond payable	10,000,000	
Discount on bonds payable		183,334
Gain on early extinguishment of debt		216,666
Cash		9,600,000
To record open-market acquisition of entire issue of 10% bonds at 96.		

BONDS SOLD BETWEEN INTEREST DATES

Bond interest payments are typically made semiannually. Suppose the company in our example had its $10 million worth of 10% bonds printed and ready to be issued on December 31, 1999, but then market conditions delayed the bond issue. On January 31, 2000, one month after the originally planned issue date, the bonds were issued at par. The bond contract still requires the payment of $500,000 interest every six months, beginning June 30, 2000.

How does this delay in the issuance date affect the *investor?* Bonds sold between interest dates command the market price plus accrued interest. If an investor owns a bond for only five months but collects interest for a full six months, one month of interest is unearned. Thus the market quotations you see for bonds always mean that the investor must pay an extra amount for any unearned interest to be received at the next interest payment date. In our example, the price to be paid is:

Market price of bonds at 100 on 1/31/00	$10,000,000
Accrued interest, 0.10 × $10,000,000 × ½	83,333
Market price plus accrued interest	$10,083,333

Note that the $500,000 interest payment due on June 30, 2000, is spread over the first six months of 2000 by the straight-line method—that is, with an equal amount to each month even though the bond was in use for only five of those six months. In this instance the straight-line method is actually used because the distortion as compared to the effective interest rate is small within a six month period.

How does the issue date affect the *issuer?* Exhibit 9-8 presents an analysis of these transactions (rounded to thousands of dollars). Note that the interest expense for the first half of

Exhibit 9-8

Analysis of Bonds Sold between Interest Dates

(in thousands of dollars)

	A	=	L		+	SE
	Cash		Bonds Payable	Accrued Interest Payable		Retained Income
Issuance, 1/31/00	+10,083	=	+10,000	+83		
Interest payment, 6/30/00	−500	=		−83		−417 [Increase Interest Expense]

2000 is properly measured as $500,000 − $83,333 = $416,667, pertaining to only five months that the money was actually in use. Although the company pays out the full $500,000, this amount is lessened by the extra $83,333 paid by the buyer. The journal entries follow:

```
1/31/00   Cash ..........................   $10,083,333
              Bonds payable ................                $10,000,000
              Accrued interest payable .......                     83,333
6/30/00   Accrued interest payable ..............   83,333
          Interest expense ...................  416,667
              Cash .......................                      500,000
```

Obviously, the analysis of transactions can be made more complicated by combining the acquisitions of bonds between interest dates with discounts and premiums. However, these are mechanical details that do not involve any new concepts, so we need not cover them in detail here.

NON-INTEREST-BEARING NOTES AND BONDS

Some notes and bonds do not provide semiannual interest payments. Instead they simply pay a lump sum at a specified date. For example, consider **zero coupon** notes. These bonds provide no cash interest payments during their life. The name, zero coupon, is completely descriptive. To call such notes non-interest-bearing is a little misleading, though. Investors demand interest revenue. Otherwise, why would they bother investing in the first place? Therefore, zero coupon and similar notes are sold for less than the face or maturity value. The investor determines their market value at the issuance date by calculating the present value of their maturity value, using the market rate of interest for notes having similar terms and risks. The discount is amortized as interest expense to the borrower (issuer) and as interest revenue to the lender (investor) over the life of the note.

Instead of collecting semiannual or other periodic payments, banks often *discount* both long-term and short-term notes when making loans. Consider a two-year, "non-interest-bearing," $10,000 face-value note issued on December 31, 1998, when semiannual market interest rates were 5%. In exchange for a promise to pay $10,000 on December 31, 2000, the bank provides the borrower with cash equal to the present value (PV) of the $10,000 payment:

> PV of $1.00 from Table 9-2, 5% column, 4-period row = 0.8227
> PV of $10,000 note = $10,000 × 0.8227 = $8,227

The note requires no specific interest payments. However, there is **implicit interest** (or **imputed interest**), which is a form of interest expense that is not explicitly recognized as such in a loan agreement. The imputed interest amount is based on an **imputed interest rate,** which is the market rate that equates the proceeds of the loan with the present value of the loan payments.

zero coupon A bond or note that pays no cash interest during its life.

implicit interest (imputed interest) An interest expense that is not explicitly recognized in a loan agreement.

imputed interest rate The market interest rate that equates the proceeds from a loan with the present value of the loan payments.

Exhibit 9-9

Analysis of Transactions of Borrower, Discounted Notes

	A	=	L		+	SE
	Cash	Notes Payable	Discount on Notes Payable			Retained Income
Proceeds of loan	+ 8,227	= +10,000	−1,773	[Increase Discount]		
Semiannual amortization						
Six months ended:						
6/30/99		=	+411			−411
12/31/99		=	+432	[Decrease Discount]		−432 [Increase Interest Expense]
6/30/00		=	+454			−454
12/31/00		=	+476			−476
Payment of note	−10,000	= −10,000				
Bond-related totals	− 1,773	= + 0	+ 0		+	−1,773

In this example, the $10,000 payment on December 31, 2000 will consist of $8,227 repayment of principal and $1,773 ($10,000 − $8,227) of imputed interest. At issue, the note is shown on the borrower's balance sheet as follows:

Note payable, due December 31, 2000	$10,000
Deduct: Discount on note payable	1,773
Net liability	$ 8,227

Exhibit 9-9 shows how interest expense is recognized for each semiannual period. Each amortization of the discount decreases the discount account and increases the net carrying amount. The appropriate journal entries follow:

12/31/98	Cash	8,227	
	Discount on note payable	1,773	
	Note payable		$10,000
6/30/99	Interest expense	411	
	Discount on note payable		411
12/31/99	Interest expense	432	
	Discount on note payable		432
6/30/00	Interest expense	454	
	Discount on note payable		454
12/31/00	Interest expense	476	
	Discount on note payable		476
	Note payable	10,000	
	Cash		10,000

ACCOUNTING FOR LEASES

Objective 4
Value and account for long-term lease transactions.

Leasing is a big business. Any asset imaginable, from television sets to cars to buildings, can be acquired via a lease contract. A **lease** is a contract whereby an owner (**lessor**) grants the use of property to a second party (**lessee**) in exchange for rental payments. Our discussion focuses on leasing from the lessee's point of view.

Some lease payments are recorded as expense each time a payment is made. This would surely be true of a month to month lease on an apartment for example. But other leases are actually recorded as liabilities and as assets when the contract is signed. Why? Because, although the ownership of a leased item has not been legally transferred, the lessee has full legal rights to use the item and full legal responsibility for maintaining it and paying for it. To see this most clearly, imagine the lease of a BMW that obligated you to payments of $800 per month for four years and gave you the right to buy the BMW at the end of the lease for $1.00. Perhaps you made a $5,000 down payment to enter into the lease. Under the lease contract, you promise to maintain, license and insure it. These rights and responsibilities are equivalent to ownership, so the leased item is considered an asset even though the lessee does not own it. In fact, you are almost certain to pay the $1.00 and take ownership at the end of the lease.

If this lease were just treated as $800 of expense each month, the reader of your financial statement might think you had more cash available than you really do. You have committed $800 per month to these payments. This obligation is no different than the obligation to make a loan payment, so accountants decided to treat this transaction *as if* the lessee owns it and *as if* the money to buy it had been borrowed.

lease A contract whereby an owner (lessor) grants the use of property to a second party (lessee) for rental payments.

lessor The owner of property who grants usage rights to the lessee.

lessee The party that has the right to use leased property and makes lease payments to the lessor.

OPERATING AND CAPITAL LEASES

The names given to the two types of lease accounting are: capital leases and operating leases. **Capital leases** (or **financing leases**) transfer most of the risks and benefits of ownership to the lessee. They are equivalent to installment sales in which the purchase price of an item is paid over time along with interest payments. The leased item must be recorded as if it were sold by the lessor and purchased by the lessee. The BMW lease would be a capital lease.

All other leases are **operating leases.** An example is a room or a car rented by the day, week, or month. Operating leases are accounted for as ordinary rent expenses. No balance sheet accounts are affected by operating leases.

Consider a simple example to see how the accounting differs for operating and capital leases. Suppose the Bestick Company can acquire a truck that has a useful life of four years and no residual value under either of the following conditions:

capital lease (financing lease) A lease that transfers substantially all the risks and benefits of ownership to the lessee.

operating lease A lease that should be accounted for by the lessee as ordinary rent expenses.

Buy Outright	**or**	**Capital Lease**

Cash outlays, $50,000
Borrow $50,000 cash to be repaid
  in four equal installments at 12%
  interest compounded annually
		Rental of $16,462 per year, payable
		  at the end of each of four years

There is no basic difference between an outright purchase or an irrevocable (noncancellable) capital lease for four years. The Bestick Company uses the asset for its entire useful life and must pay for repairs, property taxes, and other operating costs under either plan.

Most lease rentals are paid at the start of each payment period, but to ease our computations we assume that each payment of $16,462 will occur at the end of the year. To make the comparison between capital leasing and purchasing, we need to calculate payments on the $50,000 loan in the purchase option:

$$\text{Let } X = \text{loan payment}$$
$$\$50,000 = \text{PV of annuity of } X \text{ per year for 4 years at 12\%}$$
$$\$50,000 = 3.0373X$$
$$X = \$50,000 \div 3.0373$$
$$X = \$16,462 \text{ per year}$$

Note that this loan payment is exactly equal to the lease payment. Thus, from Bestick's perspective as lessee, both buying outright and capital leasing create an obligation for four $16,462 payments that have a present value of $50,000.

Now suppose this lease contract were treated as an *operating lease.* Each year the journal entry would be:

```
        Rent expense ......................  16,462
            Cash ..........................            16,462
        To record lease payment.
```

No leasehold asset or lease liability would appear on the balance sheet.

Suppose the lease described must be accounted for as a *capital lease*. Then both a leasehold asset and a lease liability must be placed on the balance sheet at the present value of future lease payments, $50,000 in this illustration. The signing of the capital lease requires the following journal entry:

```
        Truck leasehold .....................  50,000
            Capital lease liability .............            50,000
        To record lease payment.
```

At the end of each of the four years, the asset must be amortized. Straight-line amortization, which is used almost without exception, is $50,000 ÷ 4 = $12,500 annually.

The yearly journal entries for the leasehold expense are:

```
        Leasehold amortization expense ......  12,500
            Truck leasehold ................            12,500
```

In addition, the annual lease payment must be recorded. Each lease payment consists of interest expense plus an amount that reduces the outstanding liability. The effective-interest method is used, as Exhibit 9-10 demonstrates. Study the exhibit before proceeding.

The yearly journal entries for lease payments are:

	YEAR 1		YEAR 2		YEAR 3		YEAR 4	
Interest expense	6,000		4,745		3,339		1,764	
Lease liability	10,462		11,717		13,123		14,698	
Cash		16,462		16,462		16,462		16,462

Leasehold assets and lease liabilities are illustrated by the following items from the annual report of Kmart for the year ending January 30, 1997:

Kmart Company Footnotes
(Selected Items in millions)

| | End of January | |
	1997	*1996*
Assets:		
Leased property under capital leases,	$2,820	$2,875
less accumulated amortization	1,541	1,489
	$1,279	$1,386
Liabilities:		
Obligations under capital leases	$1,478	$1,586

Kmart's 1997 annual report reveals that "Kmart conducts operations primarily in leased facilities. Kmart store leases are generally for terms of 25 years with multiple five-year renewal options which allow the company the option to extend the life of the lease up to 50 years beyond the initial noncancellable term." Many of these leases also require Kmart to pay taxes, maintenance, and insurance. GAAP in the United States accounts for such lease or rental contracts "as if" Kmart borrowed money and purchased the leased stores. Kmart records both an asset (called "leased property under capital leases") and a liability called a "capital lease obligation" and shows them on the balance sheet.

But treatment varies across the globe. If Kmart were incorporated and issuing financial reports in seventeen of the forty-four countries whose accounting practices were recently surveyed by the Center for International Financial Analysis & Research, no dis-

Exhibit 9-10

Analytical Schedule of Capital Lease Payments

End of Year	(1) Capital Lease Liability at Beginning of Year	(2) Interest Expense at 12% Per Year	(3) Cash for Capital Lease Payment	(3) − (2) Reduction in Lease Liability	(5) (1) − (4) Capital Lease Liability at End of Year
1	$50,000	$6,000	$16,462	10,462	$39,538
2	39,538	4,745	16,462	11,717	27,821
3	27,821	3,339	16,462	13,123	14,698
4	14,698	1,764	16,462	14,698	0

Exhibit 9-11

Comparison of Annual Expenses: Operating versus Capital Leases

	Operating-Lease Method	Capital-Lease Method			Differences	
Year	(a) Lease Payment*	(b) Amortization of Asset†	(c) Interest Expense‡	(d) (b) + (c) Total Expense	(e) (a) − (d) Difference in Pretax Income	(f) Cumulative Difference in Pretax Income
1	$16,462	$12,500	$ 6,000	$18,500	$(2,038)	$(2,038)
2	16,462	12,500	4,745	17,245	(783)	(2,821)
3	16,462	12,500	3,339	15,839	623	(2,198)
4	16,462	12,500	1,764	14,264	2,198	0
Cumulative expenses	$65,848	$50,000	$15,848	$65,848	$ 0	

*Rent expense for the year under the operating-lease method.
†$50,000 ÷ 4 = $12,500.
‡From Exhibit 9-10.

closure of these long-term lease commitments would be required. These countries include Austria, Brazil, Sri Lanka, and Taiwan. Most other countries follow lease disclosure practices similar to those in the United States.

DIFFERENCES IN INCOME STATEMENTS

Exhibit 9-11 summarizes the major differences between the accounting for operating leases and the accounting for capital leases. The cumulative expenses are the same, $65,848, but the timing differs. In comparison with the operating-lease approach, the capital-lease approach tends to bunch heavier charges in the early years. The longer the lease, the more pronounced the differences will be in the early years. Therefore, immediate reported income is hurt more under the capital-lease approach.

An operating lease affects the income statement as rent expense, which is the amount of the lease payment. A capital lease affects the income statement as amortization (of the asset) plus interest expense (on the liability).

CRITERIA FOR CAPITAL LEASES

Prior to 1976, almost all leases in the United States were reported in financial statements as operating leases. However, many companies were criticized for keeping "invisible debt" or using "off-balance sheet financing" by treating noncancellable leases, which created a liability, merely as a monthly rent payment and not reporting them on the balance sheet under either assets or liabilities. The accounting procedures we have reviewed for capital leases were created as a way of more fairly representing these leases on the balance sheet.

The lease structure determines whether a lease is operating or capital. Under U.S. GAAP, a capital lease exists if one or more of the following conditions are met:

1. Title is transferred to the lessee by the end of the lease term.
2. An inexpensive purchase option is available to the lessee at the end of the lease.
3. The lease term equals or exceeds 75% of the estimated economic life of the property.
4. At the start of the lease term, the present value of minimum lease payments is at least 90% of the property's fair value.

Managers cannot choose how to treat an existing lease. However, some managers do seek to structure leases so that they do not meet any of the criteria of a capital lease and therefore are not shown on the balance sheet.

PENSIONS AND OTHER POSTRETIREMENT BENEFITS

Objective 5
Evaluate pensions and other postretirement benefits.

pensions Payments to former employees after they retire.

other postretirement benefits Benefits provided to retired workers in addition to a pension, such as life and health insurance.

Most U.S. companies provide retired employees with reduced wages after they stop working. Such payments are commonly called **pensions.** Retirees may also continue to receive health insurance, life insurance, or other employee benefits, which are commonly called **other postretirement benefits.**

Why are pensions and postretirement benefits liabilities? Because of accrual accounting's system of matching expenses with their associated revenues. Workers "earn" the right to postretirement payments and benefits during their working years. Financial analysts and accountants agree that these benefits should be recognized and recorded as they are earned, years before they are disbursed. As a result, the obligation to provide postretirement benefits is reported as an unpaid liability on the balance sheet. The long time between when the liability is recorded and when it is finally paid causes us to use present value techniques to measure the obligation.

To see how the accounting for pensions and postretirement benefits works, imagine a firm with a 45-year-old employee who has worked for 20 years earning $50,000 per year. She will receive a pension of $25,000 per year after retirement at age 65. To calculate the firm's liability for this pension, assume an interest rate of 10% and a life expectancy of 20 years after retirement. The employee will collect a 20-year annuity, which will have a present value of $212,840 (8.5136 from Table 9-3, p. 359, times $25,000) at retirement. Today, 20 years before retirement, the present value is $31,628 (0.1486 from Table 9-2 times $212,840). Firms must disclose this present value calculation of their liability in the notes to their financial statements.

To calculate present values for pensions, firms must estimate employee life expectancy, future work lives, ages at retirement, and levels of future pension payments to retirees. Also, the firm must choose an interest rate. The formal calculations are normally done by actuaries, specialists at making such predictions.

In fact, pension liabilities are effectively provided for each year by setting some money aside as the liability grows. Companies do not just accrue huge pension liabilities during the career of each employee and then pay out the money after retirement. What would happen if the company went out of business before it paid off accrued employee pensions? There would be a lot of angry, and poorer, retirees. Because this problem really occurred in the 50s and 60s, U.S. tax law now provides incentives for companies to make payments into a pension fund that is separate from the company's assets and controlled by a trustee. These payments are made during the employees' working years to assure that assets will be available to meet the pension obligation at retirement. Because significant assets are set aside on behalf of the employees, the major disclosures about pensions occur in footnotes. The footnotes reveal both the present value of the obligation and the current level of assets that are set aside to meet the obligation. IBM's footnotes disclose that in 1996, $34 billion of assets were set aside to cover approximately $28 billion of obligations.

How, then, do companies account for pensions? Suppose a company's current pension expense is $100,000, $90,000 of which is paid in cash to a pension fund. Note the two parts, an expense that represents the increase in the obligation during the current year, and a recording of the cash paid, which is not always equal to the expense. The accounting for pensions has the following basic framework:

	A	=	L	+	SE
	Cash		Accrued Pensions Payable		Retained Income
Current pension expense	−90,000	=	+10,000		−100,000 [Increase Pension Expense]

The journal entry would be:

```
Pension expense..........................   100,000
    Cash...............................              90,000
    Accrued pensions payable .............              10,000
To record pension expense for the year.
```

Accounting for the expense of life insurance, health insurance, and similar postretirement benefits is similar to accounting for pensions. The key difference is that congress has not created a special tax incentive to set money aside. Most companies do not set aside specific assets on behalf of employees and therefore the full amount is recorded as a liability. Financial analysts and accountants treat the present value of expected payments as a liability. Increases in the liability are recognized as a current expense.

Suppose the present value of postretirement benefits is $100,000 at the beginning of 19X1 and $120,000 at the end of the year. The summary journal entry to record the $20,000 increase for 19X1 is:

```
Other postretirement
    benefits expense..................   $20,000
    Accrued postretirement
        benefits payable .............              $20,000
```

The balance sheets thus include the following:

	December 31,	
	19X1	19X0
Long-Term Liabilities:		
Other postretirment benefits	$120,000	$100,000

Internationally, practice regarding pensions and other postretirement benefits varies widely, mainly because of differences in business practices. For example, many countries provide the majority of retirement income through individual savings or through tax-supported government programs akin to the U.S. Social Security Administration. In these cases, actual company pensions are either extremely small or do not exist, so there is nothing that needs to be reported. In roughly half of the 45 countries examined in a recent survey, it was common practice for pensions to be managed by an independent outside trustee with funding from the sponsoring company through periodic payments to the trustee, in accord with U.S. practice. This separate fund provides substantial security to employees that their future pensions claims will be honored. In the United States, prior to the 1970s it was very common for companies to go out of business and for their current and future retirees to be left without pensions. Today outside trustees maintain financial assets on behalf of current workers, and the Pension Benefit Guarantee Corporation provides some "pension insurance" for workers.

SUMMARY PROBLEMS FOR YOUR REVIEW

PROBLEM ONE

Suppose that on December 31, 1999, Exxon issued $12 million of 10-year, 10% debentures. Assume that the annual market interest rate at issuance was 14%.

1. Compute the proceeds from issuing the debentures.
2. Prepare an analysis of the following items: (a) issuance of the debentures; (b) the first two semiannual interest payments; and (c) the payment of the maturity value. Use the balance sheet equation (similar to the presentation in Exhibit 9-4, p. 365). Round to the nearest thousand dollars. Use a bond discount account.
3. Prepare journal entries for the items in requirement 2. Use a bond discount account.

SOLUTION TO PROBLEM ONE

1. Because the market interest rate exceeds the nominal rate, the proceeds will be less than the face amount. This can be computed as the present value (PV) of the twenty $600,000 interest payments and the $12 million maturity value at 7% per semiannual period:

PV of interest payments: 10.5940 × $600,000	$6,356,400
PV of maturity value: 0.2584 × $12,000,000	3,100,800
Total proceeds	$9,457,200

2. See Exhibit 9-12.

3.

12/31/99:	Cash	9,457,200	
	Discount on bonds payable	2,542,800	
	Bonds payable....................		12,000,000
6/30/00:	Interest expense	662,004	
	Discount on bonds payable...........		62,004
	Cash............................		600,000
12/31/00:	Interest expense	666,344	
	Discount on bonds payable...........		66,344
	Cash............................		600,000
12/31/09:	Bonds payable	12,000,000	
	Cash............................		12,000,000

PROBLEM TWO

Xerox Corporation plans to enter some new communications business. The company expects to accumulate sufficient cash from its new operations to pay a lump sum of $200 million to Prudential Insurance Company at the end of five years. Prudential will lend

Exhibit 9-12

Analysis of Exxon's Bond Transactions: Problem Two

(rounded to thousands of dollars)

	A	=	L		+	SE
	Cash	*Bonds Payable*	*Discount on Bonds Payable*			*Retained Income*
Exxon's records:						
1. Issuance	+9,457	+12,000	−2,543	[Increase Discount]		
2. Semiannual interest						
Six months ended:						
6/30/00	−600		+62	[Decrease	−662*	[Increase
12/31/00	−600		+66	Discount]	−666*	Interest Expense]
3. Maturity value						
(final payment)	−12,000	−12,000				
Bond-related totals†	−14,543	0				−14,543

*7% × 9,457 = 662; 7% × (9,457 + 62) = 666.

†Totals after payment at maturity and all 20 entries for discount amortization and interest payments are made.

money on a promissory note now, will take no payments until the end of five years, and desires 12% interest compounded annually.

1. How much money will Prudential lend Xerox?
2. Prepare journal entries for Xerox at the inception of the loan and at the end of each of the first two years.

SOLUTION TO PROBLEM TWO

The initial step in solving present value problems focuses on a basic question, Which table should I use? No computations should be made until you are convinced that you are using the correct table.

1. Use Table 9-2. The $200 million is a future amount. Its present value is

$$PV = \$200,000,000 \times \frac{1}{(1 + 0.12)^5}$$

The conversion factor, $1/(1 + 0.12)^5$, is in row 5 and the 12% column. It is 0.5674.

$$PV = \$200,000,000 \times 0.5674 = \$113,480,000$$

2.

Cash	113,480,000	
Long-term note payable (or long-term debt)		113,480,000
To record borrowing that is payable in a lump sum at the end of five years at 12% interest compounded annually.		
Interest expense	13,617,600	
Long-term note payable		13,617,600
To record interest expense and corresponding accumulation of principal at the end of the first year: 0.12 × $113,480,000 = $13,617,600.		
Interest expense	15,251,712	
Long-term note payable		15,251,712
To record interest expense and corresponding accumulation of principal at the end of the second year: 0.12 × ($113,480,000 + $13,617,600).		

Reflect on the entries for interest. Note how the interest expense becomes larger if no interest payments are made from year to year. This mounting interest expense occurs because the unpaid interest is being added to the principal to form a new higher principal each year.

PROBLEM THREE

Refer to the preceding problem. Suppose Xerox and Prudential agree on a 12% interest rate compounded annually. However, Xerox will pay a total of $200 million in the form of $40 million annual payments at the end of each of the next five years. How much money will Prudential lend Xerox?

SOLUTION TO PROBLEM THREE

Use Table 9-3. The $40 million is a uniform periodic payment at the end of a series of years. Therefore it is an annuity. Its present value is:

$$\begin{aligned} PV_A &= \text{Annual payment} \times \text{Present value factor} \\ &= \$40 \text{ million} \times \text{Present value factor for 5 years at 12\%} \\ &= \$40 \text{ million} \times 3.6048 \\ &= \$144,192,000 \end{aligned}$$

In particular, note that Prudential is willing to lend more than in Problem Two even though the interest rate is the same. Why? Because Prudential will get its money back more quickly.

PROBLEM FOUR

Suppose the Philbrick company enters into a lease to use a machine for three years with payments at the end of each year. Lease payments for the three-year term of the lease are as follows, for a total of $120,000. The lease is treated as a capital lease and an interest rate of 10% is used.

year 1	$ 40,000
year 2	40,000
year 3	40,000
Total minimum rentals	$120,000

1. Calculate the amount to be recorded as the carrying value of the capital leased asset and the capital lease liability as of the beginning of the lease on 12/31/X0.
2. How will the first year's payment be recorded?
3. How will the first year's income statement be affected by the lease?

SOLUTION TO PROBLEM FOUR

1. The present value of a three year annuity of $40,000 per year at 10% will be the initial value of the asset and the liability. From Table 9-3, 2.4869 is the present value factor.

$$2.4869 \times \$40,000 = \$99,476$$

2. The first year's payment will be for $40,000, part of which is interest and part of which is principal repayment. The interest portion is $.10 \times 99,476 = 9,948$. The journal entry would be

Interest expense	9,948	
Capital lease obligation	30,052	
Cash		40,000

3. The first year's income statement will show an expense of $9,948 for interest. It will also show depreciation on the capital leased asset of 33,159 calculated on a straight line basis ($99,476 ÷ 3 yrs).

Highlights to Remember

The time value of money is a critical concept for understanding many long-term liabilities. Present value concepts can be used to value future cash obligation in today's dollars. Bonds are a common long-term liability. Their current economic value can be calculated by combining the present value of their future interest payments and of their principal payment. Investors use this procedure to decide on how much to pay for a bond. Companies originally record the bond liability at the amount received from investors upon issue. During the life of the bond, interest expense is recognized each period. The effective interest rate method is used to calculate the interest expense each period. Bond discounts increase interest expense and bond premiums decrease it. The market interest rate depends on the risk associated with the bond. Third parties such as S&P and Moody's evaluate bonds to help investors decide how much a bond is worth.

Leases are contracts that grant the lessee the right to use property owned by the lessor. Because many leases involve long time periods and place many of the risks of ownership upon the lessee, GAAP contains rules to classify some leases as capital leases. A capital lease is accounted for as if the asset were purchased. Both an asset and a liability are created when a capital lease is created. The value is based on the present value of payments required under the lease. The asset is amortized and the payments are treated as payments on a loan using the effective interest amortization of interest.

The matching principal leads companies to calculate their liability for future obligations for pensions and other postretirement benefits annually. The change in the liability is recorded as an expense during the current period. Pension disclosures involve footnote presentations of the present value of the obligation as well as the value of pension assets set aside with a trustee on behalf of the employees. For life and health insurance obligations to future retirees, no assets are typically set aside. Thus, financial statements typically present a significant liability equal to the present value of anticipated future payments for life and health insurance. Both pensions and insurance obligations depend on complex forecasts of future costs, retiree life expectancies, and so forth.

Accounting Vocabulary

annuity, p. 358
capital lease, p. 371
compound interest, p. 353
compound interest method, p. 364
coupon rate, p. 361
current yield, p. 361
discount amortization, p. 364
discount on bonds, p. 360
discount rates, p. 356
effective-interest amortization, p. 364

effective interest rate, p. 361
financing lease, p. 371
future value, p. 353
implicit interest, p. 369
imputed interest, p. 369
imputed interest rate, p. 369
lease, p. 371
lessee, p. 371
lessor, p. 371
market rate, p. 361
nominal interest rate, p. 361

operating lease, p. 371
other postretirement benefits, p. 374
pensions, p. 374
premium on bonds, p. 360
present value, p. 356
rate of return, p. 356
simple interest, p. 353
underwriters, p. 361
yield to maturity, p. 361
zero coupon, p. 369

Assignment Material

QUESTIONS

9-1. Explain what is meant by the *time value of money.*

9-2. "Future value and present value are two sides of the same coin." Explain.

9-3. "If interest is compounded semiannually rather than annually, you get twice as much interest." Do you agree? Explain.

9-4. How are Table 9-2 (p. 357) and Table 9-3 (p. 359) related to each other?

9-5. Contrast *nominal* and *effective* interest rates for bonds.

9-6. A company issued bonds with a nominal rate of 10%. At what market rates will the bonds be issued at a discount? At what market rates will they be issued at a premium?

9-7. Why is it important for both companies and investors to assess the riskiness of bonds?

9-8. "The quoted bond interest rates imply a rate per annum, but the bond markets do not mean that rate literally." Explain.

9-9. "When a bond is issued at a discount, there are two components of interest expense." Explain.

9-10. Distinguish between *straight-line* amortization and *effective-interest* amortization.

9-11. What are the three main differences between accounting for a bond discount and accounting for a bond premium?

9-12. "A company that issues zero coupon bonds recognizes no interest expense until the bond matures." Do you agree? Explain.

9-13. Why might a company prefer to lease rather than to buy?

9-14. Certain leases are essentially equivalent to purchases. A company must account for such leases as if the asset had been purchased. Explain.

9-15. "A capital lease results in both an asset and a liability on a company's balance sheet." Explain.

9-16. We observe extensive use of capital leases by airlines as a method for financing planes. Why might this be true? Does it make the airline seem to have lower debt ratios?

9-17. "A capital lease and operating lease are recorded differently on the balance sheet, but their effect on the income statement is the same." Do you agree? Explain.

9-18. Discuss which characteristics of a lease are evaluated in deciding whether it is a capital lease.

9-19. "Because a company never knows how much it will have to pay for pensions, no pension liability is recognized. Pension obligations are simply explained in a footnote to the financial statements." Do you agree? Explain.

9-20. Variation in international practice in the accounting for pensions can be explained in part by different financial practices in different countries. Discuss.

EXERCISES

9-21 Exercises in Compound Interest

1. You deposit $6,000. How much will you have in four years at 8%, compounded annually? At 12%?

2. A savings and loan association offers depositors a lump-sum payment of $6,000 four years hence. If you desire an interest rate of 8% compounded annually, how much will you be willing to deposit? at an interest rate of 12%?

3. Repeat requirement 2, but assume that the interest rates are compounded semiannually.

9-22 Exercises in Compound Interest

A reliable friend has asked you for a loan. You are pondering various proposals for repayment.

1. Repayment of a lump sum of $20,000 four years hence. How much will you lend if your desired rate of return is (a) 10% compounded annually, (b) 20% compounded annually?

2. Repeat requirement 1, but assume that the interest rates are compounded semi-annually.

3. Suppose the loan is to be paid in full by equal payments of $5,000 at the end of each of the next four years. How much will you lend if your desired rate of return is (a) 10% compounded annually, (b) 20% compounded annually?

9-23 Compound Interest and Journal Entries

Jenkins Company acquired equipment for a $300,000 promissory note, payable five years hence, non-interest-bearing, but having an implicit interest rate of 14% compounded annually. Prepare the journal entry for (1) the acquisition of the equipment and (2) interest expense for the first year.

9-24 Compound Interest and Journal Entries

A Munich company has bought some equipment on a contract entailing a DM 100,000 cash down payment and a DM 400,000 lump sum to be paid at the end of four years. The same equipment can be bought for DM 336,840 cash. DM refers to the German mark, a unit of currency.

Required

1. Prepare the journal entry for the acquisition of the equipment.

2. Prepare journal entries at the end of each of the first two years. Ignore entries for depreciation.

9-25 Compound Interest and Journal Entries

A newspaper company bought new presses for a $100,000 down payment and $80,000 to be paid at the end of each of four years. The applicable imputed interest rate is 10% on the unpaid balance. Prepare journal entries (1) for the acquisition and (2) at the end of the first year.

9-26 Exercises in Compound Interest

a. It is your sixtieth birthday. You plan to work five more years before retiring. Then you want to spend $10,000 for a Mediterranean cruise. What lump sum do you have to invest now in order to accumulate the $10,000? Assume that your minimum desired rate of return is

(1) 5%, compounded annually.

(2) 10%, compounded annually.

(3) 20%, compounded annually.

b. You want to spend $3,000 on a vacation at the end of each of the next five years. What lump sum do you have to invest now in order to take the five vacations? Assume that your minimum desired rate of return is

(1) 5%, compounded annually.

(2) 10%, compounded annually.

(3) 20%, compounded annually.

9-27 Exercises in Compound Interest

a. At age sixty, you find that your employer is moving to another location. You receive termination pay of $80,000. You have some savings and wonder whether to retire now.

(1) If you invest the $80,000 now at 6%, compounded annually, how much money can you withdraw from your account each year so that at the end of five years there will be a zero balance?

(2) If you invest it at 10%?

b. At 16%, compounded annually, which of the following plans is more desirable in terms of present value? Show computations to support your answer.

	Annual Cash Inflows	
Year	Mining	Farming
1	$100,000	$ 20,000
2	80,000	40,000
3	60,000	60,000
4	40,000	80,000
5	20,000	100,000
	$300,000	$300,000

9-28 Basic Relationships in Interest Tables

1. Suppose you borrow $20,000 now at 16% interest compounded annually. The borrowed amount plus interest will be repaid in a lump sum at the end of six years. How much must be repaid? Use Table 9-1 and basic equation: FV = Present amount $\times$ Future value factor.

2. Repeat requirement 1 using Table 9-2 and the basic equation: PV = Future amount $\times$ Present value factor.

3. Assume the same facts as in requirement 1 except that the loan will be repaid in equal installments at the end of each of six years. How much must be repaid each year? Use Table 9-3 and the basic equation: PV_A = Future annual amounts $\times$ Conversion factor.

9-29 Deferred Annuity Exercise

It is your twenty-fifth birthday. On your thirtieth birthday, and on three successive birthdays thereafter, you intend to spend exactly $500 for a birthday celebration. What lump sum do you have to invest now in order to have the four celebrations? Assume that the money will earn interest, compounded annually, of 8%.

9-30 Discounted Present Value and Bonds

On December 31, 19X1, a company issued a three-year $1,000 bond that promises an interest rate of 12%, payable 6% semiannually. Compute the discounted present value of the principal and the interest as of December 31, 19X1, if the market rate of interest for such securities is 12%, 14%, and 10%, respectively. Show your computations, including a sketch of cash flows. Round to the nearest dollar.

9-31 Discounted Present Value and Leases

Suppose Wal-Mart signed a ten-year lease for a new store location. The lease calls for an immediate payment of $20,000 and annual payments of $15,000 at the end of each of the next nine years. Wal-Mart expects to earn 16% interest, compounded annually, on its investments. What is the present value of the lease payments?

9-32 Bond Quotations

Following is a bond quotation for American Telephone and Telegraph Company:

Description	Current Yield	Close	Net Change
AT&T 6S00	6.1	98	$-\frac{3}{8}$

1. How was the current yield of 6.1% calculated?
2. What price (in total dollars) would you have paid for one bond?
3. What was the closing price (in total dollars) for the bond on the preceding day?

9-33 Criteria for Capital Leases

Indicate which of the following leases would be a capital lease and which would be operating leases.

    a. Rental of a warehouse for $10,000 per month, renewable annually.

    b. Rental of a crane for $8,000 per month on a six-year lease, with an option to buy for $10,000 at the end of the six years.

    c. Rental of a computer for $1,000 per month on a five-year lease. At the end of five years the computer is expected to have a fair market value of $2,000.

    d. Rental of an automobile on a three-year lease for $500 per month. The auto will be returned to the dealer after the three years.

    e. Rental of 10 forklifts for $1,400 per month on a eight-year lease. The value of the forklifts at the end of 12 years is uncertain, but the total economic life is not expected to be more than 10 years.

9-34 Accounting for Pensions

A company's current pension expense is $800,000, $300,000 of which is paid in cash to a trustee. Using the balance sheet equation format, show which accounts are affected by these data. Prepare the corresponding journal entry.

PROBLEMS

9-35 Present Value and Sports Salaries

The *New York Times* reported that Jack Morris, a pitcher, signed a $4 million contract with the Detroit Tigers. His 1988 salary was $1,988,000, and his 1989 salary was $1,989,000. However, $1 million of his 1989 salary was paid in 1988. The *Times* reported that the advance payment increased the contract's value by about $50,000, pushing it over $4 million.

    Assume that the contract was signed on December 1, 1987, that the 1988 and 1989 payments were both made on December 1 of the respective years, and that the appropriate discount rate was 10%.

    1. What was the present value of the contract on the day it was signed?

    2. What would have been the present value of the contract if the $1 million advance payment had been paid in 1989 instead of 1988?

    3. How much present value (as of December 1, 1987) did Morris gain by receiving the $1 million payment in 1988 rather than in 1989?

    4. Do you agree that the contract was worth more than $4 million? Explain.

9-36 Bond Discount Transactions and Straight-Line Amortization

On December 31, 1998, ATP Technology issued $20 million of ten-year, 12% debentures. Proceeds were $19 million.

Show all amounts in thousands of dollars.

    1. Using the balance sheet equation format, prepare an analysis of bond transactions. Assume straight-line amortization. Show entries for the issuer regarding (a) issuance, (b) one semiannual interest payment, and (c) payment of maturity value.

    2. Show all the corresponding journal entries keyed as above.

    3. Show how the bond-related accounts would appear on the balance sheets as of December 31, 1998 and 2007.

9-37 Bonds Issued at Par

On December 31, 1998, Alaska Fisheries, Inc. issued $15 million of 10-year, 10% debentures at par.

Required

1. Compute the proceeds from issuing the debentures.
2. Using the balance sheet equation format, prepare an analysis of this bond transaction. Show entries for the issuer regarding (a) issuance, (b) the first semiannual interest payment, and (c) payment of maturity value.
3. Show all the corresponding journal entries keyed as in requirement 2.
4. Show how the bond-related accounts would appear on the balance sheet as of December 31, 1998, and June 30, 1999. Assume that the semiannual interest payment and amortization due on the balance sheet date have been recorded.

9-38 Bonds Issued at a Discount

On December 31, 1998, Ruzinski Construction issued $20 million of 10-year, 12% debentures. The market interest rate at issuance was 14%.

Required

1. Compute the proceeds from issuing the debentures.
2. Using the balance sheet equation format, prepare an analysis of this bond transaction. Show entries for the issuer regarding (a) issuance, (b) the first semiannual interest payment and discount amortization, and (c) payment of maturity value. Round all amounts to the nearest thousand.
3. Show all the corresponding journal entries keyed as in requirement 2.
4. Show how the bond-related accounts would appear on the balance sheets as of December 31, 1998, and June 30, 1999. Assume that the semiannual interest payment and amortization due on the balance sheet dates have been recorded.

9-39 Bond Discount Transactions

(Alternates are 9-40 and 9-41.) On February 1, 1998, an electric utility issued $100 million of 20-year, 9% debentures. Proceeds were $91,191 million, implying a market interest rate of 10%.

Required

Show all amounts in thousands of dollars.

1. Using the balance sheet equation format, prepare an analysis of bond transactions. Assume effective-interest amortization. Show entries for the issuer regarding (a) issuance, (b) the first semiannual interest payment, and (c) payment of maturity value.
2. Show all the corresponding journal entries for (a), (b), and (c) in requirement 1.
3. Show how the bond-related accounts would appear on the balance sheets as of February 1, 1998 and 1999. Assume the February 1 interest payment and amortization of bond discount have been made.

9-40 Bonds Issued at a Discount

(Alternates are 9-39 and 9-41.) On January 1, 1999, Metro Bus Company issued $5 million of five-year, 11% debentures. The market interest rate at issuance was 12%.

Required

1. Compute the proceeds from issuing the debentures.
2. Using the balance sheet equation format, prepare an analysis of this bond transaction. Show entries for the issuer regarding (a) issuance, (b) the first semiannual interest payment, and (c) payment of maturity value. Round to the nearest thousand.
3. Show all the corresponding journal entries keyed as in requirement 2.
4. Show how the bond-related accounts would appear on the balance sheets as of January 1, 1999, and July 1, 1999. Assume that the semiannual interest payment and amortization due on the balance sheet dates have been recorded.

9-41 Bond Discount Transactions

(Alternates are 9-39 and 9-40.) Assume that on December 31, 1995, Oslo Tool and Die issued NKR10 million of ten-year, 10% debentures. Proceeds were NKR7,881,000; therefore the market rate of interest was 14%. (NKR is the Norwegian Kroner.)

1. Using the balance sheet equation format, prepare an analysis of transactions for Oslo. Key your transactions as follows: (a) issuance, (b) first semiannual interest using effective-interest amortization of bond discount, and (c) payment of maturity value. Round all amounts to the nearest thousand.

2. Prepare corresponding journal entries keyed (a), (b), and (c) as in requirement 1.

3. Show how the bond-related accounts would appear on Oslo's balance sheets as of December 31, 1995, and June 30, 1996. Assume that the semiannual interest payments and amortization have been recorded.

9-42 Bonds Issued at a Premium

(Alternates are 9-43 and 9-44.) On December 31, 1998, Sayers Toyota issued $3 million of 10-year, 12% debentures. The market interest rate at issuance was 10%.

1. Compute the proceeds from issuing the debentures.

2. Using the balance sheet equation format, prepare an analysis of this bond transaction. Show entries for the issuer regarding (a) issuance, (b) the first semiannual interest payment and premium amortization, and (c) payment of maturity value. Round all amounts to the nearest thousand.

3. Show all the corresponding journal entries keyed as in requirement 2.

4. Show how the bond-related accounts would appear on the balance sheets as of December 31, 1998, and June 30, 1999. Assume that the semiannual interest payment and amortization due on the balance sheet dates have been recorded.

9-43 Bonds Issued at a Premium

(Alternates are 9-42 and 9-44.) On January 1, 1999, Melbourne Travel issued $2 million of five-year, 10% debentures. The market interest rate at issuance was 8%.

1. Compute the proceeds from issuing the debentures.

2. Using the balance sheet equation format, prepare an analysis of this bond transaction. Show entries for the issuer regarding (a) issuance, (b) the first semiannual interest payment, and (c) payment of maturity value. Round to the nearest thousand.

3. Show all the corresponding journal entries keyed as in requirement 2.

4. Show how the bond-related accounts would appear on the balance sheets as of January 1, 1999, and July 1, 1999. Assume that the semiannual interest payments and amortization due on the balance sheet date have been recorded.

9-44 Bond Premium Transactions

(Alternates are 9-42 and 9-43.) Assume that on December 31, 1998, Zurich Ski Company issued CHF10 million of ten-year, 10% debentures. Proceeds were CHF11,359,000; therefore the market rate of interest was 8%. (CHF is the Swiss franc.)

1. Using the balance sheet equation format, prepare an analysis of transactions for Zurich Ski. Key your transactions as follows: (a) issuance, (b) first semiannual interest using effective-interest amortization of bond discount, and (c) payment of maturity value. Round all amounts to the nearest thousand.

2. Prepare corresponding journal entries keyed (a), (b), and (c) as in requirement 1.

3. Show how the bond-related accounts would appear on Zurich Ski's balance sheets as of December 31, 1998, and June 30, 1999. Assume that the semiannual interest payment and amortization have been recorded.

9-45 Early Extinguishment of Debt

On December 31, 1997, Carribbean Cruises issued $20 million of ten-year, 12% debentures. The market interest rate at issuance was 14%. On December 31, 1998 (after all interest payments and amortization had been recorded for 1998), the company purchased all the debentures for $18.5 million. Throughout their life, the debentures had been held by a large insurance company.

Required Show all amounts in thousands of dollars. Round to the nearest thousand.

1. Compute the gain or loss on early extinguishment.
2. Using the balance sheet equation, present an analysis of the transaction on the issuer's books.
3. Show the appropriate journal entry.
4. At what price on December 31, 1998 could Carribbean Cruises redeem the bonds and realize a $500,000 gain?

9-46 Early Extinguishment of Debt

(Alternate is 9-45.) On December 31, 1995, a real estate holding company issued $10 million of ten-year, 12% debentures. The market interest rate at issuance was 12%. Suppose that on December 31, 1996 (after all interest payments and amortization had been recorded for 1996), the company purchased all the debentures for $9.6 million. The debentures had been held by a large insurance company throughout their life.

Required Show all amounts in thousands of dollars.

1. Compute the gain or loss on early extinguishment.
2. Using the balance sheet equation, present an analysis of the transaction on the issuer's books.
3. Show the appropriate journal entry.

9-47 Retirement of Bonds

This is a more difficult problem than others in this group.

On January 2, 1988, the Newcastle Financial Corporation sold a large issue of Series A £1,000 denomination bonds. The bonds had a stated coupon rate of 6% (annual), had a term to maturity of twenty years, and made semiannual coupon payments. Market conditions at the time were such that the bonds sold at their face value.

During the ensuing ten years, market interest rates fluctuated widely, and by January 2, 1998, the Newcastle bonds were trading at a price that provided an annual yield of 10%. Newcastle's management was considering purchasing the Series A bonds in the open market and retiring them; the necessary capital was to be raised by a new bond issue—the Series B bonds. Series B bonds were to be £1,000 denomination coupon (semiannual) bonds with a stated annual rate of 8% and a twenty-year term. Management felt that these bonds could be sold at a price yielding no more than 10%, especially if the Series A bonds were retired.

Required
1. On January 2, 1998, at what price could Newcastle Financial purchase the Series A bonds? *Hint:* The applicable factors are 5% and 20 periods.
2. Show the journal entries necessary to record the following transactions:
   a. Issue of one Series B bond on January 2, 1998.
   b. Purchase and retirement of one Series A bond on January 2, 1998.
   c. The first coupon payment on a Series B bond on July 2, 1998. Newcastle uses the effective-interest method of accounting for bond premium and discount.
   d. The second coupon payment on a Series B bond on January 2, 1999.

9-48 Non-Interest Bearing Notes

(Alternate is 9-49.) A local bookstore borrowed from a bank on a one-year note. The face value of the note was $20,000. However, the bank deducted its interest "in advance" at 18% of the face value.

Show the effects on the borrower's records at inception and at the end of the year:

Required

1. Using the balance sheet equation, prepare an analysis of transactions.
2. Prepare journal entries.
3. What was the real rate of interest?

9-49 Non-Interest Bearing Notes

(Alternate is 9-48.) On July 31, 1997, a veterinarian just beginning a new practice borrowed money from a bank on a two-year note due on July 31, 1999. The face value of the note was $50,000. However, the bank deducted interest of $10,140 "in advance." Assume annual compounding.

Show the effects on the borrower's records. Show the effects at July 31, 1998 and 1999.

Required

1. Using the balance sheet equation, prepare an analysis of transactions.
2. Prepare journal entries.
3. Calculate the effective annual rate of interest.

9-50 Zero Coupon Bonds

Since 1985, the U.S. Treasury has required issuers of "deep-discount" or "zero coupon" debt securities to use an effective-interest approach to amortization of discount rather than straight-line amortization. The Treasury claimed that the old tax law, which permitted straight-line amortization, resulted in overstatements of deductions in early years.

Required

1. Assume that General Motors issues a 10-year zero coupon bond having a face amount of $20,000,000 to yield 10%. For simplicity, assume that the 10% yield is compounded annually. Prepare the journal entry for the issuer.
2. Prepare the journal entry for interest expense for the first full year and the second full year using (a) straight-line and (b) effective-interest amortization.
3. Assume an income tax rate of 40%. How much more income tax for the first year would the issuer have to pay because of applying effective-interest instead of straight-line amortization?

9-51 Zero Coupon Bonds

Tenet Healthcare Corp. runs more than 125 hospitals and has revenue of more than $2 billion per year. The company included the following information on its balance sheet:

	August 31	
	1996	*1995*
Zero Coupon Guaranteed Bonds due 1997, and 2002, $130.6 million face value, net of $28.9 million unamortized discount at August 31, 1996	$101,700,000	$95,600,000

Assume that none of the bonds were issued or retired in fiscal 1996.

Required

1. Assume that the bonds were issued on August 31, 1995. Prepare the journal entry at issuance. Do not use a discount account.
2. Prepare the journal entry for recording interest expense on the bonds for fiscal 1996. Assume annual compounding of interest.

3. Assume that the bonds maturing in August of 1997 have a face value of $30 million and an effective annual interest rate of 6%. Assume annual compounding. Calculate their value at August 31, 1996.

4. Given your answer to number 3 above, estimate the effective interest rate on the bonds maturing in 2002. Assume semi-annual compounding. (*Hint:* These values do not correspond exactly to tabulated values; an approximation is close enough.)

9-52 Bonds Sold between Interest Dates

On December 31, 1998, a company had some bonds printed and ready for issuance. But market conditions soured. The bonds were not issued until February 28, 1999, at par. The indenture requires payment of semiannual interest on December 31 and June 30. The face value of the bonds is $20 million. The interest rate is 12%.

Required

1. Compute the total proceeds of the issue on February 28.

2. Prepare an analysis of transactions, using the balance sheet equation. Show amounts in thousands of dollars. Show the effects on the issuer's records on February 28 and June 30, 1999.

3. Prepare corresponding journal entries.

9-53 Capital Lease

The Chicago Packing Company acquired packaging equipment on a capital lease. There were annual lease payments of $400,000 at the end of each of three years. The implicit interest rate was 18% compounded annually.

Required

1. Compute the present value of the capital lease.

2. Prepare journal entries at the inception of the lease and for each of the three years. Distinguish between the short-term and long-term classifications of the lease.

9-54 Comparison of Operating and Capital Lease

Refer to the preceding problem. Suppose the capital lease were regarded as an operating lease. Ignore income taxes. Fill in the blanks (prepare supporting computations):

	Operating Lease	Capital Lease	Difference
Total expenses:			
Year 1	?	?	?
Year 2	?	?	?
Two years together	?	?	?
End of year 1:			
Total assets	?	?	?
Total liabilities	?	?	?
Retained income	?	?	?
End of year 2:			
Total assets	?	?	?
Total liabilities	?	?	?
Retained income	?	?	?

9-55 Capital or Operating Lease

On December 31, 19X8, Cesar's Wood Products Company has been offered an electronically controlled automatic lathe (a) outright for $100,000 cash or (b) on a noncancellable lease whereby rental payments would be made at the end of each year for three years. The lathe will become obsolete and worthless at the end of three years. The company can borrow $100,000 cash on a three-year loan payable at maturity at 16% compounded annually.

Required

1. Compute the annual rental payment, assuming that the lessor desires a 16% rate of return per year.
2. If the lease were accounted for as an operating lease, what annual journal entry would be made?
3. The lease is a capital lease. Prepare an analytical schedule of each lease payment. Show the lease liability at the beginning of the year, interest expense, lease payment, and lease liability at end of year.
4. Prepare an analysis of transactions, using the balance sheet equation format.
5. Prepare yearly journal entries.

9-56 Leases

The following information appeared in a footnote to the 1996 annual report of Delta Air Lines, Incorporated, a June 30 fiscal-year-end company:

At June 30, 1996, the company's minimum rental commitments under capital leases and noncancellable operating leases with initial or remaining terms of more than one year were (in millions):

Years Ending June 30	Capital Leases	Operating Leases
1997	$101	$ 871
1998	97	863
1999	96	868
2000	65	842
2001	55	823
After 2001	166	10,800
Total minimum lease payment	$580	$15,067
Less: Amounts representing interest	$146	
Present value of future minimum capital lease payments	$434	

Required

1. Suppose the minimum capital lease payments are made in equal amounts on September 30, December 31, March 31, and June 30 of each year. Compute the interest and principal to be paid on capital leases during the first half of fiscal 1997. Do calculations in millions with two decimal places. Assume an interest rate of 8% per annum, compounded quarterly.
2. Prepare the journal entries for the lease payments in requirement 1 on September 30 and December 31, 1997.
3. Suppose the operating leases were capital leases, the payments after 2001 were spread evenly over 12 years, and the payments were made annually at year-end. If operating leases were capitalized at 8% also, how much would long-term debt increase? Do calculations to closest million.

9-57 Leases

Consider footnote 4 from the 1997 annual report of Federal Express

Footnote 4:
   The company utilizes certain aircraft, land, facilities, and equipment under capital and operating leases which expire at various dates through 2025. A summary of future minimum lease payments under capital leases and noncancellable operating leases at May 31, 1997 are as follows:

(Dollars in Millions)	Capital Leases	Operating Leases
Minimum lease payments for year ending May 31,		
1998	$ 16	$ 827
1999	16	839
2000	16	789
2001	16	749
2002	16	685
Later years	340	7,789
Total minimum lease payments	420	$11,678

Required

1. Footnote 4 contains the minimum future lease payments due under Federal Express's capital and operating leases. Compute the net present value of the *operating* lease payments as of May 31, 1997. Use a 10% implicit interest rate. For ease of computation, assume that each payment is made on May 31 of the designated year (i.e., the first $827 million payment is made on May 31, 1998) and that the final payment, labeled "Later," is made on May 31, 2003.

2. Suppose Federal Express were to capitalize the operating leases examined in requirement 1. Show the journal entries necessary to

   a. Capitalize the leases on June 1, 1997. Ignore any prior period adjustments and do not break the lease obligation into current and long-term portions.

   b. Record the first payment on May 31, 1998.

9-58 Effect of Capital Leases

Deb Shops, Inc., a chain of specialty women's apparel stores, reported the following information about leases in its annual report (in thousands):

	January 31	
	1997	**1996**
Capital lease asset, gross	$1,982	$1,982
Less: Accumulated depreciation	1,387	1,288
Capital lease asset, net	$ 595	$ 694

The only asset under a capital lease is a warehouse and office building. The building has an economic life of twenty years and is being depreciated on a straight-line basis. Deb Shops had a loss before tax of $5,654,809 in fiscal 1997.

Required

1. Calculate the depreciation on the warehouse and office building for the fiscal year ending January 31, 1997.

2. On what date was the building placed into service? (*Hint:* How long would it take to build up the accumulated depreciation shown?)

3. The interest on the lease obligation was $391,000 in fiscal 1997. The total lease payment was $550,000. Reconstruct the 1997 journal entry.

4. Suppose this building had met the requirements for an operating lease rather than a capital lease. Calculate the operating loss for Deb Shops in fiscal 1997.

9-59 Capital Leases

Home Depot is the leading retailer in the home improvement industry and one of the ten largest retailers in the U.S. The company included the following on its February 2, 1997 balance sheet:

Lease assets	105,942,000
Capital lease obligations (long-term)	104,748,000
Capital lease obligations (current)	1,265,000

Total capital lease payments scheduled for the fiscal year ended February 2, 1998 are $17,071,000.

Required

1. Prepare the journal entry for the $17,071,000 lease payments. Remember that the lease payment will include the principle payments due for the year plus interest expense accrued for the year.

2. Suppose that lease assets have an average remaining life of 20 years and that no new leases are signed in the fiscal year ended February 2, 1998. Compute the balance in the lease asset account and the total in the capital lease obligations account (long-term and current combined) at February 2, 1998.

3. Explain why the amounts in the lease assets account is not equal to the amount in the lease obligations accounts.

9-60 Pension Liabilities

Bethlehem Steel had a pension liability of $870 million and a liability for postretirement benefits other than pensions of $1,695 million at the beginning of 1997. Total stockholders' equity was $996 million. The total market value of Bethlehem Steel is approximately $1.2 billion.

Required

1. Comment on the confidence that employees might have about receiving the benefits due to them.

2. Recognizing pensions and other postretirement benefits as liabilities on the balance sheet has been a controversial topic. Do you think this is important information to disclose to shareholders? Why or why not?

9-61 The Gap Annual Report

Examine the annual report for The Gap included in Appendix A, especially footnote D, Leases. Suppose that all operating leases were treated as capital leases. Assume that all the leases were for ten years and that the lease payments each year are at the same level they were in the year ended February 1, 1997, that is, $337,487,000 per year. Also assume that the implicit interest rate in the leases is 10%.

Required

1. Assume that the operating leases were all capitalized as of February 1, 1997. Compute the amount of the capitalized lease asset and the lease liability that would be added to The Gap's balance sheet.

2. Compute The Gap's debt-to-equity ratio on February 1, 1997, using the balance sheet numbers as reported. Also compute The Gap's debt to equity ratio using numbers that assume the capitalization of operating leases as computed in requirement 1.

3. Comment on the change in debt-to-equity ratio that results from capitalization of the operating leases. What information does this convey to potential investors in The Gap?

9-62 Financial Statement Research

Select any two companies from the airline industry, and find each company's footnote describing its leases. (Possible companies include Alaska Airlines, American Airlines, Continental Airlines, Delta Airlines, Northwest Airlines, Transworld Airlines, and U.S. Airways, but do not feel restricted to these.) Compute each company's debt-to-equity ratio under each of three assumptions:

1. With leases as reported.
2. With all leases treated as operating leases.
3. With all leases treated as capital leases.

For this calculation assume that all operating lease payments due after the fifth year are spread evenly over years 6 through 15. That is, one-tenth of the remaining lease payments will be made each of the next ten years. Use a 10% interest rate for computing the present value of the operating leases. Comment on the differences made by the three treatments of leases. Also, comment on the differences in ratios between the two companies.

COLLABORATIVE LEARNING EXERCISE

9-63 Accounting for Pensions

Form groups of two or more students. Divide each group into two debate teams. Each team should be assigned one of the two following positions:

1. Pensions and other postretirement benefits are legitimate liabilities of a company and should be recognized as such on their balance sheets. They are expenses of the periods in which the benefiting employees work, so the obligation to pay them should be accrued at that time.
2. Pensions and other postretirement benefits are not legal liabilities of a company and should not be included among their liabilities on the balance sheet. They are essentially expenses in the period when the benefits are paid.

One team defending each proposition can be given 5 to 10 minutes to present its case, followed by approximately 2 minutes each for rebuttals. Then a general class discussion of the issues can follow. The class might take a vote on which group made the most convincing argument.

9-64 Internet Case

Go to **http://www.pepsico.com/** to find PepsiCo, Inc.'s financial information. PepsiCo is the result of a 1965 merger between Pepsi-Cola Company and Frito-Lay, Inc. Click the icon for the most recent **Annual Report,** then **Financial Review** to locate the index of the company's current year annual report.

Answer the following questions about PepsiCo, Inc. and its long-term debt:

1. Identify the item and category in which PepsiCo reports its leases on the balance sheet. Are the leases that are reported on the balance sheet considered capital or operating leases?
2. During what year will PepsiCo's operating lease commitments expire? How do the operating lease payments affect PepsiCo's financial statements? Explain how these operating leases are considered "invisible debt."
3. Explain the change in long-term debt between the two comparative periods reported on PepsiCo's balance sheet. Did PepsiCo borrow any additional funds during the year? How did you determine this?

4. What is the nature of "current maturities of long-term debt"? Explain.

5. In what section(s) of the balance sheet are PepsiCo's bonds reported? How much is each annual interest payment on each $10,000 bond? If today's market rate of interest is 8% and these bonds were issued today at the same coupon rate as reported in the annual report, would they be issued as a premium or discount?

6. Describe who is eligible for PepsiCo's pension and/or other postretirement benefit plans. How are these items reported on the financial statements?

STATEMENT OF CASH FLOWS

Tiger Woods exits sandtraps
as gracefully as he collects his
endorsement fees from Nike.

Learning Objectives

After studying this chapter, you should be able to

1 Explain the concept of the statement of cash flows.

2 Classify activities affecting cash as operating, investing, or financing activities.

3 Use the direct method to measure cash flows.

4 Determine cash flows from income statement and balance sheet accounts.

5 Use the indirect method to calculate cash flows from operations.

6 Relate depreciation to cash flows provided by operating activities.

7 Reconcile net income to cash provided by operating activities.

8 Adjust for gains and losses from fixed asset sales and debt extinguishments in the statement of cash flows (Appendix 10A).

9 Use the T-account approach to prepare the cash flow statement (Appendix 10B).

If you watched nothing but commercials on television, you'd think the only thing Nike spends its money on is getting athletes to endorse the company's products. We're all familiar with Nike's first endorsement—Michael Jordan of Chicago Bulls basketball fame. But there have been countless others. Runners, hockey and soccer players, and college and professional football teams have all appeared in Nike's commercials or signed other endorsement deals, not to mention swimmers, tennis players, and just about any other sports figure imaginable. Golfer Tiger Woods's deal was for tens of millions over several years. Recently, Nike agreed to pay $120 million over eight years to sponsor the U.S. Soccer Federation, the governing body for the top men's, women's, and youth teams.

Of course, the company behind the famous Nike "swoosh" needs cash to make the endorsements happen. And a quick look at the company's balance sheet will tell you that they have plenty—close to $450 million at last count. But if you truly wanted to see where Nike spends its cash, you're better off ignoring the commercials and paying attention to one specific financial report—the Statement of Cash Flows.

Nike uses the indirect method of reporting its cash flows. Cash provided or used by the company for operating, investing, and financing activities is listed, giving you a much better picture of where the money has gone. For example, in recent years, operations such as selling merchandise have provided millions in cash for Nike ($323 million in 1997). Financing activities, primarily borrowing, have also added cash ($314 million in 1997). But 1997 investing activities used $496 million in cash for additions to property, plant, and equipment. The net result of all these activities in 1997 was an increase in cash and equivalents of 70% over the previous year.

So far this book has dealt mainly with financial statements based on accrual accounting. Focusing too heavily on accruals and deferrals, though, can make it easy to forget about cash. An understanding of where a company's cash comes from and where it goes is essential to keeping the company in good financial condition.

Given the primary importance of cash, it is not surprising that the statement of cash flows has become one of the central financial statements. It provides a thorough explanation of the changes that occurred in the firm's cash balances during the entire accounting period. The statements of cash flows allow both investors and managers to keep their fingers on the pulse of any company's lifeblood: cash. Companies that lose too much cash become critically ill. The business equivalent of critical illness is bankruptcy. Bankruptcy is loosely used to refer to companies that are unable to meet their obligations. It also refers to firms that seek court protection from their debts under federal law. Court protection allows a firm to delay paying certain obligations while it negotiates an agreement with all of its creditors on how to reorganize its business and its debts for the future. Montgomery Ward and Woolworth's are recent examples of relatively large and seemingly successful companies that have either liquidated entirely or terminated large portions of their business.

Every company benefits by tracing its cash flows, and every investor would be wise to check out a company's statement of cash flows before investing. Interestingly, though, not every company prepares a specific statement showing investors its cash flows. The accounting regulations in some countries, such as Austria, India, and Uruguay, do not require any formal statement of cash flows, so investors there rarely get such statements. Most countries do require a financial statement like the statement of cash flows, but the contents of these statements can vary widely from country to country. In this chapter, we will examine the contents of the statement of cash flows required in the United States and explain what these figures mean to companies and to investors.

OVERVIEW OF STATEMENT OF CASH FLOWS

Companies have not always prepared statements of cash flows. In fact, before 1971 only the balance sheet and income statement were required. That year a statement showing the changes in financial position between balance sheets was added. However, financial problems—mainly inflation—in the 1970s and 1980s caused many economists and accountants to call for a greater emphasis on cash management. In response, in 1987 the FASB required the preparation and presentation of the statement of cash flows in its present form.

PURPOSES OF CASH FLOW STATEMENT

Objective 1
Explain the concept of the statement of cash flows.

The statement of cash flows reports all the cash activities—both receipts and payments—of a company *during* a given period. It also explains the causes for the changes in cash by providing information about operating, financing, and investing activities. Why does the FASB require a statement of cash flows? Because:

1. It shows the relationship of net income to changes in cash balances. Cash balances can decline despite positive net income and vice versa.

2. It reports past cash flows as an aid to
   a. Predicting future cash flows.
   b. Evaluating the way management generates and uses cash.
   c. Determining a company's ability to pay interest and dividends and to pay debts when they are due.
3. It identifies changes in the mix of productive assets.

Balance sheets show the *status* of a company at a single point in time. In contrast, statements of cash flows and income statements show the *performance* of a company over a period of time. Both explain why the balance sheet items have changed. As the following diagram shows, these statements thus link the balance sheets in consecutive periods:

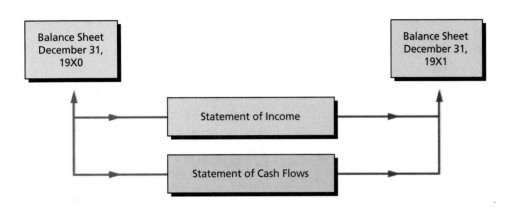

The statement of cash flows explains where cash came from during a period and where it went. We should clarify what we mean by "cash," though. Our use of the term refers not only to the bills and coins you normally think of as cash, but to cash equivalents, too. As you should recall, cash equivalents are highly liquid short-term investments that can easily be converted into cash with little delay, such as money market funds and treasury bills. Hereafter, when we refer to cash, we mean both cash and cash equivalents.

TYPICAL ACTIVITIES AFFECTING CASH

Cash affects and is affected by two primary areas of a firm: its operating management and its financial management. **Operating management** is largely concerned with the major day-to-day activities that generate revenues and expenses. **Financial management** is largely concerned with where to get cash (financing activities) and how to use cash (investing activities). For example, financial managers decide whether to issue or retire long-term debt or additional capital stock and how to invest the capital raised. The statement of cash flows covers the results of both financial management and operating management by reporting on specific operating activities, investing activities, and financing activities.

Operating activities are generally activities or transactions that affect the income statement. For example, sales are linked to collections from customers, and wage expenses are closely tied to cash payments to employees. **Investing activities** involve (1) providing and collecting cash as a lender or as an owner of securities and (2) acquiring and disposing of plant, property, equipment, and other long-term productive assets. **Financing activities** involve obtaining resources as a borrower or issuer of securities and repaying creditors and owners. You should note that financing and investing activities are really two sides of the same coin. For example, when stock is issued for cash to an investor, the issuer treats it as a financing activity and the investor treats it as an investing activity.

operating management Is mainly concerned with the major day-to-day activities that generate revenues and expenses.

financial management Is mainly concerned with where to get cash and how to use cash for the benefit of the entity.

Objective 2
Classify activities affecting cash as operating, investing, or financing activities.

operating activities
Transactions that affect the income statement.

investing activities
Activities that involve (1) providing and collecting cash as a lender or as an owner of securities and (2) acquiring and disposing of plant, property, equipment, and other long-term productive assets.

financing activities
Activities that involve obtaining resources as a borrower or issuer of securities and repaying creditors and owners.

The following are typical operating, investing, and financing activities reported in statements of cash flows:

OPERATING ACTIVITIES

Cash Inflows	*Cash Outflows*
Collections from customers	Cash payments to suppliers
Interest and dividends collected	Cash payments to employees
Other operating receipts	Interest and taxes paid
	Other operating cash payments

INVESTING ACTIVITIES

Cash Inflows	*Cash Outflows*
Sale of property, plant, and equipment	Purchase of property, plant, and equipment
Sale of securities that are not cash equivalents	Purchase of securities that are not cash equivalents
Receipt of loan repayments	Making loans

FINANCING ACTIVITIES

Cash Inflows	*Cash Outflows*
Borrowing cash from creditors	Repayment of amounts borrowed
Issuing equity securities	Repurchase of equity shares (including the purchase of treasury stock)
Issuing debt securities	Payment of dividends

To see how these activities are treated, consider the APT Company, which provides daily cleaning services for homes. Exhibit 10-1 displays APT's financial statements. The company pays all wages in cash daily, and all revenues are collected in cash daily. If these were the only transactions affecting income, APT's net income would equal cash provided by operations. But APT owns a computer, and depreciation on the computer is allocated to the income statement over the computer's anticipated three-year life. Because depreciation does not involve a cash flow, it appears on the income statement as an expense but does not affect cash provided by operations.

Cleaning supplies are purchased for cash periodically, but the supplies are not necessarily paid for upon delivery. Moreover, supplies are kept in inventory to be used as needed, so all the supplies acquired are not immediately used. The income statement reports the $3,000 of supplies used during the period, and the cash flow statement reports the $3,200 of supplies paid for during the period.

In comparing the income statement and cash flows from operations, you can see that the only differences are for supplies and depreciation. The APT Company has only one investing activity, the purchase of a computer, and one financing activity, the payment of cash dividends.

cash flows from operating activities The first major section of the statement of cash flows. It shows the cash effects of transactions that affect the income statement.

direct method In a statement of cash flows, the method that calculates net cash provided by operating activities as collections minus operating disbursements.

indirect method In a statement of cash flows, the method that adjusts the accrual net income to reflect only cash receipts and outlays.

APPROACHES TO CALCULATING THE CASH FLOW FROM OPERATING ACTIVITIES

Although cash flows from financing and investment activities are fairly easy to summarize at year end from a review of the checkbook, operating activities are more complex and the calculation of cash flow from operations is similarly complicated. Two approaches can be used to compute **cash flow from operating activities** (or operations). Computing it as collections less operating disbursements is called the **direct method.** Our APT example used this method. Adjusting the previously calculated accrual net income from the income statement to reflect only cash receipts and outlays is called the **indirect method.**

Using the direct method, the cash flow effect of each operating activity is calculated by adjusting the income statement amounts for changes in related asset and liability

Exhibit 10-1

APT Company

Financial Statements

Balance Sheets for the Years Ended December 31

Assets			Liabilities and Stockholders' Equity		
	19X1	19X0		19X1	19X0
Cash	$ 1,200	$ 4,000	Accounts payable	$ 200	$ 200
Supplies	600	400	Stockholders'		
Computer	2,000	0	equity	3,600	4,200
Total assets	$ 3,800	$ 4,400	Total Liab. and SE	$3,800	$4,400

Income Statement for the Year Ended December 31, 19X1

Sales		$35,000
Wages	$20,000	
Depreciation	1,000	
Supplies	3,000	24,000
Net income		$11,000

Statement of Cash Flows for the Year Ended December 31, 19X1

CASH FLOWS FROM OPERATING ACTIVITIES:	
Collections from customers	$ 35,000
Payments to employees	(20,000)
Payments to suppliers	(3,200)
Net cash provided by operating activities	11,800
CASH FLOWS FROM INVESTING ACTIVITIES:	
Cash investment in computer	(3,000)
Net cash used for investing activities	(3,000)
CASH FLOWS FROM FINANCING ACTIVITIES:	
Cash dividend payments	(11,600)
Net cash used for financing activities	(11,600)
Decrease in cash	(2,800)
Cash balance December 31, 19X0	4,000
Cash balance December 31, 19X1	$ 1,200

accounts. Each revenue and expense amount calculated under the accrual method is adjusted to reflect the actual cash paid or received. In contrast, the indirect method considers the same changes in related asset and liability accounts but uses them to adjust the net income number directly to a cash equivalent, rather than adjusting the individual revenue and expense items that comprise net income.

Under the direct method, we identify the cash part of each item in the income statement. Because depreciation does not use cash, it is not part of the calculation. For APT, which immediately collected the cash it was due and immediately paid out cash it owed, we have only to adjust for supplies. By examining the balance sheet, we see that supplies inventory rose from $400 to $600. This increase suggests APT bought more than it used, so cost of supplies in the income statement was smaller than purchases. But did APT pay for what it bought? Yes, the company paid for exactly the quantity purchased during the year because the Accounts Payable balance remained unchanged. Therefore the increases to accounts payable for new purchases had to be identical to the decreases for payments. So if APT paid for all it bought, and it bought $200 more than it sold, the company must have paid for $3,200. Therefore, net cash provided by operating activities must be cash sales of $35,000 less $20,000 in cash wages and $3,200 cash paid for supplies for a net of $11,800, as shown in Exhibit 10-1.

Alternatively, cash flow from operations can be calculated under the indirect method by adjusting the accrual net income figure to reflect only cash transactions. The income

Objective 3
Use the direct method to measure cash flows.

statement provides an accrual-based net income of $11,000, which will be our starting point. In calculating net income on the income statement, $1,000 of depreciation was deducted, but depreciation involved no cash, so we add it back to get $12,000 ($11,000 plus $1,000). In addition, APT spent $200 more on supplies than it used, so we subtract that $200 as an operating use of cash that does not appear in net income. Thus by adjusting the accrual net income figure, we again calculate $11,800 ($11,000 + $1,000 − $200).

The FASB prefers the direct method because it shows operating cash receipts and payments in a way that is easier for investors to understand. However, the indirect method is more common. Why? Probably because the people who generally prepare the statement are accountants and are used to thinking in terms of net income. The two approaches can be compared as follows:

APT Company Cash Flow from Operating Activities

	Direct Method		Indirect Method	
Collections from customers		$35,000	Net earnings	$11,000
Payments to employees	$20,000		Add depreciation*	1,000
Payments to suppliers	3,200	23,200	Deduct supplies†	(200)
Net cash provided by operating activities		$11,800		$11,800

*Depreciation was deducted to compute net earnings but did not involve a cash flow.

†Payments for supplies exceeded the amount charged as expense.

TRANSACTIONS AFFECTING CASH FLOWS FROM ALL SOURCES

The APT Company was an intentionally simplified illustration that gave us a first look at the principles behind the statement of cash flows. Now we will delve into more detail.

ACTIVITIES AFFECTING CASH

Exhibit 10-2 summarizes the effects of most major transactions on cash. The zeros in the "change in cash" column indicate that the transaction has no effect on cash. For example, sales and purchases on account and even the accrual recording of cost of goods sold have no effect on cash. Most of the items in the list will be familiar to you. We have included several financing transactions that will be covered in detail in Chapter 11 on stockholders' equity. However we wanted the list to be useful as a reference throughout the course.

The relationship of these activities to cash should be fairly obvious and straightforward. What is not always obvious is the classification of these activities as operating, investing, or financing. Take interest payments and dividend payments for example. Both of these represent cash flows to suppliers of capital to the firm. It would seem they might be treated the same, because both are disbursements related to financing activities. However, after much debate, the FASB decided to classify interest payments as cash flows associated with operations and dividend payments as financing cash flows. This classification maintains the long-standing distinction that dividend transactions with the owners (dividends) cannot be treated as expenses, while interest payments to creditors are expenses.

CASH FLOW AND EARNINGS

If both the income statement and the statement of cash flows reconcile the changes the company experiences during the year, you might wonder why both are required. Why not pick the best one? The problem is that each fills a critical information need. The income statement shows how the companies' owners' equity was increased (or decreased) as a result of operations. It matches revenues and expenses using the accrual concepts and pro-

Exhibit 10-2

Type of Transaction	Change in Cash
OPERATING ACTIVITIES:	
Sales of goods and services for cash	+
Sales of goods and services on credit	0
Receive dividends or interest	+
Collection of accounts receivable	+
Recognize cost of goods sold	0
Purchase inventory for cash	−
Purchase inventory on credit	0
Pay trade accounts payable	−
Accrue operating expenses	0
Pay operating expenses	−
Accrue taxes	0
Pay taxes	−
Accrue interest	0
Pay interest	−
Prepay expenses for cash	−
Write off prepaid expenses	0
Charge depreciation or amortization	0
INVESTING ACTIVITIES:	
Purchase fixed assets for cash	−
Purchase fixed assets by issuing debt	0
Sell fixed assets	+
Purchase securities that are not cash equivalents	−
Sell securities that are not cash equivalents	+
Make a loan	−
FINANCING ACTIVITIES:	
Increase long-term or short-term debt	+
Reduce long-term or short-term debt	−
Sell common or preferred shares	+
Repurchase and retire common or preferred shares	−
Purchase treasury stock	−
Pay dividends	−
Convert debt to common stock	0
Reclassify long-term debt to short-term debt	0

vides a valuable measure of economic activity. The focal point of the statement of cash flows is the net cash flow from operating activities. Frequently, this is called simply cash flow.

THE ECO-BAG COMPANY—A DETAILED EXAMPLE OF THE DIRECT METHOD FOR PREPARING THE STATEMENT OF CASH FLOWS

To see how many of the activities shown in Exhibit 10-2 would affect a real company, consider the Eco-Bag Company, whose financial statements are shown in Exhibit 10-3. The cash flow statement is prepared using the direct method.

Because the statement of cash flows explains the causes for the change in cash, the first step in developing the statement is always to compute the amount of the change (which represents the net effect):

Cash, December 31, 19X1	$25,000
Cash, December 31, 19X2	16,000
Net decrease in cash	$ 9,000

Exhibit 10-3

Eco-Bag Company

Balance Sheet as of December 31 (in thousands)

Assets			Liabilities and Stockholders' Equity		
	19X2	*19X1*		*19X2*	*19X1*
Current assets:			Current liabilities:		
			Accounts payable	$ 74	$ 6
Cash	$ 16	$ 25	Wages and		
Accounts receivable	45	25	salaries payable	25	4
Inventory	100	60			
Total current assets	161	110	Total current liabilities	99	10
Fixed assets, gross	581	330	Long-term debt	125	5
Accum. depreciation	(101)	(110)	Stockholders' equity	417	315
Net	480	220			
			Total liabilities and		
Total assets	$ 641	$ 330	stockholders' equity	$641	$330

Eco-Bag Company

Statement of Income for the Year Ended December 31, 19X2 (in thousands)

Sales		$200
Cost and expenses:		
Cost of goods sold	$100	
Wages and salaries	36	
Depreciation	17	
Interest	4	
Total costs and expenses		$157
Income before income taxes		43
Income taxes		20
Net income		$ 23

Eco-Bag Company

Statement of Cash Flows for the Year Ended December 31, 19X2 (in thousands)

CASH FLOWS FROM OPERATING ACTIVITIES:		
Cash collections from customers		$ 180
Cash payments:		
To suppliers	$ 72	
To employees	15	
For interest	4	
For taxes	20	
Total cash payments		(111)
Net cash provided by operating activities		$ 69
CASH FLOWS FROM INVESTING ACTIVITIES:		
Purchases of fixed assets	$(287)	
Proceeds from sale of fixed assets	10	
Net cash used by investing activities		(277)
CASH FLOWS FROM FINANCING ACTIVITIES:		
Proceeds from issue of long-term debt	$ 120	
Proceeds from issue of common stock	98	
Dividends paid	(19)	
Net cash provided by financing activities		199
Net decrease in cash		$ (9)
Cash, December 31, 19X1		25
Cash, December 31, 19X2		$ 16

Our Eco-Bag Company example shows how this basic calculation is often shown at the bottom of a statement of cash flows. The net change during the period is added to the beginning cash balance to compute the ending cash balance. However, beginning and ending cash balances are not required in the statement of cash flows. Explaining the net change in cash during the period is all that is necessary.

Eco-Bag Company's statement shows that the excess of cash outflows over cash inflows reduced cash by $9,000. Why does cash decline? Operating activity is contributing additional cash during the year ($69,000), but the cash required for expansion significantly exceeds what operations provides. In order to support purchases of fixed assets of $287,000 the company raised an additional $199,000 via financing activities, both borrowing and sales of stock. Business expansion usually involves numerous assets, including accounts receivable and inventories. Note that Eco-Bag experienced a significant increase in accounts receivable and inventory during the period, but these increases in current assets were more than offset by rising current liabilities.

Most importantly, this illustration demonstrates how a firm may simultaneously (1) have a significant amount of net income, as computed by accountants on the accrual basis, and yet (2) have a decline in cash that could become severe. Indeed, many growing businesses are desperate for cash even though reported net income zooms upward.

CHANGES IN THE BALANCE SHEET EQUATION

Accountants often prepare the statement of cash flows using the balance sheet approach. The balance sheet equation provides the conceptual basis for all financial statements, including the statement of cash flows. The equation can be rearranged as follows:

$$\text{Assets} = \text{Liabilities} + \text{Stockholders' equity}$$
$$\text{Cash} + \text{Noncash assets} = \text{Liabilities} + \text{Stockholders' equity}$$
$$\text{Cash} = \text{Liabilities} + \text{Stockholders' equity} - \text{Non-cash Assets}$$
$$\text{Cash} = \text{L} + \text{SE} - \text{NCA}$$

Any change (Δ) in cash must be accompanied by a change in one or more items on the right side to keep the equation in balance:

$$\Delta \text{ Cash} = \Delta \text{ L} + \Delta \text{ SE} - \Delta \text{ NCA}$$

Therefore:

$$\text{Change in cash} = \text{Change in all noncash accounts}$$

or

$$\text{What happened to cash} = \text{Why it happened}$$

The statement of cash flows focuses on the changes in the noncash accounts as a way of explaining how and why the level of cash has gone up or down during a given period. Thus, the major changes in the accounts on the right side of the equation appear in the statement of cash flows as causes of the change in cash. The left side of the equation measures the net effect of the change in cash.

Consider the following summary of 19X2 transactions for the Eco-Bag Company. In practice, a company accountant might produce this summary by carefully reviewing the general ledger accounts and combining similar transactions that occurred during the year (that is, combining all the various sales on credit, and so on). Those transactions involving cash have an asterisk (*):

1. Sales on credit, $200,000.
*2. Collections of accounts receivable, $180,000.
3. Recognition of cost of goods sold, $100,000.
4. Purchases of inventory on account, $140,000.
*5. Payments of trade accounts payable, $72,000.

6. Recognition of wages expense, $36,000.

*7. Payments of wages, $15,000.

*8. Recognition of interest accrued and paid, $4,000.

*9. Recognition and payment of income taxes, $20,000.

10. Recognition of depreciation expense, $17,000.

*11. Acquisition of fixed assets for cash, $287,000.

*12. Sale of fixed assets at book value, $10,000.

*13. Issuance of long-term debt, $120,000.

*14. Issuance of common stock, $98,000.

*15. Declaration and payment of dividends, $19,000.

Exhibit 10-4 applies the balance sheet equation to the Eco-Bag Company data. We can see, step by step, how the balance sheet equation produces and explains the statement of cash flows in Exhibit 10-3. The totals in Exhibit 10-4 show the $9,000 decrease in cash is explained by the changes in the liability, stockholders' equity, and noncash asset accounts, and that all cash transactions have been accounted for. While the information in Exhibit 10-4 summarizes the elements that caused the changes in cash, they need to be combined and reformatted for final inclusion in a cash flow statement. We turn first to calculating the elements of cash flow from operations.

COMPUTING CASH FLOWS FROM OPERATING ACTIVITIES

The first major section in Eco-Bag Company's statement of cash flows (Exhibit 10-3, p. 402) is cash flows from operating activities. Different companies will call this section

Exhibit 10-4

Eco-Bag Company

The Balance Sheet Equation (in thousands of dollars)

	Δ Cash =	Δ L	+ Δ SE	− Δ NCA
Operating activities:				
1. Sales on credit	=		+200	− (+200)
*2. Cash collections from customers	+180 =			− (−180)
3. Cost of goods sold	=		−100	− (−100)
4. Inventory purchases on account	=	+140		− (+140)
*5. Payments to suppliers	− 72 =	− 72		
6. Wages and salaries expense	=	+ 36	− 36	
*7. Payments to employees	− 15 =	− 15		
*8. Interest expense paid	− 4 =		− 4	
*9. Income taxes paid	− 20 =		− 20	
Net cash provided by operating activities, a subtotal	69			
Expenses not requiring cash:				
10. Depreciation	=		− 17	− (− 17)
Net income, a subtotal			+ 23	
Investing activities:				
*11. Acquire fixed assets	−287 =			− (+287)
*12. Dispose of fixed assets	+ 10 =			− (− 10)
Financiing activities:				
*13. Issue long-term debt	+120 =	+120		
*14. Issue common stock	+ 98 =		+ 98	
*15. Pay dividends	− 19 =		− 19	
Net changes	− 9 =	+209	+102	− (+320)

cash flow from operations, cash provided by operations, or, if operating activities decrease cash, cash used for operations.

Collections from sales to customers are almost always the major operating cash inflows. Correspondingly, disbursements for purchases of goods to be sold and operating expenses are almost always the major operating cash outflows. The amount of inflows (collections) minus the amount of outflows (disbursements) is the net cash provided by—or used up by—operating activities. In Exhibit 10-3, collections of $180,000 minus the $111,000 of operating disbursements equals net cash provided by operating activities, $69,000.

WORKING FROM INCOME STATEMENT AMOUNTS TO CASH AMOUNTS

Many accountants build the statement of cash flows from the changes in balance sheet items, a few additional facts, and a familiarity with the typical causes of changes in cash. For instance, our Eco-Bag Company example provided the "additional fact" that cash collections from customers for 19X2 was $180,000. Most accounting systems, though, do not provide such additional facts. Therefore, accountants often compute the collections and other cash flow items from figures on the income statement. Let us now examine the detailed calculations for collections and other operating items from Eco-Bag.

Objective 4
Determine cash flows from income statement and balance sheet accounts.

a. Eco-Bag Company recognized $200,000 of revenue in 19X2, but the $20,000 increase in accounts receivable suggests that only $180,000 was collected from customers:

Sales	$200,000
+ Beginning accounts receivable	25,000
Potential collections	$225,000
− Ending accounts receivable	45,000
Cash collections from customers	$180,000

or

Sales	$200,000
Decrease (increase) in accounts receivable	(20,000)
Cash collections from customers	$180,000

Note that an increase in accounts receivable means that sales exceeded collections. Conversely, a decrease in accounts receivable means collections exceeded sales.

b. The difference between the $100,000 cost of goods sold and the $72,000 cash payment to suppliers can be explained by changes in inventory and accounts payable. The $40,000 increase in inventory indicates that purchases exceeded the cost of goods sold by $40,000:

Ending inventory	$100,000
+ Cost of goods sold	100,000
Inventory to account for	$200,000
− Beginning inventory	(60,000)
Purchases of inventory	$140,000

Although purchases were $140,000, payments to suppliers were only $72,000. Why? Because some purchases were made on credit, resulting in a $68,000 increase in trade accounts payable, from $6,000 to $74,000:

Beginning trade accounts payable	$ 6,000
+ Purchases	140,000
Total amount to be paid	$146,000
− Ending trade accounts payable	(74,000)
Accounts paid in cash	$ 72,000

The effects of inventory and trade accounts payable can be combined as follows:

Cost of goods sold	$100,000
Increase (decrease) in inventory	40,000
Decrease (increase) in trade accounts payable	(68,000)
Payments to suppliers	$ 72,000

c. Cash payments to employees were only $15,000 because the wages and salaries expense of $36,000 was offset by a $21,000 increase in wages and salaries payable:

Beginning wages and salaries payable	$ 4,000
+ Wages and salaries expense	36,000
Total to be paid	$40,000
− Ending wages and salaries payable	(25,000)
Cash payments to employees	$15,000

or

Wages and salaries expense	$36,000
Decrease (increase) in wages and salaries payable	(21,000)
Cash payments to employees	$15,000

d. Notice that both interest payable and income taxes payable were zero at the beginning and at the end of 19X2. Therefore the entire $4,000 interest expense and the $20,000 income tax expense were paid in cash in 19X2.

COMPARISON OF INCOME STATEMENT AND CASH FLOW STATEMENT

Accrual-based measures of revenue and expense are reported in the income statement. Most of these are naturally linked to related asset or liability accounts and the cash effects of the revenue and expense transactions are moderated by changes in their related asset or liability accounts. The balance sheet approach relies on adjusting accrual-based income statement values for changes in asset and liability account balances. The following illustration summarizes the process.

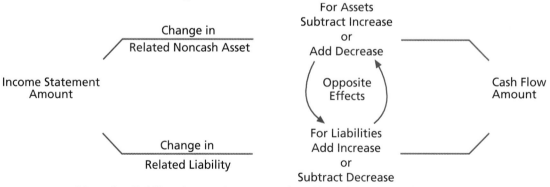

Note that liability changes have opposite effects from asset changes. Each revenue or expense account has a related asset and/or liability account, some examples of which are shown in Panel A of Exhibit 10-5.

Exhibit 10-5

Panel A. The General Case: Common Adjustments to Convert Income Statement Amounts to Cash Flow Amounts		
Income Statement Amount	*Related Noncash Asset*	*Related Liability*
Sales revenue	Accounts receivable	Unearned revenue
Cost of goods sold	Merchandise inventory	Accounts payable
Wage expense	Prepaid wages	Wages payable
Rent expense	Prepaid rent	Rent payable
Insurance expense	Prepaid insurance	Insurance payable
Depreciation expense	Plant, property, or equipment	
Amortization expense	Intangible asset	

Panel B. The Eco-Bag Company Example					
Income Statement		*Asset Change*	*Liability Change*		*Cash Flow Statement*
		−Increases +Decreases	+Increases −Decreases		
Sales revenue	$200,000	$(20,000)		=	$180,000
Cost of goods sold	(100,000)	(40,000)	$68,000	=	(72,000)
Wage and salary expense	(36,000)		21,000	=	(15,000)
Interest expense	(4,000)			=	(4,000)
Income taxes	($20,000)			=	(20,000)
Depreciation	(17,000)	17,000			
Net income	$ 23,000	$(43,000)	$89,000		$ 69,000

Panel B of Exhibit 10-5 summarizes the application of this concept to the details of the Eco-Bag Company. For example, the $20,000 increase in accounts receivable indicates that not all of the sales were collected, so sales revenue is reduced from $200,000 to $180,000, the actual cash collected. Similarly, the $40,000 increase in inventory indicates that we might have paid for more goods than we sold, an additional use of cash. This effect is offset by the increase in accounts payable of $68,000. We delayed the use of cash by increasing our trade credit.

COMPUTING CASH FLOWS FROM INVESTING AND FINANCING ACTIVITIES

The second and third major sections of the statement of cash flows show **cash flows from investing activities** and **cash flows from financing activities.** The former lists cash flows from the purchase or sale of plant, property, equipment, and other long-lived assets. The latter shows cash flows to and from providers of capital. The idea is that long-lived assets are investments, and sources of capital, such as stocks and bonds, finance the purchase of these investments. If the necessary information regarding these cash flows is not directly available by simply inspecting the cash account, accountants can determine the necessary information by analyzing changes in balance sheet items using the following rules:

- Increases in cash (cash inflows) stem from
  - Increases in liabilities or stockholders' equity
  - Decreases in noncash assets
- Decreases in cash (cash outflows) stem from
  - Decreases in liabilities or stockholders' equity
  - Increases in noncash assets

cash flows from investing activities The second major section of the statement of cash flows describing purchase or sale of plant, property, equipment, and other long-lived assets.

cash flows from financing activities The third major section of the statement of cash flows describing flows to and from providers of capital.

Consider Eco-Bag Company's balance sheet (Exhibit 10-3, p. 402). All noncash current assets and current liabilities of the company were affected only by operating activities. Three noncurrent accounts—(a) fixed assets, (b) long-term debt, and (c) stockholders' equity—affect the cash flows from investing activities ($277,000 outflow) and financing activities ($199,000 inflow).

a. Net fixed assets increased by $260,000 in 19X2. Three items usually explain changes in net fixed assets: (1) assets acquired, (2) asset dispositions, and (3) depreciation expense for the period. Therefore:

Increase in net plant assets = Acquisitions − Disposals − Depreciation expense

The elements in this equation explain the company's investing activities. Tracing the cash flow from investing activities requires some knowledge of the year's activity. Sometimes you will have only incomplete information and need to solve for the unknown values. For example, you might know the increase in net plant assets, acquisitions of new fixed assets, and depreciation expense without knowing about Eco-Bag Company's asset disposals. The book value of disposals could be computed from the preceding equation:

$$\$260,000 = \$287,000 - \text{Disposals} - \$17,000$$
$$\text{Disposals} = \$287,000 - \$17,000 - \$260,000$$
$$\text{Disposals} = \$10,000$$

Eco-Bag Company received exactly the book value for the assets sold. (Appendix 10A discusses disposals for more or less than book value.) If the amount of disposals were known, but either acquisitions or depreciation expense were unknown, the missing item could be determined by applying this same equation.

b. Long-term debt increased by $125,000 − $5,000 = $120,000. This increase was due to new long-term debt being issued—a financing activity that increased cash.

c. The $102,000 increase ($417,000 − $315,000) in stockholders' equity can be explained by three factors: (1) issuance of capital stock, (2) net income (or loss), and (3) dividends. Therefore:

Increase in stockholders' equity = New issuance + Net income − Dividends

Suppose you did not know how much new stock had been issued:

$$\$102,000 = \text{New issuance} + \$23,000 - \$19,000$$
$$\text{New issuance} = \$102,000 - \$23,000 + \$19,000$$
$$\text{New issuance} = \$98,000, \text{ an inflow of cash}$$

Both the issuance of new shares and the payment of cash dividends are financing activities that affect cash.

NONCASH INVESTING AND FINANCING ACTIVITIES

In our example, Eco-Bag Company did not have any noncash investing or financing activities. But suppose Eco-Bag Company had the following such activities:

1. Acquired a $14,000 fixed asset by issuing common stock.
2. Acquired a small building by signing a mortgage payable for $97,000.
3. Long-term debt of $35,000 was converted to common stock.

These items affect the balance sheet equation as follows:

ΔCash =	ΔL	+ ΔSE		− ΔNCA	
1. 0 =		+$14,000	[Increase Common Stock]	−(+$14,000)	[Increase Fixed Asset]
2. 0 =	+$97,000 [Increase Mortgage payable]			−(+$97,000)	[Increase Building]
3. 0 =	−$35,000 [Decrease Long-term Debt]	+$35,000	[Increase Common Stock]		

None of these transactions affects cash, and therefore they do not belong in a statement of cash flows. However, each transaction could just as easily involve cash. For example, in the first transaction, the company might issue common stock for $14,000 cash and immediately use the cash to purchase the fixed asset. The cash would then need to be traced and appear on the statement of cash flows. Because of the similarities between these noncash transactions and ones involving cash, readers of statements of cash flows should be informed of such noncash activities. Therefore such items must be included in a separate schedule accompanying the statement of cash flows. Eco-Bag Company's schedule for these additional transactions would be:

Schedule of noncash investing and financing activities:	
Common stock issued to acquire fixed asset	$14,000
Mortgage payable for acquisition of building	$97,000
Common stock issued on conversion of long-term debt	$35,000

THE CRISIS OF NEGATIVE CASH FLOW

Although investors make important economic decisions on the basis of the so-called bottom line, sometimes earnings numbers do not tell the full story of what is really happening inside a company. Take the case of Prime Motor Inns, the world's second-largest hotel operator, which reported earnings of $77 million on revenues of $410 million for 1989. That is a return on sales (net income ÷ revenues) of nearly 19%. Moreover, in 1989 revenues increased by nearly 11% from the preceding year. Despite its impressive earnings performance, though, Prime lacked the cash to meet its obligations and filed for Chapter 11 bankruptcy in September 1990. Under bankruptcy protection, a firm's obligations to its creditors are frozen as management figures out how to pay those creditors. How can a firm with $77 million in earnings file for bankruptcy about a year later?

Although the company's business was owning and operating hotels, much of Prime's reported earnings in 1989 arose from selling hotels. When outside financing for the hotel sales became harder to obtain, Prime financed the sales itself by accepting notes and mortgages receivable from buyers. Of course, Prime soon ran out of hotels to sell, if it wanted to stay in the business. Moreover, the reported gain under accrual accounting often significantly exceeded the cash received. In the year that Prime reported $77 million of net income, an astute analyst would have noted that Prime had a net cash outflow from operations of $15 million. Analyzing the cash flow statement focuses attention on important relationships such as this one.

On July 31, 1992, Prime emerged from bankruptcy with 75 hotels—roughly half of the 141 hotels it had prior to bankruptcy—and a new name, Prime Hospitality Corporation. The new company kept its great stock symbol, "PDQ," and investors who bought the new shares for about $1.50 when the reorganization occurred have done well. In May of 1998, the price was $21.00. Of course, the shareholders who bought the old company for $35 per share in 1989 watched their investment fall to under $1 in one year.

PREPARING A STATEMENT OF CASH FLOWS—THE INDIRECT METHOD

Objective 5
Use the indirect method to calculate cash flows from operations.

The Eco-Bag Company statement of cash flows in Exhibit 10-3 used the direct method to compute net cash provided by operating activities. The alternative, and often more convenient, indirect method of computing cash flows from operating activities reconciles net income to the net cash provided by operating activities. It also shows the link between the income statement and the statement of cash flows.

RECONCILIATION OF NET INCOME TO NET CASH PROVIDED BY OPERATIONS

In the indirect method, the statement of cash flows begins with net income. Then additions or deductions are made for changes in related asset or liability accounts, that is, for items that affect net income and net cash flow differently. Exhibit 10-6 shows this process for our Eco-Bag example. As we saw in Exhibit 10-5, net cash provided by operating activities exceeds net income by $46,000. If a company uses the direct method, the FASB requires a reconciliation such as Exhibit 10-6 as a supporting schedule to the statement of cash flows.

Consider the logic applied in the reconciliation in Exhibit 10-6:

1. Depreciation is added back to net income because it was deducted in the computation of net income but it does not represent a use of cash. To calculate cash provided by operations, the depreciation of $17,000 would not have been subtracted. The add-back simply cancels out the earlier deduction.

2. Increases in noncash current assets such as receivables and inventory result in less cash flow from operations. For instance, suppose the $20,000 increase in receivables was a result of credit sales made near the end of the year. The $20,000 sales figure would be included in the computation of net income, but the $20,000 would not have increased cash flow from operations. Therefore the reconciliation deducts the $20,000 from the net income to help pinpoint the effects on cash.

3. Increases in current liabilities such as accounts payable and wages payable result in more cash flow from operations. For instance, suppose the $21,000 increase in wages payable was caused by wages earned near the end of the year, but not yet paid in cash. The $21,000 wages expense would be deducted in computing net income, but the $21,000 would not yet have decreased cash flow from operations. Therefore the reconciliation adds the $21,000 to net income to offset the deduction and thereby show the effect on cash.

The general rules for additions and deductions to adjust net income using the indirect method are the same as to those for adjusting the line items of the income statement

Exhibit 10-6

Eco-Bag Company

Reconciliation of Net Income to Net Cash Provided by Operating Activities (in thousands)

Net income		$23
Adjustments to reconcile net income to net cash provided by operating activities:		
Depreciation	$ 17	
Net increase in accounts receivable	(20)	
Net increase in inventory	(40)	
Net increase in accounts payable	68	
Net increase in wages and salaries payable	21	
Total additions and deductions		46
Net cash provided by operating activities		$69

under the direct method. We focus on current assets and liabilities because they are most often tied to operations.

Objective 6
Relate depreciation to cash flows provided by operating activities.

Depreciation is an allocation of historical cost to expense and does not entail a current outflow of cash. Consider again the calculation of Eco-Bag Company's cash flows in Exhibit 10-5. Why is the $17,000 of depreciation added to net income to compute cash flow? Simply to cancel its deduction in calculating net income. Unfortunately, use of the indirect method may at first glance create an erroneous impression that depreciation is added because it, by itself, is a source of cash. If that were really true, a corporation could merely double or triple its bookkeeping entry for depreciation expense when cash was badly needed! What would happen? Cash provided by operations would be unaffected. Suppose depreciation for Eco-Bag Company is doubled:

	With Depreciation of $17,000	With Depreciation of $34,000
Sales	$200,000	$200,000
All expenses except depreciation (including income taxes)*	(160,000)	(160,000)
Depreciation	(17,000)	(34,000)
Net income	$ 23,000	$ 6,000
Nondepreciation adjustments†	29,000	29,000
Add depreciation	17,000	34,000
Net cash provided by operating activities	$ 69,000	$ 69,000

*$100,000 + $36,000 + $4,000 + $20,000 = $160,000
†From Exhibit 10-6, $(20,000) + $(40,000) + $68,000 + $21,000 = $29,000

The doubling affects depreciation and net income, but it has no direct influence on cash provided by operations, which, of course, still amounts to $69,000.

RECONCILING ITEMS

We have seen that net income rarely coincides with net cash provided by operating activities. Common additions or deductions to reconcile net income to net cash provided by operating activities are shown in Exhibit 10-7. The majority of listed items have been dis-

Objective 7
Reconcile net income to cash provided by operating activities.

Exhibit 10-7
Common Reconciling Items

ADD CHARGES (EXPENSES) NOT REQUIRING CASH:
  Depreciation
  Depletion
  Amortization of Assets
  Nonoperating Losses
  Amortization of Bond Discount
DEDUCT CREDITS TO INCOME (REVENUES) NOT PROVIDING CASH:
  Nonoperating Gains
  Amortization of Bond Premium
ADJUST FOR CHANGES IN CURRENT ASSETS AND LIABILITIES RELATING TO OPERATING ACTIVITIES

Changes in Noncash Current Assets	**Changes in Noncash Current Liabilities**
deduct increases	add increases
add decreases	deduct decreases
Examples: Accounts Receivable	Examples: Accounts Payable
Inventory	Wages Payable

Exhibit 10-8

Liz Claiborne Inc. and Subsidiaries
Consolidated Statements of Cash Flows

	Fiscal Years Ended		
	(52 weeks) December 28, 1996	(52 weeks) December 30, 1995	(53 weeks) December 31, 1994
All dollar amounts in thousands			
Cash Flows from Operating Activities:			
Net income	$155,665	$126,914	$ 82,849
Adjustments to reconcile net income to net cash provided by operating activities:			
Depreciation and amortization	42,850	39,043	35,039
Other—net	6,452	7,524	513
Change in current assets and liabilities:			
(Increase) decrease in accounts receivable—trade	(32,115)	33,713	14,669
Decrease in inventories	43,936	12,362	13,590
(Increase) in deferred income tax benefits	(676)	(416)	(15,169)
Decrease (increase) in other current assets	3,498	(846)	(7,809)
Increase (decrease) in accounts payable	24,866	219	(2,545)
(Decrease) increase in accrued expenses	(4,204)	(1,475)	59,159
(Decrease) increase in income taxes payable	(1,886)	4,754	(7,653)
Net cash provided by operating activities	238,386	221,792	172,643
Cash Flows from Investing Activities:			
Purchases of investment instruments	(348,646)	(344,626)	(181,739)
Disposals of investment instruments	524,323	227,119	121,713
Purchases of property and equipment	(23,337)	(34,357)	(70,594)
Purchase of trademarks	—	(2,595)	(3,193)
Proceeds from sale of certain shoe division assets	—	17,872	—
Other-net	3,828	2,102	2,935
Net cash provided by (used in) investing activities	156,168	(134,485)	(130,878)
Cash Flows from Financing Activities:			
Repayment of long-term debt	(119)	(112)	(107)
Proceeds from exercise of common stock options	12,878	537	297
Dividends paid	(32,318)	(33,627)	(35,304)
Purchase of common stock	(103,781)	(71,183)	(39,591)
Net cash used in financing activities	(123,340)	104,385)	(74,705)
Effect of Exchange Rate Changes on Cash	(3,055)	381	(361)
Net Change in Cash and Cash Equivalents	268,159	(16,697)	(33,301)
Cash and Cash Equivalents at Beginning of Year	54,722	71,419	104,720
Cash and Cash Equivalents at End of Year	$322,881	$ 54,722	$ 71,419

cussed above or are logical extensions. For example, depletion expense arising from natural resources are conceptually the same as depreciation.

The new item that deserves discussion is nonoperating gains and losses. Suppose the company sells 10 acres of land it has decided not to use. The land cost $20,000 and is sold for $30,000 in cash. Net income would include a gain of $10,000. The cash flow is $30,000. But note, this is not cash from operations, because for most companies ownership of land is an investing activity. To include this properly in the cash flow statement requires that all $30,000 be shown as cash provided by investing activities. The $10,000 gain is subtracted from net income in the reconciliation to avoid including elements of this transaction in both places. It was not a source of operating cash.

LIZ CLAIBORNE'S CASH FLOW STATEMENT

Exhibit 10-8 contains a statement of cash flows for Liz Claiborne, Inc., a company that designs and markets an extensive range of fashion apparel and accessories under names such as Dana Buchman, Liz Claiborne, Villager, and Russ. Statements of cash flows for other publicly held corporations may include more details, but the general format of the statement of cash flows is similar to that shown. Note that Liz Claiborne uses the indirect method in the body of the statement of cash flows to report the cash flows from operating activities. Most companies use this format. During the three years shown, Liz has had positive cash flow from operations each year. In 1996, Liz continued a three-year pattern of repurchasing common stock, spending more than $200,000 in this way. This far exceeds the total dividend payments over the three-year period. The cash flow statement reveals a number of important elements that are not highlighted as well by any other statement.

SUMMARY PROBLEMS FOR YOUR REVIEW

PROBLEM ONE

The Buretta Company has prepared the data in Exhibit 10-9.

In December 19X2, Buretta paid $54 million cash for a new building acquired to accommodate an expansion of operations. This purchase was financed partly by a new issue of long-term debt for $40 million cash. During 19X2, the company also sold fixed assets for their book value of $5 million cash. All sales and purchases of merchandise were on credit.

Because the 19X2 net income of $4 million was the highest in the company's history, Alice Buretta, the chairman of the board, was perplexed by the company's extremely low cash balance.

1. Prepare a statement of cash flows from the Buretta data in Exhibit 10-9 on the next page. Ignore income taxes. You may wish to use Exhibit 10-3 (p. 402) as a guide. Use the direct method for reporting cash flows from operating activities.

2. Prepare a supporting schedule that reconciles net income to net cash provided by operating activities.

3. What does the statement of cash flows tell you about Buretta Co.? Does it help you reduce Alice Buretta's puzzlement? Why?

SOLUTION TO PROBLEM ONE

1. See Exhibit 10-10. Cash flows from operating activities were computed as follows (in millions):

Sales	$ 100
Less increase in accounts receivable	(15)
Cash collections from customers	$ 85
Cost of goods sold	$ 73
Plus increase in inventory	32
Purchases	$ 105
Less increase in accounts payable	(25)
Cash paid to suppliers	$ 80
General expenses	$ 8
Plus increase in prepaid general expenses	1
Cash payment for general expenses	$ 9
Cash paid for interest	$ 3
Property taxes	$ 4
Less increase in accrued property tax payable	(2)
Cash paid for property taxes	$ 2

Exhibit 10-9

Buretta Co.

Income Statement and Statement of Retained Earnings for the Year Ended
December 31, 19X2 (in millions)

Sales		$100
Less cost of goods sold:		
Inventory, December 31, 19X1	$ 15	
Purchases	105	
Cost of goods available for sale	$120	
Inventory, December 31, 19X2	47	73
Gross profit		$ 27
Less other expenses:		
General expenses	$ 8	
Depreciation	8	
Property taxes	4	
Interest expense	3	23
Net income		$ 4
Retained earnings, December 31, 19X1		7
Total		$ 11
Dividends		1
Retained earnings, December 31, 19X2		$ 10

Trial Balances

	December 31 (in millions)		Increase (Decrease)
	19X2	*19X1*	
Debits			
Cash	$ 1	$20	$(19)
Accounts receivable	20	5	15
Inventory	47	15	32
Prepaid general expenses	3	2	1
Fixed assets, net	91	50	41
	$162	$92	$ 70
Credits			
Accounts payable for merchandise	$ 39	$14	$ 25
Accrued property tax payable	3	1	2
Long-term debt	40	—	40
Capital stock	70	70	—
Retained earnings	10	7	3
	$162	$92	$ 70

2. Exhibit 10-11 reconciles net income to net cash provided by operating activities.

3. The statement of cash flows shows where cash has come from and where it has gone. Operations used $9 million of cash. Why? The statement in Exhibit 10-10, which uses the direct method, shows the result clearly: $94 million in cash paid for operating activities exceeded $85 million in cash received from customers. The reconciliation using the indirect method, in Exhibit 10-11, shows why, in a profitable year, operating cash flow could be negative. The three largest items differentiating net income from cash flow are changes in inventory, accounts receivable, and accounts payable. Sales during the period were not collected in full because accounts receivable rose sharply, by $15 million—a 300% increase. Similarly, cash was spent on inventory growth, although much of that growth was

Exhibit 10-10

Buretta Company

Statement of Cash Flows for the Year Ended December 31, 19X2 (in millions)

CASH FLOWS FROM OPERATING ACTIVITIES:		
Cash collections from customers		$ 85
Cash payments:		
Cash paid to suppliers	$(80)	
General expenses	(9)	
Interest paid	(3)	
Property taxes	(2)	(94)
Net cash used by operating activities		$ (9)
CASH FLOWS FROM INVESTING ACTIVITIES:		
Purchase of fixed assets (building)	$(54)	
Proceeds from sale of fixed assets	5	
Net cash used by investing activities		(49)
CASH FLOWS FROM FINANCING ACTIVITIES:		
Long-term debt issued	$40	
Dividends paid	(1)	
Net cash provided by financing activities		39
Net decrease in cash		$(19)
Cash balance, December 31, 19X1		20
Cash balance, December 31, 19X2		$ 1

Exhibit 10-11

Supporting Schedule to Statement of Cash Flows

Reconciliation of Net Income to Net Cash Provided by Operating Activities for the Year Ended December 31, 19X2 (in millions)

Net income (from income statement)	$ 4
Adjustments to reconcile net income to net cash provided by operating activities:	
Add: Depreciation, which was deducted in the computation of net income but does not decrease cash	8
Deduct: Increase in accounts receivable	(15)
Deduct: Increase in inventory	(32)
Deduct: Increase in prepaid general expenses	(1)
Add: Increase in accounts payable	25
Add: Increase in accrued property tax payable	2
Net cash used by operating activities	$ (9)

financed by increased accounts payable. In summary, large increases in accounts receivable ($15 million) and inventory ($32 million), plus a $1 million increase in prepaid expenses, used $48 million of cash. In contrast, only $39 million (that is, $4 + $8 + $25 + $2 million) was generated. Thus $9 million was used in operations ($39 − $48).

Investing activities also consumed cash because $54 million was invested in a building, and only $5 million was received from sales of fixed assets leaving a net use of $49 million. Financing activities did generate $39 million cash, but that was $19 million less than the $58 million used by operating and investing activities. ($58 million = $9 million used in operations + $49 million used in investing.)

Alice Buretta should no longer be puzzled. The statement of cash flows shows clearly that cash payments exceeded receipts by $19 million. However, she may still be concerned about the depletion of cash. Either operations must be changed so that they do not require so much cash, or investment must be curtailed, or more long-term debt or ownership equity must be raised. Otherwise Buretta Company will soon run out of cash.

PROBLEM TWO

To understand how cash flow and net income vary during the life cycle of a business, consider the following example that portrays the four-year life of a short-lived merchandising company, Trend-2000. The first year the entrepreneurs bought twice as much as they sold because they were building their base inventory levels. Trend-2000 suppliers offered payment terms that resulted in 80% of each year's purchases being paid during that year and 20% in the next year. Sales were for cash with a 100% markup on cost. Selling expenses were constant over the life of the business and were paid in cash. At the end of the fourth year, the suppliers were paid in full and all of the inventory was sold. Use the following summary results to prepare four income statements and statements of cash flows from operations for Trend-2000, one for each year of its life.

	Year 1	Year 2	Year 3	Year 4
Purchases	2,000 units	1,500 units	1,500 units	1,000 units
$1 each	$2,000	$1,500	$1,500	$1,000
Sales	1,000 units	1,500 units	2,000 units	1,500 units
$2 each	$2,000	$3,000	$4,000	$3,000
Cost of sales	$1,000	$1,500	$2,000	$1,500
Selling expense	$1,000	$1,000	$1,000	$1,000
Payments to suppliers*	$1,600	$1,600	$1,500	$1,300

*.8 × 2,000 = 1,600; (.2 × 2,000) + (.8 × 1,500) = 1,600; (.2 × 1,500) + (.8 × 1,500) = 1,500; (.2 × 1,500) + (1.0 × 1,000) = 1,300

SOLUTION TO PROBLEM TWO

	Year 1	Year 2	Year 3	Year 4	Total
Income statement:					
Sales	$2,000	$3,000	$4,000	$3,000	$12,000
Cost of sales	1,000	1,500	2,000	1,500	6,000
Selling expenses	1,000	1,000	1,000	1,000	4,000
Net income	$ 0	$ 500	$1,000	$ 500	$2,000
Cash flows from Operations: Direct method					
Collections	$2,000	$3,000	$4,000	$3,000	$12,000
Payments on account	1,600	1,600	1,500	1,300	6,000
Payments for selling efforts	1,000	1,000	1,000	1,000	4,000
Cash flow from operations	$ (600)	$ 400	$1,500	$ 700	$ 2,000
Cash flows from Operations: Indirect method					
Net income	$ 0	$ 500	$1,000	$ 500	$ 2,000
− Increase in inventory	(1,000)				(1,000)
+ Decrease in inventory			500	500	1,000
+ Increase in accounts payable	400				400
− Decrease in accounts payable		(100)		(300)	(400)
Cash flow from operations	$ (600)	$ 400	$1,500	$ 700	$ 2,000

Balance Sheet Accounts at the end of:	Year 1	Year 2	Year 3	Year 4	
Merchandise inventory	$1,000	$1,000	$ 500	$ 0	
Accounts payable	$ 400	$ 300	$ 300	0	

This problem illustrates the difference between accrual-based earnings and cash flows. Observe that significant cash outflows occur for operations during the first year as payments to acquire inventory far exceed collections from customers. In fact, it is not until the third year that cash flow from operations exceeds net earnings for the year.

Highlights to Remember

The statement of cash flows focuses on the changes in cash and the activities that cause those changes. Accrual-based net income is a useful number, but we also ask: How did our cash position change? How much of the change in cash was caused by operating activities? By investing activities such as buying another company or new plant and equipment? By financing activities such as borrowing from a bank, issuing bonds, or paying dividends to shareholders?

The direct method of calculating net cash provided by operations requires that we restate each income element to reflect the movement of cash. We convert revenue to cash collected from customers, cost of goods sold to cash paid to suppliers, and so on. These cash items are then combined directly to yield cash from operations. The more common method in practice is the indirect method, which starts with net income and adjusts it for the differences, typically account by account, between accrual income and operating cash flow. Both methods yield the same result.

Under the indirect method, depreciation is added to net income because it is an expense not requiring the use of cash. In addition to depreciation, other items affect the reconciliation of net income to cash from operations. Examples covered in the text through Chapter 10 include depletion and amortization of bond premium and discount.

Appendix 10A: More on the Statement of Cash Flows

This appendix describes two common items that affect the statement of cash flows. You need not be familiar with these items to have a basic understanding of how the statement of cash flows generally works or is created. However, these two items occur frequently in the statements of cash flows of major corporations, so understanding these items will help you to read real financial statements.

Objective 8
Adjust for gains and losses from fixed asset sales and debt extinguishments in the statement of cash flows (Appendix 10A).

GAIN OR LOSS ON DISPOSAL OF FIXED ASSETS

In the chapter, the Eco-Bag Company sold fixed assets for their book value of $10,000. More often a fixed asset is sold for an amount that differs from its book value. Suppose the fixed assets sold by Eco-Bag Company for $10,000 had a book value of $6,000 (original cost = $36,000; accumulated depreciation = $30,000). Therefore net income would be $27,000, comprising the $23,000 shown in Exhibit 10-3, p. 402 plus a $4,000 gain on disposal of fixed assets. We are assuming no tax effects.

Consider first the disposal's effects on cash and income using the balance sheet equation:

$$\Delta \text{ Cash} = \Delta \text{ L} + \Delta \text{ SE} - \Delta \text{ NCA}$$
$$\text{Proceeds} = \qquad \text{Gain} - (-\text{Book value})$$
$$\$10,000 = \qquad \$4,000 - (-\$6,000)$$

Although the book value affects the calculation of gain, no cash is involved. The body of the statement of cash flows under the direct method would not include any gains (or losses) from the disposal of fixed assets in the section on operating activities. The disposal of fixed assets is an investing activity, thus the statement of cash flows would show the following item under investing activities:

Proceeds from sale of fixed assets	$10,000

However, consider Exhibit 10-6 on page 410, which uses the indirect method to reconcile net income to net cash provided by operating activities. If we were to produce a similar reconciliation after our gain on disposal, the new net income of $27,000 would be our starting point. However, this net income figure already includes the $4,000 gain. To avoid double counting (that is, showing inflows of $4,000 in operating activities and $10,000 in investing activities), Eco-Bag Company must deduct from net income the $4,000 gain on disposal:

Net income	$27,000
Plus adjustments in Exhibit 10-6	46,000
Less gain on disposal of fixed assets	(4,000)
Net cash provided by operating activities	$69,000

Losses on the disposal of assets would be treated similarly except that they would be added back to net income. Suppose the book value of the fixed assets sold by Eco-Bag Company was $17,000, creating a $7,000 loss on disposal and net income of $16,000. The reconciliation would show:

Net income	$16,000
Plus adjustments in Exhibit 10-6	46,000
Plus loss on disposal of assets	7,000
Net cash provided by operating activities	$69,000

Losses and gains on disposal are essentially nonoperating items that are included in net income. As such, their effect must be removed from net income when it is reconciled to net cash flow provided by operating activities.

GAIN OR LOSS ON EARLY RETIREMENT OF DEBT

Issuing and retiring debt are financing activities. Any gain or loss on early retirement of debt must be removed from net income in a reconciliation schedule. The process is conceptually the same as gains and losses on sales of fixed assets. The difference is that an outflow of cash to retire the debt is related to the book value of the debt being retired. Suppose Eco-Bag Company paid $37,000 to retire long-term debt with a book value of $34,000, generating a $3,000 loss on retirement of debt. Net income would be $23,000 − $3,000 = $20,000. The balance sheet equation would show:

$$\Delta \text{ Cash} = \quad \Delta \text{ L} \quad + \quad \Delta \text{ SE} - \Delta \text{ NCA}$$
$$-\text{Payment} = -\text{Book value} \qquad -\text{Loss}$$
$$-\$37,000 = -\$34,000 \qquad \quad -\$3,000$$

The $3,000 loss would be added back to net income to determine net cash provided by operating activities:

Net income	$20,000
Plus adjustments in Exhibit 10-6	46,000
Plus loss on retirement of debt	3,000
Net cash provided by operating activities	$69,000

The entire *payment* for debt retirement would be listed among the financing activities:

Proceeds from issue of long-term debt	$120,000
Payment to retire long-term debt	(37,000)
Proceeds from issue of common stock	98,000
Dividends paid	(19,000)
Net cash provided by financing activities	$162,000

Appendix 10B: T-Account Approach to Statement of Cash Flows

Objective 9
Use the T-account approach to prepare the cash flow statement (Appendix 10B).

Many statements of cash flows can be prepared by using the steps described in the body of the chapter. However, analysts confronted with complicated and numerous activities will find the T-account approach easier to use. When constructing any cash flow statement, we know that the increases and decreases of cash due to various activities must add up to the overall change in cash during the year. The T-account approach is simply an easier way of ensuring that all the appropriate activities are identified and treated properly.

To illustrate this approach, we will again use the Eco-Bag Company data from Exhibit 10-3, p. 402, and the summary of 19X2 transactions that appears on p. 403 and 404. Exhibit 10-12 shows the individual T-accounts for the year, as well as the overall T-account presentation of a statement of cash flows that appears in the T-account for cash.

This appendix uses T-accounts to produce cash flow information formatted to support preparation of a statement using the direct method. However, the technique helps identify financing and investing cash flows which are important under both the direct and indirect method. Ultimately, either presentation method requires an understanding of the linkages between cash flow and accrual based net income.

To employ the T-account approach, reasonably complete re-creations of the summary journal entries for the year are required. The journal entries are shown as follows, keyed to the entries in Exhibit 10-12, p. 421. Those involving cash have an asterisk (*).

1.	Sales on credit:		
	Accounts receivable	200	
	Sales		200
* 2.	Collection of accounts receivable:		
	Cash	180	
	Accounts receivable		180
3.	Recognition of cost of goods sold:		
	Cost of goods sold	100	
	Inventory		100
4.	Purchases of inventory on credit:		
	Inventory	140	
	Trade accounts payable		140
* 5.	Payment of trade accounts payable:		
	Trade accounts payable	72	
	Cash		72
6.	Recognition of wages and salaries expense:		
	Wages and salaries expense	36	
	Wages and salaries payable		36
* 7.	Payment of wages and salaries:		
	Wages and salaries payable	15	
	Cash		15
* 8.	Recognition of interest accrued and paid:		
	Interest expense	4	
	Cash		4
* 9.	Recognition and payment of income taxes:		
	Income tax expense	20	
	Cash		20

10. Recognition of depreciation expense:
   Depreciation expense 17
      Fixed assets, net   17

*11. Acquisition of fixed assets for cash:
   Fixed assets, net 287
      Cash   287

*12. Sale of fixed assets at book value:
   Cash 10
      Fixed assets, net   10

*13. Issuance of long-term debt:
   Cash 120
      Long-term debt   120

*14. Issuance of common stock:
   Cash 98
      Stockholders' equity   98

*15. Declaration and payment of dividends:
   Dividends declared and paid 19
      Cash   19

The T-account approach displayed in Exhibit 10-12 is merely another way of applying the balance sheet equation described in the body of the chapter:

$$\Delta \text{Cash} = \Delta \text{Current liabilities} + \Delta \text{Long-term liabilities} + \Delta \text{Stockholders' equity} - \Delta \text{Noncash current assets} - \Delta \text{Fixed assets, net}$$

$$\Delta \text{Cash} = \Delta \text{Accounts and wages payable} + \Delta \text{Long-term debt} + \Delta \text{Stockholders' equity} - \Delta \text{Accounts receivable and inventory} - \Delta \text{Fixed assets, net}$$

Δ Cash	Δ Accounts and wages payable	Δ Long-term debt	Δ Stockholders' equity	Δ Accounts receivable and inventory	Δ Fixed assets, net
9	68	120	102	20	260
	21			40	
	89			60	

$$-9 = 89 + 120 + 102 - 60 - 260$$

Again, we focus on the changes in the noncash accounts to explain why cash changed.

The summarized transactions for 19X2 entered in the Cash account are the basis for the preparation of the formal statement of cash flows, as can be seen by comparing the cash account from Exhibit 10-12 with the statement of cash flows in Exhibit 10-3 on page 402.

Accounting Vocabulary

cash flows from financing activities, p. 407

cash flows from investing activities, p. 407

cash flows from operating activities, p. 398

direct method, p. 398

financing activities, p. 398

financial management, p. 397

investing activities, p. 397

indirect method, p. 398

operating activities, p. 397

operating management, p. 397

Exhibit 10-12

Eco-Bag Company

T-Account Approach Using Direct Method Statement of Cash Flows for the Year Ended December 31, 19X2 (in thousands)

Cash

Bal. 12/31/X1	25		

Operating Activities

2. Collection of accounts receivable	180	5. Pay accounts payable	72
		7. Pay wages and salaries	15
		8. Pay interest	4
		9. Pay taxes	20

Investing Activities

12. Disposal of fixed assets	10	11. Acquisition of fixed assets	287

Financing Activities

13. Issue long-term debt	120	15. Pay dividends	19
14. Issue common stock	98		
Total debits	408	Total credits	417
		Net decrease	9
Bal. 12/31/X2	16		

Accounts Receivable

Bal. 12/31/X1	25			
1. Sales	200	2. Collections	180	
Net increase	20			
Bal. 12/31/X2	45			

Accounts Payable

		Bal. 12/31/X1	6
5. Payments	72	4. Purchases	140
		Net increase	68
		Bal. 12/31/X2	74

Inventory

Bal. 12/31/X1	60			
4. Purchases	140	2. Cost of goods sold	100	
Net increase	40			
Bal. 12/31/X2	100			

Wages and Salaries Payable

		Bal. 12/31/X1	4
7. Payments	15	6. Accruals	36
		Net increase	21
		Bal. 12/31/X2	25

Fixed Assets, Net

Bal. 12/31/X1	220			
11. Acquisition	287	10. Depreciation	17	
		12. Disposals	10	
Net increase	260			
Bal. 12/31/X2	480			

Long-Term Debt

		Bal. 12/31/X1	5
		13. New issue	120
		Bal. 12/31/X2	125

Stockholders' Equity

		Bal. 12/31/X1	315
3. Cost of goods sold	100	1. Sales	200
		14. New Issue	98
6. Wages	36		
8. Interest	4		
9. Income taxes	20		
10. Depreciation	17		
15. Dividends	19		
Total debits	196	Total credits	298
		Net increase	102
		Bal. 12/31/X2	417

Assignment Material

Special note: The following exercises and problems do not involve the indirect method, and therefore can be solved without reading beyond page 409: 10-26 through 10-29, 10-31 through 10-34, 10-37, 10-38, 10-39, 10-43, 10-44, 10-46, 10-48, 10-56, 10-59, 10-62, 10-63, and 10-64.

QUESTIONS

10-1. "The statement of cash flows is an optional statement included by most companies in their annual reports." Do you agree? Explain.

10-2. What are the purposes of a statement of cash flows?

10-3. Define *cash* equivalents.

10-4. Distinguish between *operating management* and *financial management.*

10-5. What three types of activities are summarized in the statement of cash flows?

10-6. Name four major operating activities included in a statement of cash flows.

10-7. Name three major investing activities included in a statement of cash flows.

10-8. Name three major financing activities included in a statement of cash flows.

10-9. What are the two major ways of computing net cash provided by operating activities?

10-10. Where does interest received or paid appear on the statement of cash flows?

10-11. "Net losses mean drains on cash." Do you agree? Explain.

10-12. Demonstrate how the fundamental balance sheet equation can be recast to focus on cash.

10-13. Why is there usually a difference between the cash collections from customers and sales revenue in a period's financial statements?

10-14. Do all changes in current assets and liabilities affect cash flows from operations? If not, give an example of an account that does not.

10-15. Explain why increases in liabilities increase cash and increases in assets decrease cash.

10-16. Why are noncash investing and financing activities listed on a separate schedule accompanying the statement of cash flows?

10-17. A company acquired a fixed asset in exchange for common stock. Explain how this transaction should be shown, if at all, in the statement of cash flows. Why is your suggested treatment appropriate?

10-18. Suppose a company paid off a $1 million short-term loan to one bank with the proceeds from an identical loan from another bank. The change in the short-term debt account would be zero. Should anything appear in the statement of cash flows? Explain.

10-19. The indirect method for reporting cash flows from operating activities can create an erroneous impression about noncash expenses (such as depreciation). What is the impression, and why is it erroneous?

10-20. An investor's newsletter had the following item: "The company expects increased cash flow in 1999 because depreciation charges will be substantially greater than they were in 1998." Comment.

10-21. "Depreciation is an integral part of a statement of cash flows." Do you agree? Explain.

10-22. XYZ Company's only transaction in 19X1 was the sale of a fixed asset for cash of $20,000. The income statement included only "Gain on sale of fixed asset, $5,000." Correct the following statement of cash flows:

Cash flows from operating activities:	
Gain on sale of fixed asset	$ 5,000
Cash flows from investing activities:	
Proceeds from sale of fixed asset	20,000
Total increase in cash	$25,000

10-23. The Lawrence Company sold fixed assets with a book value of $5,000 and recorded a $4,000 gain. How should this be reported on a statement of cash flows?

10-24. A company operated at a profit for the year, but cash flow from operations was negative. Why might this occur? What industry or industries might find this a common occurrence?

10-25. A company operated at a loss for the year, but cash flow from operations was positive. Why might this occur? What industry or industries might find this a common occurrence?

EXERCISES

10-26   Cash Received from Customers

Alpha University Press, Inc., had sales of $730,000 during 19X1, 80% of them on credit and 20% for cash. During the year, accounts receivable increased from $65,000 to $80,000, an increase of $15,000. What amount of cash was received from customers during 19X1?

10-27   Cash Paid to Suppliers

Cost of goods sold for Alpha University Press, Inc., during 19X1 was $480,000. Beginning inventory was $105,000, and ending inventory was $135,000. Beginning trade accounts payable were $24,000, and ending trade accounts payable were $45,000. What amount of cash was paid to suppliers?

10-28   Cash Paid to Employees

Alpha University Press, Inc., reported wage and salary expenses of $250,000 on its 19X1 income statement. It reported cash paid to employees of $215,000 on its statement of cash flows. The beginning balance of accrued wages and salaries payable was $18,000. What was the ending balance in accrued wages and salaries payable? Ignore payroll taxes.

10-29   Simple Cash Flows from Operating Activities

Global Strategy, Inc., provides consulting services. In 19X8, net income was $185,000 on revenues of $470,000 and expenses of $285,000. The only noncash expense was depreciation of $40,000. The company has no inventory. Accounts receivable increased by $5,000 during 19X8, and accounts payable and salaries payable were unchanged.

Required

Prepare a statement of cash flows from operating activities. Use the direct method. Omit supporting schedules.

10-30   Net Income and Cash Flow

Refer to Problem 10-29. Prepare a schedule that reconciles net income to net cash flow from operating activities.

10-31   Investing Activities

Giao Trading Company issued common stock for $300,000 on the first day of 19X8. The company bought fixed assets for $140,000 and inventory for $65,000. Late in the year it sold fixed assets for their book value of $20,000. Half of the inventory was sold for $55,000 during the year. On December 15, excess cash of $50,000 was used to purchase common stock of Franzen Company, which Giao regarded as a long-term investment.

Required

Prepare a statement of cash flows from investing activities for Giao Trading Company.

10-32   Book Value of Asset Disposals

KXYW Broadcasting Company reported net fixed assets of $47 million at December 31, 19X5, and $53 million at December 31, 19X6. During 19X6, the company purchased fixed assets for $10 million and had $3 million of depreciation. Compute the book value of the fixed asset disposals during 19X6.

10-33   Noncash Investing and Financing Activities

Seymour Company had the following items in its Statement of Cash Flows:

Retirement of long-term debt	$560,000
Common stock issued on conversion of preferred shares	340,000
Purchases of marketable securities	225,000
Mortgage assumed on acquisition of warehouse	655,000
Increase in accounts payable	42,000
Note payable issued for acquisition of fixed assets	188,000

Required Prepare a schedule on noncash investing and financing activities, selecting appropriate items from the list above.

10-34 Financing Activities

During 19X8, the Kohl Shipping Company refinanced its long-term debt. It spent DM 175,000 to retire long-term debt due in 2 years and issued DM 200,000 of 15-year bonds at par. DM signifies deutsche mark, the German monetary unit. It then bought and retired common shares for cash of DM 35,000. Interest expense for 19X3 was DM 23,000, of which DM 21,000 was paid in cash; the other DM 2,000 was still payable at the end of the year. Dividends declared and paid during the year were DM 12,000.

Required Prepare a statement of cash flows from financing activities.

10-35 Depreciation and Cash Flows

(Alternate is 10-45.) Belkview Cafe had sales of $990,000, all received in cash. Total operating expenses were $670,000. All except depreciation were paid in cash. Depreciation of $90,000 was included in the $670,000 of operating expenses. Ignore income taxes.

Required
1. Compute net income and net cash provided by operating activities.
2. Assume that depreciation is tripled. Compute net income and net cash provided by operating activities.

10-36 Gain or Loss on Disposal of Equipment

Icarus Software Company sold 5 computers. It had purchased the computers five years ago for $120,000, and accumulated depreciation at the time of sale was $90,000.

Required
1. Suppose Icarus received $30,000 cash for the computer. How would the sale be shown on the statement of cash flows?
2. Suppose Icarus received $50,000 for the computers. How would the sale be shown on the statement of cash flows (including the schedule reconciling net income and net cash provided by operating activities)?
3. Redo requirement 2 assuming cash received was $20,000.

10-37 Identify Operating, Investing, and Financing Activities

The items listed below were found on the 1996 statement of cash flows of the American Telephone and Telegraph Company (AT&T). For each item, indicate which section of the statement should contain the item—the operating, investing, or financing section. Also indicate whether AT&T uses the direct or indirect method for reporting cash flows from operating activities.

a. Proceeds from long-term debt issuance
b. Net income (loss)
c. Dividends paid
d. Capital expenditures net of proceeds from sale or disposal of property, plant, and equipment
e. Issuance of common shares
f. Retirements of long-term debt
g. Increase in inventories
h. Increase in short-term borrowing—net
i. Depreciation and amortization

PROBLEMS

10-38 Statement of Cash Flows, Direct Method

MCI Communications Corporation had cash and cash equivalents of $187 million on December 31, 1996. The following items are on the company's statement of cash flows (in millions) for the first six months of 1997.

Receipts from customers	9,311
Interest paid, net	(140)
Capital expenditures for property and equipment	(1,710)
Purchase of treasury stock	(93)
Sales of marketable securities	91
Retirement of long-term debt	(160)
Payments to suppliers and employees	(7,499)
Issuance of common stock for employee stock plans	251
Dividend payments	(17)
Issuance of long-term debt	135
Other investing activity	(134)
Taxes paid	(167)

Prepare a statement of cash flows for MCI for the first six months of 1997 using the direct method. Include the balance of cash and cash equivalents at year end. Omit the schedule reconciling net income to net cash provided by operating activities and the schedule of noncash investing and financing activities.

Required

10-39 Prepare a Statement of Cash Flows, Direct Method

(Alternate is 10-46.) Tubs, Inc. is a wholesale distributor of hot tubs and spas. Its cash balance on December 31, 19X6, was $61 thousand, and net income for 19X7 was $214 thousand. Its 19X7 transactions affecting income or cash were (in thousands):

a. Sales of $1,400, all on credit. Cash collections from customers, $1,500.

b. The cost of items sold, $800. Purchases of inventory totaled $850; inventory and accounts payable were affected accordingly.

c. Cash payments on trade accounts payable, $825.

d. Salaries and wages: accrued, $190; paid in cash, $200.

e. Depreciation, $45.

f. Interest expense, all paid in cash, $11.

g. Other expenses, all paid in cash, $100.

h. Income taxes accrued, $40; income taxes paid in cash, $35.

i. Bought plant and facilities for $435 cash.

j. Issued long-term debt for $110 cash.

k. Paid cash dividends of $39.

Prepare a statement of cash flows using the direct method for reporting cash flows from operating activities. Omit supporting schedules.

Required

10-40 Reconcile Net Income and Net Cash Provided by Operating Activities

(Alternate is 10-47.) Refer to Problem 10-39. Prepare a supporting schedule that reconciles net income to net cash provided by operating activities.

10-41 Cash Provided by Operations

Clorox Company is a leading producer of laundry additives, including Clorox liquid bleach. In 1997, net sales of $2.2 billion represented a 14% increase over 1996 and produced a 12% earnings increase to $249.4 million. To calculate net earnings, Clorox recorded $126.4 million in depreciation, and other items of revenue and expense not requiring cash decreased cash flow from operations by $1.7 million. Dividends of $110.4 million were paid during 1997. Among the changes in balance sheet accounts during 1997 were (in millions):

Accounts receivable	$ 1.7	increase
Inventories	24.3	increase
Prepaid expenses	4.5	increase
Accounts payable	26.0	decrease
Accrued liabilities	37.9	increase
Income Taxes Payable	6.6	increase

Required Compute the net cash provided by operating activities using the indirect method.

10-42 Cash Flows from Operating Activities, Indirect Method

Sumimoto Metal Industries, Ltd., is a leading diversified manufacturer of steel products. During 1996, Sumimoto earned ¥16.2 billion on revenues of approximately ¥1,057 billion (or approximately $10 billion). The following summarized information relates to Sumimoto's statement of cash flows:

	(billions of yen)
Depreciation and amortization	¥101.3
Repayments of long-term debt	185.2
Proceeds from long-term debt	110.1
Other noncash operating revenues	16.2
Increase in receivables	21.6
Decrease in inventories	17.9
Gain on sales of marketable securities	40.2
Other decreases in cash from operations due to changes in current assets and liabilities	10.7
Additions to property and equipment	115.8
Increase in payables	36.7

Required Compute the net cash provided by operating activities. All of the information necessary for that task is provided, together with some information related to other elements of the cash flow statement. Note that the format does not include parentheses to differentiate elements that increase cash from those that decrease cash, but the distinction should be clear from the captions.

10-43 Cash Flows From Investing Activities

KLM Royal Dutch Airlines transports approximately 12 million passengers and more than 460 million tons of freight annually. Its revenues in fiscal 1997 topped NLG 10 billion, where NLG is guilders, the monetary unit of the Netherlands. The company's statement of cash flows for fiscal 1997 contained the following items (in millions of guilders):

Net capital expenditure on intangible fixed assets	NLG (10)
Net income	236
Repayment of long-term debt	(618)
Net sale of investments in affiliated companies	619
Proceeds from issuance of long-term debt	176
Net capital expenditure on tangible fixed assets	(717)
Change in operating working capital	114

Required Prepare the section "Cash flows from investing activities" for KLM for the 1997 fiscal year. All the items from that section are included above, along with some items from other sections of the statement of cash flows.

10-44 Cash Flows from Financing Activities

Eli Lilly and Company is a global, research-based corporation that develops, manufactures, and markets pharmaceuticals, medical instruments, diagnostic products, and agricultural products. Its 1996 sales exceeded $7 billion. Lilly's 1996 statement of cash flows included the following items, among others (in millions):

Dividends paid	$(753.2)
Purchase of common stock and other capital transactions	(314.5)
Additions to property and equipment	(443.9)
Depreciation and amortization	543.5
Stock issuances	218.4
Decrease in short-term borrowings	(801.4)
Additions to investments	(294.3)
Net income	1,523.5
Reductions of long-term debt	(10.4)

Prepare the section "Cash flows from financing activities" from Eli Lilly's 1996 annual report. All items necessary for that section appear above. Some items from other sections have been omitted.

Required

10-45 Depreciation and Cash Flows

(Alternate is 10-35.) The following condensed income statement and reconciliation schedule are from the annual report of Cheung Company (in millions):

Sales	$371
Expenses	347
Net income	$ 24

Reconciliation Schedule of Net Income to Net Cash Provided by Operating Activities

Net income	$ 24
Add noncash expenses:	
Depreciation	25
Deduct net increase in noncash operating working capital	(17)
Net cash provided by operating activities	$ 32

A shareholder has suggested that the company switch from straight-line to accelerated depreciation on its annual report to shareholders. He maintains that this will increase the cash flow provided by operating activities. According to his calculations, using accelerated methods would increase depreciation to $45 million, an increase of $20 million; net cash flow from operating activities would then be $52 million.

Required

1. Suppose Cheung Company adopts the accelerated depreciation method proposed. Compute net income and net cash flow from operating activities. Ignore income taxes.
2. Use your answer to requirement 1 to prepare a response to the shareholder.

10-46 Prepare a Statement of Cash Flows, Direct Method
(Alternate is 10-39.) Osaka Exports, Inc., is a wholesaler of Asian goods. By the end of 19X8, the company's cash balance had dropped to ¥5 million, despite net income of ¥254 million in 19X8. Its transactions affecting income or cash in 19X8 were (in millions):

a. Sales were ¥2,510, all on credit. Cash collections from customers were ¥2,413.

b. The cost of items sold was ¥1,599.

c. Inventory increased by ¥56.

d. Cash payments on trade accounts payable were ¥1,653.

e. Payments to employees were ¥305; accrued wages payable decreased by ¥24.

f. Other operating expenses, all paid in cash, were ¥94.

g. Interest expense, all paid in cash, was ¥26.

h. Income tax expense was ¥105; cash payments for income taxes were¥108.

i. Depreciation was ¥151.

j. A warehouse was acquired for ¥540 cash.

k. Sold equipment for ¥37; original cost was ¥196, accumulated depreciation was ¥159.

l. Received ¥28 for issue of common stock.

m. Retired long-term debt for ¥25 cash.

n. Paid cash dividends of ¥88.

Required Prepare a statement of cash flows using the direct method for reporting cash flows from operating activities. Omit supporting schedules.

10-47 Reconcile Net Income and Net Cash Provided by Operating Activities
(Alternate is 10-40.) Refer to Problem 10-46. Prepare a supporting schedule to the statement of cash flows that reconciles net income to net cash provided by operating activities.

10-48 Prepare Statement of Cash Flows from Income Statement and Balance Sheet
(Alternate is 10-59.) During 19X8, Ralston Tool and Die declared and paid cash dividends of $8,000. Late in the year, the company bought new metal-working machinery for a cash cost of $125,000, financed partly by its first issue of long-term debt. Interest on the debt is payable annually. Several old machines were sold for cash equal to their aggregate book value of $5,000. Taxes were paid in cash as incurred. The following data are in thousands:

**Income Statement for the Year
Ended December 31, 19X8**

Sales		$363
Cost of sales		201
Gross margin		162
Salaries	$82	
Depreciation	40	
Cash operating expenses	15	
Interest	2	139
Income before taxes		23
Income taxes		8
Net income		$ 15

Balance Sheets

| | December 31 | | Increase |
	19X8	19X7	(Decrease)
Assets			
Cash and cash equivalents	$ 97	$ 5	$ 92
Accounts receivable	40	95	(55)
Inventories	57	62	(5)
Total current assets	194	162	32
Fixed assets, net	190	110	80
Total assets	$384	$272	$112
Liabilities and			
Stockholders' Equity			
Accounts payable	$ 21	$ 16	$ 5
Interest payable	2	—	2
Long-term debt	100	—	100
Paid-in capital	220	220	—
Retained income	41	36	5
Total liabilities and			
stockholders' equity	$384	$272	$112

Prepare a statement of cash flows. Use the direct method for reporting cash flows from operating activities. Omit supporting schedules.

Required

10-49 Indirect Method: Reconciliation Schedule in Body of Statement

Refer to Problem 10-48. Prepare a statement of cash flows that includes a reconciliation of net income to net cash provided by operating activities in the body of the statement.

10-50 Cash Flows, Indirect Method

The Ramez Company has the following balance sheet data (in millions):

| | December 31 | | | | December 31 | | |
	19X7	19X6	Change		19X7	19X6	Change
Current assets:				Current liabilities			
Cash	$ 9	$ 21	$ (12)	(detailed)	$101	$ 26	$ 75
Receivables, net	50	15	35	Long-term debt	150	—	150
Inventories	100	50	50	Stockholders' equity	208	160	48
Total current assets	$159	$ 86	$ 73				
Plant assets (net of							
accumulated depreciation)							
	300	100	200				
				Total liabilities and			
Total assets	$459	$186	$273	stockholders' equity	$459	$186	$273

Net income for 19X7 was $60 million. Net cash inflow from operating activities was $80 million. Cash dividends paid were $12 million. Depreciation was $30 million. Fixed assets were purchased for $230 million, $150 million of which was financed via the issuance of long-term debt outright for cash.

Roberto Ramez, the president and majority stockholder of the Ramez Company, was a superb operating executive. He was imaginative and aggressive in marketing and ingenious and creative in production. But he had little patience with financial matters. After examining the most recent balance sheet and income statement, he muttered, "We've enjoyed ten years of steady growth; 19X7 was our most profitable ever. Despite such profitability, we're in the worst cash position in our history. Just look at those current liabilities in relation to our available cash! This whole picture of the more you make, the poorer you get, just does not make sense. These statements must be cockeyed."

Required

1. Prepare a statement of cash flows using the indirect method. Include a schedule reconciling net income to net cash provided by operating activities in the body of the statement.

2. Using the statement of cash flows and other information, write a short memorandum to Ramez, explaining why there is such a squeeze on cash.

10-51   Prepare Statement of Cash Flows

The Goldblum Company has assembled the accompanying (a) balance sheets and (b) income statement and reconciliation of retained earnings for 19X9.

Goldblum Co.

Balance Sheets as of December 31 (in millions)

	19X9	19X8	Change
Assets:			
Cash	$ 5	$ 20	$(15)
Accounts receivable	45	33	12
Inventory	70	50	20
Prepaid general expenses	4	3	1
Plant assets, net	202	150	52
	$326	$256	$ 70
Liabilities and Shareholders' Equity:			
Accounts payable for merchandise	$ 74	$ 60	$ 14
Accrued tax payable	3	2	1
Long-term debt	50	—	50
Capital stock	100	100	—
Retained earnings	99	94	5
	$326	$256	$ 70

Goldblum Co.

Income Statement and Reconciliation of Retained Earnings for the Year Ended December 31, 19X9 (in millions)

Sales		$275
Less cost of goods sold:		
Inventory, Dec. 31, 19X8	$ 50	
Purchases	185	
Cost of goods available for sale	$235	
Inventory, Dec. 31, 19X9	70	165
Gross profit		$110
Less other expenses:		
General expense	$ 51	
Depreciation	40	
Taxes	10	101
Net income		$ 9
Dividends		4
Net income of the period retained		$ 5
Retained earnings, Dec. 31, 19X8		94
Retained earnings, Dec. 31, 19X9		$ 99

On December 30, 19X9, Goldblum paid $98 million in cash to acquire a new plant to expand operations. This was partly financed by an issue of long-term debt for $50 million in cash. Plant assets were sold for their book value of $6 million during 19X9. Because net income was $9 million, the highest in the company's history, Sidney Goldblum, the chief executive officer, was distressed by the company's extremely low cash balance.

Required

1. Prepare a statement of cash flows using the direct method for reporting cash flows from operating activities. You may wish to use Exhibit 10-3, page 402, as a guide.

2. Prepare a schedule that reconciles net income to net cash provided by operating activities.

3. What is revealed by the statement of cash flows? Does it help you reduce Mr. Goldblum's distress? Why? Briefly explain to Mr. Goldblum why cash has decreased even though net income was $9 million.

10-52 Balance Sheet Equation

Refer to Problem 10-51, requirement 1. Support your financial statement by using a form of the balance sheet equation. Step by step, show in equation form how each item in the statement of cash flows affects cash.

10-53 Noncash Investing and Financing Activities

The GameTech Company operates a chain of video-game arcades. Among GameTech's activities in 19X8 were:

1. Traded four old video games to another amusement company for one new "Flightime" game. The old games could have been sold for a total of $8,000 cash.

2. Paid off $50,000 of long-term debt by paying $30,000 cash and signing a $20,000 six-month note payable.

3. Issued debt for $60,000 cash, all of which was used to purchase new games for its Northwest Arcade.

4. Purchased the building in which one of its arcades was located by assuming the $120,000 mortgage on the building and paying $15,000 cash.

5. Debtholders converted $64,000 of debt to common stock.

6. Refinanced debt by paying cash to buy back an old issue at its call price of $21,000 and issued new debt at a lower interest rate for $21,000.

Required

Prepare a schedule of noncash investing and financing activities to accompany a statement of cash flows.

10-54 Comprehensive Statement of Cash Flows

During the past 30 years, Catskill Toys, Inc., has grown from a single-location specialty toy store into a chain of stores selling a wide range of children's products. Its activities in 19X7 included the following:

a. Purchased 40% of the stock of Seneca Toy Company for $3,846,000 cash.

b. Issued $1,906,000 in long-term debt; $850,000 of the proceeds was used to retire debt that became due in 19X7 and was listed on the books at $900,000.

c. Purchased property, plant, and equipment for $1,986,000 cash, and sold property with a book value of $576,000 for $500,000 cash.

d. Signed a note payable for the purchase of new equipment; the obligation was listed at $516,000.

e. Executives exercised stock options for 8,000 shares of common stock, paying cash of $166,000.

f. On December 30, 19X7, bought Sanchez Musical Instruments Company by issuing common stock with a market value of $297,000.

g. Issued common stock for $3,200,000 cash.

h. Withdrew $800,000 cash from a money market fund that was considered a cash equivalent.

i. Bought $249,000 of treasury stock to hold for future exercise of stock options.

j. Long-term debt of $960,000 was converted to common stock.

k. Selected results for the year:

Net income	$ 679,000
Depreciation and amortization	615,000
Increase in inventory	72,000
Decrease in accounts receivable	13,000
Increase in accounts and wages payable	7,000
Increase in taxes payable	25,000
Interest expense	144,000
Increase in accrued interest payable	15,000
Sales	9,739,000
Cash dividends received from investments	159,000
Cash paid to suppliers and employees	8,074,000
Cash dividends paid	240,000
Cash paid for taxes	400,000

Required Prepare a statement of cash flows for 19X7 using the direct method. Include a schedule that reconciles net income to net cash provided by operating activities. Also include a schedule of noncash investing and financing activities.

10-55 Statement of Cash Flows, Direct and Indirect Methods

Nordstrom, Inc., the Seattle-based fashion retailer, had the following income statement for the year ended January 31, 1997 (in millions):

Net sales		$4,453
Costs and expenses:		
Cost of sales	$3,082	
Selling, general, and administrative	1,218	
Interest	39	
Less: Other income	(129)	
Total costs and expenses		4,210
Earnings before income taxes		$ 243
Income taxes		96
Net earnings		$ 147

The company's net cash provided by operating activities, prepared using the indirect method, was (in millions):

Net earnings	$147
Adjustments to reconcile net earnings to net cash provided by operating activities:	
Depreciation and amortization	156
Changes in:	
Accounts receivable	(7)
Merchandise inventories	(94)
Prepaid expenses	(2)
Accounts payable	33
Accrued salaries and wages	8
Other accrued expenses	8
Income taxes payable	(1)
Net cash provided by operating activities	$248

Prepare a statement showing the net cash provided by operating activities using the direct method. Assume that all "other income" was received in cash and that prepaid expenses and accrued salaries and wages and other accrued expenses relate to selling, general, and administrative expenses.

Required

10-56   Statement of Cash Flows, Direct Method, for a Utility

The Columbia Gas System had operating revenues of $2.4 billion from providing gas services ranging from exploration and production to pipeline transmission to final distribution to users. The company's statement of cash flows contained the following items (some have been slightly summarized):

	(in millions)
Issuance of common stock	$ 225.3
Retirement of long-term debt	(71.7)
Dividends paid	(103.9)
Cash received from customers	2,829.8
Other operating cash receipts	161.2
Capital expenditures	(600.1)
Issuance of long-term debt	204.5
Other financing activities—net	86.0
Cash paid to suppliers	(1,319.2)
Interest paid	(172.5)
Taxes paid	(256.3)
Other investments—net	(166.3)
Cash paid to employees and for their benefit	(445.2)
Other operating cash payments	(377.7)

Required

1. Prepare the statement of cash flows for Columbia Gas using the direct method. Omit the schedule reconciling net income to net cash provided by operating activities.

2. Discuss the relation between operating cash flow and investing and financing needs.

ASSIGNMENT MATERIAL   **433**

Exhibit 10-13

Kellogg Company and Subsidiaries

Consolidated Statement of Cash Flows, Years ended December 31

(millions)	1996	1995	1994
Operating activities			
Net earnings	$531.0	$ 490.3	$ 705.4
Items in net earnings not requiring (providing) cash:			
Depreciation	251.5	258.8	256.1
Pre-tax gain on sale of subsidiaries	—	—	(26.7)
Deferred income taxes	58.0	(78.7)	24.5
Other	(51.7)	319.9	(49.3)
Change in operating assets and liabilities	(77.3)	50.7	56.8
Net cash provided by operating activities	**711.5**	**1,041.0**	**966.8**
Investing activities			
Additions to properties	(307.3)	(315.7)	(354.3)
Acquisitions of businesses	(505.2)	—	—
Proceeds from sale of subsidiaries	—	—	95.5
Property disposals	11.6	6.3	15.6
Other	14.1	0.5	7.8
Net cash used in investing activities	**(786.8)**	**(308.9)**	**(235.4)**
Financing activities			
Net borrowings of notes payable	964.6	(86.8)	(111.9)
Issuance of long-term debt	—	—	200.0
Reduction of long-term debt	(3.4)	(0.4)	(2.9)
Issuance of common stock	18.8	36.8	2.3
Common stock repurchases	(535.7)	(374.7)	(327.3)
Cash dividends	(343.7)	(328.5)	(313.6)
Other	(6.6)	(5.6)	(6.1)
Net cash provided by (used in) financing activities	**94.0**	**(759.2)**	**(559.5)**
Effect of exchange rate changes on cash	3.2	(17.3)	(3.7)
Increase (decrease) in cash and temporary investments	21.9	(44.4)	168.2
Cash and temporary investments at beginning of year	221.9	266.3	98.1
Cash and temporary investments at end of year	**$243.8**	**$ 221.9**	**$266.3**

10-57 Interpreting the Statement of Cash Flows

The Kellogg Company statement of cash flows appears in Exhibit 10-13.

Use that statement to answer two questions.

Required

1. Does Kellogg generate sufficient cash flow from operations to cover ongoing investing activities and pay dividends to its shareholders?

2. How has Kellogg changed its debt-equity ratio during the period 1994 to 1996?

10-58 Cash Flows from Operating Activities

Boise Cascade Corporation, the forest products company with headquarters in Boise, Idaho, reported net income of more than $75 million. The following data are condensed from the company's income statement and balance sheet (in thousands):

Revenues:	
Sales	$4,184,560
Costs and expenses:	
Nondepreciation expenses (summarized)	(3,737,780)
Depreciation	(212,890)
Income from operations	233,890
Interest expense	(116,620)
Interest income	4,130
Income before income taxes	121,400
Income tax provision	46,130
Net income	$ 75,270

		Increase (Decrease)
Current assets:		
Cash	$ 19,781	$ 66
Short-term investments	6,165	639
Receivables	412,558	(9,010)
Inventories	484,972	60,533
Other	74,107	13,038
Total current assets	$997,583	$ 65,266
Current liabilities:		
Current portion of long-term debt	$136,731	$106,341
Income taxes payable	140	(4,133)
Notes payable	40,000	40,000
Accounts payable	344,384	(47,158)
Accrued liabilities:		
Compensation and benefits	99,530	(14,552)
Interest payable	38,460	(1,611)
Other	99,127	1,261
Total current liabilities	$758,372	$ 80,148

You have determined that other current assets are all operating items, as are other accrued liabilities. Short-term investments are cash equivalents. Depreciation is the only noncash expense. Interest income is all in cash.

1. Prepare a statement of cash flows from operating activities. Use the direct method that begins with cash collections from customers.

2. Reconcile net income to net cash provided by operating activities. (*Hint:* The cash outflow for nondepreciation expense is an aggregation of more specific outflows. There is no way to break the total amount into its component parts.)

10-59 Prepare Statement of Cash Flows from Income Statement and Balance Sheet
(Alternate is 10-48.) Napoli S.A. had the following income statement and balance sheet items (in millions of Italian Lira)

Income Statement for the Year Ended December 31, 19X8

Sales	L.870
Cost of goods sold	(510)
Gross margin	L.360
Operating expenses	(210)
Depreciation	(60)
Interest	(10)
Income before taxes	L.80
Income taxes	(25)
Net income	L.55
Cash dividends paid	(35)
Total increase in retained earnings	L.20

Balance Sheets

	December 31 19X8	December 31 19X7	Increase (Decrease)
Assets			
Cash	L. 20	L. 60	L. (40)
Accounts receivable	240	150	90
Inventories	450	350	100
Total current assets	L. 710	L.560	L. 150
Fixed assets, gross	L. 890	L.715	L. 175
Accumulated depreciation	(570)	(550)	(20)
Fixed assets, net	L. 320	L.165	L. 155
Total assets	L.1,030	L.725	L. 305
Liabilities and Stockholders' Equity			
Trade accounts payable	L. 520	L.300	L. 220
Long-term debt	245	180	65
Stockholders' equity	265	245	20
Total liabilities and stockholders' equity	L.1,030	L.725	L. 305

During 19X8, Napoli purchased fixed assets for L.415 million cash and sold fixed assets for their book value of L.200 million. Operating expenses, interest, and taxes were paid in cash. No long-term debt was retired.

Required

Prepare a statement of cash flows. Use the direct method for reporting cash flows from operating activities. Omit supporting schedules.

10-60   Miscellaneous Cash Flow Questions

McDonald's Corporation is a well-known provider of food services around the world. McDonald's statement of cash flows for 1996 is reproduced with a few slight modifications as Exhibit 10-14. Use that statement and the additional information provided to answer the following questions:

1. In the Financing activities section, all parentheses for 1996 have been removed. Which numbers should be put in parentheses?

Exhibit 10-14

McDonald's Corporation

Consolidated Statement of Cash Flows

(in millions of dollars)	Years ended December 31, 1996	1995
Operating activities		
Net income	$1,572.6	$1,427.3
Adjustments to reconcile to cash provided by operations		
Depreciation and amortization	742.9	709.0
Deferred income taxes	32.9	(4.2)
Changes in operating working capital items		
Accounts receivable increase	(77.5)	(49.5)
Inventories, prepaid expenses and other current assets increase	(18.7)	(20.4)
Accounts payable increase	44.5	52.6
Accrued interest payable increase	5.0	13.0
Taxes and other liabilities increase	116.4	158.3
Other—net	42.9	10.1
Cash provided by operations	2,461.0	2,296.2
Investing activities		
Property and equipment expenditures	2,375.3	(2,063.7)
Sales of restaurant businesses	198.8	151.6
Purchases of restaurant businesses	137.7	(110.1)
Notes receivable additions	36.4	(33.4)
Property sales	35.5	66.2
Notes receivable reductions	59.2	31.5
Other	314.4	(151.1)
Cash used for investing activities	2,570.3	(2,109.0)
Financing activities		
Net short-term borrowings (repayments)	228.8	(272.9)
Long-term financing issuances	1,391.8	1,250.2
Long-term financing repayments	841.3	(532.2)
Treasury stock purchases	599.9	(314.5)
Common and preferred stock dividends	232.0	(226.5)
Other	157.0	63.6
Cash provided by (used for) financing activities	104.4	(32.3)
Cash and equivalents increase (decrease)	a	154.9
Cash and equivalents at beginning of year	b	179.9
Cash and equivalents at end of year	$ c	$334.8

2. In the Investing activities section, all parentheses for 1996 have been removed. Which numbers should be put in parentheses?

3. Estimate the interest expense that was originally deducted in the income statement if interest paid was $369.0 million.

4. The 1996 values for the change in cash and cash equivalents and for beginning and end-of-year balances have been omitted and replaced with the letters *a, b,* and *c.* Provide the proper values for these three missing numbers.

5. Retained earnings at December 31, 1995, was $9,831.3 million. Calculate the retained earnings balance at December 31, 1996.

6. Comment on the relation between cash flow from operations and cash used for investing activities.

7. What do you conclude about changes in McDonald's debt-to-equity ratio during this period?

10-61 Statement of Cash Flows, Direct Method, for a Bank

Bank of Granite Corporation is a North Carolina bank with total assets of about $500 million. Its statement of cash flows for the three months ended March 31, 1997, contained the following items (in thousands):

Interest received	$ 9,521
Net increase in demand deposits	1,174
Net increase in certificates of deposit	4,716
Fees and commissions received	1,365
Proceeds from security sales and maturities	3,900
Purchases of securities	(2,063)
Proceeds from disposals of fixed assets	20
Dividends paid	(811)
Net proceeds from issuance of common stock	268
Net increase in loans	(6,682)
Interest paid	(3,763)
Cash paid to suppliers and employees	(2,967)
Income taxes paid	(518)
Capital expenditures	(518)
Other financing sources of cash	514

Note: Because banks are noticeably different from manufacturing and service companies, their classifications of what constitutes operating, investing, and financing activities also differ. For example, banks treat as financing activities their sales of certificates of deposit. Similarly, the basic deposits that individuals make in the savings bank are treated as financing activities.

Prepare Bank of Granite's statement of cash flows in proper format, using the direct method. Omit the schedule reconciling net income to net cash provided by operating activities.

10-62 Statement of Cash Flows, Direct Method, Interest Expense, Australia

CSR Limited is a leading supplier of building and construction materials headquartered in Sydney, Australia. The company's revenues in fiscal 1997 exceeded A$6 billion, where A$ is the Australian dollar. The following items appeared in CSR's 1997 statement of cash flows:

Receipts from customers	A$6,165.7
Purchase of controlled entities	(59.4)
Proceeds from sale of controlled entities	61.4
Payments to suppliers and employees	(5,406.7)
Dividends received	25.0
Net cash from operating activities	670.5
Purchase of property, plant and equipment	(630.2)
Proceeds from sale of property, plant and equipment	175.0
Net proceeds from borrowings	138.7
Dividends paid	(296.0)
Other investing activities	43.9
Interest received	12.1
Income taxes paid	(125.6)
Net cash used in investing activities	(409.3)
Proceeds from issue of shares	122.3
Interest paid	(165.3)
Net cash used in financing activities	(200.3)
Net increase in cash	?

1. Prepare a statement of cash flows for CSR Limited using the direct method. Include the proper amount for the net increase in cash. One item, interest paid, is included in a different section of the statement than it would be on a U.S. statement of cash flows. Place it in the section that makes the cash flows in each section total to the amounts given. Required

2. Where would the interest paid be shown in a statement of cash flows in the U.S.?

3. Explain why CSR places interest paid where it does.

4. Explain why the FASB in the U.S. requires the interest paid to be placed in the section you indicated in requirement 2.

10-63   Statement of Cash Flows, Japan

Kansai Electric supplies power to an area of Japan that includes Osaka and Kyoto. Its operating revenues exceed ¥2.5 trillion, and its assets exceed ¥6 trillion. Instead of a statement of cash flows, Kansai Electric provides a "Statement of Receipts and Expenditures":

Statement of Receipts and Expenditures
Year Ended March 31, 1997

(in billions of yen)

Cash balance at beginning of the period	¥ 72
Receipts	
Operating revenues	2,545
Nonoperating revenues	109
Bond issue	236
Increase in loans	1,546
Total receipts	4,436
Expenditures	
Operating expenses	1,954
Nonoperating expenses	140
Repayments of bonds	262
Repayments of loans	1,419
Cost of construction	672
Total expenditures	4,447
Cash balance at end of the period	¥ 61

From the information in the statement of receipts and expenditures, prepare a statement of cash flows using the direct method. Required

10-64   British Cash Flow Statement

Lloyds TSB Group is a leading UK-based financial services group. It is the sixth largest UK company, based on market capitalization. Lloyds TSB's Consolidated Cash Flow Statement for the year ended December 31, 1996 is in Exhibit 10-15.

Discuss the differences between Lloyds TSB's cash flow statement and the statement of cash flows required for U.S. companies. Required

10-65   T-Account Approach

Study Appendix 10B. Refer to the facts concerning the Buretta Company's "Summary Problem for Your Review" in the chapter. Prepare a set of T-accounts that supports the statement of cash flows shown in Exhibit 10-10 (p. 415). Use Exhibit 10-12 (p. 421) as a guide. Key your postings by number.

Exhibit 10-15

Lloyds TSB Group plc

Consolidated Cash Flow Statement For the Year Ended 31 December 1996
(in millions of pounds)

Net cash (outflow) inflow from operating activities	£ (771)
Returns on investments and servicing of finance:	
Dividends received from associated undertakings	47
Dividends paid	(1,566)
Dividends paid to minority shareholders in group undertakings	(191)
Interest paid on subordinated liabilities (loan capital)	(265)
Interest element of finance lease rental payments	(2)
Net cash outflow from returns on investments and servicing of finance	(1,977)
Tax:	
UK corporation tax	(556)
Overseas tax	(59)
Total tax	(615)
Investing activities:	
Net disposal of (additions to) fixed asset investments	3,820
Addition to interests in associated undertakings	(4)
Disposal of group undertakings and businesses	3
Additions to tangible fixed assets	(242)
Disposals of tangible fixed assets	329
Purchase of shares from minority shareholders	(683)
Net cash inflow (outflow) from investing activities	3,223
Net cash (outflow) inflow before financing	(140)
Financing:	
Issue of subordinated liabilities (loan capital)	557
Issue of ordinary share capital	32
Repayments of subordinated liabilities (loan capital)	(320)
Capital element of finance lease rental payments	(17)
Net cash inflow (outflow) from financing	252
Increase (decrease) in cash and cash equivalents	£ 112

10-66 T-Account Approach

Study Appendix 10B. Refer to the facts concerning the Goldblum Company in Problem 10-51. Prepare a set of T-accounts that supports the statement of cash flows. Use Exhibit 10-12 (p. 421) as a guide. Key your postings by number.

10-67 Interpretation of the Statement of Cash Flows and Ethics

Fleetfoot, Inc., was a successful producer of athletic shoes in the mid-1990s. The company's peak year was 1995. Since then, both sales and profits have fallen. The following information is from the company's 1997 annual report (in thousands):

	1997	1996	1995
Net income	$1,500	$4,500	$7,500
Accounts receivable (end of year)	900	1,800	6,000
Inventory (end of year)	1,050	2,100	2,850
Net cash provided by operations	675	1,050	2,250
Capital expenditures	900	1,050	1,350
Proceeds from sales of fixed assets	2,700	1,500	2,250
Net gain on sales of fixed assets plus net extraordinary gains	2,250	1,800	2,400

During 1998, $9 million of short-term loans became due. Fleetfoot paid off only $2.25 million and was able to extend the terms on the other $6.75 million. Accounts payable continued at a very low level in 1998, and the company maintained a large investment in corporate equity securities, enough to generate $450,000 of dividends received in 1998. Fleetfoot neither paid dividends nor issued stock or bonds in 1998. Its 1998 Statement of Cash Flows was as follows:

Fleetfoot, Inc.

Statement of Cash Flows for the Year Ended December 31, 1998 (in thousands)

Cash flows from operating activities:		
Net income	$ 1,050	
Adjustments to reconcile net income to net cash provided by operating activities:		
Depreciation and amortization	600	
Net decrease in accounts receivable	150	
Net decrease in inventory	225	
Investment revenue from equity investments, less $900 of dividends received	(600)	
Gains on sales of fixed assets	(2,100)	
Extraordinary loss on building fire	1,200	
Net cash provided by operating activities		$ 525
Cash flows from investing activities:		
Purchase of fixed assets	$ (600)	
Insurance proceeds on building fire	3,000	
Sale of plant assets	3,750	
Purchase of corporate equity securities	(2,250)	
Net cash provided by investing activities		3,900
Cash flows from financing activities:		
Principal payments on short-term debt to banks	$(2,250)	
Purchase of treasury stock	(900)	
Net cash used for financing activities		(3,150)
Net increase in cash		1,275
Cash, December 31, 1997		1,800
Cash, December 31, 1998		$ 3,075

Required

1. Interpet the Statement of Cash Flows for Fleetfoot.
2. Describe any ethical issues relating to the strategy and financial disclosures of Fleetfoot.

10-68 The Gap Annual Report

Examine The Gap's statement of cash flows in Appendix A.

Required

1. Explain why The Gap's net cash provided by operating activities was $345,877,000 more in the year ended February 1, 1997, than it was in the year ended February 3, 1996. Would you expect a similar increase in the next year? Why or why not?
2. Explain to a nonaccountant what The Gap did with the $834,953,000 of cash generated by operating activities during the year ended February 1, 1997.
3. Suppose a friend of yours commented, "The Gap must have poor financial management. It made more than $450 million in the year ended February 1, 1997, and it generated more than $800 million in cash from operations, yet its cash balance decreased by nearly $94 million. Where did all that money go?" Answer your friend's question.

10-69   Financial Statement Research
Identify an industry and select two companies within that industry.

1. Determine whether cash flow from operations is stable through time.
2. Relate cash flow from operations to investing and dividend payment needs.
3. Compare cash flow from operations to net income. Explain why they differ.

COLLABORATIVE LEARNING EXERCISE

10-70   Items in the Statement of Cash Flows
Form groups of four to six students each. Each member of the group should select a different company, find its statement of cash flows for a recent year, and make a list of the items included in each section of the statement: operating, investing, and financing activities. Be ready to explain the nature of each item.

1. As a group, make a comprehensive list of all the items the companies listed under cash flows from operating activities. Identify those that are essentially the same but simply differ in terminology, and call them a single item. For each item, explain why and how it affects cash flows from operating activities. Note whether any of the companies selected uses the direct method for reporting cash flows from operating activities. (Most companies use the indirect method, despite the fact that the FASB prefers the direct method.) If any use the direct method, separate the items listed under the direct method from those listed under the indirect method.

2. Make another comprehensive list of all the items listed under cash flows from investing activities. Again, combine those that are essentially identical and differ only in terminology. For each item, explain why and how it affects cash flows from investing activities.

3. Make a third comprehensive list, this time including all the items listed under cash flows from financing activities. Again, combine those that are essentially identical and differ only in terminology. For each item, explain why and how it affects cash flows from financing activities.

4. Reconvene as a class. For each of the three sections on the statement of cash flows, have groups sequentially add one item to the list of items included in the statement, simultaneously explaining why it is included in that section. Then identify the items that appear on nearly all cash flow statements and those that are relatively rare.

10-71   Internet Case

Go to **http://www.sportsauthority.com/** to find The Sports Authority's home page. This company offers an incredible selection of athletic footwear, apparel, and equipment for team sports, fitness, hunting, fishing, camping, water sports, golf, racquet sports, cycling, and numerous other sports. To find its most recent annual report, click the *Annual Report* icon at the bottom of its home page to locate a menu. Select *Form 10-Q* for the most recent quarterly information. *Form 10-Q* is a quarterly report that is required to be filed by all public companies with the Securities and Exchange Commission. It contains financial information such as financial statements, but is not as thorough as a year-end report.

Answer the following questions about The Sports Authority's statement of cash flows:

1. From the menu, select and read **Letter to Our Shareholders.** Read also **Management's Discussion and Analysis of Financial Condition and Results of Opera-**

tions, located within the 10-Q report. The Sports Authority has been a publicly traded company only since 1994. Even now, it is clearly dedicated to expanding operations. How many new stores were opened during its most recently completed fiscal period? How do you think The Sports Authority expects to finance the cost of these new stores?

2. Find The Sports Authority's statement of cash flows in the 10-Q report. Does the company use the direct or indirect method? How can you tell?

3. Which is larger: cash provided (or used) by operations or net income for the quarter? Why is the cash provided by operations different from the amount of net income for the quarter?

4. Why does The Sports Authority add depreciation and amortization to net income in the operating activities section? Do these amounts create or use cash? Explain.

5. What is the primary reason for the increase in cash from financing activities for the most recent fiscal period?

6. How does The Sports Authority's change in working capital compare to the change in cash for the period? What conclusions can you draw?

STOCKHOLDERS' EQUITY

The public has relied on IHOP for pancakes, waffles, and more for over four decades but has only had access to IHOP stock since 1991.

Learning Objectives

After studying this chapter, you should be able to

1   Describe the rights of shareholders.

2   Differentiate among authorized, issued, and outstanding shares.

3   Contrast bonds, preferred stock, and common stock.

4   Identify the economic characteristics of stock splits and dividends.

5   Account for stock splits and both large-percentage and small-percentage stock
        dividends.

6   Interpret treasury stock transactions.

7   Record conversions of debt for equity or of preferred stock into common stock.

8   Use the rate of return on common equity and book value per share.

Pancakes, waffles, and omelettes are just a few of the choices for breakfast at the International House of Pancakes, more affectionately known as IHOP. With close to 700 locations across the United States, this popular family restaurant chain serves up breakfast—and other items—24 hours a day to satisfy hungry diners. But you can enjoy more than just a good meal at IHOP. By purchasing shares of stock in the company, you can also become an owner.

Although the company has been in business for more than four decades, public ownership is a relatively new concept to the Glendale, California-based chain. But when IHOP chose to "go public" in July of 1991, it found a receptive audience willing to pay $10 per share of common stock. The initial public stock offering generated $6.2 million, which has been used for company growth. The value of the stock has also grown to a recent high of $37 per share.

To ensure continued growth and quality to its owners, IHOP develops new restaurants one at a time. Cash generated by operations is used for this purpose. The plan seems to be working. Earnings per share and sales have increased steadily in recent years, and the company hopes to continue to open approximately 20 new stores each year. How do shareholders feel about all this? Bring on the pancakes and let's eat!

Exhibit 11-1

McDonald's Shareholders' Equity

Shareholders' equity		
Preferred stock, no par value; authorized—165.0 million shares; issued—7.2 thousand	$ 358.0	$ 358.0
Common stock, 1996—$.01 par value; 1995—no par value; authorized, 1996—3.5 billion shares; 1995—1.25 billion shares; issued—830.3 million	8.3	92.3
Additional paid-in capital	574.2	387.4
Guarantee of ESOP notes	(193.2)	(214.2)
Retained earnings	11,173.0	9,831.3
Foreign currency translation adjustment	(175.1)	(87.1)
	11,745.2	10,367.7
Common stock in treasury, at cost; 135.7 and 130.6 million shares	(3,027.0)	(2,506.4)
Total shareholders' equity	$ 8,718.2	$ 7,861.3

Thus far we have described transactions affecting assets and liabilities. Now we will examine stockholders' equity in more detail. After all, stockholders such as those of IHOP want to know details about their interests.

If the accounting equation is to balance, and if we know the amounts of assets and liabilities, the stockholders' equity must be the residual. Economically this is certainly true. When a company is liquidated, and creditors are paid out of the proceeds, the owners receive whatever is left. It is now time to address issues relating to how we classify and report transactions between a company and its shareholders and how analysts use this information to evaluate the company.

Consider McDonald's, the company that launched Chapter 1. The owners' equity section of the McDonald's annual report is reproduced as Exhibit 11-1. Some of what appears there is no surprise because common stock and retained earnings are old friends at this point. However, preferred stock, additional paid-in-capital, ESOP notes, and foreign currency are all new. Most of the issues involve explicit transactions between the company and its shareholders. For example, if you had purchased 100 shares of McDonald's in 1984, today you would have 1,350 shares. McDonald's has had five stock splits during that period. Your original investment of $700 in 1984 would have grown to $5,000.

A number of the accounting practices for shareholders' equity are based on legal characteristics of corporations, so we make frequent reference to the rights and privileges of shareholders and the consequences of various financing decisions on the firm and its owners.

Internationally there are substantial differences in the structure of corporate activity and in accounting procedures used to disclose results. We are observing the conversion of many planned economies from state-owned-and-operated business entities into private ones. In regions of the former USSR, decisions are now being made about the geographic boundaries, the form of government, and the structure of private businesses and how to own and account for those businesses. Even in the West, we increasingly observe that government is selling "public companies" to the private sector. Examples range from the United Kingdom's privatization of British Petroleum in the mid-1980s to New York City's 1994 sale of its public television station. From an accounting perspective, the key point is that many diverse legal structures worldwide lead to plentiful international variation in accounting for stockholders' equity.

BACKGROUND ON STOCKHOLDERS' EQUITY

Objective 1

Describe the rights of shareholders.

Corporations are perpetual entities created in accordance with state laws. The corporate charter specifies the rights of stockholders (or shareholders) that generally includes the right to (1) vote, (2) share in corporate profits, (3) share in any assets left at liquidation, and (4) acquire more shares of subsequent issues of stock. The extent of the stockholders' powers is determined by the number and type of shares held.

Corporations hold annual meetings of shareholders, when votes are taken on important matters. For example, the shareholders elect the board of directors. They may also vote on changing employee bonus plans, choosing outside auditors, and similar matters. Large corporations make heavy use of the proxy system. A **corporate proxy** is a written authority granted by individual shareholders to others (usually members of corporate management) to cast the shareholders' votes. By using a proxy, shareholders may express (vote) their preference without traveling to the site of the annual meeting.

corporate proxy A written authority granted by individual shareholders to others to cast the shareholders' votes.

The ultimate power to manage a corporation almost always resides with the common shareholders. But shareholders of publicly owned corporations usually delegate that power to the company's top managers. The modern large corporation frequently has a team of professional managers, from the chairman of the board downward. The chief executive officer (CEO) is frequently the chairman of the board rather than the president. Increasingly companies are requiring top managers to have a significant number of shares in the firm. When managers own shares directly or hold stock options to acquire shares, they are more likely to share a common economic interest with shareholders. When the company's stock rises in value, the managers benefit personally.

Stockholders also generally have **preemptive rights,** which are the rights to acquire a proportional amount of any new issues of capital stock. Whenever a company issues new shares of stock, more people can become owners, in which case everyone's percentage of ownership (the percent of the company held by each owner) decreases. The preemptive privilege allows present shareholders to purchase additional shares directly from the corporation before the shares can be sold to the general public. In this way, the shareholders are able to maintain their percentage of ownership.

preemptive rights The rights to acquire a pro-rata amount of any new issues of capital stock.

Perhaps the most important right of common shareholders is limited liability, which means that creditors of the corporation have claims only on the assets owned by the corporation, not on the assets of the owners of the corporation. In contrast, the creditors of a partnership have potential rights against the savings, homes, and automobiles of the individual partners.

We generally think of existing, well-established companies that issued their common stock years ago. But corporations are being formed constantly. Silicon Valley has originated thousands of new ventures, some large, some small, some successful, some not. There is a complicated marketplace in which exciting new ideas are funded. New corporations often start with a few investors and then seek additional funding as their original ideas are shown to be doable, exciting, and profitable. Groups of investors called venture capitalists support exciting ideas early in the process. If things work out, the company may issue additional shares that are registered with the SEC. This IPO (initial public offering) will be managed by an underwriting firm and the shares will be sold to individual investors and to institutional investors such as pension funds, insurance companies, mutual funds, and so on. Regardless of who is involved, and at what stage of the company's growth cycle, the accounting procedures are very similar.

Objective 2
Differentiate among authorized, issued, and outstanding shares.

AUTHORIZED, ISSUED, AND OUTSTANDING STOCK

When a company becomes a corporation, the state in which it will operate must approve its articles of incorporation, which detail the number and types of capital stock that can be issued. The total number of shares that may be issued is known as the **authorized shares.** Just because a certain number of shares is authorized does not mean that a company will ever offer that many shares to potential investors. Shares are usually offered in batches over time. When the company receives cash in exchange for stock certificates, the shares become **issued shares.** Shares that are issued and held by the stockholders are called **outstanding shares.**

authorized shares The total number of shares that may legally be issued under the articles of incorporation.

issued shares The aggregate number of shares sold to the public.

outstanding shares Shares remaining in the hands of shareholders.

treasury stock A corporation's issued stock that has subsequently been repurchased by the company and not retired.

Sometimes a company buys back shares of stock from its own shareholders. These shares are called **treasury stock.** They are issued, but because the company holds them, they are no longer outstanding. To clarify these issues let us look at an example. As of December 31, 1996, McDonald's had authorized 3.5 billion shares of which 830.3 million were issued. Over time, 135.7 million shares had been reacquired and are shown as treasury stock.

Number of Shares (in millions)	
Authorized	3,500.0
Deduct: Unissued	2,669.7
Issued	830.3
Deduct: Shares held in treasury	135.7
Total shares outstanding	694.6

ACCOUNTING FOR STOCK ISSUANCE

To account for a stock issuance, we record the receipt of cash and create a common stock account to represent the ownership interest. In 1997, McDonald's stock was selling for around $50 per share, so a stock issuance of 1 million additional shares could be recorded as:

Cash	50,000,000	
Common Stock		50,000,000

Many companies, however, separate their common stock recognition into two categories, par value and additional paid-in capital. Legally, par value was originally conceived as a measure of protection for creditors because it established the minimum legal liability of a stockholder. In this way, the creditors would be assured that the corporation would have at least a minimum amount of ownership capital (for example, $10 for each share issued). The stockholder had a commitment to invest at least the par value per share in the corporation.

McDonald's shares have a par value of $.01 each. Thus the actual entry to record issuance of 1 million additional shares would separate out par value as follows:

Cash	50,000,000	
Common Stock		10,000
Additional paid-in capital		49,990,000

In practice, the par values are usually set far below the full market price of the shares upon issuance, as is the case with McDonald's. In some cases, the minimum capital is called stated value rather than par value. Similarly, the language used to describe additional paid-in capital varies widely. For economic purposes, most of these distinctions are of little importance. However, you will encounter them in annual reports and must be aware of their meaning. The following illustrates the diversity of practice:

Company	Par Value Per Share	Name for Additional Paid-in Capital
AT&T	$1.00	Additional paid-in capital
Coca-Cola	$ .25	Capital surplus
McDonald's	$ .01	Additional paid-in capital
Motorola	$3.00	Additional paid-in capital
PepsiCo	$1.67	Capital in excess of par value

PREFERRED STOCK

There are basically two types of stock that companies can issue: common stock and preferred stock. Common stock, as the name implies, is the most basic and common type of stock. All corporations have it, and the shareholders who own it have the rights discussed above. **Preferred stock** offers owners different rights and preferential treatment. Stock represents a contract between the company and its owners and the terms of preferred stock can involve almost any arrangement the parties desire.

For example, preferred stock owners do not usually have voting rights, but they do have a preferred claim on assets. Therefore, at liquidation, preferred stockholders receive leftover company assets before common stockholders do. The most common preference terms grant preferred stockholders the right to receive dividend payments before common stockholders do.

Preferred stock is like common stock in that dividends are not a legal obligation until the board of directors declares them. With preferred shares, the amount of the dividend is generally specified and does not change over time. Consider McDonald's preferred. During the prior three years, there have been several different types of preferred outstanding, some of which is no longer outstanding. The currently outstanding preferred is 7.72% Cumulative Preferred Stock with a liquidation preference of $50,000 per share. The annual dividend on one share of this preferred is 7.72% times $50,000 or $3,860. The preferred stock usually appears in the top part of the stockholders' equity section of the balance sheet, as illustrated in the McDonald's 1996 annual report in Exhibit 11-1.

Cumulative Dividends

What happens when the board votes to skip paying a fixed preferred stock dividend one year? Just because a company can decide not to pay the dividend now does not mean that the company has completely avoided the obligation. Preferred stock dividends are often **cumulative,** which is a characteristic of preferred stock that requires that undeclared dividends accumulate and must be paid in the future before common dividends. This means that if the company does not pay a preferred dividend one year, its obligation to pay still remains and it must pay the omitted dividend before any common dividends are paid. For example, if McDonald's skipped its $3,860 preferred dividend per share one year, it must pay $7,720 for each preferred share the next year before common dividends can be paid. The holders of cumulative preferred stock would receive all accumulated unpaid dividends (called **dividend arrearages**) before the holders of common shares receive anything. Moreover, in the event of liquidation, cumulative unpaid preference dividends must be paid before common stockholders receive any cash.

To illustrate the operation of cumulative preferred stock, consider Exhibit 11-2. The stockholders' equity of Acumulado Corporation on December 31, 19X0 is shown in panel A, and the consequences of subsequent years of net income and dividends are shown in Panel B.

Acumulado's board of directors elects not to declare and pay preferred dividends in 19X1 and 19X2. This decision makes economic sense, given that Acumulado Corporation posted losses both years. You may be thinking that the company had more than enough in retained income to be able to pay the dividends despite the losses, but retained income is not the same as cash. The large retained income balance results from many prior years of profitable operations, but in those prior years the company has reinvested the cash generated by operations into productive business assets. When a firm encounters losses such as Acumulado experienced in 19X1 and 19X2, cash flow may be reduced, and there just might not be enough cash available to pay dividends.

Even though the company skipped making the $5,000,000 annual preferred dividend payments, its obligation to make those payments remained and accumulated. By the end of 19X2, the company had skipped a cumulative total of $10,000,000 of preferred dividends. When operating results improve in 19X3, the board declares and pays a partial dividend of $3,000,000. But the dividends in arrears grow by the undeclared unpaid $2,000,000 to a total of $12,000,000. In 19X4, Acumulado has a banner year and improves profitability and cash flow enough to pay a full dividend and more. Dividends to preferred shareholders of $17,000,000 cover not only the 19X4 dividend but the dividends in

Exhibit 11-2

Acumulado Corp Preferred Dividends
Panel A

Preferred stock, no par, cumulative, $5 annual dividend per share:	
Issued and outstanding, 1,000,000 shares	$ 50,000,000
Common stock, no par, 5,000,000 shares	100,000,000
Retained income	400,000,000
Total stockholders' equity	$550,000,000

Panel B

	Net Income	Preferred Dividends		Common Dividends Declared	Ending Balance, Retained Income
		Declared	*In Arrears*		
19X0					$400,000,000
19X1	$(4,000,000)	—	$ 5,000,000	—	396,000,000
19X2	(4,000,000)	—	10,000,000	—	392,000,000
19X3	21,000,000	$ 3,000,000	12,000,000	—	410,000,000
19X4	49,000,000	17,000,000	—	$ 2,000,000	440,000,000
19X5	32,000,000	5,000,000	—	17,000,000	450,000,000

arrears as well. With accumulated preferred dividends now completely paid, the firm may pay a dividend to the common shareholders for the first time in four years. Note that the ending balance in retained income in each year is equal to the beginning balance, plus net income (or minus a net loss) minus dividends declared.

Would you rather own cumulative or noncumulative preferred stock? In the preceding example, a holder of noncumulative preferred stock would not be entitled to receive more than $5 million in any single year. The cumulative feature must be explicitly included in the contract, it is not automatic. Thus, despite three years of omitted or partial dividends, the preferred dividend payment in 19X4 would have been only $5 million if the preferred stock was not cumulative. Consequently, most buyers of preferred shares insist on cumulative status, and in actual practice, such shares far outnumber the noncumulative type.

PREFERENCE IN LIQUIDATION

liquidating value A measure of the preference to receive assets in the event of corporate liquidation.

In addition to the cumulative dividend feature, preferred stock usually has a **liquidating value.** This value is the amount that preferred stock holders are supposed to receive in the event of the company liquidating. The exact liquidating value is stated on the stock certificate, but it is often the same as par value. The company would have to pay the full liquidating value to all preferred stock holders before it could distribute any assets to common stock holders. Also, any preferred dividends in arrears would have to be paid in full before common stock holders received any assets. Of course, all debt obligations have to be paid off before even preferred stock holders receive any assets.

Consider an illustration of the liquidation of assets when short- and long-term debt, preferred stock, and common stock are all present. Exhibit 11-3 shows how cash is distributed to different claimants. The priority of the claims generally decreases as you move down the chart. The first column presents the book values. The next seven columns show the distributions to each class of claimant under different circumstances.

As you can see, when there is not enough cash to go around, common stock holders are always the last to get paid and often wind up getting nothing. However, in those rare

Exhibit 11-3

Liquidation of Claims under Various Alternatives (in thousands)

	Account Balances	Assumed Total Cash Proceeds to Be Distributed						
		$ 1,500	$1,000	$500	$450	$350	$200	$100
Accounts payable	$ 100	$ 100	$100	$100	$100	$100	$100	$ 50*
Unsubordinated debentures	100	100	100	100	100	100	100	50*
Subordinated debentures	200	200	200	200	200	150		
Preferred stock ($100 par value and $120 liquidating value per share)	100	120	120	100	50			
Common stock and retained income	500	980	480					
Total liabilities and shareholders' equity	$1,000							
Total cash proceeds distributed		$1,500	$1,000	$500	$450	$350	$200	$100

*Ratio of 50:50 because each has a $100,000 claim.

instances when there is actually excess cash left over, common stock holders get that excess. In the event of liquidation, then, owning common stock is more of a gamble than is owning preferred stock. Keep in mind, though, that both types of stock holders are protected by limited liability. They do not have to add additional assets to the company in the event that the company cannot pay off its debts.

OTHER FEATURES OF PREFERRED STOCK

In addition to being cumulative and having liquidation value, preferred stock may have other features. As with our discussion of debt, each feature affects the attractiveness of the stock issue. If you add the cumulative feature to a 5% preferred, investors will pay more for it. Another way to express the same idea would be to say if you add the cumulative feature to a preferred share, you will reduce the size of the fixed dividend that investors will require to be willing to invest in the preferred stock. If given a choice between a cumulative and noncumulative preferred stock, investors will accept a lower interest rate on the safer, more desirable cumulative shares.

Each of the following features can also affect the attractiveness of the preferred. For example, a participating preferred stock ordinarily receives a fixed dividend but can receive higher dividends when the company has a very good year—one in which common stock holders receive large dividends. **Participating** means that holders of these shares participate in the growth of the company because they share in the growing amount of dividends. This might be an especially attractive feature for a company with strong growth opportunities to use to make its preferred stock more attractive and thereby lower the required dividend.

A **callable** preferred stock gives the issuing company the right to purchase the stock back from the owner upon payment of the **call price, or redemption price.** This call price is typically set 5% to 10% above the par value or issuance price of the stock, to compensate investors for the fact that the stock can be automatically bought back at any time.

A **convertible** preferred stock gives the owner the option to exchange the preferred share for shares of common stock. Because the ability to convert the stock can be quite valuable in future years when common stock prices have grown sharply, convertible securities typically carry a lower dividend rate. For example, a regular preferred offering an 8% dividend might sell for the same price as a 7% convertible preferred.

It is not possible to describe every imaginable kind of preferred stock because each investor and issuer has the opportunity to develop a unique security that exactly meets their needs, and they can adapt that security to the particular market conditions they face

participating A characteristic of preferred stock that provides increasing dividends when common dividends increase.

callable A characteristic of bonds or preferred stock that gives the issuer the right to redeem the security at a fixed price.

redemption price (call price) The price at which an issuer can buy back a callable preferred stock or bond, which is typically 5% to 10% above the par value.

convertible A characteristic of bonds or preferred stock that gives the holder the right to exchange the security for common stock.

at the time. In fact, the investment banking community works hard to develop new types of preferred stock that exactly fit the particular needs of certain investors.

COMPARING BONDS AND PREFERRED STOCK

series   Different groups of preferred shares issued at different times with different features.

Preferred stocks are actually quite similar to bonds. Like a bond, preferred stock is a contract between an investor and an issuer that spells out each party's rights and responsibilities. Also, just as some companies have many different bonds outstanding at any particular time, some companies issue a variety of preferred stock. Often each issue is called a **series** and has characteristics distinct from those of other preferred stock issued by the company. For example, in addition to its series E preferred issued in 1992 and discussed above, McDonald's issued series B and C preferreds in 1989 and 1991, respectively. These preferred shares gave owners the right to convert them to shares of common and these rights have now been fully exercised.

Preferred stocks and bonds are also similar in the sense that each pays a specific return to the investor. However, they differ greatly in those returns. The specific return to bondholders is called interest and appears on the earnings statement as an expense. In contrast, the specific return to preferred shareholders is a dividend and represents a distribution of profits, which reduces the retained income account directly.

Preferred stock and bonds also differ in that bonds have specific maturity dates, at which time they must be repaid, but preferred stock typically has an unlimited life. From the investor's perspective, preferred stock is riskier than bonds because it never matures and the company is not required to declare dividends.

CASH DIVIDENDS

Dividends are a means of proportionally distributing income among shareholders in a company. Usually these distributions are in the form of cash—it is infrequent for assets other than cash to be distributed. In the United States, dividends tend to be paid in equal amounts each quarter, although the board may declare, change, or eliminate a dividend at any time. Some firms do tend to pay a special, larger dividend once a year.

declaration date   The date the board of directors declares a dividend.

date of record   The date when ownership is fixed for determining the right to receive a dividend.

payment date   The date dividends are paid.

No dividend is automatically paid. The company's board of directors votes to approve each dividend. The date on which the board formally announces that it will pay a dividend is called the **declaration date.** The board specifies a **date of record,** a future date that determines which stockholders will receive the dividend. A person who holds the stock on the declaration date but sells before the date of record will not receive the dividend. The dividend goes to the person who owns the stock on the date of record. The actual **payment date** is the day the checks are mailed and follows the date of record by a few days or weeks.

No journal entry is required on the date of record, although the company's stock transfer agent must identify all parties to whom dividends will be paid as of that date. If a balance sheet is prepared between declaration and payment, the dividend payable will appear as a liability.

DATE OF DECLARATION

Sept. 26	Retained income	20,000	
	Dividends payable		20,000
	To record the declaration of dividends to be		
	paid on November 15 to shareholders of record		
	as of October 25.		

DATE OF PAYMENT

Nov. 15	Dividends payable	20,000	
	Cash.		20,000
	To pay dividends declared on September 26 to		
	shareholders of record as of October 25.		

The amount of cash dividends declared by a board of directors depends on many factors, primarily market expectations, the current and predicted earnings, and the corporation's current cash position and financial plans regarding spending on plant assets and repayments of debts. Remember that payment of cash dividends requires cash. Thus the single biggest factor affecting the size of dividends is the availability of cash that is not otherwise committed. It is also true that investors expect companies that have historically paid regular dividends to continue to do so. Ford and General Motors would fall in this category. Investors also expect that companies that have not paid dividends because cash was better used to finance expansion will continue to identify growth opportunities requiring additional investment. Microsoft is an example of a company that does not pay cash dividends.

The least important factor in the dividend decision is the amount of retained income. Retained income balances matter when there are legal restrictions on dividend payments in bond covenants, in cases where the company is on the brink of bankruptcy, or where the company has just been incorporated.

If a company has maintained a series of uninterrupted dividends over a span of years, it will make an effort to continue such payments even in the face of net losses. In fact, companies occasionally borrow money for the sole purpose of maintaining dividend payments. Ultimately *changes* in dividend patterns are watched very carefully by investors. Elimination and initiation of payments are big events that cause investors to pause and consider carefully what the company's decision means about the future.

ADDITIONAL STOCK ISSUANCE

After the company is formed, companies occasionally issue additional shares to investors, to executives or to current shareholders. There are several motivations and several procedures for additional stock issues. When a firm simply wishes to raise additional equity capital, the process is much like the original stock issue described above. Cash is provided by an investor and additional new shares are issued in exchange. Often shares are made available to employees under stock option contracts to encourage the employee to work harder in order to raise the market price. Sometimes shares are issued to existing shareholders to signal something about the firm, to change the market price, to alter the dividend payment or for other reasons as described subsequently.

STOCK OPTIONS

Stock options are rights granted to executives to purchase a specific number of shares of a corporation's capital stock at a specific price for a specific time period. Options are generally given to corporate officers as a form of incentive compensation. For example, suppose Company A granted its top executives options to purchase 60,000 shares of $1 par value common stock at $15 per share, the market price today (date of grant). The options can be exercised over a five-year span, beginning three years from the date of grant. Such options are valuable because the executives can gain the benefits of stock price increases without bearing the risks of price declines. However, measurement of the value of options at the time of grant is difficult because executive options may not be sold to others. As a result, there are no market prices to be used as guides. Currently accepted accounting attributes zero value to most options as long as the exercise price is the same as the market price at the date of the grant. Thus the accounting approach to recording the issuance of stock options is to make no entry at the time of grant. However, footnotes in the financial statements must reveal the number and type of options outstanding and an assessment of their value.

Suppose all options are exercised three years after the date of grant. The journal entry would be:

stock options Special rights usually granted to executives to purchase a corporation's capital stock.

```
Cash . . . . . . . . . . . . . . . . . . . . . . . . . . . . . . . .    900,000
        Common stock . . . . . . . . . . . . . . . . . . . . .                60,000
        Additional paid-in capital  . . . . . . . . . . . . .                840,000
To record issue of 60,000 shares upon exercise
of options to acquire them @ $15 per share.
```

Note that the entry is indistinguishable from the issuance of new shares at current market price to new investors. Furthermore, nothing has been said about the market price of the shares at issuance. The value of the shares being issued could be several times the $15 exercise price. We do know that the market price is at least $15, otherwise executives would let their options lapse. For example, here the options will become worthless if the price of the common stock is no higher than $15 per share during the time they may be exercised. In such a case, no journal entry is made.

The FASB has considered this reporting issue and has chosen to require extensive disclosures of options, but not to require expense recognition. The argument in favor of expense recognition is that when the company grants an executive a stock option, it is giving something of value in exchange for services rendered. At any other time that the company provides cash or other assets to the executive in exchange for services rendered, the transaction is recorded as an expense. Options should be an expense also.

While the accounting logic for this point of view is compelling, there are a number of implementation issues. Many of these implementation issues caught the attention of entrepreneurs who currently receive significant numbers of stock options and feared that markets would react unfavorably to reported option expenses. This led to significant pressure on congress and the SEC regarding the best accounting for options. Footnote disclosure of option grants without financial statement recognition was the outcome. This is an area of accounting where additional developments should be anticipated.

STOCK SPLITS AND STOCK DIVIDENDS

Objective 4
Identify the economic characteristics of stock splits and dividends.

The stock issuances discussed so far all involve the exchange of cash from an investor or executive for new shares of the company's stock. Several procedures exist for the company to issue additional shares of stock to its investors without receiving any money. For example, the company could simply issue some additional shares to current investors. In practice, such distributions of new shares take a variety of forms. We will examine two of these forms: the stock split and the stock dividend.

ACCOUNTING FOR STOCK SPLITS

stock split Issuance of additional shares to existing stockholders for no payments by the stockholders.

A **stock split** refers to the issuance of additional shares to existing shareholders without any additional cash payment to the firm. Issuance of one additional share for each share currently owned is called a "two-for-one" split. For example, suppose the Allstar Equipment Company has 100,000 shares outstanding with a market value of $150 per share and par value of $10 per share. The total market value of the stock is thus $15,000,000. If Allstar Equipment gives each shareholder an additional share for each share owned, the total number of shares would increase to 200,000. If nothing else about the company changes (assets, liabilities, and equity all stay the same), the total value of the outstanding stock should still be $15,000,000. With 200,000 shares outstanding, though, the market value per share should drop to $75. Shareholders are as well off as they were before because they have paid no additional money and they still have the same proportional ownership interest in the company.

So why bother? Good question, and one for which there is no perfect answer. Many companies do split their stock. And a common result is that stock price falls 50%. So one good explanation for issuing a split is that it causes the stock price to fall on a per share basis. If investors like to invest $1,000 to $20,000 at a time, and stocks trade in units of 100 shares, you can see that investors would be attracted to stocks trading in a range between $10 and

$200 per share. Most stocks do trade in that range and companies that split are often at the high end of that range. But it is not a requirement. Berkshire Hathaway is an example of a company whose common stock trades at over $50,000 per share at this writing.

Would the accountant need to do anything to acknowledge Allstar's stock issuance? Yes. There are now twice as many shares outstanding. If the company retains a par value of $10 per share, $1,000,000 would need to be added to common stock. Typically this is transferred from additional paid-in capital. This does not change total owner's equity, it merely rearranges it. An alternative is for the $1,000,000 to be transferred from retained income. As explained below, when this choice is made it is referred to as a stock split "accounted for as a stock dividend."

Sometimes the company decides to adjust par value by exchanging existing shares for twice as many *new* shares. Assume that Allstar does not just issue an additional share to each shareholder. Suppose that 100,000 $10 par value shares of common are returned to Allstar in exchange for 200,000 $5 par value shares of common. Nothing changes in the stockholders' equity section except the description of shares authorized, issued, and outstanding. As shown below, the aggregate par value is unchanged, no cash has changed hands, each owner has the same proportionate interest as before, and each has the same relative voting power:

	Before 2-for-1 Split	Changes	After 2-for-1 Split
Common stock, 100,000 shares @ $10 par	$ 1,000,000	−100,000 shares @ $10 par + 200,000 shares @ $5 par	$ 1,000,000
Additional paid-in capital	4,000,000		4,000,000
Total paid-in capital	$ 5,000,000		$ 5,000,000
Retained income	6,000,000		6,000,000
Stockholders' equity	$11,000,000		$11,000,000
Overall market value of stock @ assumed $150 per share	$15,000,000	@ assumed $75 per share	$15,000,000

The three alternative methods are summarized as follows:

Option 1.	Exchange 200,000 new $5.00 par value shares for the old ones	No Entry		
Option 2.	Issue 100,000 new $10.00 par value shares	Additional Paid-in Capital Common Stock	100,000	100,000
Option 3.	Issue 100,000 new $10.00 par value shares and "account for it as a stock dividend"	Retained Earnings Common Stock	100,000	100,000

ACCOUNTING FOR STOCK DIVIDENDS

Stock dividends are also issuances of additional shares to existing shareholders without additional cash payment, but the number of new shares issued is usually smaller than it is in a split, and there is no change in par value. For example, a 10% stock dividend involves issuance of one new share for every 10 currently owned.

LARGE-PERCENTAGE STOCK DIVIDENDS

With stock dividends, new shares are issued and the common stock account is increased to recognize this increase. The amount of the increase depends on the size of the "dividend." The U.S. accounting authorities require that large-percentage stock dividends (typically those 20% or higher) are accounted for at par or stated value. That means that an

stock dividends
Distribution to stockholders of additional shares of any class of the distributing company's stock, without any payment to the company by the stockholders.

Exhibit 11-4

Possible Allstar Stock Dividends; Total Market Value $15,000,000

Panel A   100% Stock Dividend

	Before 100% Stock Dividend	Changes	After 100% Stock Dividend
Common stock, 100,000 shares @ $10 par	$ 1,000,000	+ (100,000 shares @ $10 par = $1,000,000)	$ 2,000,000
Additional paid-in capital	4,000,000		4,000,000
Total paid-in capital	$ 5,000,000		$ 6,000,000
		−$1,000,000 par	
Retained income	6,000,000	value of "dividend"	5,000,000
Stockholders' equity	$11,000,000		$11,000,000

Panel B   Various Stock Dividends

Stock Dividend	Shares Original	New	Total	Price per Share
None	100,000		100,000	$150.00
20%	100,000	20,000	120,000	125.00
40%	100,000	40,000	140,000	107.14
60%	100,000	60,000	160,000	93.75
80%	100,000	80,000	180,000	83.33
100%	100,000	100,000	200,000	75.00

accounting entry is made to transfer the par or stated value of the new shares from the retained earnings account to the common stock account.

As in the case of stock splits, the market value of the outstanding shares tends to adjust completely when a stock dividend is issued. What else happens economically? When firms issue large-percentage stock dividends or splits, they usually lower the per-share dividend proportionately. Consider the Allstar Equipment Company and the effect of possible stock dividends on share price. Recall that the market value of the firm will be unchanged by simply changing the number of shares.

If the Allstar Equipment Company chose to double the outstanding number of shares by issuing a stock dividend, the total amount of stockholders' equity would still be unaffected. However, its composition would change as shown in Panel A of Exhibit 11-4. Panel B illustrates how the price per share would adjust to various stock dividends.

In substance, there is absolutely no difference between the 100% stock dividend and the two-for-one stock split. In form, the shareholder receiving a dividend has $10 par shares rather than $5 par shares. The stock dividend is accounted for as in Option 3 for stock splits—retained income is transferred to the par value account. Infrequently a company will transfer amounts from additional paid-in capital, as in Option 2 for stock splits. Regulations are not ironclad on this issue.

The company does have an economic decision to make. What happens to the cash dividend when a stock dividend or stock split is issued? One possibility is that the dividend is adjusted proportionately. For a 100% stock dividend or a two-for-one stock split, this would mean that the cash dividend per share would be cut in half and total cash dividends would remain unchanged. It is at least as common for the company to increase the total cash dividend being paid. Investors watch this issue carefully to assess the company's belief about future cash flow and future investment opportunity.

Objective 5
Account for stock splits and both large-percentage and small-percentage stock dividends.

SMALL-PERCENTAGE STOCK DIVIDENDS

When a stock dividend of less than 20% is issued, accountants require that the dividend be accounted for at market value, not at par value. This rule is not easy to defend. It is

Exhibit 11-5

2% Stock Dividend

	Before 2% Stock Dividend	Changes	After 2% Stock Dividend
Common stock, 100,000 shares @ $10 par	$ 1,000,000	+ (2,000 shares @ $10 par) = + 20,000	$ 1,020,000
Additional paid-in capital	4,000,000	+ [2,000 shares @ ($150 − $10)] = + 280,000	4,280,000
Retained income	6,000,000	−(2,000 @ $150) = −300,000	5,700,000
Stockholders' equity	$11,000,000		$11,000,000
Overall market value of stock @ assumed $150 per share	$15,000,000	@ assumed $147.06 per share*	$15,000,000
Total shares outstanding	100,000		102,000
Individual shareholder:			
Assumed ownership of shares	1,000		1,020
Percentage ownership interest	1%		Still 1%

*Many simultaneous events affect the level of stock prices, including expectations regarding the general economy, the industry, and the specific company. Thus the market price of the stock may move in either direction when the stock dividend is declared. Theory and complicated case studies indicate that a small-percentage stock dividend should have zero effect on the total market value of the firm. Accordingly, the new market price per share should be $15,000,000 ÷ 102,000 shares = $147.06.

partly the result of tradition and partly because small-percentage stock dividends are most likely to accompany increases in the total dividend payments or other changes in the company's financial policies. It is argued that the decision to increase total dividends communicates management's conviction that future cash flows will rise to support these increased distributions, and this is a positive statement about the firm's prospects.

Reconsider our example of Allstar Equipment Company (before the split). Suppose the market value of common shares is $150 at the time of issuance of a 2% stock dividend. The effect on the stockholders' equity section of the balance sheet is shown in Exhibit 11-5.

As before, the individual shareholder receives no assets from the corporation, and the corporation receives no cash from the shareholder. Also, because the overall number of shares and the number of shares held by each investor have both increased, the shareholders' fractional interest is unchanged. If the shareholders sell the dividend shares, their proportionate ownership interest in the company will decrease. The major possible economic effect of a stock dividend is to signal increased cash dividends. Suppose the board of the company in our example consistently voted to pay cash dividends of $1 per share. Often this cash dividend level per share is maintained after a small stock dividend. The recipient of the stock dividend can now expect a future annual cash dividend of $1 × 1,020 = $1,020 rather than $1 × 1,000 = $1,000. In this case, when the dividend rate per share is maintained, announcing a stock dividend of 2% has the same economic effect as announcing an increase of 2% in the cash dividend.

For small-percentage (under 20%) stock dividends, the company records the transaction by transferring the market value of the additional shares from retained income to common stock and additional paid-in capital. The entry is often referred to as being a "capitalization of retained income." It is basically a signal to the shareholders that $300,000 of retained income is being invested for the long term in productive assets such as plant, property, and equipment. In our example, the required journal entry would be:

```
Retained income  . . . . . . . . . . . . . . . . . . . . . . . . . . . . . .    300,000
    Common stock  . . . . . . . . . . . . . . . . . . . . . . . . .                    20,000
    Additional paid-in capital  . . . . . . . . . . . . . . . . . .                    280,000
To record a 2% common stock dividend, resulting in the
issuance of 2,000 shares. Retained income is reduced at the
rate of the market value of $150 per share at date of issuance.
```

U.S. practice regarding the use of market values in accounting for small-percentage stock dividends is arbitrary and is not consistently adopted worldwide. For example, in Japan these journal entries are recorded at par value. The Japanese practice is one most accountants would support. The U.S. practice compounds the false notion that the recipients are getting a dividend akin to a cash dividend.

WHY USE STOCK SPLITS AND DIVIDENDS?

Experts debate the importance of splits and stock dividends even as companies continue to use them. One observation is that most U.S. common stock sells at under $100 per share. In 1994, Wal-Mart stock sold for approximately $25 per share. During the prior 13 years, the stock split two-for-one on six occasions. An investor who purchased one share in 1981 would have 64 shares in 1994. Without any splits, one original Wal-Mart share would have been worth $1,600 in 1994. After these splits, a "round-lot" of 100 shares costs $100 \times \$25 = \$2,500$, a reasonable investment size. Without the splits, a round-lot would cost $\$1,600 \times 100 = \$160,000$. Thus splits allow the company to maintain the stock price in a trading range accessible to small investors and company employees. If one share cost $1,600, Wal-Mart might not have as many shareholders.

Often a stock split or stock dividend accompanies other announcements, such as new corporate investment strategies or changes in cash dividend levels. Suppose the firm has traditionally paid a special cash dividend at year-end but plans to substantially expand production, which will absorb available cash and make the payment of this special dividend difficult. The firm might combine the announcement of the planned expansion with an announcement of a small stock dividend. The small-percentage stock dividend will not draw on cash immediately but will provide stockholders with an increase in future cash dividends in proportion to the percentage of new shares issued.

RELATION OF DIVIDENDS AND SPLITS

Companies typically use large-percentage stock dividends to accomplish exactly the same purpose as that achieved with a stock split. That is, the companies want to reduce the market price of their shares and simultaneously they want to signal an increase in total dividend payments to shareholders. Stock splits frequently occur in the form of a stock "dividend" to save clerical costs. After all, swapping old $10-par certificates for new $5-par certificates is more expensive than merely printing and mailing additional $10-par certificates.

IBM described its 1997 two-for-one split in the following footnote to the 1996 annual report:

> On January 28, 1997, the IBM Board of Directors declared a two-for-one common stock split, subject to the approval of stockholders of an increase in the number of common shares authorized from 750 million to 1,875 million. The record date for the split is currently expected to be on or after May 9, 1997, with distribution of the split shares to follow on or after May 27, 1997.

Yes, the 1997 announcement was included in the 1996 annual report. It is a "subsequent" event. This is a significant item that arose before the financial statements were published and should be disclosed to investors. The increase in authorized shares was subsequently approved and the split occurred as planned.

FRACTIONAL SHARES

Corporations ordinarily issue shares in whole units. When shareholders are entitled to stock dividends in amounts equal to fractional units, corporations issue additional shares for whole units plus cash equal to the market value of the fractional amount.

For example, suppose a corporation issues a 3% stock dividend. A shareholder has 160 shares. The market value per share on the date of issuance is $40. Par value is $2. The shareholder would be entitled to $0.03 \times 160 = 4.8$ shares. The company would issue 4 shares plus $0.8(\$40) = \$32$ cash. The journal entry is:

Retained income (4.8 × $40)	192	
.....Common stock, at par (4 × $2)		8
.....Additional paid-in capital (4 × $38)		152
.....Cash (0.8 × $40)		32
To issue a stock dividend of 3% to a holder of 160 shares.		

THE INVESTOR'S ACCOUNTING FOR DIVIDENDS AND SPLITS

So far, we have focused on how the corporation deals with stock splits and dividends. What about the stockholder? Consider the investor's recording of the transactions described so far. Suppose Investor J bought 1,000 shares of the original issue of Allstar Equipment Company stock for $50 per share:

Investment in Allstar common stock	50,000	
Cash		50,000
To record investment in 1,000 shares of an original issue of Allstar Equipment Company common stock at $50 per share. The par value is $10 per share.		

Investor J holds the shares indefinitely. However, if Investor J sold the shares to Investor K at a subsequent price other than $50, a gain or loss would be recorded by J, and K would carry the shares at the amount paid to J. Meanwhile the stockholders' equity of Allstar Equipment Company would be completely unaffected by this sale by one investor to another. The company's underlying shareholder records would simply be changed to delete J and add K as a shareholder.

The following examples show how Investor J would record the stock split, cash dividends, and stock dividends, where each is treated as an independent event, not as sequential events. Note that several events that produced journal entries for Allstar do not provide entries for Investor J:

a. Stock split at 2-for-1:	No journal entry, but a memorandum would be made in the investment account to show that 2,000 shares are now held at a cost of $25 each instead of 1,000 shares at a cost of $50 each.		
b. Cash dividends of $2 per share:	Cash	2,000	
	Dividend income		2,000
	To record cash dividends on Allstar Equipment Company stock.		
or:	Alternatively, the following two entries might be used:		
Date of declaration:	Dividends receivable	2,000	
	Dividend income		2,000
	To record dividends declared by Allstar Equipment Company.		
Date of receipt:	Cash	2,000	
	Dividends receivable		2,000
	To record the receipt of cash dividends.		

c. Stock dividends of 2%:	No journal entry, but a memorandum would be made in the investment account to show that [assuming the stock split in (a) had not occurred] 1,020 shares are now owned at an average cost of $50,000 ÷ 1,020, or $49.02 per share.
d. Stock split in form of a 100% dividend:	No journal entry, but a memorandum would be made in the investment account to show that [assuming the stock splits and stock dividends in (a) and (c) had not occurred] 2,000 shares are now owned at an average cost of $25 instead of 1,000 shares @ $50. Note that this memorandum has the same effect as the memorandum in a above.

REPURCHASE OF SHARES

Objective 6
Interpret treasury stock transactions.

So far we have seen how companies sell shares and how they will sometimes issue additional shares to current shareholders. You should not think, though, that stocks always flow *out* of a company. Sometimes the company will bring shares back *in* by repurchasing them. Companies repurchase their own shares for two main purposes: (1) to permanently reduce shareholder claims, called retiring stock, and (2) to temporarily hold shares for later use, most often to be granted as part of employee bonus or stock purchase plans. Temporarily held shares are called *treasury stock* or *treasury shares*.

By repurchasing shares, for whatever reason, a company liquidates some shareholders' claims, and the following journal entry results:

```
Stockholders' equity . . . . . . . . . . . . . . . . .   xxx
        Cash . . . . . . . . . . . . . . . . . . . . . . . .        xxx
Repurchase of outstanding shares.
```

The purpose of the repurchase determines which stockholders' equity accounts are affected.

To illustrate the accounting behind repurchasing shares we will use the Brecht Company, whose stock has a market value of $15 per share:

Common stock, 1,000,000 shares at $1 par	$ 1,000,000
Additional paid-in capital	4,000,000
Total paid-in capital	$ 5,000,000
Retained income	6,000,000
Stockholders' equity	$11,000,000
Overall market value of stock @ assumed $15 per share	$15,000,000
Book value per share = $11,000,000 ÷ 1,000,000 = $11.	

Book value is the term we have frequently used to refer to the value at which an asset or liability is reported in the financial statements. Here book value is expressed in per share terms referring to the historical investment by the shareholders in the company. The total stockholders' equity of $11,000,000 combines the original purchase price of shares in the past (par value plus additional paid-in capital) with the periodic earnings of the firm that have remained in the business (retained income). Dividing it by the number of shares gives the average per share, in this case $11,000,000 ÷ 1,000,000 = $11. By dividing the total paid-in capital by number of shares (($1,000,000 + $4,000,000)/1,000,000 = $5) we can determine that the original shares were issued for $5 per share.

Suppose the board of directors has decided that the $15 market value of its shares is "too low." Even though the market value exceeds the book value by $4 per share ($15 − $11), the board may think the market is too pessimistic regarding the company's shares. In time, investors are expected to understand the true value of the company and the market value will rise to reflect that value. The board might believe that the best use of corporate cash would be to purchase a portion of the outstanding shares. In this way, the remaining dedicated shareholders would have the sole benefit of the predicted eventual increase in market value per share. Other motives include the desire to change the proportion of debt and equity in use to finance the firm. Buying back shares increases the relative importance of debt. Buybacks also allow the company to return cash to shareholders without creating expectations of permanent increases in dividends.

It has become very common for a firm to buy back its own stock. IBM disclosed the following in its 1996 annual report:

> *In 1996 and 1995, the Board of Directors authorized the company to purchase up to $13.5 billion of IBM common stock. During 1996 and 1995, the company repurchased 49,465,200 common shares at a cost of $5,810 million and 50,906,300 common shares at a cost of $4,864 million, respectively.*

Given that IBM had 509,070,542 shares outstanding at year end, 1996, you can see that the firm repurchased about 10% of its shares each year. Note also that the $5 billion per year being used to repurchase shares is far in excess of the $686 million paid out in dividends to shareholders each year. The buyback is similar to a dividend in that both transfer money from the firm to its shareholders and both reduce stockholder's equity. Unlike the dividend, the buyback also reduces the number of shares outstanding and will therefore tend to increase the earnings per share being reported. Consider IBM. Reported earnings per share was $10.24 in 1996. If 10% more shares had been outstanding during the year, earnings per share would have been $9.31.

A stock buyback has two additional benefits when compared to a dividend payment. The investor that receives a dividend pays income tax on the full amount at about a 35% tax rate. The investor that sells shares of stock pays tax only on the gain, the sales price less the cost of the stock, and that gain is taxed at a lower tax rate, often 20%. Moreover, the buyback is flexible. The company can increase or decrease the number of shares acquired and the cash used as circumstances dictate. In contrast, when a company increases its cash dividend payment, there is an expectation by investors that the increase will be permanent.

RETIREMENT OF SHARES

Once shares have been repurchased, they may be retired or held for reissue. Suppose the Board of Brecht Company purchases and retires 5% of its outstanding shares at $15 for a total of 50,000 × $15, or $750,000 cash. The total stockholders' equity is reduced because the $750,000 is charged against the common stock, additional paid-in capital, and retained income accounts. The stock certificates are canceled, and the shares are no longer considered either outstanding or issued as shown in Exhibit 11-6.

The journal entry reverses the original average paid-in capital per share and charges the additional amount to retained income:

Common stock	50,000	
Additional paid-in capital	200,000	
Retained income	500,000	
Cash		750,000

To record retirement of 50,000 shares of stock for $15 cash per share. The original paid-in capital was $5 per share ($1 par value + $4 additional paid-in capital), so the additional $10 per share is debited to Retained Income.

dilution Reduction in stockholders' equity per share or earnings per share that arises from some changes among shareholders' proportional interests.

Note how the book value per share of the outstanding shares has declined from $11.00 to $10.79. The phenomenon is called dilution of the common shareholders' equity. **Dilution** is usually defined as a reduction in shareholders' equity per share or earnings per share that arises from some changes among shareholders' proportionate interests. As

Exhibit 11-6

Stock Repurchase and Retirement

	Before Repurchase of 5% of Outstanding Shares	Changes Because of Retirement	After Repurchase of 5% of Outstanding Shares
Common stock, 1,000,000 shares @ $1 par	$ 1,000,000	$\left\{\begin{array}{l}-(50,000 \text{ shares @ \$1 par}) \\ =-\$50,000\end{array}\right.$	$ 950,000
Additional paid-in capital	4,000,000	$\left\{\begin{array}{l}-(50,000 \text{ shares @ \$4}) \\ =-\$200,000\end{array}\right.$	3,800,000
Total paid-in capital	$ 5,000,000		$ 4,750,000
Retained income	6,000,000	$\left\{\begin{array}{l}-(50,000 \text{ @ \$10*}) \\ =-\$500,000\end{array}\right.$	5,500,000
Stockholders' equity	$11,000,000		$10,250,000
Book value per common share:			
$11,000,000 ÷ 1,000,000	$ 11.00		
$10,250,000 ÷ 950,000			$ 10.79

*$15 − the $5 (or $1 + $4) originally paid in.

a rule, boards of directors avoid dilution. However, boards sometimes favor deliberate dilution if expected future profits will more than compensate for a temporary undesirable reduction in book value per share.

When IBM repurchased shares in 1995 and 1996, they were retired. The notes disclosed:

> *The repurchased shares were retired and restored to the status of authorized but unissued shares.*

TREASURY STOCK

Suppose the Brecht Company's Board of Directors decides that the 50,000 repurchased shares are classified as treasury stock that will be held only temporarily and then resold. Perhaps the shares are needed for an employee stock purchase plan or for executive stock options. The repurchase decreases stockholders' equity and it is not considered an asset. Why is treasury stock not an asset while it is being held by the company? Because it generates no revenues. Cash dividends are not paid on shares held in the treasury because treasury stock is not considered outstanding:

Shares issued	1,000,000
Less: Treasury stock	50,000
Total shares outstanding	950,000

If treasury stock is not an asset, then what is it? The Treasury Stock account is a contra account to Owners' Equity just as Accumulated Depreciation is a contra account to related asset accounts. As with the retirement of shares, the purchase of treasury stock decreases stockholders' equity by $750,000. Unlike the accounting for retirements, though, common stock at par value, additional paid-in capital, and retained income remain untouched by treasury stock purchases. A separate treasury stock account is a deduction from total stockholders' equity on the balance sheet. Brecht's stockholders' equity section would be affected as shown in Exhibit 11-7.

Remember that treasury stock is not an asset. A company's holding of shares in another company is an asset; its holding of its own shares is a negative element of stockholders' equity.

Exhibit 11-7

Treasury Stock Purchase

	Before Repurchase of 5% of Outstanding Shares	Changes Because of Treasury Stock	After Repurchase of 5% of Outstanding Shares
Common stock, 1,000,000 shares @ $1 par	$ 1,000,000		$ 1,000,000
Additional paid-in capital	4,000,000		4,000,000
Total paid-in capital	$ 5,000,000		$ 5,000,000
Retained income	6,000,000		6,000,000
Total	$11,000,000		$11,000,000
Deduct:			
Cost of treasury stock	—	−$750,000	750,000
Stockholders' equity	$11,000,000		$10,250,000

Why Buy Back Your Own Shares?

During the two years 1995 and 1996, total net income for The Coca-Cola Company was $6.5 billion. What did Coca-Cola do with this $6.5 billion in assets generated? It isn't surprising that some of it was distributed to shareholders in the form of cash dividends. Total cash dividends were $2.4 billion, resulting in a dividend payout ratio (cash dividends/net income) of 37%. What may be a bit surprising is that during this same period, Coca-Cola used $3.3 billion to buy back its own stock.

We often think that cash dividends are the primary method corporations employ to distribute cash to shareholders, but frequently, as in the case of Coca-Cola, cash used in stock purchases exceeds the amount paid in cash dividends. One reason firms give is that idle resources within the company could be more efficiently used by individual shareholders. If the excess cash were paid in dividends, all investors would receive cash proportional to their ownership. Some might get more cash than they want or need and would simply turn around and reinvest it. All shareholders would have increased income taxes to pay. In contrast, a share buyback allows shareholders who want cash to sell their shares and raise the cash. These same shareholders are taxed only

on their gain, the excess of the price received over the cost incurred historically to acquire the shares.

Another big advantage to the company in returning cash to investors through a buyback is that the size and timing of the buyback are both very flexible. In contrast, if the dividend is increased, it leads to an expectation of maintained high future dividends and it locks the company into the regular quarterly payment pattern.

Firms also use stock purchases to demonstrate confidence in their own prospects. Managers think that investors are more likely to believe company claims of rosy prospects if the investors see the company "putting its money where its mouth is" by buying its own shares. This tactic was employed extensively in the wake of the market crash of October 1987. At the time, in a bid to prop up falling share prices, over 600 firms announced plans to repurchase their own shares. When share prices recovered more quickly than expected, many firms decided not to complete their buyback program. As IBM noted in its 1996 annual report, "The company plans to purchase shares on the open market from time to time, depending on market conditions."

Sources: 1996 Annual Reports of The Coca-Cola Company and IBM.

DISPOSITION OF TREASURY STOCK

Treasury shares are usually resold at a later date, perhaps through an employee stock purchase plan. The sales price usually differs from the acquisition cost. Suppose the sales price is $18. The journal entry would be:

```
Cash ..........................................     900,000
    Treasury stock ..............................              750,000
    Additional paid-in capital  ...................              150,000
To record sale of treasury stock, 50,000 shares
@ $18. Cost was $15 per share.
```

Suppose the price is $13:

```
Cash .........................................     650,000
Additional paid-in capital ...........................     100,000
    Treasury stock ............................              750,000
To record sale of treasury stock, 50,000 shares
@ $13. Cost was $15 per share.
```

If the treasury shares are resold below their cost, accountants tend to debit (decrease) Additional Paid-in Capital for the difference, $2 per share in this case. Additional Paid-in Capital is sometimes divided into several separate accounts that identify different sources of capital. For example:

- Additional paid-in capital-preferred stock
- Additional paid-in capital-common stock
- Additional paid-in capital-treasury stock transactions

If such detailed accounts are used, the Additional Paid-in Capital-Treasury Stock Transactions (and no other paid-in capital account) should be debited for the excess of the cost over the resale price of treasury shares or credited if resale price exceeds historical cost. If there is no balance in such a paid-in capital account, or if the balance is not large enough to cover the full debit amount, the additional reduction to Owners' Equity should be made as a debit to Retained Income.

Suppose 25,000 of the treasury shares bought by Brecht are later sold for $17 and still later the other 25,000 shares are sold for $12. The company had no previous sales of treasury stock. The journal entries are:

Sale at $17 per share:

```
Cash .........................................     425,000
    Treasury stock .............................              375,000
    Additional paid-in capital-treasury
        stock transactions ..........................               50,000
To record sale of treasury stock, 25,000 shares @ $17.
Cost was $15 per share.
```

Sale at $12 per share:

```
Cash .........................................     300,000
Additional paid-in capital-treasury
    stock transactions .............................      50,000
Retained income .................................      25,000
    Treasury stock .............................              375,000
To record sale of treasury stock, 25,000 shares @ $12.
Cost was $15 per share.
```

The specific accounting practices for transactions in the company's own stock may vary from company to company, but one rule remains constant. Any differences between the acquisition costs and the resale proceeds of treasury stock must never be reported as losses, expenses, revenues, or gains in the income statement. Why? A corporation's own capital stock is part of its capital structure. It is not an asset of the corporation. Nor is stock intended to be treated like merchandise for sale to customers at a profit. Therefore changes in a corporation's capitalization should produce no gain or loss but should merely require direct adjustments to the owners' equity.

There is essentially no difference between unissued shares and treasury shares. In our example, Brecht Company could accomplish the same objective by (1) acquiring 50,000 shares, retiring them, and issuing 50,000 new shares, or (2) acquiring 50,000 shares and reselling them.

EFFECTS OF REPURCHASES ON EARNINGS PER SHARE

When shares are repurchased and retired or put in treasury, the number of shares outstanding is reduced. This reduction tends to increase earnings per share. For example, suppose that Brecht were generating net income of $950,000 each year. Assume further that the use of $750,000 to repurchase shares would not reduce future net income. Under these circumstances, earnings per share would rise as a result of repurchasing shares:

EPS = net income ÷ average number of shares outstanding			
Before repurchase $950,000	÷	1,000,000 shares	= $ .95
After repurchase $950,000	÷	950,000 shares	= $1.00

Note that the only time a repurchase lowers earnings per share is when using cash to repurchase shares leads to lower earnings.

OTHER ISSUANCES OF COMMON STOCK

Not all common stock is issued in exchange for cash. In some cases, a company will trade its shares for other assets. In other cases, another corporate security—a bond or preferred stock—is converted into common stock.

Objective 7
Record conversions of debt for equity or of preferred stock into common stock.

NONCASH EXCHANGES

Often a company issues its stock to acquire land, a building, or even the common stock of another company. The company can issue the stock for cash and then spend the cash on the desired assets, but the direct approach is just to trade the stock for the assets. Such exchanges, however, raise the question of the proper dollar value of the transaction to be recorded in both the buyer's and the seller's books. The proper amount is the "fair value" of either the securities or the exchanged assets, whichever is easier to determine objectively. That amount should be used by both companies.

For example, suppose Company A acquires some equipment from Company B in exchange for 10,000 newly issued shares of A's common stock. The equipment was carried on B's books at the $200,000 original cost less accumulated depreciation of $50,000. Company A's stock is listed on the New York Stock Exchange at a current market price of $18 per share. Its par value is $1 per share. In this case, the market price of A's common stock would be regarded as a more objectively determinable fair value than would be the book value or the undepreciated cost of B's equipment. The accounts are affected as shown in Exhibit 11-8.

Exhibit 11-8

Exchange of Shares for Equipment

	Assets			= Liabilities +	Stockholders' Equity	
		Equipment			*Common Stock*	*Additional Paid-in Capital*
Issuance of stock by A		+ 180,000		=	+10,000	+ 170,000
	Investment in A Common Stock	*Equipment*	*Accumulated Depreciation*		*Retained Income*	
Disposal of equipment by B	+180,000	−200,000	+50,000	=	+30,000	[gain on disposal of equipment]

The journal entries (without explanations) are:

ON ISSUER'S BOOKS (A):

Equipment	180,000	
Common stock		10,000
Additional paid-in capital		170,000

ON INVESTOR'S BOOKS (B):

Investment in A common stock	180,000	
Accumulated depreciation, equipment	50,000	
Equipment		200,000
Gain on disposal of equipment		30,000

CONVERSION OF SECURITIES

When companies issue convertible bonds or convertible preferred stock, the conversion feature makes the securities more attractive to investors and increases the price the issuer receives (or, equivalently, reduces the interest or dividend it must pay). Ultimately, the buyer or some subsequent owner may exercise the conversion privilege. For the issuer, the conversion is a transaction of form (one form of stock for another) rather than substance. The accounts are simply adjusted as if the common stock had been issued initially.

For example, suppose Company B had paid $160,000 for an investment in 5,000 shares of the $1 par value convertible preferred stock of Company A in 19X1. The preferred stock was converted into 10,000 shares of Company A common stock ($1 par value) in 19X8. The accounts of Company A (the issuer) would be affected as shown in Exhibit 11-9.

Exhibit 11-9

Analysis of Convertible Preferred Stock

	Assets	= Liabilities	+	Stockholders' Equity		
	Cash	Preferred Stock	Additional Paid-in Capital, Preferred	Common Stock	Additional Paid-in Capital, Common
Issuance of preferred (19X1)	+ 160,000 =	+5,000	+155,000		
Conversion of preferred (19X8)	=	−5,000	−155,000	+10,000	+150,000

The journal entries would be as follows:

ON ISSUER'S BOOKS (A):

19X1 Cash	160,000	
Preferred stock, convertible		5,000
Additional paid-in capital, preferred		155,000
To record issuance of 5,000 shares of $1 par preferred stock convertible into two common shares for one preferred share.		
19X8 Preferred stock, convertible	5,000	
Additional paid-in capital, preferred	155,000	
Common stock		10,000
Additional paid-in capital, common		150,000
To record the conversion of 5,000 preferred shares to 10,000 common shares.		

Company B (the investor) has also experienced a change in form of the investment, with no change in historical cost. The carrying value, or book value, of the investment remains $160,000. To show that the form of the investment is now common stock rather than preferred stock, Company B might use a journal entry to transfer the $160,000 from one investment account to another. Alternatively, it might change subsidiary records that document the composition of a single general ledger account called Investments.

RETAINED INCOME RESTRICTIONS

Boards of directors can make decisions that benefit shareholders but hurt creditors. For example, directors might pay such large dividends that payments of creditors' claims would be threatened. To protect creditors, dividend-declaring power is restricted by either state laws or contractual obligations or both. Moreover, boards of directors can voluntarily restrict their declarations of dividends.

States typically do not permit dividends to be declared if those dividends would cause stockholders' equity to be less than total paid-in capital or if stockholders' equity is already less than total paid-in capital. Therefore retained income must exceed the cost of treasury stock. If there is no treasury stock, retained income must be positive. This restriction limits dividend payments and thus protects the position of the creditors. For example, consider the following (in millions):

| | Before Dividends | After Dividend Payments of | |
		$10	$4
Paid-in capital	$25	$25	$25
Retained income	10	—	6
Total	$35	$25	$31
Deduct:			
Cost of treasury stock	6	6	6
Stockholders' equity	$29	$19	$25

Without restricting dividends to the amount of retained income in excess of the cost of the treasury stock, the corporation could pay a dividend of $10 million. This would reduce the stockholders' equity below the paid-in capital of $25 million. With the restriction, unrestricted retained income (and maximum legal payment of dividends) would be $10 million − $6 million, or $4 million. In this case the existence of treasury stock creates a restriction on the company's ability to declare dividends. The restricted retained income cannot be reduced by dividend declarations.

Most of the time, restrictions of retained income are disclosed by footnotes. Occasionally, restrictions appear as a line item on the balance sheet called **restricted retained income.** Restrictions of retained income are also sometimes called **appropriated retained income** or reserves. The term reserve can be misleading. Accountants never use the word reserve to indicate cash set aside for a particular purpose; instead they call such assets a fund. The word **reserve** has one of three broad meanings in accounting: (1) restrictions of dividend declarations, (2) offset to an asset, or (3) estimate of a definite liability of indefinite or uncertain amount. An acknowledgment of a restriction on dividend payments is contained in the following reference from Coherent, Inc.'s 1996 annual report:

> *The Company's domestic lines of credit are generally subject to standard covenants related to financial ratios, profitability and dividend payments.*

The United States' limits the use of retained earnings reserves. Restrictions tend to arise through state law or contractual agreements. Some other countries, among them France, Germany, the Netherlands, and Japan, allow purely discretionary reserves to be

restricted retained income (appropriated retained income) Any part of retained income that may not be reduced by dividend declarations.

reserve Has one of three meanings: (1) a restriction of dividend-declaring power as denoted by a specific subdivision of retained income, (2) an offset to an asset, or (3) an estimate of a definite liability of indefinite or uncertain amount.

reported. The idea is to disclose specific intentions of management. An international company might use a "reserve for plant expansion" to communicate an intention to reinvest future earnings in new technology rather than to increase dividends.

OTHER COMPONENTS OF STOCKHOLDERS' EQUITY

Two other elements commonly appear in stockholders' equity and deserve brief mention here. The McDonald's shareholders' equity included a deduction of $175.1 million labeled Foreign currency translation adjustment. These amounts arise when a company has subsidiary companies in another country. The process of translating Mexican pesos or French francs into U.S. dollars gives rise to some adjustments that affect shareholders' equity. These are discussed in chapter 14. The other element of McDonald's shareholders' equity we have not discussed explicitly is the Guarantee of ESOP notes. ESOP stands for employee stock ownership plan. McDonald's is one of many companies that enhances the commitment of its employees to hard work and provide good service by rewarding them with shares of stock. When an ESOP is set up, companies create a separate entity to hold shares on behalf of the employees and create a schedule for future allocations of shares to specific employees. The details of the accounting are beyond our scope, but these programs have become so common that it is important to realize their existence. Some companies, such as AVIS, are primarily owned by the employees, but many companies have significant employee ownership.

FINANCIAL RATIOS RELATED TO STOCKHOLDERS' EQUITY

Objective 8
Use the rate of return on common equity and book value per share.

rate of return on common equity (ROE) Net income less preferred dividends divided by average common equity.

As we have already seen, many ratios aid in evaluating the performance of a company. Not surprisingly, then, many questions pertaining to stockholders' equity can be answered with ratios. One important question is: How effectively does the company use resources provided by the shareholders? To assess this, analysts relate the net income generated by the firm to the historic investment by its shareholders. The **rate of return on common equity** (often abbreviated **ROE**) is defined as:

$$\text{Rate of return on common equity} = \frac{\text{Net income} - \text{Preferred dividends}}{\text{Average common equity}}$$

The rate of return on common equity is naturally of great interest to common stockholders. The rate focuses on the company's profitability based on the book value of the common equity. To determine the numerator of the ratio, preferred dividends are subtracted from net income to obtain net income available for common stock. The denominator is the average of the beginning and ending common equity balances. Note that the common equity balance is the total stockholders' equity less the preferred stock at book value. If the liquidating value of a company's preferred stock exceeds the stock's book value, the liquidating value is deducted from the total stockholders' equity to determine the common equity balance:

Using the data for Calvin Company in Exhibit 11-10, we can compute the company's ROE as follows:

$$\text{Rate of return on common equity} = \frac{\text{Net income} - \text{Preferred dividends}}{\text{Average common equity}}$$

$$= \frac{\$11,000,000 - \$1,000,000}{\frac{1}{2}[(\$133,000,000 - \$10,000,000) + (\$137,400,000 - \$10,000,000)]}$$

$$= \frac{\$10,000,000}{\frac{1}{2}(\$123,000,000 + \$127,400,000)}$$

$$= \frac{\$10,000,000}{\$125,200,000} = 8.0\%$$

Exhibit 11-10

Calvin Company Owners' Equity

	December 31	
	19X2	19X1
Stockholders' equity:		
$10 preferred stock, 100,000 shares,		
$100 par	$ 10,000,000	$ 10,000,000
Common stock, 5,000,000 shares,		
$1 par	5,000,000	5,000,000
Additional paid-in capital	35,000,000	35,000,000
Retained income	87,400,000	83,000,000
Total stockholders' equity	$137,400,000	$133,000,000

Net income for the year ended Dec. 31, 19X2	$11,000,000
Preferred dividends @ $10 per share	1,000,000
Net income available for common stock	$10,000,000

ROE varies considerably among companies and industries as shown below.

	1996	1995	1994	1993	1992
McDonald's	19.5	19.9	19.4	19.0	18.2
IBM	24.8	18.5	14.3	*	*
PepsiCo	16	23	27	27	24
Mobil	16.0	13.5	10.4	12.3	7.8
Chrysler	31	19	42	*	11

*Denotes a loss year.

ROE patterns can be evaluated in several ways. McDonald's demonstrates a high stable level. In contrast, Chrysler has a highly variable ROE. This is consistent with the significant variability that characterizes the automobile industry. Both IBM and Chrysler reported losses in 1993. This might arise from difficult business activity, but it is also sometimes related to changes in accounting practice. In Chapter 9, we discussed the new accounting practice for postretirement benefits. This caused many companies to record very large one-time expense items. This fact explains Chrysler's 1993 loss. Chrysler recorded a $5 billion charge for the accounting change in 1993 and would have had an ROE of more than 30% that year without the change. On the other hand, further investigation of IBM reveals that its 1993 loss had little to do with the accounting change.

The book value of a company is the stockholders' equity, often expressed on a per share basis. When preferred stock is present, the calculation of the **book value per share of common stock** adjusts for the preferred as follows:

book value per share of common stock Stockholders' equity attributable to common stock divided by the number of shares outstanding.

$$\text{Book value per share of common stock} = \frac{\text{Total stockholders' equity} - \text{Book value of preferred stock}}{\text{Number of common shares outstanding}}$$

$$= \frac{\$137,400,000 - \$10,000,000}{5,000,000} = \$25.48$$

Suppose the market value for this stock is $35. Note that the book value is much lower than the market value. Shareholders who are paying market value for the stock are paying for what they think future earning power will be rather than for the historical cost of assets. Book values are not always useful because they are based on balance sheet values, which show the historical cost of assets. The current value of those assets may differ greatly from their historical cost. As a result, some companies consistently have market prices in excess of book values, or vice versa. Comparing book values with market values is useful because it often reveals the causes behind the difference in values. Many investors express the relation between market and book value as a ratio. For example, Merck had a 1996 book value of about $9.77 and a market value per share almost ten times as large ($95). This produces a **market-to-book ratio** of 9.72 ($95 ÷ $9.77).

market to book ratio
Market value per share divided by book value per share.

What do these differences in values mean in the real world? A market value well above the book value may be appropriate if the company has many unrecorded assets or appreciated assets. For example, Merck has valuable patents on various drugs and additional research under way that are not reflected in the book values. Coca-Cola's mid-1997 market value of about $60 substantially exceeded its book value of about $2.50, producing a market-to-book ratio of 24. Why? Presumably, this difference reflects beliefs of investors that Coca-Cola will be able to continue its long-term pattern of rapid sales growth and high return on equity. Coca-Cola's return on common equity reached 60.5% in 1996.

In contrast, in mid-1992 Ford Motor Company had a $10 market value, a figure below its $11 book value. The market-to-book ratio was below one. During a series of bad years for auto sales, Ford suffered losses and cut its dividend payment sharply. The market price per share indicated a belief that Ford's production plants and other assets could not be liquidated for their book value. By 1996, Ford had recovered well with a share price ranging from $30 to $40 while book value per share had about doubled to $20.

SUMMARY PROBLEMS FOR YOUR REVIEW

PROBLEM ONE

From the following data, prepare a detailed statement of stockholders' equity for the Sample Corporation, December 31, 19X1:

Additional paid-in capital, preferred stock	$ 50,000
Additional paid-in capital, common stock	1,000,000
9% preferred stock, $50 par value, callable at $55, authorized 20,000 shares, issued and outstanding 12,000 shares	
Common stock, no par, stated value $2 per share, authorized 500,000 shares, issued 400,000 shares of which 25,000 shares are held in the treasury	
Dividends payable	90,000
Retained income	2,000,000

The 25,000 shares of treasury stock cost $250,000.

SOLUTION TO PROBLEM ONE

Dividends payable is a liability. It must therefore be excluded from a statement of stockholders' equity:

Sample Corporation Statement of Stockholders' Equity, December 31, 19X1

9% preferred stock, $50 par value, callable at $55, authorized 20,000 shares, issued and outstanding 12,000 shares	$ 600,000
Common stock, no par, stated value $2 per share, authorized 500,000 shares, issued 400,000 shares of which 25,000 shares are held in the treasury	800,000

Additional paid-in capital:

Preferred	$ 50,000	
Common	1,000,000	1,050,000*
Retained income		2,000,000
Subtotal		$4,450,000
Less: Cost of 25,000 shares of common stock		
reacquired and held in treasury		250,000
Total stockholders' equity		$4,200,000

*Many presentations would not show the detailed breakdown of additional paid-in capital into preferred and common portions.

PROBLEM TWO

B Company splits its $10 par common stock 5-for-1. How will its balance sheet be affected? Its earnings per share? Assume 2,000 shares are originally outstanding. How would your answer change if the company said it "accounted for" the split as a stock dividend?

SOLUTION TO PROBLEM TWO

The total amount of stockholders' equity would be unaffected, but there would be 10,000 outstanding shares at $2 par instead of 2,000 shares at $10 par. Earnings per share would be one-fifth of that previously reported, assuming no change in total net income applicable to the common stock.

If the question were framed as "the company recently issued a 5-for-1 stock split accounted for as a stock dividend" then the par value per share would be retained, and a journal entry would increase the par value account for common stock by $80,000 (8,000 additional shares times $10 par value per share):

Retained earnings	80,000	
Common stock at par		80,000

PROBLEM THREE

C Company distributes a 2% stock dividend on its 1 million outstanding $5 par common shares. Its stockholders' equity section before the dividend was:

Common stock, 1,000,000 shares @ $5 par	$ 5,000,000
Paid-in capital in excess of par	20,000,000
Retained income	75,000,000
Total stockholders' equity	$100,000,000

The common stock was selling on the open market for $150 per share when the dividend was distributed.

How will the stockholders' equity section be affected? If net income were $10.2 million next year, what would be the earnings per share before considering the effects of the stock dividend? After considering the effects of the stock dividend?

SOLUTION TO PROBLEM THREE

	Before 2% Stock Dividend	Changes	After 2% Stock Dividend
Common stock, 1,000,000 shares @ $5 par	$ 5,000,000	+(20,000 @ $5)	$ 5,100,000
Paid-in capital	20,000,000	+[20,000 @ ($150 − $5)]	22,900,000
Retained income	75,000,000	−(20,000 @ $150)	72,000,000
Total	$100,000,000		$100,000,000

Earnings per share before considering the effects of the stock dividend would be $10,200,000 ÷ 1,000,000, or $10.20. After the dividend: $10,200,000 ÷ 1,020,000, or $10.

Note that the dividend has no effect on net income, the numerator of the earnings-per-share computation. But it does affect the denominator and causes a mild dilution which, in theory, should be reflected by a slight decline in the market price of the stock.

PROBLEM FOUR

Metro-Goldwyn-Mayer Film Co. declared and distributed a 3% stock dividend. The applicable market value per share was $7.75. The par value of the 966,000 additional shares issued was $1.00 each. The total cash paid to shareholders in lieu of issuing fractional shares was $70,000. Prepare the appropriate journal entry.

SOLUTION TO PROBLEM FOUR

Retained income	7,556,500	
Common stock, $1.00 par value		966,000
Capital in excess of par value		6,520,500
Cash		70,000

To record 3% stock dividend. Total shares issued were 966,000 at $7.75, a total market value of $7,486,500. In addition, cash of $70,000 was paid in lieu of issuing fractional shares. Total charge to retained earnings was $70,000 + (966,000 × $7.75) = $7,556,500. The account Capital in Excess of Par Value was the description actually used by MGM.

Highlights to Remember

On the balance sheet, stockholders' equity is reported as the book values of the residual interests of a corporation's owners. By incorporating, the company provides limited liability for its owners and provides them with various rights, including the right to vote for the board of directors. Among equity holders, preferred shareholders have more senior claims to dividends and may have other special rights, including cumulative dividends, participating dividends, conversion privileges, and preference in liquidation. Preferred stocks are like bonds. However, although bonds pay legally enforceable interest and principal payments at maturity, preferred stock has an infinite life, and dividend payments to shareholders become legal obligations only if the board declares the dividend.

Stock splits and stock dividends alter the number of shares held by the owners. Accounting for these splits and dividends involves rearranging the owners' equity account balances. Par value accounts, paid-in capital accounts, and retained earnings may be rearranged without changing the total owners' equity. The exact procedure depends on whether the par value of the new shares changes and on the number of additional shares. Similarly, a rearrangement of owners' equity arises when convertible preferred shares are exchanged for common shares.

Companies sometimes acquire treasury stock, which are shares of their own stock purchased in the open market. These shares may later be retired, resold, or used to meet obligations under option agreements. Transactions in the company's own stock never give rise to gains and losses and do not affect the income statement. Such transactions with the shareholders give rise only to changes in the equity accounts.

Cash dividends to preferred and common shareholders will be declared only when cash is available for payment. But in most states, dividends may be paid legally only to the extent that retained earnings exceed the cost of treasury stock. Additional restrictions on the right to pay cash dividends are often built into debt contracts.

Security analysts use the return on common stockholders' equity as a primary ratio to assess the effectiveness of management and the profitability of the firm. Analysts often compare the market value per share with the book value per share. A higher market value should be associated with growth prospects and possibly unrecorded assets, such as internally developed patents.

Accounting Vocabulary

appropriated retained income, p. 467
authorized shares, p. 447
book value per share of common stock, p. 469
callable, p. 451
call price, p. 451
convertible, p. 451
corporate proxy, p. 447
cumulative, p. 449
date of record, p. 452
declaration date, p. 452

dilution, p. 461
dividend arrearages, p. 449
issued shares, p. 447
liquidating value, p. 450
market-to-book ratio, p. 470
outstanding shares, p. 447
participating, p. 451
payment date, p. 452
preemptive rights, p. 447
preferred stock, p. 449
rate of return on common equity, p. 468

ROE, p. 468
redemption price, p. 451
reserve, p. 467
restricted retained income, p. 467
series, p. 452
stock dividends, p. 455
stock options, p. 453
stock split, p. 454
treasury stock, p. 448

Assignment Material

QUESTIONS

11-1. What is the purpose of preemptive rights?

11-2. "Common shareholders have limited liability." Explain.

11-3. Can a share of common stock be outstanding but not authorized or issued? Why?

11-4. "Treasury stock is unissued stock." Do you agree? Explain.

11-5. "Cumulative dividends are liabilities that must be paid to preferred shareholders before any dividends are paid to common shareholders." Do you agree? Explain.

11-6. "The liquidating value of preferred stock is the amount of cash for which it can currently be exchanged." Do you agree? Explain.

11-7. What are convertible securities?

11-8. In what way is preferred stock similar to debt? To common stock?

11-9. Which are riskier, bonds or preferred stock? Why? Whose perspective are you taking, the issuer's or the investor's?

11-10. Why do some accountants want to record an expense when a company grants stock options to its employees?

11-11. Why do you suppose companies offer their employees stock options rather than simply paying higher salaries?

11-12. "The only real dividends are cash dividends." Do you agree? Explain.

11-13. "A 2% stock dividend increases every shareholder's fractional portion of the company by 2%." Do you agree? Explain.

11-14. "A stock split can be achieved by means of a stock dividend." Do you agree? Explain.

11-15. "When companies repurchase their own shares, the accounting depends on the purpose for which the shares are purchased." Explain.

11-16. "When a company retires shares, it must pay the stockholders an amount equal to the original par value and additional capital contributed for those shares plus the stockholders' fractional portion of retained earnings." Do you agree? Explain.

11-17. Why might a company decide to buy back its own shares instead of paying additional cash dividends?

11-18. "Treasury stock is not an asset." Explain.

11-19. "Gains and losses are not possible from a corporation's acquiring or selling its own stock." Do you agree? Explain.

11-20. What is the proper measure for an asset newly acquired through an exchange (e.g., an exchange of land for securities)? Explain.

11-21. Why does a conversion option make bonds or preferred stock more attractive to investors?

11-22. Restrictions on dividend-declaring power may be voluntary or involuntary. Give an example of each.

11-23. Why might a board of directors voluntarily restrict its dividend-declaring power?

11-24. "A company's return on equity (ROE) indicates how much return an investor makes on her investment in the company's shares." Do you agree? Explain.

11-25. "A common stock selling on the market far below its book value is an attractive buy." Do you agree? Explain.

EXERCISES

11-26 Distinctions Between Terms

Disposal Services, Inc., a waste-management company, had 4 million shares of common stock authorized on August 31, 19X8. Shares issued were 2.1 million. There were 300,000 shares held in the treasury. How many shares were issued and outstanding? How many shares were unissued? Label your computations.

11-27 Distinctions Between Terms

On January 1, 1997, McDonald's Corporation had 3.5 billion shares of common stock authorized. There were 830.3 million shares issued, and 135.7 million shares held as treasury stock. How many shares were issued and outstanding? How many shares were unissued? Label your computations.

11-28 Preferences as to Assets

The following are account balances of Reliable Autos, Inc. (in thousands): common stock and retained income, $300; accounts payable, $300; preferred stock (5,000 shares; $20 par and $24 liquidating value per share), $100; subordinated debentures, $300; and unsubordinated debentures, $100. Prepare a table showing the distribution of the cash proceeds upon liquidation and dissolution of the corporation. Assume cash proceeds of (in thousands): $1,500; $1,000; $790; $500; $400; and $200, respectively.

11-29 Issuance of Common Shares

Kawasaki Heavy Industries is a large Japanese company that makes ships, aircraft engines, and many other products in addition to motorcycles. Its 1997 sales of ¥1,224 billion are equivalent to $9,865 million. Kawasaki's balance sheet includes (in millions of yen):

Common stock of ¥50 par value, 1,621,760,000 shares issued in 1997	81,088
Capital surplus	24,345

Required

1. Assume that all 1,621,760,000 shares had been issued at the same time. Prepare the journal entry.

2. Is the relationship between the size of the common stock and the size of the capital surplus different from what one might expect to find for a U.S. company? Explain.

11-30 Cumulative Dividends

The Ute Data Services Corporation was founded on January 1, 19X1.

Preferred stock, no par, cumulative, $6 annual dividend per share:	
Issued and outstanding, 1,000,000 shares	$ 40,000,000
Capital stock, no par, 6,000,000 shares	90,000,000
Total stockholders' equity	$130,000,000

The corporation's subsequent net incomes (losses) were:

19X1	$(5,000,000)
19X2	(4,000,000)
19X3	14,000,000
19X4	30,000,000
19X5	13,000,000

Assume that the board of directors declared dividends to the maximum extent permissible by law. The state prohibits dividend declarations that cause negative retained earnings. **Required**

1. Tabulate the annual dividend declarations on preferred and common shares. There is no treasury stock.

2. How would the total distribution to common shareholders change if the preferred were not cumulative?

11-31 Cumulative Dividends

In recent years, the Winslow Company had severe cash flow problems. In 19X4, the company suspended payment of cash dividends on common stock. In 19X5, it ceased payment on its $4 million of outstanding 7% cumulative preferred stock. No common or preferred dividends were paid in 19X5 or 19X6. In 19X7, Winslow's board of directors decided that $1 million was available for cash dividends.

Compute the preferred stock dividend and the common stock dividend for 19X7.

11-32 Cash Dividends

If you have a credit card, you have probably dealt with First Data Corporation without knowing it. First Data maintains data for more than 150 million credit and debit cards, authorizes 2.3 billion credit and debit card transactions, and issues 100 million credit and debit cards per year. In 1996, First Data declared dividends of $.065 per share paid to an average of 447.7 million shares. First Data paid dividends every quarter, but for simplicity assume that they declared dividends only once in 1996, on November 15, payable on December 15, to stockholders of record on December 1.

Prepare the journal entries relating to the declaration and payment of dividends by First Data. Include the date on which each journal entry would be made.

11-33 Stock Options

Lyndon Systems granted its top executives options to purchase 6,000 shares of common stock (par $2) at $20 per share, the market price today. The options may be exercised over a four-year span, starting three years hence. Suppose all options are exercised three years hence, when the market value of the stock is $30 per share.

Prepare the appropriate journal entry on the books of Lyndon Systems. **Required**

11-34 Stock Split

An annual report of Dean Foods Company included the following in the statement of consolidated retained earnings:

Charge for stock split	$4,401,000

The balance sheets before and after the split showed:

	After	Before
Common stock $1 par value	$13,203,000	$8,802,000

Required Define *stock split*. What did Dean Foods do to achieve its stock split? Does this conflict with your definition? Explain fully.

11-35 Reverse Stock Split

According to a news story, "The shareholders of QED approved a one-for-ten reverse split of QED's common stock." Accounting for a reverse stock split applies the same principles as accounting for a regular stock split. QED Exploration, Inc., was an oil-development company operating in Texas and Louisiana. QED's stockholders' equity section before the reverse split included:

Common stock, authorized 30,000,000 shares, issued 23,530,000 shares	$ 287,637
Additional paid-in capital	3,437,547
Retained income	2,220,895
Less treasury stock, at cost, 1,017,550 shares	(305,250)
Total stockholders' equity	$5,640,829

Required 1. Prepare QED's stockholders' equity section after the reverse stock split.
2. Comment on possible reasons for a reverse split.

11-36 Stock Dividends

Zemex Corporation, a Toronto-based natural resource company, included the following in a footnote to its 1996 financial statements:

> On October 18, 1996, the Corporation declared a 2% stock dividend to shareholders of record on November 4, 1996, which was paid November 18, 1996. Retained earnings were charged $1,255,192 as a result of the issuance of 161,398 shares of the Corporation's common stock, and cash payments of $4,357 in lieu of fractional shares.

Required Prepare the journal entry to record Zemex's stock dividend. Assume a par value of $1 per share.

11-37 Treasury Stock

During 1996, UtiliCorp United, the electric and gas utility company based in Kansas City, repurchased 228,807 of its own shares at an average price of $27.97 per share and held them in the treasury.

Required 1. Prepare the journal entry for the purchase of treasury shares.
2. At the beginning of 1996, UtiliCorp had no treasury stock, and no treasury stock was reissued during 1996. Before accounting for treasury shares, UtiliCorp's total shareowners' equity at the end of 1996 was $1,164.4 million. Compute the total amount of shareowners' equity reported on the company's balance sheet at the end of 1996. (UtiliCorp uses the term shareowners' equity instead of stockholders' or shareholders' equity on their balance sheet.)

11-38 Book Value and Return on Equity

Reach Company had net income of $11 million in 19X8. The stockholders' equity section of its 19X8 annual report follows (in millions):

	19X8	19X7
Stockholders' equity:		
9% Preferred stock, $50 par value, 400,000		
shares authorized, 300,000 shares issued	$15.0	$15.0
Common stock, $1 par, 5 million authorized,		
2 million and 1.8 million issued	2.0	1.8
Additional paid-in capital	32.0	30.0
Retained earnings	70.0	65.0
Total stockholders' equity	$119.0	$111.8

Required

1. Compute the book value per share of common stock at the end of 19X8.
2. Compute the rate of return on common equity for 19X8.
3. Compute the amount of cash dividends on common stock declared during 19X8. (*Hint:* Examine the retained earnings T-account.)

11-39 Financial Ratios and Stockholders' Equity

Consider the following data for New York Bankcorp:

	December 31	
	19X2	*19X1*
Stockholders' equity:		
Preferred stock, 200,000 shares,		
$20 par, liquidation value $22	$ 4,000,000	$ 4,000,000
Common stock, 4,000,000 shares,		
$2 par	8,000,000	8,000,000
Additional paid-in capital	5,000,000	5,000,000
Retained income	3,000,000	1,400,000
Total stockholders' equity	$20,000,000	$18,400,000

Net income was $3 million for 19X2. The preferred stock is 10%, cumulative. The regular annual dividend was declared on the preferred stock, and the common shareholders received dividends of $.25 per share. The market price of the common stock on December 31, 19X2, was $5.25 per share.

Compute the following statistics for 19X2: rate of return on common equity, earnings per share of common stock, price-earnings ratio, dividend-payout ratio, dividend-yield ratio, and book value per share of common stock.

Required

11-40 Stockholders' Equity Section

The following are data for the Roselli Corporation.

6% cumulative preferred stock, $40 par value, callable at $42,	
authorized 100,000 shares, issued and outstanding 80,000 shares	$ 3,200,000
Treasury stock, common (at cost)	5,000,000
Additional paid-in capital, common stock	9,000,000
Dividends payable	100,000
Retained income	15,000,000
Additional paid-in capital, preferred stock	1,000,000
Common stock, $2.50 par value per share, authorized 1.8 million shares,	
issued 1.2 million shares of which 60,000 are held in the treasury	3,000,000

Required

Prepare a detailed stockholders' equity section as it would appear in the balance sheet at December 31, 19X8.

11-41 Effects on Stockholders' Equity

Indicate the effect ($+$, $-$, or 0) on *total* stockholders' equity of General Services Corp. for each of the following:

1. Operating loss for the period of $900,000.
2. Sale of 100 shares of General Services by Jay Smith to Tom Jones.
3. Declaration of a stock dividend on common stock.
4. Issuance of a stock dividend on common stock.
5. Failing to declare a regular dividend on cumulative preferred stock.
6. Declaration of a cash dividend of $50,000 in total.
7. Payment of item 6.
8. Purchase of ten shares of treasury stock for $1,000 cash.
9. Sale of treasury stock, purchased in item 8, for $1,200.
10. Sale of treasury stock, purchased in item 8, for $900.

PROBLEMS

11-42 Dividends and Cumulative Preferred Stock

Renton Interiors, Inc., maker of seats and other interior equipment for Boeing aircraft, started 19X8 with the following balance sheet.

6% cumulative convertible preferred stock, par value $10 a share, authorized 150,000 shares; issued 52,136 shares	$ 521,360
Common stock, par value $.20 a share, authorized 2,000,000 shares, issued 1,322,850 shares	264,570
Additional paid-in capital	2,063,351
Retained income	2,463,951
Less: Treasury stock, at cost:	
Preferred stock, 11,528 shares	(80,249)
Common stock, 93,091 shares	(167,549)
Total stockholders' equity	$5,065,434

Required

1. Suppose Renton Interiors had paid no dividends, preferred or common, in the prior year, 19X7. All preferred dividends had been paid through 19X6. Management decided at the end of 19X8 to pay $.05 per share common dividends. Calculate the preferred dividends that would be paid during 19X8. Prepare journal entries for recording both preferred and common dividends. Assume that no preferred or common shares were issued or purchased during 19X8.
2. Suppose 19X8 net income was $250,000. Compute the 19X8 ending balance in the Retained Income account.

11-43 Dividend Reinvestment Plans

Many corporations have automatic dividend reinvestment plans. The shareholder may elect not to receive his or her cash dividends. Instead, an equivalent amount of cash is invested in additional stock (at the current market value) that is issued to the shareholder.

The Coca-Cola Company had the following data at June 30, 1997 (in millions):

Coca-Cola Co.

Common stock: authorized 5,600,000,000 shares; $.25 par value; issued 3,438,826,444 shares	$ 860
Capital surplus	1,160
Reinvested earnings	16,735
Less treasury stock, at cost (958,700,434 shares)	10,725

1. Coca-Cola declared a quarterly cash dividend of $.14 per share. Suppose that holders of 10% of the company's shares decided to reinvest in the company under an automatic dividend reinvestment plan rather than accepting the cash. The market price of the shares upon issuance was $60 per share. Prepare the journal entry (or entries) for these transactions. (Note: No dividends are paid on shares held in the treasury.)

2. A letter to the editor of *Business Week* commented:

   Stockholders participating in dividend reinvestment programs pay taxes on dividends not really received. If a company would refrain from paying dividends only to take them back as reinvestments, it would save paperwork, and the stockholder would save income tax.

   Do you agree with the writer's remarks? Explain in detail.

11-44 Dividends
(Alternate is 11-45.)

1. The Minneapolis Company issued 400,000 shares of common stock, $4 par, for $30 cash per share on March 31, 19X1. Prepare the journal entry.

2. Minneapolis Company declared and paid a cash dividend of $2 per share on March 31, 19X2. Prepare the journal entry.

3. Minneapolis Company had retained earnings of $9 million by March 31, 19X5. The market value of the common shares was $60 each. A common stock dividend of 5% was declared; the shares were issued on March 31, 19X5. Prepare the journal entry. Also present a tabulation that compares the stockholders' equity section before and after the declaration and issuance of the stock dividend. Also include at the bottom of the tabulation the effects on the overall market value of the stock, the total shares outstanding, and the number of shares and percentage ownership of an individual owner who originally bought 6,000 shares.

4. What journal entries would be made by the investor who bought 6,000 shares of the Minneapolis common stock and held this investment throughout the time covered in requirements 1, 2, and 3?

5. Refer to requirement 4. Suppose the investor sold 200 shares for $58 each the day after receiving the stock dividend. Prepare the investor's journal entry for the sale of the shares.

11-45 Dividends
(Alternate is 11-44.)

1. Garcia Company issued 600,000 shares of common stock, $1 par, for $10 cash per share on December 31, 19X5. Prepare the journal entry.

2. Garcia Company declared and paid a cash dividend of $.50 per share on December 31, 19X6. Prepare the journal entry. Assume that only the 600,000 shares from part 1 are outstanding.

3. Garcia Company had retained earnings of $7 million by December 31, 19X9. The market value of the common shares was $30 each. A common stock dividend of 3% was declared; the shares were issued on December 31, 19X9. Prepare the journal entry. Also present a tabulation that compares the stockholders' equity section before and after the declaration and issuance of the stock dividend. Also include at the bottom of the tabulation the effects on the overall market value of the stock, the total shares outstanding, and the number of shares and percentage ownership of an individual owner who originally bought 6,000 shares.

4. What journal entries would be made by the investor who bought 5,000 shares of Garcia Company common stock and held this investment throughout the time covered in requirements 1, 2, and 3?

5. Refer to requirement 4. Suppose the investor sold 100 shares for $29 each the day after receiving the stock dividend. Prepare the investor's journal entry for the sale of the shares.

11-46 Stock Options

AIM Telephones, Inc., is one of the top five independent telecommunications equipment suppliers in the United States. Net income for a recent year was $1,018,000, and AIM paid no cash dividends. During the year, AIM issued 538,522 new shares at an average price of $7.853 per share. In addition, executives exercised stock options for 99,813 shares at an average price of $2.304 per share. The stockholders' equity at the beginning of the year was:

Common stock, par value $.01 per share	$ 39,000
Capital in excess of par value	4,962,000
Retained earnings	1,182,000
Total stockholders' equity	$6,183,000

Required

1. Prepare journal entries for (a) the newly issued shares and (b) the stock options that were exercised. Omit explanations. Round calculations to the nearest thousand dollars.

2. Prepare a statement of stockholders' equity at the end of the year.

3. Suppose all the stock options were exercised when the stock price for AIM was $7.50 per share. How much did the executives gain from exercising the stock options?

4. How much compensation expense did AIM record when the options were granted? When they were exercised?

11-47 Meaning of Stock Splits

A letter of January 31 to shareholders of United Financial, a California savings and loan company, said:

> Once again, I want to take the opportunity of sending you some good news about recent developments at United Financial. Last week the board raised United's quarterly cash dividend 12½ percent and then declared a 5-for-4 stock split in the form of a 25 percent stock dividend. The additional shares will be distributed on March 15 to shareholders of record February 15.

On March 16, the board approved a merger between National Steel Corporation and United Financial. The agreement called for a cash payment of $33.60 on each outstanding United Financial share. The original National Steel offer (in early February) was $42 per share for the 5.8 million shares outstanding.

Required

1. As a recipient of the letter of January 31, you were annoyed by the five-for-four stock split. Prepare a letter to the chairman indicating the reasons for your displeasure.

2. Prepare a response to the unhappy shareholder in requirement 1.

3. A shareholder of United Financial wrote to the chairman in early March: "I'm confused about the change in the agreed, upon price per share. I owned 100 shares and thought I'd receive $4,200. Now the price has dropped from $42.00 to $33.60." Prepare a response to the shareholder.

11-48 Stock Dividend and Fractional Shares

The Soderstrom Company declared and distributed a 2% stock dividend. The stockholders' equity before the dividend was:

Common stock, 10,000,000 shares, $1 par	$ 10,000,000
Additional paid-in capital	40,000,000
Retained earnings	50,000,000
Total stockholders' equity	$100,000,000

The market price of Soderstrom's shares was $10 when the stock dividend was distributed. Soderstrom paid cash of $30,000 in lieu of issuing fractional shares.

Required

1. Prepare the journal entry for the declaration and distribution of the stock dividend.
2. Show the stockholders' equity section after the stock dividend.
3. How did the stock dividend affect total stockholders' equity? How did it affect the proportion of the company owned by each shareholder?

11-49 Issuance and Retirement of Shares, Cash Dividends

On January 2, 19X1, Chippewa Investment Company began business by issuing 10,000 $1 par value shares for $100,000 cash. The cash was invested, and on December 26, 19X1, all investments were sold for $114,000 cash. Operating expenses for 19X1 were $5,000, all paid in cash. Therefore net income for 19X1 was $9,000. On December 27, the board of directors declared a $.35 per share cash dividend, payable on January 15, 19X2, to owners of record on December 31, 19X1. On January 30, 19X2, the company bought and retired 1,000 of its own shares on the open market for $9.50 each.

Required

1. Prepare journal entries for issuance of shares, declaration and payment of cash dividends, and retirement of shares.
2. Prepare a balance sheet as of December 31, 19X1.

11-50 Issuance, Splits, Dividends
(Alternate is 11-51.)

Required

1. Lopez Company issued 100,000 shares of common stock, $6 par, for $37 cash per share on December 31, 19X1. Prepare the journal entry.
2. Lopez Company had accumulated earnings of $5 million by December 31, 19X5. The board of directors declared a three-for-one stock split and immediately exchanged three $2 par shares for each share outstanding. Prepare the journal entry, if any. Present the stockholders' equity section of the balance sheet before and after the split.
3. Repeat requirement 2, but assume that instead of exchanging three $2 par shares for each share outstanding, two *additional* $6 par shares were issued for each share outstanding. Lopez said they issued a three-for-one stock split "accounted for as a stock dividend."
4. What journal entries would be made by the investor who bought 2,000 shares of Lopez Company common stock and held this investment throughout the time covered in requirements 1, 2, and 3?

11-51 Issuance, Splits, Dividends
(Alternate is 11-50.)

AT&T's June 30, 1997 balance sheet contained the following:

Common stock, par value $1.00 per share	$1,625,000,000

1. Suppose AT&T had originally issued 200,000 shares of common stock, $2 par, for $15 cash per share many years ago, say, on December 31, 19X1. Prepare the journal entry.

2. AT&T had accumulated earnings of $5 billion by December 31, 19X5. The board of directors declared a two-for-one stock split and immediately exchanged two $1 par shares for each share outstanding. Prepare the journal entry, if any. Present the stockholders' equity section of the balance sheet before and after the split.

3. Repeat requirement 2, but assume that one additional $2 par share was issued by AT&T for each share outstanding (instead of exchanging shares).

4. What journal entries would be made by the investor who bought 2,000 shares of AT&T common stock and held this investment throughout the time covered in requirements 1, 2, and 3?

11-52   Stock Split and 100% Stock Dividend

The Rubin Company wishes to double its number of shares outstanding. The company president asks the controller how a two-for-one stock split differs from a 100% stock dividend. Rubin has 200,000 shares ($1 par) outstanding at a market price of $30 per share.
The current stockholders' equity section is:

Common shares, 200,000 issued and outstanding	$ 200,000
Additional paid-in capital	2,300,000
Retained income	4,500,000

1. Prepare the journal entry for a two-for-one stock split.

2. Prepare the journal entry for a 100% stock dividend.

3. Explain the difference between a two-for-one stock split and a 100% stock dividend.

11-53   Treasury Stock
(Alternate is 11-60.)

Minnesota Mining and Manufacturing Company (3M) presented the following data in its 1996 annual report:

	December 31	
	1996	1995
	(in millions)	
Stockholders' Equity:		
Common stock, without par value, 500,000,000 shares authorized, with 472,016,528 shares issued in 1996 and 1995	$ 296	$ 296
Retained earnings	8,756	9,164
Other	(575)	(523)
Total	8,477	8,937
Less: Treasury stock, 55.2 million shares at December 31, 1996, and 53.3 million shares at December 31, 1995	(2,193)	(2,053)
Stockholders' Equity, Net	$ 6,284	$ 6,884

1. During 1996, 3M reacquired 9.6 million treasury shares for $532 million. Give the journal entry to record this transaction.

2. Given the information provided, calculate how many treasury shares were issued in 1996 pursuant to stock option plans.

3. Suppose that on January 7, 1997, 3M used cash to reacquire 175,000 shares for $70 each and held them in the treasury. Prepare the stockholders' equity section after the acquisition of treasury stock. Also prepare the journal entry.

4. Suppose the 175,000 shares of treasury stock are sold for $90 per share. Prepare the journal entry.

5. Suppose the 175,000 shares of treasury stock are sold for $50 per share. Prepare the journal entry.

11-54 Treasury Shares

During 1996, General Electric's outstanding common shares decreased from 1,666,512,000 to 1,644,542,000 shares. GE neither issued nor retired common shares during 1996. Treasury shares were purchased for $4,842 million and other treasury shares were sold for $2,662 million. A gain on the sale of treasury shares of $952 million was recorded. GE paid $3,138 million in dividends during the year, and retained income rose from $34,528 million to $38,670 million.

1. Compute the net increase in the number of shares of treasury stock during 1996. **Required**

2. Compute the cost of the treasury shares sold during 1996.

3. The balance in the account "common stock held in the treasury" on January 1, 1996 was $8,176 million. Compute the balance on December 31, 1996.

4. Compute GE's net income for 1996.

5. Comment on the decision to buy treasury stock rather than using the same dollars to pay additional cash dividends.

11-55 Treasury Shares in Switzerland

Nestlé N.A., the Swiss food and beverage company, reported the following in its 1996 balance sheet (in millions of Swiss francs):

Shareholders' funds	
Share capital	SF 404
Share premium and reserves	21,802
Less: Own shares	268
Total shareholders' funds	SF21,938

During 1996, Nestlé purchased 92,668 of its own shares for SF 111.2 million. Of those shares, 275 were issued on the exercise of stock options. There were no other changes in Nestlé's holdings of its own shares. The balance in the "Own Shares" account at the beginning of 1996 was SF 157.1 million.

1. Restate Nestlé's "Shareholders' Funds" section of its balance sheet using terms more commonly used in the United States. **Required**

2. Prepare journal entries for Nestlé's purchase of its own shares in 1996.

3. Prepare journal entries for Nestlé's reissue of 275 shares for the exercise of stock options. Assume that the exercise price was SF 500 per share and that the reissued shares were all among those purchased in 1996.

4. At the end of 1996, Nestlé held a total of 1,021,333 shares of its own stock. Comment on the average price paid for the shares repurchased before 1996 compared to those repurchased in 1996.

11-56 Repurchase of Shares and Book Value per Share

Mobil repurchased 2.4 million of its own common shares during 1996. The market price of Mobil shares averaged $120 per share during the year. The condensed 1996 shareholders' equity section of the balance sheet showed (dollars and shares in millions):

Common stock, no par, 446 shares issued,	
394 shares outstanding	$ 891
Retained earnings and other	20,824
Treasury stock (52 shares)	(2,643)
Total stockholders' equity	$19,072

Required

1. Prepare the journal entry to record the 1996 purchase of treasury shares.
2. Compute the book value per share at December 31, 1996.
3. Compute the book value per share, assuming that the 1996 treasury stock purchase did not occur.

11-57 Retirement of Shares

Houston Financial Systems, Inc., has the following:

Common stock, 5,000,000 shares @ $2 par	$ 10,000,000
Paid-in capital in excess of par	40,000,000
Total paid-in capital	$ 50,000,000
Retained income	10,000,000
Stockholders' equity	$ 60,000,000
Overall market value of stock @ assumed $40	$200,000,000
Book value per share = $60,000,000 ÷ 5,000,000 = $12	

Required

The company used cash to reacquire and retire 100,000 shares for $40 each. Prepare the stockholders' equity section before and after this retirement of shares. Also prepare the journal entry.

11-58 Disposition of Treasury Stock

Chirac Company bought 10,000 of its own shares for $12 per share. The shares were held as treasury stock. This was the only time Chirac had ever purchased treasury stock.

Required

1. Chirac sold 5,000 of the shares for $14 per share. Prepare the journal entry.
2. Chirac sold the remaining 5,000 shares later for $11 per share. Prepare the journal entry.
3. Repeat requirement 2, assuming the shares were sold for $8 instead of $11 per share.
4. Did you record gains or losses in requirements 1, 2, and 3? Explain.

11-59 Effects of Treasury Stock on Retained Income

Assume that Ming Company has retained income of $10 million, paid-in capital of $25 million, and cost of treasury stock of $7 million.

Required

1. Tabulate the effects of dividend payments of (a) $5 million and (b) $2 million on retained income and total stockholders' equity.
2. Why do states forbid the payment of dividends if retained income does not exceed the cost of any treasury stock on hand? Explain, using the numbers from your answer to requirement 1.

11-60 Treasury Stock

(Alternate is 11-53.)

Capetown Company has the following (in rands, the South African unit of currency):

Common stock, 2,000,000 shares @ R3 par					R 6,000,000	
Paid-in capital in excess of par					34,000,000	
Total paid-in capital					R40,000,000	
Retained income					18,000,000	
Stockholders' equity					R58,000,000	
Overall market value of stock @ assumed R35					R70,000,000	

Book value per share = R58,000,000 ÷ 2,000,000 = R29.

Required

1. The company used cash to reacquire 200,000 shares for R40 each and held them in the treasury. Prepare the stockholders' equity section after the acquisition of treasury stock. Also prepare the journal entry.

2. Suppose that all the treasury stock is sold for R50 per share. Prepare the journal entry.

3. Suppose that all the treasury stock is sold for R30 per share. Prepare the journal entry.

4. Recalculate book value after each transaction above.

11-61   Treasury Stock

The following information was provided in footnote 7 of the 1997 H. J. Heinz annual report.

7. Shareholders' Equity

	Cumulative Preferred Stock	Common Stock					Additional Capital
	$1.70 First Series $10 Par	Issued		In Treasury			
(in thousands)	Amount	Amount	Shares	Amount	Shares		Amount
Balance May 1, 1996	$271	$107,774	431,096	$ 1,500,866	62,498		$ 154,602
Reacquired	—	—	—	277,046	7,939		—
Conversion of preferred into common stock	(30)	—	—	(963)	(41)		(933)
Stock options exercised	—	—	—	(147,071)	(6,466)		21,946
Other, net	—	—	—	(377)	(18)		196
Balance April 30, 1997	$241	$107,774	431,096	$ 1,629,501	63,912		$175,811
Authorized Shares— April 30, 1997	24		600,000				

Capital Stock: The preferred stock outstanding is convertible at a rate of one share of preferred stock into 13.5 shares of common stock. The company can redeem the preferred stock at $28.50 per share.

Required

Provide summary journal entries to account for the treasury stock transactions during the period May 1, 1996, to April 30, 1997. Omit the journal entry for "Other, net."

11-62   Convertible Securities

Suppose Boston Company had paid $300,000 to Hartford Company for an investment in 10,000 shares of the $5 par value preferred stock of Hartford Company. The preferred stock was later converted into 10,000 shares of Hartford Company common stock ($1 par value).

Required

1. Using the balance sheet equation, prepare an analysis of transactions of Boston Company and Hartford Company.

2. Prepare the journal entries to accompany your analysis in requirement 1.

11-63 Issue of Common Shares

Intermec Corporation, a leader in the field of bar code data collection, issued the following common shares during a recent year:

a. 780,000 shares through a public offering for net cash of $10,765,977, an average price of $13.80 per share.

b. 16,900 shares as part of an employee stock purchase plan; $218,093, or $12.90 per share, was received.

c. 88,283 shares for the exercise of stock options; $355,275, or $4.02 per share, was received.

The stockholders' equity section of Intermec's balance sheet at the beginning of the year was the following:

Common stock: authorized 10,000,000 shares with	
$.60 par value, issued and outstanding 4,510,908 shares	$2,706,545
Additional paid-in capital	4,603,092
Retained earnings	8,128,230
Total stockholders' equity	$15,437,867

Net income for the year was $4,008,991. No dividends were paid.

Required

1. Prepare journal entries for the common stock issues in *a*, *b*, and *c*. Omit explanations.
2. Present the stockholders' equity section of the balance sheet at the end of the year.

11-64 Non-Cash Exchanges

Suppose Cartier Company acquires some equipment from Marseilles Company in exchange for issuance of 10,000 shares of Cartier's common stock. The equipment was carried on Marseilles's books at the FF520,000 original cost less accumulated depreciation of FF140,000. Cartier's stock is listed on the Paris Stock Exchange; its current market value is FF50 per share. Its par value is FF1 per share.

Required

1. Using the balance sheet equation, show the effects of the transaction on the accounts of Cartier Company and Marseilles Company.
2. Show the journal entries on the books of Cartier Company and Marseilles Company.

11-65 Covenants and Leases

Mitchell Energy and Development Corp. is one of the country's largest oil and gas producers. The notes to its 1997 financial statements reveal the existence of certain debt agreement restrictions on the level of consolidated stockholders' equity as well as on various asset-to-debt ratios:

> The bank credit agreements contain certain restrictions which, among other things, require consolidated stockholders' equity to be equal to at least $300,000,000 and require the maintenance of specified financial and oil and gas reserve and/or asset value to debt ratios.

Required

1. Given the existence of the asset-to-debt covenants, is Mitchell more likely to be able to enter into operating leases or capital leases without violating the covenants?
2. If Mitchell Energy and Development, Inc., had refused to agree to these conditions at the time of the debt issues, how would it have affected the market price of the debt they issued?

11-66 Financial Ratios

Consider the following data from two companies in very different industries. Adobe Systems is a software company that produces PageMaker, among other products. Northern

States Power is an electric utility based in Minneapolis. Neither company has preferred stock. (Amounts except earnings per share and market price are in thousands.)

	Total Assets	Total Liabilities	Net Income	Earnings per Share	Market Price per Share
Adobe Systems	$1,012,285	$305,771	$153,277	$2.04	$40
Northern States Power	6,636,900	2,667,983	231,111	3.82	47

Required

1. Compute the market-to-book ratio and the rate of return on stockholders' equity for both Adobe Systems and Northern States Power.

2. Explain what might cause the differences in these ratios between the two companies.

11-67 Shareholders' Equity Section

Enron Corp. is a worldwide energy company with annual revenues in excess of $13 billion. Its main activities are in natural gas and electricity. The following data are from the company's 1996 annual report (in millions):

For the year ended December 31	1996	1995
Additional paid-in capital	1,870	1,791
Common stock held in treasury, 821,155 shares and 2,618,034 shares, respectively	(30)	(93)
Common stock, $0.10 par value, 600,000,000 shares authorized, 255,945,304 shares and 253,860,360 shares issued, respectively	26	25
Retained earnings	2,007	1,651
Preferred stock, cumulative, $1 par value, 5,000,000 shares authorized, 1,370,714 shares and 1,375,494 shares issued, respectively	137	138

Required

1. Prepare Enron's shareholders' equity section of the 1996 balance sheet. Include the amount for total stockholders' equity.

2. Enron paid $212 million of cash dividends on common stock and $16 million of cash dividends on preferred stock in 1996. Compute Enron's net income for 1996.

3. Explain Enron's net acquisition or disposition on treasury shares during 1996. Include the increase or decrease in total number of shares and the average price per share of those acquired or sold. What is the average purchase price of the shares remaining in the treasury at the end of 1996?

11-68 International Perspective

Honda Motor Company provides the following information in its 1997 annual report:

	Yen (millions)					
	Common Stock	Capital Surplus	Legal Reserve	Retained Earnings	Other	Total Stockholders' Equity
Balance at March 31, 1996	¥86,020	¥171,910	¥25,125	¥1,243,759	(¥382,274)	¥1,144,540
Net income for the year				221,168		221,168
Cash dividends ¥14 per share (note 11)				(13,640)		(13,640)
Transfer to legal reserve (note 11)			543	(543)		—
Conversion of convertible debt (note 10)	8	—				8
Adjustments for the year					36,354	36,354
Balance at March 31, 1997	¥86,028	¥171,910	¥25,668	¥1,450,744	(¥345,920)	¥1,388,430

ASSIGNMENT MATERIAL   **487**

(10) Common Stock

During the years ended March 31, 1995, 1996, and 1997, the Company issued approximately 462 thousand, 129 thousand, and 19 thousand shares, respectively, of common stock in connection with the conversion of convertible debt. Conversions of convertible debt issued subsequent to October 1, 1982, into common stock and exercise of warrants were accounted for in accordance with the provisions of the Japanese Commercial Code by crediting one-half of the aggregate conversion price equally to the common stock account and the capital surplus account.

(11) Dividends and Legal Reserve

The Japanese Commercial Code provides that earnings in an amount equal to at least 10% of all appropriations of retained earnings that are paid in cash, such as cash dividends and bonuses to directors, shall be appropriated as a legal reserve until such reserve equals 25% of stated capital. This reserve is not available for dividends but may be used to reduce a deficit or may be transferred to stated capital. Certain foreign subsidiaries are also required to appropriate their earnings to legal reserves under laws of the respective countries of domicile.

Cash dividends and appropriations to the legal reserve charged to retained earnings during the years ended March 31, 1995, 1996, and 1997, represent dividends paid out during those years and the related appropriations to the legal reserve. The accompanying consolidated financial statements do not include any provision for the dividend of ¥8 per share aggregating ¥7,794 million to be proposed in June 1997. As at March 31, 1997, the legal reserve of Honda Motor Co., Ltd. equals 25% of stated capital.

Required

1. Give journal entries to record the items shown for fiscal 1997. Omit the item listed under "other".

2. Suppose Honda's legal reserve was still below 25% of stated capital. Give the journal entry that Honda would make for the proposed dividend and transfer to the reserve in June 1997. Assume the transfer is 10% of the dividends.

11-69 Stock Options and Ethics

Bristol-Myers Squibb is the third largest pharmaceutical company in the world. In 1996, the company granted executives options to purchase 16,179,560 shares of common stock. Suppose that all shares were granted with an exercise price of $47 per share, which was the market price of the stock on the date the options were granted, and that all options could be exercised anytime between 3 and 5 years from the grant date, provided that the executive still works for Bristol-Myers Squibb.

Assume that, at the same time the stock options were issued, Bristol-Myers Squibb also issued warrants with the same $47 exercise price that are exercisable any time in the next five years. The company received $5 for each such warrant.

Required

1. How much expense was recorded at the issue of each stock option?
2. How much value was there to the executive for each stock option issued?
3. How much did it cost the firm for each stock option that was issued?
4. Might the fact that an executive holds stock options affect his or her decisions about declaring dividends? Comment on the ethics of this influence.

11-70 The Gap Annual Report

Use The Gap's financial statements and notes contained in Appendix A to answer the following questions.

Required

1. Prepare the journal entry to record dividends declared in the year ended February 1, 1997.

2. Give the journal entry The Gap used to record the purchase of treasury stock in the year ended February 1, 1997. Do the same for the reissuance of treasury stock.

3. What was the average price per share of treasury stock purchased in the year ended February 1, 1997?

11-71 Financial Statement Research

Select a company and use its financial statements to answer the following question.

Identify each transaction that affected Stockholders' Equity during the most recent two years. Indicate which accounts were affected and by how much. List any transactions that appear unusual. For example, many companies have a change in shareholders' equity that arises from tax benefits related to stock options. This and a few other common transactions are beyond our scope in this introductory course.

COLLABORATIVE LEARNING EXERCISE

11-72 Price to Book and ROE

Form groups of three to six students each. Each student should pick two companies, preferably from different industries. Find the appropriate data and compute the market-to-book ratio and the rate of return on stockholders' equity (ROE) for each company.

Assemble the group and list the companies selected, together with their market-to-book ratio and ROE. Rank the companies from highest to lowest on price to book ratio. Then rank them on ROE.

Explain why companies rank as they do in each list. Are the rankings similar; that is, is the ranking based on market-to-book similar to the rankings on ROE? Explain why you would or would not expect similarity in the rankings.

11-73 Internet Case

Go to **http://www.us.dell.com/** to find Dell Computer Corporation's home page. Select *Company Information* under *Corporate and Careers*. Then select *Investor Information*. You will find a menu from which the current period annual report can be selected. Dell Computer Corporation was established in 1984 and today ranks among the world's largest computer systems companies.

Using the Dell Computer Corporation annual report and especially the stockholders' equity section of its balance sheet:

1. Identify the classes of stock that Dell has authorized at the end of its most recent fiscal period. What rights do the common shareholders have? (Note: *Be sure to read the Notes to the Consolidated Financial Statements.*)

2. What is the cause of the change in the *Common Stock* account during the period?

3. How many *additional* shares of common stock is Dell able to issue as of its most recent balance sheet date? Does Dell have any treasury stock?

4. Did Dell declare any stock splits or stock dividends during its most recent two year comparative reporting period? If so, what effect did these have on the number of shares of stock *outstanding?* Why do you think that Dell would want to declare a stock dividend or split?

5. Dell reports the entire issue price of its stock in one account in the stockholders' equity section of the balance sheet. How much would the company have reported in its Common Stock account if two separate accounts, both Common Stock and Additional Paid-in Capital, had been used? Why do you think Dell combines these amounts on its balance sheet?

6. During fiscal 1997, the Board of Directors authorized a common stock repurchase program. Why did Dell repurchase this stock? What happened to the stock once it was repurchased?

7. Why is the number of shares of outstanding stock at Dell's most recent balance sheet date not the same as the number of shares used in computing earnings per share?

12

INTERCORPORATE INVESTMENTS AND CONSOLIDATIONS

This GM vehicle, the Denali, is photographed in front of Mt. McKinley in Alaska, which is called Denali by Alaskans. The Denali, like any GM nameplate, can be financed with a loan from GMAC (General Motors Acceptance Corporation).

Learning Objectives

After studying this chapter, you should be able to

1 Account for short-term investments in debt securities and equity securities.

2 Report long-term investments in bonds.

3 Contrast the equity and market methods of accounting for investments.

4 Prepare consolidated financial statements.

5 Incorporate minority interests into consolidated financial statements.

6 Explain the economic and reporting role of goodwill.

7 Contrast the purchase method and the pooling-of-interests method of accounting for business combinations (Appendix 12).

Deciding to buy and finance a new car is one of the most important decisions you can make as a consumer. If you have gone through this process, you realize that automakers sell financing (auto loans) as well as automobiles. Wherever you buy a GM car you can also "buy" your financing through a fully owned subsidiary, General Motors Acceptance Corporation (GMAC). Just what is the relationship between General Motors and GMAC? They are separate entities, each with its own financial records. However, they are so closely related that authorities require them to combine financial records when preparing financial statements for the public.

Pick up the annual report of almost any major company (and even most middle-size companies) and you will find "consolidated financial statements." This term means that the books of two or more separate legal entities have been combined into the statements presented. General Motors describes its statements as follows: "The consolidated financial statements include the accounts of General Motors Corporation and domestic and foreign subsidiaries that are more than 50% owned, principally General Motors Acceptance Corporation (GMAC) and Hughes Electronics Corporation."

The process of consolidating financial statements used to be an accountant's nightmare. It took days and sometimes nights for many accountants. The consolidated statements filled pages and pages of 13-column paper spreadsheets. Today, thanks to computers and sophisticated software packages, some companies consolidate statements in hours. General Motors takes three days, but the combining of statements is really completed after the first day. The next two days are spent analyzing worldwide results for possible errors and ensuring an explanation for any deviations from the expected.

You probably know that the Ford Motor Company makes many models of cars and trucks under various Ford nameplates around the world. You may not know that Ford owns Jaguar, the prestigious British luxury car manufacturer. You also may not know that Ford owns 33% of Mazda, the popular Japanese auto manufacturer. In fact, the Ford Probe is assembled by Mazda at its Michigan plant.

Examples throughout the chapter stress the fact that investments in securities arise from many different motives. The accounting for such investments differs depending on the purpose of the investment, on whether the investment is an equity or debt security, and on the degree of control the investor has over the issuer of the security.

AN OVERVIEW OF CORPORATE INVESTMENTS

As noted previously, when a firm has an excess of cash, smart managers should invest the cash rather than let it remain idle in the company's checking account. Just as it makes sense for individuals to invest their extra money, it makes sense for a corporation to earn interest income on investments from temporarily idle cash. These investments can take on many different forms.

In many instances, companies invest in both short-term and long-term debt securities issued by governments, banks, or other corporations. For example, Ford classified $11.8 billion of marketable securities as current assets on its balance sheet and also owned $2.3 billion in debt securities classified as noncurrent investments by its Financial Services subsidiary at December 31, 1996.

In addition to debt securities, companies also invest in other corporations' equity securities. These investments are typically long-term investments, and when they are large enough, they allow the investing company varying degrees of control over the company issuing the securities. Such investments are common and arise from various motivations. Ford bought Jaguar in 1989 for approximately $2.5 billion after a fierce competition with General Motors (GM). GM already owned Lotus, and Chrysler acquired Lamborghini, so Ford was determined to acquire its own European luxury car maker. These major U.S. auto companies were all committed to a strategy that required a full range of automobile offerings, including a luxury nameplate. Ford's motives in acquiring 33% of Mazda were different. Ford does not control Mazda the way it does Jaguar. Rather, the two companies function as partners who share various production efficiencies and technical know-how.

CORPORATE MARRIAGE AND DIVORCE

Corporate mergers can be a little like marriages. The challenge is to combine and retain the right combination of people and products to succeed over the long haul. Just as not all marriages work, not all business combinations work, either. What if the combination does not work? At the worst, the combined company's assets are sold off, the proceeds are distributed to creditors, and the company disappears. But less extreme possibilities exist.

Often the parent company simply sells off a distinct business unit or subsidiary company. An interesting alternative is called a spin-off, which occurs when shares in a subsidiary are distributed to the shareholders of the parent. For example, PepsiCo recently spun-off its food operations which included Pizza Hut and KFC. The spun-off subsidiary will be a completely separate entity with its own board of directors, management, assets, liabilities, and owners. Spin-offs tend to separate dissimilar business segments to create opportunities for more creative and innovative growth or to offer managers the opportunity to invest directly in the subsidiary. Historically, companies that were spun-off have performed well and investors who held the shares they received in the spin-off or who acquired the companies when they were initially available as separate firms have earned substantial profits. A recent study of 146 spin-offs over 30 years concluded that investments in shares of spun-off firms outperform the stock market by an average of 35% in their first three years as separate companies.

Because many companies have very diverse business divisions, divorce is sometimes part of the corporate marriage plan from the start. For example, when Black & Decker purchased Emhart in 1989, the plan was to sell Emhart's information services division immediately and use the cash to reduce the significant debt Black & Decker incurred to make the purchase. However, the plan took years to execute. The sale of the information services division ultimately occurred in three stages during 1995 and 1996. By then, other actions had been undertaken to deal with the debt problem.

After companies create intercorporate linkages, their accountants must develop ways to report on the financial results of these complicated entities. In 1994, Ford increased its ownership in Hertz from 49% to 100%. That change in ownership significantly altered the way Ford accounts for the relationship. In 1996, Ford increased its ownership of Mazda from 25% to 33%, but this change did not alter the fundamental accounting for the relationship. As we will see, current accounting procedures for intercorporate linkages are tied directly to the percentage of ownership, with 20% and 50% being the critical percentages.

Once the company chooses an accounting procedure that determines how a relationship will be measured, there is also a question about where it will be reported on the balance sheet. All investments are classified on a balance sheet according to purpose or intention. An investment should be carried as a current asset if it is a short-term investment. Other investments are classified as noncurrent assets and usually appear as either (1) a separate investments category between current assets and property, plant, and equipment, or (2) a part of other assets below the plant assets category.

> **Objective 1**
> Account for short-term investments in debt securities and equity securities.

SHORT-TERM INVESTMENTS

As its name implies, a **short-term investment** is a temporary investment of otherwise idle cash in marketable securities. **Marketable securities** are notes, bonds, or stocks that can be easily sold. A company's short-term investment portfolio (total of securities owned) usually consists of short-term debt securities and short-term equity securities. The investments are highly liquid (easily convertible into cash) and have stable prices.

Ordinarily, items classified as short-term investments are *expected* to be completely converted into cash within a year after the date on the balance sheet on which they appear. But some companies hold part of their portfolio of short-term investments beyond a 12-month period. Nevertheless, these investments are still classified as current assets if management intends to convert them into cash when needed. The key point is that conversion to cash is immediately available at the option of management.

Short-term debt securities consist largely of government- and business-issued notes and bonds with maturities of one year or less. They pay a fixed amount of interest, which is usually why investors purchase them. Typically, debt security investments include short-term obligations of banks, called **certificates of deposit,** and **commercial paper,** which consists of short-term notes payable issued by large corporations with top credit ratings. They also include **U.S. Treasury obligations,** which refer to interest-bearing notes, bonds, and bills issued by the federal government. All of these debt securities may be held until maturity or may be resold in securities markets.

Short-term equity securities consist of capital stock (shares of ownership) in other corporations. Companies, as well as individuals, regularly buy and sell equity securities on the New York Stock Exchange or other stock exchanges. If the investing firm intends to sell the equity securities it holds within one year or within its normal operating cycle, then the securities are considered a short-term investment.

short-term investment A temporary investment in marketable securities of otherwise idle cash.

marketable securities Any notes, bonds, or stocks that can readily be sold. The term is often used as a synonym for short-term investments.

short-term debt securities Largely notes and bonds with maturities of one year or less.

certificates of deposit Short-term obligations of banks.

commercial paper Short-term notes payable issued by large corporations with top credit ratings.

U.S. Treasury obligations
Interest-bearing notes, bonds, and bills issued by the U.S. government.

short-term equity securities
Capital stock in other corporations held with the intention to liquidate within one year as needed.

trading securities Current investments in equity or debt securities held for short-term profit.

held-to-maturity securities
Debt securities that the investor expects to hold until maturity.

At acquisition, companies record these securities at cost. How they are reported after acquisition depends on whether they are classified as *trading securities*, *available-for-sale securities*, or *held-to-maturity securities*. You can see these three categories in the footnote to Ford's 1996 financial statements shown in Exhibit 12-1.

Trading securities are short-term investments, including both debt and equity securities, that the company buys with the intent to resell them shortly. Companies list such securities among current assets on their balance sheets and measure them at market value (or fair value). As shown in Exhibit 12-1, $412 million of Ford's short-term investments in its Financial Services operations are trading securities.

Held-to-maturity securities are debt securities that the company purchases with the intent to hold them until they mature. They are shown on the balance sheet at amortized cost, not market value. In Chapter 10, we examined the amortization of premiums and discounts on bonds payable by the issuer of the debt. Corporations that *invest* in bonds use the same approach, as illustrated later in this chapter. Unlike trading securities, which are always classified as short-term because of the owner's intention, held-to-maturity securities are classified according to the time remaining until they mature. If the time to maturity is less than one year, they are short-term investments, and thus current assets. Otherwise, they are long-term investments, and thus noncurrent assets. Only $22 million of Ford's Financial Services investments are held-to-maturity securities. Notice that the fair value of these securities is the same as the amortized cost. This would not normally be true, and the amount reported on the balance sheet (the book value) is always the amortized cost.

Exhibit 12-1

Ford Motor Company 1996 Marketable Securities Footnote

Financial Services
Investments in securities at December 31, 1996 (in millions)

	Amortized Cost	Gross Unrealized Gains	Gross Unrealized Losses	Fair Value	Memo: Book Value
Trading securities	$410	$3	$1	$412	$412
Available-for-sale securities					
Debt securities issued by the U.S. government and agencies	429	6	2	433	433
Municipal securities	14	—	—	14	14
Debt securities issued by foreign governments	42	1	—	43	43
Corporate securities	505	3	5	503	503
Mortgage-backed securities	682	3	5	680	680
Other debt securities	2	—	—	2	2
Equity securities	107	89	3	193	193
Total available-for-sale securities	1,781	102	15	1,868	1,868
Held-to-maturity securities					
Debt securities issued by the U.S. government and agencies	9	—	—	9	9
Corporate securities	13	—	—	13	13
Total held-to-maturity securities	22	—	—	22	22
Total investments in securities with readily determinable fair value	2,213	$105	$16	$2,302	2,302
Equity securities not practicable to fair value	5				5
Total investments in securities	$2,218				$2,307

Available-for-sale securities include all debt and equity securities that are neither trading securities nor held-to-maturity securities. They include equity securities that the company does not intend to sell in the near future and debt securities that the company neither plans to sell shortly nor hold to maturity. Ford provides separate lines under this category for many different types of securities held by its Financial Services operations. Note that most are debt securities of one type or another issued by the U.S. treasury, municipalities, foreign governments, or corporations. The amount reported on the balance sheet is the market value of $1,868 million, which is $87 million greater than the original cost of these securities.

Note that Ford also has $5 million of equity securities that could not be valued at fair value. These might be shares in a company that is not publicly traded, for example. These are not classified as trading, held-to-maturity, or available-for-sale securities.

The total investments by the Financial Services operations of Ford, the amount shown on Ford's balance sheet, is the $2,307 million shown at the bottom of the far right-hand column of Exhibit 12-1. It is the market value of trading securities and available-for-sale securities and the amortized cost of the held-to-maturity securities.

CHANGES IN MARKET PRICES OF SECURITIES

You now know how short-term investments are shown on the balance sheet. But how do we account for the returns on these investments?

Held-to-maturity investments are easiest to account for because interest revenue is the only return received on such securities. Changes in market value are ignored. Interest revenue appears directly on the income statement, increasing income and therefore increasing stockholders' equity.

Returns on trading securities and available-for-sale securities come in two forms: 1) dividend or interest revenue, and 2) changes in market value. The former are recorded on the income statement when earned for all securities. However, we account for changes in market value differently for trading securities than for available-for-sale securities.

As the market value of trading securities changes, companies report the gains from increases in price and losses from decreases in price in the income statement. In contrast, the gains and losses that arise as market values of available-for-sale securities rise and fall are not shown on the income statement. Instead, we add such unrealized gains and losses to a separate valuation allowance account in the stockholders' equity section of the balance sheet. This account increases stockholders' equity for securities whose price has increased since purchase. It decreases stockholders' equity for securities that have experienced a drop in prices. Ford shows $15 million of unrealized losses and $102 million of unrealized gains on available-for-sale securities, for a net increase in stockholders' equity of $87 million.

Notice that increases in prices of both trading securities and available-for-sale securities increase stockholders' equity, and decreases in prices decrease stockholders' equity. For trading securities, the increase or decrease is part of retained earnings because the gains and losses are included in net income. For available-for-sale securities, the increase or decrease is in a separate valuation account included in owners' equity.

We call this method of accounting for trading securities and available-for-sale securities the market method. Under the **market method,** the reported assets values in the balance sheet are the market values of the publicly traded securities. Suppose two companies acquire identical assets at the same price on the same day, but one company reported them as trading securities and the other reported them as available-for-sale securities. The two companies would report identical asset values on their balance sheets, but they would differ in how they report changes in those market values. Assume that the portfolio of assets purchased by the two companies cost $50 million and had the market values at the end of four subsequent periods shown in Exhibit 12-2 (in millions).

available-for-sale securities Investments in equity or debt securities that are not held for active trading but may be sold before maturity.

market method Method of accounting for trading securities changes affect the income statement; for available-for-sale securities a valuation allowance appears in owners' equity.

Exhibit 12-2

Financial Statement Presentation

Trading Securities and Available-for-Sale Securities

	End of Period			
	1	*2*	*3*	*4*
Assumed market value	50	45	47	54
Balance Sheet Presentation				
Short-term investment at cost	50	50	50	50
Valuation adjustment to market	0	(5)	(3)	4
Carrying value	50	45	47	54
For Trading securities:				
Income Statement Presentation				
Unrealized gain (loss) on changes in market	0	(5)	2	7
For Available-for-Sale-Securities:				
Additional Balance Sheet Presentation				
Valuation Allowance in Stockholders' Equity	0	(5)	(3)	4

Exhibit 12-2 shows the results for four periods. Most companies will present the market value directly as a single line on the balance sheet. The valuation adjustment provides a linkage to cost and shows that the valuation allowance in stockholders' equity for available-for-sale securities will have a balance equal to the difference between historical cost and market.

The unrealized gain (loss) for trading securities affects net income and therefore also increases (decreases) retained income. Over the four periods, the loss of $5 million and gains of $2 million and $7 million provide a net increase in retained income of $4 million ($9 million of gains less $5 million of losses).

The journal entries for the two classes of securities for periods 2, 3, and 4 would appear as follows, without explanations:

PERIOD	TRADING SECURITIES			AVAILABLE-FOR-SALE SECURITIES		
2	Unrealized loss	5		Valuation Allowance	5	
	Marketable Securities		5	Marketable Securities		5
3	Marketable Securities	2		Marketable Securities	2	
	Unrealized gain		2	Valuation Allowance		2
4	Marketable Securities	7		Marketable Securities	7	
	Unrealized gain		7	Valuation Allowance		7

LONG-TERM INVESTMENTS IN BONDS

Objective 2
Report long-term investments in bonds.

Chapter 10 explained the basic approach issuing firms use to account for bonds payable. Recall that the issuer amortizes bond discounts and premiums as periodic adjustments of interest expense. Investing firms use a similar method to account for bonds held to maturity. However, although the issuer typically keeps a separate account for unamortized discounts and premiums, investors do not (although they could if desired).

BONDS-HELD-TO-MATURITY

Exhibit 12-3 should look familiar to you. It is the same as Exhibit 9-5 except that because our perspective has changed from issuer to that of investor, the phrase net liability has been changed to book value. Recall that *book value* is a general term referring to the amount reported in financial statements under generally accepted accounting principles.

Exhibit 12-3 shows the values for 10,000 two-year bonds paying interest semiannually with a face value of $1,000 each and a 10% coupon rate (5% interest every six months).

Exhibit 12-3

Effective-Interest Amortization of Bond Discount

For Six Months Ended	(1) Beginning Book Value	(2) Effective Interest @ 6%*	(3) Nominal Interest @ 5%	(4) Discount Amortized (2) − (3)	Ending Book Value		
					Face Amount	*Unamortized Discount*	*Ending Book Value*
12/31/97	—	—	—	—	$10,000,000	$346,500	$ 9,653,500
6/30/98	$9,653,500	$579,207	$500,000	$79,207	10,000,000	267,293†	9,732,707
12/31/98	9,732,707	583,959	500,000	83,959	10,000,000	183,334†	9,816,666
6/30/99	9,816,666	588,997	500,000	88,997	10,000,000	94,337	9,905,663
12/31/99	9,905,663	594,337	500,000	94,337	10,000,000	0	10,000,000

*To avoid rounding errors, an unrounded actual effective rate slightly under 6% was used.
†$346,500 − $79,207 = $267,293; $267,293 − $83,959 = $183,334; etc.

The bonds were issued to yield 12%. Because they pay only a 10% coupon interest rate, they are sold at a discount. Therefore, despite the face value of $10,000,000, an investor acquiring the whole issue would initially pay only $9,653,500. Interest (rental payment for the $9,653,500) will take two forms—four semiannual cash receipts of $500,000 (5% × $10,000,000), plus an extra lump-sum receipt of $346,500 ($10 million face value less amount paid at issue) at maturity.

The extra $346,500 to be paid at maturity (the amount of the discount) relates to the use of the proceeds over the two years. Therefore, like the issuer, the investor amortizes the discount:

	6/30/98	12/31/98	6/30/99	12/31/99
Semiannual interest revenue:				
Cash interest payments, .05 × $10 million	$500,000	$500,000	$500,000	$500,000
Amortization of $346,500 discount*	79,207	83,959	88,997	94,337
Semiannual revenue	$579,207	$583,959	$588,997	$594,337

*For the amortization schedule, see column 4 of Exhibit 12-3. Note that $79,207 + $83,959 + $88,997 + $94,337 = $346,500.

As the preceding table shows, the discount is used to make up the difference between the stated interest rate of 12% and the actual interest rate of 10%. Amortization of a discount increases the interest revenue of investors. (Investor accounting for bonds issued at a premium is similar except that amortization of premium decreases the interest revenue of investors.)

Exhibit 12-4 shows how the investor and the issuer account for the bonds throughout the bonds' lives. Note that interest revenue and interest expense are identical in each period.

EARLY EXTINGUISHMENT OF INVESTMENT

Suppose in our example that the issuer buys back all of its bonds on the open market for $9.6 million on December 31, 1998 (after all interest payments and amortization were recorded for 1998). The investor's loss is calculated in panel A of Exhibit 12-5. The journal entries for the investor and the issuer are shown in panel B.

Recall that this same extinguishment of debt was initially analyzed from the issuer's viewpoint in Chapter 9. Note that for the issuer to extinguish the bonds early, the bond must either grant the issuer the right to repay the debt early or the investor must choose to sell the bonds back to the issuer.

Exhibit 12-4

Accounting for Bonds

		INVESTOR'S RECORDS					ISSUER'S RECORDS		
12/31/97	1.	Investment in bonds	9,653,500		1.	Cash	9,653,500	
		Cash		9,653,500		Discount on bonds payable	346,500	
						Bonds payable		10,000,000
6/30/98	2.	Cash	500,000		2.	Interest expense	579,207	
		Investment in bonds	79,207			Discount on bonds payable . . .		79,207
		Interest revenue		579,207		Cash		500,000
12/31/98		Cash	500,000			Interest expense	583,959	
		Investment in bonds	83,959			Discount on bonds payable . . .		83,959
		Interest revenue		583,959		Cash		500,000
6/30/99		Cash	500,000			Interest expense	588,997	
		Investment in bonds	88,997			Discount on bonds payable . . .		88,997
		Interest revenue		588,997		Cash		500,000
12/31/99		Cash	500,000			Interest expense	594,337	
		Investment in bonds	94,337			Discount on bonds payable . . .		94,337
		Interest revenue		594,337		Cash		500,000
12/31/99	3.	Cash	10,000,000		3.	Bonds payable	10,000,000	
		Investment in bonds .		10,000,000		Cash		10,000,000

Exhibit 12-5

Early Extinguishment

Panel A Investor's Loss

Carrying amount:			
Face or par value		$10,000,000	
Deduct: Unamortized discount on bonds*		183,334	$9,816,666
Cash received			9,600,000
Difference, loss on sale			$ 216,666

*The remaining discount is $88,997 + $94,337 = $183,334, or $346,500 − $79,207 − $83,959 = $183,334.

Panel B Journal Entries at December 31, 1998

INVESTOR'S RECORDS			ISSUER'S RECORDS		
Cash	9,600,000		Bonds payable	10,000,000	
Loss on disposal of bonds	216,666		Discount on bonds payable .		183,334
Investment in bonds . . .		9,816,666	Gain on early		
To record the sale of bonds			extinguishment		216,666
on the open market.			Cash		9,600,000

THE MARKET AND EQUITY METHODS FOR INTERCORPORATE INVESTMENTS

Objective 3
Contrast the equity and market methods of accounting for investments.

Equity securities are popular long-term investments in many companies, mainly because of the influence that can come with them. The accounting for equity securities from the issuer's point of view was discussed in Chapter 11. The investor's accounting depends on the relationship between the "investor" and the "investee." The question is: How much can the investor influence the operations of the investee? For example, the holder of a small number of shares in a company's stock cannot affect how the company invests its money, conducts its business, or declares and pays its dividends. He or she (or "it" in the case of a corporate investor) is thus known as a passive investor. Such investors use the market method, under which the investment is carried at market value and dividends are recorded as income when received.

As an investor acquires more substantial holdings of a company's stock, that investor's ability to influence the company changes. A stockholder with 2% or 3% ownership of a company will have little difficulty making appointments to speak with company management. At 5% ownership, U.S. law requires the investor to report the ownership publicly in a filing with the SEC. As ownership interest rises to 20% and beyond, the investor begins to be able to affect decisions, to appoint directors, and so on.

Once the investor has "significant influence," a term that GAAP defines as about 20% to 25% ownership, the market method no longer reflects the economic relationship between the potentially active investor and the investee (or **affiliated company**). In the United States, such an investor must use the **equity method,** which records the investment at acquisition cost and makes adjustments for the investor's share of dividends and earnings or losses experienced by the investee after the date of investment. As a result, the book value at which the investment is carried and reported is increased by the investor's share of the investee's earnings. This carrying amount is reduced by dividends received from the investee and by the investor's share of the investee's losses.

Many companies have "significant influence" stock ownership in other, usually smaller, companies. For example, Corning Inc., a technology company that is the world's leader in fiberoptic cable, holds such ownership in several companies. One such company is Samcor Glass Limited, in India in which Corning Inc. recently held a 45% interest.

Let's take a look at an example of how the market and equity methods might be applied. Suppose Buyit Corporation invests $80 million in each of two companies, Passiveco and Influential. Influential has a total market value of $200 million, generates earnings of $30 million, and pays dividends of $10 million. Because of its $80 million investment, Buyit owns 40% ($80 million ÷ $200 million) of Influential and must account for that investment using the equity method. Passiveco, however, has a total market value of $800 million, generates earnings of $120 million, and pays dividends of $40 million. Buyit thus owns only 10% ($80 million ÷ $800 million) of Passiveco and must use the market method to account for this investment.

To compare the methods, consider how Buyit is affected differently by investee earnings and dividends, as shown in Exhibit 12-6. Panel A shows the effects on the balance sheet equation and Panel B shows the different journal entries for the two cases. The example assumes that the market values of Passiveco and Influential do not change during the period.

Under the market method, Buyit recognizes income when dividends are received. While the income statement and retained earnings are affected, Buyit's investment account is unaffected by the event. Under the equity method, Buyit recognizes income as it is earned by Influential rather than when dividends are received. Cash dividends from Influential do not affect net income; they increase Cash and decrease the Investment balance. In a sense, Buyit's claim on Influential grows by its share of Influential's net income. The dividend is a partial liquidation of Buyit's "claim." The receipt of a dividend is similar to the collection of an account receivable. The revenue from a sale of merchandise on account is recognized when the receivable is created; to include the collection also as revenue would be double-counting. Similarly, it would be double-counting to include the $4 million of dividends as income after the $12 million of income is already recognized in Buyit's income statement as it is earned.

The major reason for using the equity method instead of the market method is that the equity method does a better job of recognizing increases or decreases in the economic resources that the investor can influence. The reported net income of an "equity" investor (an investor that owns more than 20% of a company and thus uses the equity method) is increased by its share of net income or decreased by its share of net loss recognized by the investee.

affiliated company A company that has 20% to 50% of its voting shares owned by another company.

equity method Accounting for an investment at acquisition cost, adjusted for the investor's share of dividends and earnings or losses of the investee subsequent to the date of investment.

Exhibit 12-6

Comparing Market and Equity Methods

Panel A Effects on the Balance Sheet Equation

	Market Method—Passiveco					Equity Method—Influential				
	A		=	L + SE		A		=	L + SE	
	Cash	Investments		Liab.	SE	Cash	Investments		Liab.	SE
1. Acquisition	−80	+80	=			−80	+80	=		
2. a. Net income of Passiveco	No entry and no effect									
b. Net income of Influential							+12	=		+12
3. a. Dividends from Passiveco	+ 4		=		+4					
b. Dividends from Influential						+ 4	− 4	=		
Effects for year	−76	+80	=		+4	−76	+88	=		+12

Passiveco: Under the market method, the investment account is unaffected. The dividend increases the cash amount by $4 million. Dividend revenue increases stockholders' equity by $4 million.

Influential: Under the equity method, the investment account has a net increase of $8 million for the year. The dividend increases the cash account by $4 million and reduces investments. Investment revenue increases stockholders' equity by $12 million.

Panel B Journal Entries

Cost Method—Passiveco			Equity Method—Influential		
1. Investment in Passiveco	80		1. Investment in Influential	80	
Cash		80	Cash		80
2. No entry			2. Investment in Influential	12	
			Investment revenue*		12
3. Cash	4		3. Cash	4	
Dividend revenue†		4	Investment in Influential		4

*Frequently called "equity in earnings of affiliated companies."
†Frequently called "dividend income."

CONSOLIDATED FINANCIAL STATEMENTS

Objective 4
Prepare consolidated financial statements.

parent company A company owning more than 50% of the voting shares of another company, called the subsidiary company.

subsidiary A corporation owned or controlled by a parent company through the ownership of more than 50% of the voting stock.

So far we have dealt with partial ownership of one company by another. Sometimes, though, as in the case of Ford and Jaguar, one company will simply buy 100% of another company. In other cases, one company will buy a majority (over 50%) share of a second company and effectively take control of that second company. In these cases, a parent-subsidiary relationship exists. The **parent company** is the owner, and the **subsidiary** is the "owned" company that is fully owned or controlled by the parent. Keep in mind that subsidiaries are not folded into the parent company but instead remain separate legal entities from their parents. One parent can have numerous subsidiaries. Ford Motor Company actually has 60 different subsidiaries just in the United States, as well as several others, including Jaguar, outside the United States.

Why have subsidiaries? Why not integrate the smaller companies into the larger parent to create a single legal entity? The reasons include limiting the liabilities in a risky venture, saving income taxes, conforming with government regulations with respect to a part of the business, doing business in a foreign country, and expanding in an orderly way. For example, there are often tax advantages in acquiring the capital stock of a going concern rather than its individual assets.

So how do we account for subsidiaries if they are their own legal entities? We must start by accounting for them separately. Each subsidiary has its own set of financial statements that are independent of the parent's statements. Of course, the financial performance of a subsidiary affects the financial performance of the parent. Therefore, anyone who owns stock in a parent company needs to know how the subsidiaries are doing. If you own stock in Ford, you probably do not want to read over 60 sets of financial statements just to find out the overall value of your stock. **Consolidated statements** solve this problem by combining the financial positions and earnings reports of the parent company with those of its subsidiaries into an overall report as *if* they were a single entity.

Consolidated statements have been common in the United States since the turn of the century, when interconnected corporate entities first began to appear in the form of "holding companies," a parent with many subsidiaries. J. P. Morgan's U.S. Steel, formed in 1901, is a classic example. As this economic form spread to Great Britain and the Netherlands, so also did consolidated accounting begin to spread. However, all countries did not embrace it. As recently as 1977, consolidated accounts were rare in Japan. In 1977, the law was changed, and now both "parent-only" and consolidated statements are publicly available although the consolidated statements are generally released later. Some countries in Europe, for example Switzerland, have been slow to adopt consolidation, but in 1992, the Seventh Company Law Directive required full implementation of consolidation by members of the European Union. Similarly, the International Accounting Standards Committee has encouraged this trend since 1976.

consolidated statements
Combinations of the financial positions and earnings reports of the parent company with those of various subsidiaries into an overall report as if they were a single entity.

THE ACQUISITION

To illustrate the concept of consolidated financial statements, consider two companies: the parent (P) and a subsidiary (S). Initially, they are separate companies with assets of $650 million and $400 million, respectively. P acquires all of the stock of S by purchasing the shares from their current owners for $213 million paid in cash. The transaction is illustrated in Panel A of Exhibit 12-7. Exhibit 12-7 shows the balance sheets of the two companies before and after this transaction in Panel B. Panel C shows the journal entries for the acquisition. Figures in this and subsequent tables are in millions.

This purchase transaction is a simple exchange of one asset for another, from P's perspective. In terms of the balance sheet equation, cash declines by $213 million, and the asset account, Investment in S, increases by the same amount. The subsidiary S is entirely unaffected from an accounting standpoint, although it now has one centralized owner with unquestionable control over all economic decisions S may make in the future. In this example, the purchase price and the "Investment in S" equal the stockholders' equity of the acquired company. Note that the $213 million purchase price is paid to the former owners of S as private investors. The $213 million is not an addition to the existing assets and stockholders' equity of S. That is, the books of S are unaffected by P's investment and P's subsequent accounting thereof. S still exists as a separate legal entity but with a new owner, P.

Each legal entity keeps its own set of books. Interestingly, no books are kept for the consolidated entity. Instead, working papers are used to prepare the consolidated statements as shown schematically in Exhibit 12-8.

How do we consolidate the financial statements? Basically, we add up the individual financial statement values of the parent and all the subsidiaries. Consider a consolidated balance sheet prepared immediately after P's acquisition of S. The consolidated statement shows the details of all assets and liabilities of both the parent and the subsidiary. The Investment in S account on P's books represent P's investment in S, which is, in essence, really composed of all the assets and liabilities of S. Of course, this same amount is represented in S's books by stockholders' equity. If the consolidated statements simply add the individual balance sheet values of S and P, the $213 amount will be represented twice, once as P's investment in S account, and again in S's stockholders' equity. The consolidated statements cannot count this amount twice because true assets and liabilities will be misstated. We can avoid this double-counting by eliminating the investment in S on P's books, and the stockholders' equity on S's books.

Exhibit 12-7

Before and After the Acquisition, Parent (P) Buys Subsidiary (S) for $213

Panel A   The Events

100% Purchase of S by P

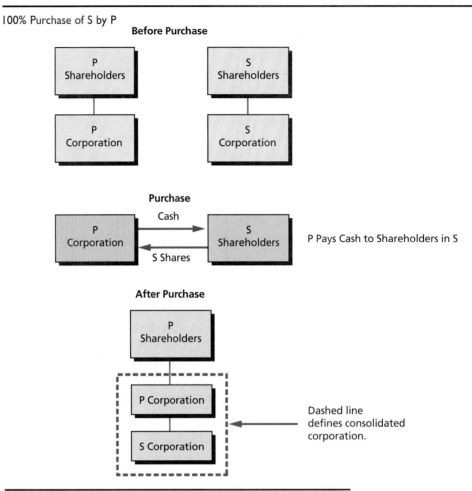

Panel B   The Balance Sheets

	Before Purchase		After Purchase	
	S	*P*	*S*	*P*
Cash	$100	$300	$100	$ 87
Net Plant	300	350	300	350
Investment in S				213
Total Assets	$400	$650	$400	$650
Accounts Payable	$187	$100	$187	$100
Bonds Payable	—	100	—	100
Stockholders' Equity	213	450	213	450
Total Liabilities and SE	$400	$650	$400	$650

The following journal entries occur:

Panel C   The Journal Entries

P BOOKS

Investment in S	213	
Cash		213

S BOOKS

No entry

502

Exhibit 12-8

Preparing Consolidated Statements

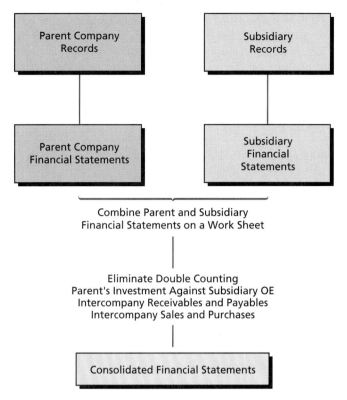

On the work sheet for consolidating the balance sheet, the entry to eliminate the double-counting of ownership interest in journal format is:

Stockholders' equity (on S books)   213
    Investment in S (on P books)   213

Separately, after the purchase, P has assets of $650 and S has assets of $400, so you might think the consolidated company would have assets totaling $1,050. However, when we consolidate and eliminate the double-counting of the investment amount in S, the consolidated assets are $1,050 − 213, or $837. The consolidated result, expressed in terms of the accounting equation, is:

100% Ownership

	Assets		=	Liabilities	+	Stockholders' Equity
	Investment in S	+	*Cash and Other Assets*	=	*Accounts Payable, etc.*	+	*Stockholders' Equity*
P's accounts, Jan. 1:							
Before acquisition		650	=	200	+	450
Acquisition of S	+213	−213	=			
S's accounts, Jan. 1		400	=	187	+	213
Intercompany						
eliminations	−213		=			−213
Consolidated, Jan. 1	0	+	837	=	387	+	450

AFTER ACQUISITION

After the initial acquisition, P accounts for its long-term investment in S by the same equity method used to account for an unconsolidated ownership interest of 20% through 50%. Suppose S has a net income of $50 million for the subsequent year (Year 1). If the parent company P were reporting alone using the equity method, it would account for the net income of its subsidiary by increasing its Investment in S account and its Stockholders' Equity account (in the form of Retained Income) by 100% of $50 million.

The income statements for the year are (numbers in millions assumed):

	P	S	Consolidated
Sales	$900	$300	$1,200
Expenses	800	250	1,050
Operating income	$100	$ 50	$ 150
Investment revenue*	50	—	
Net income	$150	$ 50	

*Pro-rata share (100%) of subsidiary net income, often called equity in earnings of affiliate or subsidiary.

P's parent-company-only income statement would show its own sales and expenses plus its proportional share of S's net income (as the equity method requires). This is shown in the leftmost column of the preceding table. The journal entry on P's books is:

```
Investment in S  . . . . . . . . . . . . . . . . . . . . . . . . . . . .    50
        Investment revenue*  . . . . . . . . . . . . . . . . .              50
```
*Or "equity in net income of subsidiary."

To avoid counting the $50 million net income twice—once as S's net income and again as P's investment revenue—P must eliminate it in consolidation. Thus, after this year's result is recorded by P, the entry to eliminate the Investment in S on the work sheet used for consolidating the balance sheets is $213 + $50 = $263.

Exhibit 12-9 reflects the changes in P's accounts, S's accounts, and the consolidated accounts (in millions of dollars). Review at this point to see that consolidated statements are the summation of the individual accounts of two or more separate legal entities. They are prepared periodically via work sheets. The consolidated entity does not have a separate continuous set of books like the legal entities. Moreover, a consolidated income statement is merely the summation of the revenue and expenses of the separate legal entities being consolidated after eliminating double-counting. The income statement for P shows the same $150 million net income as the consolidated income statement. The difference is that P's "parent-only" income statement shows its 100% share of S as a single $50 million item, whereas the consolidated income statement combines the detailed revenue and expense items for P and S.

INTERCOMPANY ELIMINATIONS

When two companies are consolidated, the accountant must be careful to avoid double-counting any items. Exhibit 12-9 emphasizes elimination of the parent's investment account and the subsidiaries owners' equity. In many cases, the parent and subsidiary do business together, which can lead to another type of double counting. For example, suppose S charges P $12 for products that cost S $10, and the sale is made on credit. The following journal entries are made by each firm on its separate books:

P'S RECORDS			S'S RECORDS		
Merchandise Inventory	12		Accounts Receivable	12	
Accounts Payable		12	Sales Revenue		12
			Cost of Goods Sold	10	
			Merchandise Inventory		10

Exhibit 12-9

Consolidation Worksheet

	Assets			=	Liabilities	+	Stockholders' Equity
	Investment in S	+	Cash and Other Assets	=	Accounts Payable, etc.	+	Stockholders' Equity
P's accounts:							
Beginning of year	+213	+	437	=	200	+	450
Operating income			+100	=			+100*
Share of S income	+50			=			+50*
End of year	263	+	537	=	200	+	600
S's accounts:							
Beginning of year			400	=	187	+	+213
Net income			+50	=			+50*
End of year			450	=	187	+	263
Intercompany eliminations	−263			=			−263
Consolidated, end of year	0	+	987	=	387	+	600

*Changes in the retained income portion of stockholders' equity.

But has anything happened economically? Not really. As far as the consolidated entity is concerned, the product is just moved from one location to another. If P paid cash to S, the cash just shifts from "one pocket to another." So this transaction is not an important one from the perspective of the consolidated company, and it should be eliminated. It is important that each separate legal entity keep track of its own transactions for its own records. The accountant can always later undo these intercompany transactions when the consolidation is done. The accountant needs to eliminate the intercompany receivable and payable, eliminate the costs and revenues, and be sure the inventory is carried at its cost to the consolidated company, $10. All of these eliminations can be made using the following consolidation journal entries on the consolidation work sheet.

Accounts Payable (P)	12	
Accounts Receivable (S)		12
Sales Revenue (S)	12	
Cost of Goods Sold (S)		10
Merchandise Inventory (P)		2

The parenthetical letters show whose records contain the account balances. But remember, these entries are not recorded on the individual records of either company, only in the consolidation work sheet.

MINORITY INTERESTS

Our example of the consolidation of P and S assumes that P purchased 100% of S. However, in reality, companies often purchase less than 100% of a subsidiary. One company can control another with just 51% of the shares. For example, Corning owns 51% of Corning Asahi Video Products Company, and the remainder is owned by Asahi Glass America, Inc. Corning consolidates Asahi Video into its consolidated financial statements. But Asahi Glass has a claim on some of the consolidated assets and has a claim on some of Asahi Video's earnings. These claims are called **minority interests.** Minority interests represent the rights of nonmajority shareholders in the assets and earnings of a company that is consolidated into the accounts of its major shareholder. On the consolidated 1996 earnings statement, Corning shows a reduction of net income of $52.6 million due to "Minority interest in earnings of subsidiaries." On the consolidated balance sheet, Corning shows

Objective 5
Incorporate minority interests into consolidated financial statements.

minority interests The outside shareholders' interests, as opposed to the parent's interests, in a subsidiary corporation.

a $310.7 million "Minority Interest in Subsidiary Companies." Some of these amounts relate to Asahi and some are related to other companies and other subsidiaries.

To apply this concept to our example, assume that our parent company (P) bought only 90% of S. Exhibit 12-10, using the basic figures of the previous example, shows the overall approach to a consolidated balance sheet immediately after the acquisition. In

Exhibit 12-10

90% Purchase of S: P Pays Cash to Some S Shareholders; Some S Shareholders Retain Minority Interest

Panel A

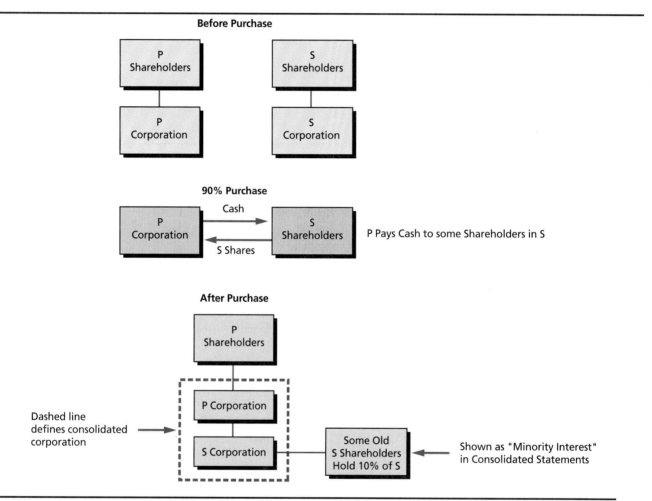

Panel B 90% Ownership

	Assets		=	Liabilities	+	Stockholders' Equity		
	Investment in S	+	Cash and Other Assets =	Accounts Payable, etc.	+	Minority Interest	+	Stockholders' Equity
P's accounts, Jan. 1:								
Before acquisition			650 =	200			+	450
Acquisition of 90% of S	+192		−192 =					
S's accounts, Jan. 1:			400 =	187			+	213
Intercompany eliminations	−192		=			+21		−213
Consolidated, Jan. 1	0		858	387		21	+	450

Panel A, the graphic shows that some shareholders of S continue to have a *minority interest* in the consolidated entity. P's 90% of S cost 0.90 × $213, or $192 million. The minority interest is 10%, or $21 million. (All dollar amounts are rounded to the nearest million.) Panel B illustrates that the investment is shown at cost on P's records and in consolidation that the minority interest appears at $21 million. You can think of the minority interest as representing the interests of those shareholders who own the 10% of the subsidiary stockholders' equity that is not owned by the parent company.

The 90% acquisition is assumed to occur on January 1. Suppose S has net income of $50 million for the year. The same basic procedures are followed by P and by S in their individual income statements regardless of whether S is 100% owned or 90% owned. P reports either 100% or 90% of S earnings as a line-item on P's income statement labeled something like *equity in earnings of subsidiary*. However, the presence of a minority interest changes the consolidated income statement. In consolidation, all of the income is combined and then the 10% share due to minority shareholders is subtracted. This is illustrated in Panel A of Exhibit 12-11. Note that the parent only income statement shows net income of $145 as does the consolidated income statement in the far right column.

Panel B shows how the minority interest from the income statement during the year serves to increase the level of the minority interest on the balance sheet at year end. Note that the minority interest of $21 that existed on January 1 has been increased by $5 during the year to reflect the minority shareholders' 10% interest in the year's net income of $50. As indicated in the intercompany elimination near the bottom of Panel B, the eliminating entry on the work sheet used for consolidating the balance sheet is:

Stockholders' equity (on S books)	263	
Investment in S (on P books)		237
Minority interest (on consolidated statements)		26

DEFINING CONTROL

Intercorporate investments occur worldwide, and different countries have made different choices about how to define control and about when to consolidate the financial results of two related companies. Consolidation is appropriate when one entity can direct the use of the assets of another company. In Australia, the definition of control and the decision to consolidate two firms is complex and relies on a combination of factors, including not only whether one firm owns 50% of another, but also whether it can control the membership of the board of directors and whether other investors own significant concentrated blocks of stock. Thus an Australian parent company might own only 40% of a subsidiary company but might control it because the parent has an influence over the board of directors or because not enough other shareholders care enough to outvote the parent.

In the United States, GAAP specifies three methods for accounting for intercorporate investments, and in 1998 "bright line" tests are used to choose among them. For ownership of less than 20% the market method is used, above 50% consolidation generally is required, and between the two the equity method is used. As this is being written, the FASB is debating whether to modify U.S. GAAP. If they do, it will no doubt move toward the more common and flexible definitions of control currently in use internationally.

Changing the rules of control can have some interesting consequences. Consider the case of USAir, a major airline in the United States that has one of the highest cost structures in the business. While United converted to employee ownership and American reached agreement on employee participation in profits during the early 1990s, USAir has struggled to engage its employees in similar agreements. The various unions have demanded representation on the board of directors as part of an arrangement to reduce wages and increase scheduling flexibility. USAir Chairman, Seth Schofield, may have

Exhibit 12-11

Effect of 90% Ownership During the Year

Panel A The Income Statement

	P	S	Consolidated
Sales	$900	$300	$1,200
Expenses	800	250	1,050
Operating income	$100	$ 50	$ 150
Investment Revenue*	45	—	
Net income	$145	$ 50	
Minority interest (10%) in subsidiary's net income			5
Net income to consolidated entity			$ 145

*Pro-rata share (90%) of subsidiary net income, often called equity in earnings of affiliate or subsidiary.

Panel B The Balance Sheet

	Assets		=	Liabilities	+	Stockholders' Equity		
	Investment in S	+ Cash and Other Assets =		Accounts Payable, etc.	+	Minority Interest	+	Stockholders' Equity
P's accounts:								
Beginning of year, before acquisition		650	=	200			+	450
Acquisition	192	−192	=					
Operating income		+100	=					+100
Share of S income	+45		=					+45
End of year	237	+ 558	=	200			+	595
S's accounts:		558						
Beginning of year		400	=	187			+	213
Net income		+50	=					+50
End of year		+ 450	=	187			+	263
Intercompany eliminations	−237		=			+26*		−263
Consolidated, end of year	0	+ 1,008	=	387	+	26*	+	595

*Beginning minority interest plus minority interest in net income: $21 + .10(50) = 21 + 5 = 26$.

favored such a plan, but could not accept it because British Airways PLC, owner of 24% of USAir, adamantly opposed any voting role for the unions. Twenty-four percent of the shares provided British Airways with significant authority.

Another interesting case of control concerns Joseph Antonini, former chairman of Kmart, a direct competitor of Wal-Mart. Ten years ago, Kmart was the bigger company, and many predicted that Wal-Mart would never exceed Kmart on any financial measure. But Sam Walton, Wal-Mart's founder, generated spectacular growth while Kmart languished. Years after Wal-Mart passed Kmart, the board still supported Antonini. What finally led to his dismissal? CALPERS, the California pension system, and other institutional holders of Kmart stock decided enough was enough. While none of them owned enough shares to individually have significant influence over the Kmart board, their collective voice was loud and clear. The Kmart board finally agreed.

The example in the previous section on consolidated financial statements assumed that the acquisition cost of Company S by Company P was equal to the book value of Company S. However, the total purchase price paid by P often exceeds the book values of the assets acquired. In fact, the purchase price also often exceeds the sum of the fair market values (current values) of the identifiable individual assets less the liabilities. Such excess of purchase price over fair market value is called **goodwill** or purchased goodwill or, more accurately, excess of cost over fair value of net identifiable assets of businesses acquired. For example, Philip Morris paid $13 billion for Kraft, but only $2 billion was assigned to identifiable individual assets. The remaining $11 billion was goodwill.

Why would Philip Morris rather buy Kraft as a going concern than pay less to buy trucks, buildings, copying machines, accounting systems, and so on that would produce the products that Kraft produces? When customers consider a purchase, they know that Kraft offers reliable quality. Customers pay more for that reputation than they would for an unbranded cheese. When grocery stores lay out their shelf space, they offer Kraft more space in better locations than they allow for unbranded, unknown products. Customers are more prone to buy well-displayed products in prime locations. These established patterns and reputations are why Kraft's goodwill is valuable.

goodwill The excess of the cost of an acquired company over the sum of the fair market value of its identifiable individual assets less the liabilities.

ACCOUNTING FOR GOODWILL

To see the impact of goodwill on the consolidated statements, refer to our initial example on consolidations, where there was an acquisition of a 100% interest in S by P for $213 million. Suppose the price were $40 million higher, or a total of $253 million cash. For simplicity, assume that the fair values of the individual assets of S are equal to their book values. This means that the entire excess of purchase price over existing book value is *goodwill*. The balance sheets immediately after the acquisition are developed in Exhibit 12-12. As suggested in the table, the eliminating entry on the work sheet for consolidating the balance sheet is:

Objective 6
Explain the economic and reporting role of goodwill.

```
Stockholders' equity (on S books) . . . . . . . . . . . . .   213
Goodwill (on consolidated balance sheet) . . . . . . . .    40
        Investment in S (on P books)  . . . . . . . . . . .          253
```

Exhibit 12-12

Creating Goodwill

	Assets		=	Liabilities	+	Stockholders' Equity
	Investment in S	+ Cash and Other Assets	=	Accounts Payable, etc.	+	Stockholders' Equity
P's accounts:						
Before acquisition		650	=	200	+	450
Acquisition	+253	−253	=			
S's accounts		400	=	187	+	213
Intercompany eliminations	−213		=			−213
Consolidated	40*	+ 797	=	387	+	450

*The $40 million "goodwill" would appear in the consolidated balance sheet as a separate intangible asset account. It is often shown as the final item in a listing of assets. It is usually amortized in a straight-line manner as an expense in the consolidated income statement over a span of no greater than 40 years.

GOODWILL AND ABNORMAL EARNINGS

As you might suspect, the final price paid by the purchaser of an ongoing business is the culmination of a bargaining process. Therefore the exact amount paid for goodwill is subject to the negotiations regarding the total purchase price. A popular logic for determining the maximum price follows.

Goodwill is fundamentally the price paid for "excess" or "abnormal" earning power. The steps to value the abnormal earning power are summarized in Panel A of Exhibit 12-13. Essentially we determine the market value of the identifiable assets of an ordinary company (M in this case) and treat that as the reasonable cost of acquiring the ordinary earnings the company generates ($80,000 in this case). The market value is 10 times earnings. Company N has identical assets worth $800,000 but also has location, human resource or reputation advantages that allow it to earn an extra $20,000 more than Company M. We calculate a price for these *abnormal* earnings using a multiple of six. These earnings are not worth as much per dollar as ordinary earnings because they are likely to be harder to maintain. The total value of Company N is $920,000, as shown in Panel B of Exhibit 12-13.

This discussion may help explain why Ford would rather buy Jaguar than start its own luxury car line. It may help explain why Ford paid $2 billion more for Jaguar than its phys-

Exhibit 12-13

Valuation of Goodwill

Panel A   Computation of Values

	Ordinary Company M	Extraordinary Company N
1. Fair market value of identifiable assets, less liabilities	$800,000	$800,000
2. Normal annual earnings on net assets at 10%	80,000	80,000
3. Actual average annual earnings for past five years (including for Co. N an excess or abnormal return of $20,000)	80,000	100,000
4. Maximum price paid for normal annual earnings is ten times line 2	800,000	800,000
5. Maximum price paid for abnormal annual earnings (which are riskier and thus less valuable per dollar of expected earnings) is six times $20,000	—	120,000*
6. Maximum price a purchaser is willing to pay for the company (line 1 plus line 5)	800,000	920,000

*This is the most the purchaser is willing to pay for goodwill.

Panel B   Value of Company N

$20,000	Abnormal Layer X 6 = $120,000
$80,000	Normal Layer X 10 = 800,000
	Total Purchase Price $920,000

ical assets were worth. Recently, several Japanese manufacturers have proven it is possible to create new prestige labels: the Lexus and the Infiniti. But these may be a notch below Jaguar in price and status. And new labels lack the generations of image building that lead people to conceive of success as being able to own a Jaguar. Ford made a strategic choice about the future extra income that the Jaguar name will provide. Only time will tell if the $2 billion investment in goodwill was worth it, not to mention the additional investment to transform Jaguar production processes made by Ford in the early 1990s. But some analysts are saying great things about the quality and performance of the Jaguars hitting the streets in 1997 and those on the drawing boards.

AMORTIZATION OF GOODWILL

Does goodwill last forever? Some might argue that it can. After all, McDonald's has enjoyed a good reputation for decades. However, take a look at a company like Atari, the old computer maker. In the early 1980s, Atari was huge as one of the first makers of home video games. Now, however, you probably do not even recognize the name. Also realize that for reputations to persist, the company must continue to advertise, to produce a quality product, and to satisfy its customers. Coke and Pepsi are internationally known, distributed, and consumed, and they command a premium price over their generic competitors. Yet if one gave up the cola wars, the other would quickly gain market share. So goodwill can be maintained by continuous effort, but it does not have perpetual life.

How do accountants reflect this limited life in financial statements? International practice ranges from immediate write-off of goodwill against stockholders' equity to treating goodwill as infinitely lived. Notice that in both cases net income was unaffected by the presence of goodwill. Current U.S. GAAP requires that goodwill purchased after 1970 be amortized as an expense against net income over the period benefited, not to exceed 40 years. The 40-year maximum is arbitrary and reflects the negotiated nature of many accounting principles. People could live with that flexibility. Footnote disclosures of amortization practices for Ford and British Petroleum are reproduced below:

Ford:

Goodwill represents the excess of the purchase price over the fair value of the net assets of acquired companies and is being amortized using the straight-line method principally over 40 years.

British Petroleum:

Goodwill is the excess of purchase consideration over the fair value of net assets acquired. It is capitalized and amortized over its estimated useful economic life, limited to a maximum period of 20 years.

Although the goodwill amounts are large and the annual amortization amounts are large in absolute terms, it is useful to keep them in perspective. For example, Ford's amortization is about $130 million per year, which was only 2% of 1996 pretax income.

PERSPECTIVE ON CONSOLIDATED STATEMENTS

Exhibit 12-14 provides summarized financial statements for Ford Motor Company for 1996. The circled items 1, 2, and 3 in the exhibit deserve special mention:

1. The headings indicate that these are consolidated financial statements.
2. Minority interests typically appear on the balance sheet, just above stockholders' equity. For Ford, the minority interest is rather small. Footnote 7 to Ford's annual report indicates that the $26,793 million of other liabilities includes "Minority interest in net assets of subsidiaries" of $93 million. In the income statement, the

Exhibit 12-14

Ford Motor Company and Subsidiaries
① Consolidated Statement of Income for the Year Ended December 31, 1996 (in millions)

AUTOMOTIVE		
Sales		$118,023
Total costs and expenses		115,507
Operating Income		2,516
Net interest income		146
③ Equity in net (loss) of affiliated companies		(6)
Net (expense)/revenue from transactions with		
Financial Services		(85)
Income before income taxes—Automotive		$ 2,571
FINANCIAL SERVICES		
Revenues		$ 28,968
Total costs and expenses		25,481
Net revenue/(expense) from transactions with		
Automotive and gain on investment		735
Income before income taxes—Financial Services		$ 4,222
TOTAL COMPANY		
Income before income taxes		$ 6,793
Provision for income taxes		2,166
Income before minority interests		4,627
② Minority interests in net income of subsidiaries		181
Net Income		$ 4,446

Ford Motor Company and Subsidiaries
① Consolidated Balance Sheet December 31, 1996 (in millions)

ASSETS	
Automotive	
Total current assets	$ 32,194
③ Equity in net assets of affilliated companies	2,483
Property, net	33,527
Other assets	11,454
Total Automotive assets	79,658
Financial services	
Total Financial Services assets	183,209
Total Assets	$262,867
LIABILITIES AND STOCKHOLDERS' EQUITY	
Automotive	
Total current liabilities	$ 33,170
Long-term debt	6,495
② Other liabilities	26,793
Deferred income taxes	1,225
Total Automotive liabilities	67,683
Financial Services	
Total Financial Services liabilities	168,422
Total stockholders' equity	26,762
Total Liabilities and Stockholders' Equity	$262,867

"Minority interests in net income of subsidiaries" appears as $181 million and is deducted to arrive at final net income of $4,446 million.

3. "Affiliated companies" are discussed in Ford's footnotes as follows: "Affiliates that are 20%–50% owned, principally Mazda Motor Corporation, and Auto Alliance International, Inc., and subsidiaries where control is expected to be temporary, principally investments in certain dealerships, are generally accounted for on an equity basis." In the balance sheet, the "Equity in net assets of affiliated companies" appears with automotive assets in the amount of $2,483 million. On the income statement, the caption "Equity in net loss of affiliated companies" describes the loss associated with these affiliates in the amount of $6 million. Recall that the equity method attributes a share of the affiliates' earnings or losses to the investor.

In 1990, these affiliates contributed a net loss of $96.6 million to Ford's consolidated income statement and in 1994, income of $271 million. These observations from prior years do not necessarily provide useful information about the performance of Mazda and Auto Alliance, however because ownership interests change over time. For example, in May of 1996, Ford increased its investment in Mazda from 24.5% to 33.4%. In the fourth quarter of 1995, the company dissolved Autolatina, a joint venture with Volkswagen in Brazil and Argentina.

To help you understand the relationship between the consolidated financial statements and Ford's actual corporate structure, consider the following simplified version of Ford Motor Company:

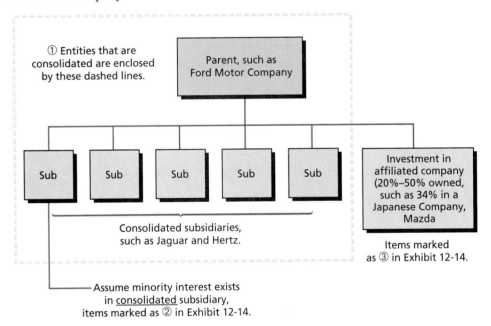

The FASB requires that all subsidiaries be consolidated. That is, all subsidiaries, regardless of their line of business or the parent company's line of business, are an integral part of the complete consolidated entity. As a result, the FASB believes that not consolidating some subsidiaries would result in significant amounts of the overall company's assets, liabilities, revenues, and expenses being left out, which would make the consolidated statements less useful.

There are exceptions to the general rule, but they are rare. One exception is that a subsidiary shall not be consolidated if control is likely to be temporary or if that control does not rest with the majority owner. This exception actually applies to Ford. As you might have noted from our discussion of item ③ for Ford's consolidated statements, the company sometimes owns dealerships that it plans to quickly resell to a new dealer. Because the ownership of these dealerships is temporary, Ford does not consolidate them. Ford's statements do reflect the consolidation of a manufacturing company with a financing company. Ford has chosen to structure the statements to clearly separate these two parts of its economic activity. The assets and liabilities of the Financial Services activity are listed separately as are the revenue and expense components. The footnotes provide additional detail on both segments of the business. Financial analysts pay particular attention to understanding the distinct parts of a business as they make predictions about the future.

EQUITY AFFILIATES AND THE STATEMENT OF CASH FLOWS

A company with equity affiliates (firms for which the investor uses the equity method) may use the direct method or the indirect method to prepare its cash flow statement. If it uses the direct method, no special problem arises because only the cash received from the affiliate as a dividend appears. However, if the indirect method is used, net earnings is increased by the investor's share of its affiliates' earnings or is decreased by its share of the affiliates' loss. To calculate cash flow from operations, we must adjust reported income. Suppose the investor had net income of $7.6 million, including equity in earnings of an affiliate of $2.5 million, and received $1.3 million in dividends from the affiliate. Cash flow is $1.3 million. Because net earnings includes $2.5 million, the indirect method must adjust net earnings by $2.5 million − $1.3 million = $1.2 million, the amount of the equity in earnings that was not received in cash. The first part of the Operating Activities section of Dow Chemical's Consolidated Statement of Cash Flows for 1996 and 1995 is reproduced below. Dow's share of the earnings of affiliated companies exceeded the dividends received by $29 million in 1996 and by $35 million in 1995. This excess is called "undistributed earnings." The income statement shows that Dow reported equity in earnings of $66 million in 1996. We can compute that dividends of $37 million were received in 1996 from equity affiliates ($66 million of equity in earnings less the $29 million undistributed portion).

The Dow Chemical Company and Subsidiaries
Consolidated Statement of Cash Flows

In Millions		1996	1995
Operating Activities (Partial)	Net income	$1,900	$1,884
	Adjustments to reconcile net income to net cash provided by operating activities:		
	Depreciation and amortization	1,298	1,442
	Undistributed earnings of related companies	(29)	(35)

SUMMARY OF ACCOUNTING FOR EQUITY SECURITIES

Exhibit 12-15 summarizes all the relationships in intercorporate investments. Take a few moments to reconcile the Ford financial statements in Exhibit 12-14 with Exhibit 12-15. In particular, note that minority interests arise only in conjunction with consolidated subsidiaries. Why? Because consolidated balance sheets and income statements assume that the parent company owns and controls 100% of the detailed assets, liabilities, sales, and expenses of the subsidiary companies. Thus, if a minority interest were not recognized, the stockholders' equity and net income of the consolidated enterprise would overstate the claims of the parent company shareholders.

In contrast, minority interests do not arise in connection with the accounting for investments in affiliated companies. Why? Because no detailed assets, liabilities, revenues, and expenses of the affiliated companies are included in the consolidated statements. The investor's interests in these companies have been recognized on a proportional basis only.

Exhibit 12-15

Summary of Accounting for Equity Securities

Item in Exhibit 12-14	Percentage of Ownership	Type of Accounting	Balance Sheet Effects	Income Statement Effects	Major Journal Entries
①	100%	Consolidation	Individual assets, individual liabilities added together. For subsidiaries purchased for more than the fair value of identifiable assets, goodwill is shown.	Individual revenues, individual expenses added together. If goodwill exists, it must be amortized against net income.	None, except in work sheets for preparing consolidated statements; to eliminate reciprocal accounts, to avoid double-counting, and to recognize any goodwill.
②	Greater than 50% and less than 100%	Consolidation	Same as 1, but recognition given to minority interest in liability section.	Same as 1, but recognition given to minority interest near bottom of statement when consolidated net income is computed.	Same as 1, but recognition of minority interests is included in work sheet entries.
③	20% to and including 50%	Equity method	Investment carried at cost plus pro-rata share of subsidiary earnings less dividends received.	Equity in earnings (losses) of *affiliated* or *associated* companies shown on one line as addition to (deduction from) income.	Investment xx / Equity in earnings xx / To record earnings. / Cash xx / Investment xx / To record dividends received.
	Below 20%	Market method	Investment carried at market.	For trading securities changes affect the income statement. For available-for-sale securities a valuation allowance appears in owners' equity.	Marketable securities xx / Unrealized Gains xx / To record appreciation. / Marketable securities xx / Valuation allowance xx / To record appreciation.

As we have seen, the accounting for investments in common stock depends on the nature of the investment:

1. Investments that represent more than a 50% ownership interest are usually consolidated. A subsidiary is a corporation controlled by another corporation. The usual condition for control is ownership of a majority (more than 50%) of the outstanding voting stock.

2. The equity method is generally used for a 20% through 50% interest because such a level of ownership creates a presumption that the owner has the ability to exert significant influence. Under the equity method, the cost at date of acquisition is adjusted for the investor's share of the earnings or losses of the investee subsequent to the date of investment. Dividends received from the investee reduce the carrying amount of the investment.

3. Marketable equity securities are generally carried at market value. These investments are typically passive in the sense that the investor exerts no significant influence on the investee.

SUMMARY PROBLEMS FOR YOUR REVIEW

PROBLEM ONE

The following is a summary of material from Dow Chemical's annual report as of December 31, 1996 (in millions):

	$
Marketable securities and interest-bearing deposits	399
Total Current Assets	9,830
Investments:	
Capital stock at cost plus equity in accumulated earnings of 20%–50% owned companies	1,387
Other investments	2,060
Noncurrent receivables	437
Total Investments	3,884
Plant Properties	23,737
Less: Accumulated depreciation	15,253
Net Plant Properties	8,484
Goodwill	899
Deferred Charges and Other Assets	1,576
TOTAL	$24,673

Note that the statements are somewhat compressed and no detail for current assets is shown. Current assets may include some smaller holdings of equity securities that are valued at market.

Dow also shows "Minority Interests in Subsidiary Companies" of $2,091 million among its liabilities.

Required

1. Suppose "Marketable Securities" included a $24 million portfolio of equity securities. Their market values on the following March 31, June 30, and September 30 were $20, $23, and $28 million, respectively. Compute the following:
   a. Carrying amount of the portfolio on each of the three dates.
   b. Gain (loss) on the portfolio for each of the three quarters.

2. Suppose the $2,060 million of "Other Investments" included a $9 million investment in the debentures of an affiliate that was being held to maturity. The debentures had a par value of $10 million and a 10% nominal rate of interest, payable June 30 and

December 31. Their market rate of interest when the investment was made was 12%. Prepare the Dow journal entry for the semiannual receipt of interest.

3. Suppose Dow's 20%–50% owned companies had net income of $200 million. Dow received cash dividends of $70 million from these companies. No other transactions occurred. Prepare the pertinent journal entries. Assume that on average Dow owns 40% of the companies.

SOLUTION TO PROBLEM ONE

1. Amounts are in millions.
   a. Market: $20, $23, and $28.
   b. $20 – $24 = $4 loss; $23 – $20 = $3 gain; $28 2 $23 = $5 gain. Gain or loss would be reported in the income statement for trading securities or in the stockholders' equity section for securities available-for-sale.

2.
Cash	500,000	
Other investments (in bonds)	40,000	
Interest revenue		540,000

Six months' interest earned is .5 × .12 × $9,000,000 = $540,000.
Amortization is $540,000 − cash received of .5 × .10 × $10,000,000 = $540,000 − $500,000.

3.
Investments in 20%–50% owned companies	80,000,000	
Investment revenue		80,000,000

To record 40% share of $200 million income.

Cash	70,000,000	
Investments in 20%–50% owned companies		70,000,000

To record dividends received from 20%–50% owned companies.

PROBLEM TWO

1. Review the section on minority interests, pages 505-507. Suppose P buys 60% of the stock of S for a cost of 0.60 × $213, or $128 million. The total assets of P consist of this $128 million plus $522 million of other assets, a total of $650 million. The S assets and equities are unchanged from the amount given in the example on page 505. Prepare an analysis showing what amounts would appear in a consolidated balance sheet immediately after the acquisition.

2. Suppose S has a net income of $50 million for the year, and P has an operating income of $100 million. Other details of their income statements are as described in the example on page 504. Prepare an analysis showing what amounts would appear in a consolidated income statement and year-end balance sheet.

SOLUTION TO PROBLEM TWO

1.

	Assets			=	Liabilities	+	Stockholders' Equity		
	Investment in S	+	Cash and Other Assets	=	Accounts Payable, etc.	+	Minority Interest	+	Stockholders' Equity
P's accounts, Jan. 1:									
Before acquisition			650	=	200			+	450
Acquisition of 60% of S	+128		−128	=					
S's accounts, Jan. 1			400	=	187			+	213
Intercompany eliminations	−128			=			+85		−213
Consolidated, Jan. 1	0	+	922	=	387	+	85	+	450

2.

	P	S	Consolidated
Sales	$900	$300	$1,200
Expenses	800	250	1,050
Operating income	$100	$ 50	$ 150
Pro-rata share (60%) of unconsolidated subsidiary net income	30	—	
Net income	$130	$ 50	
Outside interest (40%) in consolidated subsidiary net income (minority interest in income)			20
Net income to consolidated entity			$ 130

	Assets			=	Liabilities	+	Stockholders' Equity		
	Investment in S	+	Cash and Other Assets	=	Accounts Payable, etc.	+	Minority Interest	+	Stockholders' Equity
P's accounts:									
Beginning of year	128	+	522*	=	200			+	450
Operating income			+100	=				+	+100
Share of S income	+30			=					+ 30
End of year	158	+	622	=	200			+	580
S's accounts:									
Beginning of year			400	=	187			+	213
Net income			+ 50	=					+ 50
End of year			450	=	187			+	263
Intercompany eliminations	−158			=			+105†		−263
Consolidated, end of year	0	+	1,072	=	387	+	105	+	580

*650 beginning of year − 128 for acquisition = 522.

†85 beginning of year + .40 × (50) = 85 + 20 = 105.

Highlights to Remember

The accounting for intercorporate investments depends on the purpose of the investment, on whether it is an equity or debt security, and on the level of control the investor has over the issuer of the security. For short-term debt securities and short-term equity securities, accounting is at market. Trading securities are held to be resold, and the gains and losses from changes in market value go directly to the income statement. Marketable securities that are available-for-sale are reported at market in the balance sheet, but gains and losses are carried in a separate account in stockholders' equity until the securities are sold.

When the investor's intention is to hold debt securities to maturity, the investor's accounting uses the effective interest rate method in the same manner that the issuer does. That is, discount and premium are amortized to affect interest revenue. For equity securities held for the long-term, the accounting is linked to the investor's level of control of the issuer of the equity security. For ownership interests of less than 20%, accounting for equity securities requires classification as either available-for-sale or trading. The accounting is based on fair value.

As the ownership interest ranges from 20% to 50%, the increasing control the investor can exert over the issuer leads to earnings recognition in the income statement, proportional to the percentage ownership. The investment account is increased by this share of the issuer's earnings (or decreased by a proportionate share of losses). When dividends are received, the investment account is decreased with no effect on earnings. This is called the equity method.

As the ownership interest exceeds 50%, the investor controls the subsidiary. Consolidation is appropriate, which involves combining all of the assets and liabilities of the related corporate entities. For 100%-owned subsidiaries, the main concern is the elimination of intercompany transactions: sales, receivables, and payables. For less than 100%-owned subsidiaries, the rights of the minority shareholders must be recognized as a reduction of consolidated earnings on the income statement and as a liability on the balance sheet. Both amounts are calculated in proportion to the minority investors' share of the subsidiary.

Accounting Vocabulary

affiliated company, p. 499
available-for-sale securities, p. 495
certificates of deposit, p. 493
commercial paper, p. 493
consolidated statements, p. 501
equity method, p. 499
goodwill, p. 509

held-to-maturity securities, p. 494
market method, p. 495
marketable securities, p. 493
minority interests, p. 505
parent company, p. 500
pooling-of-interests method, p. 519
purchase method, p. 519

short-term debt securities, p. 493
short-term equity securities, p. 494
short-term investment, p. 493
subsidiary, p. 500
trading securities, p. 494
U.S. Treasury obligations, p. 494

Appendix 12: Pooling of Interests

NATURE OF POOLING

The business combinations described in the body of the chapter were accounted for by using the purchase method, as contrasted with the pooling-of-interests method. The **purchase method** accounts for a business combination on the basis of the market prices actually paid for the acquired company's assets. Under the purchase method, one company is obviously acquiring another and typically paying cash to do so. The shareholders of the acquired company sell their stock and go away. The owners of the purchaser now own a different, bigger company.

Sometimes two companies approach each other and agree that they would be better off combining and further agree to combine by exchanging shares of stock. Often the stock of one is exchanged for the stock of the other. Alternatively, shareholders of both companies exchange their shares for shares in a new combined company. In these instances, it is less clear who is purchasing whom. The transaction is more a union of equals.

Suppose the two companies were privately held. No market existed for the stock. After the combination, all of the previous owners remained owners. It would be hard to attach values to the shares of stock or to the assets owned by the resulting company. Such transactions are called pooling of interests. The **pooling-of-interests method** is based on the book values of the acquired company's assets, not the market values.

The purchase and pooling methods are used under different circumstances, not as alternatives for the same business combination. Pooling is a joining of ownership interests of two or more companies by the exchange of common stock. The recorded assets and liabilities of the fused companies are carried forward at their book values by the combined corporation. To use pooling-of-interests accounting, the combination must meet many specific conditions, including most importantly:

1. The acquirer must issue voting common shares (not cash) in exchange for substantially all (at least 90%) of the voting common shares of the acquired company.
2. The acquisition must occur in a single transaction.

purchase method A way of accounting for the acquisition of one company by another, based on the market prices paid for the acquired company's assets.

pooling-of-interests method A way of accounting for the combination of two corporations based on the book values of the acquired company's net assets, as distinguished from the purchase method.

If we simply combine the two companies, the following steps are required as illustrated below:

1. Sum the individual assets and liabilities of P and S, line by line.
2. Sum the individual retained incomes. By definition of pooling, the retained incomes are combined in this way.
3. Adjust common stock at par and additional paid-in capital accounts. This adjustment is usually small; it involves increasing one of the two accounts and decreasing the other by a like amount.

To illustrate, assume that the companies shown in Panel A of Exhibit 12-16 combine in a transaction in which P issues 5,000,000 shares of its $5 par value stock in exchange for the 5,000,000 outstanding shares of $4 par value stock in S. This transaction will reflect the beliefs about the economic values of the shares being exchanged, and P corporation will have negotiated the exchange ratio with the S shareholders. In this case, P gives one share for each share of S. In Panel A, the combination of assets, liabilities and retained earnings are very straightforward; just add them together. We are assuming that there are no receivables or payables between the companies.

The only awkward step is in combining the contributed capital. Five million additional shares of P were issued and those have a par value of $25,000,000 ($5 × 5,000,000 shares). The old shares of S only had a par value of $20,000,000. The total par value of outstanding P shares after the pooling must be $65,000,000 including the original 8,000,000 shares plus the 5,000,000 newly issued shares. The effect is to transfer $5,000,000 from Additional Paid-In Capital to Common Stock at Par. Panel B shows the reconciliation of the allocations within owners' equity.

Pooling and purchase accounting are determined by the nature of the transaction. However, companies considering a business combination often decide how to structure

Exhibit 12-16

Pooling of Interest

Panel A Parent and Subsidiary and Consolidated

	P	+	S	=	Consolidated
Assets	650		400		1,050
Liabilities	200		187		387
Common stock ($5 par)	40	($4 par)	20	($5 par)	65
Additional Paid-in Capital	110		140		245
Retained Earnings	300		53		353
	650		400		1,050

Panel B Reconciliation of Consolidated Owners' Equity

Common stock at par	Old P, 8,000,000 shares @ $5 =	40
	New P, 5,000,000 shares @ $5 =	25
	New total	65*
Additional paid-in capital	Old P	110
	Old S	140
	Adjustment	(5)
	New total	245*
Retained earnings	Old P	300
	Old S	53
	New total	353

*Total paid-in capital = 65 + 245 = 40 + 110 + 20 + 140 = 310.

Exhibit 12-17

Contrasting Pooling and Purchase

Panel A Balance Sheet

	Pooling	**Purchase Compared with Pooling**
1. Assets	No goodwill No fair value of other assets	Higher because of goodwill and fair values of other assets such as property, plant, and equipment
2. Retained income	P and S added together	Lower because S retained income not added; the consolidated retained income equals P retained income
3. Common stock at par	Sum of all P shares	Same as pooling
4. Additional paid- in capital	Adjusted to accom- modate changes in par values	Higher because new shares affect equity at market values at time of acquisition of S

Panel B Income Statement

	Pooling	**Purchase Compared with Pooling**
Revenue and expenses	Added together for entire year regardless of when acquisition occurred during the year	Added together only for time span subsequent to date of acquisition
Goodwill amortization	No goodwill	Amortized for time span subsequent to acquisition
Depreciation expense	Based on old book values	Based on fair values at date of acquisition

the transaction after considering what the financial accounting results would be. Therefore it is useful to contrast the balance sheet and income statement effects of a stock-for-stock pooling transaction with a cash-for-stock transaction accounted for using purchases accounting. Exhibit 12-17 provides a comparison. Note that generally total assets are higher with purchase accounting because goodwill is recognized and net income is lower because goodwill is amortized. Also note that income is combined for different periods using the two methods. The entire year is combined in a pooling while the purchaser only includes the subsidiary from the acquisition date under purchase accounting.

Assignment Material

QUESTIONS

12-1. Why is *marketable securities* an ill-chosen term to describe short-term investments?

12-2. Distinguish among trading securities, available-for-sale securities, and held-to-maturity securities.

12-3. "The cost method is applied to investments in short-term securities." Do you agree? Explain.

12-4. "Increases in the market price of short-term investments become gains on the income statement; decreases become losses." Do you agree? Explain.

12-5. Suppose an investor buys a $1,000 face value bond for $950, a discount of $50. Will amortization of the discount increase or decrease the investor's interest income? Explain.

12-6. What is the equity method?

12-7. "The equity method is usually used for long-term investments." Do you think this is appropriate? Explain.

12-8. Contrast the *market* method with the *equity* method.

12-9. What criterion is used to determine whether a parent-subsidiary relationship exists?

12-10. Why have subsidiaries? Why not have the corporation take the form of a single legal entity?

12-11. Suppose Company A buys 100% of the common shares of Company B for cash. How does Company B record the receipt of this cash on its books?

12-12. Why does a consolidated balance sheet require "eliminating entries"?

12-13. "A consolidated income statement will show more income than a parent-company-only statement when both the parent and subsidiary have positive net income." Do you agree? Explain.

12-14. What is a minority interest?

12-15. Distinguish between *control of* a company and *significant influence over* a company.

12-16. "Goodwill is the excess of purchase price over the book values of the individual assets acquired." Do you agree? Explain.

12-17. Why does GAAP require amortization of goodwill against net income? What other options might exist?

12-18. Why might a company prefer to own 19.9% interest in an affiliate rather than a 20.1% interest?

12-19. When is there justification for not consolidating majority-owned subsidiaries?

12-20. Suppose P company received $20,000 in cash dividends from Y company, a 40%-owned affiliated company. Y company's net income was $80,000. How will P's statement of cash flows show these items using the direct method?

12-21. Why do minority interests arise in connection with consolidated statements, but not with investments in affiliated companies?

12-22. Would you expect the consolidated income statement to report higher net income if a business combination is accounted for as a pooling or as a purchase? Explain.

EXERCISES

12-23 Trading Securities

The McMillan Company has a portfolio of trading securities consisting of common and preferred stocks. The portfolio cost $160 million on January 1. The market values of the portfolio were (in millions): March 31, $150; June 30, $138; September 30, $152; and December 31, $168.

Required

1. Prepare a tabulation showing the balance sheet presentations and income statement presentations for interim reporting purposes.
2. Show the journal entries for quarters 1, 2, 3, and 4.

12-24 Available-For-Sale Securities

The MacGregor Company has a portfolio of securities identical to that of the McMillan Company (see Exercise 12-23). However, MacGregor classified the portfolio as available-for-sale securities. The portfolio cost $160 million on January 1. The market values of the portfolio were (in millions): March 31, $150; June 30, $138; September 30, $152; and December 31, $168.

Required

1. Prepare a tabulation showing the balance sheet presentations and income statement presentations for interim reporting purposes.
2. Show the journal entries for quarters 1, 2, 3, and 4.

12-25 Bond Discount Transactions

On December 31, 1998, a company purchased $1 million of ten-year, 10% debentures for $885,295. The market interest rate was 12%.

Required

1. Using the balance sheet equation format, prepare an analysis of bond transactions. Assume effective-interest amortization. Show entries for the investor

regarding (a) purchase, (b) the first semiannual interest payment, and (c) payment of maturity value.

2. Show the corresponding journal entries for (a), (b), and (c) above.

3. Show how the bond investment would appear on the balance sheets as of December 31, 1998, and June 30, 1999.

12-26 Bond Premium Transactions

On December 31, 1998, the Guzman Company purchased $1 million of ten-year, 10% debentures for $1,135,915. The market interest rate was 8%.

1. Using the balance sheet equation format, prepare an analysis of transactions for the investor's records. Key your transactions as follows: (a) purchase, (b) the first semiannual interest payment using effective-interest amortization of bond premium, and (c) payment of maturity value.

2. Prepare sample journal entries keyed as above.

3. Show how the bond-related accounts would appear on the balance sheets as of December 31, 1998, and June 30, 1999.

12-27 Market Method or Equity Method

Yukon Outdoor Equipment acquired 25% of the voting stock of Bearpaw Snowshoes for $40 million cash. In Year 1, Bearpaw had a net income of $32 million and paid a cash dividend of $20 million.

1. Using the equity and the market methods, show the effects of the three transactions on the accounts of Yukon Outdoor Equipment. Use the balance sheet equation format. Also show the accompanying journal entries. Assume constant market value for Bearpaw.

2. Which method, equity or market, would Yukon use to account for its investment in Bearpaw? Explain.

12-28 Equity Method

Company X acquired 30% of the voting stock of company Y for $90 million cash. In Year 1, Y had a net income of $50 million and paid cash dividends of $30 million.

Prepare a tabulation that uses the equity method of accounting for X's investment in Y. Show the effects on the balance sheet equation. What is the year-end balance in the Investment in Y account under the equity method?

12-29 Consolidated Statements

Able and Baker Companies had the following balance sheets at December 31, 19X8 (in thousands):

	Able	Baker
Assets:		
Cash	$ 400	$100
Net plant	1,800	500
Total assets	$2,200	$600
Liabilities and stockholders' equity:		
Accounts payable	175	$ 80
Long-term debt	425	220
Stockholders' equity	1,600	300
Total liabilities and stockholders' equity	$2,200	$600

On January 1, 19X9 Able purchased 100% of the common stock of Baker for $300,000.

1. Prepare a balance sheet for Able Company immediately after its purchase of Baker Company.

2. Prepare a balance sheet for the consolidated entity immediately after the purchase of Baker Company.

3. Suppose Able Company had net income of $250,000 in 19X9 and Baker Company had net income of $60,000 in 19X9. Neither company sold items to the other. What was the 19X9 consolidated net income?

12-30 Minority Interest

Suppose P company owns 90% of S company and S company earns $100,000. What is the amount of the minority interest shown in P company's consolidated income statement? What is the amount of the minority interest shown in S company's individual income statement?

12-31 Goodwill

Megasoft, Inc. purchased 100% of the common shares of Zenatel for $670,000 on January 1, 19X7. Zenatel's balance sheet just before the acquisition was (in thousands):

Cash	$ 90
Net fixed assets	220
Total assets	$310
Liabilities	$240
Stockholders' equity	70
Total liabilities and stockholders' equity	$310

The fair market value of Zenatel's assets and liabilities was equal to their book values.

1. Compute the amount of goodwill Megasoft would recognize on this purchase. Where would this goodwill appear on Megasoft's financial statements?

2. Suppose Megasoft elected to amortize this goodwill over 20 years. Megasoft's 19X7 net income from all operations excluding those of Zenatel were $150,000. Zenatel had a net loss of $10,000. Compute consolidated net income for 19X7.

12-32 Amortization of Goodwill

On January 2, 19X1, Company X acquires Company Y for $45 million and can assign only $35 million to identifiable individual assets. What is the minimum amount of amortization of goodwill for 19X1? Could the entire amount be written off in 19X1? Why?

12-33 Affiliated Companies

Suppose P company owns 40% of S company. S company earns $200,000 and pays total dividends of $60,000 to its shareholders. What appears in the consolidated income statement of P company as a result of S company's activity? What would be the change in the account titled Investment in equity affiliates on P company's balance sheet?

12-34 Consolidations in Japan

A few years ago, Japan's finance ministry issued a directive requiring the six hundred largest Japanese companies to produce consolidated financial statements. The previous practice had been to use parent-company-only statements. A story in *Business Week* said: "Financial observers hope that the move will help end the tradition-honored Japanese practice of 'window dressing' the parent company financial results by shoving losses onto hapless subsidiaries, whose red ink was seldom revealed. . . . When companies needed to show a bigger profit, they would sell their product to subsidiaries at an inflated price. . . . Or the parent company charged a higher rent to a subsidiary company using its building."

Required

Could a parent company follow the quoted practices and achieve window dressing in its parent-only financial statements if it used the equity method of accounting for its intercorporate investments? Explain.

PROBLEMS

12-35 Trading Securities

On a recent December 31, Pennzoil Company held a portfolio of trading equity securities that cost $660,100,000 and had a market value of $955,182,000. Assume that the same portfolio was held until the end of the first quarter of the subsequent year. The market value of the portfolio was $980,160,000 at January 31, $941,187,000 at February 29, and $959,550,000 at March 31.

Required

1. Prepare a tabulation showing the balance sheet presentation and income statement presentation for monthly reporting purposes.
2. Show the journal entries for January, February, and March.
3. How would your answer to (1) change if the securities were classified as available-for-sale?

12-36 Short-Term Investments

The VanDankan Company has the following footnote to its financial statements:

Note 4: Short-Term Investments
The company holds the following short-term investments at December 31 (in thousands):

	Cost	Market Value
Trading securities:		
U.S. Government Bonds	680,000	675,000
Held-to-maturity securities:		
Bonds issued by Beta Corp.	540,000	560,000
Available-for-sale securities:		
Common shares of Gamma Corp.	300,000	770,000

Required

1. Compute the amount that VanDankan would show on its balance sheet for short-term investments.
2. Suppose the market values of the three securities at the beginning of the year had been:

U.S. Government Bonds	685,000
Bonds issued by Beta Corp.	550,000
Common shares of Gamma Corp.	710,000

Prepare journal entries to recognize the changes in market values that would be recorded in VanDankan's books during the year.

12-37 Early Extinguishment of an Investment

On December 31, 1997, an insurance company purchased $10 million of ten-year, 10% debentures for $8,852,950. On December 31, 1998 (after all interest payments and amortization had been recorded for 1998), the insurance company sold all the debentures for $9.3 million. The market interest rate at issuance was 12%.

1. Compute the gain or loss on the sale for the insurance company (i.e., the investor).
2. Prepare the appropriate journal entries for the insurance company (i.e., the investor).

12-38 Consolidated Statements

Consider the following for Chow Company (the parent) as of December 31, 19X8:

	Chow	Subsidiary*
Assets	$800,000	$200,000
Liabilities to creditors	$300,000	$ 80,000
Stockholders' equity	500,000	120,000
Total equities	$800,000	$200,000

*70 percent owned by Chow.

The $800,000 of assets of Chow include an $84,000 investment in the subsidiary. The $84,000 includes Chow's pro-rata share of the subsidiary's net income for 19X8. Chow's sales were $870,000 and operating expenses were $802,000. These figures exclude any pro-rata share of the subsidiary's net income. The subsidiary's sales were $550,000 and operating expenses were $510,000. Prepare a consolidated income statement and a consolidated balance sheet.

12-39 Consolidated Financial Statements and Minority Interest

The Parent Company owns 90% of the common stock of Company S-1 and 60% of the common stock of Company S-2. The balances as of December 31, 19X4, in the condensed accounts follow:

	(in thousands of dollars)		
	Parent	S-1	S-2
Sales	300,000	80,000	100,000
Investment in subsidiaries*	72,000	—	—
Other assets	128,000	90,000	20,000
Liabilities to creditors	100,000	20,000	5,000
Expenses	280,000	90,000	95,000
Stockholders' equity, including current net income	100,000	70,000	15,000

*Carried at equity in subsidiaries.

Prepare a consolidated balance sheet as of December 31, 19X4, and a consolidated income statement for 19X4 (in millions of dollars).

12-40 Consolidated Financial Statements

Company P acquired a 100% voting interest in Company S for $110 million cash at the start of the year. Immediately before the business combination, each company had the following condensed balance sheet accounts (in millions):

	P	S
Cash and other assets	$500	$150
Accounts payable, etc.	$200	$ 40
Stockholders' equity	300	110
Total liab. & stk. eq.	$500	$150

1. Prepare a tabulation of the consolidated balance sheet accounts immediately after acquisition. Use the balance sheet equation format.

2. Suppose P and S have the following results for the year:

	P	S
Sales	$600	$180
Expenses	450	160

Prepare income statements for the year for P, S, and the consolidated entity. Assume that neither P nor S sold items to the other.

3. Present the effects of the operations for the year on P's accounts and on S's accounts, using the balance sheet equation. Also tabulate the consolidated balance sheet accounts at the end of the year. Assume that liabilities are unchanged.

4. Suppose S paid a cash dividend of $10 million. What accounts in requirement 3 would be affected and by how much?

12-41 Minority Interests

This alters the preceding problem. However, this problem is self-contained because all the facts are reproduced below. Company P acquired an 80% voting interest in Company S for $88 million cash at the start of the year. Immediately before the business combination, each company had the following condensed balance sheet accounts (in millions):

	P	S
Cash and other assets	$500	$150
Accounts payable, etc.	$200	$ 40
Stockholders' equity	300	110
Total liab. & stk. eq.	$500	$150

1. Prepare a tabulation of the consolidated balance sheet accounts immediately after acquisition. Use the balance sheet equation format.

2. Suppose P and S have the following results for the year:

	P	S
Sales	$600	$180
Expenses	450	160

Prepare income statements for the year for P, S, and the consolidated entity. Assume that neither P nor S sold items to the other.

3. Using the balance sheet equation format, present the effects of the operations for the year on P's accounts and on S's accounts. Also tabulate consolidated balance sheet accounts at the end of the year. Assume that liabilities are unchanged.

4. Suppose S paid a cash dividend of $10 million. What accounts in requirement 3 would be affected and by how much?

12-42 Goodwill and Consolidations

This alters Problem 12-40. However, this problem is self-contained because all the facts are reproduced below. Company P acquired a 100% voting interest in Company S for $150 million cash at the start of the year. Immediately before the business combination, each company had the following condensed balance sheet accounts (in millions):

	P	S
Cash and other assets	$500	$150
Accounts payable, etc.	$200	$ 40
Stockholders' equity	300	110
Total liab. & stk. equity	$500	$150

Assume that the fair values of the individual assets of S were equal to their book values.

Required

1. Prepare a tabulation of the consolidated balance sheet accounts immediately after the acquisition. Use the balance sheet equation format.

2. If goodwill is going to be amortized over forty years, how much was amortized for the first year? If over five years, how much was amortized for the first year?

3. Suppose the book values of the S individual assets are equal to their fair market values except for equipment. The net book value of equipment is $30 million and its fair market value is $50 million. The equipment has a remaining useful life of four years. Straight-line depreciation is used.

   a. Describe how the consolidated balance sheet accounts immediately after the acquisition would differ from those in requirement 1. Be specific as to accounts and amounts.

   b. By how much will consolidated income differ in comparison with the consolidated income that would be reported in requirement 2? Assume amortization of goodwill over a 40-year period.

12-43 Purchased Goodwill

Consider the following balance sheets (in millions of dollars):

	Company A	Company B
Cash	150	15
Inventories	60	25
Plant assets, net	60	30
Total assets	270	70
Common stock and paid-in surplus	70	30
Retained income	200	40
Total liab. & stk. equity	270	70

A paid $100 million to B stockholders for all their stock. The "fair value" of the plant assets of B is $60 million. The fair value of cash and inventories is equal to their carrying amounts. A and B continued to keep separate books.

Required

1. Prepare a tabulation showing the balance sheets of A, of B, intercompany eliminations, and the consolidated balance sheet immediately after the acquisition.

2. Suppose that only $50 million rather than $60 million of the total purchase price of $100 million could logically be assigned to the plant assets. How would the consolidated accounts be affected?

3. Refer to the facts in requirement 1. Suppose A had paid $110 million rather than $100 million. State how your tabulation in requirement 1 would change.

12-44 Amortization of Goodwill

Consider the following:

1. Philip Morris purchased General Foods for $5.6 billion. Philip Morris could assign only $1.7 billion to identifiable individual assets. What is the amount of

goodwill created by the acquisition? What is the minimum amount of amortization in the first year?

2. The Gannett Co., Inc., publisher of many newspapers, including *USA Today,* purchased radio stations KKBQ-AM and FM in Houston and WDAE-AM in Tampa for a total of $41 million. A footnote in the annual report stated that goodwill is "amortized over a period of 40 years." Assume that both purchases were made on January 2 and that Gannett could assign only $33 million to identifiable individual assets. What is the minimum amount of amortization of goodwill for the first year? Could the entire amount be written off immediately? Explain.

12-45 Amortization and Depreciation
Refer to problem 12-43, requirement 3. Suppose a year passes, and A and B generate individual net incomes of $19 million and $13 million, respectively. The latter is after a deduction by B of $6 million of straight-line depreciation. Compute the consolidated net income if goodwill is amortized (a) over 40 years and (b) over 10 years. Ignore income taxes.

12-46 Allocating Total Purchase Price to Assets
Two Hollywood companies had the following balance sheet accounts as of December 31, 19X7 (in millions):

	Cinemon	Bradley Productions		Cinemon	Bradley Productions
Cash and receivables	$ 30	$ 22	Current liabilities	$ 50	$ 20
Inventories	120	3	Common stock	100	10
Plant assets, net	150	95	Retained income	150	90
Total assets	$300	$120	Total liab. and stk. eq.	$300	$120
Net income for 19X7	$ 19	$ 4			

On January 4, 19X8, these entities combined. Cinemon issued $180 million of its shares (at market value) in exchange for all the shares of Bradley, a motion picture division of a large company. The inventory of films acquired through the combination had been fully amortized on Bradley's books.

During 19X8, Bradley received revenue of $21 million from the rental of films from its inventory. Cinemon earned $20 million on its other operations (that is, excluding Bradley) during 19X8. Bradley broke even on its other operations (that is, excluding the film rental contracts) during 19X8.

1. Prepare a consolidated balance sheet for the combined company immediately after the combination on a purchase basis. Assume that $80 million of the purchase price was assigned to the inventory of films.   **Required**

2. Prepare a comparison of Cinemon's net income between 19X7 and 19X8 where the cost of the film inventories would be amortized on a straight-line basis over four years. What would be the net income for 19X8 if the $80 million were assigned to goodwill rather than to the inventory of films and goodwill were amortized over 40 years?

12-47 Prepare Consolidated Financial Statements
From the following data, prepare a consolidated balance sheet and an income statement for Midlands Data Corporation. All data are in millions and pertain to operations for 19X2 or to December 31, 19X2:

Short-term investments at cost, which approximates current market	$ 35
Income tax expense	90
Accounts receivable, net	110
Minority interest in subsidiaries	90
Inventories at average cost	390
Dividends declared and paid on preferred stock	10
Equity in earnings of affiliated companies	20
Paid-in capital in excess of par	82
Interest expense	25
Retained income	218
Investments in affiliated companies	100
Common stock, 10 million shares, $1 par	10
Depreciation and amortization	20
Accounts payable	200
Cash	55
First-mortgage bonds, 10% interest, due December 31, 19X8	80
Property, plant, and equipment, net	120
Preferred stock, 2 million shares, $50 par, dividend rate is $5 per share, each share is convertible into one share of common stock	100
Accrued income taxes payable	30
Cost of goods sold and operating expenses, exclusive of depreciation and amortization	710
Subordinated debentures, 11% interest, due December 31, 19X9	100
Minority interest in subsidiaries' net income	20
Goodwill	100
Net sales and other operating revenue	960

12-48   Minority Interest

The consolidated financial statements of Anchor Gaming, Inc., include the accounts of Colorado Grande Enterprises, Inc., an 80%-owned subsidiary. Anchor Gaming makes gambling machines and runs casinos. Colorado Grande Enterprises operates the Colorado Grande Casino in Cripple Creek, 45 miles from Colorado Springs. Colorado Grande Enterprises is Anchor Gaming's only consolidated subsidiary with minority interests. Anchor Gaming's 1997 income statement contained the following:

Income before minority interest and taxes	$56,987,737
Taxes	21,000,702
Minority interest in earnings of consolidated subsidiary	310,607
Net income	$35,676,428

Anchor Gaming's account "Minority Interest in Consolidated Subsidiary" listed $672,955 at the beginning of 1997. Colorado Grande Enterprises paid no dividends in 1997. Anchor Gaming did not buy or sell any of its interest in Colorado Grande Enterprises during 1997.

Required

1. Compute the 1997 net income of Colorado Grande Enterprises.
2. What proportion of Anchor Gaming's $35,676,428 net income was contributed by Colorado Grande Enterprises?
3. Compute Anchor Gaming's balance in "Minority Interest in Consolidated Subsidiary" at the end of 1997.
4. Comment on the reason for including a line for minority interest in the income statement and balance sheet of Anchor Gaming.

12-49 Acquisition of RCA

The stockholders of RCA approved the sale of 100% of RCA's common stock to General Electric for $66.50 per share. Of the votes cast, over 90% were in favor of the $6.28 billion cash sale, the largest non-oil acquisition at the time. Assume that the $6.28 billion price was twice RCA's book value.

Required

1. Suppose the fair market values of RCA's net assets totaled $6.28 billion. Prepare the journal entry or entries to record the acquisition on General Electric's books.

2. Suppose the fair market values of RCA's tangible assets were equal to their book values. Fair market value of identifiable intangible assets was $800 million; their useful life was eight years. None of the intangible assets appeared on RCA's balance sheet. Prepare the journal entry or entries to record the acquisition on General Electric's books.

3. Refer to requirement 2. Assume that the acquisition took place on January 2. Prepare the December 31 journal entry or entries to recognize the first year's amortization of goodwill and other intangible assets. Assume that goodwill is amortized as slowly as possible.

4. Assume that the acquisition occurred on July 1 and that RCA's net income for the year was $500 million. RCA's net income was earned at a constant rate per unit of time during the year. How much of that net income would appear in General Electric's consolidated net income for the year ended December 31?

12-50 Equity Method and Cash Flows

Moscow Resources Company owns a 30% interest in Siberia Mining Company. Moscow uses the equity method to account for the investment. During 19X6, Siberia had net income of 100 million rubles and paid cash dividends of 70 million rubles. Moscow's net income, including the effect of its investment in Siberia, was 486 million rubles.

Required

1. In reconciling Moscow's net income with its net cash provided by operating activities, the net income must be adjusted for Moscow's pro-rata share of the net income of Siberia. Compute the amount of the adjustment. Will it be added to or deducted from net income?

2. Under the direct method, the dividends paid by Siberia will affect the amounts Moscow lists under operating, investing, or financing activities. Which type(s) of activity will be affected? By how much? Will the amount(s) be cash inflows or cash outflows?

12-51 Effect of Transactions Under the Equity Method

Coca-Cola's footnotes to its 1996 financial statements revealed (in millions):

	December 31	
	1996	*1995*
Equity method investments	$3,432	$2,395

Coca-Cola's share of the net income of these equity method investments was $211 million in 1996, and it received dividends from those companies of $122 million. During 1996, Coca-Cola sold its French and Belgian bottling and canning operations for $936 million. These operations had been included in the equity method investments. Assume that there was no gain or loss on the sale and that this was the only sale of equity method investments during 1996.

1. Compute the additional investment that Coca-Cola made in its equity affiliates during 1996. *Hint:* Use a T-account to aid your analysis.

2. Describe how the income and dividends from equity investments would affect the cash flow statement. Coca-Cola uses the indirect method for cash flows from operations.

12-52 Equity Method, Consolidation, and Minority Interest

On January 2, 19X6, Jordan Shoe Company purchased 30% of Sports Clothing Company (SCC) for $1.5 million cash. Before the acquisition, Jordan had assets of $10 million and stockholders' equity of $8 million. SCC had stockholders' equity of $5 million and liabilities of $1 million, and the fair values of its assets were equal to their book values.

SCC reported 19X6 net income of $400,000 and declared and paid dividends of $200,000. Assume that Jordan and SCC had no sales to one another. Separate income statements for Jordan and SCC were as follows:

	Jordan Shoe Company	Sports Clothing Company
Sales	$12,500,000	$4,400,000
Expenses	11,100,000	4,000,000
Operating income	$ 1,400,000	$ 400,000

1. Prepare the journal entries for Jordan Shoe (a) to record the acquisition of SCC and (b) to record its share of SCC net income and dividends for 19X6.

2. Prepare Jordan Shoe's income statement for 19X6 and calculate the balance in its investments in SCC as of December 31, 19X6.

3. Suppose Jordan had purchased 80% of SCC for $4 million. Using the balance sheet equation format, prepare a tabulation of the consolidated balance sheet immediately after acquisition. Prepare the journal entries for both Jordan and SCC to record the acquisition. Omit explanations.

4. Prepare a consolidated income statement for 19X6, using the facts of requirement 3.

12-53 Equity Investments

Corning Inc.'s 1996 Consolidated Statements of Income reported equity in earnings of associated companies of $85.1 million. Its Consolidated Balance Sheets included investments in associated companies of $313.8 million in 1996 and $341.0 million in 1995. The Consolidated Statements of Cash Flow indicated that the equity in earnings of associated companies were less than dividends received from these companies in 1996 by $2.9 million.

1. Compute the amount of net investment or disinvestment in associated companies, if any, during 1996.

2. Suppose these associated companies were 40% owned and that Corning had acquired another 40% of these companies on the last day of 1996. Describe how the financial statements for 1996 would change as a result. Your answer should identify the accounts that would probably change and the direction of the probable change.

12-54 Intercorporate Investments and Statements of Cash Flow

The 19X6 balance sheet of Global Resources Corp. contained the following three assets:

	19X6	19X5
Long-term debt investments held-to-maturity	$ 166,000	$ 166,000
Investment in Alberta Mining Company, 43% owned	$ 981,000	$ 861,000
Investment in Sutter Gold Company, 25% owned	$1,145,000	$1,054,000

The long-term-debt investments were shown at cost, which equaled maturity value. Interest income was $14,000 for these debt investments, which had been owned for several years. The equity method was used to account for both Alberta Mining and Sutter Gold. Results for 19X6 included:

	Alberta Mining Company	Sutter Gold Company
Global Resources Corp. pro-rata share of net income	$120,000	$91,000
Cash dividends received by Global Resources Corp.	$ 50,000	$ 0

Global Resources reported net income of $687,000 and depreciation of $129,000 in 19X6.

A schedule that reconciles net income to net cash provided by operating activities contained the following:

Net income	$687,000
Depreciation	129,000
Increase in noncash working capital	(16,000)

Note: The increase in non-cash working capital is the net change in current assets and liabilities other than cash.

Given the available data, complete the reconciliation.

Required

12-55 Pooling-of-Interest Accounting
Study Appendix 12. Refer to problem 12-46.

Calculate the following values assuming pooling-of-interests accounting is used.

Required

1. Consolidated total assets, January 1, 19X8.
2. Retained income, January 1, 19X8.
3. 19X8 consolidated net income.

12-56 Purchase or Pooling
Study Appendix 12. Two companies had the following condensed balance sheet accounts at December 31, 19X6.

	P	S
Cash and other assets	$800	$220
Accounts payable, etc.	$300	$100
Stockholders' equity	500	120
Total liab. & stk. eq.	$800	$220

The fair value of the individual S assets is the same as their book values.

Required

1. Company P issued stock for $180 million cash at the beginning of 19X7 and then immediately used the cash to acquire all the shares of Company S. Prepare a consolidated balance sheet after the acquisition of S by P.

2. Instead of issuing its shares for $180 million cash, suppose P exchanges the same number of its shares for the shares of S. Assume that all conditions of pooling are met. Prepare a consolidated balance sheet.

3. Which set of future consolidated income statements will show higher income, the ones resulting from purchasing or from pooling? Explain.

12-57 More on Pooling of Interests
Study Appendix 12. Two companies had the following condensed balance sheet accounts at December 31, 19X7 (in millions):

	P	S
Cash and other assets	$700	$220
Accounts payable, etc.	$300	$100
Stockholders' equity:		
Common stock:		
8 million shares @ $2 par	16	
12 million shares @ $1 par		12
Additional paid-in capital	84	40
Retained income	300	68
Total stockholders' equity	$400	$120
Total liab. and stk. eq.	$700	$220

The fair values of the individual assets are the same as their book values.

Required

1. Company P issues 10 million shares of stock @ $20 for $200 million cash at the beginning of 19X8 and then immediately used the cash to acquire all the shares of Company S. Prepare a consolidated balance sheet after the acquisition of S by P.

2. Instead of issuing its shares for $200 million cash, suppose P exchanges the same number of its shares for the shares of S. Assume that all conditions of pooling are met. Prepare a consolidated balance sheet.

3. List the major differences between the two consolidated balance sheets immediately after the acquisition.

4. Suppose the acquisition occurred on December 1, 19X8. All other information is unchanged. How will the purchase and the pooling income statements differ for 19X8? Respond by listing the major differences. No numerical differences are required.

12-58 Intercorporate Investments and Ethics
Hans Rasmussen and Alex Renalda were best friends at a small undergraduate college and they fought side-by-side in the jungles of Vietnam. Upon returning to the United States, they went their separate ways to pursue MBA degrees, Hans to a prestigious East Coast business school and Alex to an equally prestigious West Coast school. But 25 years later, their paths crossed again.

By 1995, Alex had become president and CEO of Medusa Electronics after 21 years with the firm. Hans had started working for American Airlines, but had left after nine years to start his own firm, Rasmussen Transport. In April of 1995, Rasmussen Transport was near bankruptcy when Hans approached his old friend for help. Alex Renalda answered his friend's call, and Medusa Electronics bought 19% of Rasmussen Transport.

In 1998, Rasmussen was financially stable and Medusa was struggling. In fact, Alex Renalda thought his job as CEO might be in jeopardy if Medusa did not report income up to expectations. Late in 1998, Alex approached Hans with a request—quadruple Rasmussen's dividends so that Medusa could recognize $760,000 of investment income. Medusa had listed its investment in Rasmussen as an available-for-sale security, so changes in the market value of Rasmussen were recorded directly in stockholders' equity. However, dividends paid were recognized in Medusa's income statement.

Although Rasmussen had never paid dividends of more than 25% of net income, and it had plenty of use for excess cash, Hans felt a deep obligation to Alex. Thus he agreed to a $4 million dividend on net income of $4.17 million.

Required

1. Why does the dividend policy of Rasmussen Transport affect the income of Medusa Electronics? Is this consistent with the intent of the accounting principles relating to the market and equity methods for intercorporate investments? Explain.

2. Comment on the ethical issues in the arrangements between Hans Rasmussen and Alex Renalda.

12-59 The Gap Annual Report

The Gap includes the following two items on its balance sheet for the year ended February 1, 1997 (in thousands):

Short-term investments	$135,632
Long-term investments	36,138

Required

1. How does The Gap determine whether an investment is short-term or long-term?
2. How does The Gap measure the balance sheet value of these investments?
3. Suppose the market value of The Gap's short-term investments on February 1, 1997, was $136,632,000. During the next year, all of the investments matured, and The Gap received the face value of $135,632 for the securities. Prepare the journal entry or entries required by the securities transactions during the year. Include any gains or losses that would be recognized by The Gap.

12-60 Financial Statement Research

Select five companies in any industry. Review each company's financial statements to determine whether an acquisition occurred during the most recent year. For each acquisition, identify as much as possible regarding each of the following:

Required

1. Did the company use cash or stock?
2. What percentage of the target was purchased?
3. Can you determine whether the acquired company was previously either a customer or a supplier of the acquiring company? If so, which one?

COLLABORATIVE LEARNING EXERCISE

12-61   International Perspective on Consolidation

Form groups of four to six students. Each student should pick a country from the following list:

Australia

France

Germany

Italy

Japan

Sweden

United Kingdom

Find out the policy on consolidating financial statements in the country you select. If possible, find out when consolidated statements were first required and what criteria are used to determine what subsidiaries should be consolidated.

Meet as a group and share your information. What generalizations can you draw from the policies you found? Propose explanations for the differences you find among countries. Discuss the effect of consolidation policies on comparisons of financial statements across countries.

12-62   Internet Case

Go to **http://www.pg.com/** to find Procter & Gamble's home page. Chances are you have used several of this company's numerous products produced by its various consolidated subsidiaries. To find its annual report, click the Globe icon near the bottom of the page and then select *Financial Center*, listed under the *Information Center* icon. Select the company's most recent annual report.

Answer the following questions about Procter & Gamble:

1. What business segments do the consolidated financial statements of Procter & Gamble include? How are the operations of these segments interrelated?

2. Read *Note 1* to the financial statements. What criteria have Procter & Gamble applied in choosing which investments to account for using the equity method?

3. Did Procter & Gamble acquire any new companies during the current fiscal period? What are they?

4. Where are investments in equity securities reported on Procter & Gamble's financial statements?

5. Did Procter & Gamble report any goodwill? Why would Procter & Gamble want to pay more than the value of the net assets of a company it acquires? Over what period of time is goodwill amortized? For what reason did accumulated amortization on the company's balance sheet decline during the current fiscal period?

6. Does Procter & Gamble use the market method for any of its investments? Where are these investments reported on Procter & Gamble's financial statements, if any? Where are any earnings resulting from these investments reported by Procter & Gamble?

7. Has Procter & Gamble reported any "minority interest"? How do you know the answer to this? Why does Procter & Gamble not report an amount for "intercompany eliminations"?

13

FINANCIAL STATEMENT ANALYSIS

Competition for the fast food dollar on this Chicago street is just one example of a battle fought city-by-city and country-by-country, around the world.

Learning Objectives

After studying this chapter, you should be able to

1 Locate and use the many sources of information about company performance.

2 Analyze the components of a company using trend analysis and other techniques.

3 Use the basic financial ratios to guide your thinking.

4 Evaluate corporate performance using ROA and ROE.

5 Calculate EPS under complex circumstances.

6 Adjust for nonrecurring items.

Chapter 1 opened with a discussion of McDonald's, and we should now consider some additional questions an investor might ask in evaluating this company. During the 12 months from September 1996 through September 1997, McDonald's shares traded as low as $42.50 and as high as $54.88. McDonald's shares closed at the end of September at the middle of the range around $48, up about 13% from its low point. McDonald's was selling at a price-earnings ratio of about 20.

What happened to cause investor sentiment to change during the year and therefore to cause McDonald's price to move? Some events were economywide. The stock market did well through September 1997, supported by world peace, low inflation, a strong dollar, high employment, and so forth. McDonald's benefited as did most companies. The federal budget was moving toward balance, taxes had been reduced, and life was good.

For McDonald's specifically, there was good news and bad news. *Business Week* labeled the three-day, $5.00, 9% decline in the value of a McDonald's share in February 1997 "the discount dip." McDonald's dropped the price of Big Macs and McMuffins to 55 cents. As a consumer, you probably thought "great," more value, but investors figured it was bad news if McDonald's had to nearly give away burgers to increase sales. Investors want rising sales, yes, but more than that, they want rising profits. Analysts estimated that sales would have to rise 2% just to cover the effect of lower prices and noted that Burger King would not sit still while this happened.

This sales campaign also raised questions as to whether it made sense for McDonald's to continue its U.S. expansion in the face of tightening markets. After opening 1,130 units in 1995 and 726 stores in 1996, plans to open 720 more in 1997 worried investors. Adding almost 10% more stores each year in a crowded market worried investors who still remembered the failed 1996 launch of "Deluxe" sandwiches. These were the high-priced adult sandwiches that did not attract a lot of business and seriously injured the McDonald's image of a pro-kid happy-meal haven.

Adding stores should increase sales. But a good question would be: How are sales in existing McDonald's going? The answer in 1997 was that "same store" sales had fallen in 9 of the last 10 quarters. McDonald's share of the U.S. burger market had fallen slightly over two years, while Burger King's rose one percentage point. Of course, the analyst would also figure out that some 60% of McDonald's operating income in 1997 came from overseas business. Separate forecasts of international growth and profitability could then be performed and combined with U.S. forecasts to guide investment decisions.

Of course, good financial analysis requires that we understand how the business works. Much of McDonald's business is done through franchises. If the people owning and running the franchises are not happy, they will not be delivering the focused quality service and product that makes people associate McDonald's with the break they deserve today. Interviews with franchise owner's revealed only 26% supported some policies, down from 86% two years earlier. One owner of four franchises pointed out that her third franchise lost money and the fourth was 42% below sales projections.

McDonald's is a great company with one of the world's most recognized brands. But investors want to know where the company is on its growth curve. Potential franchise investors want to decide whether 1997 or 2001 is the right year to buy. The analysis methods in this chapter summarize many of the techniques such investors use to answer these questions.

In prior chapters, we concentrated on how to collect financial data, and how to prepare and evaluate financial statements. You know that the accountant's goal in preparing financial statements is to provide usable information to anyone who wants it. Here we must focus exclusively on how to interpret that information so that we fully understand the story it tells about the company.

Different people read financial statements for different reasons. Suppliers might want to see if a customer can afford a price hike. Customers might want to know if a company will still be around in a year to honor a warranty. Managers, creditors, investors, and the CEO's mother all have their purposes for reading the statements. Our focus will be on the investor. Investors read financial statements either to check on their current investments or to plan their future ones. Investors analyze financial statements to determine whether their beliefs about the company have been borne out and to develop expectations about the future.

How do we get the future out of financial statements? Throughout the book we have shown you various ratios and other tools of analysis, so you should have at least a clue as to how it is done. Ratios focus your attention and direct your questions. This chapter will integrate the tools you have already seen and teach you several new ones as we focus on financial statement analysis. Most of the chapter deals with ratios and how to understand the financial statements as prepared under GAAP.

SOURCES OF INFORMATION ABOUT COMPANIES

financial statement analysis
Using financial statements to assess a company's performance.

Financial statement analysis, whether conducted by managers inside the company or investors outside the company, uses the same basic methods. Our focus is more on the investment decisions of external investors who rely primarily on publicly available information.

Publicly available information takes on many forms. The now familiar annual report is important because of its completeness and its reliability, given the attestation of an independent third-party auditor. In addition to the financial statements (income statement, balance sheet, statement of cash flows, and statement of stockholders' equity) we have already seen, annual reports usually contain:

1. Footnotes to the financial statements.
2. A summary of the accounting principles used.
3. Management's discussion and analysis of the financial results.
4. The auditor's report.
5. Comparative financial data for a series of years.
6. Narrative information about the company.

The Gap annual report included in Appendix A of this book provides examples of each of the items listed. In addition to the annual reports distributed to shareholders, companies also prepare reports for the Securities and Exchange Commission (SEC). Form 10-K presents financial statement data in greater detail than do the financial statements in annual reports. Form 10-Q includes quarterly financial statements, so it provides more timely, although less complete, information than do the annual reports. Other SEC reports are required for specific events, such as the issuance of common shares or debt. All SEC filings are available to any investor and most are available on the World Wide Web. See the Prentice Hall web site for easy access to Edgar, the SEC electronic information source.

Both annual reports and SEC reports are issued well after the events being reported have occurred. More timely information can be found in periodic company press releases, which provide the public with news about company developments, including the following:

1. Changes in personnel.
2. Changes in dividends.
3. Issuance or retirement of debt.
4. Acquisition or sale of assets or business units.
5. New products.
6. New orders.
7. Changes in production plans.
8. Financial results.

Press releases provide the basis for articles appearing in the financial press, such as local newspapers, *The Wall Street Journal, Business Week, Forbes, Fortune,* and *Barron's.* Members of the financial press decide which information in press releases will be interesting and important. For example, the *Tulsa World* newspaper in Oklahoma may report in great detail about local oil exploration and production. The *Washington Post* in Washington, DC, probably would not cover these issues but would instead provide up-to-date news on local companies and government business. National publications, such as the *Wall Street Journal,* would not provide as much detail in these specific areas as either the *Tulsa World* or *The Washington Post.*

Investors also rely on the other articles, reports, and analyses that appear in the financial press. Services such as Value Line, Moody's Investors Services, and Standard and Poor's Industrial Surveys also provide investors with useful information, as do credit agencies such as Dun & Bradstreet. In addition, stockbrokers prepare company analyses for their clients, and private investment services and newsletters supply information to their subscribers. Internet competitors such as Bloomberg News are providing competing services electronically.

Investors should always get information before they invest, and the sources we have described tend to provide plenty. Of course, some large investors can demand even

pro forma statement A carefully formulated expression of predicted results.

more information. For example, banks or other creditors making multimillion-dollar loans can ask for a set of projected financial statements or other estimates of predicted results, known as **pro forma statements.** Not every investor can demand pro forma statements, but not every investor needs to. There is so much information available to the public that wading through it all can take a good deal of time. Although there is much to be gained from other sources, our discussion will focus on analyzing the information contained in the financial statements themselves. But sometimes examining that information necessarily directs the analyst to other information that is required to resolve an issue.

OBJECTIVES OF FINANCIAL STATEMENT ANALYSIS

Different types of investors expect different types of returns. Equity investors expect both dividends and an increase in the value of the stock they hold. Creditors, however, expect to receive interest and the return of their loan principal. Although the types of returns they expect are different, equity investors and creditors both risk not receiving those returns. Therefore, both types of investors use financial statement analysis to (1) predict their expected returns and (2) assess the risks associated with those returns.

Creditors mainly want to know about short-term liquidity and long-term solvency. **Short-term liquidity** refers to how much cash a company has on hand to meet current payments, such as interest, wages, taxes, and so on, as they become due. Conversely, **long-term solvency** refers to a company's ability to generate cash to repay the principals on long-term debts to creditors as they mature.

short-term liquidity An organization's ability to meet current payments as they become due.

long-term solvency An organization's ability to generate enough cash to repay long-term debts as they mature.

In contrast, equity investors are more concerned with profitability and future security prices. Why? Because dividend payments depend on how profitable operations are, and stock prices depend on the market's assessment of the company's future prospects. Investors gain when they receive dividends and when the values of their securities rise. Rising profits spur both events. Actually, creditors also want to know about profitability because the profitable operations that drive stock prices to higher levels also provide the cash to repay loans and finance growth.

Both creditors and equity investors are interested in the what will happen in a company's future. What good to them, then, is financial statement analysis, which deals solely with past events? Financial statement analysis helps creditors and equity investors because past performance is often a good indicator of future performance. The same trends in past sales, operating expenses, and net income may continue, so financial statement analysis of past performance gives clues to future returns. This is perhaps most significant when past trends are downward and an abrupt, significant reversal of the trends is required to make the company attractive.

EVALUATING TRENDS AND COMPONENTS OF THE BUSINESS

Objective 2
Analyze the components of a company using trend analysis and other techniques.

There are several ways of looking at financial statement information. One of the most popular methods involves comparing financial trends from one year to the next. A second method focuses on examining the components of the business. At one level, the composition of the business involves the relationship among elements reported in the financial statements. We have already examined many ratios that do this; the current ratio, the inventory turnover ratio, ROE, and so on. Components can also be thought of as business units or geographic segments. For example, Philip Morris has a food business and a tobacco business and operates in the United States and many other regions of the world. Investors and analysts could focus on any one, or better yet, all of these dimensions in trying to predict the future of Philip Morris.

TREND ANALYSIS

Annual reports contain financial statements for the current and previous year, the amounts of key financial items for at least the last five years and often for 10 or 11. Not surprisingly, the longer histories of information tend to be published by the companies whose 10 year histories are impressive. In evaluating trends, these numbers may or may not be adequate. Many supplemental sources provide much longer and richer access to information by archiving and adjusting older information. Many colleges and universities now have Compustat PC, a CD-ROM data collection that provides 20 years of financial information extracted from the financial statements. Multiple services are arising to provide rich information for financial analysis. Trends are nothing more than predictable patterns that have been observed in the past and are expected to continue into the future. The aging composition of the U.S. population is a classic example of a trend.

The essence of trend analysis in accounting is to identify a pattern in the past, a trend. Then you ask yourself why that trend exists and whether you expect it to continue. Often this pattern of questions forces you to ask more questions. If sales have been growing steadily, but inventories have not, can this continue or will future inventory growth require substantial additional investment? If inventories have been growing steadily but sales have not, why is someone buying so much inventory?

To see how trend analysis works, let's examine the income statements and balance sheets from the Oxley company, a retailer of nursery products for lawns and gardens, shown in Exhibits 13-1 and 13-2. The first two columns show Oxley's information for the last two years. The third column shows the amount of the change in each item from 19X1 to 19X2. Finally, the fourth column shows the percentage change, computed as follows:

Exhibit 13-1

Oxley Company
Statement of Income (in thousands except earnings per share)

	For the Year Ended December 31, 19X2	For the Year Ended December 31, 19X1	Increase (Decrease) Amount	Percentage
Sales	$999	$800	$199	24.9%
Cost of goods sold	399	336	63	18.8
Gross profit (or gross margin)	$600	$464	$136	29.3
Operating expenses:				
Wages	$214	$150	$ 64	42.7
Rent	120	120	0	0.0
Miscellaneous	100	50	50	100.0
Depreciation	40	40	0	0.0
Total operating expenses	$474	$360	$114	31.7
Operating income (or operating profit)	$126	$104	$ 22	21.2
Other revenue and expense:				
Interest revenue	36	36	0	0.0
Deduct: Interest expense	(12)	(12)	0	0.0
Income before income taxes	$150	$128	$ 22	17.2
Income tax expense	60	48	12	25.0
Net income	$ 90	$ 80	$ 10	12.5
Earnings per common share*	$.45	$.40	$.05	12.5%

*Dividends per share, $.40 and $.20, respectively. For publicly held companies, there is a requirement to show earnings per share on the face of the income statement, but it is not necessary to show dividends per share. Calculation of earnings per share: $90,000 ÷ 200,000 = $.45, and $80,000 ÷ 200,000 = $.40

$$\text{Percentage change 19X1 to 19X2} = \frac{\text{Amount of change}}{\text{19X1 amount}} \times 100$$

For example, Oxley's accounts receivables increased 35.7%:

$$\text{Percentage change} = \frac{\$95,000 - \$70,000}{\$70,000} \times 100 = 35.7\%$$

Both the amount and the percentage changes are needed to recognize trends and understand their true meaning. For example, although the sales increase of $199,000 is larger than the $22,000 increase in operating income, the percentage increase is only slightly larger—24.9% to 21.2%. Similarly, the 140% increase in accrued wages payable seems large, but the increase is only $14,000, a relatively small amount in the overall picture. Remember that unlike the amounts of change, the percentage changes cannot be added or subtracted to obtain subtotals.

Exhibit 13-2

Oxley Company Balance Sheet
(in thousands)

	December 31		Increase (Decrease)	
	19X2	*19X1*	*Amount*	*Percentage*
ASSETS				
Current assets:				
Cash	$150	$ 57	$ 93	163.2%
Accounts receivable	95	70	25	35.7
Accrued interest receivable	15	15	0	0.0
Inventory of merchandise	20	60	(40)	(66.7)
Prepaid rent	10	—	10	*
Total current assets	$290	$202	$ 88	43.6
Long-term assets:				
Long-term note receivable	288	288	0	0.0
Equipment, less accumulated depreciation of $120 and $80	80	120	(40)	(33.3)
Total assets	$658	$610	$ 48	7.9%
LIABILITIES AND STOCKHOLDERS' EQUITY				
Current liabilities:				
Accounts payable	$90	$ 65	$ 25	38.5%
Accrued wages payable	24	10	14	140.0
Accrued income taxes payable	16	12	4	33.3
Accrued interest payable	9	9	0	0.0
Unearned sales revenue	—	5	(5)	(100.0)
Note payable—current portion	80	—	80	*
Total current liabilities	$219	$101	$118	116.8
Long-term note payable	40	120	(80)	(66.7)
Total liabilities	$259	$221	$ 38	17.2
Stockholders' equity:				
Paid-in capital†	$102	$102	$ 0	0.0
Retained income	297	287	10	3.5
Total stockholders' equity	$399	$389	$ 10	2.6
Total liabilities and stockholders' equity	$658	$610	$ 48	7.9%

*When the base-year amount is zero, no percentage change can be computed.

†Details are often shown in a supplementary statement or in footnotes. In this case, there are 200,000 common shares outstanding, $.25 par per share, or 200,000 × $.25 = $50,000. Additional paid-in capital is $52,000.

Changes in dollar amount and percentage terms help analysts to see patterns, such as a rise in sales or a decrease in inventories. Although recognizing patterns is key, understanding what caused those patterns is even more important. In our example, why did current assets increase by 43.6% while equipment decreased by 33.3%? Why did cash and accounts receivable increase, while inventories plummeted? Why did current liabilities increase 116.8% while long-term liabilities decreased 66.7%? The answers to these questions say a lot about how a company is run, how it will perform in the future, and whether or not it would be a good investment.

An analyst would note that Oxley Company's sales increase of 24.9%, exceeds the 18.8% increase in cost of goods sold, causing a 29.3% increase in gross profit. That is good news. But operating expenses increased by 31.7% with only two items, wages and miscellaneous expenses, causing the increase. In total, the nearly 25% increase in sales led to only a 12.5% increase in net income. Investors know that the most powerful growth occurs because people are dying to acquire your product. Top-line, revenue growth that leads to increasing net income is highly desirable. But when sales grow 25% and net income grows less, something is wrong. Has the company gotten top-heavy, hiring too many managers and not enough production and sales people?

Good analysts develop pictures in their heads about how changes in one financial statement item should affect another. When relationships do not look as good as expected, the issue is whether a crisis exists. When relationships look better than expected, the question is whether this excellent situation can be sustained. To see how trends develop over time, analysts often look at several years' worth of a company's financial information. Exhibit 13-3 shows a five-year summary of key items for Oxley Company with selected percentage growth rates. For example, percentage changes in sales are:

19X2
$$\left(\frac{\$999 - \$800}{\$800}\right) \times 100 = 24.9\%$$

19X1
$$\left(\frac{\$800 - \$765}{\$765}\right) \times 100 = 4.6\%$$

19X0
$$\left(\frac{\$765 - \$790}{\$790}\right) \times 100 = (3.2\%)$$

19Y9
$$\left(\frac{\$790 - \$694}{\$694}\right) \times 100 = 13.8\%$$

Applying the present value techniques of Chapter 9, we can see that the four-year average compound growth rate has been 9.53%. This precise value was obtained with a calculator. Using the tables in Chapter 9 we can approximate the value. The future value multiple is 1.44 ($999 ÷ $694 = 1.44). In Table 9-1 in Chapter 9, p. 355, the future value factor for 4 years for 8% is 1.3605 and for 10% is 1.4641. The observed value of 1.44 falls near the upper end of this range, so it must be closer to 10% than to 8%. Our 9.53 value qualifies.

What caused these highly variable sales growth rates? Thoughtful analysts might conclude that weather and rates of new home construction play a role. Perhaps the sales decline in 19X0 was caused by a recession, and 19X2's sales increase involved a new product. Understanding these causes can help in assessing how Oxley has performed and how it might perform in the future.

COMMON-SIZE STATEMENTS

To aid comparisons with a company's prior years or comparisons of companies that differ in size, income statements and balance sheets are often analyzed using **common-size statements** in which the components are assigned a relative percentage. Oxley's common-size statements appear in Exhibit 13-4, side by side with the income statements from Exhibit 13-1 and the condensed balance sheets from Exhibit 13-2.

The income statement percentages are based on sales = 100%. Then each element of the income statement is expressed as a percentage of sales. In 19X1, gross margin was

common-size statements
Financial statements expressed in component percentages.

Exhibit 13-3

Oxley Company

Five-Year Financial Summary (in thousands, except per share amounts)

	For the Year Ended December 31				
	19X2	*19X1*	*19X0*	*19Y9*	*19Y8*
Income Statement Data:					
Sales	$999	$800	$765	$790	$694
Gross profit	600	464	448	460	410
Operating income	126	104	85	91	78
Net income	90	80	62	66	56
Earnings per share	.45	.40	.31	.33	.28
Dividends per share	.40	.20	.20	.20	.15
Balance Sheet Data (as of December 31):					
Total assets	$658	$610	$590	$585	$566
Total liabilities	259	221	241	258	265
Stockholders' equity	399	389	349	327	301

Exhibit 13-4

Oxley Company

Common-Size Statements (in thousands except percentages)

	For the Year Ended December 31			
	19X2		*19X1*	
Statement of Income				
Sales	$999*	100%	$800	100%
Cost of goods sold	399	40	336	42
Gross profit (or gross margin)	$600*	60%	$464	58%
Wages	$214	21%	$150	19%
Rent	120	12	120	15
Miscellaneous	100	10	50	6
Depreciation	40	4	40	5
Operating expenses	$474	47%	$360	45%
Operating income	$126	13%	$104	13%
Other revenue and expense	24	2	24	3
Pretax income	$150	15%	$128	16%
Income tax expense	60	6	48	6
Net income	$ 90	9%	$ 80	10%

	December 31			
	19X2		*19X1*	
Balance Sheet				
Current assets	$290	$44%	$202	33%
Long-term note receivable	288	44	288	47
Equipment, net	80	12	120	20
Total assets	$658	100%	$610	100%
Current liabilities	$219	33%	$101	16%
Long-term note	40	6	120	20
Total liabilities	$259	39%	$221	36%
Stockholders' equity	399	61	389	64
Total liab. and stk. eq.	$658	100%	$610	100%
Working capital	$ 71		$101	

*Note the use of dollar signs in columns of numbers. Frequently, they are used at the top and bottom only and not for every subtotal. Their use by companies depends on the preference of management.

58%, rising to 60% in 19X2. To understand the importance of this improvement in Oxley's gross margin, we might compare them to a specific competitor's values, or to industry averages. It is good to realize that gross margins improved, but did they improve as much as a competitor's did? Did they improve as much as most industry members did? The common-size statements translate raw dollar values for gross margins into percentage values that can be compared easily to the performance of others.

The behavior of each expense in relation to changes in total revenue is often revealing. That is, which expenses go up or down as sales fluctuate? For example, during these two years, rent, depreciation, and interest have been fixed in total but have decreased in relation to sales. In contrast, the wages have increased in total and as a percentage of sales. The latter is not a welcome sign. Exhibit 13-4 indicates that wages in 19X1 were $150 ÷ $800 = 19% of sales, whereas wages in 19X2 were $214 ÷ $999 = 21% of sales. A manager confronted with this information might ask who was hired and what they were doing. An investor would ask similar questions but would have a slightly harder time finding the answers. If we learned that wages rose because we hired some people to open a new location where no revenues were yet being generated, we might view this pattern as very reasonable. Alternatively, if we had more people working in the same locations with no greater business, we might conclude that management had gotten lazy.

The balance sheet percentages in Exhibit 13-4 are based on total assets = 100%. They are often referred to as **component percentages** because they measure each component of the financial statements as a percentage of the total. Current liabilities are more prominent as a percent of the total assets at the end of 19X2. What is the cause of the change? In 19X2, $80,000 of the long-term note came due and became a current liability.

component percentages Elements of financial statements that express each component as a percentage of the total.

MANAGEMENT'S DISCUSSION AND ANALYSIS

Both trends and component percentages are generally discussed in a required section of annual reports called **management's discussion and analysis** (often called **MD&A**). The MD&A section explains the major changes in the income statement, liquidity, and capital resources. Space devoted to MD&A has increased dramatically in recent years.

Exhibit 13-5 contains excerpts from the chairman's letter and the Industry Segment disclosure included in MD&A in the annual report of PepsiCo. The annual report is 52 pages long. The first 18 pages are colorful, graphical introductory information about the company, followed by about six pages of discussion and the remainder includes the financial statements, notes, and other financially related data. The letter is from Roger A. Enrico, who had just accepted the role of chairman of the board. It identifies a number of significant changes in PepsiCo, especially the spin-off of the restaurants into a stand-alone business called Tricon Global Restaurants.

management's discussion and analysis (MD&A) A required section of annual reports that concentrates on explaining the major changes in the income statement, liquidity, and capital resources.

SEGMENT REPORTING

Panel B of Exhibit 13-5 provides useful information regarding business segments by type of business—restaurant, snack foods, and beverages as well as breaking the information down by geographic region. In the text, PepsiCo indicates that this element of the MD&A is newly structured to follow management practice and does not follow perfectly the rules in FASB Statement No. 14, which is summarized in Exhibit 13-6. The FASB is currently reconsidering how its segment rules will be written. The approach taken by PepsiCo based on how the business is managed has a lot of support. Note that the PepsiCo manages its restaurants as a United States activity and combines all of North America for beverages and snack foods.

Exhibit 13-7 contains the geographic segment information from PepsiCo's footnote disclosures required by Statement No. 14. Here the information breaks out the three largest international areas, Europe, Canada, and Mexico. It also includes information on

Roger A. Enrico
Chairman and
Chief Executive Officer

Dear Friends

This is my first Annual Report as your Chairman and CEO, and it comes at the end of a tough year, certainly by PepsiCo standards.

On one hand, we earned more than a billion dollars, we generated record cash flow and many of our businesses posted big gains in sales, profit and market share. On the other, our total earnings declined, our international beverage business had big problems and our U.S. restaurants underperformed.

We also made some major strategic decisions: to spin off our restaurant business and to sell our restaurant supply distribution company and smaller restaurant chains—but more about that later.

A Look at 1996

For the year, our sales rose 5%, to nearly $32 billion, but earnings fell 28% to $1.1 billion. If you exclude one-time charges, earnings declined 6%, to $1.9 billion.

On the plus side:

- We contributed far more to the growth of U.S. super-market sales than any other company. Of the top-20 manufacturers, Frito-Lay's supermarket sales grew fastest; Pepsi-Cola ranked number two.
- Our free cash flow grew to a very robust $1.5 billion.
- We repurchased 54 million shares of PepsiCo stock.
- Pepsi-Cola North America increased sales by 4% and operating profit by 14%.
- Frito-Lay worldwide posted a 13% gain in both sales and profit.
- PepsiCo Restaurants International posted a 10% sales gain and a whopping 37% increase in profit.
- And in a sluggish U.S. restaurant industry, KFC increased same store sales by a remarkable 6%, making it one of the best-performing big chains in the country.

On the minus side:

- Pepsi-Cola International had dramatic losses, as we found it necessary to completely restructure the business, our Venezuelan bottler was bought by our competitor, and a big bottler in Brazil and Argentina in which we had an ownership interest ran into major financial difficulties.
- Pizza Hut and Taco Bell suffered volume declines, resulting in lower sales and profits in our U.S. restaurant business.

A Look Ahead

So what does all this mean for our future? Can we put PepsiCo on a sustainable, consistent 15% annual earnings growth trajectory?

I believe we can. And I believe we need to do three things to achieve that goal:

- Sharply focus our financial and management resources on our core business: restaurant management on restaurants, packaged goods management on beverages and snacks.
- Ruthlessly prioritize to be sure we employ our greatest sustaining efforts on the biggest opportunities within our core businesses. In beverages, for example, the lion's share of our investment dollars and management attention will go to high-potential markets where no company dominates—like China, India, and Russia—and to markets where we lead or are a strong number two.
- Build our success upon our key functional strengths: 1) day-to-day management of operationally intensive businesses; 2) manufacturing, selling and distribution infrastructure development; and 3) marketing and new product R&D.

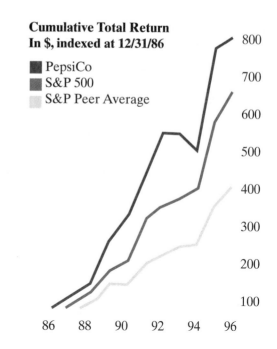

**Cumulative Total Return
In $, indexed at 12/31/86**

■ PepsiCo
■ S&P 500
  S&P Peer Average

Focus works miracles. By putting our greatest resources behind a few big opportunities, we expect to achieve our historic mid-teens profit growth, only with more predictability and consistency.

We look forward to delivering a terrific future.

Roger A. Enrico
Chairman of the Board and Chief Executive Officer

Panel B

Industry Segments—Management Basis

($ in millions)	Growth Rate 1991–1996(a)	1996	1995	1994	1993	1992
NET SALES						
Beverages						
North America (b)	7%	$ 7,725	$ 7,400	$ 7,031	$ 6,404	$5,932
International	15%	2,799	2,982	2,535	2,148	1,589
	9%	10,524	10,382	9,566	8,552	7,521
Snack Foods						
North America (b)	12%	6,618	5,863	5,356	4,674	3,922
International	15%	3,062	2,682	2,908	2,353	2,210
	13%	9,680	8,545	8,264	7,027	6,132
Restaurants						
U.S.	8%	9,110	9,206	8,696	8,025	7,112
International	22%	2,331	2,122	1,825	1,331	1,120
	10%	11,441	11,328	10,521	9,356	8,232
Combined Segments	10%	$31,645	$30,255	$28,351	$24,935	$21,885
OPERATING PROFIT						
Beverages						
North America (b)	12%	$ 1,428	$ 1,249	$ 1,115	$ 1,019	$ 759
International	NM	(846)	117	136	97	45
	6%	582	1,366	1,251	1,116	804
Snack Foods						
North America (b)	13%	1,286	1,149	1,043	914	762
International	12%	346	301	354	285	221
	13%	1,632	1,450	1,397	1,199	983
Restaurants						
U.S.	4%	370	726	637	682	594
International	7%	153	112	86	109	134
	4%	523	838	723	791	728
Combined Segments— Management Basis	8%	$ 2,737	$ 3,654	$ 3,371	$ 3,106	$ 2,515

(a)Five-year compounded annual growth rate. Operating profit growth rates excluded the impacts of the unusual impairment, disposal and other charges in 1996 and 1991.

(b)North America is composed of operations in the U.S. and Canada.

NM—Not Meaningful.

1996 Net Sales
Total: $31,645
$ in Millions

1996 Segment Operating Profits
Total: $2,737*
$ in Millions

*On Management Basis—included unusual charges of $576 and $246 in Beverages and Restaurants, respectively.

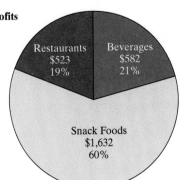

Exhibit 13-6

Main Provisions of FASB Statement No. 14

Type of Disclosure	Criteria Disclosure	Items to Be Disclosed
1. Industry segment	a. Revenue at least 10% of company revenue, b. Profit at least 10% of company profit, or c. Assets at least 10% of company assets	a. Segment revenue b. Segment profit c. Segment assets d. Other (e.g., segment depreciation and capital expenditures)
2. Geographic segment	a. Foreign operations contribute at least 10% of company's revenue, or b. Foreign operations use more than 10% of the company's assets	a. Segment revenue b. Segment profit c. Segment assets
3. Export disclosures	At least 10% of revenues from export sales	Export sales by geographic area
4. Major customers	Any customer providing more than 10% of company's revenue	Customer identity and amount of revenue

the identifiable assets that are associated with these areas. The same footnote included additional industry segment information by business on acquisitions, amortization of intangibles, depreciation, and so on as required by Statement No. 14.

FINANCIAL RATIOS

Objective 3
Use the basic financial ratios to guide your thinking.

time-series comparisons
Comparisons of a company's financial ratios with its own historical ratios.

bench marks General rules of thumb specifying appropriate levels for financial ratios.

cross-sectional comparisons
Comparisons of a company's financial ratios with the ratios of other companies or with industry averages.

Although many analysis methods exist, the cornerstone of financial statement analysis is the use of ratios. Exhibit 13-8 groups some of the most popular ratios into four categories. Most of these ratios have been introduced in earlier chapters, as indicated in the second column (a dash in the column means that the ratio is being introduced in this chapter for the first time). We provide this summary to avoid the need to search for definitions in prior material.

EVALUATING FINANCIAL RATIOS

There are three main types of comparisons used to evaluate financial ratios: (1) with a company's own historical ratios (called **time-series comparisons**), (2) with general *rules of thumb* or **bench marks,** and (3) with ratios of other companies or with industry averages (called **cross-sectional comparisons**).

Annual reports typically support *time-series* trend analysis by providing a table of comparative ratios for 5 or 10 years. For example, some of the items listed in the 1996 annual report of PepsiCo are:

	1996	1995	1994	1993	1992
Income per share	$.72	$1.00	$1.11	$.98	$.81
Debt as a percentage of total capitalization	48%	46%	49%	50%	49%
Return on common stockholders' equity	16%	23%	27%	27%	24%

Exhibit 13-7

Data from 1996 PepsiCo Annual Report

Industry Segment

GEOGRAPHIC AREAS[a]

	Net Sales			Segment Operating Profit (Loss)			Identifiable Assets		
	1996	1995	1994	1996[b]	1995[b]	1994	1996	1995	1994
Europe	$ 2,865	$ 2,783	$ 2,177	$ (90)	$ (65)	$ 17	$ 3,159	$ 3,127	$ 3,062
Canada	1,340	1,299	1,244	134	86	82	1,354	1,344	1,342
Mexico	1,334	1,228	2,023	116	80	261	661	637	995
Other	3,658	3,437	2,782	(73)	342	258	2,628	2,629	2,196
Total International	9,197	8,747	8,226	87	443	618	7,802	7,737	7,595
United States	22,448	21,508	20,125	2,922	2,728	2,706	14,728	14,505	14,218
Combined Segments	$31,645	$30,255	$28,351	$3,009	$3,171	$3,324	22,530	22,242	21,813
Investments in Unconsolidated Affiliates							1,375	1,635	1,295
Corporate							607	1,555	1,684
							$24,512	$25,432	$24,792

[a]The results of centralized concentrate manufacturing operations in Puerto Rico and Ireland have been allocated based upon sales to the respective geographic areas.

[b]The unusual impairment, disposal and other charges reduced combined segment operating profit by $822 (United States–$246, Europe–$69, Mexico–$4, Other–$503) in 1996 and $503 (United States–$302, Europe–$119, Mexico–$21, Canada–$30, Other–$31) in 1995.

Exhibit 13-8

Some Typical Financial Ratios

Typical Name of Ratio	Introduced In Chapter	Numerator	Denominator	Using Appropriate Oxley Numbers Applied to December 31 of Year	
				19X2	19X1
Short-term liquidity ratios:					
Current ratio	4	Current assets	Current liabilities	$290 \div 219 = 1.3$	$202 \div 101 = 2.0$
Quick ratio	4	Cash + marketable securities + receivables	Current liabilities	$(150 + 0 + 95) \div 219 = 1.1$	$(57 + 0 + 70) \div 101 = 1.3$
Average collection period in days	5	Average accounts receivable × 365	Sales	$[1/2(95 + 70) \times 365] \div 999 = 30$†	Unknown*
Inventory turnover	6	Cost of goods sold	Average inventory at cost	$399 \div 1/2(20 + 60) = 10$	Unknown*
Long-term solvency ratios:					
Total debt to total assets	8	Total liabilities	Total assets	$259 \div 658 = 39.4\%$	$221 \div 610 = 36.2\%$
Total debt to equity	8	Total liabilities	Stockholders' equity	$259 \div 399 = 64.9\%$	$221 \div 389 = 56.8\%$
Interest coverage	8	Income before interest and taxes	Interest expense	$(150 + 12) \div 12 = 13.5$	$(128 + 12) \div 12 = 11.7$
Profitability ratios:					
Return on stockholders' equity (ROE)	4, 11	Net income	Average stockholders' equity	$90 \div 1/2(399 + 389) = 22.8\%$	Unknown*
Gross profit rate or percentage	4	Gross profit or gross margin	Sales	$600 \div 999 = 60\%$	$464 \div 800 = 58\%$
Return on sales	4	Net income	Sales	$90 \div 999 = 9\%$	$80 \div 800 = 10\%$
Asset turnover	—	Sales	Average total assets available	$999 \div 1/2(658 + 610) = 1.6$	Unknown*
Pretax return on operating assets	—	Operating income	Average total assets available	$126 \div 1/2(658 + 610) = 19.9\%$	Unknown*
Earnings per share	2	Net income less dividends on preferred stock, if any	Average common shares outstanding	$90 \div 200 = \$.45$	$80 \div 200 = \$.40$
Market price and dividend ratios:					
Price-earnings	2	Market price of common share (assume $4 and $3)	Earnings per share	$4 \div 45 = 8.9$	$3 \div 40 = 7.5$
Dividend-yield	2	Dividends per common share	Market price of common share (assume $4 and $3)	$.40 \div 4 = 10.0\%$	$.20 \div 3 = 6.7\%$
Dividend-payout	2	Dividends per common share	Earnings per share	$.40 \div .45 = 89\%$	$.20 \div .40 = 50\%$

*Insufficient data available because the *beginning* balance sheet balances for 19X1 are not provided. Without them, the *average* investment in receivables, inventory, total assets, or stockholders' equity during 19X1 cannot be computed.

†This may be easier to see as follows: Average receivables = 1/2(95 + 70) = 82.5. Average receivables as a percentage of annual sales = 82.5 ÷ 999 = 8.25%. Average collection period = 8.25% × 365 days = 30 days.

RATIOS

Ratios are useful for financial analysis by investors because ratios capture critical dimensions of the economic performance of the entity. How might ratios pay off for managers? Increasingly ratios are a tool that managers use to guide, measure, and reward workers. If managers compensate workers for actions that make the company more profitable, workers are likely to do the right thing. Thus some companies give workers a bonus if the company generates an ROE of more than 20% or if earnings per share exceeds a specific number. Hewitt Associates, a compensation consulting firm, reports that 60% of the 1,941 large companies they surveyed had profit-sharing programs. Such programs are based on the solid view that when profits rise, workers are doing the right thing and should share in the benefits.

Duke Power Co. decided that profit may not be the right measure for rewarding employees. Suppose profit increases because you raise more capital and expand the company? Should the workers necessarily earn more? Duke Power decided to reward workers based on two factors: success in meeting goals and the return on stockholders' equity (ROE). For one worker, the goal might be defined as reduced injuries and for another as improved customer service. But everyone earns more for meeting ROE targets. ROE is a good measure of efficiency because it can be improved by increasing profitability (the return on sales) and also by increasing the efficiency with which assets are employed (asset turnover).

In 1991, many Duke Power workers had never heard of ROE, but by 1996, they were watching the monthly financial results as carefully as their children look both ways before crossing the street. Now workers participate, and bonuses can exceed the base pay. As a result, a $9.00 per hour worker can earn $20.00 per hour by achieving targets. Management is delighted to pay these bonuses because they are only paid when worker productivity is exceptional. The surprise is that workers can and do turn in exceptional performances when they know it will be recognized—not just by kind words, but by a management that puts its money where its mouth is.

Compare the ratios for Oxley Company in Exhibit 13-8 to some of the Dun & Bradstreet ratios for 1,712 retail nurseries and garden stores:

Dun and Bradstreet Ratios

	Current Ratio	Quick Ratio	Average Collection Period (Days)	Total Debt to Stockholders' Equity (Percent)	Return on Sales (Percent)	Return on Stockholders' Equity (Percent)
1,712 companies:						
Upper quartile	4.2	1.5	5.5	32.3	6.1	30.2
Median	2.0	0.5	11.3	92.8	2.5	12.6
Lower quartile	1.3	0.2	23.0	230.7	0.5	2.6
Oxley*	1.3	1.1	30.0	64.9	9.0	22.8

*Ratios are from Exhibit 13-8. Please consult that exhibit for an explanation of the components of each ratio.

Dun and Bradstreet ranks the individual ratios from best to worst. The ratio ranked in the middle is the *median*. The upper quartile is the ratio ranked halfway between the median and the best value. The lower quartile is the ratio ranked halfway between the median and the worst value. The concept of best and worst must be taken with a grain of salt. Different analysts may have different ideas about what is good and what is bad. For example, a short-term creditor would think that a very high current ratio was good, because it means the assets are there to repay the debt. From management's perspective, however, a very high current ratio may be bad and show that the company is maintaining higher levels of inventory and receivables than it should. Let's take a look at how analysts would interpret some of the main types of ratios.

Oxley is above the median level of net-income-based ratios and has a reasonable debt level. The long collection period means Oxley has a lot of receivables. It is unclear whether the long collection period is a problem or just an odd practice of Oxley's. The analyst must ask management about it. What are the possibilities? Oxley could have a lot of deadbeat customers. Bad news. Alternatively, most companies similar to Oxley may require bank cards and not have any "real" receivables while Oxley actually lets local buyers have credit terms on their large purchases. You must understand the business and be aware of what the norms are before you evaluate the specifics of one company.

Although the current ratio is low, the quick ratio is high, which means Oxley should have enough liquid funds to manage current obligations.

How might analysts think about specific liquidity ratios? Changes in average collection period and inventory turnover can alert investors and creditors to problems. For example, a decrease in inventory turnover may suggest that a company's sales staff is no longer doing a very good job or that the company's products have fallen out of favor with the buying public. An alternative to the "sales are falling" explanation is the "inventory is rising" explanation. Suppose manufacturing is producing product at a rapid pace beyond what current buyers want. Inventory builds faster than sales, and the turnover falls.

Similarly, an increase in the average collection period of receivables may indicate that the company has started selling to buyers who are credit risks or that the company has gotten lazy in its collection efforts. Whether the inventory turnover of 10 and the average collection period of 30 days are "fast" or "slow" depends on past performance and the performance of similar companies. Inventory turnover is not available from Dun & Bradstreet on an industry-comparable basis. The average collection period for Oxley is nearly three times as long as the industry median of 11.3 days. Perhaps most firms give large discounts for prompt payment and Oxley does not.

A company with many cash sales may have a short average collection period for total sales, even though there may be long delays in receiving payments for items sold on credit. Suppose half of Oxley's sales were for cash and half were on open credit. The average collection period for credit sales would be

$$\frac{(1/2)(95 + 70) \times 365}{(1/2)(999)} = 60 \text{ days}$$

To compare this average for credit sales with the given industry average collection period, we must adjust the industry average for credit sales. Suppose only one-fourth of the sales in retail nurseries are on credit. The industry median collection period for credit accounts would be $11.3 \div (1/4) = 45.2$ days. Many analysts use sales *on account* in the denominator of the average collection period to remove this interpretation problem.

Oxley's debt-to-equity ratio of 64.9% is below the industry median of 92.8%, which suggests that the company has a better than average ability to pay its debts on time. Typically, companies with heavy debt in relation to ownership capital are in greater danger of suffering net losses or even insolvency when business conditions sour. Why? Because revenues and many expenses decline, but interest expenses and maturity dates do not change.

Oxley's ROE of 22.8% is above the industry median of 12.6%. What explains Oxley's superior performance? Two additional profitability ratios help explain it. The return on sales has fallen from 10% to 9% but still places Oxley well above the upper quartile for nurseries and garden stores according to Dun & Bradstreet. Also, Oxley is very efficient when using its assets to generate sales. Various additional ratios can be used to assess the role of operating performance and financial performance in the overall success of the company.

OPERATING PERFORMANCE AND FINANCIAL PERFORMANCE

Measures of overall profitability such as ROE are affected by both operating and financing choices. *Financial management* is concerned with where the company gets cash and how it uses that cash to its benefit. *Operating management* is concerned with the day-to-day activities that generate revenues and expenses. Ratios to assess operating efficiency should not be affected by financial management performance.

Objective 4
Evaluate corporate performance using ROA and ROE.

OPERATING PERFORMANCE

In general, we evaluate the overall success of an investment by comparing what the investment returns to us with the amount of investment we initially made:

$$\text{Rate of return on investment} = \frac{\text{Income}}{\text{Invested capital}} \qquad (1)$$

In various settings, we find it useful to define income differently, sometimes as net earnings and sometimes as either pretax income from operations or earnings before interest and taxes (**EBIT**). We also define invested capital differently, sometimes as the stockholders' equity and other times as the total capital provided by both debt and equity sources. These choices are determined by the purpose of the analysis. For example, an investor in common stock would be more concerned about the ROE, whereas a lender is more concerned with how effectively borrowed capital is being used to generate cash in support of interest payments.

EBIT Earnings before interest and taxes.

  Because the measurement of *operating* performance should not be influenced by how assets are financed, it is best measured by **pretax operating rate of return on total assets** also called simply **return on total assets (ROA)**:

$$\begin{array}{c}\text{Pretax operating rate}\\ \text{of return on total assets}\end{array} = \frac{\text{Operating income}}{\text{Average total assets available}} \qquad (2)$$

pretax operating rate of return on total assets (return on total assets— ROA) Operating income divided by average total assets available.

The right side of Equation 2 consists of two important ratios:

$$\frac{\text{Operating income}}{\text{Average total assets available}} = \frac{\text{Operating income}}{\text{Sales}} \times \frac{\text{Sales}}{\begin{array}{c}\text{Average total}\\ \text{assets available}\end{array}} \qquad (3)$$

These relationships are displayed for Oxley Company in Exhibit 13-9.

  The right-side terms in Equation 3 are often called the **operating income percentage on sales** and the **total asset turnover (asset turnover),** respectively. Equation 3 may be re-expressed:

operating income percentage on sales Operating income divided by sales.

$$\begin{array}{l}\begin{array}{c}\text{Pretax operating rate}\\ \text{of return on total assets}\end{array} = \text{Operating income percentage on sales} \times \text{Total asset turnover:}\\ \qquad\qquad 19.9\% = 12.6\% \times 1.576 \text{ times} \qquad\qquad\qquad\qquad (4)\end{array}$$

total asset turnover (asset turnover) Sales divided by average total assets available.

Equation 4 highlights that operating income percentage and turnover will, by themselves, each increase the rate of return on total assets. Unfortunately, these ratios are sometimes calculated on after-tax amounts, so peculiarities of the income tax laws may sometimes distort results. You will know how you calculate a number but may not always be sure how published numbers are calculated.

FINANCIAL PERFORMANCE

Good financial performance requires an appropriate balance of debt and equity financing. In addition to deciding how much debt is appropriate, a firm must choose how much to borrow short-term (for example, accounts payable and some bank debt) and how much to borrow by issuing bonds or other longer-term debt. Short-term debt must be quickly

Exhibit 13-9

Major Ingredients of Return on Total Assets

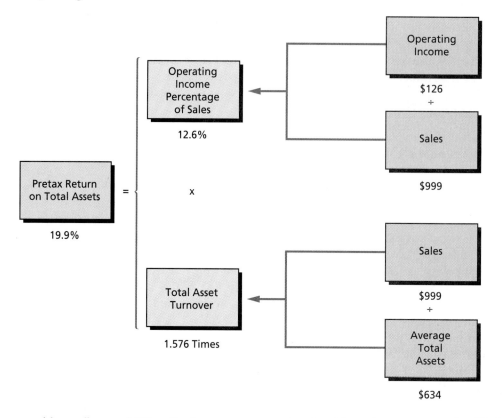

repaid or refinanced. When the borrower encounters trouble and cannot repay, it will also be difficult to refinance. Lenders prefer healthy, profitable borrowers, not troubled ones. Such problems are especially severe during periods when interest rates are rising, because each new refinancing occurs at a higher interest rate, and the cash flow needed to cover interest payments rises.

Long-term investments are usually financed by long-term capital: debt or stock. Debt is often a more attractive vehicle to companies than is common stock because (1) interest payments are deductible for income tax purposes, but dividends are not, and (2) the ownership rights to voting and profits are kept by the present shareholders.

TRADING ON THE EQUITY

capitalization (capital structure) Owners' equity plus long-term debt.

Most companies have two basic types of long-term financing: long-term debt and stockholders' equity. The total of long-term financing is often called the **capitalization,** or simply **capital structure** of a corporation. Suppose a company has long-term debt (bonds payable) and common stock as its capital structure. The common shareholders enjoy the benefits of all income in excess of interest on the bonds.

trading on the equity (financial leverage, leveraging, gearing) Using borrowed money at fixed interest rates with the objective of enhancing the rate of return on common equity.

Trading on the equity (also referred to as using **financial leverage, leveraging,** or in the U.K., **gearing**) means using money borrowed at fixed interest rates to try to enhance the rate of return on common shareholders' equity. There are costs and benefits to shareholders from trading on the equity. The costs are interest payments and increased risk, and the benefits are the larger returns to the common shareholders—as long as overall income is large enough.

To illustrate, imagine the companies, A, B, and C shown in Exhibit 13-10. Each is in the same industry, with $80,000 of assets and with the same rate of return on total assets (ROA) each year. However, the annual ROA varies from 20% in Year 1, to 10% in Year 2, and 5% in Year 3. The three companies have chosen very different capital structures. Company A has

Exhibit 13-10

Trading on the Equity-Effects of Debt on Rates of Return

	(1) Income before Interest	(2) Interest Expense	(3) Net Income	(4) Stockholders' Equity	(5) Return on Equity
	$(ROA \times Assets)^*$	$(Debt \times Interest\ Rate)^\dagger$	$(1) - (2)$		$(3) \div (4)$
Year 1: 20% ROA					
Company A	$16,000	$ 0	$16,000	$80,000	20%
Company B	16,000	3,000	13,000	50,000	26%
Company C	16,000	7,200	8,800	20,000	44%
Year 2: 10% ROA					
Company A	$ 8,000	$ 0	$ 8,000	$80,000	10%
Company B	8,000	3,000	5,000	50,000	10%
Company C	8,000	7,200	800	20,000	4%
Year 3: 5% ROA					
Company A	$ 4,000	$ 0	$ 4,000	$80,000	5%
Company B	4,000	3,000	1,000	50,000	2%
Company C	4,000	7,200	(3,200)	20,000	(16%)

*All three companies have $80,000 in assets.

†Company A, no debt; Company B, $30,000 in debt at 10%; Company C, $60,000 in debt at 12%.

no debt, Company B has $30,000 in debt, and Company C has $60,000 in debt. Company B pays 10% interest, while the more heavily indebted Company C must pay 12%. How do the shareholders fare in these three companies in different years? The results are summarized in Exhibit 13-10.

The first column of Exhibit 13-10 gives the income before interest expense. To focus clearly on leverage, this example ignores taxes. Recall that the return on assets is calculated as

$$\text{Pretax operating rate of return on total assets} = \frac{\text{Operating income (income before interest and taxes)}}{\text{Average total assets}}$$

Therefore, income before interest and taxes equals rate of return on total assets (ROA) times average total assets. In this instance, we assume a constant ROA for each firm, but we vary the ROA from one year to the next. We can calculate operating income by multiplying ROA times the constant asset level of $80,000. The values are the same for all three companies within a year but vary from year to year. The interest expense differs by company because each has a different level of debt, but for any company it does not change from year to year. Our primary interest is the effect of leverage on the level of the rate of return on common stockholders' equity (ROE).

What do we learn from Exhibit 13-10? First, a debt-free, or unlevered, company has identical ROA and ROE. Note that equity-financed, unlevered Company A's ROE and ROA are identical in each year: 20%, 10%, and 5%. Second, when a company has an ROA greater than its interest rate, ROE exceeds ROA. This situation is called favorable financial leverage and describes both companies B and C in Year 1. They earn 20% on their assets and pay either 10% or 12% on their debt. The earnings in excess of the interest cost increase earnings available to shareholders. Year 2 is interesting because Company B has an ROA of 10%, which equals its interest rate. Thus, like Company A, Company B has an ROE of 10%. In contrast, Company C experiences unfavorable financial leverage. Because its 10% ROA is less than its 12% interest cost, its ROE falls sharply to 4%.

Year 3 further stresses the effects of leverage in poor years. When ROA falls noticeably below the firm's interest cost, ROE falls sharply as well. Company B falls to an ROE of 2%, while the more highly leveraged Company C faces a loss year and negative ROE.

When a company is unable to earn at least the interest rate on the money borrowed, the return on equity will be lower than it would be for the debt-free company. If earnings are low enough that the interest and principal payments on debt cannot be made, a company may be forced into bankruptcy. The possibility of bankruptcy increases the risk to the common stockholders even more than it does to debtholders. Remember, debtholders collect their claims before stockholders do.

Obviously, the more stable the income, the less dangerous it is to trade on the equity. Therefore, regulated utilities such as electric, gas, and telephone companies tend to have a much heavier proportion of debt than do manufacturers of computers or steel. Historically, these regulated companies have had a stable customer base and were somewhat protected from competition. Government regulations helped assure that prices would be sufficiently high to ensure a profit. The breakup of AT&T as the dominant national phone company and current efforts to introduce more competition among electric utility companies may produce changes in these historical patterns of leverage. The prudent use of debt is part of intelligent financial management.

INCOME TAX EFFECTS

Because interest payments are deductible as an expense for income tax purposes but dividends are not, if all other things are equal, the use of debt is less costly to the corporation than is equity. Consider raising additional capital of $10 million either through long-term debt or through preferred stock. The typical preferred stock is a part of shareholders' equity, and the dividend thereon is not deductible for income tax purposes. Moreover, the rate of preferred dividends is usually higher than is the rate of interest because the preferred stockholders have a greater risk due to their lower-priority claim on the total assets of a company. Assume an interest rate of 10% for debt and a preferred dividend rate of 11%. The income tax rate is 40%. Compare the effects in net income of these two methods shown in the accompanying table.

	$10 Million Long-Term Debt	$10 Million Preferred Stock
Income before interest expense (assumed)	$5,000,000	$5,000,000
Interest expense at 10% of long-term debt	1,000,000	—
Income before income taxes	$4,000,000	$5,000,000
Income tax expense at 40%	1,600,000	2,000,000
Net income	$2,400,000	$3,000,000
Dividends to preferred shareholders at 11%	—	1,100,000
Net income less dividends	$2,400,000	$1,900,000
Pretax cost of capital raised	10%	11%
After-tax cost of capital raised:		
$600,000* ÷ $10,000,000	6%	
$1,100,000 ÷ $10,000,000		11%
*Interest expense	$1,000,000	
Income tax savings because of interest deduction:		
.40 × $1,000,000	400,000	
Interest expense after tax savings	$ 600,000	

You should note three points:

1. Interest is tax deductible, so its after-tax cost can be considerably less than that of dividends on preferred stock. In other words, net income attributable to common shareholders can be substantially higher if debt is used.

2. Interest is an expense, whereas preferred dividends are not. Therefore net income is higher if preferred shares are used. Note that trading on the equity can

benefit the common stockholders by the issuance of either long-term debt securities or preferred stock, provided that there are sufficient earnings on the additional assets acquired.

3. Failure to pay interest is an act of bankruptcy, which gives creditors rights to control or liquidate the company. Failure to pay dividends has less severe consequences.

MEASURING SAFETY

Investors in debt securities want assurance that future operations will easily provide enough cash for the company to make the scheduled payments of interest and principal. Corporate borrowers do not like to take on too much risk by borrowing. While both lenders and borrowers try to avoid excessive risks from debt, the issue is most important to lenders.

Debt securities often have provisions aimed at reducing investor risk, such as the right to repossess assets or the right to receive payment before common stockholders do. However, because they kick in only when the company is in danger of defaulting on the loans, these provisions are nowhere near as valuable as a pattern of growing earnings. Bondholders would like to avoid the trouble and costs of foreclosure or bankruptcy litigation. They would much rather have a steady stream of interest and repayments of principal provided by a company with good, steady earnings.

Debt-to-equity ratios are popular measures of risk. But they do not focus directly on the major concern of the holders of long-term debt: the ability to make debt payments on schedule. A ratio that focuses on interest-paying ability is *interest coverage* (see, p. 335, also called **times interest earned**), calculated as income before interest expense and income taxes divided by interest expense. For example, in the table on page 558, interest coverage is:

times interest earned
Income before interest expense and income taxes divided by interest expense. Synonym for interest coverage.

$$\text{Interest coverage} = \frac{\text{Income before interest expense and income taxes}}{\text{Interest expense}}$$

$$= \frac{\$5,000,000}{\$1,000,000} = 5.0 \text{ times}$$

The equation is self-explanatory. A rule of thumb or bench mark for debt investors is that the interest coverage should be at least five times, even in the poorest year in a span of 7 to 10 years. The numerator in this equation does not deduct income taxes because interest expense is deductible for income tax purposes. In effect, income taxes, as a periodic "claim" on earnings, have a lower priority than does interest. For instance, if the numerator were only $1 million, interest would be paid, leaving a net taxable income of zero. This tax-deductibility feature is a major reason why bonds are used much more widely than preferred stock.

PROMINENCE OF EARNINGS PER SHARE

Throughout this text, we have viewed earnings as a basic reporting element in the financial statements. We have noted that earnings are often expressed on a per share basis (EPS) and that EPS is itself a component in the price-earnings ratio. Up to this point, though, we have kept EPS simple by considering only common stock. In reality, EPS can be a bit more complicated. We now turn to three issues that might complicate it: preferred stock, stock issues and redemptions, and the possibility of exercise of options or various convertible securities.

WEIGHTED-AVERAGE SHARES AND PREFERRED STOCK

When the outstanding shares are all common stock, the primary complication is the calculation of weighted-average shares in the following equation:

$$\text{Earnings per share of common stock} = \frac{\text{Net income}}{\text{Weighted-average number of shares outstanding during the period}}$$

$$= \frac{\$1,000,000}{800,000} = \$1.25$$

How would the 800,000 average shares be calculated? Suppose 750,000 shares were outstanding at the beginning of a calendar year, and 200,000 of additional shares were issued on October 1 (three months before the end of the year). The weighted average is based on the number of months that the shares were outstanding during the year. The basic computation can be accomplished in two different ways:

750,000 × weighting of 12/12 = 750,000		750,000 × 9/12 = 562,500
200,000 × weighting of 3/12 = 50,000	*or*	950,000 × 3/12 = 237,500
Weighted average shares 800,000		800,000

In this example, the number of shares outstanding rose because additional shares were issued. This might have occurred because some executives exercised some stock options and acquired more shares. The company might have simply issued a block of additional shares to outside investors at the current market price. The number of shares could also decline during the year due to purchase of shares for the treasury.

A second complication arises if shares of nonconvertible preferred stock are outstanding. The dividends on preferred stock for the current period, whether or not paid, should be deducted in calculating earnings applicable to common stock (figures assumed):

$$\text{Earnings per share of common stock} = \frac{\text{Net income} - \text{Preferred dividends}}{\text{Weighted-average number of shares outstanding during the period}}$$

$$= \frac{\$1,000,000 - \$200,000}{800,000} = \$1.00$$

Historical summaries of EPS must be made comparable by adjusting for changes in capitalization structure (for example, stock splits and stock dividends). For example, PepsiCo had a 2-for-1 stock split in 1996. In the 1996 historical summary, 1995 earnings per share are reported to be $1.00. If you actually looked at the 1995 annual report, the EPS reported there would be $2.00. Why? Because there were half as many shares outstanding in 1995. The investor wants to be able to compare the year-to-year performance and 1995 EPS must be adjusted to allow meaningful comparisons.

BASIC AND DILUTED EPS

Objective 5
Calculate EPS under complex circumstances.

EPS calculations become a bit more complex when companies have convertible securities, stock options, or other financial instruments that can be exchanged for or converted to common shares. For example, suppose a firm has some convertible preferred stock outstanding:

5% convertible preferred stock, $100 par, each share convertible into 2 common shares	100,000 shares
Common stock	1,000,000 shares

The basic EPS computation follows (numbers assumed):

Computation of earnings per share:	
Net income	$10,500,000
less Preferred dividends	500,000
Net income to common stock	$10,000,000
Earnings per share of common stock:	
$10,000,000 ÷ 1,000,000 shares	$ 10.00

However, note how EPS would be affected if the preferred stock were converted, that is, exchanged for common stock. EPS will be "diluted," or reduced. We can calculate EPS as if conversion had occurred at the beginning of the period and thus no preferred dividends were paid:

Net income	$10,500,000
less Preferred dividends	0
Net income to common stock	$10,500,000
Earnings per share of common stock—assuming conversion:	
$10,500,000 ÷ 1,200,000 shares	$ 8.75

The dilution of common stock caused by the conversion is $10.00 − $8.75 = $1.25 per share. Diluted EPS assumes the conversion of all potentially dilutive securities.

DISCLOSURE OF NONRECURRING ITEMS

Objective 6
Adjust for nonrecurring items.

As we have said, one of the main ideas behind financial statement analysis is evaluating or estimating a firm's future prospects. When estimating the future, though, we need to distinguish the elements of the current financial statements that reflect recurring aspects of the firm from those that represent one-time events or items that will not continue. These nonrecurring items fall into four major categories: special items, extraordinary items, discontinued operations, and accounting changes.

SPECIAL ITEMS

special items Expenses that are large enough and unusual enough to warrant separate disclosure.

Special items are large and unusual items. They appear in the income statement as a separately identified amount. Companies have substantial flexibility in deciding when to treat something as a *special item*. Recently, the most common special item has been restructuring charges. A restructuring occurs when a firm decides to substantially change the size or scope or location of a part of the business. It often involves relocation, plant closings, and reductions in personnel. The costs will typically be incurred over an extended period of time, often several years, but GAAP requires that the total costs be estimated and recorded when the plan is made. In 1994, the FASB and the SEC acted to assure that restructuring changes did not include costs that will benefit future periods. Specifically, restructuring cannot include relocation and training costs for people who will continue to work for the firm. These costs must still be properly matched to future revenues. A special item would appear as a separate line item among operating expenses, with any necessary discussion or explanation in the footnotes. The following example is taken from PepsiCo's 1996 annual report.

(in millions except per share amounts)	1996 (52 Weeks)	1995 (52 Weeks)
Net Sales	$31,645	$30,255
Costs and Expenses, net		
Cost of sales	15,383	14,886
Selling, general and administrative expenses	12,593	11,546
Amortization of intangible assets	301	316
Unusual impairment, disposal and other charges	822	520
Operating Profit	$ 2,546	2,987

How would an analyst use this information to project future earnings? Because a restructuring of such magnitude is rare, the analyst might argue that the expense of $822 million is nonrecurring. Continuing operating profit projections would be based on 1996 levels of $2,546 million + $822 milion or $3,368 million.

Notice that because special items are reported with other expenses, they are reported before tax. Taxable income is thus reduced as is income tax expense. If we assume a 40% tax rate, the special item reduced taxable income by $822 million and therefore reduced the tax provision by 40% of $822 million, or $329 million. The special item's after-tax effect would be $822 − (.40 × 822) = $493 million. In estimating future net income, the analyst would add back $493 million to reported net income.

In 1996, however, life would not be quite that easy for the equity analyst trying to assess the future earnings of PepsiCo. The biggest issue is that PepsiCo was in the midst of selling off a number of the companies in its food division and by mid-1997 had spun-off the remainder. California Pizza Kitchen, Chevys and East Side Mario's were among the units sold. Pizza Hut, KFC and Taco Bell were packaged in the spun-off subsidiary. So forecasting 1997 earnings will require a careful focus on PepsiCo's segment disclosures as well as sorting out unusual, nonrecurring items.

EXTRAORDINARY ITEMS

extraordinary items Items that are unusual in nature and infrequent in occurrence that are shown separately, net of tax, in the income statement.

Extraordinary items result from events that must have both an *unusual nature* and an *infrequency of occurrence*. Therefore, write-downs of receivables and inventories are ordinary items, as are gains or losses on the sale of fixed assets. The effects of a strike and many foreign currency revaluations are also ordinary items. However, the financial effects of an earthquake or government expropriation are likely to qualify as extraordinary items. Interestingly enough, the effects of most floods are not considered extraordinary. Why not? Because most floods occur in areas that are prone to certain amounts of flooding, thus a flood there is not an unusual occurrence. Basically, an event or transaction should be presumed to be ordinary unless the evidence clearly supports its classification as extraordinary.

The few events and items that are considered extraordinary must be excluded from regular net income calculations. Extraordinary items are presented separately on the income statement. They are reported net of tax, which means that the figure presented includes any tax effect an item might have (remember, any items that increase/decrease income also increase/decrease taxes).

In an average year, fewer than 10% of major U.S. companies report an extraordinary item. Fewer than 5% have an extraordinary item greater than 10% of their net income. Most of the extraordinary items arise from extinguishment of debt. For example, consider the following extract from the 1996 income statement of Chrysler (in millions):

Income before extraordinary item	$3,720
Extraordinary item—Loss on early extinguishment of debt, net of taxes	(191)
Net earnings	$3,529

A tragic illustration of an extraordinary charge was caused by criminal tampering with Tylenol capsules. People died as a result of cyanide being put into the product. The manufacturer, Johnson & Johnson, took immediate action to pull all product from store shelves while tracing the source of the problem. J&J reported the following on its income statement (in millions):

Earnings before extraordinary charge	$146.5
Extraordinary charge—costs associated with the withdrawal of TYLENOL capsules (less applicable tax relief of $50.0)	50.0
Net earnings	$ 96.5

DISCONTINUED OPERATIONS

Discontinued operations involve the termination (closing or sale) of a segment of the business, not just of a single plant or location. Many large companies have several discrete business segments. For example, RJR Nabisco has a tobacco business and a food business. The results of continuing operations should be reported separately from discontinued operations, although both must be reported on the income statement. Any gain or loss from the disposal of a segment of a business must be reported with the related results of discontinued operations and not as an extraordinary item. As were extraordinary items, discontinued operations are shown on the income statement net of tax.

> **discontinued operations**
> The termination of a business segment. The results are reported separately, net of tax, in the income statement.

In a comparative income statement, the income or loss of the discontinued segment's operations needs to be shown separately for all past years that segment operated. Otherwise, the company's current financial status, which no longer includes the discontinued segment, would not be comparable to its past financial status.

The Sears Roebuck and Company income statement for 1995 showed the following:

Income from continuing operations	$1,025
Discontinued operations	776
Net Income	1,801

Exhibit 13-11 gives an integrated example of special items, discontinued operations, and extraordinary items.

ACCOUNTING CHANGES

The presentation of the effects of an accounting change is net of tax and is separated from ongoing operations in the same section of the income statement that contains discontinued operations. Changes of accounting method that are treated this way arise from FASB requirements. When the FASB changes its rules, it often requires a major one-time recognition. Such a change in reporting for postretirement insurance and health costs affected many U.S. companies in 1992 and 1993. This led to large charges against income. At the same time, many companies adopted the new FASB rule on taxes that caused some companies to realize one-time additional expense and caused other companies to show increased income. Significant accounting changes have not been recorded by very many companies in 1995 and 1996, but the following examples illustrate the importance of some of the 1992/1993 accounting changes (in millions of dollars):

	Bethlehem Steel	IBM	PepsiCo
Income before accounting change	$(260.2)	$(6,865)	$1,302
After-tax effect of change	(290.1)	1,900	(928)
Net Income	$(550.3)	$(4,965)	$ 374

Exhibit 13-11

Illustrated Partial Income Statement (in millions, data assumed)

Revenue		$ 800
Operating expenses		700
Special items		50
Income from continuing operations before income taxes		$ 50
Deduct applicable income taxes		20
Income from continuing operations		$ 30
Discontinued operations:		
Income from operations of discontinued Division X		
(less applicable income taxes of $4)	$ 6	
Loss on disposal of Division X, including provision of		
$3 for operating losses during phase-out period		
(less applicable income taxes of $6)	(9)	(3)
Income before extraordinary items		$ 27
Add extraordinary items:		
Loss from earthquake (less applicable income taxes of $2)	(3)	
Gain from early extinguishment of debt		
(less applicable income taxes of $8)	12	9
Net income		$ 36
Per share amounts (in dollars), assuming 4 million shares		
of common stock outstanding:		
Income from continuing operations		$7.50
Loss on discontinued operations		(.75)
Income before extraordinary items		$6.75
Extraordinary items		2.25
Net income		$9.00

Bethlehem Steel's loss on the accounting change almost doubled its loss, IBM's gain on the accounting change reduced its loss, while PepsiCo's loss on the accounting change dropped its income by some 75%.

Internationally, financial statement analysis is significantly complicated by a variety of factors. Throughout the text, we have considered differences in accounting methods used. In addition, we should stress the obvious but easily forgotten differences in the language of reporting and the currency of measurement. For example, most U.S. analysts cannot read financial statements in Japanese and do not readily "have a feel for" the value of yen versus dollars. Last, but not least, is the fact that different structures for security markets, different tax laws, and different preferences among citizens of different countries all affect the relative value of financial assets.

SUMMARY PROBLEM FOR YOUR REVIEW

PROBLEM

Exhibit 13-12 contains a condensed income statement and balance sheet for The Timberland Company, the company that designs, engineers, and markets premium quality footwear, apparel, and accessories.

1. Compute the following ratios: (a) current ratio, (b) quick ratio, (c) average collection period, (d) inventory turnover, (e) total debt to total assets, (f) return on sales, and (g) return on stockholders' equity.

2. Compare your computed values to the values provided below for Nike.

Nike 1996	
Current ratio	2.05
Quick ratio	1.18
Average collection period	61.59
Inventory turnover	4.85
Total debt to total assets	.41
Return on sales	.09
ROE	.28

SOLUTION

1. **a)** Current ratio = current assets ÷ current liabilities
= 371,468 ÷ 101,865 = 3.65

b) Quick ratio = (cash + marketable securities + receivables)
÷ current liabilities
= (93,336 + 100,556) ÷ 101,865 = 1.90

c) Average collection period = (average accounts receivable × 365) ÷ sales
= [((100,556 + 95,786) ÷ 2) × 365] ÷ 689,973
= 51.93

d) Inventory turnover = cost of goods sold ÷ average inventory
= 438,064 ÷ [(159,058 + 180,636) ÷ 2]
= 2.58

e) Total debt to total assets = total liabilities ÷ total assets
= (total asssets − stockholders' equity)
÷ total assets
= (449,586 − 165,360) ÷ 449,586
= .63

f) Return on sales = net income ÷ sales
= 20,419 ÷ 689,973
= .03

g) ROE = net income ÷ average stockholders' equity
= 20,419 ÷ [(165,360 + 142,221) ÷ 2]
= .13

2. Timberland has higher current and quick ratios for higher short term liquidity. This could also suggest that current assets are excessive. Accounts receivable levels are favorable for Timberland compared to Nike, given the shorter collection period. On the other hand, Timberland may have excessive inventories because its inventory turnover is much lower than Nike. This problem appears to be in process of improvement. Timberland inventories declined from 1995 to 1996 while sales increased.

Timberland has significantly more debt than Nike and a much lower return on sales. Collectively these comparisons help explain why Nike has an ROE twice as high as Timberland's.

Highlights to Remember

Financial and operating information is available from many sources, including daily newspapers. Various regulations in the United States require the issuance of annual reports and govern their content. In addition, publicly traded companies must disclose particular information by filing 10-K, 8-K, and other forms with the SEC on a periodic basis.

Financial information is provided to aid investors in assessing the risk and return of a potential investment. Investors in debt are particularly concerned about the solvency and liquidity of the issuer, while equity investors are more interested in profitability.

Exhibit 13-12

The Timberland Company
(Amounts in thousands except per share data)

	For the Years Ended	
Consolidated Statements of Operations	*December 31, 1996*	*December 31, 1995*
Revenues	$689,973	$ 655,138
Cost of goods sold	438,064	451,741
Gross profit	251,909	203,397
Operating expenses		
Selling	152,834	145,924
General and administrative	46,502	46,721
Amortization of goodwill	1,684	1,685
Restructuring charge	—	16,000
Total operating expenses	201,020	201,330
Operating income (loss)	50,889	(6,933)
Other expense (income)		
Interest expense	20,582	22,861
Other, net	(631)	(11,028)
Total other expense	19,951	11,833
Income (loss) before income taxes	30,938	(18,766)
Provision (benefit) for income taxes	10,519	(7,131)
Net income (loss)	$ 20,419	$ (11,635)
Earnings (loss) per share	$ 1.81	$ (1.04)
Weighted average shares outstanding and share equivalents	11,255	11,171

(continued)

Trend analysis is a form of financial statement analysis that concentrates on changes in the financial statements through time. It involves comparing relationships for a period of years or quarters. Common-size financial statements are constructed by expressing the elements of the balance sheet as a percentage of total assets and the elements of the income statement as a percentage of total revenue. They enhance the ability to compare one company with another or to conduct a trend analysis over time.

The basic financial ratios allow us to put numbers in perspective. By relating one part of the financial statements to another, they facilitate questions such as "Given the change in revenues, was the change in accounts receivable reasonable?" and "Is the company's inventory level, given its size, comparable to industry norms?" The chapter reviews the ratios presented throughout the text.

Liquidity ratios deal with the immediate ability to make payments. Solvency ratios deal with the longer-term ability to meet obligations. Both are often incorporated into debt covenants to ensure lenders' rights. Profitability ratios are used to assess operating efficiency and performance.

Return on equity (ROE) is the most fundamental profitability ratio because it relates income to the shareholder's investment. Return on assets is one of several related elements that focuses on the profitable use of all assets. It can be further divided into the return on sales and the total asset turnover.

Earnings per share (EPS) is a fundamental measure of performance. In this chapter, three complexities in calculating this measure were identified and incorporated into the calculation. Since preferred shares receive preference to dividends, their dividends are deducted from earnings in the numerator. Since shares outstanding may change during the year, the denominator is calculated as a weighted average over the year. The presence of options and convertible securities creates a potential to issue

Exhibit 13-12 (continued)

The Timberland Company

(Amounts in thousands except per share data)

	As of	
Consolidated Balance Sheets	*December 31, 1996*	*December 30, 1995*
Assets		
Current assets		
Cash and equivalents	$ 93,336	$ 38,389
Accounts receivable, net of allowance for doubtful accounts		
of $3,540 in 1996 and $2,658 in 1995	100,556	95,786
Inventories	159,058	180,636
Prepaid expenses	9,351	12,752
Deferred and refundable income taxes	9,167	10,267
Total current assets	371,468	337,830
Property, plant and equipment	103,650	95,937
Less accumulated depreciation and amortization	(54,666)	(43,533)
Net property, plant and equipment	48,984	52,404
Excess of cost over fair value of net assets acquired, net	22,587	24,271
Other assets, net	6,547	6,903
Total assets	$449,586	$ 421,408
Liabilities and Stockholders' Equity		
Current liabilities		
Current maturities of long-term debt	$ 17,778	$ 7,733
Accounts payable	21,348	25,207
Accrued expenses		
Payroll and related	15,173	7,882
Interest and other	35,753	28,001
Income taxes payable	11,813	892
Total current liabilities	101,865	69,715
Long-term debt, less current maturities	171,676	199,454
Deferred income taxes	10,685	10,018
Commitments and contingencies	—	—
Stockholders' equity		
Class A Common Stock	84	83
Class B Common Stock	27	27
Additional paid-in capital	61,806	59,716
Retained earnings	100,600	80,181
Cumulative translation adjustment	2,963	2,334
Less treasury stock at cost; 18,369 shares at December 31, 1996		
and 1995	(120)	(120)
Total stockholders' equity	165,360	142,221
Total liabilities and stockholders' equity	$449,586	$ 421,408

new shares as a result of the actions of others. Therefore, basic EPS is calculated, and EPS is also reported on a diluted basis when significant options and conversion features exist.

Special items, extraordinary items, discontinued operations and accounting changes are categories of unusual and possibly nonrecurring items. Separately disclosing these allows analysts to refine forecasts of future performance based on current operations. Special items are included with other expenses but identified separately. Extraordinary items, discontinued items and accounting changes are shown separately below earnings from operations and net of their individual tax effects.

Accounting Vocabulary

asset turnover, p. 555
bench marks, p. 550
capital structure, p. 556
capitalization, p. 556
common-size statement, p. 545
component percentages, p. 547
cross-sectional comparisons, p. 550
discontinued operations, p. 563
EBIT, p. 555
extraordinary items, p. 562
financial leverage, p. 556

financial statement analysis, p. 540
gearing, p. 556
leveraging, p. 556
long-term solvency, p. 542
management's discussion and analysis (MD&A), p. 547
operating income percentage on sales, p. 555
pretax operating rate of return on total assets, p. 555

pro forma statement, p. 542
return on total assets (ROA), p. 556
short-term liquidity, p. 542
special items, p. 561
time-series comparisons, p. 550
times interest earned, p. 559
total asset turnover, p. 555
trading on the equity, p. 556

Assignment Material

QUESTIONS

13-1. Why do decision makers use financial statement analysis?

13-2. In addition to the basic financial statements, what information is usually presented in a company's annual report?

13-3. Give three sources of information for investors besides accounting information.

13-4. "Financial statements report on *history*. Therefore they are not useful to creditors and investors who want to predict *future* returns and risk." Do you agree? Explain?

13-5. How do information demands of creditors differ from those of equity investors?

13-6. "It's always a bad sign when revenues increase at a faster percentage rate than does net income." Do you agree? Explain.

13-7. Suppose you wanted to evaluate the financial performance of IBM over the last 10 years. What factors might affect the comparability of a firm's financial ratios over such a long period of time?

13-8. How do common-size statements aid comparisons with other companies?

13-9. What information is presented in the "management's discussion and analysis" (MD&A) section of annual reports?

13-10. Ratios are often grouped into four categories. What are the categories?

13-11. Suppose you compared the financial statements of an airline and a grocery store. Which would you expect to have the higher values for the following ratios: debt-to-equity ratio, current ratio, inventory turnover ratio, average collection period, and return on equity? Explain.

13-12. Name three types of comparisons that are useful in evaluating financial ratios.

13-13. Suppose you worked for a small manufacturing company and the president said that you must improve your current ratio. Would you interpret this to mean that you should increase it or decrease it? How might you do so?

13-14. Suppose the current ratio for your company changed from 2-to-1 to become 1.8-to-1. Would you expect the level of working capital to increase or to decrease? Why?

13-15. Suppose you work for a small local department store that manages its own accounts receivable with a private charge card. Your boss has told you to improve the average collection period from thirty to twenty days. How would you go about this? What are the risks in your proposal that might affect the company negatively?

13-16. Distinguish between operating management and financial management.

13-17. What two measures of operating performance are combined to give the pretax operating return on total assets?

13-18. "Trading on the equity means exchanging bonds for stock." Do you agree? Explain.

13-19. "Borrowing is a two-edged sword." Do you agree? Explain.

13-20. Why are companies with heavy debt in relation to ownership capital in greater danger when business conditions sour?

13-21. "The tax law discriminates against preferred stock and in favor of debt." Explain.

13-22. "Any company that has income before interest and taxes greater than its interest expense is a relatively safe investment for creditors." Do you agree? Explain.

13-23. What causes the "dilution" in diluted EPS?

13-24. How does the accounting for special items differ from the accounting for extraordinary items?

13-25. "Separate reporting of the results of discontinued operations aids predicting future net income." Do you agree? Explain.

13-26. Suppose you wanted to compare the financial statements of Colgate-Palmolive and Procter & Gamble. What concerns might you have in comparing their various ratios?

EXERCISES

13-27 Common-Size Statements

Following are condensed income statements for Netscape and Microsoft, two companies battling for supremacy of the Internet:

	Netscape (in thousands)	Microsoft (in millions)
Total revenues	$346,195	$11,358
Total cost of revenues	49,965	1,085
Gross profit	296,230	10,273
Total operating expenses	273,515	5,143
Operating income	22,715	5,130
Other income, net	6,738	184
Income before income taxes	29,453	5,314
Provision for income taxes	8,545	1,860
Net income	$ 20,908	$ 3,454

Prepare common-size income statements for Netscape and Microsoft. Compare the two companies using the common-size statements.

Required

13-28 Computation of Ratios

MCI, the long-distance telephone company, included the income statement and balance sheets in Exhibit 13-13 in its 1996 annual report. Additional information includes: average common shares outstanding in 1996, 695 million; dividends per share, $.05; and market price per share, $30.

Compute the following ratios:

Required

1. Current ratio
2. Quick ratio
3. Average collection period
4. Total debt to total assets
5. Total debt to equity
6. Interest coverage
7. Return on stockholders' equity
8. Gross profit rate
9. Return on sales
10. Asset turnover
11. Pretax return on operating assets
12. Earnings per share
13. Price-earnings ratio
14. Dividend-yield
15. Dividend-payout

Exhibit 13-13
MCI Income Statement

	For the Year Ended December 31, 1996
Revenue	$18,494
Operating expenses	
Cost of services	9,489
Sales, operations and general	5,028
Depreciation	1,664
	16,181
Income from operations	2,313
Interest expense	(196)
Other expense, net	(127)
Income before income taxes	1,990
Income tax provision	753
Net income	1,237
Preferred stock dividends	35
Net income available to common stockholders	$ 1,202

	As of December 31	
Balance Sheet	*1996*	*1995*
ASSETS		
Current assets:		
Cash and cash equivalents	$ 187	$ 471
Marketable securities	161	373
Receivables	3,480	2,912
Other current assets	888	749
Total current assets	4,716	4,505
Property and equipment, at cost	17,372	14,243
Accumulated depreciation	(6,535)	(5,238)
Construction in progress	1,337	1,304
Total property and equipment, net	12,174	10,309
Other assets	6,088	487
Total assets	$22,978	$19,301
LIABILITIES AND STOCKHOLDERS' EQUITY		
Current liabilities:		
Accounts payable	$ 992	$ 706
Accrued telecommunications expense	2,045	1,936
Other accrued liabilities	1,806	1,728
Long-term debt due within one year	203	500
Total current liabilities	5,046	4,870
Noncurrent liabilities:		
Long-term debt	4,798	3,444
Deferred taxes and other	1,723	1,385
Total noncurrent liabilities	6,521	4,829
Manditorily redeemable preferred stock	750	
Stockholders' equity:		
Class A comon stock, $.10 par value, authorized		
500 million shares, issued 136 million shares	14	14
Common stock, $.10 par value, authorized 2 billion		
shares, issued 593 million shares	60	60
Additional paid in capital	6,410	6,405
Retained earnings	5,231	4,063
Treasury stock, at cost, 44 and 43 million shares	(1,054)	(940)
Total common stockholders' equity	10,661	9,602
Total liabilities and stockholders' equity	$22,978	$19,301

13-29 Common Stock Ratios and Book Value

The Somar Corporation has outstanding 500,000 shares of 8% preferred stock with a $100 par value and 10.5 million shares of common stock of $1 par value. The current market price of the common is $24, and the latest annual dividend rate is $2 per share. Common treasury stock consists of 500,000 shares costing $7.5 million. The company has $150 million of additional paid-in capital, $15 million of retained income, and $12 million of investments in affiliated companies. Net income for the current year is $20 million.

Compute the following:

Required

1. Total stockholders' equity.
2. Common price-earnings ratio.
3. Common dividend-yield percentage.
4. Common dividend-payout percentage.
5. Book value per share of common.

13-30 Rate-of-Return Computations

1. Sapporo Company reported a 4% operating margin on sales, an 8% pretax operating return on total assets, and 3 billion of total assets. Compute (a) operating income, (b) total sales, and (c) total asset turnover.
2. Glasgow Corporation reported £900 million of sales, £48 million of operating income, and a total asset turnover of 4 times. Compute (a) total assets, (b) operating margin percentage on sales, and (c) pretax operating return on total assets.
3. Compare the two companies.

13-31 Return on Assets

The Home Depot, Inc. is the leading retailer in the home improvement industry and ranks among the 10 largest retailers in the United States. Some data from the company's financial statements for the years ended February 2, 1997 and January 28, 1996 follow (in millions):

	1997	1996
Sales	$19,539	$15,470
Operating income	1,534	1,180
Net income	9	14
Property, plant and equipment, net	5,437	4,461
Total assets	9,342	7,354
Stockholders' equity	5,955	5,005

Required

1. Compute Home Depot's pretax operating return on total assets for the year ended February 2, 1997.
2. Compute the operating income percentage on sales and total asset turnover. Show how these two ratios determine the pretax operating return on total assets.

13-32 Trading on the Equity

Bayol Company has assets of $600 million, bonds payable of $400 million, and stockholders' equity of $200 million. The bonds bear interest at 10% per annum. Carmody Company, which is in the same industry, has assets of $600 million and stockholders' equity of $600 million. Prepare a comparative tabulation of Carmody Company and Bayol Company for each of three years. Show income before interest, interest, net income, return on assets, and return on stockholders' equity. The income before interest for both companies was: Year 1, $60 million; Year 2, $30 million; and Year 3, $90 million. Ignore income taxes. Show all monetary amounts in millions of dollars. Comment on the results.

13-33 Using Debt or Equity

The O'Hare Corporation is trying to decide whether to raise additional capital of $40 million through a new issue of 12% long-term debt or of 10% preferred stock. The income tax rate is 40%. Compute net income less preferred dividends for these alternatives, assuming that income before interest expense and taxes is $12 million. Show all dollar amounts in thousands. What is the after-tax cost of capital for debt and for preferred stock expressed in percentages? Comment on the comparison. Compute times interest earned for the first year.

13-34 Debt Versus Preferred Stock

Bell Atlantic Corporation provides telephone services to several middle-Atlantic states. In 1996, the company had operating income before taxes and interest of $3,228.5 million. Interest expense was $477.9 million on long-term debt of $5,960.2 million. The company has no preferred stock outstanding, although 10 million shares are authorized.

Suppose $4,000 million of preferred stock with a dividend rate of 12% had been issued instead of $4,000 million of the long-term debt. The debt had an effective interest rate of 8.02%. Assume that the income tax rate is 40%.

Required Compute net income and net income attributable to common shareholders under (a) the current situation with $5,960.2 million of long-term debt and no preferred stock, and (b) the assumed situation with $4,000 million of preferred stock and $1,960.2 million of long-term debt.

13-35 Earnings Per Share

Ford Motor Company had net income of $4,446 million and paid preferred dividends of $65 million in 1996. An average of 1,179 million common shares were outstanding during the year.

Required
1. Compute Ford's earnings per share of common stock in 1996.
2. Suppose all preferred stock was convertible into 42 million shares of common stock. Compute diluted earnings per share.

13-36 EPS and Times Interest Earned Computations

Baltimore Shipping Co. has outstanding 500,000 shares of common stock, $4 million of 8% preferred stock, and $8 million of 10% bonds payable. Its income tax rate is 40%.

1. Assume the company has $6 million of income before interest and taxes. Compute (a) EPS and (b) number of times bond interest has been earned.
2. Assume $4 million of income before interest and taxes, and make the same computations.

13-37 Discontinued Operations

Nokia, a Finnish company based in Helsinki, is a leading international telecommunications company that employs 31,700 people in 45 countries. The company's 1996 income statement ended with the following three lines (in millions of Finnish marks):

Profit from continuing operations	FIM 3,044
Discontinued operations	219
Net profit	FIM 3,263

Required Suppose the operations in place at the end of 1996 continued into 1997 with exactly the same results in 1997 as in 1996. What net profit would you expect Nokia to report in 1997? Explain.

13-38 Interpretation of Changes in Ratios

Consider each of the following as an independent case:
   a. Increase in current ratio.
   b. Decrease in interest-coverage.

c. Increase in return on sales.

d. Increase in the price-earnings ratio.

e. Reduction in accounts receivable turnover.

f. Increase in cash dividends.

Required

1. From the point of view of a manager of the company, indicate which of these items indicate good news and which indicate bad news. Explain your reasoning for each.

2. Would any of these items be viewed differently by an investor than by a manager? If so, which ones? Why?

13-39 Common-Size Statements

(Alternate is 13-46.) Price-Break and Low-Cost are both discount store chains. Condensed income statements and balance sheets for the two companies are shown in Exhibit 13-14. Amounts are in thousands.

Exhibit 13-14

Financial Statements for Price-Break and Low-Cost

Income Statements for the Year Ended December 31, 19X9

	Price-Break	Low-Cost
Sales	$905,600	$491,750
Cost of sales	602,360	301,910
Gross profit	303,240	189,840
Operating expenses	184,130	147,160
Operating income	119,110	42,680
Other revenue (expense)	(21,930)	6,270
Pretax income	97,180	48,950
Income tax expense	38,870	19,580
Net income	$ 58,310	$ 29,370

Balance Sheets

	Price-Break		Low-Cost	
	December 31		December 31	
	19X9	19X8	19X9	19X8
Assets				
Current assets				
Cash	$ 9,100	$ 10,700	$ 8,200	$ 6,900
Marketable securities	8,300	8,300	4,100	3,800
Accounts receivable	36,700	37,100	21,300	20,500
Inventories	155,600	149,400	105,100	106,600
Prepaid expenses	17,100	16,900	8,800	8,400
Total current assets	226,800	222,400	147,500	146,200
Property and equipment, net	461,800	452,300	287,600	273,500
Other assets	14,700	13,900	28,600	27,100
Total assets	$703,300	$688,600	$463,700	$446,800
Liabilities and Stockholders' Equity				
Liabilities				
Current liabilities (summarized)	$ 91,600	$ 93,700	$ 61,300	$ 58,800
Long-term debt	156,700	156,700	21,000	21,000
Total liabilities	248,300	250,400	82,300	79,800
Stockholders' equity	455,000	438,200	381,400	367,000
Total liabilities and stockholders' equity	$703,300	$688,600	$463,700	$446,800

1. Prepare common-sized statements for Price-Break and Low-Cost for 19X9.
2. Compare the financial performance for 19X9 and financial position at the end of 19X9 for Price-Break with the performance and position of Low-Cost. Use only the statements prepared in requirement 1.

13-40 Financial Ratios

(Alternate is 13-42.) This problem uses the same data as 13-39, but it can be solved independently. Price-Break and Low-Cost are both discount store chains. Condensed income statements and balance sheets for the two companies are shown in Exhibit 13-14. Amounts are in thousands.

Additional information:

- Cash dividends per share: Price-Break, $2.00; Low-Cost, $1.50
- Market price per share: Price-Break, $30; Low-Cost, $40
- Average shares outstanding for 19X9: Price-Break, 15 million; Low-Cost, 7 million

1. Compute the following ratios for both companies for 19X9: (a) current, (b) quick, (c) average collection period, (d) inventory turnover, (e) total debt to total assets, (f) total debt to total equity, (g) return on stockholders' equity, (h) gross profit rate, (i) return on sales, (j) asset turnover, (k) pretax return on assets, (l) earnings per share, (m) price-earnings, (n) dividend yield, and (o) dividend payout.
2. Compare the liquidity, solvency, profitability, and market price and dividend ratios of Price-Break with those of Low-Cost.

13-41 Trend Analysis

Merck & Co., the pharmaceutical company, has frequently been ranked America's most admired company by *Fortune* magazine. The 1995 and 1996 income statements and balance sheets are in Exhibit 13-15. A few categories are slightly condensed.

1. Prepare an income statement and balance sheet for Merck & Co. that has two columns, one showing the amount of change between 1995 and 1996 and the other showing the percentage of change.
2. Identify and discuss the most significant changes between 1995 and 1996.

Exhibit 13-15

Merck & Co., Inc. and Subsidiaries

Consolidated Statement of Income (in millions)

Years Ended December 31	1996	1995
SALES	$19,828.7	$16,681.1
Costs, Expenses, and Other		
Materials and production	9,319.2	7,456.3
Marketing and administrative	3,841.3	3,297.8
Research and development	1,487.3	1,331.4
Other (income) expense, net	(359.9)	(201.6)
	14,287.9	11,883.9
Income before taxes	5,540.8	4,797.2
Taxes on income	1,659.5	1,462.0
Net income	$ 3,881.3	$ 3,335.2
Earnings Per Share of Common Stock	$ 3.20	$ 2.70

(continued)

Exhibit 13-15   (continued)

Merck & Co., Inc. and Subsidiaries

Consolidated Balance Sheet

December 31	1996	1995
ASSETS		
Current Assets		
Cash and cash equivalents	$ 1,352.4	$ 1,847.4
Short-term investments	829.2	1,502.4
Accounts receivable	2,655.9	2,495.7
Inventories	2,148.8	1,872.5
Prepaid expenses and taxes	740.3	899.5
Total current assets	7,726.6	8,617.5
Investments	2,499.4	1,969.6
Property, Plant, and Equipment (at cost)	8,726.4	7,709.0
Less allowance for depreciation	2,799.7	2,439.9
	5,926.7	5,269.1
Goodwill and other intangibles, net	6,736.6	6,826.3
Other Assets	1,403.8	1,149.3
	$24,293.1	$23,831.8
LIABILITIES AND STOCKHOLDERS' EQUITY		
Current Liabilities		
Accounts payable and accrued liabilities	$ 2,937.8	$ 3,105.2
Loans payable	606.1	423.1
Income taxes payable	802.6	800.8
Dividends payable	482.7	418.2
Total current liabilities	4,829.2	4,747.3
Long-term debt	1,155.9	1,372.8
Deferred income taxes and noncurrent liabilities	4,027.3	3,689.7
Minority Interests	2,310.2	2,286.3
Stockholders' Equity		
Common Stock		
Authorized—2,700,000,000 shares		
Issued—1,483,619,311 shares—1996	4,967.5	4,742.5
—1,483,463,327 shares—1995		
Retained earnings	14,817.7	12,740.6
	19,785.2	17,483.1
Less treasury stock, at cost		
227,016,963 shares—1996		
254,614,794 shares—1995	7,814.7	5,747.4
Total stockholders' equity	11,970.5	11,735.7
	$24,293.1	$23,831.8

13-42   Financial Ratios

(Alternate is 13-40.) Merck & Co. is the largest company in the health-care industry in the United States. Two recent income statements and balance sheets are in Exhibit 13-15. Additional 1996 data are:

- Cash dividends, $1.42 per share
- Market price per share, $80
- Average common shares outstanding, $1,213,600,000

Compute the following ratios for Merck & Co. for 1996: (a) current, (b) quick, (c) average collection period, (d) total debt to total assets, (e) total debt to total equity, (f) return on stockholders' equity, (g) return on sales, (h) asset turnover, (i) pretax return on assets, (j) earnings per share, (k) price-earnings, (l) dividend yield, and (m) dividend payout. Total debt includes current liabilities, long-term debt, and deferred income taxes and noncurrent liabilities.

ASSIGNMENT MATERIAL   **575**

Exhibit 13-16

Ryan Company

Balance Sheets and Income Statements (in thousands)

	December 31		
	19X3	*19X2*	*19X1*
Cash	$ 30	$ 25	$ 20
Accounts receivable	90	70	50
Merchandise inventory	80	70	60
Prepaid expenses	10	10	10
Land	30	30	30
Building	70	75	80
Equipment	60	50	40
Total assets	$370	$330	$290
Accounts payable	$ 50	$ 40	$ 30
Taxes payable	20	15	10
Accrued expenses payable	15	10	5
Long-term debt	45	45	45
Paid-in capital	150	150	150
Retained income	90	70	50
Total liab. and stk. eq.	$370	$330	$290

	Year Ended December 31	
	19X3	*19X2*
Sales (all on credit)	$800	$750
Cost of goods sold	(440)	(410)
Operating expenses	(300)	(295)
Pretax income	60	45
Income taxes	(20)	(15)
Net income	$ 40	$ 30

13-43 Trend Analysis and Common-Size Statements

Ryan Company furnished the condensed data shown in Exhibit 13-16.

Required

1. Prepare a trend analysis for Ryan's income statement and balance sheet that compares 19X3 with 19X2.

2. Prepare common-size income statements for 19X3 and 19X2 and balance sheets for December 31, 19X3 and December 31, 19X2 for Ryan Company.

3. Comment on Ryan Company's performance and position for 19X3 compared with 19X2.

13-44 Financial Ratios

Consider the data for Ryan Company in Exhibit 13-16.

Required

1. Compute the following ratios for each of the last two years, 19X2 and 19X3:
   a. Current ratio
   b. Gross profit rate
   c. Percent of net income to sales
   d. Ratio of total debt to stockholders' equity
   e. Inventory turnover
   f. Percentage of net income to stockholders' equity
   g. Average collection period for accounts receivable

2. For each of the following items, indicate whether the change from 19X2 to 19X3 for Ryan Company seems to be favorable or unfavorable, and identify the ratios you computed above that most directly support your answer. The first two items below are given as an example.

  a. Return to owners, favorable, f

  b. Gross margin, favorable, b

  c. Ability to pay current debts on time

  d. Collectibility of receivables

  e. Risks of insolvency

  f. Salability of merchandise

  g. Return on sales

  h. Overall accomplishment

  i. Future stability of profits

  j. Coordination of buying and selling functions

  k. Screening of risks in granting credit to customers

13-45   Computation of Financial Ratios

The financial statements of the Ito Co. are shown in Exhibit 13-17.

Exhibit 13-17

The Ito Co.

Balance Sheets (in millions of yen)

	December 31	
	19X8	*19X7*
Assets		
Current assets:		
Cash	¥ 2,000	¥ 2,000
Short-term investments		1,000
Receivables, net	5,000	4,000
Inventories at cost	11,000	8,000
Prepayments	1,000	1,000
Total current assets	¥19,000	¥16,000
Plant and equipment, net	22,000	23,000
Total assets	¥41,000	¥39,000
Liabilities and Stockholders' Equity		
Current liabilities:		
Accounts payable	¥10,000	¥ 6,000
Accrued expenses payable	500	500
Income taxes payable	1,500	1,500
Total current liabilities	¥12,000	¥ 8,000
8% bonds payable	¥10,000	¥10,000
Stockholders' equity:		
Preferred stock, 12%, par value		
$100 per share	¥ 5,000	¥ 5,000
Common stock, $5 par value	4,000	4,000
Premium on common stock	8,000	8,000
Unappropriated retained earnings	1,000	3,000
Reserve for plant expansion	1,000	1,000
Total stockholders' equity	¥19,000	¥21,000
Total liab. and stk. eq.	¥41,000	¥39,000

(*continued*)

Exhibit 13-17 (continued)

The Ito Co.

Statement of Income and Reconciliation of Retained Earnings for the Year Ended December 31, 19X8
(in thousands of dollars)

Sales (all on credit)		¥44,000
Cost of goods sold		32,000
Gross profit on Sales		¥12,000
Other operating expenses:		
Selling expenses	¥5,000	
Administrative expenses	2,000	
Depreciation	1,000	8,000
Operating income		¥ 4,000
Interest expense		800
Income before income taxes		¥ 3,200
Income taxes at 40%		¥ 1,280
Net income		¥ 1,920
Dividends on preferred stock		600
Net income for common stockholders		¥ 1,320
Dividends on common stock		3,320
Net income retained		¥(2,000)
Unappropriated retained earnings, December 31, 19X7		3,000
Unappropriated retained earnings, December 31, 19X8		¥ 1,000

Required

Compute the following for the 19X8 financial statements.

1. Pretax return on total assets.

2. Divide your answer to requirement 1 into two components: operating income percentage of sales and total asset turnover.

3. After-tax rate of return on total assets. Be sure to add the *after-tax* interest expense to net income.

4. Rate of return on total stockholders' equity. Did the preferred and common stockholders benefit from the existence of debt? Explain fully.

5. Rate of return on *common* stockholders' equity. This ratio is the amount of net income available for the common stockholders, divided by total stockholders' equity less the par value of preferred stock. Did the common stockholders benefit from the existence of preferred stock? Explain fully.

13-46 Common-Size Statements

(Alternate is 13-39.) Exhibit 13-18 contains the slightly condensed income statement and balance sheets of 3M (Minnesota Mining and Manufacturing Company), a multinational company with sales over $6.5 billion in the United States and over $7.5 billion abroad.

Required

1. Prepare common-size statements for 3M for 1995 and 1996.
2. Comment on the changes in component percentages from 1995 to 1996.

13-47 Liquidity Ratios

Exhibit 13-18 contains the slightly condensed income statement and balance sheets of Minnesota Mining and Manufacturing Company (3M), maker of Scotch brand tapes.

Required

1. Compute the following ratios for 1996: (a) current, (b) quick, (c) average collection period, and (d) inventory turnover.
2. Assess 3M's liquidity compared with the following industry averages:

Exhibit 13-18

Minnesota Mining and Manufacturing Company (3M) and Subsidiaries

Consolidated Statement of Income for the Years Ended December 31, 1996 and 1995
(amounts in millions, except per-share data)

	1996	1995
Net Sales	$14,236	$13,460
Operating Expenses		
Cost of goods sold	8,099	7,720
Selling, general, and administrative expenses	3,646	3,440
Restructuring Charge	—	79
Total	11,745	11,239
Operating Income	2,491	2,221
Other Income and Expense		
Interest Expense	79	102
Investment and Other Income—Net	(67)	(49)
Total	12	53
Income before Income Taxes and Minority Interest	2,479	2,168
Provision for Income Taxes	886	785
Minority Interest	77	77
Income from Continuing Operations	1,516	1,306
Discontinued Operations	10	(330)
Net Income	$ 1,526	$ 976
Average Shares Outstanding	418.2	419.8

Consolidated Balance Sheet as of December 31, 1996 and 1995
(dollars in millions)

	1996	1995
Assets		
Current Assets		
Cash and cash equivalents	$ 583	$ 485
Other securities	161	287
Accounts receivable—net	2,504	2,398
Inventories	2,264	2,206
Other current assets	974	1,019
Total current assets	6,486	6,395
Investments	585	565
Property, Plant, and Equipment—net	4,844	4,638
Other Assets	1,449	2,585
Total	$13,364	$14,183
Liabilities and Stockholders' Equity		
Current Liabilities		
Accounts payable	$ 895	$ 762
Payroll	300	298
Income taxes	201	214
Short-term debt	1,117	822
Other current liabilities	1,276	1,628
Total current liabilities	3,789	3,724
Other Liabilities	2,440	2,372
Long-Term Debt	851	1,203
Stockholders' Equity—net	6,284	6,884
Shares outstanding—1996: 416,836,008: 1995: 418,702,754		
Total	$13,364	$14,183

Current ratio	1.8 times
Quick ratio	1.0 times
Average collection period	41.6 days
Inventory turnover	4.5 times

13-48 Solvency Ratios

Exhibit 13-18 contains the income statement and balance sheets of Minnesota Mining and Manufacturing Company (3M), a diversified manufacturing company with operations in the United States and fifty-one other countries.

Required

1. Compare the following ratios for 1996: (a) total debt to total assets and (b) total debt to total equity.

2. Assess 3M's solvency compared with the following industry averages:

Total debt to total assets	57.4%
Total debt to total shareholders' equity	115.3%

13-49 Profitability Ratios

Exhibit 13-18 contains the income statement and balance sheets of Minnesota Mining and Manufacturing Company (3M), a technology company with over one hundred technologies. A corporate objective is for significant sales to be generated by new products introduced in the last five years.

Required

1. Compute the following ratios for 1996: (a) return on stockholders' equity, (b) gross profit rate, (c) return on sales, (d) asset turnover, (e) pretax return on assets, and (f) earnings per share.

2. Assess 3M's profitability in 1996 compared with the following industry averages:

Return on stockholders' equity	12%
Gross profit rate	32%
Return on sales	3.2%
Asset turnover	2.66 times
Pretax return on assets	7.7%
Earnings per share	$1.94

13-50 Market Price and Dividend Ratios

Exhibit 13-18 contains the income statement and balance sheets of Minnesota Mining and Manufacturing Company (3M), a leader in bringing new technology-based products to the market. In 1996, 3M paid cash dividends of $1.92 per share, the market price was $80 per share and EPS was $3.65.

Required

1. Compute the following ratios for 1996: (a) price-earnings, (b) dividend-yield, and (c) dividend-payout.

2. Assess 3M's market price and dividend ratios compared with the following industry averages:

Price-earnings	16.0
Dividend-yield	2.8%
Dividend-payout	46%

13-51 Income Ratios and Asset Turnover

The following data are from the 1996 and 1995 annual reports of McDonald's Corporation. There are more than 21,000 McDonald's restaurants in 101 countries:

	1996	1995
Rate of return on stockholders' equity	18.97%	19.36%
Operating income percentage on sales	24.63%	26.56%
Total asset turnover (sales ÷ average assets)	.65	.68
Average total assets	$16,400 million	$14,504 million
Interest and other nonoperating expenses	$ 382 million	$ 432 million
Income tax expense	$ 678 million	$ 742 million

Required

1. Complete the following condensed income statement for 1996. Round to the nearest million.

1996	
Sales	$?
Operating expenses	?
Operating income	$?
Interest and other nonoperating expenses	?
Pretax income	$?
Income tax expense	?
Net income	$?

2. Compute the following:
   a. Pretax operating rate of return on total assets
   b. Rate of return on sales
   c. Average stockholders' equity
3. Compare the values for 1996 to 1995.

13-52   Income Ratios and Asset Turnover

Tribune Company, publisher of the *Chicago Tribune* and owner of the Chicago Cubs baseball team, included the following data in its 1996 annual report to stockholders (in millions of dollars expect percentages):

Net income	$ 372
Total assets:	
Beginning of year	3,288
End of year	3,701
Net income as a percent of:	
Total revenue	15.5%
Average stockholders' equity	25.5%

Using only the above data, compute

Required

1. Net income as a percentage of average assets
2. Total revenues
3. Average stockholders' equity
4. Asset turnover, using two different approaches
5. Compare the 1994 net income percentages of 11.2 and 19.9 to their 1996 values of 15.5% and 25.5%

13-53   Special Items, Discontinued Operations, and Extraordinary Items

Westinghouse Electric Corporation reported net income of $95 million for the year ended December 31, 1996, as shown in the following condensed income statement (in millions):

ASSIGNMENT MATERIAL   **581**

Sales of services and products	$8,605
Cost of services and products sold	(5,868)
Gross margin	2,737
Restructuring, litigation and other matters	(979)
Marketing, administration and general expenses	(2,406)
Operating loss	(648)
Other expenses, net	(125)
Loss from continuing operations	(773)
Discontinued operations, net of tax	961
Extraordinary items	(93)
Net income	$ 95

Required

1. Point out the items in this income statement that ordinarily would not be expected to recur in 1997.

2. Which items in the income statement would be called "special items"? Explain how Westinghouse accounts for these special items differently than it accounts for the other items listed in your response to requirement 1.

3. Do you think the $95 million net income is a good predictor of future net income? If so, why? If not, explain how you would adjust it to get a better predictor of future net income.

13-54 Diluted EPS

Microsoft reported 1997 net income of $3,454 million and had an average of 1,199 million common shares outstanding. Dividends on 12.5 million shares of convertible preferred stock were $15 million. Conversion of preferred shares into common shares and exercise of stock options and warrants would result in the equivalent of issuance of 114 million additional common shares.

Required

1. Compute basic earnings per share.

2. Compute diluted earnings per share.

3. Explain what an investor can learn from the two earnings per share numbers.

13-55 Industry Identification

Exhibit 13-19 presents common-size financial statements and selected ratio values for nine companies from the following industries:

1. Department Store
2. Telecommunications
3. Pharmaceutical
4. Petroleum
5. Newspaper
6. Grocery
7. Consumer Products
8. Utility
9. Home Building

Required

Use your knowledge of general business practices to match the industries to the company data.

Exhibit 13-19

(for Problem 13-55)

(Columns may not add due to rounding.)

	A	B	C	D	E	F	G	H	I
	%	%	%	%	%	%	%	%	%
Balance Sheet									
Cash & Marketable Securities	13.86	3.71	1.28	1.67	1.32	0.00	1.21	1.57	3.54
Current Receivables	13.85	14.52	15.73	18.30	7.90	3.87	2.94	0.00	17.09
Inventories	0.00	10.78	7.95	19.23	0.97	2.48	22.62	34.90	11.62
Other Current Asets	2.16	11.20	1.96	2.73	2.93	0.69	1.85	0.67	3.20
Total Current Assets	29.87	40.20	26.91	41.93	13.12	7.04	28.63	37.15	35.46
Net Property, Plant, & Equip.	55.35	48.14	61.39	43.22	36.93	84.64	49.91	1.41	32.37
Other Noncurrent Assets	14.78	11.66	11.69	14.86	49.95	8.31	21.47	61.45	32.18
Total Assets	100.00	100.00	100.00	100.00	100.00	100.00	100.00	100.00	100.00
Current Liabilities	19.17	46.90	32.30	21.91	14.38	9.35	36.31	29.84	24.90
Long-Term Liabilities	25.82	16.70	26.43	48.69	36.37	50.64	50.87	51.85	45.43
Owners' Equity	55.02	36.40	41.27	29.40	49.25	40.02	12.82	18.31	29.68
Total Liabilities & Owners' Eq	100.00	100.00	100.00	100.00	100.00	100.00	100.00	100.00	100.00
Income Statement									
Revenue	100.00	100.00	100.00	100.00	100.00	100.00	100.00	100.00	100.00
Cost of Sales	51.85	20.58	54.41	61.71	53.56	32.11	72.80	76.81	51.57
Gross Profit	48.15	79.42	45.59	38.29	46.44	67.89	27.20	23.19	46.43
Interest Expense	1.15	1.21	0.68	3.15	1.19	5.28	1.42	6.39	1.14
Research & Development	0.00	13.21	0.77	0.00	0.00	0.00	0.00	0.00	0.00
Selling, General, & Admin.	28.42	35.89	8.09	27.25	37.48	23.03	21.19	11.79	31.50
Other Expenses (Income)	0.17	−0.43	27.00	0.50	−8.66	9.57	−0.15	1.05	1.09
Depreciation & Amortization	8.82	3.38	4.60	3.40	0.00	13.35	2.09	1.56	3.10
Income Taxes	3.64	6.25	2.85	1.73	7.37	6.04	1.11	0.91	3.95
Net Income	5.96	19.80	1.60	2.26	9.05	10.63	1.53	1.49	7.65
Ratios									
Current Ratio	1.56	0.86	0.83	1.91	0.91	0.75	0.79	1.24	1.42
Long Term Debt as % of Equity	33.29	11.80	27.49	124.44	30.64	75.70	314.43	274.09	96.08
Return on Sales	5.96	19.80	1.62	2.26	9.05	10.63	1.53	1.49	7.65
Return on Assets	5.75	21.34	2.62	1.90	6.72	4.79	4.75	1.22	9.75
Return on Equity	11.59	58.42	6.28	6.34	13.56	12.27	46.69	8.08	31.37
Inventory Turnover	INF	2.20	9.83	2.88	32.45	5.66	10.05	2.33	5.62
Times Interest Earned	9.37	22.59	8.98	2.26	14.63	4.16	2.91	1.36	11.15

13-56 MD&A and Ethics

If certain conditions are met, the SEC requires companies to disclose information about future events that are reasonably likely to materially affect the firm's operations. Many companies are understandably reluctant to disclose such information. After all, positive predictions may not materialize and negative predictions may unduly alarm the investors. What ethical considerations should a company's managers consider when deciding what prospective information to disclose in the MD&A section of the annual report?

13-57 The Gap Annual Report

Use the financial statements and notes of The Gap in Appendix A to respond to the following questions:

Required

1. Calculate return on common stockholders' equity for the year ended February 1, 1997. Compare it to the value for the year ended February 3, 1996.
2. Calculate the current ratio for the year ended February 1, 1997 and compare it to the value for the year ended February 3, 1996.
3. Calculate debt-to-total-assets for the year ended February 1, 1997. Compare it to the value for the year ended February 3, 1996.

13-58 Financial Statement Research

Choose two companies in each of two industries.

Required

Calculate the return on assets, return on equity, and return on sales for each of the companies. Compare and contrast the two companies in each industry and the averages for each industry.

COLLABORATIVE LEARNING EXERCISE

13-59 Operating Return on Total Assets

Form groups of four to six students. Each student should choose an industry (a different industry for each student in the group) and pick two companies in that industry. Compute the following for each of the companies:

1. Operating income percentage on sales
2. Total asset turnover
3. Pretax operating rate of return on total assets

Get together as a group and list the industries and the three ratios for each company in the industry. Examine how the ratios differ between the two companies within each industry compared with the differences between industries. As a group, prepare two lists of possible explanations for the differences in ratios. The first list should explain why ratios of two companies within the same industry might differ. The second list should explain why ratios differ by industry.

13-60 Internet Case

Go to **http://www.intel.com/intel/** to find Intel Corporation's home page. Select *Contents* from the icons at the top of the screen, then select *Investor Relations* to get a menu of the company's financial information. The company's most recent annual report can be found by selecting *Annual Report* from the menu bar at the left of the screen. Today, Intel supplies the computing industry with the chips, boards, systems, and software that are the "ingredients" of computer architecture.

Answer the following questions to apply some of the financial statement analysis tools you learned about in this chapter.

1. What type of investor, equity or creditor, would Intel most likely attract based on its current financial position and profitability? Explain.
2. Where in Intel's annual report would you expect to find a trend and component percentage analysis?
3. What pattern or trend do you observe in evaluating the amount of dividends declared for the fiscal period reported in Intel's annual report? What questions would this trend cause you to ask of Intel's management?

4. Which items has Intel reported that are considered "special" items? Why are these items reported differently?

5. Where do you expect to find geographic segment information in Intel's annual report? Describe Intel's business and geographic segments.

6. How are Intel's long-term investments (plant and equipment, etc.) financed—with debt or equity? Suppose Intel needs additional financing. Would you recommend more debt or more equity financing? Explain. What impact does additional financing have on net income?

7. What is the amount of Intel's EPS for the most recent fiscal reporting period? Identify the cause of the increase or decrease during the year.

14 CONCEPTUAL FRAMEWORK AND MEASUREMENT TECHNIQUES

At Dell Computer Corporation a technician tests a new personal computer (PC). Elsewhere at Dell financial analysts are using various techniques to evaluate the financial condition of customers and suppliers.

Learning Objectives

After studying this chapter, you should be able to

1 Describe the FASB's conceptual framework.

2 Identify the qualities that make information valuable.

3 Explain how accounting differences could produce differing income for similar companies.

4 Differentiate between financial capital and physical capital.

5 Incorporate changing prices into income measurement using four different methods.

6 Compare U.S. GAAP with other countries' standards.

There is an old saying that "beauty is in the eye of the beholder." Depending on who you are, you may find beauty and meaning in places others do not. When looking at accounting information, its usefulness is like beauty—meaning is found in the eye of the beholder. The information serves a purpose in decision making, but the types of decisions made will differ with the individual user.

When an organization prepares financial statements, it recognizes that the reported results will be used by different people in different ways. For example, investment analysts, brokers, and investors look at reported performance to determine whether a particular company is worthy of investment. At Piper Jaffray, corporate financial data is analyzed regularly so that recommendations can be made to clients to buy, sell, or hold stocks. Banks such as Bank of America use financial reports to determine creditworthiness. When an organization seeks a line of credit or loans, the financial statements are used to get a picture of the applicant's economic health. Even businesses use financial reports to examine the status of current and potential business partners. Dell Computer Corporation employs analysts who are charged with keeping an eye on how their suppliers are doing. If a problem arises with one, it could seriously affect whether Dell meets its own commitments and financial targets.

The analyses may differ among decision makers, but they all rely on the same conceptual framework that guides the creation of the financial reports. When prepared according to generally accepted accounting principles, investors, bankers, analysts, and others can count on finding meaning, value, and reliability in the accounting information. However, it is important to conduct your analysis with a careful eye toward choices that a company makes among permitted principles! When the companies under analysis include non–U.S. companies, the range of possible variability in principles grows substantially.

The essence of the related topics in this chapter involves the questions: What are we trying to measure and what principles should we bring to the task? Throughout the book, we have included some international examples and some discussion of basic principles. In this chapter, we integrate these discussions. You have now considered enough details of the accounting process to address some underlying issues in a more integrated manner. Many countries have confronted the problem of selecting accounting principles, and they have reached different conclusions. In the United States, we allow a wide range of choices in method. In this chapter, we will examine some of the reasons for this practice.

CONCEPTUAL FRAMEWORK OF ACCOUNTING

For years, accountants have sought a consistent set of concepts underlying accounting practice. But GAAP remains a patchwork that has evolved slowly over many years. The key element of this patchwork is that people accept it. Some accounting rules seem inconsistent with others and changes occur one at a time. For example, the lower-of-cost-or-market basis was applied differently to inventories, to short-term investments, and to long-term investments in prior years. The recent acceptance of the market method of accounting for most short-term investments has made the conservatism of lower-of-cost-or-market relevant only in the inventory arena.

FASB's Conceptual Framework

Objective 1
Describe the FASB's conceptual framework.

Between 1978 and 1984, the Financial Accounting Standards Board (FASB) issued four Statements of Financial Accounting Concepts (SFACs) relating to business enterprises. The statements provide the conceptual framework used by the FASB. The FASB makes accounting policy by choosing the accounting measurements and disclosure methods for financial reporting. The board's function might be called rule making, standard setting, or regulation, but the essence is that the FASB exercises judgment in choosing among alternatives. Because there are no objective criteria to guide the FASB in making its decisions, the conceptual framework summarized in Exhibit 14-1 was created to guide the exercise of judgment and increase the consistency between standards.

Are the statements in Exhibit 14-1 the final word in U.S. accounting practice? No. Accounting policy is too complex to remain fixed over time. The FASB has to adjust it to changes in the world of business, such as changes in technology, business practice, economics, and so on. Progress comes in fits and starts and will always be considered too fast by some and too slow by others. One person's improvement is often another person's impairment. A key for the FASB, then, is getting everyone to accept its decisions and statements.

The FASB has a good batting record. Of the more than 130 statements it has issued, only a few have been opposed. How does the FASB get such compliance? For one reason, the board involves various constituencies at every stage of the debate, including the public accounting firms, corporate preparers, and the analysts who use the information. So it solicits opinions and works to create a consensus around good accounting. It also compromises when necessary to get acceptance. Of course, a conceptual framework, plausible logic, and compelling facts all increase the odds of winning support from diverse interests.

Exhibit 14-1

Statements of Financial Accounting Concepts for Business Enterprises

Statement	Highlights
SFAC No. 1, Objectives of Financial Reporting by Business Enterprises	• Accounting should provide information useful for making economic decisions • Statements should focus on external users, such as creditors and investors • Information should aid the prediction of cash flows • Earnings based on accrual accounting provide a better measure of performance than do cash receipts and disbursements
SFAC No. 2, Qualitative Characteristics of Accounting Information	• Usefulness is evaluated in relation to the purposes to be served • Different information is useful for different decisions • Decision usefulness is the primary characteristic in the hierarchy of desirable characteristics • Both relevance and reliability are necessary for information to be useful • Relevance requires timeliness and either predictive or feedback value • Reliable information must faithfully represent the item being measured and be verifiable and neutral • Comparability and consistency aid usefulness • To be useful, information must be material, that is, reported amounts must be large enough to make a difference in decisions • Benefits from using information should exceed its cost
SFAC No. 3, Elements of Financial Statements of Business Enterprises	• Defines the ten building blocks that comprise financial statements: (1) assets, (2) liabilities, (3) equity, (4) investments by owners, (5) distributions to owners, (6) comprehensive income, (7) revenues, (8) expenses, (9) gains, and (10) losses
SFAC No. 5, Recognition and Measurement in Financial Statements of Business Enterprises	• Specifies what information should be included in financial statements and when • All components of financial statements are important, not just a single "bottom-line" number • A statement of financial position provides information about assets, liabilities, and equity; it does not show the market value of the entity • Earnings measure periodic performance; comprehensive income recognizes all effects on equity except investments by or distributions to owners • Financial statements are based on the concept of financial capital maintenance • Measurement is and will continue to be based on nominal units of money • Revenue is recognized when it is earned and realized (or realizable) • Information based on current prices, if reliable and more relevant than alternative information, should be reported if costs involved are not too high

*SFAC Nos. 4 and 6 relate to nonbusiness entities and are not summarized here.

Until the early 1930s, when the Securities and Exchange Commission was created by Congress, accounting practices in the United States evolved in accordance with the best professional judgment of CPAs and managers. Then private and public regulators entered the picture. Today, the Securities and Exchange Commission is legally charged with setting accounting standards but has delegated that responsibility to the FASB.

The term *generally accepted* is a key part of the familiar term generally accepted accounting principles. When the FASB considers a financial accounting standard, assorted interested parties present arguments to support their favored choices. The standards issued are often compromises among the contending interests. Therefore, the standards are not necessarily products of airtight logic.

The FASB's task is not only technical, but also political in the sense that the FASB must convince interested persons about the wisdom of the board's decisions. The FASB has encountered only an occasional failure to obtain acceptance. One early example was Statement No. 19 in which the FASB mandated specific accounting standards for oil and gas exploration, only to be overturned by SEC action requiring that firms be granted continued opportunity to choose between two methods.

More recently, the board issued an exposure draft that would have required firms to record an expense in their income statements when they issued stock options to executives. In the face of strong opposition from managers around the country and spirited discussion in Congress, the FASB ultimately decided to accept disclosure of such costs in footnotes rather than in the income statement itself.

Of course, in retrospect, the FASB probably won more than it lost. True, they did not require expense recognition in the income statement, but on the other hand, they did require substantially increased disclosure in the footnotes. When the information is in the footnotes to be read and interpreted, the security analysts and interested investors will quickly understand what is going on.

CHOOSING AMONG REPORTING ALTERNATIVES

Objective 2
Identify the qualities that make information valuable.

The FASB must make difficult decisions about reporting requirements. For example, should stock options for executives be treated as an expense? How should the expense for nonpension retirement benefits be measured and disclosed? Should assets and liabilities be shown at historical cost or current market value? The list could go on and on.

How does the FASB decide that one level of disclosure or one measurement method is acceptable and another is not? The main decision criterion is always cost versus benefit. Accounting should improve decision making. This is a benefit. But accounting information is an economic good that is costly to produce. The FASB must choose rules whose decision-making benefits exceed their costs. Unfortunately, these costs and benefits are hard to measure and sometimes even hard to identify

Many would say that the United States has the best accounting standards in the world. Because our standards are good, they would argue U.S. corporations have very easy and cheap access to both debt and equity financing. Investors have confidence in the disclosures. Others would point out that because the United States requires more disclosure than any other country, many international companies list their shares in exchanges in London, Tokyo, and other capital cities where the accounting regulations are less difficult to meet. This costs the New York Stock Exchange and other U.S. exchanges a lot of business and it makes it harder for U.S. investors to buy shares in some premier international companies.

The costs of providing information include costs to both providers and users. Providers incur costs for data collecting and processing, auditing, and educating preparers. In addition, disclosure of sensitive information can lead to lost competitive advan-

Exhibit 14-2
Qualities that Increase the Value of Information

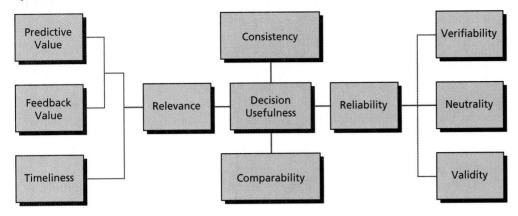

Source: Adapted from *Qualitative Characteristics of Accounting Information* (Stamford, CT: FASB, 1980), p. 15.

tages or increased labor union pressures. These provider costs are often passed along to the user via higher prices. They then become user costs. User costs also include the costs of education, analysis, and interpretation.

The benefits of accounting information are sometimes harder to pinpoint than are the costs. A major effort by countries in the former Soviet Union and in other emerging market economies has been to create an infrastructure of financial markets and relevant information to guide the economy. But the specific benefits of a particular proposal are harder to articulate than the general benefits of an intelligent system of accounting rules and procedures.

Because these broad benefits can be hard to measure or even see, the FASB has come up with a set of easily identified characteristics of information that lead to increased benefits, as shown in Exhibit 14-2. The main characteristic is decision usefulness. If accounting information is not useful in making decisions, it provides no benefit. The rest of the characteristics are aspects of decision usefulness.

ASPECTS OF DECISION USEFULNESS

You might notice that accuracy is not a quality that is mentioned explicitly. This is intentional. Note that materiality is a fundamental concept of accounting. We want to know the important issues. Tell us things that might change our mind. Do so in a consistent, comparable way so we can compare one company to another and trace a company through time. We do not expect IBM to report its earnings to the penny. We settle for hundreds of millions as being precise enough and accurate enough. So the qualities emphasized in Exhibit 14-2 have to do with meaningful, valuable, reliable information on which people can agree.

Relevance and reliability are the two main qualities that make accounting information useful for decision making. **Relevance** refers to whether or not the information will make a difference to the decision maker. **Reliability** means that the information can be counted on to represent faithfully the condition of the company, given the rules in use. Accounting is filled with trade-offs between relevance and reliability. Consider the balance sheet value of Weyerhaeuser Company's timberlands, which are recorded at original cost. Most of the land was purchased more than 50 years ago. The historical cost is reliable, but not very relevant. In contrast, the current value of the land is more relevant, but estimates of this current value are subjective and thus might not be reliable. Which quality is more important? That answer depends on the specific decision being made. How-

relevance The capability of information to make a difference to the decision maker.

reliability A quality of information meaning that it can be counted on to represent faithfully the condition of the company.

ever, the most desirable information is both reliable and relevant. The prevailing view in the United States is that many current market value estimates are not sufficiently reliable to be included in the accounting records, even though they are more relevant. However, in some countries, current market values are routinely used. For example, British Petroleum used market values when it subtracted the "replacement cost of sales" in obtaining "replacement cost operating profit" of £1,884 million in 1996.

As you can see in Exhibit 14-2, relevance and reliability each have their own characteristics. For information to be relevant, it must help decision makers either predict the outcomes of future events (predictive value) or confirm or update past predictions (feedback value). Relevant information must also be available on a timely basis, that is, before a decision maker has to act.

Reliability is characterized by verifiability (or objectivity), neutrality, and validity. **Verifiability** means that information can be checked to make sure it is correct. It also means that measured amounts will have the same value each time the measurement is made. The historical cost of an item is verifiable because we can easily check records to verify that the amounts are correct. In contrast, estimates or appraisals are not verifiable. **Validity** (also called **representational faithfulness**) means the information provided represents the events or objects it is supposed to represent. **Neutrality,** or freedom from bias, means that information is objective and is not weighted unfairly. For example, information that focuses heavily on the benefits of one option while ignoring the benefits of another option is not neutral and will not help lead to a fair decision. Neutrality suggests that allowable depreciation methods should effectively match depreciation expense with revenue but should not be chosen to encourage or discourage investment.

The final items affecting decision usefulness are comparability and consistency. Information is more useful if it can be compared with similar information about other companies or with similar information for other reporting periods. For example, financial results for two companies are hard to compare if one company uses FIFO and the other uses LIFO. These comparisons cannot be made over time if a company keeps changing its accounting methods.

verifiability A quality of information meaning that it can be checked to make sure that it is correct.

validity (representational faithfulness) A correspondence between the accounting numbers and the objects or events those numbers purport to represent.

neutrality A quality of information meaning that it is objective and free from bias.

OVERVIEW OF KEY CONCEPTS

Exhibit 14-3 presents an overview of key accounting concepts covered in this text, where in the text they appear, and a concrete example of each. This table should be a handy guide for recalling and comparing major ingredients of accounting's conceptual framework.

MEASURING INCOME

Measuring income is easily the most controversial subject in accounting. The most popular approach to income measurement, the historical-cost method, is based on actual costs of acquiring assets. This is the primary method underlying U.S. GAAP. However, the label "historical cost" does not completely define the way income is measured. Disputes often occur in applying the historical-cost method. The majority of these disputes center on timing. For example, when are revenues recognized? When do the costs of assets become expenses? In addition, in recent years a few exceptions to historical cost have worked their way into GAAP, most notably in the valuation of marketable securities. Let's take a look at some of the issues regarding the historical-cost method.

Objective 3
Explain how accounting differences could produce differing income for similar companies.

REVENUE RECOGNITION

Under accrual accounting, revenue is usually recorded when goods or services are delivered to customers. However, there are some exceptions to this rule. For example, companies taking on long-run construction projects often recognize revenue using a percentage-

Exhibit 14-3

Frequently Encountered Terminology in Conceptual Frameworks of Accounting

Term	Short Description	Example	Chapters in this Text*
Cost and Benefits	Accounting information is an economic good. It should be gathered as long as its benefits exceed its costs.	Decisions must be improved sufficiently to justify recording current values in addition to historical costs.	Mainly in 4, 7
Relevance	Capability of information to make a difference to the decision maker.	Report of cash in bank is essential to determine how much money to borrow.	3, 14
Reliability	Dependability of information as representing what it purports to represent.	The cost of the land was $1 million 1998 dollars.	4, 14
Verifiability (objectivity)	Characteristic of information that allows it to be checked to be sure it is correct.	Cash has high verifiability, accounts receivable less, inventories less yet, depreciable assets even less, and so on.	1, 3, 14
Validity (representational faithfulness)	Correspondence between numbers and objects or events portrayed.	The historical cost/constant dollar cost of the land described above may be $1.2 million 1998 dollars, but the $1.2 million does not represent the current cost of market value of the land.	14
Consistency	Applying the same accounting methods over a series of reporting periods.	Use of FIFO inventory over a series of years, not FIFO for two years, LIFO for three, and so on.	6
Neutrality (evenhandedness)	A quality of information implying that it is objective and without bias.	An example of lack of neutrality may clarify: The MACRS system used for depreciation for tax purposes is constructed from arbitrary economic lives and an accelerated schedule intended to encourage investment and reduce conflict with tax payers.	14
Materiality	An item is material if the judgment of a reasonable person would have been changed or influenced by its omission or misstatement.	An error of $100 of revenue would be immaterial for a firm with $100,000 of revenue but material for a firm with $1,000.	4
Conservatism	Way of dealing with uncertainties. Avoids recognition of income on the basis of inadequate evidence but requires recognition of losses when assets have been impaired or liabilities incurred. In short, when in doubt, write it off.	Charging all research and development costs to expenses as incurred. Applying lower-of-cost-or-market methods to asset valuation.	5, 7, 12

(continued)

593

Exhibit 14-3

Frequently Encountered Terminology in Conceptual Frameworks of Accounting (*continued*)

Term	Short Description	Example	Chapters in this Text*
Continuity (going concern)	Assumption that an entity will continue indefinitely or at least will not be liquidated in the near future.	Letterhead stationery on hand is classified as supplies or rubbish, depending on the going concern assumption.	4
Entity	The unit of accountability.	A parent corporation, a subsidiary, a retail store.	1, 12
Accrual accounting	Record financial effects in the periods affected regardless of when cash is received or paid.	Recognize receivables and payables when promise to pay is made and match expenses with revenues.	2, 3, 4
Recognition	Formally recording or incorporating an item in accounts and financial statements. An element may be recognized (recorded) or unrecognized (unrecorded).	Recognition requires revenues to be earned and realized. Increases or decreases in the value of land may be earned but unrealized. Advance payments on subscriptions may be realized but not earned.	1, 2, 4, 5
Matching and cost recovery	Matching is relating revenues and expenses to each other in a particular period.	Sales commission expenses are "matched" directly against related sales. Sales salaries, costs of heating, and depreciation on equipment are "matched" indirectly against current revenues because their benefits are considered to be exhausted in the current period.	2, 4, 5, 14

*Many of these criteria or basic ideas underlie this entire textbook.

of-completion method. Consider the builder of an ocean liner. Such a company might take well over a year to finish and deliver a given product. Spreading expected costs and revenues over the life of the contract, based on the work accomplished, allows income recognition in each year and realistically portrays the economic process. Otherwise, all the net income would appear in one chunk upon completion of the project, as if it had been earned on a single day.

Also, in very rare cases, revenue can be recorded in proportion to cash collections under long-run installment contracts. An illustration is the retail sales of undeveloped lots. The receivables may be collectible over decades rather than months, and there is no reliable basis for estimating how likely it is that the full amount will ever be collected.

Not knowing whether a receivable will be collected does not always delay the recording of revenue. Many accountants regard the revenue as realized but provide an ample allowance for uncollectible accounts. For example, hospitals can recognize revenue on the accrual basis as their services are delivered. However, because many hospital debts go unpaid, hospitals must offset some of this revenue with an account for bad debts expense.

EXPENSE RECOGNITION

Generally accepted accounting principles also allow accountants to choose when to recognize certain expenses. Comparing two companies can be difficult if each chooses a different method for recognizing major expenses. To achieve comparability, analysts often reconstruct a company's financial statements to place them on a basis consistent with other companies in the same industry.

Suppose two companies, Miami Marine (MM) and Sarasota Sailboats (SS), began business in the same industry in 19X1. Each company would have reported amounts from Exhibit 14-4, depending on the accounting method chosen.

For stockholder reporting purposes, the choice of accounting policies can have a dramatic effect on operating income before taxes. Assume that MM takes one extreme stance; SS takes the other extreme. As Exhibit 14-5 shows, the choices of LIFO, accelerated depreciation, and immediate write-off of product introduction costs will cause MM's operating income to be $50. In contrast, SS's operating income will be $120.

Exhibit 14-4

Accounting Differences

	Amount	Difference
Beginning inventory	$ 0	
Purchases	270,000	
Ending inventory, if FIFO is used	110,000 }	$40,000
Ending inventory, if LIFO is used	70,000 }	
Depreciation, if MACRS is used	20,000 }	10,000
Depreciation, if straight-line is used	10,000 }	
Product introduction costs, original total amount	30,000 }	20,000
Product introduction costs, amortized amount	10,000 }	
Revenue	400,000	
Other expenses	100,000	

	Individual Effects				
	(1) Miami Marine (LIFO, Accelerated, Immediate Write-off)	(2) Change from LIFO to FIFO	(3) Change from Accelerated to Straight-line	(4) Change from Immediate Write-off to Amortization	(5) Sarasota Sailboat (FIFO, Straight-line, Amortization)
Revenue	400				400
Expenses:					
Cost of goods sold	200	40			160
Depreciation	20		10		10
Product introduction					
costs	30			20	10
Other expenses	100				100
Total expenses	350	—	—	—	280
Operating income before					
income taxes	50	40	10	20	120

Many managers seek to maximize reported earnings by choosing the accounting policies favored by SS. Others tend to be more conservative and choose the MM policies. The point here is that similar operations may be portrayed differently in income statements. Note that all the data are the same as far as the underlying cash flows are concerned.

Someday accounting procedures may become more standardized and financial statements will be easier to compare. Until then, though, companies will have to disclose all of the practices used in creating their financial statements. Why? Because once analysts know what methods are in use by different companies, the analysts can revise the financial statements to put them on a comparable basis so comparisons are meaningful.

STATEMENT OF ACCOUNTING POLICIES

How and where do companies disclose the accounting methods they used to create their financial statements? The disclosure usually appears as a separate Summary of Significant Accounting Policies preceding the footnotes of financial statements. Exhibit 14-6 displays some of the items in a typical summary, that of Procter & Gamble Company from its 1996 annual report. Many of the items identified have been discussed in this book, although a few, including accounting changes and currency translation, are topics for subsequent courses.

INCOME MEASUREMENT WHEN PRICES CHANGE

Objective 4
Differentiate between financial capital and physical capital.

Sometimes historical costs do not measure income properly. Accountants tend to agree that income is best described as the return on capital invested by shareholders. By examining the relationship of income to capital in greater detail, we can discover circumstances when historical cost leads to incorrect and misleading measures of income.

INCOME OR CAPITAL

At first glance, the concept of income seems straightforward. Income is a company's increase in wealth during a period. It is the amount that could be paid out to shareholders at the end of the period, while still leaving the company as *well off* as it was at the beginning of the period. In essence, shareholders invest capital and expect a return *on* the

1. Summary of Significant Accounting Policies (Millions of Dollars Except Per Share Amounts)

Basis of Presentation: The consolidated financial statements include The Procter & Gamble Company and its controlled subsidiaries (the Company). Investments in companies that are at least 20% to 50% owned, and over which the Company exerts significant influence but does not control the financial and operating decisions, are accounted for by the equity method. These investments are managed as integral parts of the Company's segment operations, and the Company's share of their results is included in net sales and in earnings for the related segments.

Use of Estimates: The preparation of financial statements in conformity with generally accepted accounting principles requires management to make estimates and assumptions that affect the amounts reported in the consolidated financial statements and accompanying disclosures. Although these estimates are based on management's best knowledge of current events and actions the Company may undertake in the future, actual results ultimately may differ from the estimates.

Accounting Changes: In 1996, the Company adopted FASB Statement No. 121, "Accounting for the Impairment of Long-Lived Assets and for Long-Lived Assets to Be Disposed Of," which requires review for possible impairment whenever events or changes in circumstances indicate that the carrying amount of an asset may not be recoverable. The effect of the adoption was not material. In 1997, the FASB issued Statement No. 130, "Reporting Comprehensive Income," and Statement No. 131, "Disclosures about Segments of an Enterprise and Related Information." These statements, which are effective for periods beginning after December 15, 1997, expand or modify disclosures and, accordingly, will have no impact on the Company's reported financial position, results of operations or cash flows.

Currency Translation: The financial statements of subsidiaries outside the U.S. generally are measured using the local currency as the functional currency. Translation adjustments are accumulated in a separate component of shareholders' equity. For subsidiaries operating in highly inflationary economies, the U.S. dollar is the functional currency. Remeasurement and other transactional exchange gains/(losses) reflected in earnings were $1, $(28) and $(38) for 1997, 1996 and 1995, respectively.

Cash Equivalents: Highly liquid investments with maturities of three months or less when purchased are considered cash equivalents.

Inventory Valuation: Inventories are valued at cost, which is not in excess of current market price. Cost is primarily determined by either the average cost or the first-in, first-out method. The replacement cost of last-in, first-out inventories exceeds carrying value by approximately $122.

Goodwill and Other Intangible Assets: The cost of intangible assets is amortized, principally on a straight-line basis, over the estimated periods benefited (not exceeding 40 years). The average remaining life is 30 years. The realizability of goodwill and other intangibles is evaluated periodically as events or circumstances indicate a possible inability to recover the carrying amount. Such evaluation is based on various analyses, including cash flow and profitability projections that incorporate the impact on existing Company businesses. The analyses necessarily involve significant management judgment to evaluate the capacity of an acquired business to perform within projections. Historically, the Company has generated sufficient returns from acquired businesses to recover the cost of the goodwill and other intangible assets.

Property, Plant, and Equipment: Property, Plant, and equipment are recorded at cost reduced by accumulated depreciation. Depreciation expense is provided based on estimated useful lives using the straight-line method.

Selected Operating Expenses: Research and development costs are charged to earnings as incurred and were $1,282 in 1997, $1,221 in 1996 and $1,148 in 1995. Advertising costs are charged to earnings as incurred and were $3,468 in 1997, $3,254 in 1996, and $3,284 in 1995.

Net Earnings Per Common Share: Net earnings less preferred dividends (net of related tax benefits) are divided by the weighted average number of common shares outstanding during the year to calculate net earnings per common share. Fully diluted net earnings per common share are calculated to give effect to stock options and convertible preferred stock. In 1997, the FASB issued Statement No. 128, "Earnings Per Share," which revises the manner in which earnings per share is calculated. The statement is effective for the reporting period ending December 31, 1997 and is not expected to have a significant impact on the Company's earnings per share.

Stock Split: In July 1997, the Company's board of directors approved a two-for-one stock split that is effective for common and preferred shareholders of record as of August 22, 1997. The financial statements, notes and other references to share and per share data have been retroactively restated to reflect the stock split for all periods presented.

Fair Values of Financial Instruments: Fair values of cash equivalents, short and long-term investments, and short-term debt approximate cost. The estimated fair values of other financial instruments, including debt and risk management instruments, have been determined using available market information and valuation methodologies, primarily discounted cash flow analysis. These estimates require considerable judgment in interpreting market data, and changes in assumptions or estimation methods may significantly affect the fair value estimates.

Major Customer: The Company's largest customer, Wal-Mart Stores, Inc. and its affiliates, accounted for 10% of consolidated net sales in 1997.

Reclassification: Certain reclassifications of prior years' amounts have been made to conform with the current year presentation, primarily related to the segment information.

capital and an eventual return *of* the capital. To measure the shareholders' return on capital, the company first measures the resources required to maintain invested capital at its original level. Any profit above and beyond this level of maintained capital is income. Traditional historical-cost accounting would state that maintaining capital requires keeping resources equal to the dollar value of the original investment. Under this *financial concept* of income, any excess dollar amount is income, the return on capital.

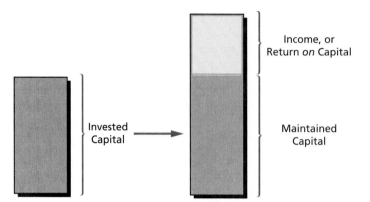

In contrast to the financial concept, some accountants and managers define capital as a physical concept, based on the company's real productive capacity. They identify the physical resources that make up capital at the beginning of the period, such as plant, property, equipment and inventory. To maintain that capital, the company must set aside enough end-of-period resources (dollars) to replace the beginning-of-period physical capacity. Only resources in excess of those required to replicate the initial productive capacity are considered income.

Consider an example in which a company begins with owners' investment (capital) of $1,000. That $1,000 is used immediately to purchase 500 units of inventory. The inventory is sold a year later for $1,500. The cost of replacing the 500 units of inventory has risen to $1,200. The year began with financial capital of $1,000 which is immediately transformed into 500 units of physical capital (inventory). At the end of the year, there is $1,500 and no inventory. Suppose management wanted to keep the initial level of capital to begin a new year but also to pay investors a return on their investment. How much can the company pay out?

The simple answer is that the company can pay out its *income*—all of the $1,500 not needed to maintain the initial level of capital. But what capital are we maintaining? If we are maintaining financial capital, income is based on the $1,500 sales less the $1,000 level of financial investment, which equals $500. Calculating income based on maintaining financial capital is known as **financial capital maintenance.** Conversely, if we are maintaining physical capital, income is based on the $1,500 less the cost of maintaining a 500-unit inventory. That cost is now $1,200, so income would be only $300 ($1,500 − $1,200). Calculating income based on maintaining physical capital is known as **physical capital maintenance.** Do you see how using historical costs to determine income might be a problem in this example? Historical cost is a financially driven concept. In a world of changing prices in which physical capital maintenance is important, historical cost overstates income. If dividend distributions are based on historical cost, $500 will be distributed, inventories will not be fully replaced, and prior levels of activity will not be maintainable.

financial capital maintenance A concept of income measurement whereby income emerges only after financial resources are recovered.

physical capital maintenance A concept of income measurement whereby income emerges only after recovering an amount that allows physical operating capability to be maintained.

	Financial Capital Maintenance	Physical Capital Maintenance
Sales	$1,500	$1,500
Cost of goods sold	1,000	1,200
Income	$ 500	$ 300

COMPLAINTS ABOUT HISTORICAL COST

A pet theme of politicians and other critics of business is the "unconscionable" or "obscene" profits reported by American companies. In response, many business executives insist that our traditional historical-cost basis for measuring income overstates profits during a time of rising prices. These overstated profits also cause their companies to pay more income taxes than they should.

The importance of this issue varies to some extent by industry. Industries with huge investments in plant and equipment tend to be most affected. For instance, consider NYNEX, a telephone company that emerged from the breakup of the Bell system, and subsequently merged into Bell Atlantic. In a recent period of high inflation NYNEX reported net income of $1,095 million. This would have been a net loss of $82 million if depreciation had been adjusted for inflation. In 1998, inflation was fairly low, around 3% per year, so annual effects are small. Even so, if an asset was purchased in 1978, its historical cost would probably be about half of its replacement cost. This would mean its depreciation would be half of what depreciation should be under a physical capital maintenance concept.

The soaring inflation of the late 1970s in the United States raised many questions about the usefulness of traditional historical-cost financial statements. The FASB responded by issuing Statement No. 33. "Financial Reporting and Changing Prices." The statement required no changes in the primary financial statements. However, it required large companies to include supplementary inflation-adjusted schedules in their annual reports.

Statement No. 33 was experimental, and its requirements were in place for eight years. By 1987 inflation had subsided, and the FASB decided that inflation-adjusted disclosures would no longer be required. Although U.S. companies do not need to report inflation-adjusted numbers, a basic knowledge about reporting the effects of changing prices is useful for at least four reasons: (1) high inflation is still present in many countries, and most accounting reports in those countries report the effects of inflation; (2) if history is any indication, higher inflation rates will return to the United States sooner or later, and when they do, readers of financial statements will again become concerned with inflation-adjusted statements; (3) the cumulative effect of even a 2% or 3% rate is substantial; (4) understanding the limitations of traditional financial statements is enhanced by knowing how inflation affects (or does not affect) such financial statements.

ALTERNATIVES TO HISTORICAL-COST INCOME MEASUREMENT

When prices of resources do not change, financial and physical capital maintenance give identical measures of income. But price changes are a fact of life. Some price changes are a result of **inflation,** a general decline in the purchasing power of the dollar (or other monetary unit) or a general increase in the average cost of goods and services. Other price changes are specific to a product. For example, the price of computing power has been declining steadily for decades as a result of improved technology, although most products were stable in price or rising.

Changing prices, and particularly inflation, have caused accountants to consider two types of changes in financial reporting: (1) Switch from measuring transactions in **nominal dollars,** which are dollar measurements that are not restated for fluctuations in the general purchasing power of the monetary unit, to **constant dollars**, which are dollar values restated in terms of current purchasing power. (2) Instead of reporting the **historical cost** of an asset, which is the amount originally paid to acquire it, use the **current cost,** which is generally the cost to replace it. As we saw in our previous example, using historical costs implies financial capital maintenance, and using current costs implies physical capital maintenance. Traditional accounting uses nominal (rather than constant) dollars and historical (rather than current) costs. Such accounting has almost exclusively dominated financial reporting in the United States throughout this century.

inflation A general decline in the purchasing power of the monetary unit.

nominal dollars Those dollars that are not restated for fluctuations in the general purchasing power of the monetary unit.

constant dollars Dollar measurements that are restated in terms of current purchasing power.

historical cost The amount originally paid to acquire an asset.

current cost Generally, the cost to replace an asset.

<table>
<tr><td></td><td>The two proposed changes, which can be applied separately or in combination, address separate but related problems caused by changing prices: (1) constant-dollar disclosures account for general changes in the purchasing power of the dollar, and (2) current-cost disclosures account for changes in specific prices. The two approaches create the following four alternatives for measuring income:</td></tr>
</table>

Objective 5
Incorporate changing prices into income measurement using four different methods.

The two proposed changes, which can be applied separately or in combination, address separate but related problems caused by changing prices: (1) constant-dollar disclosures account for general changes in the purchasing power of the dollar, and (2) current-cost disclosures account for changes in specific prices. The two approaches create the following four alternatives for measuring income:

	Historical Cost	Current Cost
Nominal Dollars	1 Historical cost/ nominal dollars	2 Current cost/ nominal dollars
Constant Dollars	3 Historical cost/ constant dollars	4 Current cost/ constant dollars

We will use the Greystone Company situation to compare these four basic methods of income measurement. Greystone has the following comparative balance sheets at December 31 (based on historical costs in nominal dollars):

	19X1	19X2
Cash	$ 0	$10,500
Inventory, 400 and 100 units, respectively	8,000	2,000
Total assets	$8,000	$12,500
Original paid in capital	$8,000	$8,000
Retained income	—	4,500
Stockholders' equity	$8,000	$12,500

The company acquired all 400 units of inventory at $20 per unit (total of $8,000) on December 31, 19X1, and held the units until December 31, 19X2. Three hundred units were sold for $35 per unit (total of $10,500 cash) on December 31, 19X2. The replacement cost of the inventory at that date was $30 per unit. The government monitors price levels by calculating how much a particular collection of items, called a market basket, would cost at various points in time. Suppose the market basket cost $300 on December 31, 19X1 and $330 on December 31, 19X2. You can see that the cost rose 10%. The $30 change is 10% of the original value of $300 ($330 − $300/$300 = 10%).

For ease of reference, an index is often created, so future price levels can be expressed in terms of a base year. If we set December 31, 19X1 as the base year and set the index to 100 on that date, we can express the index value on December 31, 19X2 as 110. This is calculated by dividing the 19X2 value by the 19X1 dollar value ($330/$300 = 110). This means that a bundle of goods that cost $100 on December 31, 19X1 will cost $110 on December 31, 19X2. You could also predict that, because of inflation, a bundle of goods that cost $200 in 19X1 would cost $220 in 19X2 ($200 × 110 = $220). We assume that these are the company's only transactions, and for simplicity, we ignore income taxes. Exhibit 14-7 shows Greystone's balance sheets and income statements prepared according to each of the four methods for measuring income.

HISTORICAL COST/NOMINAL DOLLARS

The first two columns of Exhibit 14-7 show financial statements prepared using the time-honored historical cost/nominal dollars approach (Method 1). Basically, this method measures invested capital in nominal dollars. It is the most popular approach to income measurement and is the primary method in U.S. GAAP, which we have referred to as historical-cost. Operating income (which equals net income in this case) is $4,500, the excess of realized revenue ($10,500 in 19X2) over the "not restated" $6,000 historical

Exhibit 14-7

Greystone Company
Four Major Methods to Measure Income and Capital (in dollars)
Assumptions: Inventory, historical cost—$20/unit; Inventory, current cost—$30/unit;
Beginning index—100; Ending index—110

	Nominal Dollars*				Constant Dollars*			
	(Method 1) Historical Cost		(Method 2) Current Cost		(Method 3) Historical Cost		(Method 4) Current Cost	
Balance sheets as of								
December 31	**19X1**	**19X2**	**19X1**	**19X2**	**19X1**	**19X2**	**19X1**	**19X2**
Cash	—	10,500	—	10,500	—	10,500	—	10,500
Inventory, 400 and 100								
units, respectively	8,000	2,000 ᵇ	8,000	3,000 ᶜ	8,800 ᵉ	2,200 ᵉ	8,800 ᵉ	3,000 ᶜ
Total assets	8,000	12,500	8,000	13,500	8,800	12,700	8,800	13,500
Original paid-in capital	8,000	8,000	8,000	8,000	8,800 ᶠ	8,800 ᶠ	8,800 ᶠ	8,800 ᶠ
Retained income (confined to income from continuing operations)		4,500		1,500		3,900		1,500
Revaluation equity (accumulated holding gains)				4,000				3,200
Total liab. & stk. eq.	8,000	12,500	8,000	13,500	8,800	12,700	8,800	13,500
Income statements for 19X2								
Sales, 300 units @ $35		10,500		10,500		10,500		10,500
Cost of goods sold, 300 units		6,000 ᵇ		9,000 ᶜ		6,600 ᵉ		9,000 ᶜ
Income from continuing operations (to retained income)		4,500		1,500		3,900		1,500
Holding gains (losses)ᵃ								
On 300 units sold				3,000 ᵈ				2,400 ᵍ
On 100 units sold				1,000 ᵈ				800 ᵍ
Total holding gainsᵃ (to revaluation equity)				4,000				3,200

*Nominal dollars are not restated for a general price index, whereas constant dollars are restated.

ᵃMany advocates of the current-cost method favor showing these gains in a completely separate statement of holding gains rather than as a part of the income statement. Others favor including some or all of these gains as a part of income for the year.

ᵇ100 × $20, 300 × $20.
ᶜ100 × $30, 300 × $30.
ᵈ300 × ($30 − $20), 100 × ($30 − $20).
ᵉ110/100 × $8,000, 110/100 × $2,000, 110/100 × $6,000.
ᶠ110/100 × $8,000.

ᵍ$9,000 − [(110/100) × $6,000] = $2,400
or
300 × [30 − (110/100) × $20] = $2,400.

$3,000 − [(110/100) × $2,000] = $800
or
100 × [$30 − (110/100) × $20] = $800.

costs of assets used in obtaining that revenue. As we know, when this conventional accrual basis of accounting is used, an exchange transaction is ordinarily necessary before revenues (and resulting incomes) are recognized. Thus no income generally appears until the asset is sold, and intervening price fluctuations are ignored.

CURRENT COST/NOMINAL DOLLARS

The second set of financial statements in Exhibit 14-7 illustrates a current-cost method that has especially strong advocates in the United Kingdom and Australia (Method 2). This method uses current cost/nominal dollars. The focus is on income from continuing operations. This model emphasizes that operating income should be income that is "distributable" to shareholders while maintaining physical capital. That is, Greystone could pay dividends in an amount of only $1,500, leaving enough assets to allow for replacement of the inventory that has just been sold.

Critics of traditional accounting claim that the $4,500 historical-cost measure of income from continuing operations is misleading because it overstates the net amount of distributable assets. If a $4,500 dividend were paid, the company would not be able to continue operations at the same level as before. The current cost statement reports only the $1,500 profit available after replacing the inventory. The $3,000 difference between the two operating incomes ($4,500 − $1,500 = $3,000) is frequently referred to as an "inventory profit" or an "inflated profit." Why? Because under the traditional method 1, this amount counts as profit, although it will actually need to be spent on inventory. The $3,000 can be considered an overstatement of profit because the extra inventory replacement cost is being ignored.

HOLDING GAINS AND PHYSICAL CAPITAL

The current-cost method stresses a separation between income from continuing operations, which is defined as the excess of revenue over the current costs of the assets consumed in obtaining that revenue, and holding gains (or losses), which are increases (or decreases) in the replacement costs of the assets held during the current period. The current-cost method recognizes the impact of intervening price fluctuations on a company when the values of its assets change.

Accountants differ sharply on how to account for holding gains. The "correct" accounting depends on distinctions between capital and income. That is, income cannot occur until invested capital is "recovered" or "maintained." The issue of capital versus income is concretely illustrated in Exhibit 14-7. The advocates of a physical concept of capital maintenance claim that all holding gains (both those gains related to the units sold and the gains related to the units unsold) should be excluded from income and become a part of stockholders' equity called **revaluation equity.** Why? Because holding gains represent the amount that must be reinvested to maintain physical capital at its beginning-of-the-year level. Holding gains become part of capital, not a return on capital.

Some U.S. companies, especially real estate companies, present current cost/nominal dollar financial statements as a supplement to their historical cost statements. An example is Catellus Development Co. of San Francisco, one of the country's largest publicly held real estate companies. The company's reasoning is explained in a footnote to its financial statements:

> ### Current Value Reporting
> *Current value basis consolidated balance sheets presented as of December 31, 1994 and 1993 provide supplemental information about the economic condition of the Company. Because of the low historical cost basis of the Company's real estate assets, management believes that the historical cost basis presentation used in customary financial statements does not reflect the true economic value of the Company's holdings. Current value reporting provides recognition that, over time, real property generally appreciates in value, and that value may be realized through the development process and effective management of income producing assets. It does not represent the net realizable value of the Company as a whole, nor does it contemplate liquidation or a distressed sale of the Company's assets. Management believes that current value information provides meaningful information regarding the Company's economic condition and the value of its holdings in today's real estate market.*
>
> *Current value accounting continues to represent an experimental approach; authoritative criteria have not been established for its prepara-*

revaluation equity A part of stockholders' equity that includes all holding gains that are excluded from income.

tion and presentation. As experimentation continues, preparation and presentation methods may be modified in future reporting periods.

The company's 1994 condensed current cost balance sheet and statement of changes in revaluation equity are in Exhibit 14-8. Notice that the current value of the company's properties exceeds the historical book value by $1,781,182,000 − $1,087,119,000 = $694,063,000. Further, revaluation equity, which represents the difference between current-cost and historical-cost values for all assets and liabilities, not just properties, adds $524,907 to the stockholders' equity. Finally, from the statement of changes in revaluation equity, you can see the revaluation equity includes holding gains on both properties sold and those still held.

The Catellus current cost disclosure was voluntary. In 1995, Catellus reduced these disclosures significantly, replacing full supplemental financial statements with briefer footnote disclosure. In 1996, Catellus eliminated the supplemental disclosures because of significant production costs and because calculated current values "fluctuate resulting from changes in interest rates, capitalization rates, and development assumptions."

HISTORICAL COST/CONSTANT DOLLARS

Method 3 of Exhibit 14-7 shows the results of applying general index numbers to historical costs. Essentially, the income measurements in each year are restated in terms of constant dollars (which possess the same general purchasing power of the current year) instead of the nominal dollars (which possess different general purchasing powers of various years).

Because of inflation, dollars spent or received in 19X2 have a different value than do dollars spent or received in 19X1. Adding 19X1 dollars to 19X2 dollars is like adding apples and oranges. Constant-dollar accounting measures all items on the 19X2 financial statements, including the items from previous years, in 19X2 dollars to aid comparability.

Consider the objections to Method 1. Deducting 6,000 19X1 dollars from 10,500 19X2 dollars to obtain $4,500 is akin to deducting 60 centimeters from 105 meters and calling the result 45 meters. That sort of nonsensical arithmetic can get you in trouble, but accountants have been paid well for years for performing similar arithmetic. It has worked because inflation rates have been relatively low.

Method 3, historical cost/constant dollars, shows how to remedy the foregoing objections. General indexes may be used to restate the amounts of historical-cost/nominal-dollar Method 1. Examples of such indexes are the Gross National Product Implicit Price Deflator and the Consumer Price Index for All Urban Consumers (CPI). You may have noticed in the popular press continuing discussion about whether the CPI is being measured properly. This obscure issue turns out to be very important because the increases that many retirees get in their Social Security payments are tied directly to such indices. Index numbers are used to gauge the relationship between current conditions and some norm or base condition (which is assigned the index number of 100). For our purpose, a **general price index** compares the average price of a group of goods and services at one date with the average price of a similar group at another date.

A price index is an average. It does not measure the behavior of the individual component prices. Some individual prices may move in one direction, and some may move in another. For example, the general consumer price level may soar while the prices of eggs and chickens decline. During 1997, the CPI rose slightly while crude oil prices fell sharply.

Do not confuse general indexes, which are used in constant-dollar accounting, with specific indexes. The two have entirely different purposes. Sometimes **specific price indexes** are used as a means of approximating the current costs of particular assets or types of assets. That is, companies use specialized indexes to inexpensively approximate current costs without hiring professional appraisers. For example, Inland Steel has used the Engineering News Record Construction Cost Index to value most of its property, plant, and equipment for purposes of using the current-cost method.

general price index An index that compares the average price of a group of goods and services at one date with the average price of a similar group at another date.

specific price index An index used to approximate the current costs of particular assets or types of assets.

Exhibit 14-8

Current Cost Financial Statements Catellus Development Corporation

Historical Cost Basis and Supplemental Current Value Basis
(In thousands, except share data)

December 31,		94
	Supplemental Current Value Basis (Note 2)	*Historical Cost Basis*
Assets		
Properties	$1,826,853	$1,248,398
Less accumulated depreciation	—	(161,279)
Less estimated disposition costs	(45,671)	—
	1,781,182	1,087,119
Other assets	63,729	103,324
Cash and cash equivalents	16,920	16,920
Total	$1,861,831	$1,207,363
Liabilities and stockholders' equity		
Mortgage and other debt	$530,641	$530,641
Accounts payable and accrued expenses	38,876	38,876
Deferred credits and other liabilities	15,446	25,495
Deferred income taxes	252,272	112,662
Stockholders' equity		
Preferred stock	322,500	322,500
Common stock	730	730
Paid-in capital	220,338	220,338
Accumulated deficit	(43,879)	(43,879)
Revaluation equity	524,907	—
Total stockholders' equity	1,024,596	499,689
Total	$1,861,831	$1,207,363

Consolidated Statement of Changes in Revaluation Equity
(In thousands)

Supplemental Current Value Basis

Year Ended December 31	94
Revaluation equity at beginning of year	$476,171
Revaluation equity attributable to properties sold	(21,564)
Increase (reduction) in value of properties held at beginning and end of year	127,915
Other decrease (increase) in historical cost of properties, net	(30,905)
Decrease (increase) in estimated disposition costs	(1, 768)
Decrease (increase) in deferred taxes, net of historical cost	(9,323)
Decrease in value of other assets, net of liabilities	(15,619)
Revaluation equity at end of year	$524,907

MAINTAINING INVESTED CAPITAL

The historical-cost/constant-dollar approach (Method 3) is not a fundamental departure from historical costs. Instead it maintains that all historical costs to be matched against revenue should be restated on some constant-dollar basis so that all revenues and all expenses are expressed in dollars of the same (usually current) purchasing power. The restated figures are actually historical costs expressed in constant dollars via the use of a general price index.

The current dollar is typically employed because readers of financial statements tend to think in such terms instead of in terms of old dollars with significantly different purchasing power. The original units in inventory would be updated on each year's balance sheet along with their effect on stockholders' equity. For example, the December 31, 19X1 balance sheet would be restated for comparative purposes on December 31, 19X2:

	Not Restated Cost	Multiplier	Restated Cost
Inventory	$8,000	110/100	$8,800
Original paid-in capital	8,000	110/100	8,800

To extend the illustration, suppose all the inventory was held for two full years. The general price index rose from 110 to 132 during 19X3. The December 31, 19X2 balance sheet items would be restated for comparative purposes on December 31, 19X3, using 19X3 dollars:

	Not Restated Cost 12/31X2	Multiplier	Restated Cost 12/31X3
Inventory	$8,800	132/110	$10,560*
Original paid-in capital	8,800	132/110	10,560*

*The same restated 19X3 result could be tied to 19X1, the year of acquisition:
Inventory $8,000 × 132/100 = $10,560
Original paid-in capital $8,000 × 132/100 = $10,560

The restated amount is just that—a restatement of original cost in terms of current (19X3) dollars. It is not a gain in any sense. Therefore, this approach should not be confused with "current-cost" accounting. Using this approach, if the specific current cost of the inventory goes up or down but the average price level remains unchanged, the restated cost also remains unchanged.

The restated historical-cost approach fits with the concept of maintaining the general purchasing power of the invested capital in total rather than maintaining "specific invested capital" item by item. You could think of it as a financial concept of capital maintenance.

CURRENT COST/CONSTANT DOLLARS

Method 4 of Exhibit 14-7 shows the results of applying general index numbers together with current costs. As the footnotes of the exhibit explain in more detail, the nominal gains reported under Method 2 are adjusted so that only gains in constant dollars are reported. For example, suppose you buy 100 units on December 31, 19X1 for $2,000 cash. If the current replacement cost of your inventory at December 31, 19X2 is $3,000 but the general price index has risen from 100 to 110, your nominal gain is $1,000, but your "real" gain in constant dollars in 19X2 is only $800: the $3,000 current cost minus the restated historical cost of $2,000 × 1.10 = $2,200.

Suppose the 100 units are held throughout 19X3 while the general price index rises from 110 to 132. The replacement cost rises from $30 to $34, a nominal holding gain for 19X3 of $4 × 100 = $400. However, the current-cost/constant-dollar approach (Method 4) would report a real holding loss in 19X3:

	December 31		
	19X1	*19X2*	*19X3*
Original cost restated for changes in the price level	$2,000	$2,200	$2,640
Current cost	2,000	3,000	3,400
Increase in current cost		1,000 *	400 *
Increase due to price level		200 †	440 †
Holding gain (loss)		$ 800	$ (40)

*3,000 − 2,000 = 1,000, and 3,400 − 3,000 = 400
†2,200 − 2,000 = 200 and 2,640 − 2,200 = 440

Many accountants disagree on the relative merits of using historical-cost approaches versus using current-cost approaches to income measurement. However, most accountants agree that using constant dollars would be an improvement if for no other reason than improved comparability.

ACCOUNTING STANDARDS THROUGHOUT THE WORLD

Objective 6
Compare U.S. GAAP with other countries' standards.

This text has focused on U.S. GAAP while mentioning practices of other countries throughout. The most basic aspects of accounting are consistent throughout the world. For example, double-entry systems, accrual accounting, and the income statement and balance sheet are used worldwide. However, as you have already seen in some cases, there are many differences in accounting around the world. Accounting practices differ among countries for a variety of reasons, such as differences in government, economic systems, culture, and traditions. We will briefly discuss how accounting in the United Kingdom, France, Germany, and Japan differs from that in the United States.

DIFFERENCES IN TAX AND INFLATION ACCOUNTING

One major area of differences in financial reporting is the influence of the income tax law on reporting to shareholders. Methods in the United States for reporting to tax authorities differ from those used for reporting to shareholders. In contrast, tax reporting and shareholder reporting are identical in many countries. For example, France has a "Plan Compatible" that specifies a National Uniform Chart of Accounts that is used for both tax returns and reporting to shareholders. German financial reporting is also determined primarily by tax laws. If accounting records are not kept according to strict tax laws, the German tax authorities can reject the records as a basis for taxation. Similarly, in Japan, certain principles are allowed for tax purposes only if they are also used for shareholder reporting. When such principles provide tax advantages, there is a tendency for companies to use them for reporting to shareholders. This "tax conformity" concept appears occasionally in the United States as in the LIFO/FIFO conformity rule, but it is uncommon.

In addition to the influence of the tax law, financial reporting of income taxes differs among countries. For example, in Argentina, income tax expenses are recognized in financial statements only when payments are made to the government; in contrast, most countries, including the United States, Great Britain, the Netherlands, and Canada, accrue taxes when the related income is recognized. This process of deferred tax accounting was discussed in Chapter 8. Sweden and Switzerland are two other countries that do not recognize deferred taxes.

Another significant difference among countries is the extent to which financial statements account for inflation. In the 1980s, the FASB experimented with requiring supplementary disclosure of inflation-adjusted numbers. After years of accounting research on the value of these disclosures, the FASB concluded that the costs exceeded the benefits. Now no requirements for such supplementary disclosure exist in the United States. In contrast, many countries require full or partial adjustments for inflation for reporting to both shareholders and tax authorities. For example, until recently, Brazil experienced persistent double- and triple-digit inflation rates and required all statements to be adjusted for changes in the general price level in the manner described earlier in this chapter. Such inflation-adjusted statements are used for both tax and shareholder reporting. In many countries, the requirement is linked to the level of inflation being experienced.

The Netherlands has been a leader in the application of current replacement-cost measurements to financial accounts, although it has no formal requirement mandating either historical cost or replacement cost. French financial statements include a partial inflation adjustment, using replacement cost for fixed assets. Similarly, Sweden allows (but does not require) the revaluation of certain property, plant, and equipment. Mexico requires inflation adjustments, but allows either price-level adjustments or current-cost statements.

Not surprisingly, countries that have experienced the lowest inflation rates have been the slowest to recognize inflation in their accounting statements. Japan has no recognition of inflation, and Germany has recommended supplementary disclosures, but few companies have responded.

ACCOUNTING PRINCIPLES IN SELECTED COUNTRIES

The Companies' Laws in the United Kingdom provide general guidance for accounting standards, and details are specified by the Accounting Standards Board, a private-sector body sponsored by the accountancy profession. U.K. companies can use either historical-cost or current-cost accounting, or a mixture of the two. For example, British Petroleum reports both "Historical cost operating profit" and "Replacement cost operating profit" on its income statement. LIFO is not allowed for either tax or shareholder reporting. Research expenditures are charged to expense, but development expenses can be capitalized. Purchased goodwill is usually written off immediately.

France leads the way in standardizing accounting. Companies must use a National Uniform Chart of Accounts and abide by extensive financial reporting requirements. Accounting records are considered legal control devices more than they are considered sources of information for decision makers. Accounting methods such as pooling-of-interests, LIFO, and capitalization of leases are not allowed. Research and development costs can be capitalized but must be amortized over no more than 5 years, and goodwill is amortized over 5 to 25 years. Future pension obligations are not recognized as liabilities. Two reporting requirements are unique to France: (1) companies must publish an annual social balance sheet relating to environmental matters and employee conditions and benefits, and (2) companies must publish comprehensive financial forecasts.

Tax law dominates financial reporting in Germany. Whatever is reported to shareholders must also be reported to tax authorities. Therefore, accounting standards are based on statutes and court decisions, and they are not necessarily directed at producing statements useful for decision making. Both FIFO and LIFO are allowed, but they must correspond to the physical flow of inventory. Goodwill must be written off over 15 years. Depreciation is based on specific tax-depreciation schedules. Cash flow statements are not required, but many companies provide them anyway. Consolidated statements are required, but exceptions are granted for many companies. Although German accounting standards have grown closer to U.S standards since World War II, they remain significantly different.

Accounting and finance play a smaller role in Japanese companies and in the Japanese economy than they do in other industrialized countries. Accounting is dominated by the central government, especially the Ministry of Finance. There is extensive cross-ownership among Japanese firms, and banks are often heavily involved with companies to whom they lend money. Debt capital is used much more than is equity capital. Because large creditors can obtain extensive information easily, there is less need for public financial disclosure to capital market participants such as individual investors. Japan almost reveres historical-cost accounting. Current-cost data cannot be given even as supplementary information. Consolidated statements are required, though many significant subsidiaries are still excluded from the consolidated statements. There is often a significant delay between the initial publication of parent-only financial statements and the subsequent publication of consolidated statements. Goodwill is based on the difference between purchase price and book value (not fair market value) of net assets acquired. Goodwill, research and development expenditures, and many other intangible assets must be written off over five years or less. Few leases are capitalized, and pension obligations are not recognized as liabilities.

In general, Japanese accounting standards are very conservative. One study showed that the average net income for a Japanese firm is 58% below the amount that would be reported using U.S. accounting standards. This is one of the reasons that price-earnings ratios of Japanese firms average more than double those of U.S. firms.

This section has presented only a sample of the differences in international accounting standards. Until recently, few people were very concerned about these differences. But the growing globalization of business is creating much current interest in common, worldwide standards. There are too many cultural, social, and political differences among countries to expect complete worldwide standardization of financial reporting in the near future. In fact, complete standardization could be harmful, because it could mask true cultural and economic differences among countries. However, the trend is clear. The International Federation of Accountants (IFAC) is leading the way toward more standardization of accounting measurement and reporting practices throughout the world.

FOREIGN-CURRENCY ISSUES

Today, companies conduct business in various countries and so must learn to do business using different currencies. Two problems arise. One problem is accounting for day-to-day transactions that occur in foreign currencies. Another problem is consolidating a subsidiary that exists in another country and does its own accounting in the currency of that country.

foreign-currency exchange rates The number of units of one currency that can be exchanged for one unit of another currency.

These issues are important because of fluctuating **foreign-currency exchange rates.** The foreign-currency exchange rate specifies how many units of one currency are required to obtain one unit of another currency. Recently, the conversion rate of Japanese yen into U.S. dollars has been approximately .0075. This means that one yen buys .75 cents. The relation could be expressed as the conversion rate of U.S. dollars into Japanese yen, which would be ¥133. If conversion rates were constant, no accounting problems would arise, but the rates often change significantly. Forty years ago, the conversion rate of dollars into yen was ¥360. In the spring of 1991 it was around ¥138, and in the spring of 1995 around ¥90. From 1981 to 1995 the value of the yen increased relative to the value of the dollar. From 1995 to 1998 the yen fell in value and the exchange rate returned to ¥133.

ACCOUNTING FOR TRANSACTIONS IN FOREIGN CURRENCIES

If a U.S. firm exports an automobile to Japan for $10,000, the sale will often be on credit and *denominated* in yen. The customer owes ¥1,330,000 (because the conversion rate at the time of the sale was ¥133). The U.S. firm will record the sale in dollars, and the receivable would be $10,000 on its books. After one month, the Japanese buyer remits ¥1,330,000 to the U.S. seller. Suppose the yen has fallen (or weakened) against the dollar, and the new exchange rate is ¥140. When the yen is converted to dollars the seller ends up with only $9,500 (¥1,330,000 ÷ ¥140). The transaction has given rise to a loss for the U.S. seller of $500.00, which would be recorded as follows:

Cash	$9,500	
Loss on currency fluctuation	500	
Accounts receivable		$10,000.00

Not surprisingly, the currency exchange rate could move in the other direction and give rise to a gain. Many companies use sophisticated financial transactions to eliminate the effect of currency fluctuations, but these hedging transactions and their accounting are covered in more advanced courses.

CONSOLIDATING INTERNATIONAL SUBSIDIARIES

The previous section dealt with a company in one country doing business with a company in another country. A more complex problem arises in an international parent-subsidiary relationship. Suppose a U.S. company (parent) owns a Japanese company (subsidiary, or sub) doing business in Japan in yen. At the end of the year the parent must consolidate the sub's financial data with its own and create a single set of statements. What exchange rate should be used?

GAAP requires that different exchange rates be used for different elements of the financial statements. Assets and liabilities of the sub are translated at the year-end exchange rate. The common stock account is translated at the historic rate existing when the sub was created. The average exchange rate during the year is used to account for the transactions in the income statement. These translated net income figures annually increase the retained earnings of the parent. Over time, the parent's retained earnings reflect yen translations of annual incomes at different exchange rates. The problem is apparent. If the assets of the sub equal its liabilities plus its owners' equity in yen, and different rates are used to translate assets, liabilities, and equity, then the consolidated balance sheet is forced out of balance. To bring it back in balance a **translation adjustment** is created, which is reported as part of stockholders' equity. Details of computing this translation adjustment are beyond the scope of this text.

translation adjustment
A contra-account in stockholders' equity that arises when a foreign subsidiary is consolidated.

The stockholders' equity sections of most multinational firms include foreign-currency translation adjustments. The title and amount of the translation adjustment and total stockholders' equity for some international companies follow:

Company	Account Name	Amount	Total SE
Mobil	Cumulative foreign exchange translation adjustment	(73)	19,072
IBM	Translation adjustments	791	19,816
McDonald's	Foreign currency translation adjustment	(175)	8,718

SUMMARY PROBLEMS FOR YOUR REVIEW

PROBLEM ONE

In 1970, a parcel of land (parcel 1) was purchased for $1,200. An identical parcel (parcel 2) was purchased today for $3,600. The general-price-level index has risen from 100 in 1970 to 300 now. Fill in the blanks in the table below.

Parcel	(1) Historical Cost Measured in 1970 Purchasing Power	(2) Historical Cost Measured in Current Purchasing Power	(3) Historical Cost as Originally Measured
1	_____	_____	_____
2	_____	_____	_____
Total	_____	_____	_____

1. Compare the figures in the three columns. Which total presents a nonsense result. Why?
2. Does the write-up of parcel 1 in column 2 result in a gain? Why?
3. Assume that these parcels are the only assets of the business. There are no liabilities. Prepare a balance sheet for each of the three columns.

Solution to Problem One

Parcel	(1) Historical Cost Measured in 1970 Purchasing Power	(2) Historical Cost Measured in Current Purchasing Power	(3) Historical Cost as Originally Measured
1	$1,200	$3,600	$1,200
2	1,200	3,600	3,600
Total	$2,400	$7,200	$4,800

1. The addition in column 3 produces a nonsense result. In contrast, the other sums are the results of applying a standard unit of measure. The computations in columns 1 and 2 are illustrations of a restatement of historical cost in terms of a common dollar, a standard unit of measure. Such computations have frequently been called adjustments for changes in the general price level. Whether the restatement is made using the 1970 dollar or the current dollar is a matter of personal preference. After all, columns 1 and 2 yield equivalent results. Restatement in terms of the current dollar (column 2) is most popular because the current dollar has more meaning than does the old dollar to the reader of the financial statements.

2. The mere restatement of identical assets in terms of different but equivalent measuring units cannot be regarded as a gain. Expressing parcel 1 as $1,200 in column 1 and $3,600 in column 2 is like expressing parcel 1 in terms of, say, either 1,200 square yards or $9 \times 1,200 = 10,800$ square feet. Surely, the "write-up" from 1,200 square yards to 10,800 square feet is not a gain. It is merely another way of measuring the same asset. That is basically what general-price-level accounting is all about. It says you cannot measure one plot of land in square yards and another in square feet and add them together before converting to some common measure. Unfortunately, column 3 fails to perform such a conversion before adding the two parcels together; hence the total is meaningless.

3. The only items on the balance sheets would be:

	(1)	(2)	(3)
Land	$2,400	$7,200	$4,800
Paid-in Capital	$2,400	$7,200	$4,800

Note that (1) is expressed in 1970 dollars, (2) is in current dollars, and (3) is a mixture of 1970 and current dollars.

Note that the construction of this problem forces current cost and constant dollar equivalence. The general price index rose by a factor of 3 from an index value of 100 to 300 while the specific price of the land rose by exactly the same amount from $1,200 to $3,600.

Problem Two

Reexamine Exhibit 14-7, page 601. Suppose the replacement cost at December 31, 19X2 had been $25 instead of $30. Suppose also that the general price index had been 120 instead of 110. All other facts are unchanged. Use four columns to prepare balance sheets as of December 31, 19X2 (only) and income statements for 19X2 under the four concepts shown in Exhibit 14-7.

Solution to Problem Two

The solution is in Exhibit 14-9. In particular, compare Methods 2 and 4. The current cost of inventory items has risen 25% during a period when the general level has risen 20%.

Exhibit 14-9

Solution Exhibit for Summary Problem Two

	Nominal Dollars		Constant Dollars*	
	(Method 1) Historical Cost[a]	(Method 2) Current Cost	(Method 3) Historical Cost	(Method 4) Current Cost
Balance sheets, December 31, 19X2				
Cash	10,500	10,500	10,500	10,500
Inventory, 100 units	2,000	2,500[b]	2,400[d]	2,500[b]
Total assets	12,500	13,000	12,900	13,000
Original paid-in capital	8,000	8,000	9,600[e]	9,600[e]
Retained income (confined to income from continuing operations)	4,500	3,000	3,300	3,000
Revaluation equity (accumulated holding gains)	—	2,000	—	400
Total stockholders' equity	12,500	13,000	12,900	13,000
Income statements for 19X2				
Sales, 300 units @ $35	10,500	10,500	10,500	10,500
Cost of goods sold, 300 units	6,000	7,500[b]	7,200[d]	7,500[b]
Income from continuing operations	4,500	3,000	3,300	3,000
Holding gains (losses):				
On 300 units sold		1,500[c]		300[f]
On 100 units unsold		500[c]		100[f]
Total holding gains		2,000		400

[a]All numbers are the same as in Exhibit 14-7.

[b]$100 \times \$25$ [c]$300 \times (\$25 - \$20)$ [d]$120/100 \times \$2,000$ [e]$120/100 \times \$8,000$

  $300 \times \$25$ $100 \times (\$25 - \$20)$ $120/100 \times \$6,000$

[f]$\$7,500 - [(120/100) \times 6,000] = \$300$

 $\$2,500 - [(120/100) \times 2,000] = \$100$

Note too that the historical-cost/constant-dollar concept restates the old historical-cost amounts in 19X2 dollars rather than 19X1 dollars by multiplying the old dollars by 120/100.

Highlights to Remember

Accountants have sought a conceptual framework for years, but financial accounting standards are still largely set on a piecemeal basis. The FASB is in charge of setting standards and determining accounting practice. This is no easy task because the FASB not only needs to choose the best possible practices, but also needs to get companies to comply with the standards. The FASB is responsible only for U.S. accounting standards.

The generally accepted accounting principles in the United States allow managers and accountants to choose a company's exact accounting policies. Publicly held companies must publish a statement of their accounting policies as a part of their annual financial reports.

The matching of historical costs with revenue is the generally accepted means of measuring net income. However, this method is often criticized in times of changing prices. Some critics suggest using general price indexes to adjust historical costs so that all expenses are measured in current dollars of the same purchasing power. Such adjustments do not represent a departure from historical cost. A more fundamental change is to base net income computations on some version of current costs. Proponents claim that such a measure is a better gauge of the distinctions between income (the return on capital) and capital maintenance (the return of capital).

Accounting standards vary from country to country and probably will for years to come.

Accounting Vocabulary

constant dollars, p. 599
current cost, p. 600
financial capital maintenance, p. 598
foreign currency exchange rate, p. 608
general price index, p. 603
historical cost, p. 599

inflation, p. 599
neutrality, p. 592
nominal dollars, p. 599
physical capital maintenance, p. 598
relevance, p. 591
reliability, p. 591

representational faithfulness, p. 592
revaluation equity, p. 602
specific price index, p. 603
translation adjustment, p. 609
validity, p. 592
verifiability, p. 592

Assignment Material

QUESTIONS

14-1. "A conceptual framework is too theoretical to be of practical value." Do you agree? Explain.

14-2. What are the major objectives of financial reporting as chosen by the FASB?

14-3. "Now that the FASB has a conceptual framework, accounting policy making is simply a matter of mechanically applying the framework to issues that arise." Do you agree? Explain.

14-4. "Accounting policy making is a political endeavor." Do you agree? Explain.

14-5. What is the fundamental cost-benefit test in accounting policy making?

14-6. Name three types of costs of producing accounting information.

14-7. "It is better to be roughly right than precisely wrong." Interpret this statement in light of the qualitative characteristics of accounting.

14-8. "The ability of a dozen independent accountants to apply the same measurement methods and obtain the same result is an example of validity." Do you agree? Explain.

14-9. "Neutrality underscores a fundamental approach that should be taken by the FASB." Describe the approach.

14-10. "Timing of expense recognition is not important. The important thing is that all expenses eventually be recognized on the income statement." Do you agree? Explain.

14-11. What is a statement of accounting policies?

14-12. Distinguish between the physical and the financial concepts of maintenance of invested capital.

14-13. "The FASB no longer requires reporting of inflation-adjusted data in annual reports. Therefore there is no reason to study inflation-adjusted financial statements." Do you agree? Explain.

14-14. "The choice among accounting measures of income is often expressed as either historical-cost accounting or general-price-level accounting or current-cost accounting." Do you agree? Explain.

14-15. What is the common meaning of current cost?

14-16. Explain how net income is measured under the current-cost approach.

14-17. "All holding gains should be excluded from income." What is the major logic behind this statement?

14-18. Explain what a general price index represents.

14-19. Distinguish between general indexes and specific indexes.

14-20. "Specific indexes are used in nominal-dollar accounting but not in constant-dollar accounting." Do you agree? Explain.

14-21. "Accounting policies differ so much from country to country that accountants trained in one country have difficulty practicing in another, even if there is no language barrier." Do you agree? Explain.

14-22. How have high inflation rates influenced accounting policies in many countries?

14-23. Do you expect common, worldwide accounting standards within the next decade? Explain.

EXERCISES

14-24 Statements of Financial Accounting Concepts
Using your own words, describe the basic contents of *Statements of Financial Accounting Concepts* Numbers 1, 2, 3, and 5. Use only *one sentence* for each statement. Make each sentence as informative as possible.

14-25 Costs and Benefits of Information
The FASB requires companies to include a liability for postretirement benefits on their balance sheets. Postretirement benefits are items such as health insurance that are provided to retired employees. Many companies argued against such a requirement. They maintained that the costs would exceed the benefits.

Required

1. Discuss the potential costs and benefits of mandatory reporting of a liability for postretirement benefits on companies' balance sheets.
2. Assess the relevance and reliability of measuring and reporting such a liability.

14-26 Characteristics of Information
International Paper Company shows the following under long-term assets in its balance sheet (in millions):

Forestlands	$3,342

A footnote described the forestlands as 6.4 million acres in the United States and 800,000 acres in New Zealand that are "stated at cost, less accumulated depletion." The average cost of the timberlands is $464 per acre. Suppose the current market price is estimated to be between $600 and $1,000 per acre, providing a best estimate of total market value of $800 × 7.2 million = $5,760 million.

Required

1. Which measure, the $3,342 million or $5,760 million, is more relevant? What characteristics make it relevant?
2. Which measure is more reliable? What characteristics make it reliable?
3. If you were an investor considering the purchase of common stock in International Paper, which measure would be most valuable to you? Explain.

14-27 Effect of Inventory and Depreciation Methods on Income
Langdon Building Supply began business on January 2, 19X1, with a cash investment by shareholders of $100,000. Management immediately purchased inventory for $60,000 and a machine for $40,000. The machine has a useful life of four years and no salvage value.

The inventory was sold during 19X1 for $120,000, and it was replaced at a cost of $80,000. Ignore taxes.

Required

1. Compute operating income assuming Langdon uses FIFO and straight-line depreciation.
2. Compute operating income assuming Langdon uses LIFO and double-declining-balance depreciation.
3. Compare the answers in requirements 1 and 2. Does the choice of accounting method make a difference? Explain.

14-28 Effects of Transactions on Financial Statements
For each of the following numbered items, select the lettered transaction that indicates its effect on the corporation's financial statements. If a transaction has more than one effect, list all applicable letters. Assume that the total current assets exceed the total current liabilities both before and after every transaction described.

NUMBERED TRANSACTIONS

1. Purchase of inventory on open account.
2. Payment of trade account payable.
3. Sale on account at a gross profit.
4. Collection of account receivable.
5. Issuance of additional common shares as a stock dividend.
6. Sale for cash of a factory building at a selling price that substantially exceeds the book value.
7. The destruction of a building by fire. Insurance proceeds, collected immediately, slightly exceed book value.
8. The appropriation of retained earnings as a reserve for contingencies.
9. Issue of new shares in a three-for-one split of common stock.

LETTERED EFFECTS

a. Increases working capital.
b. Decreases working capital.
c. Increases current ratio.
d. Decreases current ratio.
e. Increases the book value per share of common stock.
f. Decreases the book value per share of common stock.
g. Increases total retained earnings.
h. Decreases total retained earnings.
i. Increases total stockholders' equity.
j. Decreases total stockholders' equity.
k. None of the above.

14-29 Financial and Physical Capital Maintenance

Natalie's Neighborhood Grocery began business on January 2, 19X8, with a cash investment of $140,000, which was used to immediately purchase inventory. One-half of the inventory was sold for $110,000 during January and was not replaced before the end of the month. The cost to replace the inventory would have been $80,000 on January 31.

Required

1. Using the financial capital maintenance concept, compute operating income for January.
2. Using the physical capital maintenance concept, compute income for January.

14-30 Holding Gains

Suquamish Cedar Mill had cedar logs that were purchased for $40,000 on March 1, 19X8. During March, Congress passed a law severely restricting the cutting of cedar trees, so the replacement cost of the logs jumped to $68,000. On March 31, half of the logs were sold for $34,000.

Required

Compute the holding gain on the logs for the month of March under (a) the historical-cost/nominal-dollar method and (b) the current-cost/nominal-dollar method.

14-31 Inventory in Constant Dollars

On December 31, 19X1, Hannon Company bought inventory for $18,000. During 19X2, half of the inventory was sold, and on December 31, 19X2, the inventory that was sold was replaced at a cost of $10,000. The price index was 110 on 12/31/X1 and 121 on 12/31/X2.

Required

Compute the inventory reported on the balance sheets of 12/31/X1 and 12/31/X2 assuming that Hannon uses (a) the historical cost/nominal dollar method of accounting and FIFO and (b) the historical-cost/constant-dollar method of accounting.

14-32 Meaning of General Index Applications and Choice of Base Year

Alamo County Hospital acquired land in mid-1978 for $4 million. In mid-1998, it acquired a substantially identical parcel of land for $8 million. The general-price-level index annual averages were:

1998—210.0   1988—100.0   1978—60.0

Required

1. In four columns, show the computations of the total cost of the two parcels of land expressed in (a) costs as traditionally recorded, (b) dollars of 1998 purchasing power, (c) 1988 purchasing power, and (d) 1978 purchasing power.
2. Explain the meaning of the figures that you computed in requirement 1.

PROBLEMS

14-33 Revenue Recognition and Percentage-of-Completion

Van Danken Company contracted to build a large river bridge for the city of Amsterdam. The board of directors is about to meet to decide whether to adopt the completed-contract or the percentage-of-completion method of accounting. The percentage-of-completion method recognizes income based on incurred costs to date, divided by these known costs plus the estimated future costs to complete the contract. It computes an applicable percentage as follows:

$$\text{Percentage of completion} = \frac{\text{Costs incurred to date}}{\left(\begin{array}{c}\text{Cost incurred} \\ \text{to date}\end{array}\right) + \left(\begin{array}{c}\text{Estimated additional} \\ \text{costs to compute}\end{array}\right)}$$

The percentage is applied to the total contract price to determine the recognized revenue for the period.

Van Danken began business on January 1, 19X8. Construction activity for the year ended December 31, 19X8, revealed (in millions of Netherlands guilders, NG):

Total contract price	NG 88
Billings through December 31, 19X8	35
Cash collections	28
Contract costs incurred	45
Estimated additional costs to complete the contract	15

Any work remaining to be done is expected to be completed in 19X9. Ignore selling and other expenses as well as income taxes.

Required

Prepare a schedule computing the amount of revenue and income that would be reported for 19X8 under

a. The completed-contract method
b. The percentage-of-completion method (based on estimated costs)

14-34 Recognition Criteria

Fortune reported on a recent Supreme Court decision related to accrual accounting. The Internal Revenue Service (IRS) and several casinos disagreed on when to recognize revenue and expenses for progressive slot machines. These slot machines have no limit to the payoff. They pay a lucky winner the money others have put into the machine since the last payoff (less the house takeout, of course). The longer since the last win, the larger the jackpot. Progressive slots pay off on average every four and one-half months.

Suppose that on December 31, 1998, Harrah's Casino had a progressive slot machine that had not paid off recently. In fact, $900,000 had been placed in the machine since its last payoff on February 13, 1998. Assume that the house's takeout is 5%.

The IRS regarded the $900,000 as revenue but allowed no expense until a payoff occurred. The casinos argued that an expense equal to 95% of the revenue will eventually be incurred, and accrual accounting would require recognition of the expense at the same time as the revenue is recorded.

Required

1. How much revenue should Harrah's recognize in 1998 from the machine? Explain fully.

2. How much expense should Harrah's recognize in 1998 from the machine? Explain fully.

3. The IRS argued that no expense should be recognized until a payoff to the winner had been made. What do you suppose was the basis for their argument?

4. Suppose you are a gambler who uses accrual accounting. How would you account for $1,000 placed into the progressive slot machine described above? Is this consistent with your answers to requirements 1 and 2? Why or why not?

14-35 Nature of Capital, Income, Revenue

(M. Wolfson, adapted) Here is a letter written by the financial vice president of Acurex Corporation, a manufacturer of energy, environmental, and agricultural equipment:

> *Dear Professor:*
>
> *We are engaged in a somewhat unusual government contract with the Department of Energy as a demonstration, or "showcase," program. We are designing and constructing a fuel delivery system for industrial boilers in which we will cost-share 35% of the total cost with the government. In return, we are awarded immediate title to all the equipment involved, including the government's 65% portion.*
>
> > *It seems to me that there is some real logic in reflecting the government's gift of 65% of total cost in current earnings, subject only to a test of net realizable value. I'd appreciate your thoughts.*
>
> > *Sincerely,*

The company's net income the previous year was $1,007,000.

Required

Suppose the cost of the fuel delivery system is $1.2 million. This consists of about $600,000 in "hard assets" (equipment, etc.) and about $600,000 in designing costs. Via journal entries, show at least two ways in which the government contract could be reflected in Acurex's books, assuming the costs are all incurred prior to the end of the year. What is the effect of your two ways on the year's pretax income?

14-36 Japanese Annual Reports

Ishikawajima-Harima Heavy Industries Co., Ltd. is a large Japanese manufacturing firm with sales of more than ¥1 trillion (equivalent to more than $10 billion at current exchange rates). Ishikawajima-Harima Heavy Industries maintains its records and prepares its financial statements in accordance with generally accepted accounting principles and practices in Japan. Selected parts of the company's footnote on "Significant Accounting Policies" follow:

> #### Basis of financial statements
> *The accompanying consolidated financial statements of Ishikawajima-Harima Heavy Industries Co., Ltd. and consolidated subsidiaries have been prepared from the financial statements filed with the Minister of Finance as required by the Japanese Securities and Exchange Law in accordance with accounting principles and practices generally accepted in Japan.*
>
> #### Sales recognition
> *Net sales from contracts are recognized at the time the contracts are completed.*

Allowance for doubtful receivables

The allowance for doubtful receivables is provided by adding amounts estimated individually for uncollectible receivables to the maximum amount permitted by the Corporate Income Tax Law of Japan.

Inventories

Finished goods, work in process and contracts in process are stated principally at identified cost, and raw materials and supplies are stated principally at the lower of cost or market, cost being determined by the moving-average method.

Marketable securities and investment securities

Marketable securities and investment securities, other than common stocks listed on stock exchanges, are stated principally at cost as determined by the moving-average method. Common stocks listed on stock exchanges are stated principally at the lower of cost or market, cost being determined by the moving-average method.

Property, plant and equipment and intangible assets

Depreciation of plant and equipment is computed principally by the declining-balance method based on the estimated useful lives of the assets as stipulated by the Corporate Income Tax Law and regulations of Japan.

Income taxes

The Companies record income taxes currently payable based upon taxable income determined in accordance with the applicable tax laws, and do not recognize deferred income taxes arising from timing differences in the recognition of income and expenses for financial statement and income tax purposes.

Leases

Noncancellable lease transactions of the Companies are accounted for as operating leases regardless of whether such leases are classified as operating leases or finance leases, except that lease agreements which stipulate the transfer of ownership of the leased property to the lessee are accounted for as finance leases.

Identify the accounting policies used by Ishikawajima-Harima Heavy Industries that would not generally be used in the United States. **Required**

14-37 Effects of Various Accounting Methods on Net Income

You are the manager of Tsumagari Company, a profitable new company that has high potential growth. It is nearing the end of your first year in business and you must make some decisions regarding accounting policies for financial reporting to stockholders. Your controller and your certified public accountant have gathered the following information (all figures in millions except tax rate):

Revenue	¥42,000
Beginning inventory	0
Purchases	21,000
Ending inventory—if LIFO is used	6,000
Ending inventory—if FIFO is used	8,000
Depreciation—if straight-line is used	1,500
Depreciation—if double-declining-balance is used	3,000
Store-opening costs	4,000
Store-opening costs (amortized amount)	800
Other expenses	5,000
Income tax rate	40%
Common shares outstanding	2,000

Double-declining-balance depreciation will be used for tax purposes regardless of the method chosen for reporting to stockholders. For all other items, assume that the same method is used for tax purposes and for financial reporting purposes.

Required

1. Prepare a columnar income statement such as in Exhibit 14-5 on page 596. In column 1, show the results using LIFO, double-declining-balance depreciation, and direct write-off of store-opening costs. Show earnings per share as well as net income. In successive columns, show the separate effects on net income and earnings per share of substituting the alternative methods: column 2, FIFO inventory; column 3, straight-line depreciation; column 4, amortization of store-opening costs. In column 5, show the total results of choosing all the alternative methods (columns 2 through 4). Note that in columns 2 through 4 only single changes from column 1 should be shown; that is, column 3 does not show the effects of columns 2 and 3 together, nor does column 4 show the effects of columns 2, 3, and 4 together.

2. As the manager, which accounting policies would you adopt? Why?

14-38 Effects of Various Accounting Methods on Income

General Electric had the following data in its 1996 annual report (in millions of dollars except for earnings per share):

Total revenues	$79,179
Cost of goods and services sold	32,869
Depreciation and amortization	3,785
Other expenses (summarized here)	31,719
Total expenses	68,373
Earnings before income taxes	10,806
Provision for income taxes	3,526
Net earnings	$ 7,280
Net earnings per share (in dollars)	$ 4.40

Inventories on December 31, 1996, were $4,473 million and on December 31, 1995, were $4,395 million. If FIFO had been used instead of LIFO, the FIFO inventories would have been higher by $1,217 million at December 31, 1996, and $1,345 million at December 31, 1995.

The company stated that most depreciation is computed by accelerated methods, primarily sum-of-the-years'-digits.

General Electric's marginal 1996 income tax rate was 35%

Required

Suppose General Electric had used straight-line depreciation for reporting to shareholders, resulting in depreciation and amortization expense of $2,785 million rather than $3,785 million in 1996. Also, suppose the company had used FIFO instead of LIFO. Recast all the above data for 1996, including the amount earned per common share. Show supporting computations.

14-39 Four Versions of Income and Capital

Asia Pacific Trading Company has the following comparative balance sheets as of December 31 (based on historical costs in nominal dollars):

	19X4	19X5
Cash	$ —	$4,500
Inventory, 100 and 40 units, respectively	5,000	2,000
Total assets	$5,000	$6,500
Paid-in capital	$5,000	$5,000
Retained income	—	1,500
Stockholders' equity	$5,000	$6,500

The general-price-level index was 140 on December 31, 19X4, and 161 on December 31, 19X5. The company had acquired 100 units of inventory on December 31, 19X4, for $50 each and held them throughout 19X5. Sixty units were sold on December 31, 19X5, for $75 cash each. The replacement cost of the inventory at that date was $60 per unit. Assume that these are the only transactions. Ignore income taxes.

Required

Use four sets of columns to prepare comparative balance sheets as of December 31, 19X4 and 19X5, and income statements for 19X5 using (1) historical cost/nominal dollars, (2) current cost/nominal dollars, (3) historical cost/constant dollars, and (4) current cost/constant dollars.

14-40 Concepts of Income
Suppose you are in the business of investing in land and holding it for resale. On December 31, 19X7, a parcel of land had a historical cost of $200,000 and a current value (measured via use of a specific price index) of $600,000; the general price level had doubled since the land has acquired. Suppose also that the land was sold a year later on December 31, 19X8, for $720,000. The general price level rose by 5% during 19X8.

Required

1. Prepare a tabulation of income from continuing operations and holding gains for 19X8, using the four methods illustrated in Exhibit 14-7.
2. In your own words, explain the meaning of the results, giving special attention to what income represents.

14-41 LIFO and Current Costs
Inman Company began business on December 31, 19X1, when it acquired 100 units of inventory for $40 per unit. It held the inventory until December 31, 19X2, when it acquired 100 more units for $60 per unit and sold 150 units for $70 each. Assume that these are the company's only transactions, and ignore income taxes.

Required

1. Compute operating income using the historical-cost/nominal-dollars method and a FIFO inventory method.
2. Compute operating income using the historical-cost/nominal-dollars method and a LIFO inventory method.
3. Compute operating income using the current-cost/nominal-dollars method.
4. Explain the differences in operating income in requirements 1, 2, and 3.
5. Does historical-cost/nominal-dollars operating income using LIFO give results that approximate current-cost operating income? Why or why not?

14-42 Reporting on Changing Prices
Transamerica Corporation, a large diversified company, reported operating income of $151 million on sales of $5,399 million. After adjusting for changes in specific prices (current costs), operating income was $107 million. Three other amounts reported were related to holding gains (in millions):

Effect of increase in general price level	$64
Excess of increase in specific prices over increase in general price level	23
Increase in specific prices of inventories and property and equipment held during the year	$87

Required

1. Identify the holding gain under the current-cost/nominal-dollars method.
2. Identify the holding gain under the current-cost/constant-dollars method.
3. Explain why the holding gain in requirement 1 differs from that in requirement 2.

14-43 Depreciation and Price-Level Adjustments

Shreck Legal Services purchased a computer with networking services for $400,000. This computer has an expected life of four years and an expected residual value of zero. Straight-line depreciation is used. The general price index is 100 at the date of acquisition; it increases 20 points annually the next three years. The results follow:

Year	Price-Level Index	Historical-Cost/ Nominal-Dollars Depreciation	Multiplier	Historical-Cost/ Constant-Dollars Depreciation as Recorded
1	100	$100,000	$\frac{100}{100}$	$100,000
2	120	100,000	$\frac{120}{100}$	120,000
3	140	100,000	$\frac{140}{100}$	140,000
4	160	100,000	$\frac{160}{100}$	160,000
		$400,000		

Required

1. Convert the figures in the last column so that they are expressed in terms of fourth-year dollars. For example, the $120,000 second-year dollars would have to be restated by multiplying by 160/120.

2. Suppose in requirement 1 that revenue easily exceeds expenses for each year and that cash equal to the annual depreciation charge was invested in a noninterest-bearing cash account. If amounts equal to the unadjusted depreciation charge were invested each year, would sufficient cash have accumulated to equal the general purchasing power of $400,000 invested in the asset four years ago? If not, what is the extent of the total financial deficiency measured in terms of fourth-year dollars?

3. Suppose in requirement 2 that amounts equal to the constant-dollar depreciation for each year were used. What is the extent of the total financial deficiency?

4. Suppose in requirement 3 that the amounts were invested each year in assets that increased in value at the same rate as the increase in the general price level. What is the extent of the total financial deficiency?

14-44 Revenues in Constant Dollars

Alcoa, the aluminum company, reported the following total revenues (in millions):

	1996	1995	1994	1993	1992
Historical basis	$13,061	$12,500	$9,904	$9,056	$9,492
In average 1996 dollars	13,061	12,869	10,485	9,833	?

The average Consumer Price Index was 156.9 in 1996 and 140.3 in 1992.

Compute the following:

Required

1. Total revenues for 1992 in average 1996 dollars. Round to the nearest million.

2. Percentage increase in revenues between 1992 and 1996 on a historical-cost basis.

3. Percentage increase in revenues between 1992 and 1996 in average 1996 dollars.

4. Average Consumer Price Index for 1994.

14-45 Effects of General Versus Specific Price Changes

The following data are from the annual reports of Gannett Co., owner of 120 newspapers; Zayre Corporation, operator of 290 discount stores; and Goodyear Tire and Rubber Company:

(in millions)	Gannett	Zayre	Goodyear
Increase in specific prices of assets held during the year*	$45.8	$ 24.9	$ (4.7)
Less effect of increase in general price level	37.5	55.5	252.0
Excess of increase in specific prices over increase in the general price level†	$ 8.3	$(30.6)	$(256.7)

*Holding gain using current-cost/nominal-dollars method.

†Holding gain using current-cost/constant-dollars method.

Required

Compare and contrast the relationship between changes in the general price level and changes in the prices of the specific assets of each of the three companies.

14-46 Ethics and Business Practices

Ethical considerations affect business decisions of many companies. Consider the brief descriptions of how ethics affects each of the following three companies:

> A. *Baxter International, Inc.*—*This health-care company adopted an aggressive environmental and ethical policy in 1990. The company met its goal of having all its facilities in the United States achieve "state of the art" environmental status by 1993. Between 1990 and 1993 it reduced emissions of 17 toxic substances by 94%. In three years it reduced hazardous waste by 49%. In 1993 the company increased the percentage of women in its work force from 46% to 52% and the percentage of minorities from 28% to 29%. The company has a Corporate Responsibility Office that benchmarks Baxter's policies against companies known to have exemplary business practices. Baxter's commitment is to "assure that the company follows, at all times, the highest standards of corporate responsibility." (Note: All this information is contained in Baxter's annual report.)*

> B. *SC Johnson Wax*—*Since its founding in 1896, Johnson Wax has been committed to putting something back into the community. As described in* Management Accounting, *the company contributes a minimum of 5% of pretax profits to charities. It also promotes employee involvement in community service activities. Two areas where Johnson Wax has been especially supportive are education and the environment. From elementary schools through colleges and universities, a variety of programs improve the quality of education and thereby the quality of Johnson Wax's workforce. For the environment, Johnson Wax first makes its operations as environmentally friendly as possible. In addition, the company supports numerous outside environmental activities that improve the communities in which it operates. Underlying the philanthropic vision is the belief that Johnson Wax will eventually benefit from contributing to worthy social causes.*

> C. *Calvert Social Investment Fund*—*Calvert is the largest of approximately 33 U.S. mutual funds devoted to "ethical investing." Calvert directs more than $1 billion into companies who "make a significant contribution to society through their products and services and through the way they do business." Total assets in "ethical" mutual funds exceed $4 billion. These funds avoid companies for a variety of reasons, among them companies that damage the environment, make weapons, sell tobacco or alcohol, dis-*

criminate in employment, or use animals in testing products. Each fund has its own standards.

Required Describe how ethical issues might affect the decisions of each company. Do you believe these firms view ethical behavior as primarily a cost or a benefit? List some specific costs for each company and some potential benefits.

14-47 Comprehensive Review: Reconstruct Transactions

Childrobics, Inc. was incorporated in New York State on May 7, 1993. The company owns and operates indoor recreation facilities for children and their families in the New York metropolitan area. The company prepared financial statements on February 28, 1994, for the period since incorporation. Slightly revised versions of the company's balance sheet and statement of cash flows are in Exhibit 14-10. Footnotes pointed out that, in exchange for a note payable of $250,000, the creditors supplied $146,000 in cash and $104,000 in property and equipment.

Required Compute amounts to replace each of the question marks in Childrobic's balance sheet.

14-48 Comprehensive Review: Reconstruct Transactions

Interlinq Software Corporation develops, sells, and supports PC-based systems for residential mortgage loan management. Its products are used by approximately 2,000 companies in all fifty states. Its main product is called MortgageWare.

Interlinq's balance sheets for 1996 and 1997 and statement of cash flows for 1997, are in Exhibit 14-11. Note that the tax benefit on stock options increased paid-in capital by the $10,967.

Required
1. Compute the amount to replace each of the question marks in Interlinq's balance sheet and statement of cash flows. You might find it helpful to begin with the Statement of Cash Flows.

2. Assess the performance of Interlinq during 1997.

Exhibit 14-10

Childrobics, Inc.
Balance Sheet February 28, 1994

ASSETS			
Current assets:			
Cash			$?
Property and equipment:			
At cost	$?		
Accumulated depreciation	?		
Net			?
Other assets			25,300
Total assets			$?
LIABILITIES AND STOCKHOLDERS' EQUITY			
Current liabilities:			
Accounts payable and accrued expenses	$?		
Deferred revenue	?		
Note payable	?		
Total current liabilities			$?
Stockholders' equity:			
Common stock—$.01 par value, 25,000,000 shares authorized, 975,000 shares issued and outstanding		?	
Additional paid-in capital		?	
Retained Earnings		?	
Total stockholders' equity			?
Total liabilities and stockholders' equity			$?

(continued)

Exhibit 14-10 (continued)

Childrobics, Inc.
Statement of Cash Flows for the Period Ended February 28, 1994

OPERATING ACTIVITIES:		
Net income	$ 2,516	
Adjustment to reconcile net income to net cash provided by operating activities:		
Depreciation	10,947	
Change in assets and liabilities:		
Accounts payable and accrued expenses	59,871	
Deferred revenue — customer deposits	13,450	
Net cash — operating activities		$ 86,784
INVESTING ACTIVITIES:		
Purchases of property and equipment	$(192,583)	
Expenditures for other assets	(25,300)	
Net cash — investing activities		(217,883)
FINANCING ACTIVITIES:		
Loans	$ 146,000	
Common stock	25,000	
Net cash — financing activities		171,000
Net increase in cash		39,901
Cash — beginning of period		0
Cash — end of period		$ 39,901

14-49 The Gap Annual Report

Examine the income statement of The Gap. The cost of goods sold is based on the FIFO inventory method. Assume that the operating expenses include all $214,905,000 of depreciation and amortization, which is computed using the straight-line method.

Suppose The Gap had switched to LIFO and accelerated depreciation on February 4, 1996. Prior-year results were not restated. Therefore, balance sheet amounts for February 3, 1996, were unaffected by the changes. As a result of the change, the ending inventory amount at February 1, 1997, was $478,765,000 instead of $578,765,000 and depreciation and amortization charged during the year ended February 1, 1997, was $264,905,000 instead of $214,905,000. For requirements 1 and 2, assume that the changes were made for shareholder reporting only; no change was made in tax statements.

Required

1. Compute the revised income before income taxes for the year ended February 1, 1997.

2. The effective tax rate is 39.5%. Compute the revised provision for income taxes and net income for The Gap for the year ended February 1, 1997.

14-50 Financial Statement Research

Select any company. Be sure that amounts are available for both beginning and ending inventory and depreciation and amortization for the most recent fiscal year.

Suppose your company changed its inventory and depreciation methods beginning with the start of the most recent fiscal year. Prior-year results were not restated. Therefore, balance sheet amounts at the beginning of the year were unaffected by the changes.

The changes caused the ending inventory value to be 10% lower than the amount shown in the statements and the annual depreciation and amortization to be 20% greater. (Such changes might result from a switch from FIFO to LIFO and from straight-line to accelerated depreciation. However, assume the given changes regardless of the inventory and depreciation methods currently being used.)

1. Compute the revised income before taxes for the most recent fiscal year.
2. Determine the company's effective tax rate. Then compute the revised provision for income taxes, net income, and net income per share for your company in the most recent fiscal year.
3. Assume that your company reports the same cost of sales on its tax and shareholder income statements. However, the tax statement includes the new depreciation and amortization (that is, it is 20% higher on the tax statement than on shareholder reports). Now assume that the inventory method is changed as specified in the problem for both tax and shareholder reports, while the depreciation and amortization is changed in the shareholder report only. This makes tax and

Exhibit 14-11

Interlinq Software Corporation

Balance Sheets as of June 30, 1997 and 1996

Assets	1997	1996
Current assets:		
Cash and cash equivalents	$?	$ 6,511,041
Short-term investments	?	7,706,846
Accounts receivable, less allowance for doubtful accounts of $176,000 in 1997 and $187,007 in 1996	1,602,220	1,971,507
Inventory	55,246	72,644
Prepaid expenses	?	331,026
Deferred income taxes	267,660	172,041
Total current assets	?	16,765,105
Property and equipment, at cost	?	5,289,836
Less accumulated depreciation and amortization	4,364,628	3,253,190
Net property and equipment	?	2,036,646
Capitalized software costs, less accumulated amortization of 1,718,683 in 1997 and 1,509,305 in 1996	?	3,493,563
Other assets	70,899	26,021
Total Assets	$?	$22,321,335
Liabilities and Shareholders' Equity		
Current liabilities		
Accounts payable	$?	$ 158,226
Accrued compensation and benefits	?	402,701
Other accrued liabilities	498,276	380,435
Customer deposits	199,636	363,703
Deferred software support fees	?	2,637,500
Total current liabilities	?	3,942,565
Noncurrent liabilities, excluding current installments:		
Deferred rent	160,443	383,750
Deferred software support fees	6,746	10,233
Deferred income taxes	306,950	213,548
Total noncurrent liabilities	?	607,531
Shareholders' equity		
Common stock, $.01 par value. Authorized 30,000,000 shares; issued and outstanding 5,416,512 shares in 1997 and 6,038,550 shares in 1996	?	60,386
Additional paid-in capital	?	13,167,629
Retained earnings	?	4,543,224
Total shareholders' equity	?	17,771,239
Total Liabilities and Shareholders' Equity	$?	$22,321,335

(*continued*)

Exhibit 14-11 (continued)

Interlinq Software Corporation

Statement of Cash Flows for the Year Ended June 30, 1997

Assets	1997
Cash flows from operating activities:	
Net income	$ 1,109,877
Adjustments to reconcile net income to net cash	
provided by operating activities:	
Depreciation and amortization of property and equipment	1,111,438
Amortization of capitalized software costs	1,287,881
Deferred income tax benefit	(2,217)
Tax benefit on stock options	10,967
Change in certain assets and liabilities	
Decrease in accounts receivable	?
Increase in inventory and prepaid expenses	(60,485)
Increase in other assets	?
Increase in accounts payable	77,669
Increase in accrued compensation and benefits, other	
accrued liabilities, and deferred rent	47,235
Increase in customer deposits	?
Increase in deferred software support fees	411,835
Net cash provided by operating activities	?
Cash flows from investing activities:	
Purchases of property and equipment	(547,059)
Capitalized software costs	(877,334)
Purchase of source code	(275,000)
Purchase of short-term investments	(14,511,012)
Proceeds from sales and maturities of investments	16,180,313
Net cash used in investing activities	(30,092)
Cash flows from financing activities:	
Proceeds from issuance of common stock	17,520
Repurchase of common stock	(2,859,250)
Net cash used in financing activities	(2,841,730)
Net increase in cash and cash equivalents	$?

shareholder reports identical. What would be the effect of the change in tax reporting on the income taxes shown on the income statement for shareholder reporting? What would be the effect on the taxes currently payable and the deferred taxes on the reports to shareholders?

4. Assume that the changes in requirement 3 are allowed for both tax and shareholder reporting. What factors would affect your company's decision about whether or not to make the changes?

COLLABORATIVE LEARNING EXERCISE

14-51   Understanding Financial Statements

Form groups of four to six students each. Each group should pick a company that has a corporate or division headquarters in the local or regional area. Contact a top financial person at the company to arrange an interview. The person should have some responsibility for the company's financial statements. The person might be the chief financial officer (CFO), controller, accounting manager, or even treasurer at some companies.

Before the interview, the group should meet and study the company's annual report, focusing on the financial statements. Prepare at least six questions about the financial statements.

The questions can form the basis of the interview. The goal, besides answering the questions, is to determine how the company decides on the accounting policies and practices to be used in the financial statements. For example, how does the company decide on an inventory policy (FIFO, LIFO, or weighted-average), depreciation method (especially if it uses something other than straight-line), amount of allowance for uncollectible accounts, and classification of short-term investments (trading securities, available-for-sale securities, and held-to-maturity securities)?

Each group should be prepared to share with the entire class what it learns about accounting policy choices at the company it selected.

14-52 Internet Case

Go to **http://www.bp.com/bpfinance/annual_report/** to learn about The British Petroleum Company. This company prepares its financial statements using different GAAP from Untied States corporations. From the green icon bars at the top of the menu at the right of the screen, select *Annual Report and Accounts* for the current fiscal period, then select *Accounts*. Financial statements and notes can be selected from the green menu bar on the right of the screen again.

Answer the following questions about The British Petroleum Company and how it differs from companies that use U.S. GAAP:

1. What type of "GAAP" does The British Petroleum Company (BP) use in the preparation of its financial statements? Why does it not use U.S. GAAP?

2. Examine BP's balance sheet. What differences exist between the British balance sheet and a U.S. balance sheet concerning the order in which items are reported?

3. Identify the major differences between British GAAP and U.S. GAAP in measuring income. How is this method different from the method required by U.S. GAAP? What advantages does the method that BP uses have over the method of measuring income in the United States? What accounting concept is justification for using historical-cost accounting?

4. One item of disclosure provided by BP is a summary of adjustments to profit for the year-end which would have been required if the statements were prepared using U.S. GAAP. Of what interest would this be to users? How much does shareholders' equity differ between British and U.S. GAAP?

5. Does BP have any holding gains and losses? If so, where are they reported? What do these amounts represent? How does the British concept of reporting revenue (and therefore income) differ from U.S. revenue recognition?

BANANA REPUBLIC

The Gap, Inc. 1996 Annual Report

Financial Highlights

($000 except per share amounts)	Fiscal 1996 52 weeks	Fiscal 1995 53 weeks	Fiscal 1994 52 weeks
Operating Results			
Net sales	$5,284,381	$4,395,253	$3,722,940
Earnings before income taxes	748,527	585,199	529,322
Net earnings	452,859	354,039	320,240
Per Share Data(a)			
Net earnings	$1.60	$1.23	$1.10
Cash dividends	.30	.24	.23
Financial Position			
Total assets	$2,626,927	$2,343,068	$2,004,244
Long-term debt, less current installments	—	—	—
Working capital	554,359	728,301	555,827
Current ratio	1.72:1	2.32:1	2.11:1
Stockholders' equity	1,654,470	1,640,473	1,375,232
Statistics			
Weighted-average number of shares outstanding(a)	283,330,290	288,062,430	291,141,076
Number of shares outstanding at year-end, net of treasury stock(a)	274,517,331	287,747,984	289,529,498
Net earnings as a percentage of net sales	8.6%	8.1%	8.6%
Return on average assets	18.2%	16.3%	17.0%
Return on average stockholders' equity	27.5%	23.5%	25.6%
Number of stores open at year-end	1,854	1,680	1,508
Comparable store sales growth (52-week basis)	5.0%	0.0%	1.0%

(a) Reflects the two-for-one split of common stock in the form of a stock dividend to stockholders of record on March 18, 1996.

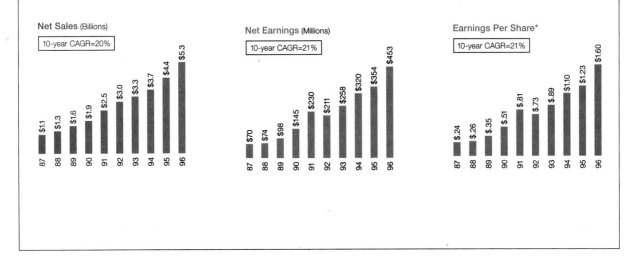

Net Sales (Billions) — 10-year CAGR=20% — $1.1, $1.3, $1.6, $1.9, $2.5, $3.0, $3.3, $3.7, $4.4, $5.3 (87–96)

Net Earnings (Millions) — 10-year CAGR=21% — $70, $74, $98, $145, $230, $211, $258, $320, $354, $453 (87–96)

Earnings Per Share* — 10-year CAGR=21% — $.24, $.26, $.35, $.51, $.81, $.73, $.89, $1.10, $1.23, $1.60 (87–96)

How do you build a **brand**? Start with an environment where creative **people** can flourish, sharpen it with discipline and **focus**, then support it with a well-developed **infrastructure**.

Result: powerful and extendable brands. Gap, Banana Republic, and Old Navy are three of the strongest apparel brands on the market today.

Dear Shareholders

For the fourth year in a row—and tenth out of the last eleven—we are delighted to report that Gap, Inc. has achieved record sales and earnings. Across the board, all of our key financial indicators—including net sales, net earnings, and return on equity—increased meaningfully in 1996. Needless to say, we are proud to have created such outstanding results for our shareholders.

But 1996 was about more than setting financial records. It was also an important year in the evolution of our brands. Through four quarters and eight seasons of new merchandise, we approached our business not only as retailers, but as the builders of three strong, distinctive brands—Gap, Banana Republic, and Old Navy.

Instead of seeing limits—in the product categories we could extend into, the real estate we could manage, the advertising media we could use—we searched for new opportunities to increase the reach of our brands. All the while, we emphasized quality, value, style, and service—the core elements that have made this Company famous for 27 years. And, finally, we came closer to striking that delicate but powerful balance between innovation and operating discipline.

The result was that in 1996, Gap, Banana Republic, and Old Navy returned superior results, each one combining the necessary quickness and flexibility of a good retailer with the long-term perspective of a growth-oriented brand. We're not yet as ubiquitous as we hope to be, but with Old Navy penetrating the huge mass apparel market, Gap occupying the all-important middle segment (with GapKids looking out for the youngsters), and

Banana Republic addressing the sophisticated upscale market, Gap, Inc. now represents a balanced portfolio of brands committed to building long-term shareholder value.

None of this is to suggest, of course, that we have somehow found a way to rise above the inherently unpredictable nature of the apparel industry. If only it were possible. We're in the fashion business, after all, and will always be subject to the vagaries of popular taste. From time to time, we'll miss a trend. We'll bet on the wrong color palette or over-invest in a dud. It happens. But as our long-term performance demonstrates, over time, our talented and passionate people have gotten pretty good at getting the right product into our stores at the right time.

That track record also has a lot to do with our organizational strength, or infrastructure. At Gap, Inc., we see this as a real competitive advantage. Over the years, we've been admired for our quality products, distinctive stores, and attentive salespeople, but our success has just as much to do with what goes on behind the scenes. Our corporate support functions—including Sourcing (with nearly 600 production and quality assurance employees based in North America, Europe, and Asia), Distribution (with eight shipment-processing facilities on three continents), Real Estate (with people scouting locations around the world), and Information Systems (with the technology and know-how to keep our stores and headquarters connected and communicating around the clock)—are Gap, Inc.'s quiet enablers. They provide a foundation for creativity, making it possible for our product designers, visual merchandisers, and marketing managers to immerse themselves in the details that ultimately define the Gap, Banana Republic, and Old Navy brands. Every day, their strength can be leveraged across all divisions of the corporation.

To ensure that Gap, Inc.'s infrastructure gets the attention it needs to support our growth, in 1996 we hired John Wilson as Chief Administrative Officer. Working closely with us, Chief Operating Officer Bob Fisher, and the senior management team, John now oversees most of the Company's support functions, plus Gap's U.S. sales organization.

Of course, customers tend to care more about things they can see and feel: store designs, displays, merchandise, marketing concepts. In 1996, we looked for—and frequently found—new ways to get consumers to connect with our brands. You could sense it walking into our stores, where our visual merchandising was simpler, bolder, more direct. You could feel it in our product assortments, which featured better balance between basics and fashion items. You could see it in our increased brand-oriented marketing activity, which included our first national babyGap TV ads, Old Navy radio and television spots, and the debut of Gap's interactive World Wide Web site. It all added up to an aggressive push to increase awareness of our brands.

At Gap, the Company's original brand and the vehicle for our GapKids, babyGap, and Gap Outlet spin-offs, we are testing new strategies to meet the challenges of what many perceive to be a mature retail concept. We threw out the rigid devotion to 6,000- and 7,000-square-foot Gap stores and tested smaller formats, men's- and women's-only shops, airport locations, and babyGap stand-alones. Inside, we created new interest for customers by expanding our personal care collections and introducing items such as women's intimates and bedding for babies.

Admittedly, in pursuit of greater ubiquity for the Gap brand, we embarked on a few too many new initiatives. We lost focus on some of our franchise businesses, especially in men's, and paid the price when our customers found that our assortment had moved too far from what we've come to stand for at Gap. By year's end, however, we had recognized these problems, and began working to get back on track by renewing investments in the core categories that made us famous. In 1997 and beyond, we will look to strike the right balance between fashion and franchise items, and make certain that extending the reach of our brands does not become an exercise in stretching ourselves too thin.

Banana Republic truly came into its own in 1996. Shaking off a past marred by image inconsistency, the brand honed its identity as the source for casual but sophisticated lifestyle apparel. Customers and employees alike rallied around a simple concept known as "relaxed style," as Banana Republic continued to meet the needs of its demanding but loyal client base while adding excitement with brand enhancements like jewelry, shoes, gifts, and home accessories. In 200-plus stores—including a few men's- and women's-only formats—strong sales and profit margins made it clear that we had hit on a refreshing combination of specialty apparel accessibility and contemporary design attitude.

To be sure, the secret of Old Navy got out in 1996. Having jumped to almost 200 stores in three years, and now occupying approximately one-quarter of Gap, Inc.'s total retail space, our newest brand is being called the fastest growing specialty apparel concept in the world. Originally conceived as a category-killer that could help the corporation maintain the lower-priced business being siphoned off by Gap imitators, Old Navy has since developed into our primary U.S. growth vehicle. It has also become something of a corporate proving ground for fun products and unusual merchandising innovations—like Item of the Week℠ promotions, music CDs customers can sample in converted telephone booths, and headset walkie-talkies that help our salespeople serve shoppers more efficiently. Its growth fueled largely by employees transferred from Gap, Inc.'s other divisions, Old Navy's success is a testament to our people and their ability to redirect their skills, energy, and creativity to an entirely new concept.

While we are looking to Old Navy to help drive our next phase of growth in the United States, we continue to count on Gap to introduce our brands to the rest of the world. In 1996 we added 40 new stores to our international portfolio, which now includes more than 200 locations in Canada, the United Kingdom, France, Germany, and Japan. Though our global expansion has not been as rapid as some might expect, we feel we've done it in a way that reflects discipline. Eschewing start-up speed for quality, consistency, and control, we are learning to manage the considerable cultural, legal, and operational challenges of overseas business development. We are delighted to report that our Gap brand travels well outside the United States, and that returns from Banana Republic's Canadian stores are also promising.

Going forward, we intend to focus our growth within the countries where we already operate and continue to take a cautious approach to opening new markets. With Gap, Inc. footholds now established in five nations outside the United States—and a strong, centralized corporate infrastructure back home—we believe our brands are well-positioned to grow internationally in the years to come.

It's all part of our desire to achieve ubiquity on a global scale. We'll do it the way we have tried to do everything at Gap, Inc.: with quality, passion, and an unshakable commitment to building, enhancing, and protecting the value of our brands.

Millard S. Drexler
President and Chief Executive Officer

Donald G. Fisher
Chairman and Founder

Our **brands** deliver great quality, value, style, and service to our customers. Each of our brands—Gap, Banana Republic, and Old Navy—occupies a unique place in the hearts and minds of customers worldwide.

Gap offers separates or complete outfits. Gap is like a 'fashion safety net'.

every age...

There is nothing quite like the Gap. Our customers tell us that Gap clothes are like social passports. Almost *everyone*—from infant to adult—has something from Gap in a drawer or closet. As a product innovator, each season the Gap offers **modern American classics with a twist**: maybe it's some detailing on the pocket, or a more relaxed silhouette, or an unusual fabric. Our customers take those basics and create style statements all their own. How would we describe the Gap brand? Classic, casual, stylish, fun. Our customers think Gap is indispensable.

Indeed, we're striving to ensure that the Gap label is

every stage...

on every item customers want it to be on. Each season we offer our wardrobe basics, like jeans, khakis, white shirts, denim shirts, and T-shirts, so that our customers, regardless of stage in life or lifestyle, can find those basics in a style and size that suit their needs. And we continue to extend the Gap brand—into new items like personal care products—to complement our assortment of modern American classics.

only gap.

We believe our customers should be able to find Gap wherever they happen to be. There are six miles of Gap storefronts around the world, and in 1997 a new store will open more than once a week. The variety of places where people can buy Gap has expanded, too. Breaking away from our traditional regional mall and street locations, we've opened several Gap stores in strip malls. Additionally, we debuted men's- and women's-only stores to help customers simplify their shopping experiences.

GAP

821 Stores

5.5 Million Square Feet

70 New Stores Planned '97

Personal Care
Om is our sixth scent in this popular category.

GAP
KIDS

great style and value is kid stuff

We think that kids clothes should offer the same quality, style, and value as other Gap products. GapKids and babyGap merchandise is made of comparable materials with equal attention to both function and detail. Affordably priced, every collection includes outerwear, shoes, accessories, and even stuffed toys, in addition to casual basics, in beautiful colors and modern, durable designs.

creating opportunities for growth

Innovation is the hallmark of creativity. Through babyGap and Gap-Kids, first-time partnerships helped to extend the Gap brand in 1996. Working with the National Basketball Association, we created a sportswear collection for babies and children featuring the logos of three prominent NBA teams. We also created a limited edition Gap Barbie for Holiday 1996. Adding to our range of merchandise is also key. New babyGap product lines include linens, diaper bags, and other baby essentials in addition to clothes.

getting off to a good start in life

Launched in 1986, there are already more than 400 GapKids stores around the country. A decade later, we introduced 17 freestanding babyGap stores in major metropolitan shopping areas, including New York City, San Francisco, Chicago, and Dallas. These smaller baby-only stores enable us to test a new concept: providing a high-quality, tasteful source for apparel and gift items. And it seems like a good idea: In 1997, we plan to open a total of 70 GapKids and babyGap stores.

babyGap
Durable, adorable clothes and accessories for any occasion.

GAP
KIDS
413
Stores
1.8
Million
Square Feet
70
New Stores
Planned '97

GapKids
Quality, style, and variety are elementary.

going  places

baby
GAP

BANANA REPUBLIC

Stores – 218; Square Feet – 1.3 Million; New Stores Planned '97 – 30

Banana Republic reflects an **American sensibility, a sophisticated style, a relaxed attitude, an adventurous spirit.** Those same words could be used to describe an important trend in fashion: the casual work wardrobe. Naturally, Banana Republic is leading the way. By designing comprehensive collections for men and women, incorporating everything from shoes and hosiery to lingerie and outerwear, Banana Republic is redefining what it means to be confident, comfortable, and in command at the office, or out of it. ~ The shopping experience is as important as our merchandise for Banana Republic customers. We have an obsession with style and quality. That drives us to provide an environment that looks like the kind of place in which our customers can be comfortable. New store interiors, incorporating diffused lighting, leather, stone, quality woods, and modern fixtures, have created an ambiance that matches the

Banana Republic spirit of relaxed American style. ~ Providing the Banana Republic customer with a variety of shopping venues is another of our priorities. In 1997, we will increase the number of men's- and women's-only stores. New product extensions include watches, sunglasses, shoes, and accessories for the home. ~ Building and reinforcing the Banana Republic brand has demanded the kind of resources and support that only a large, well-established corporation like Gap, Inc. can provide. Relying on the power and reach of Gap, Inc. for sourcing, distribution, and other operational support leaves Banana Republic free to pursue its individual agenda: **an integrated vision of the store as the brand.** In 1997, Banana Republic plans to open 30 new stores and remodel or expand 15 more. Four of the new locations will be "flagships" of 20,000–30,000 square feet, offering a more complete selection of styles and fits.

Banana Republic collections for men and women include key elements for relaxed style, from shoes and jewelry to outerwear—and everything in between.

OLD NAVY

☞ Today many Americans shop for value-priced apparel at large discount stores and in strip malls. Okay, but how much fun is that? Plenty, if you've been to Old Navy. Old Navy is Gap, Inc.'s newest brand and represents a tremendous opportunity for growth. Its hallmarks: innovative design, a creative and fun shopping experience, great prices and extraordinary value, exceptional customer service, and something for everyone—adults, kids, and baby.

☞ Old Navy pushes the creative boundaries. By offering new merchandise every four to six weeks, new products like shoes, small gifts, music, and personal care, and the now-famous Item of the Week[SM], Old Navy guarantees that shopping really is fun again. In fact, Old Navy is fast becoming a destination store. Some 80% of Old Navy merchandise retails for under $25, a level that is accessible for the value-conscious shopper.

☞ In just three years, building from Gap, Inc.'s solid base, we've opened 193 Old Navy stores in 30 states, and we plan to open 75 more throughout 1997. Already Old Navy stores have over one-half the square footage of all U.S. Gap stores.

Shopping is fun again!

look!

☑ **Amazing! We have 193 stores!**   ☑ **Astounding! 2.9 million square feet!**

☑ **Opening '97! 75 new stores planned!**

personas

Nothing sells like American Style. Each of the Gap, Inc. brands has tremendous potential abroad. The international apparel markets we've targeted for our initial expansion add up to twice the size of the U.S. apparel market. Except for Canadian locations, the population densities in areas with Gap stores are higher than those of U.S. cities. What's more, customers in all of these markets are likely to spend as much or more than Americans on comparable apparel items. We are experimenting with both freestanding and department store models to determine what is most appropriate for each market.

le focus

International expansion can be complex. Our strategy is simple: build a strong support base to fuel profitability as the foundation for future growth. We are taking the necessary steps to ensure that we master doing business in each

Shibuya

The opening of the Shibuya flagship store in Tokyo was the most successful international Gap debut to date.

infrastruktur

of the countries we enter before accelerating our long-term growth. We've targeted the most attractive markets first, and have already established flagship stores in several major metropolitan areas: Tokyo, Cologne, Stuttgart, Toronto, Paris, and London. At year end, we had 68 stores in the United Kingdom, 109 in Canada, 17 in France, 9 in Japan, and 6 in Germany, totaling over 1.2 million square feet. Our greatest success in 1996 was the debut of our Japan flagship store in the Shibuya shopping district of Tokyo. This year we plan to open at least 30 new international stores.

1-800-OLD-NAVY

OLD NAVY
CLOTHING CO.
GIVING A LIFT TO LONG ISLAND

701

FREE FOR PUBLIC SCHOOLS
ON LONG ISLAND.
CALL 1-800-OLD-NAVY.

Magic

Old Navy Bus Program

GAP KIDS
LAUREL VILLAGE, is
involved in the fight
against AIDS

GAP

GAP
BANANA REPUBLIC
OLD NAVY
CLOTHING CO.
GAP
KIDS

AIDS Walk

Volunteers

COMMUNITY INVOLVEMENT

"Giving something back" is more than a slogan at Gap, Inc. In 1996 we contributed cash and merchandise totaling $7.2 million. In addition, eligible employees are given paid time off to do volunteer work in the community. As a corporation, we strive to support projects that supply critical resources to people in need, underscoring the Company's essential commitment to customers and our communities. Our continuing efforts encompass both onetime projects and ongoing commitments. Here's a sampling:

Volunteers

In October, the New York Product Development group employed Gap's corporate values as well as its creative skills to throw a Halloween party for 40 children ranging in age from 2 to 12 who live in a homeless shelter in East Harlem. Employees made costumes for each child, and the party featured a jack-o-lantern piñata and cloth goodie bags filled with candy and small gifts.

Special Events

For World AIDS Day, Gap Foundation hosted an in-house fund-raiser for the AIDS Emergency Fund, an agency that provides critical financial assistance to people throughout the San Francisco Bay Area living with HIV and AIDS. Headquarters employees were invited to a special sale of select leather, suede, and specialty Gap and Banana Republic sample items. The sale generated close to $14,000, which was paid directly to the AIDS Emergency Fund.

Old Navy Bus Program

Public schools are central to family and community life. The Old Navy Bus Program, launched last autumn in Long Island, helps schools meet critical transportation needs by providing buses free of charge for field trips to museums, planetariums, parks, nature centers, hospitals, performances, community events, tournaments, and other destinations. The bus is also available for use by groups like the Girl Scouts and by Old Navy employees for community service activities. So far, the Old Navy Bus Program has provided 6,000 students and 1,100 adults with transportation to special events. In 1997, Old Navy will extend the program with buses in Chicago and San Francisco.

ENVIRONMENT

At Gap, Inc., being a good corporate citizen involves more than volunteer programs and charitable activities—we also strive to operate in an environmentally responsible manner. We believe that business profitability and environmental responsibility are not mutually exclusive. To protect the environment, we encourage employees to improve the environmental performance of our suppliers, stores, and offices worldwide.

Financial Contents

Key Financial Statistics

Net Sales (Billions)

10-year CAGR=20%

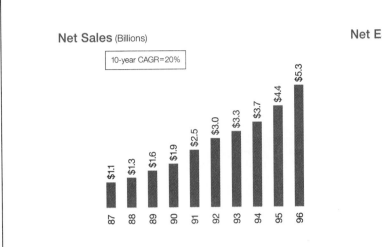

87	88	89	90	91	92	93	94	95	96
$1.1	$1.3	$1.6	$1.9	$2.5	$3.0	$3.3	$3.7	$4.4	$5.3

Net Earnings (Millions)

10-year CAGR=21%

87	88	89	90	91	92	93	94	95	96
$70	$74	$98	$145	$230	$211	$258	$320	$354	$453

Earnings Per Share*

10-year CAGR=21%

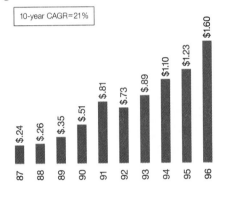

87	88	89	90	91	92	93	94	95	96
$.24	$.26	$.35	$.51	$.81	$.73	$.89	$1.10	$1.23	$1.60

Return on Equity (%)

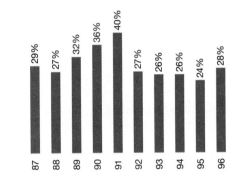

87	88	89	90	91	92	93	94	95	96
29%	27%	32%	36%	40%	27%	26%	26%	24%	28%

Dividends Per Share*

10-year CAGR=22%

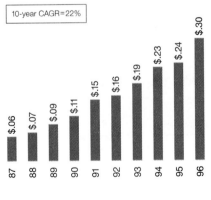

87	88	89	90	91	92	93	94	95	96
$.06	$.07	$.09	$.11	$.15	$.16	$.19	$.23	$.24	$.30

Sales Per Average Gross Square Foot**

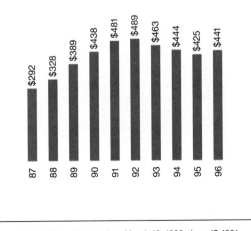

87	88	89	90	91	92	93	94	95	96
$292	$328	$389	$438	$481	$489	$463	$444	$425	$441

*Reflects the two-for-one splits of common stock in the form of a stock dividend to stockholders of record on March 18, 1996, June 17, 1991, September 17, 1990, and June 30, 1986.

**52-week basis.

Ten-Year Selected Financial Data

	Compound Annual Growth Rate			1996 52 weeks	1995 53 weeks
	3-year	5-year	10-year		
Operating Results ($000)					
Net sales	17.0%	16.0%	20.1%	$5,284,381	$4,395,253
Cost of goods sold and occupancy expenses, excluding depreciation and amortization	—	—	—	3,093,709	2,645,736
Percentage of net sales	—	—	—	58.5%	60.2%
Depreciation and amortization(a)	—	—	—	191,457	175,719
Operating expenses	—	—	—	1,270,138	1,004,396
Net interest (income) expense	—	—	—	(19,450)	(15,797)
Earnings before income taxes(b)	20.8%	15.1%	18.5%	748,527	585,199
Percentage of net sales	—	—	—	14.2%	13.3%
Income taxes	—	—	—	295,668	231,160
Net earnings	20.6%	14.5%	20.9%	452,859	354,039
Percentage of net sales	—	—	—	8.6%	8.1%
Cash dividends	16.5%	15.3%	23.0%	83,854	66,993
Capital expenditures(c)	—	—	—	375,838	309,599
Per Share Data(d)					
Net earnings(e)	21.6%	14.6%	20.9%	$1.60	$1.23
Cash dividends	—	—	—	.30	.24
Stockholders' equity (book value)(f)	—	—	—	6.03	5.70
Financial Position ($000)					
Property and equipment (net)	15.3%	15.7%	25.5%	$1,135,720	$ 957,752
Merchandise inventory	20.5%	13.0%	14.8%	578,765	482,575
Total assets	14.2%	18.0%	21.9%	2,626,927	2,343,068
Working capital	3.9%	18.7%	17.4%	554,359	728,301
Current ratio	—	—	—	1.72:1	2.32:1
Total debt, less current installments	—	—	—	—	—
Ratio of long-term debt to stockholders' equity	—	—	—	N/A	N/A
Stockholders' equity	13.7%	19.5%	22.8%	1,654,470	1,640,473
Return on average assets	—	—	—	18.2%	16.3%
Return on average stockholders' equity	—	—	—	27.5%	23.5%
Statistics					
Number of stores opened	23.4%	7.9%	9.0%	203	225
Number of stores expanded	—	—	—	42	55
Number of stores closed	—	—	—	30	53
Number of stores open at year-end(g)	10.6%	8.8%	9.9%	1,854	1,680
Net increase in number of stores	—	—	—	10.4%	11.4%
Comparable store sales growth (52-week basis)	—	—	—	5.0%	0.0%
Sales per square foot (52-week basis)(h)	—	—	—	$441	$425
Square footage of gross store space at year-end	18.8%	17.5%	14.1%	12,645,000	11,100,200
Percentage increase in square feet	—	—	—	13.9%	21.1%
Number of employees at year-end	14.5%	15.6%	18.6%	66,000	60,000
Weighted-average number of shares outstanding(d)	—	—	—	283,330,290	288,062,430
Number of shares outstanding at year-end, net of treasury stock(d)	—	—	—	274,517,331	287,747,984

(a) Excludes amortization of restricted stock.

(b) 1989 includes a non-recurring pretax charge of $10,785 ($.02 per share after tax) taken in the fourth quarter for costs associated with closing the Hemisphere stores. 1988 includes a non-recurring pretax charge of $6,800 ($.01 per share after tax) taken in the first quarter for costs associated with the restructuring of Banana Republic's operations.

(c) Includes property and equipment, as well as lease rights.

(d) Reflects the two-for-one splits of common stock in the form of a stock dividend to stockholders of record on March 18, 1996, June 17, 1991, September 17, 1990, and June 30, 1986.

(e) Based on weighted-average number of shares outstanding at year-end.

(f) Based on actual number of shares outstanding at year-end.

(g) Includes the conversion of GapKids departments to their own separate stores. Converted stores are not classified as new stores.

(h) Based on weighted-average gross square footage.

	Fiscal Year							
	1994 52 weeks	1993 52 weeks	1992 52 weeks	1991 52 weeks	1990 52 weeks	1989 53 weeks	1988 52 weeks	1987 52 weeks
	$3,722,940	$3,295,679	$2,960,409	$2,518,893	$1,933,780	$1,586,596	$1,252,097	$1,062,021
	2,202,133	1,996,929	1,856,102	1,496,156	1,187,644	1,006,647	814,028	654,361
	59.2%	60.6%	62.7%	59.4%	61.4%	63.4%	65.0%	61.6%
	148,863	124,860	99,451	72,765	53,599	39,589	31,408	24,869
	853,524	748,193	661,252	575,686	454,180	364,101	277,429	254,209
	(10,902)	809	3,763	3,523	1,435	2,760	3,416	3,860
	529,322	424,888	339,841	370,763	236,922	162,714	125,816	124,722
	14.2%	12.9%	11.5%	14.7%	12.3%	10.3%	10.0%	11.7%
	209,082	166,464	129,140	140,890	92,400	65,086	51,585	55,127
	320,240	258,424	210,701	229,873	144,522	97,628	74,231	69,595
	8.6%	7.8%	7.1%	9.1%	7.5%	6.2%	5.9%	6.6%
	64,775	53,041	44,106	41,126	29,625	22,857	18,244	17,328
	236,616	215,856	213,659	244,323	199,617	94,266	68,153	67,307
	$1.10	$ .89	$ .73	$ .81	$ .51	$ .35	$.26	$.24
	.23	.19	.16	.15	.11	.09	.07	.06
	4.75	3.88	3.08	2.38	1.65	1.20	.98	.95
	$ 828,777	$ 740,422	$ 650,368	$ 547,740	$ 383,548	$ 238,103	$ 191,257	$ 156,639
	370,638	331,155	365,692	313,899	247,462	243,482	193,268	194,886
	2,004,244	1,763,117	1,379,248	1,147,414	776,900	579,483	481,148	434,231
	555,827	494,194	355,649	235,537	101,518	129,139	106,210	129,988
	2.11:1	2.07:1	2.06:1	1.71:1	1.39:1	1.69:1	1.70:1	2.01:1
	—	75,000	75,000	80,000	17,500	20,000	22,000	18,500
	N/A	.07:1	.08:1	.12:1	.04:1	.06:1	.08:1	.05:1
	1,375,232	1,126,475	887,839	677,788	465,733	337,972	276,399	272,912
	17.0%	16.4%	16.7%	23.9%	21.3%	18.4%	16.2%	17.4%
	25.6%	25.7%	26.9%	40.2%	36.0%	31.8%	27.0%	28.7%
	172	108	117	139	152	98	106	110
	82	130	94	79	56	7	N/A	N/A
	34	45	26	15	20	38	21	19
	1,508	1,370	1,307	1,216	1,092	960	900	815
	10.1%	4.8%	7.5%	11.4%	13.8%	6.7%	10.4%	12.6%
	1.0%	1.0%	5.0%	13.0%	14.0%	15.0%	8.0%	9.0%
	$444	$463	$489	$481	$438	$389	$328	$292
	9,165,900	7,546,300	6,509,200	5,638,400	4,762,300	4,056,600	3,879,300	3,644,500
	21.5%	15.9%	15.4%	18.4%	17.4%	4.6%	6.4%	8.0%
	55,000	44,000	39,000	32,000	26,000	23,000	20,000	16,000
	291,141,076	289,682,274	287,345,848	284,279,154	283,001,776	282,160,400	289,178,240	285,836,104
	289,529,498	290,497,456	288,370,476	285,046,668	282,528,060	281,102,808	281,050,912	286,959,704

Management's Discussion and Analysis

of Results of Operations and Financial Condition

Results of Operations

Net Sales

	Fiscal Year Ended		
	Feb. 1, 1997 (Fiscal 1996) 52 Weeks	Feb. 3, 1996 (Fiscal 1995) 53 Weeks	Jan. 28, 1995 (Fiscal 1994) 52 Weeks
Net sales ($000)	$5,284,381	$4,395,253	$3,722,940
Total net sales growth percentage	20	18	13
Comparable store sales growth percentage (52-week basis)	5	0	1
Net sales per average gross square foot (52-week basis)	441	425	444
Square footage of gross store space (000)	12,645	11,100	9,166
Number of:			
New stores	203	225	172
Expanded stores	42	55	82
Closed stores	30	53	34

The total net sales growth reflected above for 1996, 1995, and 1994 was attributable to the opening of new stores (net of stores closed), the expansion of existing stores, and in 1996, to an increase in comparable store sales. During 1995, an additional week of operations compared to fiscal 1994 contributed one percent to sales growth.

Net sales per average square foot were $441 in 1996, $425 in 1995, and $444 in 1994. The increase in net sales per average square foot in 1996 compared to 1995 was primarily attributable to increases in comparable store sales aided by the smaller size of new stores. The decline in net sales per average square foot in 1995 compared to 1994 was primarily attributable to continued store growth in the Old Navy division, with lower-priced merchandise and significantly larger stores, and to increases in the average size of new stores in other divisions in connection with the Company's store expansion program. During 1995, the Company increased the average size of its new stores and expanded existing stores as a long-term investment.

Cost of Goods Sold and Occupancy Expenses

Cost of goods sold and occupancy expenses as a percentage of net sales were 62.2 percent in 1996, 64.2 percent in 1995, and 63.2 percent in 1994.

The resulting 2.0 percentage point increase in gross margin net of occupancy expenses in 1996 from 1995 was attributable to a 1.2 percentage point increase in merchandise margin as a percentage of net sales combined with a .8 percentage point decrease in occupancy expenses as a percentage of net sales. The increase in merchandise margin in 1996 from 1995 was driven by increases in initial merchandise margin and in the percentage of merchandise sold at regular price.

The 1.0 percentage point decrease in gross margin net of occupancy expenses in 1995 from 1994 was attributable to a 1.2 percentage point decrease in merchandise margin as a percentage of net sales offset by a .2 percentage point decrease in occupancy expenses as a percentage of net sales. The decrease in merchandise margin in 1995 from 1994 was driven by a decline in initial merchandise margin in the first three quarters partially offset by better regular-priced selling in the second half.

The Company reviews its inventory levels in order to identify slow-moving merchandise and broken assortments (items no longer in stock in a sufficient range of sizes) and uses markdowns to clear merchandise. Such markdowns may have an adverse impact on earnings, depending upon the extent of the markdown and the amount of inventory affected.

The decrease in occupancy expenses as a percentage of net sales between 1996 and 1995 was primarily attributable to the effect of the growth of the Old Navy division, which carries lower occupancy expenses as a percentage of net sales when compared to other divisions, and leverage achieved through comparable store sales growth.

The decrease in occupancy expenses as a percentage of net sales between 1995 and 1994 was attributable to leverage obtained from the 53rd week of sales. Without this extra week, occupancy expenses as a percentage of net sales would have been essentially flat.

Operating Expenses

Operating expenses as a percentage of net sales were 24.0 percent for 1996 and 22.9 percent for 1995 and 1994.

During 1996, the 1.1 percentage point increase was primarily attributable to a planned .3 percentage point increase in advertising/marketing costs to support the Company's brands and a .5 percentage point increase in incentive bonus expense. The Company awarded bonuses for 1996 due to strong earnings performance measured against annual targets.

During 1995, a .3 percentage point increase in advertising costs as a percentage of net sales was offset by a .4 percentage point decrease in bonus expense as a percentage of net sales. Advertising costs increased to support the Company's brands and included marketing expense related to the opening of stores in Germany, Japan, and the Old Navy store in Manhattan. Due to the Company's performance relative to financial targets, less bonus expense was recognized in 1995 as compared to 1994.

Net Interest Income

Net interest income was $19.5, $15.8, and $10.9 million for 1996, 1995, and 1994, respectively. The change in 1996 from 1995 was primarily attributable to an increase in gross average investments. The change in 1995 from 1994 was attributable to an increase in income from higher average interest rates.

Income Taxes

The effective tax rate was 39.5 percent in 1996, 1995, and 1994.

A24

Liquidity and Capital Resources

The following sets forth certain measures of the Company's liquidity:

	Fiscal Year		
	1996	1995	1994
Cash provided by operating activities ($000)	$834,953	$489,087	$504,450
Working capital ($000)	554,359	728,301	555,827
Current ratio	1.72:1	2.32:1	2.11:1

For the fiscal year ended February 1, 1997, the increase in cash provided by operating activities was attributable to an increase in net earnings exclusive of depreciation and the timing of certain year-end payables and accrued expenses. For the fiscal year ended February 3, 1996, the decrease in cash provided by operating activities was attributable to an increased investment in inventory partially offset by a decrease in income tax payments. Merchandise inventories at February 3, 1996 increased primarily as a result of new products, new store growth, and early receipt of Spring merchandise to accommodate a one-week shift in the Spring selling season.

The Company funds inventory expenditures during normal and peak periods through a combination of cash flows provided by operations and normal trade credit arrangements. The Company's business follows a seasonal pattern, peaking over a total of about ten to twelve weeks during the late Summer and Holiday periods. During 1996 and 1995, these periods accounted for approximately 33 and 34 percent, respectively, of the Company's annual sales.

The Company has a credit agreement which provides for a $250 million revolving credit facility through June 30, 2001. In addition, the credit agreement provides for the issuance of letters of credit on a committed basis of up to $450 million at any one time. The Company has arrangements providing the issuance of letters of credit on an uncommitted basis of up to an additional $200 million at any one time. The Company had outstanding letters of credit of approximately $429 million at February 1, 1997.

Capital expenditures, net of construction allowances and dispositions, totaled approximately $359 million in 1996. These expenditures resulted in a net increase in store space of approximately 1.5 million square feet or 14 percent due to the addition of 203 new stores, the expansion of 42 stores, and the remodeling of certain stores. Capital expenditures for 1995 and 1994 were $291 million and $220 million, respectively, resulting in a net increase in store space of approximately 1.9 million square feet or 21 percent in 1995, and approximately 1.6 million square feet or 21 percent in 1994.

The increase in capital expenditures in 1996 from 1995 was primarily attributable to the construction of two distribution centers and an administrative facility. The increase in capital expenditures in 1995 from 1994 was due to an increase in the number of stores opened and expanded. Expenditures in 1996, 1995, and 1994 also included costs for equipment.

For 1997, the Company expects capital expenditures to total approximately $400 to $450 million, net of construction allowances, representing the addition of at least 275 new stores, the expansion of approximately 65 to 75 stores, and the remodeling of certain stores. Planned expenditures also include amounts for administrative facilities, distribution centers, and equipment. The Company expects to fund such capital expenditures with cash flow from operations. Square footage growth is expected to be approximately 18 percent before store closings. New stores are generally expected to be leased.

During 1996, the Company completed construction of a distribution center in Gallatin, Tennessee for approximately $55 million. The facility became fully operational in September 1996. Additionally, in May 1996, the Company purchased land and a building in the Netherlands for approximately $10 million to relocate its European distribution center. The distribution center, which began operating in June 1996, provides a central shipping location to the European continent.

In February 1996, the Company exercised an option to purchase land for $9 million in San Bruno, California to expand its headquarters facilities. Construction commenced in April 1996 for an estimated cost at completion of $55 to $60 million. The facility is expected to be in operation in late fiscal 1997.

On February 27, 1996, the Company's Board of Directors authorized a two-for-one split of its common stock effective by a distribution on April 10, 1996, in the form of a stock dividend for stockholders of record at the close of business on March 18, 1996. Per share amounts in the accompanying consolidated financial statements give effect to the stock split.

In October 1996, the Board of Directors approved a program under which the Company may repurchase up to 30 million shares of its outstanding common stock in the open market over a three-year period. During 1996, 4.7 million shares were repurchased for $140 million. The program announced in October 1996 an earlier 18 million share repurchase program, which was completed in November 1996. Under this program, 10.9 million shares were acquired in fiscal 1996 for approximately $329 million. The cost for the entire 18 million share repurchase program was approximately $450 million.

Per Share Data

Fiscal	Market Prices				Cash Dividends	
	1996		1995		1996	1995
	High	Low	High	Low		
1st Quarter	$30½	$23⅕	$17¾	$15⅜	$.075	$.06
2nd Quarter	36⅛	27¼	18¾	14⅞	.075	.06
3rd Quarter	36½	26	20¼	15⅞	.075	.06
4th Quarter	33½	27⅞	25½	19¼	.075	.06
Year					$.30	$.24

The information above has been adjusted to reflect the two-for-one split of common stock in the form of a stock dividend to stockholders of record on March 18, 1996.

The principal markets on which the Company's stock is traded are the New York and Pacific Stock Exchanges. The number of holders of record of the Company's stock as of March 24, 1997 was 6,785.

Management's Report on Financial Information

Management is responsible for the integrity and consistency of all financial information presented in the Annual Report. The financial statements have been prepared in accordance with generally accepted accounting principles and necessarily include certain amounts based on Management's best estimates and judgments.

In fulfilling its responsibility for the reliability of financial information, Management has established and maintains accounting systems and procedures appropriately supported by internal accounting controls. Such controls include the selection and training of qualified personnel, an organizational structure providing for division of responsibility, communication of requirement for compliance with approved accounting control and business practices, and a program of internal audit. The extent of the Company's system of internal accounting control recognizes that the cost should not exceed the benefits derived and that the evaluation of those factors requires estimates and judgments by Management. Although no system can ensure that all errors or irregularities have been eliminated, Management believes that the internal accounting controls in use provide reasonable assurance, at reasonable cost, that assets are safeguarded against

loss from unauthorized use or disposition, that transactions are executed in accordance with Management's authorization, and that the financial records are reliable for preparing financial statements and maintaining accountability for assets. The financial statements of the Company have been audited by Deloitte & Touche LLP, independent auditors. Their report, which appears below, is based upon their audits conducted in accordance with generally accepted auditing standards.

The Audit and Finance Committee of the Board of Directors is comprised solely of directors who are not officers or employees of the Company. The Committee is responsible for recommending to the Board of Directors the selection of independent auditors. It meets periodically with Management, the independent auditors, and the internal auditors to assure that they are carrying out their responsibilities. The Committee also reviews and monitors the financial, accounting, and auditing procedures of the Company in addition to reviewing the Company's financial reports. Deloitte & Touche LLP and the internal auditors have full and free access to the Audit and Finance Committee, with and without Management's presence.

Independent Auditors' Report

To the Stockholders and Board of Directors of The Gap, Inc.:

We have audited the accompanying consolidated balance sheets of The Gap, Inc. and subsidiaries as of February 1, 1997 and February 3, 1996, and the related consolidated statements of earnings, stockholders' equity, and cash flows for each of the three fiscal years in the period ended February 1, 1997. These financial statements are the responsibility of the Company's management. Our responsibility is to express an opinion on these financial statements based on our audits.

We conducted our audits in accordance with generally accepted auditing standards. Those standards require that we plan and perform the audits to obtain reasonable assurance about whether the consolidated financial statements are free of material misstatement. An audit includes examining, on a test basis, evidence supporting the amounts and disclosures in the financial statements. An audit also includes assessing the accounting principles used and significant estimates made by management, as well as evaluating the overall financial statement presentation.

We believe that our audits provide a reasonable basis for our opinion.

In our opinion, such consolidated financial statements present fairly, in all material respects, the financial position of the Company and its subsidiaries as of February 1, 1997 and February 3, 1996, and the results of their operations and their cash flows for each of the three fiscal years in the period ended February 1, 1997 in conformity with generally accepted accounting principles.

Deloitte & Touche LLP

San Francisco, California

February 27, 1997

A26

Consolidated Statements of Earnings

($000 except per share amounts)	Fifty-two Weeks Ended February 1, 1997		Fifty-three Weeks Ended February 3, 1996		Fifty-two Weeks Ended January 28, 1995	
Net sales	$5,284,381	100.0%	$4,395,253	100.0%	$3,722,940	100.0%
Costs and expenses						
Cost of goods sold and occupancy expenses	3,285,166	62.2%	2,821,455	64.2%	2,350,996	63.2%
Operating expenses	1,270,138	24.0%	1,004,396	22.9%	853,524	22.9%
Net interest income	(19,450)	(0.4%)	(15,797)	(0.4%)	(10,902)	(0.3%)
Earnings before income taxes	748,527	14.2%	585,199	13.3%	529,322	14.2%
Income taxes	295,668	5.6%	231,160	5.2%	209,082	5.6%
Net earnings	$ 452,859	8.6%	$ 354,039	8.1%	$ 320,240	8.6%
Weighted-average number of shares[a]	283,330,290		288,062,430		291,141,076	
Earnings per share[a]	$1.60		$1.23		$1.10	

See Notes to Consolidated Financial Statements.

(a) Reflects the two-for-one split of common stock in the form of a stock dividend to stockholders of record on March 18, 1996.

THE GAP, INC.

Consolidated Balance Sheets

($000)	February 1, 1997	February 3, 1996
Assets		
Current Assets		
Cash and equivalents	$ 485,644	$ 579,566
Short-term investments	135,632	89,506
Merchandise inventory	578,765	482,575
Prepaid expenses and other current assets	129,214	128,398
Total Current Assets	1,329,255	1,280,045
Property and Equipment		
Leasehold improvements	836,577	736,879
Furniture and equipment	960,516	763,673
Construction-in-progress	101,520	62,030
	1,898,613	1,562,582
Accumulated depreciation and amortization	(762,893)	(604,830)
	1,135,720	957,752
Long-term Investments	36,138	30,370
Lease rights and other assets	125,814	74,901
Total Assets	$2,626,927	$2,343,068
Liabilities and Stockholders' Equity		
Current Liabilities		
Notes payable	$ 40,050	$ 21,815
Accounts payable	351,754	262,505
Accrued expenses	282,494	194,426
Income taxes payable	91,806	66,094
Deferred lease credits and other current liabilities	8,792	6,904
Total Current Liabilities	774,896	551,744
Long-Term Liabilities		
Deferred lease credits and other liabilities	197,561	150,851
Stockholders' Equity		
Common stock $.05 par value(a)		
Authorized 500,000,000 shares; issued 317,864,090 and 315,971,306 shares; outstanding 274,517,331 and 287,747,984 shares	15,895	15,799
Additional paid-in capital(a)	442,049	335,193
Retained earnings	1,938,352	1,569,347
Foreign currency translation adjustment	(5,187)	(9,071)
Restricted stock plan deferred compensation	(47,838)	(48,735)
Treasury stock, at cost	(688,801)	(222,060)
	1,654,470	1,640,473
Total Liabilities and Stockholders' Equity	$2,626,927	$2,343,068

See Notes to Consolidated Financial Statements.

(a) Reflects the two-for-one split of common stock in the form of a stock dividend to stockholders of record on March 18, 1996.

Consolidated Statements of Cash Flows

($000)	Fifty-two Weeks Ended February 1, 1997	Fifty-three Weeks Ended February 3, 1996	Fifty-two Weeks Ended January 28, 1995
Cash Flows from Operating Activities			
Net earnings	$452,859	$354,039	$320,240
Adjustments to reconcile net earnings to net cash provided by operating activities			
Depreciation and amortization[a]	214,905	197,440	168,220
Tax benefit from exercise of stock options by employees and from vesting of restricted stock	47,348	11,444	19,384
Deferred income taxes	(28,897)	(2,477)	(24,431)
Change in operating assets and liabilities			
Merchandise inventory	(93,800)	(113,021)	(39,860)
Prepaid expenses and other	(16,355)	(15,278)	(10,989)
Accounts payable	88,532	1,183	46,031
Accrued expenses	87,974	9,427	21,953
Income taxes payable	25,706	24,806	(29,241)
Deferred lease credits and other long-term liabilities	56,681	21,524	33,143
Net cash provided by operating activities	834,953	489,087	504,450
Cash Flows from Investing Activities			
Net maturity (purchase) of short-term investments	(11,774)	116,134	(36,474)
Purchase of long-term investments	(40,120)	(30,370)	(85,669)
Purchase of property and equipment	(371,833)	(302,260)	(232,776)
Acquisition of lease rights and other assets	(12,206)	(6,623)	(4,938)
Net cash used for investing activities	(435,933)	(223,119)	(359,857)
Cash Flows from Financing Activities			
Net increase (decrease) in notes payable	18,445	20,787	(4,583)
Payments on long-term debt	—	—	(75,000)
Issuance of common stock	37,053	17,096	12,849
Net purchase of treasury stock	(466,741)	(71,314)	(58,292)
Cash dividends paid	(83,854)	(66,993)	(64,775)
Net cash used for financing activities	(495,097)	(100,424)	(189,801)
Effect of exchange rate changes on cash	2,155	(465)	(637)
Net increase (decrease) in cash and equivalents	(93,922)	165,079	(45,845)
Cash and equivalents at beginning of year	579,566	414,487	460,332
Cash and equivalents at end of year	$485,644	$579,566	$414,487

See Notes to Consolidated Financial Statements.

(a) Includes amortization of restricted stock.

Consolidated Statements of Stockholders' Equity

($000 except per share amounts)	Common Stock[a]	
	Shares	Amount
Balance at January 29, 1994	311,466,512	$15,573
Issuance of common stock pursuant to stock option plans	1,249,612	63
Net issuance of common stock pursuant to management incentive restricted stock plans	1,229,430	61
Tax benefit from exercise of stock options by employees and from vesting of restricted stock		
Foreign currency translation adjustment		
Amortization of restricted stock		
Purchase of treasury stock		
Net earnings		
Cash dividends ($.23 per share)		
Balance at January 28, 1995	313,945,554	$15,697
Issuance of common stock pursuant to stock option plans	994,372	50
Net issuance of common stock pursuant to management incentive restricted stock plans	1,031,380	52
Tax benefit from exercise of stock options by employees and from vesting of restricted stock		
Foreign currency translation adjustment		
Amortization of restricted stock		
Purchase of treasury stock		
Reissuance of treasury stock		
Net earnings		
Cash dividends ($.24 per share)		
Balance at February 3, 1996	315,971,306	$15,799
Issuance of common stock pursuant to stock option plans	1,591,174	81
Net issuance of common stock pursuant to management incentive restricted stock plans	301,610	15
Tax benefit from exercise of stock options by employees and from vesting of restricted stock		
Foreign currency translation adjustment		
Amortization of restricted stock		
Purchase of treasury stock		
Reissuance of treasury stock		
Net earnings		
Cash dividends ($.30 per share)		
Balance at February 1, 1997	317,864,090	$15,895

See Notes to Consolidated Financial Statements.

(a) Reflects the two-for-one split of common stock in the form of a stock dividend to stockholders of record on March 18, 1996.

Additional Paid-in Capital[a]	Retained Earnings	Foreign Currency Translation Adjustment	Restricted Stock Plan Deferred Compensation	Treasury Stock[a]		Total
				Shares	Amount	
$232,869	$1,026,836	($8,314)	($48,035)	(20,969,056)	($ 92,454)	$1,126,475
10,842						10,905
27,470			(25,587)			1,944
19,384						19,384
		(6)				(6)
			19,357			19,357
				(3,447,000)	(58,292)	(58,292)
	320,240					320,240
	(64,775)					(64,775)
$290,565	$1,282,301	($8,320)	($54,265)	(24,416,056)	($150,746)	$1,375,232
9,616						9,666
19,556			(16,191)			3,417
11,444						11,444
		(751)				(751)
			21,721			21,721
				(4,192,800)	(72,717)	(72,717)
4,012				385,534	1,403	5,415
	354,039					354,039
	(66,993)					(66,993)
$335,193	$1,569,347	($9,071)	($48,735)	(28,223,322)	($222,060)	$1,640,473
19,732			(9,648)			10,165
32,807			(12,903)			19,919
47,348						47,348
		3,884				3,884
			23,448			23,448
				(15,523,100)	(468,246)	(468,246)
6,969				399,663	1,505	8,474
	452,859					452,859
	(83,854)					(83,854)
$442,049	$1,938,352	($5,187)	($47,838)	(43,346,759)	($688,801)	$1,654,470

Notes to Consolidated Financial Statements

For the Fifty-two Weeks ended February 1, 1997, the Fifty-three Weeks ended February 3, 1996 and the Fifty-two Weeks ended January 28, 1995.

Note A: Summary of Significant Accounting Policies

The Company is an international specialty retailer which operates stores selling casual apparel, shoes, and other accessories for men, women, and children under a variety of brand names including: Gap, GapKids, babyGap, Banana Republic, and Old Navy Clothing Co. Its principal markets consist of the United States, Canada, Europe, and Asia with the United States being the most significant.

On February 27, 1996, the Company's Board of Directors authorized a two-for-one split of its common stock effective April 10, 1996, in the form of a stock dividend for stockholders of record at the close of business on March 18, 1996. Per share amounts in the accompanying consolidated financial statements give effect to the stock split.

The consolidated financial statements include the accounts of the Company and its subsidiaries. Intercompany accounts and transactions have been eliminated.

The preparation of financial statements in conformity with generally accepted accounting principles requires management to make estimates and assumptions that affect the reported amounts of assets and liabilities and disclosure of contingent assets and liabilities at the date of the financial statements and the reported amounts of revenue and expenses during the reporting period. Actual results could differ from those estimates.

Cash and equivalents represent cash and short-term, highly liquid investments with original maturities of three months or less.

Short-term investments include investments with an original maturity of greater than three months or a remaining maturity of less than one year. Long-term investments include investments with an original and remaining maturity of greater than one year and less than five years. The Company's short- and long-term investments consist primarily of debt securities which have been classified as held to maturity and are carried at amortized cost, which approximates fair market value.

Merchandise inventory is stated at the lower of FIFO (first-in, first-out) cost or market.

Property and equipment are stated at cost. Depreciation and amortization are computed using the straight-line method over the estimated useful lives of the related assets or lease terms, whichever is less.

Lease rights are recorded at cost and are amortized over 12 years or the lives of the respective leases, whichever is less.

Costs associated with the opening or remodeling of stores, such as pre-opening rent and payroll, are charged to expense as incurred. The net book value of fixtures and leasehold improvements for stores scheduled to be closed or expanded within the next fiscal year is charged against current earnings. The Company adopted Statement of Financial Accounting Standards (SFAS)

No. 121, *Accounting for the Impairment of Long-Lived Assets and Long-Lived Assets to Be Disposed Of,* as of January 29, 1995. The adoption of SFAS No. 121 had no material effect on the Company's consolidated financial statements.

Costs associated with the production of advertising, such as writing copy, printing, and other costs, are charged to expense when incurred. Costs associated with communicating advertising that has been produced, such as magazine and billboard space, are charged to expense when the advertising first takes place. Advertising costs were $96 million, $64 million, and $44 million in fiscal 1996, 1995, and 1994, respectively.

Deferred income taxes arise from temporary differences between the tax basis of assets and liabilities and their reported amounts in the consolidated financial statements.

Translation adjustments result from the process of translating foreign subsidiaries' financial statements into U.S. dollars. Balance sheet accounts are translated at exchange rates in effect at the balance sheet date. Income statement accounts are translated at average exchange rates during the year. Resulting translation adjustments are included in stockholders' equity.

Restricted stock awards represent deferred compensation and are shown as a reduction of stockholders' equity. The Company adopted SFAS No. 123, *Accounting for Stock-Based Compensation*, as of February 4, 1996. The Company elected to continue the intrinsic value-based method under Accounting Principles Board (APB) Opinion No. 25, *Accounting for Stock Issued to Employees*, and has provided pro forma disclosures of net earnings and earnings per share in accordance with the provisions of SFAS No. 123.

In February 1997, the Financial Accounting Standards Board issued SFAS No. 128, *Earnings per Share*. SFAS No. 128 requires dual presentation of basic earnings per share (EPS) and diluted EPS on the face of all statements of earnings issued after December 15, 1997, for all entities with complex capital structures. Basic EPS is computed as net earnings divided by the weighted-average number of common shares outstanding for the period. Diluted EPS reflects the potential dilution that could occur from common shares issuable through stock-based compensation including stock options, restricted stock awards, warrants, and other convertible securities. The Company does not anticipate the effect on earnings per share to be material.

Earnings per share are based upon the weighted-average number of shares of common stock outstanding during the period.

Certain reclassifications have been made to the 1994 and 1995 financial statements to conform with the 1996 financial statements.

Note B: Debt and Other Credit Arrangements

The Company has a credit agreement with a syndicated bank group which provides for a $250 million revolving credit facility through June 30, 2001. The revolving credit facility contains both auction and fixed spread borrowing options and may serve as support for the Company's commercial paper program. In addition, the credit agreement provides, on a committed basis, for the issuance of letters of credit through July 1, 1997 of up to $450 million at any one time.

At February 1, 1997, the Company had outstanding letters of credit, including committed and uncommitted lines of credit, totaling $428,600,000.

Borrowings under the Company's loan and credit agreements are subject to the Company maintaining certain levels of tangible net worth and financial ratios. Under the most restrictive covenant of these agreements, $1,074,062,000 of retained earnings were available for the payment of cash dividends at February 1, 1997.

Gross interest payments were $2,800,000, $2,274,000, and $7,032,000 in fiscal 1996, 1995, and 1994, respectively.

Note C: Income Taxes

Income taxes consisted of the following:

($000)	Fifty-two Weeks Ended Feb. 1, 1997	Fifty-three Weeks Ended Feb. 3, 1996	Fifty-two Weeks Ended Jan. 28, 1995
Currently Payable			
Federal income taxes	$269,648	$180,597	$182,811
Less tax credits	(3,585)	(4,397)	(12,692)
	266,063	176,200	170,119
State income taxes	36,167	40,111	45,807
Foreign income taxes	22,335	17,348	17,587
	324,565	233,659	233,513
Deferred			
Federal	(23,980)	(7,169)	(19,911)
State	(4,917)	4,670	(4,520)
	(28,897)	(2,499)	(24,431)
Total provision	$295,668	$231,160	$209,082

The foreign component of pretax earnings before eliminations and corporate allocations in fiscal 1996, 1995, and 1994 was $82,220,000, $71,545,000, and $66,701,000, respectively. Deferred federal and applicable state income taxes, net of applicable foreign tax credits, have not been provided for the undistributed earnings of foreign subsidiaries (approximately $123,489,000 at February 1, 1997) because the Company intends to permanently reinvest such undistributed earnings abroad.

The difference between the effective income tax rate and the United States federal income tax rate is summarized as follows:

($000)	Fifty-two Weeks Ended Feb. 1, 1997	Fifty-three Weeks Ended Feb. 3, 1996	Fifty-two Weeks Ended Jan. 28, 1995
Federal tax rate	35.0%	35.0%	35.0%
State income taxes, less federal benefit	4.4	5.0	5.1
Other	.1	(.5)	(.6)
Effective tax rate	39.5%	39.5%	39.5%

Deferred tax assets (liabilities) consisted of the following at February 1, 1997 and February 3, 1996:

($000)	Feb. 1, 1997	Feb. 3, 1996
Compensation and benefits accruals	$ 31,640	$ 28,872
Scheduled rent	40,834	34,077
Inventory capitalization	16,459	13,243
Nondeductible accruals	18,705	17,011
Other	24,224	10,022
Gross deferred tax assets	131,862	103,225
Depreciation	(13,611)	(14,318)
Other	(5,404)	(4,957)
Gross deferred tax liabilities	(19,015)	(19,275)
Net deferred tax assets	$112,847	$ 83,950

Income tax payments were $249,968,000, $197,802,000, and $232,869,000 in fiscal 1996, 1995, and 1994, respectively.

Note D: Leases

The Company leases virtually all of its store premises, office facilities, and some of its distribution centers.

Leases relating to store premises, distribution centers, and office facilities expire at various dates through 2035.

The aggregate minimum annual lease payments under leases in effect on February 1, 1997 are as follows:

Fiscal Year	($000)
1997	$ 335,774
1998	330,712
1999	324,824
2000	318,642
2001	311,492
Thereafter	1,740,731
Total minimum lease commitment	$3,362,175

For leases that contain predetermined fixed escalations of the minimum rentals, the Company recognizes the related rental expense on a straight-line basis and records the difference between the recognized rental expense and amounts payable under the leases as deferred lease credits. At February 1, 1997 and February 3, 1996, this liability amounted to $110,633,000 and $93,081,000, respectively.

Cash or rent abatements received upon entering into certain store leases are recognized on a straight-line basis as a reduction to rent expense over the lease term. The unamortized portion is included in deferred lease credits.

Some of the leases relating to stores in operation at February 1, 1997 contain renewal options for periods ranging up to 30 years. Most leases also provide for payment of operating expenses, real estate taxes, and for additional rent based on a percentage of sales. No lease directly imposes any restrictions relating to leasing in other locations (other than radius clauses).

Rental expense for all operating leases was as follows:

($000)	Fifty-two Weeks Ended Feb. 1, 1997	Fifty-three Weeks Ended Feb. 3, 1996	Fifty-two Weeks Ended Jan. 28, 1995
Minimum rentals	$337,487	$300,171	$255,202
Contingent rentals	30,644	22,464	20,955
	$368,131	$322,635	$276,157

Note E: Foreign Exchange Contracts

The Company enters into foreign exchange contracts to reduce exposure to foreign currency exchange risk. These contracts are primarily designated and effective as hedges of commitments to purchase merchandise for foreign operations. The market value gains and losses on these contracts are deferred and recognized as part of the underlying cost to purchase the merchandise. At February 1, 1997, the Company had contracts maturing at various dates through 1997 to purchase the equivalent of $60,598,000 in foreign currencies (35,900,000 Canadian dollars through July 3, 1997, 17,100,000 British pounds through May 29, 1997, and 759,000,000 Japanese yen through July 3, 1997) at the contracted rates. The deferred gains and losses on the Company's foreign exchange contracts at February 1, 1997 are immaterial.

Note F: Employee Benefit and Incentive Programs

Retirement Plans

The Company has a qualified defined contribution retirement plan, called GapShare, which is available to employees who meet certain age and service requirements. This plan permits employees to make contributions up to the maximum limits allowable under the Internal Revenue Code. Under the plan, the Company matches all or a portion of the employee's contributions under a predetermined formula; the Company's contributions vest on behalf of the employee progressively over a seven-year period. Company contributions to the retirement plan in 1996, 1995, and 1994 were $11,427,000, $9,839,000, and $8,281,000, respectively.

A nonqualified Executive Deferred Compensation Plan was established on January 1, 1994 and a nonqualified Executive Capital Accumulation Plan was established on April 1, 1994. Both plans allow eligible employees to defer compensation up to a maximum amount defined in each plan. The Company does not match employees' contributions.

Employee Benefits Plan

The Company has an Employee Benefits Plan to provide certain health and welfare benefits. Payments made to the plan relating to benefits payable in future periods are included in prepaid expenses.

Incentive Compensation Plans

The Company has a Management Incentive Cash Award Plan (MICAP) for key management employees. The MICAP empowers the Compensation and Stock Option Committee to award compensation, in the form of cash bonuses, to employees based on the achievement of Company and individual performance goals. Awards can also be made in the form of nonqualified stock options or restricted shares of the Company's stock under the 1996 Stock Option and Award Plan. Restrictions on shares generally lapse in one to five years. Compensation expense is recorded during the vesting period. The nonqualified stock options generally have a maximum term of ten years and vest over a period of three to four years.

An Executive Management Incentive Cash Award Plan (Executive MICAP) was established on March 22, 1994 for key executive officers. The Executive MICAP empowers the Compensation and Stock Option Committee to award compensation in the form of cash bonuses to executives based on the achievements of Companywide or divisional earnings goals for that fiscal year.

An Executive Long-Term Cash Award Performance Plan (ELCAPP) was established in January 1996. The ELCAPP empowers the Compensation and Stock Option Committee to award compensation in the form of cash bonuses to key officers based on the achievement of multiyear financial goals, as determined by the Committee for each participant in the plan. Payouts are determined based upon the achievement of performance goals over a three-year period.

The 1996 Stock Option and Award Plan (the Plan), was established on March 26, 1996. The Board authorized 20,000,000 shares for issuance under the Plan. The Plan superseded a Management Incentive Restricted Stock Plan (MIRSP) and an earlier stock option plan established in 1981. The Plan empowers the Compensation and Stock Option Committee to award compensation primarily in the form of nonqualified stock options or restricted stock to key employees. Nonqualified stock options are generally issued at fair market value but may be issued at prices less than the fair market value at the date of grant or at other prices as determined by the Board of Directors. Total compensation cost for the Plan and MIRSP was $22,248,000, $23,743,000, and $20,317,000 in 1996, 1995, and 1994, respectively.

Employee Stock Purchase Plan

An Employee Stock Purchase Plan was established on December 1, 1994. Under this plan all eligible employees may purchase common stock of the Company at 85 percent of the lower of the closing price of the Company's common stock on the grant date or the purchase date on the New York Stock Exchange Composite Transactions Index. Employees pay for their stock purchases through payroll deductions at a rate equal to any whole percentage from 1 percent to 15 percent. There were 399,663 shares issued under the plan during fiscal 1996 and all shares were acquired from reissued treasury stock. At February 1, 1997, there were 3,214,803 shares reserved for future subscriptions.

Note G: Stockholders' Equity and Stock Options

Common and Preferred Stock

The Company is authorized to issue 60,000,000 shares of Class B common stock which is convertible into shares of common stock on a share-for-share basis; transfer of the shares is restricted. In addition, the holders of the Class B common stock have six votes per share on most matters and are entitled to a lower cash dividend. No Class B shares have been issued.

The Board of Directors is authorized to issue 30,000,000 shares of one or more series of preferred stock and to establish at the time of issuance the issue price, dividend rate, redemption price, liquidation value, conversion features, and such other terms and conditions of each series (including voting rights) as the Board of Directors deems appropriate, without further action on the part of the stockholders. No preferred shares have been issued.

In October 1994, the Board of Directors approved a program under which the Company repurchased 18,000,000 shares of its outstanding stock in the open market over a two-year period. In fiscal 1996, 10,860,000 shares were acquired for $328,695,000. All 18,000,000 shares were purchased for $449,672,000. In October 1996, the Board of Directors approved a second share-buyback program under which the Company may repurchase up to 30,000,000 shares of its outstanding stock in the open market over a three-year period. Under this program, 4,663,000 shares were repurchased for $140,031,000 in fiscal 1996.

Stock Options

Under the Company's Stock Option Plans, nonqualified options to purchase common stock are granted to officers and key employees at exercise prices equal to the fair market value of the stock at the date of grant or at other prices as determined by the Board of Directors.

Outstanding options at February 1, 1997 have expiration dates ranging from March 20, 1997 to January 29, 2007 and represent grants to 1,793 key employees.

At February 1, 1997, the Company reserved 34,239,852 shares of its common stock for the exercise of stock options. There were 14,749,234 and 190,602 shares available for granting of options at February 1, 1997 and February 3, 1996, respectively. Options for 2,915,481 and 2,946,164 shares were exercisable as of February 1, 1997 and February 3, 1996, respectively, and had a weighted-average exercise price of $13.52 and $12.38 for those respective periods.

The Company accounts for its Stock Option and Award Plans in accordance with APB Opinion No. 25, under which no compensation cost has been recognized for stock option awards granted at fair market value. Had compensation cost for the Company's three stock-based compensation plans been determined based on the fair value at the grant dates for awards under those plans in accordance with the provisions of SFAS No. 123, *Accounting for Stock-Based Compensation*, the Company's net earnings and earnings per share would have been reduced to the pro forma amounts indicated below. The effects of applying SFAS No. 123 in this pro forma disclosure are not indicative of future amounts. SFAS No. 123 does not apply to awards prior to fiscal year 1995. Additional awards in future years are anticipated.

		1996	1995
Net earnings ($000)	As reported	$452,859	$354,039
	Pro forma	$437,232	$348,977
Earnings per share	As reported	$1.60	$1.23
	Pro forma	$1.54	$1.21

The weighted-average fair value of the stock options granted during fiscal 1996 and 1995 was $11.21 and $6.27, respectively. The fair value of each option granted is estimated on the date of the grant using the Black-Scholes option-pricing model with the following weighted-average assumptions for grants in 1996 and 1995: dividend yield of 1.0 percent for all years; expected price volatility of 30 percent; risk-free interest rates ranging from 5.5 percent to 6.5 percent; and expected lives between 3.5 and 6 years.

Stock option activity for all employee benefit plans was as follows:

	Shares	Weighted-Average Exercise Price
Balance at January 29, 1994	7,151,086	$12.12
Granted	2,310,800	22.45
Exercised	(1,249,612)	8.73
Cancelled	(465,730)	19.97
Balance at January 28, 1995	7,746,544	$15.27
Granted	9,484,400	17.91
Exercised	(994,372)	9.72
Cancelled	(596,148)	18.41
Balance at February 3, 1996	15,640,424	$17.11
Granted	6,242,740	30.90
Exercised	(1,591,174)	12.45
Cancelled	(799,072)	22.28
Balance at February 1, 1997	19,492,918	$21.69

The following table summarizes information about stock options outstanding at February 1, 1997:

Range of Exercise Prices	Options Outstanding			Options Exercisable	
	Number Outstanding at 2/1/97	Weighted-Average Remaining Contractual Life (in years)	Weighted-Average Exercise Price	Number Exercisable at 2/1/97	Weighted-Average Exercise Price
$ 4.76 to $15.69	2,825,688	4.31	$12.38	2,173,888	$11.42
15.72 to 16.94	4,001,690	6.09	16.10	97,023	16.29
17.09 to 22.59	7,186,470	6.10	20.23	593,970	19.81
22.69 to 35.44	5,479,070	9.25	32.51	50,600	24.36
$ 4.76 to $35.44	19,492,918	6.72	$21.69	2,915,481	$13.52

Note H: Related Party Transactions

The Company has an agreement with Fisher Development, Inc. (FDI), wholly owned by the brother of the Company's chairman, setting forth the terms under which FDI may act as general contractor in connection with the Company's construction activities. FDI acted as general contractor for 177, 204, and 159 new stores' leasehold improvements and fixtures during fiscal 1996, 1995, and 1994, respectively. In the same respective years, FDI supervised construction of 38, 54, and 79 expansions, as well as remodels of existing stores. FDI construction also included

administrative offices. Total cost of this construction was $111,871,000, $164,820,000, and $142,791,000, including profit and overhead costs of $10,751,000, $11,753,000, and $10,738,000. At February 1, 1997 and February 3, 1996, amounts due to FDI were $6,456,000 and $12,491,000, respectively. The terms and conditions of the agreement with FDI are reviewed annually by the Audit and Finance Committee of the Board of Directors.

During the first quarter of fiscal 1995, the Company repurchased 250,000 shares of its common stock for $8,438,000 from a senior executive of the Company.

Note I: Quarterly Financial Information (Unaudited)

Fiscal 1996 Quarter Ended

($000 except per share amounts)	Thirteen Weeks Ended May 4, 1996	Thirteen Weeks Ended August 3, 1996	Thirteen Weeks Ended Nov. 2, 1996	Thirteen Weeks Ended Feb. 1, 1997	Fifty-two Weeks Ended Feb. 1, 1997
Net sales	$1,113,154	$1,120,335	$1,382,996	$1,667,896	$5,284,381
Gross profit	413,840	400,170	545,221	639,984	1,999,215
Net earnings	81,573	65,790	134,310	171,186	452,859
Net earnings per share	.28	.23	.48	.62	1.60

Fiscal 1995 Quarter Ended

($000 except per share amounts)	Thirteen Weeks Ended April 29, 1995	Thirteen Weeks Ended July 29, 1995	Thirteen Weeks Ended Oct. 28, 1995	Fourteen Weeks Ended Feb. 3, 1996	Fifty-three Weeks Ended Feb. 3, 1996
Net sales	$848,688	$868,514	$1,155,929	$1,522,122	$4,395,253
Gross profit	280,557	259,193	458,050	575,998	1,573,798
Net earnings	50,113	32,414	116,875	154,637	354,039
Net earnings per share	.17	.11	.41	.54	1.23

Corporate Officers

Donald G. Fisher
Chairman of the Board

Millard S. Drexler
President and
Chief Executive Officer

Robert J. Fisher
Chief Operating Officer

John B. Wilson
Chief Administrative Officer

Dennis M. Connors
Senior Vice President
Chief Information Officer

Charles K. Crovitz
Senior Vice President
Strategic Planning and
Business Development

James P. Cunningham
Senior Vice President
Offshore Sourcing and
Managing Director of
Gap International Sourcing

Anne B. Gust
Senior Vice President
General Counsel

Warren R. Hashagen, Jr.
Senior Vice President and
Chief Financial Officer

Adrienne M. Johns
Senior Vice President
Human Resources

George A. Joseph
Senior Vice President
Distribution

Steven B. Kaplan
Senior Vice President
Real Estate

Gary L. McNatton
Senior Vice President
Personal Care

Stanley P. Raggio
Senior Vice President
Sourcing and Logistics

Alan J. Barocas
Vice President
Real Estate

David G. Bergen
Vice President
Information Technology

George P. Blankenship
Vice President
Real Estate

Carrie Brooks-Brown
Vice President
Assistant Controller

James A. Brownell
Vice President
Information Technology

Susan L. Cooper
Vice President
Human Resources

Charles J. Cristella
Vice President
Real Estate

Stephen M. Dillon
Vice President
Consulting and
Auditing Services

Robert W. Engel
Vice President
Store Design

Claude Frattini
Vice President
European Sourcing

Joanne K. Garrison
Vice President
Associate General Counsel

William R. Jaeger
Vice President
Distribution

Barbara J. Johnson
Vice President
Taxes

Michelle M. Lantow
Vice President
Corporate Controller

James M. LaRocco
Vice President
Human Resources

Paula L. Levitan
Vice President
Associate General Counsel

John A. Minor
Vice President
Distribution

Ayliffe B. Mumford
Vice President
Human Resources

Stephen L. Pearson
Vice President
Sourcing

Sheila S. Peters
Vice President
Human Resources

John A. Sabol
Vice President
Corporate Administration

Lauri M. Shanahan
Vice President
Associate General Counsel

Laurence S. Shushan
Vice President
Corporate Communication and
Public Affairs

Thomas D. Stromberg
Vice President
Information Technology

Eugene Torchia, Jr.
Vice President
Corporate Architecture

John Michael Whisman
Vice President
Associate General Counsel

Steven Winningham
Vice President
Information Technology

Gap International Sourcing

K.L. Szetoh
Vice President
General Manager
Southeast Asia Region

Hansel Wong
Vice President
Operations

Divisional Officers

Gap

Dennis R. Parodi
*Division Executive
Vice President
Stores*

Elizabeth H. Salamone
*Division Executive
Vice President
Merchandising*

Lisa A. Schultz
*Division Executive
Vice President
Product Design
and Development*

Richard F. Eastwick
*Senior Vice President
Merchandise Planning
and Distribution*

Michael McCadden
*Senior Vice President
Marketing*

Kenneth S. Pilot
*Senior Vice President
Outlet and New Business
Development*

Kenneth R. Rapp
Senior Zone Vice President

Ed Stair
*Senior Vice President
Operations*

June A. Beckstead
*Vice President
Product Design*

Joanne Calabrese
Vice President Merchandising

Lorraine C. Christensen
Regional Vice President

Mary Ellen Coyne
*Vice President
Product Design*

Mark E. Dvorak
*Vice President
Visual Design*

John Farugia
*Vice President
Store Operations
and Control*

Carmen T. Gennuso
Regional Vice President

Jayne Greenberg
*Vice President
Advertising Media*

Amy Hennisch
*Vice President
Product Design
and Development*

Thomas E. Hurney
Zone Vice President

Lanny Israel
*Vice President
Visual Merchandising*

Douglas C. Marker
*Vice President
Loss Prevention*

Robert D. Muncey
Regional Vice President

Rhonda L. Schladerbach
Zone Vice President

GapKids

Ronald G. Franks
*Division Executive
Vice President
Stores*

Paula Flynn
*Senior Vice President
Product Design
and Development*

Michael D. Tucci
Senior Vice President Merchandising

Nancy Blok-Anderson
Regional Vice President

Jane E. Dolan Rizzo
*Vice President
Merchandising*

Nancy M. Green
*Vice President
Merchandising*

Margaret G. Hopkins
*Vice President
Merchandising*

Robin R. Rice
*Vice President
Merchandising*

Johanna Sedman
*Vice President
Merchandise Planning
and Distribution*

Steven Yacker
Regional Vice President

Banana Republic

Jeanne Jackson
Chief Executive Officer

Marie Holman-Rao
President

Michael J. Dadario
*Division Executive
Vice President
Stores and Operations*

Ronald R. Beegle
*Senior Vice President
Finance, Planning and
Administration*

Jerome M. Jessup
*Senior Vice President
Product Design
and Development*

Gary P. Muto
*Senior Vice President
Merchandising*

Mary M. Anderson
Regional Vice President

Jody L. Austin
*Vice President
Product Design
and Development*

Kathleen H. Boyer
*Vice President
Merchandising*

Stacey K. Brown
Regional Vice President

Deborah T. Corsiglia
*Vice President
National Sales*

Lisa Kay Engler
*Vice President
Merchandising*

Dorothy B. Hardesty
*Vice President
Product Design
and Development*

Jill McCoy
*Vice President
Visual Merchandising
and Design*

Mary Mitchell
*Vice President
Merchandise Control*

Robert J. Mulholland
*Vice President
Product Sourcing*

Paul Price
*Vice President
Merchandising*

Amy Schoening
*Vice President
Marketing*

Jayme R. Witman
Regional Vice President

Daniel J. Worden
*Vice President
Store Design*

John L. Zannini
*Vice President
Product Design*

Old Navy

Kevin M. Lonergan
*Division Executive
Vice President
Stores and Operations*

Jenny J. Ming
*Division Executive
Vice President
Merchandising*

Jeffrey A. Pfeifle
*Division Executive
Vice President
Product Design
and Development*

Richard Crisman
*Senior Vice President
Marketing*

Richard Anders
Zone Vice President

Patricia A. Barkin
*Vice President
Product Design
and Development*

Maureen Chiquet
*Vice President
Merchandising*

Lori David
*Vice President
Merchandising*

Kevin L. Finnegan
Zone Vice President

John Fontana
*Vice President
Planning and Distribution*

Catherine C. Guiley
*Vice President
Merchandising*

Robert A. Hodges
Zone Vice President

Charlotte Marshall
*Vice President
Product Design
and Development*

Richard S. McKinley
*Vice President
Finance*

Jody E. Patraka
*Vice President
Visual Merchandising
and Design*

James C. Petty
*Vice President
Operations*

International

William S. Fisher
President

Richard M. Lyons
*Division Executive
Vice President
Brand Development*

Marka V. Hansen
*Senior Vice President
Merchandising*

Edward F. Dunlap
*Vice President
Finance and Business
Development*

Christopher Garek
*Vice President
Japan*

Jerome S. Griffith
*Vice President
Managing Director
Europe*

Alain Moreaux
*Vice President
Country Manager
France*

Carl A. Seletz
*Vice President
Country Manager
United Kingdom*

Pascal Somarriba
*Vice President
Marketing*

Stephen Sullivan
*Vice President
Administration*

Janelle Van Rensselaer
*Vice President
Merchandise Planning
and Distribution*

Directors

Adrian D. P. Bellamy†□
*Chairman of the Gucci Group N.V.;
Director of The Body Shop
International PLC; and
Paragon Trade Brands, Inc.
Director since 1995.*

John G. Bowes†□
*Former Chairman of
Kransco Group Companies.
Director since 1974.*

Millard S. Drexler
*President and Chief Executive Officer
of the Company; and Director of
Williams-Sonoma, Inc.
Director since 1983.*

Donald G. Fisher□
*Chairman and founder of
the Company; Director of
The Charles Schwab Corporation;
and AirTouch Communications.
Director since 1969.*

Doris F. Fisher
*Merchandising consultant
and founder of the Company.
Director since 1969.*

Robert J. Fisher
*Chief Operating Officer of the Company;
and Director of Sun Microsystems, Inc.
Director since 1990.*

Lucie J. Fjeldstad†□
*President of Video and Networking,
Tektronix, Inc.; Formerly President of
Fjeldstad International; Vice President
and General Manager of Multimedia, IBM;
Director of Keycorp, Entergy; and
Bolt Beranek & Newman.
Director since 1995.*

William A. Hasler*□
*Dean, Haas Graduate School of Business,
University of California, Berkeley; Formerly
Vice Chairman of KPMG Peat Marwick;
Director of Tenera Inc.; Aphton, Inc.; Walker
Interactive Systems Inc.; and TCSI.
Director since 1991.*

John M. Lillie†□
*Former Chairman and Chief Executive
Officer of American President Companies,
Ltd.; Director of Vons Companies;
Consolidated Freightways, Inc.;
The Harper Group, Inc.; and Walker Inter-
active Systems Inc.
Director since 1992.*

Charles R. Schwab*□
*Chairman and Chief Executive Officer of
The Charles Schwab Corporation; Director
of Transamerica Corporation; AirTouch
Communications; and Siebel Systems, Inc.
Director since 1986.*

Brooks Walker, Jr.*□
*General Partner of Walker Investors;
Director of Pope & Talbot, Inc.; and AT&T
Capital Corporation.
Director since 1972.*

* Audit and Finance Committee
† Compensation and Stock Option Committee
□ Corporate Governance Committee

A39

Corporate Information

Corporate Offices

Gap, Inc.
One Harrison Street
San Francisco, CA 94105
415-952-4400

Annual Meeting

The annual meeting of stockholders will be held at 1:30 p.m., Tuesday, May 20, 1997, at the Delancey Street Foundation Town Hall, 600 Embarcadero, San Francisco, California 94107. Each stockholder is cordially invited to attend.

Common Stock

The common stock of Gap, Inc., is listed for trading on the New York and Pacific Stock Exchanges, ticker symbol "GPS."

Fiscal 1997 Quarterly Earnings Release Dates

1st quarter:	May 15, 1997
2nd quarter:	August 14, 1997
3rd quarter:	November 13, 1997
4th quarter and fiscal year:	February 26, 1998

Information Resources

Publications

A copy of the Company's Annual Report to the Securities and Exchange Commission (Form 10-K) for the fiscal year ended February 1, 1997, will be available after May 5, 1997, by calling 1-800-GAP-NEWS (1-800-427-6397).

Web site

Our Web site at www.gap.com offers information about our Company and stock, as well as online versions of our Annual Report, SEC reports, quarterly earnings results and monthly sales reports.

Hotline

The Company's Investor Relations Hotline, 1-800-GAP-NEWS, offers recorded highlights from the most recent quarter and month, as well as upcoming news release dates, and may be used to request mailed copies of the most recently published financial information. The hotline is accessible from within the United States.

Duplicate mailings

If you are receiving duplicate or unwanted copies of our publications, please contact us at 1-800-GAP-NEWS.

Stockholder Assistance

Registered Stockholders
(shares held by you in your name):
Questions about your statement, dividend payments, registration changes, lost stock certificates, stock holdings, or related matters should be directed to the Transfer Agent and Registrar:

Harris Trust Company of California, Chicago
311 West Monroe Street
Chicago, IL 60606
312-461-5139

Beneficial Shareholders
(shares held by your broker in the name of the brokerage house):
Questions should be directed to your broker on all administrative matters.

Independent Auditors

Deloitte & Touche LLP
San Francisco, California

Design: Frankfurt Balkind Partners, NY/LA/SF. Photography: Chris Felver (pg. A6, bottom), Thibault Jenson (pgs. A8, A14, & A18).

GLOSSARY

accelerated depreciation Any depreciation method that writes off depreciable costs more quickly than the ordinary straight-line method based on expected useful life.

account A summary record of the changes in a particular asset, liability, or owners' equity.

account format A classified balance sheet with the assets at the left.

account payable A liability that results from a purchase of goods or services on open account.

accounting The process of identifying, recording, summarizing, and reporting economic information to decision makers.

accounting controls The methods and procedures for authorizing transactions, safeguarding assets, and ensuring the accuracy of the financial records.

Accounting Principles Board (APB) The predecessor to the Financial Accounting Standards Board.

accounting system A set of records, procedures, and equipment that routinely deals with the events affecting the financial performance and position of the entity.

accounts receivable (trade receivables, receivables) Amounts owed to a company by customers as a result of delivering goods or services and extending credit in the ordinary course of business.

accounts receivable turnover Credit sales divided by average accounts receivable.

accrual basis Accounting method that recognizes the impact of transactions on the financial statements in the time periods when revenues and expenses occur.

accrue To accumulate a receivable or payable during a given period even though no explicit transaction occurs.

accumulated depreciation (allowance for depreciation) The cumulative sum of all depreciation recognized since the date of acquisition of the particular assets described.

adjustments (adjusting entries) End of period entries that assign the financial effects of implicit transactions to the appropriate time periods.

administrative controls All methods and procedures that facilitate management planning and control of operations.

affiliated company A company that has 20% to 50% of its voting shares owned by another company.

aging of accounts receivable An analysis that considers the composition of year-end accounts receivable based on the age of the debt.

AICPA American Institute of Certified Public Accountants, the leading organization of the auditors of corporate financial reports.

allowance for uncollectible accounts (allowance for doubtful accounts, allowance for bad debts, reserve for doubtful accounts) A contra asset account that measures the amount of receivables estimated to be uncollected.

allowance method Method of accounting for bad debt losses using estimates of the amount of sales that will ultimately be uncollectible and a contra asset account, allowance for doubtful accounts.

amortization When referring to long-lived assets, it usually means the allocation of the costs of intangible assets to the periods that benefit from these assets.

annual report A combination of financial statements, management discussion and analysis, and graphs and charts that is provided annually to investors.

annuity Equal cash flows to take place during successive periods of equal length.

APB Opinions A series of thirty-one opinions of the Accounting Principles Board, many of which are still the "accounting law of the land."

assets Economic resources that are expected to benefit future cash inflows or help reduce future cash outflows.

audit An examination of transactions and financial statements made in accordance with generally accepted auditing standards.

audit committee A committee of the board of directors that oversees the internal accounting controls, financial statements, and financial affairs of the corporation.

auditor A person that examines the information used by managers to prepare the financial statements and attests to the credibility of those statements.

auditor's opinion (independent opinion) A report describing the auditor's examination of transactions and financial statements. It is included with the financial statements in an annual report issued by the corporation.

authorized shares The total number of shares that may legally be issued under the articles of incorporation.

available-for-sale securities Investments in equity or debt securities that are not held for active trading but may be sold before maturity.

bad debt recoveries Accounts receivable that were written off as uncollectible but then collected at a later date.

bad debts expense The cost of granting credit that arises from uncollectible accounts.

balance The difference between the total left-side and right-side amounts in an account at any particular time.

balance sheet (statement of financial position, statement of financial condition) A financial statement that shows the financial status of a business entity at a particular instant in time.

balance sheet equation Assets = Liabilities + Owners' equity

basket purchase The acquisition of two or more types of assets for a lump-sum cost.

bench marks General rules of thumb specifying appropriate levels for financial ratios.

bonds Formal certificates of indebtedness that are typically accompanied by (1) a promise to pay interest in cash at a specified annual rate plus (2) a promise to pay the principal at a specific maturity date.

book of original entry A formal chronological record of how the entity's transactions affect the balances in pertinent accounts.

book value (net book value, carrying amount, carrying value) The balance of an account shown on the books, net of any contra accounts. For example, the book value of equipment is its acquisition cost minus accumulated depreciation.

book value per share of common stock Stockholders' equity attributable to common stock divided by the number of shares outstanding.

call premium The amount by which the redemption price of a callable bond exceeds par.

callable A characteristic of bonds or preferred stock that gives the issuer the right to redeem the security at a fixed price.

callable bonds Bonds subject to redemption before maturity at the option of the issuer.

capital A term used to identify owners' equities for proprietorships and partnerships.

capital lease (financing lease) A lease that transfers substantially all the risks and benefits of ownership to the lessee.

capitalization (capital structure) Owners' equity plus long-term debt.

capitalized A cost that is added to an asset account, as distinguished from being expensed immediately.

capital stock certificate (stock certificate) Formal evidence of ownership shares in a corporation.

cash basis Accounting method that recognizes the impact of transactions on the financial statements only when cash is received or disbursed.

cash discounts Reductions of invoice prices awarded for prompt payment.

cash dividends Distributions of cash to stockholders that reduce retained income.

cash equivalents Highly liquid short-term investments that can easily be converted into cash.

cash flows from financing activities The third major section of the statement of cash flows describing flows to and from providers of capital.

cash flows from investing activities The second major section of the statement of cash flows describing purchase or sale of plant, property, equipment, and other long-lived assets.

cash flows from operating activities The first major section of the statement of cash flows. It shows the cash effects of transactions that affect the income statement.

certificates of deposit Short-term obligations of banks.

certified public accountant (CPA) In the United States, a person earns this designation by a combination of education, qualifying experience, and the passing of a two-day written national examination.

charge A word often used instead of debit.

chart of accounts A numbered or coded list of all account titles.

classified balance sheet A balance sheet that groups the accounts into subcategories to help readers quickly gain a perspective on the company's financial position.

common-size statements Financial statements expressed in component percentages.

commercial paper A short-term debt contract issued by prominent companies that borrow directly from investors.

Commercial paper Short-term notes payable issued by large corporations with top credit ratings.

common stock Stock representing the class of owners having a "residual" ownership of a corporation.

compensating balances Required minimum cash balances on deposit when money is borrowed from banks.

component percentages Elements of financial statements that express each component as a percentage of the total.

compound entry A transaction that affects more than two accounts.

compound entry An entry for a transaction that affects more than two accounts.

compound interest For any period, interest rate multiplied by a changing principal amount. The unpaid interest is added to the principal to become the principal for the new period.

conservatism Selecting the methods of measurement that yield lower net income, lower assets, and lower stockholders' equity.

consistency Conformity from period to period with unchanging policies and procedures.

consolidated statements Combinations of the financial positions and earnings reports of the parent company with those of various subsidiaries into an overall report as if they were a single entity.

constant dollars Dollar measurements that are restated in terms of current purchasing power.

contingent liability A potential liability that depends on a future event arising out of a past transaction.

contra account A separate but related account that offsets or is a deduction from a companion account. An example is accumulated depreciation.

contra asset A contra account that offsets an asset.

convertible A characteristic of bonds or preferred stock that gives the holder the right to exchange the security for common stock.

convertible bonds Bonds that may, at the holder's option, be exchanged for other securities.

copyrights Exclusive rights to reproduce and sell a book, musical composition, film, and similar items.

corporate proxy A written authority granted by individual shareholders to others to cast the shareholders' votes.

corporation A business organization that is created by individual state laws.

cost-benefit criterion As a system is changed, its expected additional benefits should exceed its expected additional costs.

cost of goods available for sale Sum of beginning inventory plus current year purchases.

cost of goods sold (cost of sales) The original acquisition cost of the inventory that was sold to customers during the reporting period.

cost recovery The concept by which some purchases of goods or services are recorded as assets because their costs are expected to be recovered in the form of cash inflows (or reduced cash outflows) in future periods.

cost valuation Process of assigning specific historical costs to items counted in the physical inventory.

coupon rate The rate of interest to be paid on a bond.

credit An entry or balance on the right side of an account.

creditor A person or entity to whom money is owed.

cross-sectional comparisons Comparisons of a company's financial ratios with the ratios of other companies or with industry averages.

cumulative A characteristic of preferred stock that requires that undeclared dividends accumulate and must be paid in the future before common dividends.

current assets Cash plus assets that are expected to be converted to cash or sold or consumed during the next twelve months or within the normal operating cycle if longer than a year.

current cost Generally, the cost to replace an asset.

current liabilities Liabilities that fall due within the coming year or within the normal operating cycle if longer than a year.

current ratio (working capital ratio) Current assets divided by current liabilities.

current yield Annual interest payments divided by the current price of a bond.

cutoff error Failure to record transactions in the correct time period.

data processing The totality of the procedures used to record, analyze, store, and report on chosen activities.

date of record The date when ownership is fixed for determining the right to receive a dividend.

days to collect accounts receivable (average collection period) 365 divided by accounts receivable turnover.

debenture A debt security with a general claim against all assets rather than a specific claim against particular assets.

debit An entry or balance on the left side of an account.

debt-to-equity ratio Total liabilities divided by total shareholders' equity.

debt-to-total-assets ratio Total liabilities divided by total assets.

debtor A person or entity that owes money to another.

declaration date The date the board of directors declares a dividend.

deferred charges Similar to prepaid expenses, but they have longer-term benefits.

depletion The process of allocating the cost of natural resources to the periods in which the resources are used.

depreciable value The amount of the acquisition cost to be allocated as depreciation over the total useful life of an asset. It is the difference between the total acquisition cost and the predicted residual value.

depreciation The systematic allocation of the acquisition cost of long-lived or fixed assets to the expense accounts of particular periods that benefit from the use of the assets.

depreciation schedule The listing of depreciation amounts for each year of an asset's useful life.

dilution Reduction in stockholders' equity per share or earnings per share that arises from some changes among shareholders' proportional interests.

direct method In a statement of cash flows, the method that calculates net cash provided by operating activities as collections minus operating disbursements.

discontinued operations The termination of a business segment. The results are reported separately, net of tax, in the income statement.

discount amortization   The spreading of bond discount over the life of the bonds as expense.

discount on bonds   The excess of face amount over the proceeds upon issuance of a bond.

discount rates   The interest rates used in determining present values.

dividend arrearages   Accumulated unpaid dividends on preferred stock.

dividend-payout ratio   Common dividends per share divided by earnings per share.

dividend-yield ratio   Common dividends per share divided by market price per share.

double-declining-balance depreciation (DDB)   The most popular form of accelerated depreciation. It is computed by doubling the straight-line rate and multiplying the resulting DDB rate by the beginning book value.

double-entry system   The method usually followed for recording transactions, whereby at least two accounts are always affected by each transaction.

Earnings per share (EPS)   Net income divided by average number of common shares outstanding.

EBIT   Earnings before interest and taxes.

effective-interest amortization (compound interest method)   An amortization method that uses a constant interest rate.

entity   An organization or a section of an organization that stands apart from other organizations and individuals as a separate economic unit.

equity method   Accounting for an investment at acquisition cost, adjusted for the investor's share of dividends and earnings or losses of the investee subsequent to the date of investment.

expenditures   The purchases of goods or services, whether for cash or on credit.

expenses   Decreases in owners' equity that arise because goods or services are delivered to customers.

explicit transactions   Events such as cash receipts and disbursements, credit purchases, and credit sales that trigger nearly all day-to-day routine entries.

extraordinary items   Items that are unusual in nature and infrequent in occurrence that are shown separately, net of tax, in the income statement.

F.O.B. destination   Seller pays freight costs from the shipping point of the seller to the receiving point of the buyer.

F.O.B. shipping point   Buyer pays freight costs from the shipping point of the seller to the receiving point of the buyer.

FASB Statements   The FASB's rulings on generally accepted accounting principles (GAAP).

financial accounting   The field of accounting that serves external decision makers, such as stockholders, suppliers, banks, and government agencies.

Financial Accounting Standards Board (FASB)   A private-sector body that determines generally accepted accounting standards in the United States.

financial capital maintenance   A concept of income measurement whereby income emerges only after financial resources are recovered.

financial management   Is mainly concerned with where to get cash and how to use cash for the benefit of the entity.

financial statement analysis   Using financial statements to assess a company's performance.

financing activities   Activities that involve obtaining resources as a borrower or issuer of securities and repaying creditors and owners.

finished goods inventory   The accumulated costs of manufacture for goods that are complete and ready for sale.

first-in, first-out (FIFO)   This method of accounting for inventory assigns the cost of the earliest acquired units to cost of goods sold first.

fiscal year   The year established for accounting purposes.

franchises (licenses)   Privileges granted by a government, manufacturer, or distributor to sell a product or service in accordance with specified conditions.

freight in (inward transportation)   An additional cost of the goods acquired during the period, which is often shown in the purchases section of an income statement.

freight out   The transportation costs borne by the seller of merchandise and often shown as a "shipping expense."

future value   The amount accumulated, including principal and interest.

general journal   The most common example of a book of original entry; a complete chronological record of transactions.

general ledger   The collection of accounts that accumulates the amounts reported in the major financial statements.

general price index   An index that compares the average price of a group of goods and services at one date with the average price of a similar group at another date.

generally accepted accounting principles (GAAP)   A term that applies to the broad concepts or guidelines and detailed practices in accounting, including all the conventions, rules, and procedures that make up accepted accounting practice at a given time.

going concern convention (continuity convention)   The assumption that in all ordinary situations an entity persists indefinitely.

goodwill   The excess of the cost of an acquired company over the sum of the fair market value of its identifiable individual assets less the liabilities.

gross profit (gross margin)   The excess of sales revenue over the cost of the inventory that was sold.

gross profit percentage (gross margin percentage)   Gross profit divided by sales.

gross profit percentage Gross profit as a percentage of sales.

gross sales Total sales revenue before deducting sales returns and allowances.

held-to-maturity securities Debt securities that the investor expects to hold until maturity.

historical cost The amount originally paid to acquire an asset.

holding gain (inventory profit) Increase in the replacement cost or other measure of current value of the inventory held during the current period.

implicit interest (imputed interest) An interest expense that is not explicitly recognized in a loan agreement.

implicit transactions Events (such as the passage of time) that are temporarily ignored in day-to-day recording procedures and are recognized via end-of-period adjustments.

improvement (betterment, capital improvement) An expenditure that is intended to add to the future benefits from an existing fixed asset.

imputed interest rate The market interest rate that equates the proceeds from a loan with the present value of the loan payments.

income (profit, earnings) The excess of revenues over expenses.

income statement (statement of earnings, operating statement) A report of all revenues and expenses pertaining to a specific time period.

indirect method In a statement of cash flows, the method that adjusts the accrual net income to reflect only cash receipts and outlays.

inflation A general decline in the purchasing power of the monetary unit.

intangible assets Rights or economic benefits, such as franchises, patents, trademarks, copyrights, and goodwill, that are not physical in nature.

interest-coverage ratio Pretax income plus interest expense divided by interest expense.

interest rate The percentage applied to a principal amount to calculate the interest charged.

interim periods The time span established for accounting purposes that are less than a year.

internal control System of checks and balances that assumes that all actions ocurring within the company are in accordance with organizational objectives.

International Accounting Standards Committee (IASC) An organization representing over one hundred accountancy boards from over seventy-five countries that is developing a common set of accounting standards to be used throughout the world.

inventory Goods held by a company for the purpose of sale to customers.

inventory shrinkage Inventory reductions from theft, breakage, or losses of inventory.

inventory turnover The cost of goods sold divided by the average inventory held during the period.

investing activities Activities that involve (1) providing and collecting cash as a lender or as an owner of securities and (2) acquiring and disposing of plant, property, equipment, and other long-term productive assets.

invoice A document issued by the seller to a buyer indicating the number of items shipped, their price, and any additional costs such as shipping along with payment terms, if any.

issued shares The aggregate number of shares sold to the public.

journal entry An analysis of the effects of a transaction on the accounts, usually accompanied by an explanation.

journalizing The process of entering transactions into the journal.

keying of entries (cross-referencing) The process of numbering or otherwise specifically identifying each journal entry and each posting.

last-in, first-out (LIFO) This inventory method assigns the most recent costs to cost of goods sold.

lease A contract whereby an owner (lessor) grants the use of property to a second party (lessee) for rental payments.

leasehold The right to use a fixed asset for a specified period of time, typically beyond one year.

leasehold improvement Investments by a lessee in items that are not permitted to be removed from the premises when a lease expires, such as installation of new fixtures, panels, walls, and air-conditioning equipment.

ledger The records for a group of related accounts kept current in a systematic manner.

lessee The party that has the right to use leased property and makes lease payments to the lessor.

lessor The owner of property who grants usage rights to the lessee.

liabilities Economic obligations of the organization to outsiders or claims against its assets by outsiders.

LIFO layer (LIFO increment) A separately identifiable additional segment of LIFO inventory.

LIFO reserve The difference between a company's inventory valued at LIFO and what it would be under FIFO.

limited liability A feature of the corporate form of organization whereby corporate creditors ordinarily have claims against the corporate assets only. The owners' personal assets are not subject to the creditors' grasp.

line of credit An agreement with a bank to provide automatically short-term loans up to some preestablished maximum.

liquidating value A measure of the preference to receive assets in the event of corporate liquidation.

liquidation Converting assets to cash and terminating or paying off outside claims.

long-lived assets Resources that are held for an extended time, such as land, buildings, equipment, natural resources, and patents.

long-term-debt-to-total-capital ratio Total long-term debt divided by total shareholders' equity plus long-term debt.

long-term liabilities Obligations that fall due beyond one year from the balance sheet date.

long-term solvency An organization's ability to generate enough cash to repay long-term debts as they mature.

lower-of-cost-or-market method (LCM) The superimposition of a market-price test on an inventory cost method.

management accounting The field of accounting that serves internal decision makers, such as top executives, department heads, college deans, hospital administrators, and people at other management levels within an organization.

management reports Explicit statements in annual reports of publicly held companies that management is responsible for all audited and unaudited information in the annual report.

management's discussion and analysis (MD&A) A required section of annual reports that concentrates on explaining the major changes in the income statement, liquidity, and capital resources.

marketable securities Any notes, bonds, or stocks that can readily be sold. The term is often used as a synonym for short-term investments.

market rate The rate available on investments in similar bonds at a moment in time.

market to book ratio Market value per share divided by book value per share.

matching The recording of expenses in the same time period as the related revenues are recognized.

materiality convention The concept that states that a financial statement item is material if its omission or misstatement would tend to mislead the reader of the financial statements under consideration.

minority interests The outside shareholders' interests, as opposed to the parent's interests, in a subsidiary corporation.

mortgage bond A form of long-term debt that is secured by the pledge of specific property.

multiple-step income statement An income statement that contains one or more subtotals that highlight significant relationships.

negotiable Legal financial contracts that can be transferred from one lender to another.

net income The remainder after all expenses have been deducted from revenues.

net loss The name given to the difference between revenues and expenses when expenses exceed revenues.

net sales Total sales revenue reduced by sales returns and allowances.

neutrality A quality of information meaning that it is free from bias.

nominal dollars Those dollars that are not restated for fluctuations in the general purchasing power of the monetary unit.

nominal interest rate (contractual rate, coupon rate, stated rate) A contractual rate of interest paid on bonds.

nominal interest rate Synonym for coupon rate.

notes payable Promissory notes that are evidence of a debt and state the terms of payment.

open account Buying or selling on credit, usually by just an "authorized signature" of the buyer.

operating activities Transactions that affect the income statement.

operating cycle The time span during which cash is used to acquire goods and services, which in turn are sold to customers, who in turn pay for their purchases with cash.

operating income (operating profit) Gross profit less all operating expenses.

operating income percentage on sales Operating income divided by sales.

operating lease A lease that should be accounted for by the lessee as ordinary rent expenses.

operating management Is mainly concerned with the major day-to-day activities that generate revenues and expenses.

other postretirement benefits Benefits provided to retired workers in addition to a pension, such as life and health insurance.

outstanding shares Shares remaining in the hands of shareholders.

owner' equity The residual interest in the organization's assets after deducting liabilities.

paid-in capital The total capital investment in a corporation by its owners at the inception of business and subsequently.

paid-in capital in excess of par value When issuing stock, the difference between the total amount received and the par value.

parent company A company owning more than 50% of the voting shares of another company, called the subsidiary company.

participating A characteristic of preferred stock that provides increasing dividends when common dividends increase.

partnership A form of organization that joins two or more individuals together as co-owners.

par value (stated value) The nominal dollar amount printed on stock certificates.

patents Grants by the federal government to an inventor, bestowing (in the United States) the exclusive right for 17 years to produce and sell the invention.

payment date The date dividends are paid.

pensions Payments to former employees after they retire.

percentage of accounts receivable method An approach to estimating bad debts expense and uncollectible accounts at year end using the historical relations of uncollectibles to accounts receivable.

percentage of sales method An approach to estimating bad debts expense and uncollectible accounts based on the historical relations between credit sales and uncollectibles.

period costs Items identified directly as expenses of the time period in which they are incurred.

periodic inventory system The system in which the cost of goods sold is computed periodically by relying solely on physical counts without keeping day-to-day records of units sold or on hand.

permanent differences Revenue or expense items that are recognized for tax purposes but not recognized under GAAP, or vice versa.

perpetual inventory system A system that keeps a running, continuous record that tracks inventories and the cost of goods sold on a day-to-day basis.

physical capital maintenance A concept of income measurement whereby income emerges only after recovering an amount that allows physical operating capability to be maintained.

physical count The process of counting all the items in inventory at a moment in time.

pooling-of-interests method A way of accounting for the combination of two corporations based on the book values of the acquired company's net assets, as distinguished from the purchase method.

posting The transferring of amounts from the journal to the appropriate accounts in the ledger.

preemptive rights The rights to acquire a pro-rata amount of any new issues of capital stock.

preferred stock Stock that offers owners different rights and preferential treatments.

premium on bonds The excess of the proceeds over the face amount of a bond.

present value The value today of a future cash inflow or outflow.

pretax income Income before income taxes.

pretax operating rate of return on total assets (return on total assets (ROA)) Operating income divided by sales.

price-earnings ratio (P-E) Market price per share of common stock divided by earnings per share of common stock.

principal (face amount, par value) The loan amount that a borrower promises to repay at a specific maturity date.

private accountants Accountants who work for businesses, as well as government agencies, and other nonprofit organizations.

privately owned A corporation owned by a family, a small group of shareholders, or a single individual, in which shares of ownership are not publicly sold.

private placement A process whereby notes are issued by corporations when money is borrowed from a few sources, not from the general public.

product costs Costs that are linked with revenues and are charged as expenses when the related revenue is recognized.

profitability The ability of a company to provide investors with a particular rate of return on their investment.

pro forma statement A carefully formulated expression of predicted results.

promissory note A written promise to repay principal plus interest at specific future dates.

protective covenant (covenant) A provision stated in a bond, usually to protect the bondholders' interests.

public accountants Accountants who offer services to the general public on a fee basis including auditing, tax work, and management consulting.

public accounting The field of accounting where services are offered to the general public on a fee basis.

publicly owned A corporation in which shares in the ownership are sold to the public.

purchase method A way of accounting for the acquisition of one company by another, based on the market prices paid for the acquired company's assets.

purchase order A document that specifies the items ordered and the price to be paid by the ordering company.

rate of return The amount earned by an investor expressed as a percentage of the amount invested.

rate of return on common equity (ROE) Net income less preferred dividends divided by average common equity.

raw material inventory Includes the cost of materials held for use in the manufacturing of a product.

receiving report A document that specifies the items received by the company and the condition of the items.

recognition A test for determining whether revenues should be recorded in the financial statements of a given period. To be recognized, revenues must be earned and realized.

reconcile a bank statement To verify that the bank balance for cash is consistent with the accounting records.

redemption price (call price) The price at which an issuer can buy back a callable preferred stock or bond, which is typically 5% to 10% above the par value.

relevance The capability of information to make a difference to the decision maker.

reliability A quality of information meaning that it can be counted on to represent faithfully the condition of the company.

reliability   The quality of information that assures decision makers that the information captures the conditions or events it purports to represent.

replacement cost   The cost at which an inventory item could be acquired today.

report format   A classified balance sheet with the assets at the top.

reserve   Has one of three meanings: (1) a restriction of dividend-declaring power as denoted by a specific subdivision of retained income, (2) an offset to an asset, or (3) an estimate of a definite liability of indefinite or uncertain amount.

residual value (terminal value, disposal value, salvage value, scrap value)   The amount received from disposal of a long-lived asset at the end of its useful life.

restricted retained income (appropriated retained income) Any part of retained income that may not be reduced by dividend declarations.

restructuring   A significant makeover of part of the company typically involving the closing of plants, firing of employees, and relocation of activities.

retailer   A company that sells items directly to the final users, individuals.

retained income (retained earnings, reinvested earnings) Additional owners' equity generated by income or profits.

return on sales ratio   Net income divided by sales.

return on stockholders' equity ratio   Net income divided by invested capital (measured by average stockholders' equity).

revaluation equity   A part of stockholders' equity that includes all holding gains that are excluded from income.

revenues (sales)   Increases in owners' equity arising from increases in assets received in exchange for the delivery of goods or services to customers.

sales allowance (purchase allowance)   Reduction of the original selling price.

sales returns (purchase returns)   Products returned by the customer.

Securities and Exchange Commission (SEC)   The agency designated by the U.S. Congress to hold the ultimate responsibility for authorizing the generally accepted accounting principles for companies whose stock is held by the general investing public.

series   Different groups of preferred shares issued at different times with different features.

short-term debt securities   Largely notes and bonds with maturities of one year or less.

short-term equity securities   Capital stock in other corporations held with the intention to liquidate within one year as needed.

short-term investment   A temporary investment in marketable securities of otherwise idle cash.

short-term liquidity   An organization's ability to meet current payments as they become due.

simple entry   An entry for a transaction that affects only two accounts.

simple interest   For any period, interest rate multiplied by an unchanging principal amount.

single-step income statement   An income statement that groups all revenues together and then lists and deducts all expenses together without drawing any intermediate subtotals.

sinking fund   Cash or securities segregated for meeting obligations on bonded debt.

sinking fund bonds   Bonds with indentures that require the issuer to make annual payments to a sinking fund.

sole proprietorship   A separate organization with a single owner.

solvency   An entity's ability to meet its immediate financial obligations as they become due.

source documents   The supporting original records of any transaction.

special items   Expenses that are large enough and unusual enough to warrant separate disclosure.

specific identification method   This inventory method concentrates on the physical linking of the particular items sold.

specific price index   An index used to approximate the current costs of particular assets or types of assets.

specific write-off method   This method of accounting for bad debt losses assumes all sales are fully collectible until proved otherwise.

statement of cash flows (cash flow statement)   A required statement that reports the cash receipts and cash payments of an entity during a particular period.

statement of income and retained income   A statement that includes a statement of retained income at the bottom of an income statement.

statement of retained income   A statement that lists the beginning balance in retained income, followed by a description of any changes that occurred during the period, and the ending balance.

stock dividends   Distribution to stockholders of additional shares of any class of the distributing company's stock, without any payment to the company by the stockholders.

stock options   Special rights usually granted to executives to purchase a corporation's capital stock.

stock split   Issuance of additional shares to existing stockholders for no payments by the stockholders.

stockholders' equity (shareholders' equity)   Owners' equity of a corporation. The excess of assets over liabilities of a corporation.

straight-line depreciation   A method that spreads the depreciable value evenly over the useful life of an asset.

subordinated debentures Debt securities whose holders have claims against only the assets that remain after the claims of general creditors are satisfied.

subsidiary A corporation owned or controlled by a parent company through the ownership of more than 50% of the voting stock.

T-account Simplified version of ledger accounts that takes the form of the capital letter T.

tangible assets (fixed assets, plant assets) Physical items that can be seen and touched, such as land, natural resources, buildings, and equipment.

tax rate The percentage of taxable income paid to the government.

times interest earned Income before interest expense and income taxes divided by interest expense. Synonym for interest coverage.

time-series comparisons Comparisons of a company's financial ratios with its own historical ratios.

timing differences (temporary differences) Differences between net income and taxable income that arise because some revenue and expense items are recognized at different times for tax purposes than for reporting purposes.

total asset turnover (asset turnover) Sales divided by average total assets available.

trade discounts Reductions to the gross selling price for a particular class of customers.

trademarks Distinctive identifications of a manufactured product or of a service taking the form of a name, a sign, a slogan, a logo, or an emblem.

trading on the equity (financial leverage, leveraging, gearing) Using borrowed money at fixed interest rates with the objective of enhancing the rate of return on common equity.

trading securities Current investments in equity or debt securities held for short-term profit.

transaction Any event that both affects the financial position of an entity and can be reliably recorded in money terms.

treasury stock A corporation's issued stock that has subsequently been repurchased by the company and not retired.

trial balance A list of all accounts in the general ledger with their balances.

trust indenture A contract whereby the issuing corporation of a bond promises a trustee that it will abide by stated provisions.

turnover A synonym for sales or revenues in many countries outside the United States.

U.S. Treasury obligations Interest-bearing notes, bonds, and bills issued by the U.S. government.

uncollectible accounts (bad debts) Receivables determined to be uncollectible because debtors are unable or unwilling to pay their debts.

underwriters A group of investment bankers that buys an entire bond or stock issue from a corporation and then sells the bonds to the general investing public.

unearned revenue (revenue received in advance, deferred revenue, deferred credit) Revenue received and recorded before it is earned.

unit depreciation A depreciation method based on units of service when physical wear and tear is the dominating influence on the useful life of the asset.

unsubordinated debenture A bond that is unsecured by specific pledged assets, giving its owner a general claim with a priority like an account payable.

useful life (economic life) The time period over which an asset is depreciated.

validity (representational faithfulness) A correspondence between the accounting numbers and the events or objects those numbers purport to represent.

verifiability A quality of information meaning that it can be checked to make sure that it is correct.

weighted-average method This inventory method computes a unit cost by dividing the total acquisition cost of all items available for sale by the number of units available for sale.

wholesaler An intermediary that sells inventory items to retailers.

work in process inventory Includes the cost incurred for partially completed items, including raw materials, labor, and other costs.

working capital The excess of current assets over current liabilities.

write-down A reduction in the assumed cost of an item in response to a decline in value.

yield to maturity (effective interest rate) The interest rate that equates market price at issue to the present value of principal and interest.

zero coupon A bond or note that pays no cash interest during its life.

INDEX

statement of revenues and. *See* Income statement

transactions to, 90–93

Expired assets, recognition of, 49–50

Explicit transactions, 126

Extinguishment of debt

early, 497, 498

gain or loss on in statement of cash flows, 418–19

Extraordinary items, 562–63, 564

Face amount. *See* Principal

FASB. *See* Financial Accounting Standards Board

FASB Statements. *See under* Financial Accounting Standards Board

FICA taxes, 322–23

FIFO (first-in, first-out). *See* Inventory valuation methods

Financial accounting, 4

Financial Accounting Standards Board (FASB), 64, 148–49, 232, 332, 396, 400, 454, 507, 513, 561, 563, 588–90, 591, 606, 612

Statements of, 148, 547, 550, 551, 599

Statements of Financial Accounting Concepts (SFACs), 588–89, 590

Financial capital maintenance, 598

Financial leverage. *See* Trading on the equity

Financial management, 397, 555

Financial performance, 555–56

Financial position/condition, statement of. *See* Balance sheet

Financial ratios, 61–64, 550, 552–54. *See also* Earnings per share (EPS)

book value per share of common stock, 469–70

dividend-payout ratio, 63–64, 552

dividend-yield ratio, 62–63, 552

evaluating, 550

long-term solvency ratios, 452, 552, 554

market-to-book ratio, 470

price-earnings ratio (P-E), 62, 552

profitability ratios, 552, 553, 554

rate of return on common equity, 468

short-term liquidity ratios, 552, 553, 554

stockholders' equity and, 468–70

Financial statement analysis, 538–84. *See also* Financial ratios

common-size statements in, 545–47

disclosure of nonrecurring items and, 561–64

earnings per share (EPS) and, 552, 559–61

financial performance and, 555–56

foreign currency issues and, 564

income tax effects and, 558–59

management's discussion and analysis (MD&A) and, 547, 548–49

measuring safety in, 559

objectives of, 542

operating performance and, 555, 556

segment reporting and, 547, 549–50

trading on the equity and, 556–58

trend analysis and, 543–45, 550

Financial statements, 4, 7. *See also* Balance sheet; Income statements; Statement of cash flows; Statement of retained income

credibility of, 20–21

customs of presentation of, 59–60

deriving from trial balance, 97–98, 99

financial ratios and, 61–64

for governmental units, 152

with incomplete records, 101–2, 106

inventory errors and, 239–41

for not-for-profit organizations, 151–52

Financing activities, 397, 398

in statement of cash flows, 52–53, 397, 398, 399, 401, 402, 407–9

Financing lease. *See* Capital lease

Finished goods inventory, 252

First-in, first-out (FIFO). *See* Inventory valuation methods

Fiscal year, 43

Fisher, Don, 277

Fixed assets. *See* Tangible assets

F.O.B. destination, 225

F.O.B. shipping point, 225

Forbes, 152, 541

Ford, Henry, II, 21

Foreclosure, 559

Foreign currencies, financial statements and, 564

Foreign currency translation adjustment, 468

Form 10-K, 541

Form 10-Q, 541

Fortune, 541, 614

Fractional shares, 459

France, accounting in, 606–7

Franchises, 290

revenue recognition and, 129

Fraud. *See* Internal control

Freight in, 225, 226

Freight out, 225–26

Fringe benefits, 322

Fully diluted EPS, 561

Future value, 353–56

GAAP. *See* Generally accepted accounting principles (GAAP)

Gains, on sales of of tangible assets, 287–88

Gearing. *See* Trading on the equity

General journal. *See* Journal

General ledger, 83

Generally accepted accounting principles (GAAP), 148–51, 237, 283, 290, 331, 332, 372, 374, 499, 507, 511, 561, 588, 592, 595, 600

concepts and conventions of, 149–51

cost-benefit criterion, 151

entity concept, 150

going concern convention, 150

materiality convention, 151

reliability concept, 150

stable monitory unit, 151

standard-setting bodies for, 148–49

General price index, 603

Germany, accounting in, 606, 607

Going concern convention, 150, 594

GoodEarth Products, Inc. example, 227–28

Goodwill, 509–11

abnormal earnings and, 509, 510, 511

accounting for, 509, 510

amortization of, 511

fair values of individual assets and, 509

purchased, 509–11

Governments

accrual-based accounting for, 64

financial statements for, 64

Greystone Company example, 600–601

Griffey, Ken, Jr., 127

Gross margin. *See* Gross profits

Gross margin percentage (gross profit percentage). *See* Gross profits

Gross National Product Implicit Price Deflator, 603

Gross profit percentage. *See* Gross profits

Gross profits, 143, 144, 226–27, 241–46

adjusting from LIFO to FIFO and, 244–45

gross profit percentage and, 146–47, 241

inventory turnover and, 242–44

inventory and estimating intraperiod, 242–43

inventory shrinkage and, 246–47

inventory valuation and, 222–23

percentage and inventory turnover, 552

reports to stockholders and, 245–46

Gross sales, 175

Harbor Electronics example, 234–35, 236

Harmonization of accounting principles, 149

Health insurance, 375

Held-to-maturity securities, 494, 495

Historical cost accounting, 592, 597–99

Historical cost/constant dollars method of income measurement, 600, 603

Historical cost/nominal dollars method of income measurement, 600–601

Holding companies, 501

Holding gains (or losses), 233–34, 602–3, 604

Hughes, Don, 125–26

IASC. *See* International Accounting Standards Committee

Immediate-liquidation assumption, 150

Implicit interest. *See* Imputed interest

Implicit transactions, 126. *See also* Adjustments

Improvements, repairs and maintenance *versus,* 286–87

Imputed interest, 369

Imputed interest rate, 369

Income, 44. *See also* Gross profits

cash flow *versus,* 52

measurement of, 41–50, 592, 593–625. *See also* Accrual-basis accounting

cash-basis, 42

current cost/constant dollars method, 600, 605–6

current cost/nominal dollars method, 600, 601–2

fiscal year and, 43

historical cost, 592, 597–99

Payment date, 452
Payroll taxes, 322
P-E. *See* Price-earnings ratio
Pension Benefit Guarantee Corporation, 376
Pensions, 374–76, 563
Percentage of accounts receivable method, 185–86
Percentage of sales method, 184–85
Period costs, 46
Periodic inventory systems. *See* Inventory systems
Permanent differences, 331
Perpetual inventory system. *See* Inventory systems
Perry, Glen, 214
Personnel, internal controls and, 191, 246
Philbrick company example, 378–79
Physical capital maintenance, 598
Physical count, of inventory, 223, 224
Physical inventory, 224–25
Physical safeguards, internal control and, 192
Plant assets. *See* Tangible assets
P & L statement. *See* Income statements
Pooling of interests, 519–21
    purchase method compared to, 519, 520–21
Posting, 87, 88
Postretirement insurance, 374–76, 563
Preemptive rights, 447
Preferred stock. *See* Stock
Premium on bonds, 362, 366, 367, 368
Prepaid costs, adjustments for expiration of, 127
Present value, 352, 356–60
    of annuity, 358–60
Press releases, 541
Pretax income, 132–33
Pretax operating rate of return on total assets, 555, 556
Pretax return on operating assets, 552
Price-earnings (P-E) ratio, 62, 552
Principal, bonds and, 327
Private accounting, 23
Privately owned corporation, 16
Private placements, 327
Procedure manuals, internal control and, 192
Product costs, 46
Product warranties, 324
Profit, 44. *See also* Gross profits; Income
Profitability evaluation, 146
Profitability evaluation ratios, 146–47, 552, 553, 554
    gross profit percentage, 146–47
    return on sales ratio, 147
    return on stockholders' equity ratio, 147
Profit margin. *See* Gross profits
Pro forma statements, 452
Promissory note, 321
Protective covenants, 329
Public accounting, 23, 24
Publicly owned corporation, 16
Purchase allowance. *See* Sales allowance
Purchase method, 519, 520–21
Purchase order, 325
Purchase returns, 175

Quick ratio, 552, 553, 554

RAO. *See* Return on total assets
Rate of return, 356
Rate of return on common equity (ROE), 468–69
Rate of return on stockholders' equity (ROE), 557
Ratings, of bonds, 361–62
Ratio analysis, debt levels and, 335–36
Raw material inventory, 252
Realization test, of sales revenue, 174
Receivables. *See* Accounts receivable
Receiving report, 325
Recognition, 594
    of expenses, 595–96
    of expired assets, 49–50
    of revenues, 45–46, 592, 595
    of sales revenue, 174
Reconciliation
    bank statements and, 180, 196–98
    internal control and, 189
    statement of cash flows and, 410–12
Recording, internal control and, 189
Redemption price, 451
Reinvested earnings (retained income/earnings). *See* Income
Relevance, 591–92, 593
Reliability, 150, 591–92, 593
Repairs, improvements *versus*, 287
Replacement cost, 233, 236–37
    in other countries, 606–7
Report format, balance sheets and, 141, 142
Reports
    annual, 7–8, 320, 541
    audit committee, 190
    management, 190
    stockholders, 245–46, 284
Representational faithfulness. *See* Validity
Repurchase of shares, 460–61, 462, 463, 465
Reserve, 467
Reserve for doubtful accounts. *See* Allowance for uncollectible accounts
Residual value, 280
Responsibility, internal controls and, 191
Restricted retained income, 467
Restructuring, 330
Results of operations. *See* Income statements
Retailers, 241
Retained earnings/income. *See* Income
Retirement, pensions and other postretirement benefits and, 374–76, 563
Retirement of debt (early), in statement of cash flows, 418–19
Retirement of shares, 461–62
Returnable deposits, 324–25
Return on investment ratio, 555
Return on sales ratio, 147, 552, 553, 554
Return on stockholders' equity ratio, 147, 552, 553, 555, 557
Return on total assets (ROA), 556–57
Returns of merchandise, accounting for, 175–77
Revaluation equity, 602
Revenue received in advance. *See* Unearned revenue

Revenues, 43–45
    adjustments for accrual of unrecorded, 133–35
    deferred. *See* Unearned revenues
    measurement of, 175–80
        accounting for net sales, 178–79
        compensating balances, 179
        management of cash, 179–80
        merchandise returns and allowances, 175–77
        recording charge card transactions, 177–78
    other, 143
    recognition of, 45–46, 174, 592, 595
        franchises and, 129
        tests of, 174
        timing of, 174
    statement of expenses and. *See* Income statements
    transactions to, 90–93
    unearned, 325
Revenues collected in advance. *See* Unearned revenues
Ripley Company example, 237–38
ROE. *See* Rate of return on common equity; Rate of return on stockholders' equity
Rotation of duties, internal control and, 192–93
Running balance column, 88–89

Safeguards, internal control and, 189
Safety, financial statement analysis measuring, 559
Salad Oil Swindle, 225
Sales. *See also* Revenues
    cost of. *See* Cost of goods sold
    on credit, 13
Sales allowance, 175–77
Sales returns, 175–77
Sales revenues. *See* Revenues
Sales tax, 323–24
Salvage value. *See* Residual value
Sample Corporation example, 470–71
Samuels, Patrice Duggan, 8
San Francisco Chronicle, 212–13
Sarasota Sailboats example, 595–96
Schillit, Howard, 210–11
Schofield, Seth, 507–8
Scrap value. *See* Residual value
Securities and Exchange Commission (SEC), 148–49, 447, 454, 499, 541, 561, 582–83, 590
Segment reporting, 547, 549–50
Separation of duties, internal controls and, 191–92
Series, preferred stock and, 452
Shareholders. *See also under* Stock; Stockholders
Shareholders' equity. *See* Stockholder's equity
Short-term debt securities, 493
Short-term equity securities, 493–94
Short-term investments, 492, 493–95, 514–16
Short-term liquidity, 452
Short-term liquidity ratios, 552, 553, 554
Shrinkage. *See* Inventory shrinkage
Simple entry, 89

INDEX OF COMPANIES

PHOTO CREDITS